HAROLD WILSON
THE WINNER

Nick Thomas-Symonds

WEIDENFELD & NICOLSON

First published in Great Britain in 2022 by Weidenfeld & Nicolson
This paperback edition first published in Great Britain in 2023
by Weidenfeld & Nicolson,
an imprint of The Orion Publishing Group Ltd
Carmelite House, 50 Victoria Embankment
London EC4Y 0DZ
An Hachette UK Company

1 3 5 7 9 10 8 6 4 2

A CIP catalogue record for this book is
available from the British Library.

ISBN (Mass Market Paperback) 978 1 476 1196 1
ISBN (eBook) 9781474611978

Typeset by Input Data Services Ltd, Somerset

Printed in Great Britain by Clays Ltd, Elcograf S.p.A.

www.weidenfeldandnicolson.co.uk
www.orionbooks.co.uk

Praise for *Harold Wilson: The Winner*

'Nick Thomas-Symonds' excellent new biography puts Harold Wilson in his rightful place as a crucial figure in Labour Party history, winning four General Elections and introducing important reforms that have endured. It deserves to be widely read not only as a fine work of history but also for its lessons in how Labour wins'
Keir Starmer

'The Labour frontbencher Nick Thomas-Symonds – a rare parliamentarian who can write – offers an unashamedly revisionist and readable account of the man who led Labour to four election victories. So often derided as a shameless opportunist, Wilson here shines through as a quick-witted, silver-tongued master strategist'
Patrick Maguire, *The Times*, Books of the Year

'Wilson was one of the most remarkable British political figures of the 20th century . . . Nick Thomas-Symonds, in his entertaining and assured biography, paints a portrait of a man who embodied all the contradictions of the movement he led'
Daniel Finkelstein, *The Times*

'This comprehensive, carefully researched and very readable biography aims to establish Wilson's place in history – not as the neurotic schemer often reported during his sad last years, which were blighted by dementia, nor even as the supreme political fixer portrayed by Pimlott, but as a decent, honourable man, as well as a very clever one, who was in politics to do something, not just to be someone. He was, Thomas-Symonds concludes, one of our greatest prime ministers, who, given the political circumstances, had a remarkable record of solid achievement'
Francis Beckett, *Spectator*

'Excellent'   Andrew Marr, *New Statesman*

'A timely new biography'   Andrew Pierce, *Daily Mail*

Also by Nick Thomas-Symonds

Nye: The Political Life of Aneurin Bevan
Attlee: A Life in Politics

For my grandparents, my parents,
Matilda Olwyn, Florence Elizabeth Mary,
William Nicklaus and Pippa

Contents

Introduction

Forged in white heat

It was on Tuesday, 1 October 1963 that James Harold Wilson gave the speech that defined his political times. Elected Labour Party leader earlier that year after the death of Hugh Gaitskell, Wilson, then leader of the Opposition, addressed his party conference. The text was produced as the deadline approached, an all-night effort on which he had started work shortly before midnight. At first he wrote but, with time running out, he started dictating. At breakfast, his highly efficient political secretary, Marcia Williams, was still typing it up, with him expected on the podium at 10 a.m.

Wilson was downbeat, convinced that it would lead to disappointment. His ambition was modest, hoping that those in the hall might at least react sympathetically to a newly elected party leader. His worry was that those 'expecting a tub-thumping speech about Tory iniquities . . . would hardly welcome a disquisition on science and technology'.[1] This was because Wilson intended to define Labour's mission in the 1960s as harnessing technological advancement for the benefit of people.[2] Wilson wanted science to be the word most associated with modern-day socialism. Automation in industry would continue at speed: computers 'with an impulse cycle of three millionths of a second, already technically obsolete and giving place to machines a thousand times faster'. Machine tools would themselves develop new, more efficient machine tools. Human agency would no longer be required to assemble cars. This, he argued, presented the choice for the country: 'a choice between unrivalled misery or unrivalled prosperity'. If government chose to be an observer in this, rather than an active participant, the

I

technological revolution would lead to profits for a few people, and unemployment for those no longer needed. However, with an active government, planning the economy and protecting jobs, people could instead use technology to improve their lives, see living standards rise and increased leisure time.[3]

The Grand Hall of Scarborough's Spa complex, built on the location of the natural waters discovered in the seventeenth century, was an unusual location for a speech about the cutting edge of the future. Yet, as people watched Wilson's speech in black and white on their television sets, it was modernity to which he appealed. Leaning forward, energetic, his tie tucked neatly into his waistband, he grasped either side of the box in front of him:

> . . . in this Conference, in all our plans for the future, we are re-defining and we are re-stating our Socialism in terms of the scientific revolution. But that revolution cannot become a reality unless we are prepared to make far-reaching changes in economic and social attitudes which permeate our whole system of society.

He lifted his right hand momentarily to emphasise the signature line:

> The Britain that is going to be *forged in the white heat of this revolution* [author's emphasis] will be no place for restrictive practices or outdated methods on either side of industry.[4]

In this single sentence that prompted immediate applause, Wilson combined vision and hard politics. He intended to show that Labour was the party ready to grasp the opportunities of a changing society, while sending a message to business and trade unions that he expected them not to obstruct the project of modernisation.

Wilson's concern about how the speech would be received proved to be unfounded. Robert McKenzie, reporting on the BBC's lunchtime news, said that 'Harold Wilson has moved the Labour Party forward fifty years in fifty minutes.'[5] The reason for the success of the speech was not only its focus on the future; it was also because both its intended target and its speaker personified the central message. Britain was being held back by the old boy network approach to life. That industry was under the control of 'men whose only claim is their aristocratic connections or the power of inherited wealth or speculative finance is as irrelevant to the twentieth century as would be the continued purchase of commissions in the armed forces by lowly amateurs'.[6] The Conservatives, whom Wilson hoped to displace from power, were led by the patrician, old Etonian Harold Macmillan who, within less than three weeks, would be replaced by the aristocrat Alec Douglas-Home, another old Etonian who disclaimed his hereditary peerage in order to enter the House of Commons to become prime minister. In contrast, Wilson, the grammar school boy who had risen to the top by dint of his own abilities and efforts, would make Britain a meritocracy at home and abroad: 'From now on Britain will have as much influence in the world as we can earn, as we can deserve.'[7]

It was an inspiring vision. A year later, in October 1964, Wilson won a general election and was elected prime minister. One writer, Christopher Bray, has argued that it was during the following year when modern Britain was made: '. . . 1965 planted bomb after bomb under the hidebound, stick-in-the-mud, living-on-past-glories Britain that preceded it – and gave us the country we live in today.' The newly elected Labour government was part of this: 'Everywhere you looked, from the House of Commons to the school common room, from the recording studio to the television screen, from the railways to the rear-view mirror, from the inner space of the tortured mind to the outer space of the moon, the country was (as Bob Dylan put it that year) "busy being born". Change wasn't just in the air – it *was* the air, the air everyone breathed all day long.'[8]

Wilson captured this zeitgeist. His ordinary background and his folksy image – the Yorkshire accent, the love of HP Sauce, the pipe, the witty speeches – made him the ideal Labour leader for the time. In March 1963, the month after Wilson was elected to the leadership, the Beatles released their first album, *Please Please Me*, that was to launch a phenomenon, propelling George Harrison,

John Lennon, Paul McCartney and Ringo Starr to worldwide stardom.

'Beatlemania' swept the country as the working-class boys from Liverpool delivered songs in simple lyrics with a huge popular appeal. Wilson, too, was amiable and accessible, not hidebound by excessive formality. He often stayed at the Adelphi Hotel in Liverpool: walking the streets with his wife Mary on the night of the 1964 general election, the people seeing the couple chanted 'Wilson, Yeah Yeah Yeah' to the tune of the Beatles' hit 'She Loves You'.[9] The Labour leader was an instantly recognisable figure who had mastered the art of the new mode of communication: the television. Labour MP Tony Benn, a former television producer, was brought into his inner circle to handle public relations. As David Frost's great TV political satire *That Was The Week That Was* lampooned the end of Harold Macmillan's premiership, Wilson became a familiar face on the small screen, relaxed and confident in making the case for electing a Labour government to unleash the talents of the country's people.

Wilson was to win four of the five general elections he contested, spending nearly eight years in Downing Street. He is the only post-war party leader to have served as prime minister on two separate occasions from 1964 to 1970 and 1974 to 1976, when he brought Labour back to power after only one term in opposition, a feat no other leader has accomplished. He led his party and the country through a period of acute economic difficulty and profound social change. With a brilliant mind, sure-footed political moves and an instinctive feel for public opinion, Wilson was a survivor who emerged from crises to defeat political opponents time and time again.

His governments shaped our modern-day United Kingdom: from our family and sexual laws, to the transition from grammar to comprehensive schools and the opening up of lifelong learning through the Open University. The change spanned different spheres of modern life: the first anti-discrimination laws, a durable framework for employment protections and safety in the workplace, equal pay for women, the humanising of our criminal justice system through the abolition of capital punishment and the bar-baric practice of birching. In housing, social services and health, his governments focused on helping the poorest. In his stewardship of the economy, Wilson sought to minimise unemployment, his politics shaped by his own family's experience of joblessness. He was by instinct a conciliator who sought industrial peace, prefer-ring to work with the unions and to avoid open confrontation if possible.

Yet it was his governments' economic record that brought criticism. In Anthony King and Ivor Crewe's *The Blunders of Our Governments*, Wilson features prominently: 'Probably the single biggest blunder created by Harold Wilson's post-1964 Labour gov-ernment was its decision not to devalue the pound, if not immedi-ately, then at least within a year or two of taking office. Ministers were divided on the issue . . . Eventually, in 1967, amidst mounting market pressures, Wilson and [James] Callaghan did devalue it.'[10] Wilson then compounded the problem with a television broadcast widely thought to be misleading in which he argued that the pound in people's pockets, purses and banks at home in Britain *had not been devalued*. As prime minister, the charge against Wilson is that he focused on short-term tactics rather than long-term strategy. Against a difficult economic backdrop, the accusation is that his governments were beset with crises and under-achieved, failing to implement a longer-term economic model despite creating a spe-cific Department for Economic Affairs for this purpose in 1964 and publishing a National Plan the following year.

Wilson's political rivals were not kind in their assessments. When Wilson was elected Labour leader in February 1963, Mac-millan was acerbic: 'Wilson is an able man . . . He is good in the House and in the country – and, I am told, on T.V. But he is a fundamentally dishonest – even "crooked" man – almost of the "3 Card Trick" kind. This may, sooner or later, find him out.'[11] Edward Heath, Conservative prime minister from 1970 to 1974, who faced Wilson across the Commons dispatch boxes for a decade, criticised him for a lack of core beliefs. In a 1985 interview, he said Wilson's approach could not even be described as tactics over strategy: 'It was just opportunism. He wasn't my style.'[12] The view that Wilson was inauthentic had long roots. In the 1950s, when Wilson spoke about his origins as being 'forged' in Sheffield steel, Aneurin Bevan had quipped: 'I always thought there was something counterfeit about you!'[13] The remark contained what was a truth for many fellow politicians: that Wilson was calculating his own self-interest in every situation rather than looking to the national interest. Wilson's phrase that 'a week is a long time in politics' was meant to convey that political leaders should not be diverted from long-term aims by short-term crises, but came to mean the opposite: that his moves were designed to survive the next week with little care for the long-term consequences.[14]

Heath's view did not improve significantly as the years passed. In 1998, he damned Wilson with faint praise: 'Harold Wilson's lasting achievements are difficult to discern, except for the fact that he held the Labour Party together for nearly fifteen years, whereas under his successors it collapsed, thereby helping to sustain eighteen years of Conservative government. Harold was, above all else, a great political survivor, a fine politician if, perhaps, never truly a statesman.'[15] By then, Wilson's reputation was very low. This fall can be traced back to the publication of Wilson's resignation honours list after he left office in 1976: the 'Lavender List', named after the coloured paper on which Marcia Williams noted down the suggested names containing businessmen with no Labour Party links, some of whom turned out to be convicted fraudsters.

The passage of time did not help. The former civil servant Clive Ponting wrote in 1989 that Wilson's period in office represented a breach of promise and was a comparative failure. In comparison to Clement Attlee's reforming Labour government of 1945 to 1951, its achievements 'were limited and outweighed by the failures. It proved unable to write an enduring and significant contribution to the second chapter of the socialist story. The promise remained unfulfilled.'[16] Roy Jenkins, who served in Wilson's governments, twice as home secretary and once as chancellor of the exchequer, wrote in 1992 that if prime ministerial shares existed, he could buy

'Wilson's at a low value, with room for a very sharp recovery . . . before they begin to approach par.'[17]

Over two decades later, with Wilson having died in 1995, and another Labour government having been in office from 1997 to 2010, trenchant critics remained. The historian Dominic Sandbrook penned an article in the *Daily Mail* on 25 January 2013, after the then Conservative prime minister David Cameron's announcement of a renegotiation of the UK's relationship with the EU followed by a referendum on membership. This was the same approach Wilson had used in 1975, when he had adjusted the British terms of entry into what was then the European Economic Community (EEC) and held a referendum to stay in. Sandbrook's piece was entitled, 'Beware the ghost of slippery Harold: David Cameron's European referendum speech was hailed as a masterstroke, but we've been here before'. He was harsh on Wilson: 'in the second decade of the twenty-first century, with Britain facing dreadful economic challenges at home and extraordinary turmoil abroad, the last thing we need is a second Harold Wilson.'[18]

Yet two events in the new century should reshape views of Wilson. First, it was the fact that Cameron, after his renegotiation, sought to keep Britain in Europe in the 2016 referendum, exactly as Wilson had done over forty years before. Cameron was to fail in his aim, and announced his resignation as prime minister the day after the poll. Wilson, in contrast, secured Britain's place in Europe with a two-to-one majority. On the face of it, though, Wilson had been inconsistent on the issue. He had been sceptical when Macmillan had applied to join the EEC in 1961, then, as prime minister, made an unsuccessful application in 1967. In both cases, the French president, Charles de Gaulle, had blocked British entry. By the time Heath was in power from 1970, de Gaulle had left office. Yet, with the path to entry clear, Wilson came out against entry on the agreed Conservative terms, to keep his party, which was deeply divided on the issue, together. However, to dismiss Wilson's approach on Europe as short-termist is to miss what Wilson's real view was: a hard-headed pragmatic analysis that Britain was better off in what was then known as the Common Market, and to avoid

Labour becoming openly opposed to membership. As can be seen in this biography, on this issue, Wilson was to prove a successful strategist, not a lucky tactician.

A week before Cameron left office, Sir John Chilcot's Iraq inquiry report was published. The Iraq War of 2003 should also change our analysis of Wilson as it illustrates what the consequences are of a prime minister committing ground troops alongside a United States president. When Wilson supported the American war in Vietnam and protesters thronged the streets in 1968, he was decried as a sell-out. Yet he did not send in British soldiers, sought to broker a peace and maintained the Anglo-American Alliance. Tony Blair's involvement in the Iraq War had already been described by his biographer Anthony Seldon as 'the biggest disappointment, and failure, of his premiership'.[19] Chilcot concluded it was 'an intervention which went badly wrong, with consequences to this day.'[20] From 2003 to 2009, 178 British soldiers were killed, as was a Ministry of Defence civilian. In Iraq, the carnage was terrible. Chilcott cited one study that concluded that there had been 461,000 excess deaths from 2003 to 2011: 'Most . . . were due to direct violence but about a third resulted from indirect causes, such as the failures of health, sanitation, transportation, communication and other systems . . . About a third of the deaths due to direct violence were attributed to coalition forces (some 90,000), and a third to militias.'[21] Perhaps a second Harold Wilson might not have been such a bad thing for the country after all.

Some less critical views have started to emerge. In a collection of essays edited by Andrew S. Crines and Kevin Hickson, published in 2016 to commemorate the centenary of his birth, *Harold Wilson: The Unprincipled Prime Minister? Reappraising Harold Wilson*, Gerald Kaufman pointed out that Wilson had not been given credit for avoiding committing British troops to the Vietnam War.[22] This, according to George Howarth, MP for the successor constituency to Wilson's Huyton, was still a matter of some pride locally.[23] The academic Gillian Peele argued that Wilson's 'achievement in keeping Britain in Europe after the intense urge to reject Heath and all his works in Labour ranks should also be recognised.'[24] Yet negative views remain. In 2021, Seldon still declared Wilson 'Labour's most disappointing prime minister [who] caved in to the left and unions, failed to provide strong leadership, and largely squandered Labour's landslide election victory in 1966.'[25]

When he left office, Wilson told the BBC's political editor David Holmes that he wished he 'could have been prime minister in happier times and easier times'.[26] The challenges he faced are set out in the two substantial books he produced defending the record of his own governments. In *The Labour Government 1964–1970*, running to nearly 800 pages, Wilson wrote in the foreword: 'This book is the record of a Government all but a year of whose life was dominated by an inherited balance of payments problem which was nearing a crisis at the moment we took office; we lived and governed during a period when that problem made frenetic speculative attack on Britain both easy and profitable.' He added: 'It was a Government that faced disappointment after disappointment, and none greater than the economic restraints on our ability to carry through the social revolution to which we were committed at the speed we would have wished.' Yet, 'despite those restraints and the need to transfer resources from domestic expenditure, private and public, to the needs of our export markets, we carried through an expansion in the social services, health, welfare and housing, education and social security unparalleled in our history.'[27] In *Final Term: The Labour Government 1974–1976* he explained why he tried to keep the Labour Party in one piece: 'To produce a policy on which the party could remain united, despite unhappiness on one wing or the other wing – or both – inevitably evoked the phrase "devious". But in my view a constant effort to keep his party together, without sacrificing either principle or the essentials of basic strategy, is the very stuff of political leadership.'[28] While both books follow a chronological approach that lends itself to narrative at the expense of analysis, they also illustrate the day-to-day pressures on the prime minister, whose ability to focus on a single issue for a sustained period is limited. Instead, Wilson, like all occupants of the office, had to move quickly between different issues as they arose.

There are two major biographies of Harold Wilson: by Ben Pimlott, first published in 1992;[29] and Philip Ziegler's authorised biography in 1993.[30] Both provide a considered assessment of Wilson, though neither captures his full significance in British politics. Both biographers accept the charge that Wilson was a short-term tactician, and seek to mitigate it, rather than challenge it. Pimlott noted: 'Wilson went to great pains to defend himself against the charge of being inconsistent, although there is no clear reason why – in politics or in life – people should not vary their remarks and opinions according to the circumstances.'[31] Ziegler argued that: 'there is a need for the compromiser, the trimmer, the politician who puts first the business of keeping government on the road and views principles with the beady eye of a pragmatist who decides what must be done and only then considers whether it can be modified to serve some long-term end.'[32] He then draws this conclusion about Wilson's limited utility: 'A succession of Wilsons as leader would doom any nation to decline; a Wilson from time to time to let the dust settle while the demolition squads of the radicals gather strength for this next enterprise can be positively beneficial.'[33] This is to underestimate the constructive achievements of Wilson's administrations. It is telling that the reforms introduced by Wilson's 1964–70 governments do not even merit their own chapter in either book.

In fairness, neither author had access to a full range of primary sources, and both books were written during Wilson's lifetime, without a longer-term perspective. Ziegler wrote that Wilson's third volume of autobiography, *Memoirs 1916–64: The Making of a Prime Minister* was 'largely a compilation of Brian Connell's with the titular author contributing little beyond a string of anecdotes'.[34] Actually, it was partly based upon Wilson's own handwritten notes, typed up in the early 1980s: this previously unpublished material was deposited in the Bodleian Library in Oxford by Wilson's son Robin in 2018, alongside other papers that were in the possession of the Wilson family.[35] This biography has made use of that material, and the full set of Wilson government papers at the National Archives that had not been released when Pimlott and

Ziegler were writing. There are also newly released papers available in the Lyndon Johnson Presidential Library, including the record (declassified in June 1999) of a meeting in December 1964 between Johnson and Wilson that both parties agreed to say had never occurred, during which the two leaders discussed devaluation. This biography also relies on new, first-hand interviews with those who knew him, which are particularly valuable since so little of Wilson's time in parliament was broadcast.[36]

At the cabinet meeting at which Wilson announced his resignation, on 16 March 1976, James Callaghan, then foreign secretary and Wilson's successor as prime minister, said that 'history would deal even more kindly with the Prime Minister than his contemporaries.'[37] Two weeks later, Wilson faced Prime Minister's Questions for the last time with his wife, Mary, watching on in the public gallery. At the end of the session, in a finale fitting of any stage play, the lights went out at the exact moment Wilson sat down after answering the last question.[38] Thus, Wilson's final appearance in the House of Commons in high office ended in a darkened chamber, as MPs heard the distinctive Welsh accent of the speaker, George Thomas, reassuring them that efforts would be made to restore light.[39] Over four decades later, the time has now come to illuminate the significance of Harold Wilson as one of the shapers of post-war Britain.

Chapter 1

The fourteenth Mr Wilson

Childhood and Early Years, 1916–34

The first Labour prime minister, Ramsay MacDonald, was born in Lossiemouth, Scotland, the illegitimate son of a farm labourer who left school at fifteen.[1] The second, Clement Attlee, was born in Putney and educated at Haileybury public school: his father an esteemed solicitor who went on to become the president of the Law Society.[2] The third, James Harold Wilson, was a grammar school boy, the son of a manager at a dyestuffs factory. If the first two represented, respectively, backgrounds of poverty and wealth, Wilson represented what a later Labour leader, Ed Miliband, called the 'squeezed middle', with his father James Herbert Wilson often moving to find work and a secure income.[3]

Harold Wilson's background became a matter of public interest when Alec Douglas-Home succeeded Harold Macmillan as prime minister in October 1963. Home disclaimed his hereditary peerage before winning election to the House of Commons at the Kinross and Western Perthshire by-election on 7 November, meaning there was a short period when he held the office of prime minister but was a member of neither house of parliament. Wilson, then leader of the opposition, declared the process 'the machinery of an aristocratic cabal' before adding: 'This is a counter-revolution. After half a century of democratic advance, of social revolution, of rising expectations, the whole process has ground to a halt with a fourteenth Earl.'[4] Home's riposte, while failing to deflect the criticism, was at least witty: 'I suppose, when you come to think of it, he is the fourteenth Mr Wilson.[5] Home had, however, got his numbers wrong.

Wilson was a proud Yorkshireman. His ancestry can be traced to the Cistercian Abbey of Rievaulx, near Helmsley in North Yorkshire. The Helmsley Archaeological Society's study of Wilson's genealogy led to an agricultural labourer: 'The surname Wilson was handed down through several generations after its establishment to one Thomas Wilson whose father farmed his feudal strip, a peasant tied to the soil, on the lands of the great Abbey of Rievaulx five hundred years ago . . .'[6] Wilson's male ancestors tilled the soils of Rievaulx for decades during the fifteenth century, so when 'Alexander Lord Home was created the first Earl of Home and Lord Dunglas in 1605, there had already been seven or eight Wilsons in direct line of succession at Rievaulx. Mr Harold Wilson is at least the 24th Mr Wilson, and probably 30th of his name line!'[7]

Wilson later bemoaned that: 'one blot on my impeccable Yorkshire connection . . . was a recent one. My father and mother had been born in Openshaw, Manchester, a digression due on my father's side to his father's move to Manchester in the early 1860s.'[8] Herbert Wilson, as he was known, was born on 12 December 1882, at Chorlton-upon-Medlock. There was a strong progressive political influence in his life. Herbert's older brother Jack had been Keir Hardie's election agent in 1895 and 1900. Wilson's great-uncle, Alderman Herbert Thewlis, was lord mayor of Manchester. In the 1906 general election, with local areas able to choose polling day, Thewlis chose a Saturday, to allow the working classes who had the vote the best chance of doing so. Herbert was going through one of his periodic bouts of unemployment in the dyestuffs industry, so he used the freedom to serve on the election staff of John Hodge, Labour candidate for Gorton, for whom the Liberals had stood aside to give a free run against the Conservatives. Hodge was elected one of twenty-nine members forming the Independent Labour Party.[9]

Having spare time was, however, no substitute for a steady job. Herbert had started in the dyestuffs industry at the age of sixteen at Levinstein's of Manchester, before winning a scholarship to the

Manchester Technical School where he studied from 1897 to 1899.[10] There he met Chaim Weizmann, 'the founder of modern Israel, who was working, though obviously at a higher level, in dyestuffs and associated chemical products'.[11] This was a fact treasured by his son, who was to become one of Israel's greatest friends. The Technical School provided a solid foundation for Herbert's career, but it did not yield consistent employment. What sustained him during the periods of worklessness was his family: he married Ethel Seddon on 14 March 1906 at the Congregational Church in Openshaw. Ethel was born on 10 April 1882, the daughter of William and Elizabeth Seddon, and one of seven children. The family had strong railway connections. Her grandfather had been an engine driver on the Manchester, Sheffield and Lincolnshire Railway, the line on which her father became a ticket clerk.[12] Their first child, Marjorie, was born on 12 March 1909.

Three years later, the family was on the move. At this time, the town of Huddersfield, twenty-two miles north-east of Manchester, was prospering. Dominated by the fabric industry, by the early twentieth century it had a 'global reputation for the manufacture of fine woollen and worsted cloth'.[13] This industry had, in turn, encouraged the growth of others linked to it, including a chemical industry in which L.B. Holliday and Company was dominant, and an engineering sector that developed machine-making to diversify into a range of products.[14] It was in a related industry, in nearby Colne Valley, that Herbert secured a job in 1912 that took him away from Manchester: running the explosives department at John W. Leitch and Company in Milnsbridge. When the First World War broke out in 1914, the demand for incendiary devices soared, and Herbert prospered: 'His salary, paid monthly by cheque, compared favourably with the weekly wages earned by local engineering workers . . . who were paid according to time.'[15]

This had two major consequences for his family. The first was the decision to have a second child: Harold was born on 11 March 1916 in the two-up, two-down terraced house the family were renting: 4 Warneford Road, Cowlersley, in the Colne Valley, three miles south-west of Huddersfield. The second was that, the following year, the Wilson family could afford to buy a house: 40 Western Road, Milnsbridge, a semi-detached property with a garden, less than a mile away. Herbert also secured a pay rise with a new job at L.B. Holliday, again in charge of a department, but this time it was back to dyestuffs. His starting salary of £425 was, for the time, considerable: 'He still regarded himself as lower middle-class, but always described himself as "working class" to Tory friends.' While he was doing well, Herbert retained a social conscience. After the war ended in 1918, he felt bitter about what he regarded as the betrayal of the aims of Prime Minister David Lloyd George and his colleagues.[16] Any positive feelings towards the Liberal Party that had worked with the Labour Party before the war in multi-member constituencies, and which had been the Conservatives' main competitors for power in general elections before the war, were extinguished. Herbert, expecting Lloyd George's promise of 'homes fit for heroes' to be fulfilled, was 'greatly shocked by social injustice, especially the bad housing conditions ... spreading unemployment and the constant attempts to cut down wages ... Henceforth he was a full-blooded supporter of the Labour Party.'[17]

In 1920, as Lloyd George, then in his fourth year as prime minister, grappled with multiple domestic and international political problems, the young Harold Wilson began his formal education. At the age of four, he started at New Street Elementary School, Milnsbridge, within walking distance of home. His early memories were not positive: 'Every one of us, boys and girls, were terrified of the class mistress, who was head of the infants department. Looking back on it I would have to conclude that Miss Oddy was either an incompetent teacher or a sadist, probably both.' Her mode of teaching involved leaving the class at lunchtime to each write the longest word they knew on the blackboard: given his future roles in the civil service, party politics and government, it was appropriate that the word Wilson remembered writing was 'committee'. He never forgot his unhappiness. Decades later he still concluded: 'It was a miserable year'.[18]

Wilson's ability stood out at a very early stage. He was top of the class: 'Two things in particular aided him in achieving this supremacy. One was his prodigious reading ability, and the other his intense interest in every subject. He thoroughly enjoyed school work, and astonished and delighted his teachers by his apparently effortless ability to learn and remember every thing.'[19] These were talents Wilson drew on throughout his working life. Wilson's progress at school was not, however, entirely smooth. A lengthy break from his education came when he had an operation for appendicitis and he missed the term from Christmas 1923 to Easter in 1924.

The surgery itself took place on the day of the 1923 general election, 6 December: 'That evening my parents came to see me in hospital as I came round from the anaesthetic. As they lingered, I kept urging them to leave so that they would be in time to vote for Philip – my hero Philip Snowden.'[20] That Snowden was so admired by the young Wilson is unsurprising. He was a Yorkshireman, born in Cowling, and, since 1922, he had been the local MP for Colne Valley. Victor Grayson, the firebrand socialist orator, had been elected for the same constituency at a 1907 by-election, but he had lost the seat before Wilson was born. Snowden was to go on to be Labour's first chancellor of the exchequer, first in 1924, and then from 1929 until 1931, when the second Labour government fell. Snowden was to follow the first Labour prime minister, Ramsay MacDonald, in abandoning the party and joining the National Government. At this point, though, Snowden was a Labour pioneer, and undoubtedly influenced Wilson in his ambition to emulate him and become chancellor himself.[21] This said, Snowden and Wilson were very different characters. According to Wilson, though they both identified strongly as Yorkshiremen, he found it 'difficult to tabulate our common characteristics. A judicious calm perhaps . . . never coming to hurried conclusions.' Wilson said he never lost his temper unless it was for effect.[22]

A shared sense of pride in regional heritage was, however, a strong bond. Wilson felt his Yorkshire background gave rise to an 'intense feeling of family loyalty . . . reinforced in my younger days by regular chapel-going and a sense of community which found expression in countless voluntary organisations. We also have a capacity for protracted hard work, and a sturdy and uncomplaining defiance of setbacks that afflicted too many livelihoods.' History mattered: 'By tradition we were solid dyers and weavers of wool. We [Yorkists] used to look down on the Lancastrians on the other side of the Pennines because their staple was cotton, a weak yarn compared with wool. Our chief joy was to beat them at cricket . . .' The Wars of the Roses might have ended in 1485, but local rivalry remained strong: 'We were happy that the conflict continued in our favour.'[23] Huddersfield Town Football Club was also in the ascendant, winning three English top division league titles in succession from 1923 to 1926. Two of these, and the Football Association Cup of 1922, were secured under legendary manager Herbert Chapman; Wilson became a lifelong fan. Going to watch a home game was a weekly treat. As prime minister, making small talk with his officials, he often turned to tales of the footballing exploits of his beloved white-and-blue Terriers.[24]

None of this, however, is to explain what made Wilson tick. To understand that, it is necessary to consider the whole atmosphere of his childhood, and the values that shaped him. First, there was religious conviction. Herbert and Ethel were committed Congregationalists, a denomination of Protestant dissenters with local groups of believers asserting autonomy without hierarchy: 'that principle of church polity according to which the unit of sovereignty in church government is the individual congregation of Christian disciples meeting habitually for worship and fellowship'.[25] Central to this was the idea of the 'priesthood of believers' with every member of the church an equal, with the knowledge and power to make a difference. Helping others was crucial: 'The crowning glory of the Story of the Congregationalists is the record of what they have done . . . for the glory of God in the service of his creatures.'[26] There was no local chapel, so the Wilsons attended the Milnsbridge Baptist church. Yet they continued to live in the Congregationalist tradition. Central to the Wilson family conception of what faith meant in practice was, firstly, personal morality, and Wilson always remained a social conservative with a strong sense of right and wrong. Equally important was helping others through wider community work. Herbert and Ethel were both Sunday school teachers; Herbert ran the church amateur operatic society and Ethel founded the local Women's Guild. Faith in and of itself was personal and understated. In his political career, Wilson rarely gave speeches of high moral principle but instead sought to use his skills to achieve the result he wanted. It was not that he practised what he preached, for he was not given to preaching; rather, he got on with the job of securing the best possible outcome in the circumstances he faced.

It is in this context that Wilson's passion for the Boy Scout movement should be viewed. Founded in 1908 by Robert Baden-Powell with the publication of *Scouting for Boys*, the Scout movement spread through the British Empire. The Scouts' motto 'Be prepared' could be applied to Wilson's careful approach to his progress throughout his life, but it was the combination of a duty to God with practical action that perfectly summed up the principles imbued in him during his youth. Duty and honour are at the core of the Scout movement. Peter Duncan, chief scout of the UK from 2004 to 2009, captured this: 'Scouts were encouraged to live their lives by a code of honour. In doing their duty to God, to themselves and, in particular, to other people, the first Scouts set themselves apart from their peers.'[27]

Wilson joined the Wolf Cubs as soon as he was eligible, at the age of eight. His family threw themselves into it: Herbert, and, later, Marjorie, became district commissioners; Ethel became a Guide captain, and Wilson himself became a King's Scout. He enjoyed camping, and, in the band, he played the triangle and side drum. As a patrol leader, planning activities and taking the lead in ceremonies, Wilson was able to demonstrate a sense of responsibility and his ability to be a role model for others. Decades later, in 1963, a few weeks after Wilson had been elected Labour Party leader he spoke as chief guest at the Scout Commissioners' Dinner in London, and declared that the Scout movement inspired moral purpose, and its values gave people 'elemental truths which, once absorbed, were never forgotten throughout their whole lifetime'.[28]

Christianity and scouting reinforced each other, not least through the figure of W.H. Potter, who was minister of the Baptist church and group scoutmaster. Widely respected, he extolled the virtues of living a life following Christian principles, and closed meetings with a prayer. He inspired loyalty; Wilson and his fellow scouts wanted to please him as much for who he was as for his moralistic approach. When Wilson was president of the Board of Trade in Attlee's post-war Labour government, in 1948, he spoke at Milnsbridge on the anniversary of the Baptist Church Sunday school, and declared: 'Nobody should be in a political party unless he believes that party does represent his own highest religious and moral ideals.'[29] In 1962, Wilson put this in a slightly different way when he addressed the Labour Party conference: 'No socialist party can ever be satisfied with an electoral victory based on a mere swing against the Government. This party is a moral crusade or it is nothing.'[30]

Wilson's parents also found time away from scouting to broaden his horizons. While his mother and sister were away at a summer Guide camp in 1924, his father took him away for a break to London on his motorcycle and sidecar. They stayed at a bed and breakfast in Russell Square and saw the sights. Wilson looked at Big Ben through a pavement telescope and went to Downing Street, where Herbert took a photograph of him outside Number Ten's black door that was to become so famous in later years when Wilson moved in as prime minister. In 1926, he went with his mother to Australia for six months – an incredible experience for any ten-year-old, particularly in the 1920s, when long-haul travel was not commonplace. The Seddon family had emigrated: William had sought a warmer climate to help with his breathing problems. Had his mother not remained behind, a consequence of her engagement, Wilson, as he told Gough Whitlam seven decades later, could have had his job as Australian prime minister. When news came through that Ethel's father was mortally ill, Herbert insisted his wife go to Perth, and she left on HMS *Temperance Bay*, one of the five ships owned by the nationalised Australian Commonwealth government shipping line.[31]

Wilson soaked up knowledge, remembering every aspect of what he saw and experienced, preparing a lecture, filling a school notebook, and writing numerous articles. He was always fascinated by detail. He visited Mundaring Weir, a dam on the River Helena just over twenty miles from Perth. He noted that the pipe laid from there to the gold-mining centre of Kalgoorlie, 300 miles away, was 'six inches in diameter and withstood pressure of 400 pounds to the square inch'.[32] Politics was not far away, either: Wilson saw his uncle – also called Harold, his mother's brother – become a member of the Legislative Council of Western Australia. On his return home, Wilson delivered his lecture to every class in Milnsbridge.

He was a brilliant pupil, and won a scholarship to Royds Hall (Grammar) School in Huddersfield, where he started in September 1927. There he flourished, not only academically, but by throwing himself into extra-curricular activity with varying degrees of success: as an unexceptional goalkeeper for his form's football team and using his 'shrill treble voice' in the school choir. Wilson was nothing if not determined: '. . . behind the piping shrillness lay a staunch effort to overcome the inadequacy he felt. His toughest ordeal had come at an evening service at the Baptist Church, when he had to sing a solo at the age of eleven.'[33] He was a student of prodigious energy: as an actor, he won 'high praise' for his portrayal of Shylock in William Shakespeare's *The Merchant of Venice* and 'in the school production of *She Stoops to Conquer*, he stole the show'. After a quiet performance on the first night, Wilson was advised to be more demonstrative. Accepting this advice, he showed an early ability to perform and make his audience laugh. In Oliver Goldsmith's comedy, he 'took his part with gusto, in fast over-acting in places . . . He was very amusing . . .'[34]

In the summer of 1928, Herbert and Ethel took Wilson on a holiday to Scotland. At Stirling, Herbert took Wilson to see the statue of his own political hero, Sir Henry Campbell-Bannerman, MP for the Stirling Burghs, and Liberal prime minister from 1905 to 1908. It was under Campbell-Bannerman that the pre-war New Liberal reforms began that started to establish the welfare state, including free school meals. Yet it was another aspect of Campbell-Bannerman's leadership that piqued Wilson's interest. He remembered his 'tour of obeisance' to the statue and

Campbell-Bannerman's emphasis on holding his party together: 'Perhaps no one but Campbell-Bannerman could have kept his party in a state of even nominal unity through the Boer War, and the period persisted right up to and after the Liberal landslide [of 1906] . . .' Wilson saw this as essential to the achievements of the Liberals in government, and to the wider progressive cause in the twentieth century.[35] The importance of promoting unity was a lesson he learned at a young age.

Back in school at Royds Hall, Wilson completed an essay, 'Myself in 25 Years', by describing an interview between the chancellor of the exchequer and a reporter about a budget. He was convinced he would reach 11 Downing Street, and it was not long before he started telling his friends he could also see himself next door, summarising his ambition pithily: 'I should like to be Prime Minister.'[36] It was a grand ambition, and, to show the part that chance would play in whether it was achieved, Wilson became seriously ill. In his fourth year, he contracted typhoid from a glass of milk he had drunk from a local farm while on a scout trip. He spent thirteen weeks in the Colne and Holme Joint Isolation Hospital, near Meltham, some five miles from home. There were over a dozen cases of typhoid there causing six deaths. Wilson, living on boiled milk and water, pulled through.

It was a tough time for the family. Herbert lost his job at L.B. Holliday while his son was in hospital and endured a miserable two-year period without work, relying on savings to survive. Until the debate on appeasement prompted by the rise of fascism in the 1930s, unemployment was the dominant issue in British politics, and it had a profound impact on the teenage Wilson. For a family so involved in the local community, it was a chastening, humiliating experience. The memory of it clouded the future prime minister's life: 'For years I never forgave myself for asking my father at some scout function in Wakefield if I could have 3s.6d. to buy a sheath knife. I still remember his expression and his words: "I can't just now – you know how things are."'[37] Later, Wilson identified 'Unemployment more than anything else' as what made him politically aware.[38] He saw his father's continuous, yet fruitless, search for work and the impact it had on his family. His sister Marjorie had progressed through her education from New Street Council School, Milnsbridge, to Greenhead High School and then Leeds University.[39] But she then failed her exams – in chemistry – and it is difficult to conclude that the situation at home did not have an adverse effect on her performance, and her having to abandon her ambition to follow her father's path in life. Later, as Wilson proudly set out in his memoirs, she turned to teacher training and 'became a gifted children's teacher',[40] but such success was in the future: at the time it was another crushing blow to the Wilson household.

On a positive note, Wilson began to settle down to his education with renewed determination, with his first task to catch up on the two terms he had missed through illness. He looked back with gratitude on his mathematics teacher, F.S. Wilmut, an active supporter of the Huddersfield Labour Party, who remained behind after school-time for half an hour each day to help him catch up on geometry and algebra. Wilson thought the arrangement a great success: 'The cramming worked and I was a willing pupil. No one was more pleased than he when I received a distinction in the School Certificates examination.'[41] More good news was to follow: in late 1932, Herbert Wilson finally found another job, as chief chemist at Brotherton's Chemical Works on the Wirral. That November, the Wilson family left Colne Valley and moved to live in a company flat, the ground floor of a Victorian period house on Spital Road in the town of Bromborough, south of Birkenhead, over sixty miles from Huddersfield.

Harold Wilson always remained a provincial figure. He had an instinctive feel for what voters across the country, away from Westminster, were thinking, and that arose from his background in a northern town. He always had the sense of being an outsider as well, caused by moving from one place to another. Wilson's biographer Leslie Smith, writing in the 1960s, wrote: 'In a town of textile workers like Milnsbridge . . . [the Wilson family were] . . . regarded as slightly apart, being relative newcomers to the district . . . The feeling of being newcomers faded only gradually as the years passed.'[42] The uprooting of the Wilson family was necessitated by the search for work: that unemployment was a social evil was seared on his mind. He understood the importance of local, quality jobs and the dignity that came with employment. The moves also gave him a sense of detachment: the ability to observe a scene, understand the personalities, and develop a strategy to achieve an outcome.

The crucial choice for Wilson was his next school. On the advice of Herbert's brother Jack, who had been HM Inspector of Technical Colleges, Wilson, now sixteen, was sent to Wirral Grammar School. Founded only a year before, in 1931, Jack's feeling was the staff there had 'got their name to make'. He was right: the school was staffed by ambitious young teachers. With the exception of the headteacher, none was over thirty years old. Wilson also had the unique advantage of being the school's first, and sole, sixth-former, with the individual attention that came with it. In the post-16 education system as it then existed, Wilson chose History, with English and French, as subjects to be taken at 'principal level'; at 'subsidiary level' he chose Latin and Maths. Wilson later reflected that he had pushed to do Maths as he wanted to study economics. His interests were developing. History was his passion, and he was inspired by his teacher, Mr P.L. Norrish, a Devonian who pushed Wilson from his comfort zone of nineteenth-century history, which he had previously studied, to learning about the seventeenth century.[43] At home, the Wilsons read the *Manchester Guardian*: 'We had taken it in our family from the time of my grandfather's arrival in Manchester in 1860, and it was a matter of family pride that we were in part descended from the Taylors of Radcliffe, Lancashire, who were among the paper's founders.'[44]

Another favourite teacher was Frank Allen, senior classics master, who had a great influence: 'He had more effect on my political development in my later school years than anyone else. He was a Socialist, and a pacifist I would think . . .'[45] Allen took Wilson to hear Sir Norman Angell speaking at Birkenhead after he had been awarded the Nobel Peace Prize in 1933. The international landscape was changing dramatically that year with Adolf Hitler appointed German chancellor on 30 January. Angell's theory, expressed in his book *The Great Illusion*, seemed more important than ever. Angell's argument was that the interconnected nature of the world meant that the idea that one state invading another with military force made the aggressor country richer was a fantasy: '. . . the conqueror is unable to take the wealth of a conquered territory, owing to the delicate interdependence of the financial world (an outcome of our credit and banking systems), which makes the financial and industrial security of the victor dependent upon financial and industrial security in all considerable civilized centres; so that widespread confiscation or destruction of trade and commerce in a conquered territory would react disastrously upon the conqueror.'[46] Angell had also been a founder member of the Union of Democratic Control in 1914 that was convinced the cause of the war was a lack of democratic influence on international norms. MacDonald had been a leading light. Wilson was fascinated by Angell: 'His speech made a more lasting impression on me than anything else I heard over the years.'[47] As prime minister, Wilson, though never a pacifist, certainly had a reluctance to commit troops to actions abroad. Allen also inspired Wilson's lifelong love of the D'Oyly Carte Opera Company, which staged Gilbert and Sullivan Savoy Operas around the country and internationally.

Allen had a further influence on Wilson, too. He was a fine cricketer and the school games coach.[48] Now fully recovered physically after his typhoid scare, Wilson threw himself into sport at Wirral Grammar. The rugby involved a change of code: from the rugby league of Huddersfield to rugby union. It was a culture shock at first. It was not the '"Kick him, he's still breathing" rugby league game I had often played . . . As the biggest boy around I was directed into the forward line and in the scrum I was penalized a number of times for tactics that would have won acclaim in the thirteen-a-side version of the game.'[49] Wilson found athletics more to his liking, winning the Wirral Athletics Club's Junior Cross Country Championship, and captaining the Wirral junior team in the Merseyside Championships. He had the build for it: he was light, with a long stride.[50]

Wilson also delivered his first public speech at Wirral Grammar

School's prize-giving at the Hulme Hall building in Port Sunlight in December 1933. Named after its 'Sunlight Soap' product, this was a model village built by Lever Brothers to accommodate soap-factory workers for a new works, expanding from its existing Warrington site. The guest of honour, Brigadier General Sir Harold Hartley, an expert in physical chemistry who later went into industry, was then an academic at Balliol College, Oxford. He commented that 'This young man's speech showed great promise' on account of its factual content and touches of humour.[51] Mastery of detail and wit were to become features of Wilson's speeches in later life, and Wirral Grammar undoubtedly had a formative influence, but he always remained a Yorkshireman.

As time passed at Wirral Grammar, another great influence in Wilson's life began to loom into view: Oxford University, where he was to read for a degree at Jesus College from 1934. On one level, Jesus College was an unusual destination for Wilson. It was closely associated with Wales, with historic endowments funding scholarships and exhibitions reserved for students from the Principality.[52] Wilson's application had arisen because Oxford colleges were grouped for the purposes of admissions: if there were insufficient places for the number of suitable candidates at one college, surplus students could be moved to another college within the set. Wilson had applied to a group of six colleges led by Merton College. His headteacher, James Moir, who was something of an intellectual snob, decided that his star pupil, Wilson, should apply for a place at Oxford on an Open Scholarship. Surprisingly, perhaps, Wilson's teacher Mr Norrish was against this, on the basis that he thought that if Wilson did badly, it would count against him in a future application. After all, Wilson was applying during his second year at Wirral Grammar School, a year earlier than he needed to, the proper time in the education system of the 1930s being after the third year when he would have received his Higher School Certificate. Eventually, Norrish relented, and facilitated a few days of revision for Wilson before he went up for interview.

As with many state school Oxford applicants, Wilson later identified an element of chance in making a good impression on his interviewer, Norrish once again playing a significant role: 'It had been my good fortune that my history master was himself working for a London University external degree, writing a thesis on Robert Spencer, third Earl of Sunderland . . . and he used to borrow the relevant books by post from some university library.'[53] Spencer is an ancestor of both Winston Churchill and Princess Diana; Charles II, King from 1660 to 1685, had been on the throne when he was born in 1675. Wilson remembered a point about Charles II but could not recall where he had read it. About to leave the interview, he suddenly remembered the author, and the conversation continued for a further ten minutes, when he was convinced he made a favourable impression. On the following Monday, a proud Herbert and Ethel opened their *Manchester Guardian* to discover that their son had been offered a £60 Open Exhibition to read Modern History at Jesus College.

There was still a problem, since the estimated cost of living at Oxford, taking into account the need for board and lodging, was £300 per year. Wilson had a £240 shortfall to make up. Norrish got cold feet again, thinking Wilson should remain at school for a further year. It was Moir who intervened, and spoke to the county education authorities to press for more money for Wilson, who had missed out on a more lucrative county scholarship. A dozen had been awarded and Wilson had been placed tenth on the list, but, since at least three had to go to girls and the top nine were boys, he had not qualified. Moir succeeded, and Wilson was awarded a grant. Herbert did all he could too, and Brotherton's increased his salary by a couple of pounds a week so he could assist. When Wilson later won prizes at Oxford, it not only made his parents proud, it also vindicated Moir, who, remembering the efforts he had had to make, telephoned the county authorities and said, 'Will you [just] listen to me next time?'[54]

The chance of an Oxbridge education, with all the transformative effect that had, was accompanied by another change that was to dramatically alter Wilson's personal life. During his Higher School Certificate examinations Wilson met Gladys Mary Baldwin. Given that another of his life's loves was to be statistics, it was fitting that they met as a consequence of a bet on numbers. Wilson was seeking a break from revising with a visit to a local tennis club to watch his father compete. The match was not, however, of the type that involved a racquet. Rather, his father's remarkable gift for mental arithmetic was being tested. Herbert could – within a matter of seconds – multiply two numbers of up to five digits each. When the senior chemist at rival firm Lever Brothers reacted with disbelief that anyone could do this, a five-shilling wager was offered, to be settled at the tennis club. Herbert duly answered five questions within fifteen seconds each, and the bet was won. For Wilson himself, the event offered more than entertainment and vindication for his father. He saw his future wife playing tennis. His gift for finding a strategic route to a particular objective was already in evidence as he purchased a racquet and joined the club. Within a week, he and Mary were, as he put it, 'walking out'.[55] He later told his friend, the journalist Ernest Kay, that it was truly love at first sight: 'She looked lovely in white. It was in the summer of 1934. We met regularly and we became engaged just three weeks after our very first meeting.'[56]

Mary – as she became known later, ending the use of the first name 'Gladys' – was from Diss, a small market town in Norfolk, where she had been born on 12 January 1916.[57] Her father, Rev. Daniel Baldwin, was the Congregationalist minister there. Like Wilson, her childhood had involved moving home on more than one occasion. First, the family moved to Cambridgeshire, then on to Nottinghamshire. There, she became ill, before being sent away to the now-closed Milton Mount College, a boarding school at Worth Park, near Crawley, founded for the purpose of educating the daughters of Congregationalist ministers. Her father, meanwhile, moved on to Penrith in the Lake District in Cumbria. Mary left school in 1932. She did not think her parents could afford to send her to university, so she instead spent two years learning shorthand and typing. Forced to move to find work, she secured employment as a typist at the Lever Brothers works in Port Sunlight.

A committed Congregationalist like Wilson, Mary attended the same church as him on Sundays, at nearby Rockferry, but they had not met as he and his sister Marjorie had been frequenting the morning service, she the evening. If their faith was what they had in common, they were temperamentally very different. Mary's passion was poetry: she was a private person, not drawn to the public life that was Wilson's aim. Wilson reflected that, had she genuinely thought he would achieve his ambitions in life, she might have run away at the start. It was 4 July 1934, the day King George V opened the Mersey Tunnel. Wilson was eighteen, and he told Mary he was going to become an MP, and then prime minister.[58] Fortunately for him, Mary thought that this was unlikely to happen.

Chapter 2

Owed it to his family to be a success

Oxford and Beveridge, 1934–42

Harold Wilson arrived at Jesus College, Oxford, in October 1934 with great opportunities in front of him. His commitment was crucial to his success at Oxford, as he put in the hours needed to excel. He later judged that it was when he 'speedily learnt what hard work meant'.[1] College life transformed Wilson from a student of great potential into an academic of the highest rank, as he achieved the top mark across Oxford University in his final examinations in the school of Politics, Philosophy and Economics. It was a stunning achievement for anyone; for the boy from Colne Valley, it was a source of great pride, and he added to it prestigious university prizes that marked him out as one of most gifted scholars of his generation in any field. This, in turn, led to his association with the great social reformer and administrator William Beveridge, and a job in the wartime civil service.

Wilson's phenomenal memory gave him a major advantage over other students: 'He could remember an incredible amount of detail with uncanny accuracy for dates, figures and statistics.'[2] Yet, as with so many of Wilson's achievements in life, determination and adaptability were crucial in allowing him to make the most of his innate ability. He could always learn from his mistakes. His initial attempt to win an award at Oxford ended in failure. When he submitted an essay for the Cecil Peace Prize on the private manufacture of armaments, his 'entry was submitted more in the form of a declamatory sermon than a serious study and brought him no success'.[3] It did not take him long to work out what he needed to do to succeed, under the tutelage of Albert – Bert – Goodwin. Born in Sheffield, he was, like Wilson, a Yorkshire grammar school boy who had won financial assistance, in the form of a scholarship, to Jesus College in 1924. In 1931, he had become a fellow of the college; Wilson was one of his first students. A tall, thin man with horn-rimmed spectacles, he had a deadpan humour and down-to-earth manner.[4] Wilson was inspired to emulate his tutor in another important respect. Goodwin had won the Gladstone Memorial Prize as an undergraduate in 1926 with an essay on the Abbey of St Edmundsbury; Wilson was to win it ten years later. Awarded for a thesis on British history, politics or economics, and established in memory of four-time Victorian era Liberal prime minister William Gladstone, it was, and is, one of the most prestigious academic prizes in universities across the world. Competition to win it is incredibly fierce; no less a historian than A.J.P. Taylor missed out on it in 1929. With a nod to his mother's family, Wilson chose as his subject 'The State and the Railways 1823–63'. Goodwin provided a reading list; Wilson mined the references in the publications to find more and more information. There was a clear link to Gladstone himself, who, as president of the Board of Trade from 1843 to 1845, had piloted through the House of Commons what became the Railway Act 1844. He was attempting to provide co-ordination to the various railways that had been constructed around the country, and reserved the power of nationalisation to the government as an option if private enterprise failed.[5]

Two of the three terms in Wilson's second year were spent producing his 18,000-word essay. The rules specified 12,500 words as the length, but Goodwin told Wilson that meant no more than 18,000: 'an early example of academic inflation' as he later reflected.[6] Utilising Liverpool's Picton Library during vacations, Wilson produced a remarkable piece of work. Tightly structured, and argued with authority, it draws on a wide-ranging bibliography of primary and secondary sources with no fewer than four hundred footnotes. Wilson traces the development of railways back to the early days when everything was left to private enterprise: while this meant that tracks would appear in certain parts of the country, it was no way to produce a national network. This laissez-faire attitude was changed decisively by the Gladstone Act.

Wilson's case was that 'into the unsettled England of the eighteen-twenties the locomotive burst its way, heralding the new industrial order of which it was to form so important a part. It was an answer to the demand of the age, for an efficient means of preserving the new division of labour, between industry and industry, district and district, and in its wider aspect, town and country.' The work of Gladstone at the Board of Trade was seminal: 'It is not because of this reform or that proposal that his work will go down in history, but because he realised that the whole railway question must be considered in its relation to the state.' Wilson observed: 'The railway system was the first privately-owned public utility of its size and importance in this country . . . the tentative policy of the state over the period of railway development was therefore of great importance in determining the attitude of the state to future public utilities, which in the twentieth century have come to play an increasingly important part in national life.' Wilson then drew a broader conclusion about the significance of his research: 'It is a tendency with many people – and politicians are not immune – to regard "history as complete", that is, to think of the present time as unique in world history, and to think that what has been said, and that what has been done in connection with a particular social or economic problem, is all that can be said and done about it. If the study of the growth of the British railway system contributes to the undermining of this tendency, it is well worth while.'[7] A detailed, careful piece of work that was well-argued and pragmatic, recognising the wider significance of particular events, it showcased many of the skills that Wilson relied on in his political career.

It also drove Wilson on to further achievements. Such was the esteem in which the winner of the Gladstone essay prize was held that the award was given on Honorary Degree Day, at which Wilson read a one-page extract from the essay. Among those listening was the then foreign secretary and future prime minister, Anthony Eden. Also there were his parents Herbert and Ethel, together with Mary: an incredibly proud moment for them. Yet Wilson did not rest. Next he secured the George Webb Medley Junior Economic Scholarship, for which he sat an exam in October 1936, at the start of Oxford University's Michaelmas term. He struggled with economic theory but excelled in economic organisation, focusing on the Co-operative movement in Colne Valley: he always preferred practically applied ideas to abstract theory. He opened his first bank account with the £100 prize.[8] Later, he added the Senior Economics Scholarship: he now had the formula for success and made the most of it.

Wilson was also assisted by the change of undergraduate course he made in January 1935. Oxford University degrees required the passing of two sets of examinations. For Wilson, the preliminary examination was taken at the end of his first term, then his final examinations ('Finals') at the end of his third year in 1937. On arrival at Oxford, his economics set books included the future Labour chancellor of the exchequer Hugh Dalton's *Public Finance* and he had to grapple with heavy Latin set texts. His ferocious work ethic carried him through, and, by December 1934, as he contemplated what his interests were for the next two years, he was seriously considering swapping subjects. Philosophy, Politics and Economics (PPE) was known as 'Modern Greats'. Founded in 1921, it was to become the quintessential Oxford degree, with its students going on to senior positions in the professions, politics, government, and public life in Britain and across the world. With his political ambitions and passion for economics, it seemed an ideal choice for Wilson. Oxford did not offer the opportunity to study economics on its own, only in combination with other subjects. PPE allowed him to develop his interest in economics while also giving him the chance to continue his study of history through the politics section of the course: 'Not least because of my political ambitions I wanted to go on to read economics, which in the Oxford of those days meant a Final Honours course called Philosophy, Politics and Economics (PPE). But of course my scholarship was in history.'[9]

The college principal at the time, Alfred Hazel, whose permission Wilson needed to make the change, was a lawyer who had held a parliamentary seat for four years, having been elected in the Liberal Party landslide of 1906. While sympathetic to Wilson's request, he and the other college dons made the switch conditional upon Wilson passing an examination in German at the start of Oxford's Hilary term after the Christmas holiday. That was because PPE required its entrants to pass two languages; Wilson had French but no other. Over the festive season he worked away at unseen German texts before scraping through the examination itself: in itself a piece of luck as Goodwin gave him a paper he had already completed with the help of a dictionary as part of his preparation. Wilson learned from the scare, and wisely switched to Italian, which he found much easier to learn, building on his Latin and French.

Alongside the pressures of work Wilson had to cope with being away from home for extended periods in a way he had not done previously: a common issue for state school students at Oxford who have not been to private boarding schools. He shared a room with a Welsh Foundation Scholar, A.H.J. Thomas from Tenby, who met with his approval. Thomas' father was a plumber, and, like Wilson, he had a distinct accent. Wilson wrote home: 'He is an exceptionally nice fellow and we get on well. We seem to have similar tastes – both keen on running, neither on smoking or drinking and have similar views on food.' His experience at Scout camps at least gave him some practice of managing his affairs independently, and he busied himself with the laundry and other domestic chores.[10] He kept up his participation in sport, including football and tennis, and maintained his passion for athletics, running regularly on the famous Iffley Road track where Roger Bannister was to run the first sub-four-minute mile in 1954. Wilson was never close to achieving a 'Blue' – a place in the Varsity team – but he did manage a creditable seventh place in a field of sixteen for the second Varsity team in a competition against Reading Athletics Club.

Wilson's work-hard, play-hard approach was not unusual in Oxford, but he was not someone who also built a network of contacts for use in later life. His later political opponents and colleagues Edward Heath, Denis Healey and Roy Jenkins took full advantage of the Oxford social scene at Balliol College, as did the likes of Richard Crossman, Hugh Gaitskell and Douglas Jay at New College. Wilson focused on his academic work. One reason for this was his background. His loyalty was to his parents: he knew the sacrifices they had made to give him the opportunity to study at Oxford, and he never wanted to let them down. Eric Sharpe, a future Baptist minister, who lived in a room beneath Wilson's in his first year at Oxford, observed: 'he felt he owed it to his family to be a success'.[11]

That is not to say Wilson remained a total outsider to student politics. Once he had finished his very intense first term and moved across to PPE, he started to attend party meetings on a regular basis. First, he tried the Oxford University Labour Club, but was unimpressed: 'What I felt I could not stomach was all those Marxist public school products rambling on about exploited workers and the need for a socialist revolution.' Wilson – even in retirement – continued to claim that he had never read Marx, and said that when he purported to quote him in trade discussions with leaders of the Soviet Union, he was making it up! When nobody noticed, Wilson assumed any inaccuracies were blamed on translation issues.[12] Wilson was always impatient with those who would put their own desire for ideological purity above the need for realistic, practical action to improve people's lives.

Nonetheless, his next political move raised questions: becoming a member of the Liberal Club, where he met Frank Byers, later a Liberal MP.[13] Byers served as president, with Wilson as treasurer. Some commentators have used this to claim that Wilson was never a true Labour tribalist and that he really *was* a Liberal. The journalist Paul Foot advanced this view in an assessment of Wilson published in 1968, when his premiership was at a low point: 'The moral force of Campbell-Bannerman, the grandeur of Gladstone, the electoral weakness of the Labour Party, even after 1935, the Marxism of the Labour Club, which absorbed the communist October Club in December 1935, the facts of parliamentary life as taught by Mr McCallum – all these combined to maintain Harold Wilson's Liberal allegiances.'[14] R.B. McCallum was a politics don at Pembroke College who had taught Wilson political institutions in his final two years as an undergraduate, and the *Manchester Guardian*'s Oxford correspondent. He wrote to Foot identifying two important aspects of Wilson's views as expressed in tutorials: '. . . the moral force (I suppose it would now be called charismatic) of Campbell-Bannerman . . . [and] . . . I probably drew his attention to the case for specialist committees in the House of Commons . . . .'[15] Wilson had already paid homage to the statue of the Liberal prime minister, as a boy, and was fascinated by detail: that he was intrigued by the mechanics of government scrutiny in the House of Commons is no surprise. Yet such points do not explain why Wilson was drawn to the Liberal Club. One of Wilson's critical biographers, Dudley Smith, wrote that he had 'joined the Liberal Club hoping, no doubt, to convert the faithfuls to Socialism. He was unsuccessful – his art of persuasion had still not reached a sufficiently high state of professionalism.'[16] Wilson himself was honest in his own assessment: 'Ignorance and vanity persuaded me that I might convert them to a middle-of-the road Colne Valley standpoint. I failed . . .'[17]

Yet it would be wrong to suggest Wilson's politics was only about pragmatism. His interest in the battle of ideas found expression in regular discussion classes that he attended with G.D.H. Cole. Cole linked the intellectual base of politics with its frontline: an economics don at University College when Wilson met him, he had also served on the National Economic Advisory Council set up by MacDonald's second Labour government. Cole was a thin, bird-like, all-knowing, slightly eccentric academic. His nephew, Oliver Postgate, created the children's television animation *Bagpuss*, in which the character of the wooden woodpecker, Professor Yaffle, was based partly on his uncle.[18]

Wilson thoroughly enjoyed sitting in Cole's room in groups of eight to ten students, smoking and talking about great intellectual questions. Cole's socialism had strong elements in common with Wilson's, most obviously the distrust of Marxism. There were differences: Cole was a guild socialist who believed in workers themselves controlling industry, which would be organised in trade-related 'guilds'. He argued that this was not 'purely Utopian, but constructive and practical.'[19] Wilson did not agree, but remained persuaded of the power of the state to intervene in the economy, not least because of the issue of unemployment, which he felt in a very personal sense.

The defining feature of Wilson's undergraduate years was, in any event, his remarkable academic achievement. He secured the top overall mark in PPE Finals. Until recent years, Oxford used a grading system based on the Greek alphabet, with an alpha mark as the top level. Wilson was awarded seventeen alpha or alpha-minus marks, and a 'beta ?plus plus plus'. In economic theory, he achieved the first-ever alpha-plus mark in PPE Finals.[20] Typically, it was for a quantitative analysis: a geometric diagram had to be used as a proof, rather than an analysis of abstract ideas. As with so many Wilson accomplishments, others sought to offer less than charitable reasons for his success. One of the examiners, Maurice Allen, said his papers were unoriginal and that he played to the views of the dons who he knew were marking specific papers.[21] The allegation that he was cunning was never far from Wilson, even at this early stage. But this analysis does not bear great scrutiny. He may well have researched the interests and views of those dons who would consider his answers. Propounding arguments on an academic's specialist field carries risk, though: they will, almost inevitably, know more about that area than any student – even one as brilliant as Wilson. It is not credible to suggest that so many high marks came about because Wilson repeatedly gave the arguments of his markers back to them. There is a much simpler explanation: he had comprehensive knowledge for every paper, the ability to apply it to the particular question set, and the critical skills to provide in-depth analysis of the academic debate under timed conditions.

His euphoria was, unfortunately, short-lived as he received the news that his father had lost his job at Brotherton's. Herbert was to endure another period of unemployment, this time for eighteen months, before securing a job as a supervisor at an explosives manufacturer in Liskeard in Cornwall, a 300-mile journey from the Wirral, and another place to which the Wilsons would be incomers with no prior links, reinforcing Wilson's sense of being slightly apart from the community. Though his Webb Medley Junior Scholarship offered £300 per year, Wilson could not take it for granted that he would win, so, in 1937, he applied for a job as a journalist at the *Manchester Guardian*. McCallum provided the recommendation for him to the editor William P. Crozier. Wilson was offered a temporary holiday job with a view to something permanent, but turned it down as soon as news came through that he had secured the Webb Medley. Wilson immediately set about paying back his parents for all their support by helping with the rent on the Brotherton's company flat that they still occupied despite Herbert ceasing his employment with the firm. This support continued when his father moved to Cornwall, with his mother joining him on a permanent basis in 1939.

Wilson's academic performance was outstanding, but he was also in the right place at the right time that summer. Beveridge had just taken over as master of University College, having left the London School of Economics (LSE). He asked two other former lecturers at LSE, now at Oxford, to recommend a research assistant: Wilson was their stand-out choice. Beveridge's ambition was sweeping. In February 1936, John Maynard Keynes had published his *General Theory of Employment, Interest and Money*. Beveridge was unimpressed as he regarded Keynes as a theorist, so he responded with his *Analysis of Unemployment*: as he put it, 'an example of studying unemployment by observations and not by concepts.'[22] Now, Beveridge wanted to 'begin applying the same procedure to the Trade Cycle, the mysterious alternation between boom and depression which dominated economic life till World War II.'[23] He thought highly of Wilson, whom he described as a '. . . first-rate research student doing just what I am going about saying all research students should do: that is, working on a problem that I want solved and on which I am working myself, in place of writing a thesis to please himself.'[24] Wilson did register a title for a doctoral thesis: 'Aspects of the Demand for Labour in Great Britain'. He never completed it, though he did try to pursue an academic career.

On two occasions, he applied to Oxford's All Souls' College. Founded in 1438, All Souls has no undergraduates; rather, Oxford graduates and postgraduates compete for the prestigious fellowships. Had he succeeded, Wilson would have had a quiet but challenging academic life. In 1937, after Finals, he applied by sitting an examination. He completed a history paper and lunched with another candidate, Arthur Brown, who recalled: 'Harold scared me by talking all the time about his answers to the questions on this morning's history paper'.[25] Brown secured a fellowship; Wilson did not. The following year, 1938, Wilson tried again, this time via the method of submitting a thesis. Wilson sent in his Gladstone prize-winning essay. Again, he failed. Given the level of competition, Wilson's failure is not as surprising as it may seem. But it did hurt him. He did not speak of it in public, and he did not mention anything about it in his own published works. Perhaps his style was too formulaic; perhaps it was the case that others simply displayed more effective analytical skills. Either way, All Souls was not for him. It clearly rankled: when it came to his autobiography and writing about his academic career, it is not even mentioned.[26]

In contrast, the Beveridge approach of gathering voluminous facts was, on the face of it, ideally suited to him. With his love of numbers, he should have been his element, assisting Beveridge in seeking to explain why economies moved between phases of boom and slump using a statistical analysis of changes since 1870. His personality and mode of working was, however, less congenial to Wilson. While Beveridge, with his long nose, white hair and neat suits, had the look of a wise uncle, he had an extraordinary self-assurance and was a difficult person to manage. Wilson thought he was 'a devil to work for'.[27] Kingsley Martin, editor of the *New Statesman*, described Beveridge as a 'despot who resented criticism'.[28]

Beveridge, who had been an assistant commissioner helping Sidney and Beatrice Webb on the royal commission on the Poor Law from 1906 to 1909, had ingrained views. He thought that there was no army of people 'genuinely seeking work'. Wilson disproved this by visiting labour exchanges and poring over the vacancy records. He found that the issue was not that unemployed people were failing to obtain work; rather, the statistics showed that fewer than one in twenty of advertised vacancies actually led to a job.[29] This ability to challenge an argument using facts was a major strength of Wilson's, and gave him the confidence to stand up to the self-assured Beveridge.

In the long four-month Oxford summer vacation, Beveridge gave Wilson three weeks' holiday before settling into his exhausting routine at his Wiltshire cottage in Avebury. Beveridge started the day with a cold swim, then roused Wilson at seven o'clock with a cup of tea before they began work in a crammed room above a barn, with two hours completed before breakfast. If that was stifling, worse still was Beveridge's cousin Jessie Mair who was also at the house: 'Where Beveridge was difficult to live with, she was almost impossible,' Wilson recalled.[30] She was an intimidating presence, and Wilson was left having to partner her at bridge every evening, being subjected to her ferocious assessment after each hand.

Wilson sought solace in teaching. He was recommended for a lecturing post at New College and notched up another remarkable academic achievement: he was an Oxford don at the age of twenty-one. Great ability doesn't necessarily equate to fine teaching quality, but Wilson flourished in the role. Teaching at such a young age brings challenges. Students are closer in age than academic colleagues, meaning that authority needs to be established quickly.[31] His first pupil was someone who was the same age as him: a mathematics graduate, David Worswick, who was studying for a one-year economics diploma prior to taking the entrance examination for the civil service. Wilson also taught third-year PPE undergraduates – characteristically, the more practical 'Economic Organisation' rather than economic theory – and they would only have been a year younger than him. In addition, New College had a strong link to the expensive Winchester private school. Wilson found its former pupils difficult, observing that they 'shared one trait in common: they were all extremely bright and, after a couple of tutorials with me, more or less allowed it to be known that they knew more economics than I would ever know.'[32] At least it meant Wilson had some experience of dealing with Wykehamists before they played such a significant part in his political career. His discomfiture was in any event short-lived as, after two terms, he moved to University College in a more senior role as a research fellow, allowing him to continue his work with Beveridge, but also retaining some teaching duties. With it came an annual stipend of £400, rooms in college and free meals. Wilson now had the opportunity of an academic career if he wanted one.

Yet his eye remained on politics, as he left the Liberals and joined the Oxford University Labour Club. In February 1938, Wilson resigned from the Eighty Club: a now-closed London gentleman's club aligned to the Liberal Party. The Labour Party was shifting. It was in a desperate situation in the 1931–35 parliament, when the triumvirate of George Lansbury, the party leader from 1932, Stafford Cripps and Clement Attlee shared the duties of leader of the opposition between them to keep the office functioning in parliament. With Attlee as leader – initially on a temporary basis when George Lansbury resigned – Labour started to develop a policy programme. Hugh Dalton wrote *Practical Socialism for Britain* in 1935; Douglas Jay wrote *The Socialist Case* in 1937. Yet it was G.D.H. Cole's powerful arguments about poverty as a great ill in society, and his libertarian version of socialism, as distinct from Marxism, that inspired Wilson. Later, he wrote: 'It was G.D.H. Cole as much as any man who finally pointed me in the direction of the Labour Party. His social and economic theories made it intellectually respectable. My attitudes had been clarifying for some time and the catalyst was the unemployment situation.'[33] He added: 'My religious upbringing and practical studies of economics and unemployment in which I had been engaged in Oxford combined in one single thought: unemployment was not only a severe fault of government, but it was in some way evil, and an affront to the country it afflicted.'[34]

Late-1930s British politics was dominated by debate on Prime Minister Neville Chamberlain's policy of appeasement. The national became local in the Oxford by-election of 27 October 1938 held after the death of the sitting Conservative MP. Labour's Patrick Gordon Walker, later a cabinet minister under Wilson, and the Liberals' Ivor Davies, stood down to give a clear run to A.D. Lindsay, the master of Balliol, who stood as an Independent Progressive. He faced Quintin Hogg, later Lord Hailsham, a supporter of Chamberlain. On 30 September 1938, Chamberlain had concluded his Munich Agreement with Adolf Hitler, ceding the Czechoslovakian German-speaking Sudetenland to the Nazis, before returning to Heston Aerodrome to declare that he had secured 'peace for our time'. With Winston Churchill denouncing the agreement in the House of Commons, Lindsay's campaign was a full-throated attack: 'A Vote for Hogg is a Vote for Hitler'. Future top-rank politicians such as Edward Heath and Roy Jenkins threw themselves into the campaign for Lindsay. Hogg held the seat with a reduced majority of 3,434 votes, down from 6,645 in 1935. Yet there is no sign of Wilson playing an active part in this. When he recalled it for his memoirs he had all the details of the by-election – even the year – wrong.[35] This is an indication of Wilson's state of mind at the time: while he had completed his conversion to Labour from the Liberals, it was the progress of his academic career that took precedence.

Wilson's reputation as an expert in the field of unemployment was confirmed as he travelled to Dundee to give a paper on unemployment at the annual gathering of the British Association for the Advancement of Science. Mary, to whom he had become formally engaged in the summer of 1938, was living at Preesall near Fleetwood, with her father in charge of the local Congregational Church. Wilson called there on the way to Scotland in his Wolseley Hornet. However, his idea of delivering an impressive lecture to an admiring hall of people was upset by Hitler invading Poland on 1 September. The room emptied: 'There was little to hear but the roar of car exhausts as I read my paper.' Wilson returned south to Oxford, knowing his life was about to change irrevocably, picking up Mary on the way.[36]

On 3 September, Britain and France declared war on Nazi Germany. Wilson registered at the local employment exchange under the Military Service Act. He was categorised as a 'specialist' and after some days 'war work' was found for him. The old Potato

Marketing Board, now titled Potato Control at the Ministry of Food, was being evacuated to Oxford. With the trade channels functioning normally in this period of the 'phoney war' with no immediate Luftwaffe bombing, there was a job to do: Wilson was registered as a temporary clerk; Mary took a job at the same place.[37] The outbreak of war also led Wilson to bring forward the date of his marriage to Mary, to New Year's Day 1940.

A quarter of a century later, the *Sunday Times* journalist Hunter Davies interviewed Mary and wrote a feature on the Wilsons' wedding as they were spending their silver wedding anniversary at their bungalow in the Isles of Scilly. The ceremony was 'really a rush job. They hadn't intended to get married till the spring. They thought then it would be nice to have a fairly big wedding and a honeymoon in the Isles of Scilly. But the war had begun. Nobody knew what was going to happen.' Wilson was expecting to be called up for military service; in the meantime, he and Mary took up residence in a one-room flat on South Parks Road in Oxford. They were to experience married life with him as an Oxford don for a brief time: Mary loved it, and, in the many years ahead when she sought to guard her family's privacy, it was a period she looked back on as to how their life might have been. These were always the halcyon days as far as she was concerned, and it is easy to see why. Wilson had a role that made him happy, and Mary could support him without any concern about how the couple were perceived by anyone else. Oxford, with its exquisite architecture and layers of history, was an ideal location for Mary to have lived a thoughtful, contemplative life. In the community of the university's scholars, there was intellectual stimulation, but it was protected from the prying eyes of the outside world.

The wedding was in the chapel at Mansfield College, the venue demonstrating the continuing significance of Congregationalism in Wilson's life, given the roots of the institution. Initially based in Birmingham as Spring Hill College, it moved to Oxford and was opened in 1889, with the primary reason for its establishment to 'provide a high-class theological education for men who intended to enter the Congregational Ministry'.[38] The service was conducted by the College Principal, Dr Nathaniel Micklem, with Mary's father, Rev. David Baldwin, assisting. Mary did not say 'I obey': she said 'I'm a great feminist, not for myself, just for all women to be treated as equals.' The reception was at the Park Royal, a nearby private hotel. There was no champagne: both sides of their religious family being teetotal. Wilson, and the majority of the guests, were in academic dress. Beveridge could not make it, and sent two red Venetian glass bowls. The best man was an Oxford friend, Patrick Duncan, who was at that time waiting to join the Indian civil service. He was killed on the North-West Frontier just after the war. The honeymoon was spent at the Cotswold village of Minster Lovell: the happy couple had to leave early as it was getting foggier – the driver of the hire car issued an ultimatum. It was not romantic. They both had colds and brought a stack of books. Mary read *Busman's Honeymoon*, by Dorothy Sayers. Sadly, her own honeymoon was interrupted after a week by a telegram from Beveridge calling Wilson back to help with research on the trade cycle.[39]

Ironically, as Wilson began to publish his own work, Beveridge's property at Avebury closed for the duration. His first academic article appeared in *Economica* in May 1940: he considered industrial production between 1717 and 1786 with the aim of establishing the concept of a trade cycle.[40] The method of analysing detailed statistics to establish economic phenomena was pure Beveridge: Wilson was learning from the master in the field. The link to Beveridge also helped with Wilson becoming a wartime civil servant. After only a few weeks back in Oxford, Wilson was invited for interview at the Ministry of Supply. The director of statistics questioned whether he had seen the article in that week's *Economist* about mobilisation of the wartime economy, and how he would summarise it for a ministerial brief. Wilson answered fluently before confessing that he had written the article. A job offer followed; he and Mary moved to London, with temporary rooms in Earl's Court and then Dolphin Square, Pimlico, before they settled in a rented flat in Twickenham. However, Wilson was not inspired by the work. He tried to move to the Ministry of Food but was blocked by the department, which could not spare him.[41]

Then, unexpectedly, Wilson was rewarded for his trip to Dundee. Not all his listeners had dashed back home during his speech. In April 1940, he received a telephone call from Stanley Dennison, economics professor at Newcastle, who remembered Wilson from the event. Dennison was working in the Cabinet Office as economic adviser to Jean Monnet, chairman in London of the Anglo-French Co-ordinating Committee, concerned with the economic and trade aspects of the alliance. He needed a research statistician: Wilson was ideal, and became its joint secretary, moving into the extension to the Scotland Yard buildings opposite Downing Street. His role was to report on available supply routes as ports and territory were taken by the invading German armies. It turned out that Dennison was not the only significant link Wilson made in Dundee. Also there was Alec Cairncross, an economist who was then also a wartime civil servant who was willing to recommend him to colleagues.[42] With a remarkable mind and his rimmed spectacles on his sharp nose, Cairncross exuded authority.

The appointment was short-lived. On 10 May 1940, with the Wehrmacht sweeping through the Low Countries, Winston Churchill had taken over as prime minister, putting together a war cabinet of five along with Lord Halifax, his predecessor Neville Chamberlain, Labour leader Clement Attlee and his deputy Arthur Greenwood. The month after the fall of France at the end of June 1940, the Anglo-French Co-ordinating Committee collapsed. Yet, a strength of the civil service between 1939 and 1945 was the way it adapted to mobilising the whole of society for the war effort, both in its changing structures and its personnel, blending capable outsiders like Wilson with existing staff. The historian Peter Hennessy wrote that the Second World War was the 'high point of achievement in the history of the British Civil Service'.[43]

Thus, Wilson found Dennison and himself merged with the economic section of the Cabinet Secretariat led by John Jewkes, an economics professor at Merton College, Oxford. Wilson's task was to assess the capacity to supply the war effort, bringing an economist's eye to manpower requirements across industry. He served with other economists, including another future Labour MP, Evan

Durbin. He was very worried: '. . . in the principal munitions fact-ories, in aircraft and tank production above all, there was a chronic shortage of skilled engineers and a considerable lack even of semi-skilled.'[44] His concern deepened as the Blitz began with an average of two hundred Luftwaffe aeroplanes bombing London daily from 7 September to 3 November. Initially, Mary stayed with Wilson's parents in Cornwall, then moved to Oxford. When Wilson was working overnight, he either watched the fires from the roof or slept with other civil servants on mattresses in a building on Rich-mond Terrace at the heart of Whitehall: 'in a makeshift dormitory . . . more or less fully clothed and rolled up in an army blanket'.[45] When Mary returned to London, they decided to move from the top-floor flat in Twickenham. It was dangerous: Mary had become a shelter warden, and, for safety, she and Wilson were sleeping on a mattress in the ground-floor hall. Thus, they moved to a flat on the Little Green in Richmond. They remained unscathed, though their cat Kubla Khan was killed one night in a bombing raid that hit the local cattery, while Wilson and Mary were back at Oxford for the weekend.

By then, Wilson had moved to a new role. The general secretary of the Transport and General Workers' Union, Ernest Bevin, had entered parliament unopposed in the Wandsworth Central by-election on 22 June 1940. Churchill had appointed him as minister for Labour and National Service and wished to secure a seat for him. A thick-set man, Bevin had an imposing physique and a powerful personality. Having risen through the ranks of the trade union movement, he was dominant in any company. He turned to Beveridge to carry out a study of how effectively workers were being utilised in the economy, and, on 28 June, Beveridge was confirmed as commissioner for Manpower Survey, and, in August, was ap-pointed as chair of a cross-departmental Manpower Requirements Committee. Beveridge immediately turned to his old research as-sistant for help, so Wilson became its joint secretary. Douglas Jay, who had started work as a civil servant at the Ministry of Supply in December 1940, observed Beveridge presiding over the Man-power Requirements Committee with Wilson as secretary: 'There they both were across the table in a large Whitehall committee room, rather like an owl and a sparrow: Beveridge, august, white-haired, venerable and dogmatic; and Wilson diminutive, chubby and chirpy.'[46] Later, Beveridge reflected that their work had been crucial in the war effort: 'The most important recommendation was that, whatever the size formally approved for each of the fighting forces, the actual calling up of men should depend on the supply of munitions for them.'[47] In January 1941, Bevin adopted this principle as war cabinet policy.

By then, Beveridge himself had moved on. An under-secretary at the Ministry of Labour had fallen ill, so, at Christmas 1940, Beveridge was asked to provide cover, in charge of the Military Service Department. Beveridge then asked Wilson to become head of the ministry's Manpower, Statistics and Intelligence branch. Wilson accepted, and was joined by another familiar face, G.D.H. Cole, who was responsible for local fieldwork. This did not, how-ever, bring stability for Wilson. Beveridge and Bevin were soon to clash: both were strong-willed, single-minded men. The issue of contention was the compulsory call-up of women to the armed forces. As Beveridge recalled: 'Ernest Bevin's answer to my argu-ment for immediate conscription of women was to procrastinate – and to part from me.'[48] Bevin looked for other roles for Beveridge to move him out of the way, and, in doing so, was to find one that was to result in a fundamental shift in the whole direction of post-war domestic policy. On 9 June 1941, Beveridge left the Ministry of Labour and National Service for two new roles. The first was as chair of the Committee on Skilled Men in Services, considering whether engineers were being best utilised in the armed forces, and whether more needed to be called up. Wilson – again – became secretary. It was with regard to the second post found for Beveridge that Wilson made an uncharacteristic error. Beveridge was asked to chair an inter-departmental committee on Social Insurance and Allied Services. He was keen to appoint Wilson as the secretary, but this time his former research assistant decided his other work was simply too much to allow him to take it on.

The final work, published in December 1942, came to be known by just the surname of its author. The Beveridge Report shaped the welfare policy of Clement Attlee's post-war Labour government and the whole post-war social security settlement. Ironically, it was probably political calculation that caused Wilson to turn down the role. Another opportunity had arisen at the Mines Department, which was looking for a head of its statistics branch. For an aspiring Labour politician, knowledge of the coal industry – employing hundreds of thousands of miners across the country and at the heart of working-class communities – would be invaluable for the future. With Wilson being asked to apply all the skills he had learned with Beveridge to compile and analyse detailed statistics, it seemed ideal.

Beveridge's impact on Wilson was profound. He had an unrivalled understanding of administration: not only a unique ability to interpret information, and to devise the action that was required to enhance performance, but also a feel for what data needed to be collected in the first place. Like many highly talented people, Beveridge was irascible and difficult to manage. After all his efforts in tolerating his behaviour, patiently assisting him in the many tasks he took on, it was an irony that Wilson missed out on contributing to Beveridge's greatest achievement. The man frozen out at the Ministry of Labour had managed to produce his most influential piece of writing from outside. As Wilson put it: 'He became, for the first time, not a Whitehall expert, but a national figure, in some ways the harbinger of the kind of post-war world people wanted to see. Public opinion forced the adoption of his report by Parliament . . .'[49] Wilson, however, could comfort himself with the fact that he was to thrive in the Mines Department, and his work was to contribute to his entry into parliament in the 1945 general election.

Chapter 3

New deal for coal

Into Parliament, 1942–45

In February 1942, Winston Churchill restructured his government. Hugh Dalton, minister for Economic Warfare, was moved to the Board of Trade. Then fifty-four, the Bishop Auckland MP was a veteran of 1930s Labour politics. As spokesperson on foreign policy, he had contributed to shifting the party from the pacifism of George Lansbury, leader from 1932 to 1935, to a position of opposition to appeasement only a few years later. Dalton also saw himself as a mentor to talented young politicians. His protégé at the time was Hugh Gaitskell, his principal private secretary at Economic Warfare, whom he persuaded to move with him to the Board of Trade. There, he appointed him his personal assistant. Aged only thirty-five, with dark wavy hair and a sharp mind, Gaitskell was one for the future.

It was not long before Wilson's ability with statistics caught Dalton's eye: 'Among junior officials at the Mines Department was Harold Wilson, a don at University College, Oxford, who had worked with Beveridge, and was now showing a gift for forecasting, with quite uncanny accuracy, our monthly coal input.'[1] The Board of Trade had three sub-ministries: Mines, Petroleum and Overseas Trade. Each had a political head: in the case of mining, it was David Grenfell, MP for the Welsh constituency of Gower. Every month, Grenfell chaired the Coal Production Council. Wilson's job was to provide it with the figures.

There was a major issue with producing coal. As Dalton wrote:

'We were producing too little and consuming too much, and the labour force in the industry was falling. Too many miners had joined the Army, and the average age left was too high.'[2] While all this was correct, there was a more complex set of problems in the industry itself. In their seminal history of the South Wales miners during the twentieth century, Hywel Francis and Dai Smith thought that the cause of periodic fuel crises between 1941 and 1944 was 'rooted in the indiscriminate closure of pits during the inter-war period, the depletion of the labour force by lack of opportunities, migration, now a military call-up which further increased the age of remaining miners, as well as the inadequate technical standards of Britain's collieries.'[3]

Wilson's attention to detail and eye for statistics proved vital in understanding the true cause of the problems. The European market for exporting coal had collapsed with the Nazi conquest of France. While this at first caused a labour surplus in the coalfields, those men left without work quickly moved to other industries such as munitions. This led to a mass of workers leaving the pits. In May 1941, Ernest Bevin tried to stem the flow with an essential work order, preventing colliers moving to other industries unless there was permission from the National Service Department.[4] In July 1941, he broadcast an appeal for former miners to return to the pits. Wilson studied every statistic he could lay his hands on for the period from 1938 to 1941, considering events in the final year of peacetime as well as the situation in wartime.

Wilson saw through the coal owners, whose deceptively simple explanation was that not enough coal was being produced because men were not turning up for work. With support from the Conservative benches in the Commons, this issue of absenteeism was turned into a question of patriotism: the miners who were not getting out of bed in the mornings were not serving their country in time of peril. Wilson applied the Beveridge method: ask the right questions, collect detailed statistics and then draw conclusions. He dismissed the 'innumerate owners' whose arguments he dismantled skilfully. He found that the output 'per man shift worked at the coal face . . . was only marginally lower, 2.94 against 2.95. The main explanation of the decline in output lay in the proportion of total shifts actually worked at the coalface, which in 1938–41 was down from 38.03 to 35.96 per cent.'[5] The miners were turning up at pitheads, and those underground were working as hard as ever. The issue was that, as the number of miners working in the industry had reduced, a *larger proportion* of the loss was on the coalface, hence the issue with output. Since there was a minimum number of men required for safety work and other essential duties, it was at the coalface where the fall in numbers was most severe.

Brilliant though his analysis was, Wilson quickly worked out that flattery was the way to impress Dalton, who recorded in his diary in March 1942: 'I hear tonight it is being said in the Mines Department, at least by [Harold] Wilson and his friends, that my paper on coal is "the best ever".'[6] The central question Dalton had to answer was on the organisation of the industry. There were three competing interests. First, there were the miners themselves, seeking better conditions and higher wages, looking on as other workers, often including the women in their own households, took home decent pay-packets from what they regarded as unskilled work in munitions factories. Second, there were the coal owners, looking for profit. As Grenfell himself later argued: 'Colliery owners have done well out of coal. They have drawn high dividends from the old mines. Little new capital has been invested and few new mines have been opened since 1913, when the industry reached its highest level of employment and production.'[7] Third, there was the government, seeking to raise output for the war effort.

Dalton was in favour of requisitioning the mines for the duration of the war, but the situation did not lend itself to a simple solution. In March, he commissioned Beveridge to provide a report on fuel rationing, but its proposals were met with widespread opposition, and eventually had to be shelved. On the one side, Will Lawther, then president of the Miners' Federation of Great Britain, told the press that 'the miners are all against coal rationing' while the Tory backbench 1922 Committee launched a fierce revolt in parliament. R.A. Butler, then president of the Board of Education, told Dalton that 'the Tories are against fuel rationing because they are afraid that it will mean that they won't get enough for their country houses.'[8]

Something had to be done to maintain coal supplies at an adequate level. In July 1940, the TUC had agreed the Conditions of Employment and National Arbitration Order making strikes illegal, but this did not prevent various stoppages in the coal industry during the war. The problems in early 1942 led to a crisis that forced the government to act. In Durham, South Wales, Lancashire and Yorkshire, there were mass walkouts in April and May. Another wave of strikes – again in Durham, Lancashire and Yorkshire, but this time also in Cumberland – led to a board of investigation being set up under the master of the rolls, Lord Greene, with Wilson as its joint secretary.

Greene held a series of private court sittings over ten days in June 1942. Wilson claimed a great deal of the credit for its recommendations, citing a conversation over lunch with Greene once all the evidence had been given.[9] The general secretary of the Miners' Federation, Ebby Edwards, had spoken for the colliers, emphasising the importance of a co-ordinated national approach to miners' wages, arguing for a four-shilling increase in pay. Greene was minded to split the difference and award two shillings. Wilson counselled against, on the basis that the more militant of the miners would then blame Edwards for not asking for more. He suggested a 2/6d. increase to avoid this, and, with his eye on popular feeling, because he thought the term 'Greene half-crown' would catch on.

On the issue of a national minimum wage, Greene's instinct was to shy away, on the basis that the miners would not expect such a finding. Wilson, conscious of civil service neutrality, initially agreed with this, then moved on to argue that a national approach would mark a step-change away from the days when mining districts were pitted against each other to a unifying approach. Green listened, then sought Wilson's views on the level of the minimum wage. Wilson had accumulated pay sheets for tens of collieries in a range of coalfields, and formulated a proposal that would leave fewer than 2 per cent of workers earning less than the minimum. Greene adopted Wilson's proposals; the Miners' Federation accepted them on 23 June, and the owners' Mining Association adopted them two days later. The implementation of the proposals would be overseen by a new government ministry: on 4 June 1942, the government had announced the creation of a Ministry of Fuel and Power under Gwilym Lloyd George, taking over responsibility for coal production. It was also another move within Whitehall for Wilson, who became director of Economics and Statistics at the new department.

By any standards, Greene's report was a remarkable piece of work, allowing the focus of the mining industry to turn to output. Wilson could claim great influence over the recommendations. Not only that, he had come into direct contact with both sides of the industry. On the one side, there was Evan Williams who spoke for the coal owners. On the other – and most importantly, given their influence in Labour Party politics – he now understood the union leaders: men like Lawther, Ebby Edwards, Jim Bowman, Arthur Horner and Ernest Jones.

At the Labour Party conference in 1943, Lawther heaped praise on Dalton and Bevin, whom, he said, had 'done more for the mining industry than all the governments which have preceded it.' There was a specific minister for Fuel and Power and the principle of a National Wages Board had been established.[10]

Wilson knew, though, that this was not all that was sought by the miners and continued to make the case for full-scale nationalisation. It was fertile political ground to choose. In the House of Commons, Nye Bevan, then a backbencher, questioned whether full nationalisation would ever happen. Even in wartime, he argued, this was not possible, since the state was operating a private industry, the coal owners 'still in charge of the revenues of the industry, and so all these people are still to be paid out of the bloody sweat of the miners . . .'[11] Wilson's consideration of the future of the coal industry was based on the approach he had perfected: looking at which data was *not* being gathered, and ensuring it was collected: 'It seems incredible to me, though true, that no one ever thought in peace-time of asking certain questions . . . on the price of coal, the elasticity of demand for coal and other types of fuel, the importance of coal in manufacturing costs . . . without this information much of our post-war planning must be blind.'[12]

There would be no further progress towards state ownership in wartime. Churchill accepted that government control would continue for the duration of the war, but said the question of long-term nationalisation would be one for the next administration to decide upon after a general election.[13] Within government, the debate continued. Gwilym Lloyd George was unconvinced by Churchill's position: 'the assumption of full State control during the war would be ineffective if the long-term position remained uncertain . . .'[14] On the other hand, it was questioned whether nationalisation would make any difference on issues such as output and absenteeism.[15] Wilson remained firm, producing a paper entitled 'Nationalisation the Answer' arguing that it would mean pit amalgamations could be directed, adequate finance provided, risks taken in new pits and methods, providing a recruitment service guaranteeing employment and for adequate funds for research.[16] His pragmatic approach chimed with that of the National Council of Labour, which emphasised the problem of an industry operating in twenty-five areas: 'Each district exercises considerable autonomy; this applies both to the owners and the miners . . . The difficulty of obtaining speedy decisions is therefore obvious.'[17] Wilson broadened the argument for state ownership into other sectors, with a nod back to his Gladstone Memorial Prize essay. In March 1945, he produced a further substantial paper on 'The Finance of Railway Nationalisation' in which he suggested that 'consideration be given to the establishment by a Socialist Government of a "Compensation Claims Tribunal" to deal with all the industries passing into public ownership'.[18]

Such debates about post-war Britain were, however, subordinated to the ultimate task: winning the war. As the Allies began to plan the invasion of Western Europe, attention turned to coal supply for the enormous logistical exercise that would be required. In early 1943, Wilson was appointed to his by now familiar role of joint secretary of a committee: this time a sub-committee of the Anglo-American Combined Chiefs of Staff. The idea was to increase coal stocks at the ports from which the attacks were to be launched, and to ensure that all establishments – like power stations – that relied on two tons per day, had twenty weeks in reserve, meaning that ships used for supply were freed up. The sub-committee had an American equivalent and Sam Berger, the State Department's first Labour attaché, was Wilson's opposite number in the US embassy in London. Since there was little in the way of effective co-ordination between London and Washington on this key issue, Wilson and Berger were dispatched to the other side of the Atlantic to find agreement on the estimates needed.

The journey in wartime was a hazardous one. Wilson took the train to RAF Hurn, an airfield that was later to become Bourne-mouth airport, from where he was flown by seaplane to Foynes in County Limerick, the last port of call on the eastern side of the Atlantic before the long journey across the ocean began. Due to a headwind, and the need for more fuel, half of the travelling party had to be left behind to fly another day. Wilson was amused that his American visa entitled him to a place on the first flight, ahead of more senior civil servants, including a permanent secretary. After a rough flight, they made it to the Hudson River at around midnight, where Berger 'took me on a tour of the brilliantly lit streets. Officially there was a "brownout" for fear of U-boats, but no Briton visiting the United States for the first time would have imagined that New York could have been even more resplendently illuminated.'[19] The next day he went on to Washington, where he at first stayed in a suite of rooms at the sumptuous Hotel Roosevelt but, conscious of his 'mission allowance' of nine dollars per day, he soon moved to somewhere cheaper.

Wilson was struck by the number of telephone calls he received from various US officials, each seemingly unaware of each other's contact, asking him to set out the British approach. He drafted a single memorandum on the position to hand out to save time and ensure consistency as he conducted meetings over ten days. Wilson's mastery of detail was important but it was a contact that proved crucial in reaching an agreement. A new department in the US Administration had been created headed by a statistician,

Harlan Cleveland, a former pupil of Wilson's who had been a Rhodes Scholar at University College, Oxford. Wilson and Cleveland thrashed out an agreement on the British coal needs for the invasion of Western Europe. Wilson wrote home to Mary, having been shown – off the record – a memorandum sent from the American side to the head of the British Supply Mission: 'He said my handling of them was superlative . . . What he said to *me* was that it was a good thing they hadn't gold fillings in their teeth or I would have had them as well as four million dollars' worth of mining machinery and a US commitment for coal in the Mediterranean.'[20]

The trip was a great success. Wilson had worked hard and played hard, enjoying spending his dollars on new clothes including a new dark-blue navy tweed suit. He was, however, keener than usual to return home. Mary was in the late stages of pregnancy: their first child, a son, Robin, was to be born on 5 December 1943. Mary dedicated a poem to him: 'To Robin, when a Baby'. Its final lines are touching: 'Soundly he sleeps, heavy upon the pillow/Knees bent in comfort, fingers tightly curled/Gently quiescent, helpless, unprotected/Man of the future – heir to all the world!'[21] When Wilson managed a meeting in America with film producer Sir Alexander Korda, he gave him a white silk layette for the baby's impending arrival. The journey eastward back across the Atlantic was arduous. At first they were stuck for three days at Gander in Newfoundland before flying to Scotland on a seatless Hudson bomber that had no pressurised cabin, leaving Wilson having to breathe through an oxygen mask.

To protect Robin from the risk of air raids, Mary left London to stay with Herbert and Ethel in Cornwall before joining her own parents in Duxford in Cambridgeshire. She was back in the capital by the time the Germans started their attacks on London with V1 flying bombs – 'doodlebugs', as they became known – in June 1944. Wilson, sometimes sleeping in the shelter accommodation at Whitehall, often listened to Gwilym Lloyd George's stories about his father David: 'We also had many talks about the politics of the post-war world and my own rapidly forming decision to sit as a Labour candidate as soon as a general election was called.'[22] Mary's view was that Wilson had it in mind all along, which he undoubtedly did: 'His plan was to get established as a don, then try for a seat at thirty . . . He enjoyed his pupils and the Oxford life. But he always intended to go into politics. He didn't want to spend the next fifty years lecturing about politics. He wanted to take part . . . If the war had not happened, Harold would probably have stayed at Univ. He would have consolidated his donnish career and then tried to find a seat.'[23]

The process for selection as a Labour candidate was chaotic. Party politics had been suspended for the duration of the war, with the electoral truce meaning that the Conservatives and Labour did not compete in by-elections. There had been no general election since 1935. In 1944, as it became clear that it was a matter of time before Nazi Germany was finally defeated, pressure built within the Labour Party for a return to electoral competition. While there was still a debate to be had about the continuation of cross-party government into peacetime, as had happened with the Lloyd George coalition in 1918, the Labour constituency parties set about seeking candidates.

Having influential people onside mattered, as it almost always does. In Wilson's case, they were contacts he had made through his work, rather than a network he had been born into: 'John Parker MP, the General Secretary of the Fabian Society, together with Tom Smith, a mining MP who had been appointed by Churchill as parliamentary secretary to the Ministry of Fuel and Power, both sounded me out about standing as a Labour candidate.'[24] Once a miner himself, Smith was on one of the lower governmental rungs as parliamentary secretary at the Ministry of Fuel and Power. Wilson's wartime work was impressive but his wider political activities were restricted by the requirement of civil service neutrality. The evidence suggests he did stretch the rule. He told Cairncross, then at the Ministry of Aircraft Production, 'that he was dividing his time between his duties as a civil servant in the Ministry and addressing Miners' gatherings in the North at the weekend.'[25] Wilson had also been approached in 1943 by Dr W.A. Robson of

London University, whom he had met before the war, to ask him to accept nomination to the Fabian Society's executive committee.[26]

Smith's work with Wilson also involved dealing with parliament and the intricacies of answering queries accurately but without causing embarrassment. He sought Wilson's help in dealing with an enquiry from Viscount Castlereagh, who had written on 5 May 1944 in support of the miners, who were again being accused of failing to turn up for work: 'Many of the criticisms I hear I resent.' Castlereagh asked about a comparison with the level of absenteeism in aircraft production. Wilson observed, in a note to Smith six days later: 'It is often found that in the aircraft industry absenteeism amongst women is very high, but this is largely due, we are told, to domestic ties . . .' Wilson's analysis was that the Ministry of Labour figures 'by and large show coal mining higher [in absenteeism] than other industries, with one or two exceptions, principally the married women.' Such figures were not, however, published. Wilson advised Smith to reply to Castlereagh, indicating that the Ministry had no comparable figures and that 'the Ministry of Labour have nothing available for publication', which he did on 15 May.[27]

Smith pressed for Wilson to be placed on an approved list of candidates at Labour Party headquarters – the 'B' list of those without trade union sponsorship. Parker's support of Wilson was based upon his involvement with the Fabian Society. When the Elections Sub-committee of the Labour Party's National Executive granted Wilson a place on the approved list on 9 February 1944, alongside another Oxford graduate and then serving army officer, Anthony Crosland, he was listed as a member of the Liskeard and Oxford University Labour Parties.[28] But his involvement in local Labour Party campaigning on the ground was at this time non-existent. During another period, this would have been a problem, but the unique circumstances in the final months of the war changed things. The existing Parliamentary Labour Party had just over 150 MPs, so hundreds of constituencies were looking for candidates.

The great advantage of being an approved candidate was that your name, along with the others, would be sent to local constituency Labour parties who would then, in turn, send invitations to prospective candidates on the list to appear before them in order to secure the parliamentary nomination for that area. Wilson was first invited to Peterborough, where he finished as runner-up. As it happened, the winning candidate was later disqualified on the grounds that the length of his Labour Party membership was only three weeks. As runner-up, Wilson would have captured the nomination but, by then, he had been selected elsewhere. For Wilson had applied for the candidacy at Ormskirk, a large constituency running from the outer edges of the city of Liverpool in the south nearly as far as Preston in the north. It was in some ways an unappealing prospect. Its voting history was, to say the least, varied. Labour's James Bell, a trade unionist in the cotton industry, had won the seat in 1918, but lost it at the next general election in 1922. Labour won the seat back in 1929: the candidate, Samuel Rosbotham, had chaired the Lancashire Farmers Association for two decades, no doubt widening his appeal. Then, in 1931, Rosbotham left the Labour Party to join MacDonald under the 'National Labour' label. With MacDonald leading the Conservative-dominated National Government, Rosbotham had no Tory opponent in the general election that year, and heavily defeated the official Labour candidate by over 20,000 votes. This also meant there was no Tory challenge in 1935, as the National Government continued under Stanley Baldwin. In 1939, Rosbotham retired, and was replaced, in an uncontested by-election, on 27 October, by another National Labour candidate, Stephen King-Hall, a naval officer and playwright. He founded the Hansard Society in 1944, a cross-party organisation promoting parliament and democracy. This was an indication of his political journey: he was by now a more or less independent critic of the government.

From the city voters of Liverpool to rural Lancashire to the mining constituencies of Skelmersdale and Upholland, this was a decidedly mixed constituency. This had two great disadvantages for Wilson: first, while it looked a fine prospect for a victory in a good Labour year, it would be very hard to hold the seat in the longer term; second, its very diversity made it a prime candidate for future boundary changes. The obvious advantage for Wilson was that localism almost always matters in parliamentary selections. The Ormskirk constituency, or at least its southernmost tip, was not too far from the Wirral. Wilson could claim a link. His major rival was Clifford Kenyon, who went on to win the Chorley seat in 1945. As a farmer, Kenyon was a strong candidate for the constituency.[29] A railway ticket-collector and an organiser at the General Workers' Union made up a four-strong shortlist of candidates for a selection hustings in September 1944 at the Congregational school in Ormskirk, a fitting venue for Wilson. In his speech, he drew on his experience in the coal industry, promising 'a new deal in regard to the basic industry of coal, and the miners of Skelmersdale now knew that they and their sons could look forward to an industry of which they could be proud under national ownership.'[30] No doubt his fine grasp of detail stood him in good stead, and the link to the Wirral was enough to avoid a backlash against him as a carpetbagger. He won the nomination with Kenyon second. The *Daily Telegraph* reported that he was seen by socialists as 'a coming President of the Board of Trade or Chancellor of the Exchequer'.[31]

As he could not be both a neutral civil servant and a parliamentary candidate, Wilson returned to Oxford, as a fellow and lecturer in Economics at University College, a post he had wisely secured prior to his selection victory at Ormskirk, no doubt with the possibility of having to leave the civil service in mind. The problem was that, in wartime, there were few students to teach, so he took on the role of home bursar and junior dean, responsible for, of all things, the catering budget and the senior common room drinks cupboard: 'In so far as self-indulgences were allowed (on Sunday nights only) the dons in residence were drinking from the 1895 stocks.'[32] For Wilson, it was a rare break from the privations of wartime. He also had something to celebrate: the 1945 New Year's Honours List brought the standard reward for a civil servant of his mark, an OBE. Then, at Easter, Mary and Robin moved into college rooms. It was a brief return to an Oxford life he had left behind six years ago.

Wilson used the time to produce a work that was the culmination of his wartime study of the mining industry: *New Deal for*

Coal. This short tract was significant for three reasons. First, it showcased Wilson's argument for socialism on pragmatic, rather than ideological grounds. It was not only the case 'that socialism and efficiency are compatible, but also that socialism, properly applied, is the only means to full efficiency. . . .'[33] Second, it showed Wilson's technical expertise in exploring the structure of nationalised industries. Third, Wilson chose to accept what became known as the 'Morrisonian' model of public ownership: industries run by boards. Herbert, who led the London County Council from 1934 to 1940, drew on the London Passenger Transport Board of the 1930s. Lawther was helpful in describing the piece as 'one of the most important statements issued' on the coal industry.[34] The pamphlet was also significant due to its publisher: George Weidenfeld, who was to become Wilson's friend and regular publisher in future years, after founding the firm Weidenfeld and Nicolson with Nigel Nicolson in 1949. Born to a Jewish family in Vienna in 1919, Weidenfeld had escaped to Britain in 1938 after Hitler's annexation of Austria. *New Deal for Coal* had been rejected a number of times before Wilson sent it to a magazine called *Contact*, which had been founded by Weidenfeld as a vehicle to publish short books. For a £50 advance, Weidenfeld secured the book, and a long-term association with Wilson.[35]

Wilson, knowing he had an opportunity to win a parliamentary seat, threw himself into the public meetings that were the staple of political campaigning at the time. In his capacity as the prospective Labour candidate for Ormskirk, he also attended the Labour Party conference of 1945 that opened in Blackpool on 21 May. In reply to a letter from Churchill, Attlee avoided giving a firm commitment to the continuation of the wartime coalition, leaving the prime minister having to call a general election. The wartime government was at an end.[36] With the mindset of generals fighting the last war, Westminster politicians expected Churchill to secure a resounding victory as 'the man who won the war' as David Lloyd George had done in 1918.

The reality was very different, partly hidden by the wartime political truce: there were no Conservative–Labour contests in by-elections, only sole government candidates. Nonetheless, Independent Labour candidates did well in by-elections in the final years of the war, as did the Common Wealth Party, founded in June 1942. Paul Addison's study of Second World War by-elections concluded: 'failure to sense Labour's growing majority was a measure of the lack of communication between the world of Westminster . . . and the mood of the public . . . polls conducted by the British Institute of Public Opinion predicted a Labour victory on six occasions after June 1943.'[37]

In Ormskirk, Wilson was also assisted by the Conservative decision to field a candidate, unlike in 1931 and 1935. Stephen King-Hall standing as a 'National Independent', drew the ire of the local Conservatives for his perceived disloyalty to Churchill's leadership of the wartime coalition. Since 1941, King-Hall had been producing a 'National News-Letter': after the election, he wrote that 'a small section of the [local] Conservative Party' had spouted 'meaningless claptrap' about him. Churchill even sent a telegram to his Conservative opponent, A.C. Greg, saying he did not want King-Hall in the new parliament.[38] Wilson did not get involved and let them fight it out. King-Hall later commented that he was 'a highly intelligent young man, who made the stereotyped party promises'.[39] That he stuck to the party line was a wise choice for Wilson in his first general election: he caused no controversy for the national party, and meant he had full benefit of the pro-Labour tide. That is not to say he had it easy. He still spoke too often in the 'academic-intellectual jargon common among the denizens of Oxford and Whitehall' which led some miners' leaders to call him 'college boy'. His agent, Huddersfield man Arthur Waite, told him after one speech: 'Can't you talk down to the people, so they can understand what you're talking about?' Wilson reflected: 'Looking back, my orations were painfully dull, factual, and over-weighted with statistics . . . .'[40] However, he could also draw on his contacts in the National Union of Mineworkers, who sent their big guns to Ormskirk: Lawther, as president, and Bowman, as vice-president, came to speak for him in Skelmersdale.[41]

The general election was held on 5 July 1945, but, due to the need to count the votes of service personnel still stationed at various locations around the globe, the result was not declared until three weeks later. Nationally, Labour had won a landslide victory, with nearly 12 million votes, 47.8 per cent, taking 393 seats. The Conservatives secured just under 10 million votes, 39.8 per cent, and 213 seats. Labour had a commanding overall majority of 146 seats. Wilson won the Ormskirk seat, polling 30,126 votes, representing 46.3 per cent of the votes. Greg took 23,104; King-Hall trailed in with 11,848. The Labour surge and the split opposition had given Wilson his victory, but it was a reminder that a single opponent would most likely have beaten him. His position was far from secure, but he was, at the age of twenty-nine, a member of parliament.

Chapter 4

Said you tried to kill him

Joining the Government, 1945–47

Two days after the declaration of the general election results, on Saturday, 28 July, every Labour MP was summoned to a meeting of the new Parliamentary Labour Party at the Beaver Hall in the City of London. The reason for the meeting was not, however, for parliamentarians to introduce themselves and meet their new colleagues. It had come about because of the manoeuvring of Herbert Morrison, who had, as Wilson put it, advanced the 'bogus constitutional argument that when Attlee had been the leader of the Parliamentary Labour Party for the previous Parliament, now there was a new Parliament. A fresh election was needed, he asserted.'[1]

Morrison was man of great determination who overcame adversity to succeed. Within three days of his birth, he had gone blind in his right eye, the centre of which became a circle of grey, apparently due to the negligence of a midwife in failing to clean it.[2] In photographs, he tended to stand at an angle to hide the eye, and he was bullied at school, being called 'one eye' and 'ball of fat'. Yet, as he later reflected: 'Still, my one eye served me well.'[3] His clear ambition was to be party leader and prime minister.

When the constituency results had come through, with Attlee, Bevin, Morrison and party secretary Morgan Phillips in Labour Party headquarters at Transport House, it was Ernest Bevin who had urged his party leader to go to Buckingham Palace. He was convinced that rather than the personal, charismatic leadership of MacDonald, the party needed someone like Attlee who would hold a team together. Accordingly, Attlee had kissed hands, and set about appointing his cabinet. Initially, it was dominated by him and four other figures: Hugh Dalton, who went to the Treasury as chancellor of the exchequer; Stafford Cripps became president of the Board of Trade; Herbert Morrison was given overall responsibility for domestic policy as lord president of the council; and Ernest Bevin became foreign secretary, dealing with the immediate issue of the ongoing conference of international powers at Potsdam to discuss the future of Europe after the defeat of Germany.

It was Bevin who, once again, saw off Morrison at the Saturday meeting. The chief whip, William Whiteley, took the chair and immediately called Bevin to speak. For the first time, Wilson saw Bevin's dominance as a government minister: 'In the fewest possible words Ernie formally moved that Clem Attlee be confirmed as the leader of the Parliamentary Party. It was accepted with acclamation: no one would have dared to moved an amendment.'[4] Attlee and Bevin then left for Potsdam, catching an aeroplane from Northolt. Wilson, meanwhile, offered a lift home to George Tomlinson, MP for the neighbouring Lancashire seat of Farnworth, and a senior party figure. The car broke down near the Watford Gap filling station, over a hundred miles from Tomlinson's house, so Wilson borrowed a replacement from the garage owner. He quickly discovered the brakes did not work, so had no choice but to move forward slowly and drive the car into the nearest pavement when he wanted to stop. The nightmare journey endured: Tomlinson was not dropped off until after midnight.[5]

Wilson returned to London for a dinner on the Monday evening, 30 July, hosted by Dalton at St Ermin's Hotel. The new chancellor did not wear glasses, and, with his high forehead, had an open face that seemed to hide little. Yet he was a notorious gossip, fascinated by political machinations. He was also a keen talent-spotter, and chose thirteen members of the new Commons intake as guests, including Wilson, Gaitskell, Evan Durbin, Woodrow Wyatt, John Freeman and Dick Crossman, together with George Brown – 'the only non-University man, [who] kept rather quiet.'[6] Dalton asked all those present to give their views of the issues facing the government. Wilson's answer was substantial, if occasionally technocratic. He agreed with the previous speaker, Evan Durbin, about the slowness of parliamentary draughtsmen impeding the bringing forward of legislation, then said that he thought the new government needed to emphasise that the problems of coal supply and housing were due to the war and not the fault of ministers. There should be an 'announcement of urgent, even desperate measures, to deal with the situation. It would also be helpful to announce at the same time a speed-up in Demobilisation. As regards the problem of Redundancy, he would like to see the government, if necessary, placing orders for refrigerators and vacuum cleaners. He also favoured the maintenance of a guaranteed wage.'[7]

Wilson had an ability to understand what would please people of power, though he perhaps went a bit too far with Dalton. Durbin made the point that newly elected MPs could go straight into government jobs; Wilson disagreed on the principle, but said 'I'd make one exception – on sheer merit Hugh Gaitskell.'[8] Flattering Gaitskell was one thing, but the remark was no doubt aimed at Dalton, who saw Gaitskell as his prize protégé. In any event, Gaitskell was temporarily unavailable for a stressful position. In March 1945, out with his wife Dora at the Gargoyle Club in Soho, he had suffered a heart attack and was recovering.

In any event, Wilson was offered a role very quickly. He took the oath and signed in as a Member of Parliament on 2 August. While in the Palace of Westminster, 'A Whip approached him and said that Emmanuel ('Manny') Shinwell wanted him as his PPS.'[9] Wilson was a natural fit. Shinwell was appointed minister of Fuel and Power; Wilson could use his wartime experience to assist him, and, while not a minister, he would be taking on the first step to becoming one, as a parliamentary private secretary, the eyes and ears of Shinwell in the House of Commons. With this good news Wilson returned to Oxford, where he intended to teach at University College on a Saturday and Sunday, allowing Mary and Robin to continue to live there. Wilson's parents were in the Richmond flat: Herbert was working temporarily at the Ministry of Supply.

As it happened, a more senior role was in the offing. On the

Saturday morning, 4 August, returning from shopping, the head porter on the gate at University College told Wilson that the prime minister had been trying to contact him. Wilson had memorised the Downing Street telephone number and rang back. Attlee was typically brief: 'Forming a government. Want you to be Parliamentary Secretary, Ministry of Works. George Tomlinson will be your Minister. Said you tried to kill him, but doesn't hold it against you. Report to him.'[10]

The prime minister was always terse in his use of words. This clipped style was part of Attlee's calm approach to leadership, holding together a team of big personalities around him. Bald on the top of his head with a trimmed moustache, Attlee looked like a reassuring, competent administrator who would not have been out of place as a town clerk keeping rowdy elected councillors in line. Yet it was another aspect of Attlee that Wilson thought relevant in his appointment: he was convinced that the fact he and Attlee had studied at the same college was a factor in the prime minister's thinking.[11] Attlee himself later said: 'I had heard of him as a don at my old College and knew of the work he had done for the Party. I therefore put him into the Government at once . . .'[12] Wilson's rise through the ministerial ranks was also assisted by Attlee's model of leadership, which provided great opportunities for him. He did not see himself as someone who should be personally driving forward policy, or out on the stump making great speeches to move public opinion this way and that. Rather, he was a quintessential chair of cabinet, finding a consensus among colleagues upon which to move forward. Attlee – provided he thought the argument was sound and expressed in few words – would listen, particularly on policy areas where he was weak in knowledge himself. Wilson later wrote that Attlee was 'tone deaf' on economics.[13] This allowed Wilson to become influential as one of the 'Young Economists'[14] in the government, alongside Gaitskell and Douglas Jay, upon whom Attlee relied, and who were in contention to be appointed chancellor of the exchequer in the administration's final year.

Wilson could hardly have been better prepared to serve. His years in the wartime civil service had given him a unique insight into how the government machine operated. Allied to that was his work with Beveridge: Wilson not only had the ability to analyse information put before him, he also had a keen sense of the data he required. It meant that, as a government minister, he could get the very best out of his public servant and make informed decisions. His ferocious intelligence and remarkable memory were great assets. None of this meant that he would get everything right: far from it. For, ultimately, decisions are always a question of judgement. But it did mean that Wilson would have more evidence upon which to base his assessments.

Wilson received a call from the permanent secretary at the Ministry of Works, Sir Percival Robinson, and threw himself into his new job. It was an awkward beginning. Wilson's primary concern was the government's house-building programme, but Robinson's priority was to protect the department's reputation: 'Cheerfully, Sir Percival told me that the Ministry was a long way behind schedule in supplying the shells of the houses, but this was not a matter for concern since the Ministry of Health had failed to provide the sites and concrete slabs known as foundations.' He and Wilson clashed immediately. Wilson sent for an official to brief him from an administrative grade rather than the executive level. Such distinctions mattered to the hierarchical Robinson, who had spent the war working at Buckingham Palace. Wilson dealt with his permanent secretary decisively, if inelegantly: '. . . I told him I had had more (expletive deleted) government experience than he had.'[15] Attlee did have Robinson shifted: he became a government director of the board of the Suez Canal Company.

The Ministry of Works was responsible for building and other public works, the materials industry including timber supply, and the construction engineering sector. In reality, its work was dominated by the minister of Health and Housing, Aneurin Bevan. A brilliant, charismatic orator, with a Welsh lilt, Bevan, with his distinctive side-parted hair, greying as he aged, could be at turns passionate, humorous, and sarcastic. He was the master of his government department, giving it firm, strategic direction. Attlee had shown great magnanimity in appointing Bevan to the role: the

Ebbw Vale MP had been the wartime coalition's foremost critic, first on its military strategy and then on its curtailment of civil liberties for the war effort. Bevan's twin tasks were the creation of the National Health Service and providing places to live for families. There was a shortage of housing, with the stock severely depleted by war damage. He was a strong advocate of public ownership who brought his experience as a local councillor to the issue of constructing homes.

It was a challenging task. Bevan's Conservative predecessor, Henry Willink, had issued an order in June 1945 to 'secure the erection of the largest possible number of houses as quickly as possible' and to make full use of all available agencies and workers.[16] An apparently simple instruction caused consternation in Wilson's department, and showed the problem of a lack of constructive co-operation across government. In order to ensure a regular supply of labour for urgent housing needs, workers would often need to move around, meaning that accommodation and travel allowances had to be paid. The Ministry of Works, Health and Housing, Scotland and the Treasury were all involved. One despairing civil servant wrote in frustration: 'This is about as grim a subject as any with which I have tried to deal. On the one hand it is extremely complicated and singularly uninteresting, but on the other it may well, if not settled, hold up the housing programme . . .'[17] Eventually, a solution was found by local authorities making an allowance for such expenses in the up-front sums they agreed in standard building contracts, but the involvement of the four departments showed the difficulty in making swift decisions.

The Ministry of Works was expected to stimulate the production and distribution of building materials. The government could agree to specific quantities being manufactured and offer to buy any surplus. The role of ministers was key: 'Only the Government is in a position to organise mass production and place wholesale orders.'[18] Thus, the task for Wilson was to source material for the housing programme and to ensure that the building sector was working as efficiently as it could be. The new parliamentary secretary was determined to get out of London: 'Houses were not built in Whitehall . . . or at our headquarters across the river in Lambeth Bridge House.' He thought that building a relationship with the employers was particularly important since few, if any, had voted Labour in 1945, and they were suspicious of Bevan's emphasis on investment in council houses in preference to the private sector. Wilson's efforts were rewarded: 'their co-operation could not be faulted, though many of them, in public and private, expressed considerable criticism of Aneurin Bevan, and particularly of his decision to concentrate all available resources on building houses for local authorities, with only a small margin for the more profitable construction of houses for sale. Before long my relations with them were as warm as my contacts with the trade unions.'[19]

In order to streamline decision-making, Bevan set up a housing executive of ministers from three relevant departments: Housing, Works, and Town and Country Planning, headed by Lewis Silkin, who had campaigned against urban sprawl in pre-war days. To avoid this happening now, his focus was on developing what became known as New Towns instead: rather than houses springing up on major roads out of London, areas would be designated for new settlements.[20] Thus, the focus of the Ministry of Works was on implementation of this policy. As Tomlinson made clear: with the Ministry of Supply and the Board of Trade, his own department had to ensure that 'the [housing] programme . . . [would] . . . not fail for want of particular materials or items of equipment.'[21]

While Wilson immersed himself in the detail of his ministerial work, he still had to complete his rite of passage as a new MP: his maiden speech. The moment is approached with a mixture of pride and nervousness, but there were distinct differences about the occasion for the new member for Ormskirk. The House of Commons had been destroyed by bombing in the war, meaning there was a lack of facilities for newly elected MPs. The Ministry of Works was responsible for its restoration, so Wilson was sent to answer for the government in a debate on the standard of accommodation on 9 October 1945. Since, unusually, Wilson was making his first speech from the dispatch box rather than the backbenches, ordinary rules had to be ignored. He could not pay tribute to his predecessor as MP, nor could he speak in glowing terms about his constituency. Crucially, the convention that the new member is heard in silence, uninterrupted, did not apply. Thus, Wilson was berated by angry interventions from his own side to which he struggled to respond. Gilbert McAllister, the new Labour MP for Rutherglen, pressed him on the issue of the chamber not having enough seats and on the details of construction of the new chamber. Wilson did not have the details at his fingertips: 'My hon. Friend has raised a rather wide question, which I will bring to the attention of the leader of the House, and to which he will not expect me to reply now.'[22] Ian Mikardo, then the newly elected MP for Reading, challenged him on commandeering offices outside the precincts of the Palace of Westminster. Wilson tried to argue that the number of rooms available to ministers was the same as in 1939; another Labour MP, Alfred Edwards, who sat for Middlesbrough East, and who was leading the debate from the backbenches, told him he had been misled.[23] Edwards was unrelenting: 'I understand that he himself a short time ago could not find accommodation and was driven to a room in his Ministry.'[24] As it happened, the debut edition of BBC Radio's *Today in Parliament* was broadcast that day, ending with a feature on the speech: 'Mr J.H. Wilson, Parliamentary Secretary to the Ministry, in a maiden speech, said that everything was being done to get better amenities in the House.'[25] What was not said on the radio was that Wilson had been taught a harsh lesson. The House of Commons can be a difficult and unforgiving place, keen to test newly appointed frontbenchers, who, however able, can be caught out on issues with which they are not fully familiar.

In contrast, Wilson's understanding of the Whitehall machine made him a highly competent departmental minister. He did not wield great power in such a junior role, but he had a fine command of the situation on the ground. He served on the cabinet committee on housing, chaired by Bevan, giving him a strategic view of the problem. He created progress charts, and was summoned by Attlee to explain the problems with getting things moving more quickly. Wilson saw the scale of the problem: of 12.5 million houses in the country in 1939, a third had been damaged in the war. He thought that unrealistic expectations had been raised by Churchill in the final months of the coalition, encouraging a belief that building hundreds of thousands of houses per year was straightforward. Wilson pointed out that, after the First World War, an annual target of 300,000 new houses was not achieved by the private sector until 1933, fifteen years after the Armistice. The building industry had been, in Wilson's view, 'cosseted' during the war, with generous contracts in place, making it harder to enforce larger agreements for mass building. He felt that the extent of pre-war overcrowding, and increased post-war demand with increases in the birth rate and number of marriages, were underestimated.

Wilson's relationship with Bevan became closer. The two men had a pre-existing connection through Herbert Wilson: A.R. Davies, who had known Bevan when he was growing up, was a sales director supervised by Wilson's father at the small Cornish chemicals business where he was working. In addition, the minister of health distrusted the civil servants at the Ministry of Works, so he dealt with Wilson directly. Wilson's grasp of detail meant that circumventing his civil servants was not disadvantageous. The problem for the housing drive in the early years of the Attlee government was the lack of access to raw materials, particularly timber. Wilson could do little about this issue in his position: it was being grappled with at cabinet level, and never fully resolved. As Wilson told the Commons on 25 March 1946: 'All we can guarantee is that timber will be available for essential permanent houses, but we will do as much as we possibly can to make timber available for repairs and maintenance.'[26] However, Wilson, on his own initiative did try to source timber from Canada.[27]

Attlee was impressed, and Wilson was an obvious candidate for further promotion. In May 1946, his and Gaitskell's paths were to cross again. 'I hear you are going to a place I'm interested in,' Wilson said to Gaitskell, now recovered from his heart attack and ready to serve in government. Tomlinson had told Wilson he would be moving to the Ministry of Fuel and Power under Shinwell, a prospect Wilson welcomed, meaning he would be able to return to the issue of the mines. He assumed Gaitskell would take his job at Works. In the event, Wilson stayed put and Shinwell chose Gaitskell, who recorded in his diary: 'I suspect . . . Shinwell . . . chose me because he did *not* want anyone who was supposed to know about Mining to be his Parliamentary Secretary!'[28] In September 1946, Dalton pressed for Wilson to become minister of transport in place of Alfred Barnes but his reputation as a poor House of Commons performer told against him as the chief whip blocked the appointment.[29] Another Dalton attempt to promote Wilson by bringing him into the Treasury as an additional minister was blocked by Ernest Bevin on grounds that this could not be done unless Tomlinson could be given a good minister as a replacement.[30]

Attlee, who had a good eye for opportunities to develop his younger ministers, found a different task for Wilson in October 1946. The Food and Agriculture Organization (FAO) was a specialist agency of the United Nations set up to tackle food shortages around the world. Sir John Boyd Orr, Independent MP for the Scottish Universities, was its first director general, and was to win the Nobel Peace Prize for his work in 1949. Boyd Orr wanted to appoint a working commission of the FAO comprised of sixteen countries chaired by former Australian prime minister Stanley Bruce. Attlee appointed Wilson as the head of the UK delegation. This meant three months in Washington working twelve-hour days managing a talented cross-departmental team that included John Wall, from the Ministry of Food, who was later ennobled by Wilson as prime minister, and Eugene Melville, a talented diplomat at the Colonial Office. Wilson had to try to find an agreed solution to the problem of the world overproducing and wasting food while simultaneously causing food shortages, particularly in the world's poorer countries. The solution that emerged was the use of formal agreements between countries around commodities. Managing a group like this was invaluable experience. The trip was also significant because it brought Wilson in contact with Tom Meyer for the first time. Tom was the son of Montague Meyer, and had succeeded his father as head of Montague L. Meyer Ltd, the largest timber-exporting firm in Britain. Time with his family was always important to Wilson, and he ensured that the period away was not an extended one, with Mary and Robin joining him in Washington for the last few weeks.

Over Christmas, Wilson updated Attlee on developments in Washington over lunch at Chequers, and the timber shortage at home. Cripps' advice from the Board of Trade was that there were no softwoods in the USA available for export. A purchasing commission was being dispatched to Canada only. Meyer, a friend of Tomlinson and Ernest Bevin, was on a tour of the USA and Canada looking for supplies. He confirmed to Wilson there was timber available in the USA, in contradiction of the civil service advice. Wilson found an ingenious solution. F.W. ('Bomber') Smith had been in charge of making the bombers at the Ministry of Aircraft Production in the Second World War; Wilson had had him brought into the Ministry of Works, in charge of building materials as director general. Now, Wilson had him added to the Board of Trade purchasing commission, and put him in touch with Tom Meyer. Smith adopted a two-stage approach: first, persuade the purchasing commission to find time to travel to the USA after completing timber purchases in Canada; second, contrive a meeting with Tom Meyer and purchase American timber. This was all done successfully, and the additional timber was secured for the housing programme.[31]

Wilson reported back on the Washington talks to the House of Commons on 6 February 1947. The commission had produced a substantial 75-page report that Wilson knew cover-to-cover. While he was still some years away from mastery of the chamber, it was a far more assured performance than he had produced previously. Richard Law, responding for the Conservatives, called his speech 'straightforward, lucid and brief'.[32] His argument was measured: 'I want to make it quite clear at the outset that this Report does nothing or, at any rate, very little to deal with the present acute world food shortage. What it does aim at doing is to ensure that the shortage of food for the ordinary people of the world will come to an end as food production increases, and not continue for 25 years, as it did after the last war.'[33] The agreement was known as the 'buffer stocks scheme' whereby countries would agree to purchase from each other to create price stability between set maximum and minimum prices.[34]

Weeks later, in March 1947, Wilson's long-awaited promotion arrived. Hilary Marquand moved to the role of paymaster general, with Wilson taking his place as secretary for Overseas Trade. While not in the cabinet, it was one of the most senior positions outside it. It made him the second-in-command to Cripps at the Board of Trade. It was a job worth waiting for. Wilson's first task was to attend the International Trade Organisation in Geneva at the end of the month. There, he immersed himself in the detail, but he had to wait until later in the year for any firm progress; eventually, the General Agreement on Tariffs and Trade (GATT) was signed by twenty-three nations on 30 October 1947. More pressing was the task of securing more timber: to do this, Attlee asked Wilson to travel to Moscow to join Ernest Bevin, who had suffered a recent heart attack and needed support in his work.

Wilson left on 18 April for three weeks of initial negotiations, before returning again on 20 June for final talks. Accompanied by his secretary Eileen Lane and civil servants, Wilson arrived in Moscow that spring to be treated to a bargaining style he had never encountered before. Bevin quickly departed, leaving the thirty-one-year-old Wilson to it. His opposite number was the wily Anastas Mikoyan, an Armenian political survivor who held on to senior roles from the time of Lenin to that of Brezhnev. As minister for Foreign Trade, he was formidable. He was also ruthless, perhaps even a cold-blooded killer. In 1975, when Wilson visited Moscow as prime minister, he was discussing the execution of Lavrentiy Beria. Beria was part of a triumvirate that, briefly, led the Soviet Union after the death of Stalin in 1953, before being overthrown by Nikita Khrushchev, tried and condemned to death. Wilson had been told by Mikoyan that two army generals had shot Beria in the throat. He was now told: 'When Beria came into the room, Mikoyan pulled a pearl-handled revolver from up his sleeve and shot him through the throat.'[35]

The first thing Wilson learned with Mikoyan was that there

were no rules. The British delegation stayed in the National Hotel in Moscow, kept under close surveillance. Food was hardly plentiful, and negotiations took place from the late evening to the early hours, when the Soviets thought opposing delegations were more likely to make concessions. On 22 April, the two sides met for the first time, with Wilson having to establish himself quickly as a match for a tough opponent. Mikoyan opened the negotiation on a positive note: 'Russia was ready to supply timber, timber products, cellulose, grain, salmon and crab.' He then added that 'quantities would be settled later', keeping that particular bargaining chip in his pocket. The timber supplies were offered in return for equipment from Britain. There would, however, be a cost to this: 'Mr Mikoyan said that in order to expand Anglo-Soviet trade on a basis of cash payment both ways, it would be necessary for Russia to secure some modification of the terms of repayment, which were onerous for Russia, of the credit advanced under the Civil Supplies Agreement of 1941.' Referring to this wartime arrangement was to raise the stakes; Wilson was canny in response, saying that he had no authority to discuss it.[36]

At the meeting of the delegations two days later, it remained the sticking point: 'Mr Wilson said that he had . . . sent an account of Mikoyan's proposals to London for information, but that he had received no instructions.' It became testy: 'Mr Mikoyan replied that this was . . . a question of the commodity credit granted during the war and affecting current trade. Without a settlement of this question we would not be able to reach agreement.' Wilson continued to argue that the delegation had no authority to deal with the issue, and 'did not think it was likely that London would authorise us to deal with it.' The response was firm: 'Mr Mikoyan said that these were attempts to put aside discussion of this question . . .' Wilson was equally strong, and 'asked Mr Mikoyan whether he was making a modification of the 1941 Agreement a prior condition of trade talks. If so, Mr Wilson had no doubt what the reaction of the Government would be, namely to instruct him to return home.' At this point Mikoyan budged and 'said that the Russian side would [only] insist on their proposal being discussed.'[37]

Wilson's advice from his civil servants was that he should aim at securing the supply of 100,000 standards of softwood. While a smaller quantity would help, he was told he 'should not be too ready to accept any Russian protestations that they can only make small quantities available.'[38] Wilson achieved an offer of 50,000 standards from Mikoyan, which meant enough for around 30,000 houses. However, despite the information Wilson had been given, this was thought to be the maximum Russia could offer in 1947 without being 'at the expense of Russia's own real needs'.[39] In exchange, Mikoyan wanted assistance with the mechanisation for the Russian timber industry. Wilson discussed the equipment that Britain could supply for this, including cutters and excavators, and also offered to assist with technological development by supplying jet engines.[40] No agreement was reached on the repayments of the wartime credit. Wilson cabled back to Cripps to confirm that he presumed he was still instructed not to discuss the issue of the credit.[41] This did not change and, on 6 May, in a meeting lasting over two and a half hours: '. . . we were unable to shake Mikoyan far from his previous attitude.'[42] Wilson and the delegation left two days later.

When Wilson reported to the Commons in a written statement on 12 May, he summarised the position as the Russian government offering 'moderate quantities of timber and timber products' for export in 1947, with a suggestion of a steadily increasing supply. In return, the UK would supply equipment. The Russians also offered food from 1948, including wheat and coarse grains. As regards the longer term, he was less optimistic: 'The Russian Government expressed the view that a healthy development of Anglo-Soviet trade would not be possible unless some further adjustment of the terms of the credits advanced under the Civil Supplies Agreement of 1941 were made and that any general agreement about the development of trade between the two countries should be linked with an agreement on the credit question.'[43]

Yet it was Wilson's decision to offer to supply jet engines to the Soviet Union that was to cause the greatest controversy, and proved to be the start of a relationship of deep suspicion, and at times, hostility, between him and the security services. The Armed Forces Chiefs of Staff issued a 'Top Secret' memorandum put together by MI5 which argued against East–West trade on the basis that the Soviet trade delegations were likely to include intelligence officers. Of particular concern was 'the Russian Wood Agency concerned with timber exports and the Soviet trade delegation itself' who should be refused visas to come to Britain. There should be a list of items embargoed for export.[44] Thus, the 'Chiefs were annoyed by the decision of the President of the BOT, Cripps, and Attlee – against the advice of the Cold War advocates – to sell the Soviets twenty Rolls-Royce Nene and Derwent jet engines. Wilson played absolutely no part in this decision. They were more angry at the offer of jet aircraft as bargaining chips in Wilson's search for timber and grain supplies in the Soviet Union.'[45]

The case against Wilson was that 'the Soviet Union wishes to buy jet aircraft engines which had strategic uses – the turbine blades were made of a secret steel called "Mnemonic 80" . . . the Foreign Office "fought like cats" to prevent this, but the Board of Trade believed that exports were more important than ideology; that the minister approved the idea in the absence of Ernest Bevin in Moscow; and the engines were subsequently copied in the new MIG fighters used by the Russians.'[46] The Rolls-Royce jet engines were world-leading and Wilson's agenda was, apparently, to assist the communist regime against the West. A document allegedly by MI5, sent to *Private Eye* in 1974, stated that the export, in 1947, of the two Rolls-Royce engines – the Nene and the Derwent – had significant consequences: 'This give-away not only enabled the Russians to catch up very rapidly with the superior technology in jets then possessed by the British, but also enabled her to save the enormous R & D costs that the British people had spent in developing such products.'[47]

It is certain from the government papers that Wilson did offer the Soviet delegation jet engines. There is, however, absolutely nothing to show that this was done because of some desire to give the communist Soviet Union a competitive advantage in the Cold War against the capitalist West. In the context of the negotiation, it was entirely rational and sensible: aside from the discounted repayments on the wartime loan, on which Wilson had no instructions to concede, what the Soviet Union needed was machinery and technological advancement. Offering the jet engines was unsurprising in this context.

The second stage of the negotiations was a disappointment. Wilson had not wanted to return to Moscow so soon as it looked desperate, but two issues tipped the balance: the continuing need for timber, and the opening up of a new source of raw materials for Britain, strengthening its hand in the ongoing trade talks in Geneva. There were some notable triumphs. On feeding grain, Wilson was tasked with securing 700,000 tonnes. Mikoyan offered 500,000 tonnes; Wilson demanded 2 million. When Mikoyan failed to move, he decided to call for his return aircraft and reclaimed all the washing from the laundry at the hotel. Mikoyan called him to a midnight meeting before the aeroplane was due to depart and offered 1.25 million. 'Weeks of hard bargaining has produced many fluctuations between hope and disappointment,' reported *The Times* on 24 July. 'A part of the agreement providing for the export of a small quantity of Soviet timber to this country has been concluded . . .'

Cripps reported to the Commons on 28 July: 'After several difficulties, we had succeeded in reaching agreement on all matters within the trade field, including quantities, prices and terms and conditions of shipment . . . But, unfortunately, with so wide an agreement on trade matters, we were unable to reach agreement on the terms of repayment of the 1941 Credit.'[48] Though Britain had offered concessions, including the rate of interest, there was a limit to the loss to the economy the government was willing to accept.[49] Mikoyan followed up by only paying £1 million of the £2.4 million instalment due on the credit agreement on 1 August 1947. At cabinet on 7 August, as a consequence, Ernest Bevin said there was 'no question of reopening discussions' until this was paid in full.[50]

The negotiations with the Soviet Union having broken down, Wilson returned to Geneva where non-discrimination in trade between countries was the issue of the day. He was uncompromising:

Britain would protect its interests and *would* discriminate in favour of the Commonwealth. Invited to cabinet on 19 August, he declared: 'The United States Delegation has now accepted our view on the matter.'[51] He then left for a holiday in Cornwall with Mary and Robin, enjoying some fishing at Mullion Cove on the Lizard Peninsula. While there, he was summoned back by the prime minister for lunch at Chequers. Wilson knew it had to be for a good reason so boarded the train at Penzance as soon as he could.

For Wilson personally, 1947 was a year of political progress. For the government as a whole, it was a different story. The Conservative slogan of 'Shiver with Shinwell' was coined as the minister of Fuel and Power took the blame for the fuel shortage during the deep freeze of January to March 1947. As the snow built up, coal movement became impossible. By early February, power stations were on the verge of total closure.[52] Whole villages were cut off, offices and factories had to close and unemployment spiked. The fuel shortage also contributed to a fall in exports, causing the balance of payments position to deteriorate.[53] That summer, there was a full-blown currency crisis. In November 1945, to fund the postwar recovery, the government had agreed a loan of $3.75bn with the United States of America, a condition of which was subject to a 'convertibility clause' meaning that, on 15 July, sterling became freely available for exchange into dollars.[54] Countries that used the pound sterling, or had currencies pegged to it, had not been directly paid for goods and services provided to Britain in wartime. This meant that recompense could be demanded in dollars, not pounds, and then spent outside Britain, which would be spending far more dollars than it was earning.[55] By 1 August, $2.75bn of the whole $3.75bn had been used, and drawings continued.[56] Eventually, on 20 August, the free convertibility of sterling was suspended. But the damage was done. The balance of payments issue was addressed with a reduction in imports, meaning a raft of unpopular measures including a cut in the meat ration from 7 September, and restrictions on foreign travel. Attlee's leadership style, leaving his cabinet members to get on with their jobs without prime ministerial interference, brought criticism, particularly with him on holiday in North Wales for most of the August crisis. The press asked Morrison, deputising for the prime minister, if Attlee intended to retire.[57]

Wilson was to profit from the political situation that resulted. Attlee was in trouble, and Cripps sought to depose him. Matters came to a head on 5 September when Cripps approached Dalton: 'He [Cripps] said we *must* now shift Attlee and replace him by Bevin. Otherwise the Government, the Party and the country were all sunk. There was no leadership, no grip, no decision.'[58] The plot had two major flaws. First, the senior members of the government could not agree on who Attlee should be replaced with. Though he had become ill with a thrombosis in the leg and pneumonia, Morrison remained highly ambitious and would not agree to Ernest Bevin becoming prime minister. 'He thought that *he* should be Prime Minister . . . He wouldn't serve under Bevin.'[59] Second, the main candidate to take over was loyal to Attlee. On 9 September, when Cripps went to visit Attlee alone to suggest he be replaced by Bevin, Attlee telephoned his foreign secretary who confirmed he did not want to change jobs. This ended the attempted coup, and Attlee then bought off Cripps with the offer of being minister in charge of Economic Affairs, which he accepted.

This opened up the opportunity for Wilson to be promoted to the post of president of the Board of Trade. At Chequers, Attlee, in his usual clipped tones, told Wilson that Cripps was being given an overall, supervisory responsibility for Economic Affairs and that he wanted Wilson to take his old job. Morrison was supportive of this, but Cripps' recommendation was crucial: Attlee later wrote that he was 'fortified' by Cripps in his choice of Wilson.[60] Wilson respected Cripps, and often referred to a speech he gave in that testing 1947 summer as an example of a piece of outstanding oratory.[61] On 7 August, Cripps spoke in the Commons on the need to increase production and used his peroration to refer to 'the deep spiritual values that we acknowledge in our Christian faith, that we shall be enabled and inspired to move the present mountains of our difficulties, and so emerge into that new and fertile plain of prosperity which we shall travel in happiness only as the result of

our own efforts and our own vision.'[62] Given his own Congregationalist background, it is easy to see why this struck a chord with
Wilson, who, given his own issues with making a positive impression in the Commons with his speeches, had a model to look to.

With his elegant suits and rimless spectacles, Cripps was a man
of precision. He was an austere, detached figure: a vegetarian and
teetotaller who held himself to the highest standards of personal
integrity. Churchill is said to have remarked of him: 'There, but
for the grace of God, goes God himself!'[63] Yet he and Wilson both
had their religion, together with a firm grasp of administrative
detail: their motivations and their minds were similar. Wilson
himself described Cripps' thinking as 'that of a trainee lawyer, a
master of speedy reactions in the middle of a cross-examination;
moreover in his case the master-stroke was planted in his mind by
the Almighty.'[64] They also had political experiences in common.
As Wilson battled with Mikoyan, Cripps also knew the Soviet
negotiating style well: his reputation as a man of the left had led to
his appointment by Churchill as British ambassador to the Soviet
Union from 1941 to 1942. When Wilson saw Cripps the day after
his appointment, there was genuine warmth: 'Well, my boy . . .
You've seen Clem. Let me say I'm very glad indeed – and happy for
you.'[65] Thus, in his first two government roles, Wilson had developed a closeness to two of its most left-wing members in Aneurin
Bevan and Stafford Cripps.

Gaitskell was also a big winner as he replaced the under-pressure
Shinwell at Fuel and Power. This left an uneasy situation with
Cripps in charge of 'Economic Affairs' with Dalton still chancellor, though this was to resolve itself in weeks. On 12 November,
before his budget, Dalton leaked its principal measures to the *Star*'s
lobby correspondent John Carvel. By the standards of the time, it
was a major scandal. Wilson recalled it was the only time he 'ever
saw Attlee rattled'.[66] Dalton was removed, and Cripps took over as
chancellor, the post of Economic Affairs abolished. The economic
crisis was also easing. On 5 June, US Secretary of State George
Marshall set out what became known as the 'Marshall Plan' in
a speech at Harvard University: financial assistance to improve

social and economic conditions to support free institutions. On 12 July, a conference on European construction began in Paris: Soviet foreign minister Molotov walked out. Between April 1948 and December 1951, Britain was to receive around 3 billion dollars in aid. A further currency crisis was staved off, at least for the time being. By the time another one came, in 1949, Wilson was a far more senior member of the government.

Chapter 5

Aircraft engines revved up

President of the Board of Trade, 1947–51

Harold Wilson was delighted to be the youngest cabinet member of the twentieth century at thirty-one. Even Gladstone had not become president of the Board of Trade until thirty-three, the same age that Winston Churchill had been on entering the same office in 1908. If Wilson had done little else, it was a fine achievement in itself, and a recognition of his competence as a minister and his grip on those parts of the government machine for which he had been responsible. It also represented another step in a seamless progression from his work with William Beveridge and in the wartime civil service. He adored the job: for the remainder of his career, he referred back to his years at the Board of Trade. Wilson could indulge his interest in statistics and combine it with a boyish excitement for the public side of the role, relishing the company of the stars of the silver screen. He quoted yearly trade figures to anyone who would care to listen, and continued to take an interest in the film industry in the decades ahead.

The new president had every reason to be proud of himself, and made a positive start. On 7 October, he spent the day with Sir Raymond Streat, a Lancashire grammar school boy, who, after two decades as an officer of the Manchester Chamber of Commerce, had been appointed chairman of the Cotton Board in 1940. Streat's initial view was positive: 'I think Wilson made a good impression on my cotton friends and on me personally. He is quick in the uptake – too well versed in economics and civil service work to rant or rave like a soap-box socialist . . . he lets his mind work on lines that come naturally to a young economist with civil service experience. We shall get on easily with him.' He contrasted him favourably with Cripps: 'He is less aloof than the man of austere principles, fanaticism and Christian ideals with whom we have dealt since 1945 . . .'[1]

This was a happy period for Wilson, spoiled only by the fall of Dalton, a mentor to the younger generation of MPs, for whom Wilson had a genuine affection. He was upset to see him go. A Dalton decision in his final months as chancellor also caused Wilson some inconvenience in the cabinet room. Earlier in the year, on 15 April, Dalton had hiked customs duty on tobacco imports, increasing the price of a packet of twenty cigarettes.[2] To show a lead, and share the pain of the nation, Attlee banned smoking during cabinet meetings. Wilson was unhappy not to be able to puff on his cigarettes and was frustrated by the comings and goings during cabinet discussions. Minister after minister suddenly found they needed to use the lavatory and returned to their seats carrying a smell of tobacco. It was an issue Wilson returned to during both his periods as prime minister: 'In my own period in office from 1964 to 1970 there were no restrictions on smoking, but Mr Heath reintroduced them [from 1970–74].' In 1974, back in government, his rule was: 'Smoking is not compulsory.'[3]

Wilson inherited two parliamentary private secretaries from Cripps. The first, Barbara Castle, was to have an enduring political relationship with him lasting decades. Elected MP for Blackburn in 1945, Castle was a trailblazer for women in politics. A tenacious campaigner and a memorable, passionate speaker, with her red hair and keen sense of fashion, Castle was to become a leading member of Wilson's governments in the 1960s and 1970s, and one of the most distinctive political figures in post-war Britain. Wilson always enjoyed female company, and having a woman as parliamentary private secretary suited him. Castle reflected that: 'He liked a flirtation, but it was verbal rather than physical.'[4] She thought that one 'of Harold's endearing traits was his desire to bring women to the fore. He was an instinctive feminist: the first Prime Minister to have two women in his Cabinet. Like Ted [her husband] he never regarded women as rivals, but rejoiced in their success and was always trying to promote them to new opportunities. Such men are rare.'[5] Castle and Wilson had their ups and downs, but her loyalty to him was crucial in the many political battles that lay ahead.

Wilson's other parliamentary private secretary, Tom Cook, MP for Dundee East, provided an immediate benefit to Wilson. He was an electrician, adept at removing the covert listening devices the Soviets used on visiting overseas politicians. Wilson added Cook to his trade delegation to travel to the Soviet Union, which had had a bountiful harvest, yielding a surplus of grain that Britain could access. On the Russian side, the priority remained machinery: for mining and rails as well as the timber industry.[6] After a day's delay in Berlin due to bad weather, Wilson arrived in Moscow on 5 December to start the negotiations. Wilson and Mikoyan then started their long game of brinkmanship. Mikoyan told Wilson that Britain's politicians were too old. Wilson pointed out that he was thirty-one, and challenged Mikoyan to pick a football team: the Kremlin's first eleven versus eleven British MPs. Mikoyan said he would be on the sidelines but the tough Molotov would play in goal and nobody would score past him![7] Cook busied himself with removing bugs, including one under a bath in Wilson's room.

Wilson was so meticulous in his approach that he decided to stop puffing his way through cigarettes and took up pipe smoking instead so as to slow himself down in such tense situations. Events also helped: a telegram arrived to notify Wilson that an agreement on wheat had been concluded with Australia. This took that whole issue out of the talks with Mikoyan; Wilson now only needed to reach an agreement on coarse grains, which meant agreeing a price. It was salami-slicing at its finest. Wilson had the engines of his aircraft revved up at Vnukovo airport to add to the suspense. Wilson's upper limit was $123. He started at $97, moved to $108, then finally reached an agreement at $113 at 5 a.m. at the end of the final negotiating session. It was a job well done. On 11 December, in the House of Commons, Wilson told the Tories: 'I only wish they could have been there to see the speed and helpfulness with which quantities and prices were fixed between five o'clock and six o'clock yesterday morning.'[8]

The experience had a profound effect on Wilson, and he remained an ardent admirer of the Soviet negotiating style long afterwards. There was, no doubt, self-interest at play too: Wilson could hardly use the trips to Moscow as evidence of his own political skill if he accepted that he had inept opponents on the other side of the table. But his feeling was genuine. When he outlined his vision of a Britain forged in the white heat of the technological revolution sixteen years later, it was the economic threat of the Soviet Union that he had in mind: 'For those of us who have studied the formidable Soviet challenge in the education of scientists and technologists . . . know that our future lies not in military strength alone but in the effort, the sacrifices, and above all the energies which a free people can mobilise for the future greatness of our country.' He deplored the 'methods which Communist countries are deploying in applying the results of scientific research to industrial life' but insisted that Britain should 'use all the resources of democratic planning . . .'[9] As Neil Kinnock put it: 'Wilson – for some extraordinary reason – held the Soviet Union in awe.' Kinnock always thought his negative view of Soviet industrial power probably got him dropped off Wilson's 'promising backbenchers' list in the 1970s.[10] This is not to say that Wilson ever had any affection for the Soviet leaders. On his final day in Moscow, Stalin invited him and his colleagues for dinner at the Kremlin. Wilson did not hesitate in turning it down to fulfil an engagement with Attlee at Number Ten, celebrating the engagement of Princess Elizabeth and Lieutenant Philip Mountbatten.[11]

Alongside his new job, Wilson also found stability in his living arrangements. By 1948, Mary was again pregnant. This, together with the increase in Wilson's salary to £5,000 a year, prompted a change. Remarkably, Wilson had been managing a three-centre existence: nursing his constituency in Ormskirk; staying with his parents in London; and travelling to Oxford, where Mary and Robin had been living, first in college rooms, then in a college flat on Banbury Road, in the north of the city. Maintaining the college accommodation had necessitated Wilson continuing to teach on weekends. It was too much, and only Wilson's prodigious energy had made it possible.

Therefore, on their eighth wedding anniversary, 1 January 1948, Wilson and Mary moved to Southway in Hampstead Garden Suburb with Robin, shortly before the Wilsons' second son, Giles, was born on 7 May. They initially took number 10 Southway, then moved next door to number 12, where they remained until Wilson won the keys to 10 Downing Street in 1964. This made Wilson's life much easier, not only in terms of logistics but also in terms of family harmony. The £5,100 purchase price was partly funded by a loan of £800 from Herbert Wilson, who had just sold the family house in Milnsbridge, having relied upon its rental income.

Mary was very happy with life in Hampstead. With Golders Green station having opened in 1900, the land north of Hampstead Heath was ideal for housing. The particular type of development was the brainchild of Henrietta Barnett, a believer in social reform who wanted to create an area of quality housing for all, by creating a space of low-housing density with an emphasis on gardens and landscaped open areas. Thus, the Garden Suburb was established by a private parliamentary bill in 1906.[12] Barnett created a trust that purchased 243 acres of land – from Eton College – and her vision was made reality by the planners Barry Parker and Sir Raymond Unwin, with Sir Edwin Lutyens, arguably the finest architect of his day, laying out the central square. The Wilson family were in London, but very removed from the hustle and bustle of the capital's central streets and the cramped accommodation of other districts. No wonder Mary later said that she hoped to 'stay [there] forever'.[13] She could bring up her boys away from the goldfish bowl of politics, but close enough to Westminster for it not to be a strain on her husband. It also suited Wilson, who made himself known to the local Scouts and the Free Church. Giles, meanwhile, became quite the parliamentary baby, christened in the crypt in parliament in September 1948, with the Attlees as godparents. Wilson found time for his sons, even when his political career dominated his time, always keeping fifteen minutes in the morning to take the children to school, and eating with the family whenever he could.[14]

In contrast, Wilson's relationship with his civil servants was mixed. Some he had little to do with. Partly, this was because Wilson thought he could rely on his own knowledge. It was no coincidence that, having been a member of the Economic Section himself as a civil servant, he barely consulted its head, Robert Hall. In July 1949, after a discussion on the issue of devaluation of sterling, Hall recorded in his diary, icily, that 'he had hardly spoken to me for a year and was now anxious to get on the right side.'[15] Wilson's principal private secretary, the New Zealander Max Brown, saw Wilson as someone who 'had more of a civil service than a political background and, in these early days, he was happiest with civil servants'. But Brown damned Wilson with faint praise: 'Some people think fast and stop . . . Others think three or four times, but not fast. Wilson belonged in the first category.'[16] For all this, Wilson was always full of energy and was kind and courteous. Alec Cairncross, then advising the Board of Trade, lunched with Wilson's assistant private secretary Michael Halls who 'described . . . the President's exertions, including about six successive nights on the train, and his astonishing resiliency and good nature. Never angry.' In fact, Cairncross thought Wilson was too nice. His kindness prevented him from being more direct with people.[17]

The Board of Trade was a challenging department. The permanent secretary, John Henry Woods, a man of gravitas and authority, delivered a lecture to the Institute of Public Administration on 9 December 1947, just over two months after Wilson took office, entitled: 'Administrative Problems of the Board of Trade'.[18] Woods was worried that too much was going to be expected from civil servants, particularly with the additional need to manage Marshall Aid. Woods divided the responsibilities of the department into two categories: domestic and foreign. On the home front, the Board of Trade had to ensure a range of industries, such as steel, timber, transport, fuel and power, met the needs of the country. Others, including textiles, films, tobacco, pottery, glass, hosiery, and furniture had to meet export targets. Internationally, Woods complained that the Board of Trade had carried the burden of preparing for the trade discussions in Geneva. He had a point in terms of the work it caused for the department, but Wilson himself was always well briefed. There were two major issues: a general lowering of tariff barriers around the world, and agreeing a charter for a new world trade body. Wilson saw the issue in strategic terms, informing cabinet that the central issue was between Britain and America: the idea of an 'International Trade Organisation, to which we are fully committed . . . really stands and falls on an agreement on tariffs and preferences between ourselves and the U.S.A.'[19] This meant Britain reducing its trade preferences for the Commonwealth, and America lowering its protective barriers around its native industries like synthetic rubber manufacture. The General Agreement on Tariffs and Trade (GATT) had eventually been signed on 30 October 1947.

Wilson had the self-assurance to overrule his officials, including on one of the major issues of the day: the relaxation of wartime controls. Woods and his deputy, Sir James Helmore, thought Wilson should either leave things as they were or end rationing altogether. Wilson dismissed this, and adopted a staged approach, knowing the impact that the ration books were having on daily life: 'the Board of Trade was best known to the public as the department for clothes rationing. The miserable ration of twenty-six coupons for the period of six months still continued and the whole population was shabby and ill-clothed.'[20] Wilson was determined to change this, but was initially delayed by the economic conditions, with priority having to be given to exports to ease the balance of payments crisis.

The network of restrictions was extensive. There were measures on: prices; production, including in textiles; consumption, particularly food rationing; the need for licences for import and export; and centralised purchasing, including for raw materials. In some areas, controls had even been tightened. In October 1947, the government had issued a Control of Engagement Order preventing workers leaving certain industries, and directing the unemployed to accept work. On 6 October 1948, Wilson spoke at the Institution of Works' Managers Luncheon in London, stressing that 'he hoped to announce a considerable easing of quota controls in industry. Within the last six months a very large number of controls had disappeared.' This was 'Mr Wilson's Hint,' claimed *The Times* the next day.[21]

Though Wilson's measures met little opposition in parliament, there was disquiet on the left about sweeping away this system of state control. After the First World War, the Lloyd George coalition's decisions on ending wartime directions were widely thought to have been major errors, particularly in the case of the coal industry that was returned to private ownership. The controls were regarded as a means of bringing about equality. The *New Statesman* accused Wilson of 'bland capitulation to rationing by price'.[22] There was deep concern in cabinet as to how this all looked. A socialist government did not want to be seen to be restoring free markets. When Wilson presented a memorandum to cabinet for discussion on the relaxation of import restrictions on 20 June 1949, 'it was agreed that some alternative words should be substituted for "liberalisation" and "liberalising" in future papers and statements on this subject.'[23] Wilson was, however, sensitive to the privations of life under the Attlee governments. In this, he took a similar view to Herbert Morrison, who, with one eye on the next general election, could see how the easing of controls would lift the government's popularity.

The president of the Board of Trade took to the task with enthusiasm. From April, when he removed controls over the manufacture of mugs and babies' beakers, to October 1948, controls on everyday items were relaxed every month. In June, it was ties and stockings; in July, it was toys. It was, however, the issue of footwear that attracted controversy: the first time a furore surrounding Wilson penetrated the national consciousness. The decisions themselves were straightforward, with rationing ended for children's shoes in May and for adults in August.[24] Wilson's political argument was a sound one: that the Attlee government's comprehensive welfare provision had raised the quality of life of the nation's poorest people so that children could now go to school with quality shoes on their feet. The problem was how he expressed this, in a speech in Birmingham on 3 July 1948: 'The school I went to in the North was a school where more than half the children in my class never had boots and shoes on their feet. I have been up there again, and the children of my old school are now running about with decent shoes because their fathers are in safe jobs and got the social security which we promised our people.'[25] Wilson should never have said this unless he was sure it would be verified by others. As a statement on its own, it had two obvious weaknesses: first, it refers to a school Wilson went to, and, second, makes a specific claim about the children there. In order to undermine Wilson, all that was required was to ask staff or local people there whether it was accurate.

Whatever the situation with unemployment and poverty in inter-war Britain, civic pride remained an important factor. The mayor of Huddersfield was incensed and rejected the suggestion that Wilson's New Street Elementary School, Milnsbridge, had barefoot pupils. Wilson was probably wise to have withdrawn from the fray at this point, but he continued the argument: '. . . there were thousands of children who actually went barefoot during the war. I referred to this in terms of the slums of Liverpool and other big cities, which I can certainly confirm from my own experience.' He claimed that he 'did not say or suggest that was at all the case in Huddersfield; my only reference to barefoot children was in Liverpool, Manchester and Birmingham . . . in fact I never suggested that my school friends had to go to school barefoot, as was the case in many more depressed areas. Such a suggestion would have been quite incorrect, I agree.'[26]

The 'Barefoot Boy' speech, as it became known, was to be hung around Wilson's neck for decades. He had never said he went to school barefoot, but that was how it was portrayed. Norman Shrapnel, the *Guardian*'s parliamentary sketch writer, recalled: 'In later years he found it necessary to deny that he ever made this claim, and I remember a Conservative remarking that the only reason young Harold would ever have gone without boots would have been because he was too big for them.'[27] It was used as an example of Wilson's inauthenticity, and having scant regard for the truth in saying what was helpful to him politically. It also cemented in Wilson's mind a hatred for the press, whom he claimed had not reported his speech faithfully. Wilson's account was that, since the playground was sloping and great for sliding in frosty weather, many pupils wore clogs with iron cladding on the soles, 'which enabled them not only to raise sparks, but to outdistance those of us wearing stout leather boots . . .' At a press conference, Wilson said that at 'my school, pre-war . . . many did not wear leather shoes, they wore clogs. The Conservative press went mad with delight. In no time they were reporting me as saying that my schoolmates had nothing on their feet; then I had none . . . It was many years before the Press ceased to deride me as "Barefoot boy." But Labour Ministers must expect this literary style: as Confucius, or perhaps another philosopher said: "What do you expect from a pig but a grunt?"'[28]

Wilson's abolition of a large number of controls on 5 November 1948 also penetrated the public consciousness. With a nod to his father, he loosened restrictions on dyestuffs, and a wide variety of other household and luxury items, from fertilisers to fountain pens to gramophone records to glue, jewellery and silk.[29] Choosing Guy Fawkes Day for their implementation meant it was characterised as the day that Wilson lit a match under the apparatus of the wartime state: this was his 'Bonfire of Controls'. In the Commons, the Conservatives complained that it was a 'little bonfire' that should have been much bigger.[30] Wilson argued that he had made considerable progress, and that 200,000 fewer licences would be issued each year as a consequence of his changes.[31] There was a long way to go: petrol would not come off the ration until March 1950; food rationing did not disappear completely until July 1954.

A more pressing concern was clothing. The Conservatives accused Wilson of having raised expectations that he would loosen restrictions, though he was firm in response: 'I specifically said that there was no question of abolishing clothes rationing, or of anything of a similar kind being on that bonfire . . .'[32] Nonetheless, he knew he would have to act soon. The announcement was made with some elan: on 14 March, the president of the Board of Trade ostentatiously tore up his clothing ration book.[33]

In the British Pathé film of Wilson's announcement, he is sat behind a desk, pipe in hand, citing the increase in production in clothing and textiles as having made the difference. He appealed to people to buy only what they needed and emphasised the continued importance of the export drive.[34] While Wilson was clear in what he said, he looked awkward. He was sat stiffly, his mode of delivery formal, more in the style of giving a speech rather than speaking with watching voters. In order to develop a folksy connection with the public, it was obvious that Wilson was going to have to evolve: above all, he was going to need to become more relaxed and conversational.

The measure itself was well received. Streat welcomed the end of clothes rationing, and the removal of price controls on yarn and cloth the following month.[35] Wilson, to confirm the continuing importance of the export drive, set off for a three-week tour of Canada on 10 May with Castle and a number of civil servants, returning home to make a national broadcast calling for Britain to increase its North American exports. If his mode of speaking remained the same, his appearance did at least start to change soon afterwards. He shaved off his small moustache as Herbert Morrison kept mistaking him for pensions minister Hilary Marquand: Marquand refused to remove his own as it had been there first.[36]

The transatlantic relationship required careful management in another important area: the film industry. Wilson loved its lustre and glamour; he thoroughly enjoyed mixing with the stars of the 1940s screen. The South African actress Edana Romney, later a TV personality and writer, even came to watch Wilson speak from the House of Commons gallery.[37] Yet there was a major problem to solve. In August 1947, Dalton had slapped a 75 per cent levy on imported American films. Instead of raising much-needed revenue, it had the unintended effect of prompting a Hollywood boycott, with American film producers refusing to send new films to Britain. The British Film Producers' Association told Wilson that this would 'inflict serious financial hardship on British film producers, who cannot, except on a long-term plan, so increase production as to make British cinemas independent of imported films.'[38] In a period when the weekly visit to the cinema was part of British life, the quality and variety of films on show was of cultural and social importance. As it was, cinema-goers faced the unappealing choice of numerous repeats of past American films or more limited domestically produced offerings. With the American ambassador, Lew Douglas, protesting to the Foreign Office, Wilson announced the abolition of the levy in the Commons on 11 March 1948, indicating that the export of American films to the UK could then resume.[39]

This did not, however, solve the problem of how more films could be produced in the United Kingdom. For this, Wilson relied on a number of other measures. The first of these was to raise the quota of home-produced films shown in British cinemas from 30 per cent to 45 per cent in June 1948.[40] This was not entirely effective, and, in March 1949, Wilson reduced the quota to 40 per cent.[41] Finally, in March 1950, Wilson announced that the quota would return to 30 per cent.[42] Setting the level of the quota presented a dilemma: '. . . it is important that the quota should be fixed reasonably high, but it is also important in the interests of the quota legislation as a whole to fix the quota at a level where we can enforce a much better standard of compliance with it than we have had in recent years.'[43]

Second, Wilson's National Film Finance Corporation was incorporated in October 1948: its purpose was to distribute loans for film production. Again, this was only partially effective, since it was, in practice, offering financial support for production not distribution, an issue Wilson acknowledged.[44] The problem this created was that there was little in the way of quality control over the film-making. Wilson also worried about public money being frittered away. Alexander Korda's London Films Productions had bought a controlling interest in British Lion Films after the war, and it received substantial finance from the National Film Finance Corporation. In late October 1948, Wilson attended a party at Korda's London apartment in celebration of the premiere of his latest film, *Bonnie Prince Charlie*. Wilson told him he had enjoyed the film, but, with a cost of £750,000, it would not make £150,000 at the box office. Wilson was later told it had made £151,000, but he had made his point. Korda teased the president of the Board of Trade: 'just wait until you see my next [film]. It is being filmed in the sewers of Vienna.' Wilson pointed out it was the money of taxpayers going down the Austrian drains. On this occasion, he need not have worried, as the picture was Graham Greene's classic, *The Third Man*.[45] Wilson could also claim credit for other films financed by the National Film Finance Corporation, from *The Fallen Idol* to *Seven Days to Noon* to *State Secret*.

Wilson also made another lasting contribution: the concept of levy on box office takings, which was introduced on a voluntary basis in September 1950. The idea was to distribute the money on a 50/50 basis: half to the exhibitor, and half to subsidise the production companies via the British Film Fund Agency. Known as the 'Eady Levy' after the plan of the Treasury official, Sir Wilfred Eady, it was made compulsory in 1957. Wilson made no attempt to name the levy after himself: knowing the Treasury, as he did, he saw no harm in giving credit to a civil servant and thought there would be an advantage in it remaining in place in the long term.

If Wilson had a hands-on approach to the film industry, he also managed to create distance between himself and scandals. The first was uncomfortably close to home. In late August 1948, Wilson was told by his officials about the allegation of a bribe to withdraw a criminal prosecution. John Belcher, parliamentary secretary at the Board of Trade, was implicated.

With Attlee away, Wilson had approached Cripps, who asked Jowitt, as lord chancellor, to look into it. The Board of Trade also informed the Metropolitan Police. While there could have been questions as to how closely Wilson was supervising the actions of his junior minister, these swift actions were to his credit. On 27 October 1948, Attlee set up an inquiry, and said all 'allegations could be traced back to the activities of a certain alien'.[46] This was Sidney Stanley, a man of multiple aliases, a Polish émigré who had lost his citizenship and was stateless; he had been bankrupt more than once and made his dubious living by offering to influence public officials in return for cash. Sir George Lynskey presided over the tribunal, which opened on 15 November 1948 at Church House, Westminster, and reported on 21 January 1949. Belcher was caught by the allegation that he had, in return for gifts from Stanley, improperly withdrawn the prosecution against football pools promoter Harry Sherman who had exceeded the amount of paper licensed to his firm for coupons. Belcher resigned his parliamentary seat the following month.

The second issue was what became known as the 'groundnuts scandal' that was conceived as a piece of latter-day colonial exploitation. Frank Samuel, managing director of the Unilever subsidiary, the United Africa Company, had the idea of clearing 2.5 million acres of East African land to grow peanuts on a large scale to avert a worldwide shortage of fats. No household in the UK would have to concern itself with the prospect of cooking oil supplies running out and, it was assumed, houses and infrastructure would be built for the local workforce. At the insistence of Cripps, who thought the Colonial Office incapable of managing such a large project, responsibility for delivery was passed to John Strachey at the Ministry of Food.[47] It was a disaster, with even basic data like soil condition and rainfall not properly investigated, let alone the sourcing of appropriate machinery, like heavy tractors, and essential materials such as steel. Strachey blamed John Wakefield, a former director of agriculture in Tanganyika, who had headed a commission that, in September 1946, recommended the specific three-and-a-quarter million acres for cultivation, mostly in Tanganyika. Strachey said the Wakefield Report had underestimated the challenges.[48] His successor at the Ministry of Food, Maurice Webb, eventually had to abandon the scheme altogether in January 1951, with £37 million of public money wasted. Wilson managed to avoid any personal blame, despite the fact that he was responsible for trade policy and had not opposed the idea, principally because the Ministry of Food had been specifically tasked with delivering the scheme.

The issue for which Wilson did take a great deal of responsibility was the devaluation of the pound in September 1949. It was a seminal moment in his political career: he was at the centre of decision-making on an issue central to the government's future prospects, and introduced him to the strategic dilemmas he would later face as prime minister as a consequence of the position of sterling. The context is important. In September 1931, in the midst of the Great Depression, Britain had left the gold standard – the system by which paper currency was convertible into a fixed amount of gold. Trading partners were then encouraged to peg their currencies to the value of the pound. These were, mostly, Commonwealth countries, but other nations, too. If Britain ran a trade deficit with a particular country in the Sterling Area, that country would hold the surplus in London banks. The idea was to reduce barriers to trade, and to protect the empire, though, in 1939, exchange controls had to be introduced on the outbreak of the Second World War. At the Bretton Woods Conference in July 1944, representatives of forty-four countries met with the aim of creating a stable international monetary system after the war. This system rested on countries pegging their currencies to the US dollar, which was itself pegged to the value of gold. Yet many countries remained in the Sterling Area, including most of the Commonwealth (though Canada was a notable exception), but also nations such as Iraq, Jordan and Kuwait. The Sterling Area countries had fixed exchange rates with the pound, held their foreign-exchange reserves in sterling, and agreed to work with Britain on exchange controls to prevent flight from sterling to the dollar. In return, they had freer trade with Britain and easier access to its capital markets. The problem was that Britain, without its previous status in world affairs, now dominated by the United States and the Soviet Union, had the challenge of maintaining the international value of the pound in more difficult circumstances.

In January 1949, Hugh Gaitskell, still minister of Fuel and Power, provided a detailed paper to cabinet setting out the extent of the economic problem Britain faced.[49] An expected gap of £300 million in the dollar account had widened to between £500 million and £600 million. There was no glossing over it: dollar spending needed to be reduced and dollar earnings increased. The government had two options that would become all too familiar to Wilson. The first was deflation, which would reduce imports by lowering incomes and increase exports by cutting money costs, and, accordingly, prices. The second was devaluation. Gaitskell argued for the latter on social justice grounds, since deflation involved 'deliberately creating unemployment and that in this case it is the unemployed and those who suffer wage cuts who *pay* for the high exports, whereas with devaluation it is the people with fixed incomes who do the real paying – in the form of higher import prices.'[50]

The decision was taken by the three young ministers regarded as having economic expertise: Wilson; Gaitskell, as minister of Fuel and Power; and Douglas Jay, the economic secretary to the Treasury. Attlee took little direct interest in economics, and the strain of many years of high office on members of the government was taking its toll. In particular, Cripps' health was failing. The high-minded Cripps was also affected by having to mislead people in public. On 6 July, the chancellor told the Commons: 'His Majesty's Government have not the slightest intention of devaluing the pound.'[51] While this was necessary, as to speculate in public about a possible devaluation itself encourages selling of the currency, Cripps hated having to say it in the knowledge that it was under consideration. On 18 July, he left for the Bircher-Benner Clinic in Zurich to convalesce.

The dynamics between Wilson, Gaitskell and Jay are crucial to understanding where Wilson stood in the final two years of the Attlee governments. Jay recalled converting to the cause of devaluation on 17 July on his Sunday walk around Hampstead Heath. The next day he called on Gaitskell at his office in the Ministry of Fuel and Power, who said he had formed the same view. They then spoke to Wilson on the Thursday, with Edward Bridges, permanent secretary to the Treasury, and Henry Wilson-Smith, additional second secretary to the Treasury. Jay pronounced himself surprised that Wilson argued against devaluation: 'Astonished at this, Gaitskell and I arranged to see Wilson for a second time and again thought we had all three agreed; only to discover at the second meeting with Attlee and Morrison early in the next week [on 25 July] that he took refuge in ambiguity.'[52] Cairncross was scathing in his assessment of Wilson's role: 'What emerged during the summer of 1949 was Harold's fondness for keeping his options open, his disinclination to say unpalatable things to his colleagues, his tendency to see economic issues in purely political terms (in this case, the date of the next election) and, most of all, his deviousness.'[53]

This judgement is unfair. Wilson had told Robert Hall on 21 July that Jay and Gaitskell had now come round to devaluation: 'a view *he* had long held'.[54] Hall noted, with scepticism, that Jay had already told him the previous day that he had changed his mind to be in favour of devaluation and was working on Gaitskell.[55] He was sure Wilson had 'known for a long time what was needed but would not take a line until he was fairly sure he would not be alone.'[56] Hall's account is not, however, consistent with that of Jay: if Gaitskell told Jay he was already convinced of the case for devaluation on the Monday, Jay would not have told Hall on the Wednesday that he was still trying to persuade him. On Wilson's own account, the debate on the principle of devaluation was a short one, with it moving very quickly to the question of timing.[57]

The reality is that Wilson, Gaitskell and Jay were three ambitious young politicians who *all* wanted to come out of the situation with credit. Wilson was at a disadvantage because Gaitskell and Jay were closer to each other than they were to him. At the end of July, Gaitskell and Jay told Dalton, back in cabinet as chancellor of the Duchy of Lancaster, that they were persuaded of the case for devaluation, but had their doubts about Wilson: 'Gaitskell and Jay both explain distrust of Wilson. They don't know what he's up to. They think he's currying favour with Bridges [permanent secretary to the Treasury] and Treasury officials.' Dalton summoned Wilson to tell him: 'You three young economists must work together.' Wilson replied that he thought Cripps needed a minister of state to support him, but told Dalton that should not be Jay 'who had a few sound ideas (e.g. [regional] Development Areas) buzzing in his head to the exclusion of all else'. His sympathy was with the reluctant Cripps, who was reacting strongly against 'the very heavy pressure being brought to bear on him'.[58] This conversation was significant. Wilson was right that, if Cripps was to remain as chancellor, he needed help. Whoever was providing that assistance would become a prime candidate to succeed to the office if Cripps deteriorated further. Jay's praise of Gaitskell's role in the events as amounting to him being 'Vice-Chancellor of the Exchequer' was an indication as to who was in the strongest position to take over from Cripps.[59]

Dalton himself told Attlee he was persuaded of the case for devaluation.[60] On 29 July, a crucial joint meeting of ministers and officials took place before full cabinet. Not only was devaluation inevitable from then on, but Attlee also effectively subcontracted decision-making on the whole issue from the full cabinet, on the basis that he did not want to summon any emergency meetings during August so as to add to the impression of crisis. He regarded himself as 'fully informed for the general attitude of his Cabinet colleagues towards the problems which might arise'. He would take decisions himself, in consultation with ministers 'immediately available in or around London'.[61]

Wilson was travelling to Annecy for a meeting of GATT in any event, so was asked to call in to see Cripps, taking a letter containing a written plan for devaluation, signed by Attlee. That the 'Young Economists' were in charge was evidenced in the fact that the letter was penned by Jay.[62] Cripps replied to say that he thought there should be a general election first. When Wilson delivered the message to Attlee, he gave a characteristically terse response: 'Stafford – political goose.'[63] As it happened, Cripps himself returned for a Chequers meeting with Attlee and Bevin on 19 August, with Wilson and Gaitskell also in attendance. At cabinet on 29 August, Attlee said that Bevin and Cripps should be deputed to the meeting of the International Bank and Fund, due to open in Washington on 13 September, to discuss the amount and timing. They left by ship, with the ailing Bevin too ill to fly.[64] Cripps then made his broadcast to the nation on 18 September devaluing the pound from $4.03 to $2.80. Since devaluation made exports cheaper to dollar buyers, but increased the cost of food and raw materials bought from the dollar area, Cripps also announced a penny on the price of bread.

Wilson's job was to see what more could be done to increase exports. On 18 November, he left for two weeks in the United States, spending the first week leading the UK delegation to the Food and Agricultural Organisation conference in Washington. He met President Truman and other cabinet members including assistant secretaries at the Department of Commerce and the secretary for agriculture. He then moved on to New Orleans, Chicago and New York, where superintending trade consuls were in post. In New York, he attended a lunch organised by Eric Johnston, the Motion Picture Association chairman, with many leading businessmen present, including the presidents of Standard Oil and General Motors. He concluded that British exporters were not seizing the opportunities before them: '. . . I keep on hearing disheartening stories not only of failure to go out and get markets but of a regrettable take-it-or-leave-it attitude on the part of our exporters even when American buyers come over here with their chequebooks.'[65] Wilson was proud of what the government had achieved, and saw his role in the United States as giving proof 'that Social Democracy in Britain, so far from being a halfway house to Communism, was the most live and practical alternative to it'.[66]

It was Cripps' decision to impose another round of cuts as part of the post-devaluation package that was to start the series of events that led to Wilson's resignation from the Attlee cabinet. The focus immediately shifted to Aneurin Bevan, whose Health estimates had already been overspent by £100m. Morrison wrote that the general feeling of cabinet colleagues was that 'Nye is getting away with murder . . . The original plan was that the medical services should provide everybody with everything needed for nothing, and nothing must alter that.'[67] When, in December 1949, Bevan had accepted the introduction of a law authorising a prescription charge of one shilling, he insisted it was 'the power to enforce a charge' and no more.[68]

In January 1950, prior to Attlee starting his campaign tour for the general election on 23 February, Dalton spoke to the prime minister about the situation with his ailing chancellor, and pressed Gaitskell's claims to become minister of state at the Treasury. Dalton's loyalty was to his protégé who had been at his side in wartime: 'We agreed that Gaitskell was better for this than Wilson (though he was doing very well), or Jay, who, though very able, had not always good judgment, and wasn't very personable.' His praise was fulsome: 'I said Gaitskell had a great gift of concentration of clear thought and argument . . . In due course, he probably should be Chancellor of the Exchequer.'[69]

The general election itself, which resulted in a loss of seventy-eight Labour seats, and a slim overall majority of five, was the closest Wilson came to a premature end of his political career. The 1948 Representation of the People Act reducing the number of parliamentary seats from 640 to 625, did not favour Labour, since its overall effect was to increase the representation of rural areas (generally Conservative) compared to towns and cities (generally Labour).[70] For Wilson, the issue was deeply personal. Ormskirk, always too large to be a single constituency, was to be split up. The new Ormskirk seat was largely rural, and, without the divided opposition Wilson had faced in 1945, he had no chance of retaining it. Wilson was not well established as a popular Labour figure where constituencies were queuing up to offer him a route into parliament. He had only one realistic option, which was to seek selection for one of the other seats the old Ormskirk division was redistributed into. This at least gave him the argument that he was continuing to represent parts of his existing seat, and he gave the press the excuse that, with his ministerial duties and responsibilities as a national politician campaigning around the country: 'he was unable to give so large and scattered a division as [the new] Ormskirk the time and work required.'[71] He had been selected for the newly created Huyton division, which also included north Widnes. The sitting MP for the old Widnes constituency, Christopher Shawcross, was standing down to take up a senior judicial post, as recorder of Nottingham, so the opportunity was there to be taken. Wilson held on by only 834 votes, polling 21,536 to 20,702 for the Conservative. A Liberal trailed in on 1,905 and a Communist drew 387 votes.[72]

Wilson thought being a government minister had been a disadvantage in two ways. Not only had his absence from the constituency campaigning for the government cost him votes, he also thought the Conservative candidate, without any of the bounds of collective responsibility that came with being a minister, had been making promises to Catholic voters on how children should be educated without concerning himself with his party's official position. This had, in Wilson's view, produced a late swing against him among Catholic voters. However, he comforted himself in the belief that the vote represented the high watermark of the Conservative vote. He was to be proved correct in terms of Huyton, but wrong with regard to the Conservative vote across the country, including in the next general election.[73]

Having survived as an MP, Wilson's attention now turned back to the politics of Westminster.

In March 1950, Gaitskell duly moved to the Treasury as minister of state. Nye Bevan was under no illusions about the battle that lay ahead. He wrote to Cripps to indicate that he would no longer attend the weekly dinners organised for all the economic ministers. He received a sharp reply on 29 June that was an indication of the deteriorating relationship between him and Cripps, now on opposite sides of an argument about public expenditure cuts: 'Would it not have been more friendly to have stated your real reason for giving up our weekly meetings at dinner?' Bevan responded: '. . . you are right in your assumption that I finally made up my mind on this question because of something that happened recently.' He said he had told Cripps, Attlee and Gaitskell that if charges on any part of the Health Service were introduced, his 'resignation would automatically follow'.[74] That same month, Bevan moved to the Ministry of Labour, but on the basis of 'no further attack on the social services.'[75]

The clash between Bevan and Gaitskell was one of personalities, political rivalry and principle. Though the disagreement was ostensibly about charges for teeth and spectacles provided by the National Health Service, there were deeper issues at play. Wilson's assessment was that: 'Hugh – Winchester and New College – had many fine qualities, including unswerving loyalty to his close band of friends and to the principles of economics as he interpreted them, together with great personal charm.' But Wilson thought Gaitskell was intolerant of dissenting views.[76] Gaitskell's unwillingness to move was 'due to the fact that he, Hugh, had quickly reviewed the facts and taken a final decision, discussion of which was factious, not to say disloyal – indeed a clear case of intellectual dishonesty. In the case of Aneurin Bevan, a policy decision or political attitude came from the inner certainty he derived away from the smoky metropolis in the pure Welsh air of the moorlands.'[77]

If Gaitskell's inflexibility and Bevan's passionate views were in conflict, Wilson also thought that the opportunity this presented was grasped. Gaitskell soon linked his 'ambition with a determination to out-manoeuvre, indeed humiliate Aneurin Bevan. Hugh, for his part, despised what he regarded as emotional oratory, and if he could defeat Nye in open conflict, he would be in a strong position to oust Morrison as the heir apparent to Clement Attlee. At the same time he would ensure that post-war socialism would take a pragmatic form – totally anti-Communist, unemotional, undoctrinaire.'[78] Cripps's inevitable replacement with Gaitskell as chancellor in October 1950 sent Bevan into a rage, and he wrote to Attlee to express his 'consternation and astonishment'.[79]

A new set of commitments on rearmament necessitated even deeper expenditure cuts. After the outbreak of the Korean War in June 1950, Attlee had crossed the Atlantic to meet President Harry S. Truman, and had secured an agreement that the United States would not use its nuclear weapons without consulting Britain and Canada.[80] Attlee had averted the possibility of nuclear catastrophe, but it came at a price. Britain committed to a steep increase in defence spending, a £3,600 million programme pushed up to £4,700 million. It was a tremendous burden on the economy. As Wilson recalled: 'The expanded re-armament programme created a new tension between Gaitskell and Bevan.' Bevan was opposed on grounds of principle and practicality. This was an initiative that marked a move away from the American focus on economic support in the programme of Marshall Aid to a more confrontational foreign policy. Moreover, he did not think such a large amount of money could be spent within the three years for which it was allocated.[81] Wilson also identified this as a key reason for his resignation: 'the idea that signing cheques for an arms programme created for political purposes – mainly to impress the Americans – was unrealistic so far as industrial capacity was concerned.'[82]

The point of no return was reached at cabinet on 9 April. Gaitskell insisted on raising £13 million from charges for teeth and spectacles and went further, saying that even if he could find the saving elsewhere, he would spend it on something else rather than avoiding the NHS charges.[83] Gaitskell then delivered his budget the next day. Attlee asked Ernest Bevin, who was ill and confined to his Foreign Office flat in Carlton Gardens, to mediate. Wilson knew how to manipulate him: 'Nye's destruction I quietly suggested, was being supported, if not indeed masterminded by Morrison.' This did the trick and sent Bevin into a rage. Two days later, though, when Wilson was in the royal box at Wembley to watch the England football team lose 3–2 to Scotland, Hector McNeil, minister of state at the Foreign Office, rang to say that Ernest Bevin had died. Even this was seen as an opportunity to split Wilson and Bevan: 'Since a general election could not be long delayed – it took place six months later – it was suggested to me, without quite saying I must first break with Nye – that Ernie's seat be left vacant until the Election, and I should be adopted as candidate there, in view of my wafer-thin majority in Huyton. I stuck to Huyton.'[84]

Political decisions with immediate personal consequences, such as resignations, are rarely a product of straightforward calculation between principle and expediency. Rather, they are the consequence of a number of competing factors. For the political biographer, it is not possible to watch how the arguments loom and fade in the subject's mind day by day, but external evidence can highlight the importance of different issues. In this situation, Wilson's own instincts were far closer to those of Nye Bevan than of Gaitskell. At one level, Wilson and Gaitskell had a great deal in common: both Oxford-educated wartime civil servants immersed in the detail of policy while they served under Attlee. Wilson even lived a short distance away from Gaitskell in Hampstead. Yet in other ways they could not have been more different. Wilson did not join the dinner party sets of North London. At Frognal Gardens, Hugh Gaitskell entertained the likes of Jay and Crosland for regular dinners, political discussion and intrigue. Wilson was no Frognalite, and did not go out of his way to socialise with parliamentary colleagues. Partly, this was to spend time with his young family, but it was also his character. He *did* enjoy political discussion – he was *political* to his fingertips – but was not someone who enjoyed the society dinner party scene. For Wilson, getting on in life was not about building a network of society connections, and he was never at home in the artificial conversation-making of the dinner table.

There was a deeper point, too. Wilson thought Gaitskell's more clinical approach to politics missed something profound: the reason why people became involved in the Labour Party in the first place. Later, he wrote that Gaitskell did not realise 'a great number of converts had joined Labour because they believed Socialism was a way of making a reality of Christian principles in everyday life.'[85] In Nye Bevan, Wilson found an advocate for socialism who could appeal to emotion and to reason. In Bevan's hands, socialism had a higher purpose. Bevan's *In Place of Fear*, published in 1952, captured this: 'The capacity for emotional concern for individual life is the most significant quality of a civilised human being.'[86] Bevan was inspired by the Uruguayan writer Jose Enrique Rodo, whose critique of unrestrained capitalism was that it stymied individual fulfilment in vulgar materialism. In Gaitskell, Wilson saw a colder temperament; in Bevan he saw emotional power.

Like Bevan, Wilson was also a believer in economic planning. At its most basic level, this meant having a government that could best mobilise the resources of the country to meet the needs of its people. Bevan's sarcastic remark about the absence of such planning in Conservative thinking could have come from Wilson: 'This island is almost made of coal and surrounded by fish. Only an organising genius could produce a shortage of coal and fish in Great Britain at the same time.'[87] This was relevant to the issues of the time. By mid-1950, the debate in the Labour Party on the way forward was coming to a head. On one side were those such as Morrison and Gaitskell, 'consolidators' who believed that the changes brought about by the government in welfare and public ownership should now be seen as a platform upon which to build a further set of policies targeted at middle-class affluence. On the other were the 'radicals' such as Bevan, who believed that nationalisation had to be driven even further forward.

While Wilson believed that nationalisation should be judged on a case-by-case basis, he was a passionate advocate for wider state intervention, though not to the level that existed in wartime. He framed his thoughts in a paper, 'The State and Private Industry', that he produced in May 1950, based upon the experience of his time as president of the Board of Trade: 'There has been a tendency in certain quarters to idealise these controls and to think that they could achieve more than was in fact possible . . . [but] . . . controls over production and consumption represent the most effective and subtle means of imposing selective pressure on industry . . .'[88]

Wilson echoed Bevan's argument that it was 'of no advantage at all to a Socialist that private enterprise should be languishing.'[89] He wrote that in 'arguing and presenting the case for Socialism it was not realised that for perhaps a quarter of a century or more we should be operating a mixed economy, with the private sector of crucial importance . . .' Even voters who were not in favour of more nationalisation were 'not tolerant about inefficiency in private industry'.[90] Wilson's proposals included price control, the government operating 'factories competitive with private industry' and beefed-up machinery to tackle monopolies and restrictive practices.[91]

Wilson sent copies to Attlee and Morrison. Attlee, conscious that 'the men of my generation will before long be passing out' suggested the document be considered informally by a group of senior ministers, and by a group of 'juniors' chaired by Wilson himself, to include Gaitskell and Jay as well.[92] At the meeting Jay complained that Wilson 'made little reference to what would be achieved by persuasion rather than control.'[93] Gaitskell was also critical, pointing out that 'bulk buying of goods meant that there would have to be provision for selling the goods that were bought'. Wilson responded immediately 'and pointed out that the difficulty had been raised in the Memorandum'.[94]

It was, however, Gaitskell's career trajectory, rather than this personal hostility that was another factor in Wilson's decision to resign. On the right of the parliamentary party, Morrison remained the favourite to succeed Attlee, but the longer time went on, the better would be the chance of the younger Gaitskell, especially with him now established as chancellor of the exchequer. Wilson had shown that he was an effective cabinet minister but he had come off second-best to Gaitskell in the devaluation saga. There was, therefore, a strong political logic to allying himself to the left, where he could establish himself, behind Bevan, as a credible future leader of the party. It was also a bold stroke, marking Wilson out as decisive. Morrison wrote that Wilson's resignation had left the cabinet 'speechless with surprise'.[95] Though Wilson hated leaving the Board of Trade, it was less of a personal sacrifice than it seemed. With the government's tiny majority, another general election was imminent, and it looked likely that Labour would lose, so it did not look like Wilson could enjoy an extended period in office.

So it came to pass that Bevan, Wilson and the left-wing minister of supply, John Freeman, resigned from the government on 24 April 1951. Wilson's resignation speech was well-crafted, highlighting not only his deep differences with his former colleagues but also his continuing loyalty to the Labour government. He said that the issue was not only about more than teeth and spectacles but something more fundamental, namely: 'a re-armament programme which I do not believe to be physically practicable with the raw materials available to us'. Wilson was careful to stress that he was in favour of an *effective* defence programme: 'it is a fact which has been forced on us by the state of the world today'.[96] Wilson's pride in his time in office was obvious; he said that the approach of the government: 'provides to the world another way based neither on Communism nor on the harshness and brutalities of unregulated free enterprise.'[97] He finished on a note of unity, saying he hoped

Labour would come 'once again to a proper balance of priorities between arms expenditure and social expenditure . . . although I personally find it necessary to leave the Government I intend inside and outside this House to do everything in my power to support the party and the Government in the difficult times that lie ahead.'[98]

This constructive tone did not prevent the resignation from making him enemies. Dalton, once an ally, was disparaging: 'Some Pressmen claimed to have heard me describe him as "Nye's little dog". I had counted him as very promising some years before and there was no doubt he was very clever "but a bit of a cold fish," people said. In contrast with the other two [Bevan and Freeman], he did not seem to have much warmth or strength of character.'[99] Streat, who had been impressed with Wilson, thought he had developed too high an opinion of himself: '. . . high office had begun to go to his head . . . I think now he will become just a political jobber and adventurer.'[100] Time would prove this judgement wrong.

Chapter 6

Keep left

Bevan to Gaitskell, 1951–55

The period from his resignation alongside Aneurin Bevan, to when he reached an accommodation with Hugh Gaitskell to be appointed shadow chancellor in 1955, was seminal in Harold Wilson's political career. A move from backbencher to the most senior of the shadow cabinet portfolios would be significant in itself, but for Wilson it was about far more than that. His time with the Bevanites gave him an enduring link to the Labour left that, while it became stretched and frayed, was never fully severed. The left always preferred Wilson to his rivals from the Labour right in the years ahead. At the same time, being part of the Bevanite group raised Wilson's profile with the constituency parties, giving him popularity with party members and election to the National Executive Committee. Wilson proved himself an adept political operator, being a part of the group of MPs around Bevan, but never being *of* them. He showed a pragmatism that meant that MPs outside Bevan's circle felt they could work with him, even if – as was often the case – they were suspicious of his motives, and thought him self-interested.

On 26 April 1951, two days after his resignation speech, Wilson joined Bevan and Freeman at a meeting that marked the start of the Bevanite grouping. In addition to the three former ministers, there were seven members of the Keep Left group that had already organised on the backbenches since Richard Crossman, Michael Foot and Ian Mikardo had penned the policy programme of that name in 1947. Those three were joined by Richard Acland, Barbara

Castle, Harold Davies and Leslie Hale. Other significant figures present included Tom Driberg and Jennie Lee. Jo Richardson, who had served as secretary of Keep Left after Mikardo's election to the NEC in October 1950, became secretary of the new group. Richardson kept records, including a 'membership list' which, by 1952, listed 51 names, including 47 MPs.[1] They met weekly, with papers prepared for discussion on the political issues of the day. They were highly talented: Foot and Wilson would both go on to be party leader; and there were a number of journalists with outlets for their views. Driberg had a column in *Reynold's News*. Foot, Lee and J.P.W. Mallalieu, made up the *Tribune* editorial board. Richard Crossman, a former Oxford don, who was to become a key Wilson ally, served as deputy editor of the *New Statesman*. Around the constituencies, the Bevanite 'Brains Trusts' proved remarkably popular. Named after the BBC wartime radio show to which listeners sent in questions to a panel and advertised in advance in *Tribune* and the *New Statesman*, they attracted party members around the country.

The popularity of the Bevanite cause in the constituency parties assisted Wilson locally. On Saturday, 5 May, the Huyton divisional Labour Party gave Wilson its unanimous backing, both in his decision to resign from the government and in him being their candidate in the next general election. The resolution set out the regret of local members about the imposition of health charges and called upon the government to 'redress the balance between our rearmament expenditure and the social services, and by increasing subsidies, to check the rising cost of living.' Wilson himself called for an increase in food subsidies and the reintroduction of clothing subsidies.[2] With his local base now secured, Wilson looked beyond politics to secure his financial future. His contact with Tom Meyer paid dividends: a role as part-time economic adviser to Montague L. Meyer Limited was announced by *The Times* nine days later on 14 May 1951.[3]

This appointment, which was to last for the next decade, had four important consequences. The first was that it gave Wilson long-term financial security. He used the money to send his sons to private school, and for travel. Second, it gave him an office on the Strand, with a secretary, close to Westminster, at a time when securing office space in parliament itself was extremely difficult, and there was no money available for staff. Third, it gave him the chance to show his skills as an international negotiator, a politician with presence on the stage of world affairs. Finally, on the negative side, it heightened suspicion of him among elements of the security services as a leading Labour politician who was helping to facilitate East–West trade behind the Iron Curtain.

The consequences of this were, at this point, far in the future. The immediate priority was for the former ministers to make sure that their side of the story was heard. On 10 July 1951, a *Tribune* pamphlet, *One Way Only*, was published: Wilson, Bevan and Freeman penned the introduction. The pamphlet attacked the rearmament programme on the basis that it carried the risks of inflation and a raw materials shortage. Its scale was disproportionate to the Soviet threat and a world aid programme was more important.[4] A further pamphlet, *Going Our Way?*, appeared on 21 September, with Bevan continuing the critique: it was not possible to maintain the export drive while carrying out the rearmament programme; the assumptions the programme had been based on had been abandoned, including the projection for the balance of payments; the charges for teeth and spectacles were unnecessary. Wilson's article, entitled 'Neither Guns nor Butter', accepted that, while a critical raw material shortage had not developed since April, unless the rearmament programme was reduced to realistic levels, world inflation would gather pace, raw materials would become scarce, and import prices would rise.[5]

The pamphlet also criticised members of the National Executive Committee, pointing out that Bevan, Castle, Driberg and Mikardo were the only members to disagree with the resolution supporting the budget. This was an obvious attack on the trade union leaders of the Labour right, who, Bevan alleged, were out of step with their members. This provoked the strongest of reactions at the party conference in Scarborough, where Bevan topped the vote for the constituency section of the NEC, showing his popularity with the party rank and file; Castle came in second, with Mikardo and Driberg increasing their votes. On the night of Tuesday, 2 October, a meeting at the St Nicholas Hotel resolved to 'stop Bevan'. This gathering was led by the general secretary of the Transport and General Workers' Union, Arthur Deakin. Michael Foot described Deakin as a 'fierce, breezy, irascible, stout-hearted bison of a man who genuinely believed any proposition he could force through his union executive must be the will of the people and more especially the will of Ernest Bevin whose requirements he had normally taken the precaution of finding out in advance. But Bevin was now dead, and Deakin lacked Bevin's redeeming powers of individual imaginative rumination.' Deakin was backed by Will Lawther, president of the National Union of Mineworkers, whom Foot accused of making up his mind to 'swim with the strongest tides' and Tom Williamson, general secretary of the National Union of General and Municipal Workers, an altogether milder figure who was 'more an earnest civil servant than a trade union leader'.[6] Whatever their differing levels of hatred towards Nye Bevan, the three were united in preventing him ever becoming leader, and together held more than two million – of the fewer than three million total – union block votes at party conference. They were formidable opponents with significant power.

Internal wrangling had to be put to one side for the moment, though. Influenced by the ill health of his own MPs sustaining a government with a majority of only five, and a concern about the king being in Australia when the parliamentary situation was so uncertain (a trip the king never actually made), Clement Attlee had called a general election for 25 October. Wilson rejected a national speaking tour in favour of focusing all his energies on Huyton. In his election address, Wilson sought to make a virtue of his exit from the government: 'One of the Reasons Why I Resigned was my disagreement on the handling of the cost of living. I pressed for increasing the food subsidies, and an all-out attack to freeze the cost of living by more Socialist methods.'[7] While Bevan himself was targeted as a bogeyman by the Tories, a crypto-communist who would seek to oust Attlee, Wilson's association with him clearly helped in terms of practical assistance. The Bevanites assisted each other in campaigning, and Bevan himself visited Huyton.[8] Wilson also thought the additional council houses – built by Bevan during his time as minister of health and housing – helped, with the new tenants voting Labour in their droves.[9] With no Liberal or Communist candidate, Wilson polled 23,582 votes, a winning margin of 1,193 over a single Conservative opponent. Nationally, the result was a perverse one, with Labour winning 13.9 million votes, while the Conservatives took just over 13.7 million. The Liberals won just six seats, but their significance was in the number of candidates they ran: just 109 in comparison to the 475 they ran in 1950. In the absence of a Liberal candidate, more of their voters plumped for the Tories over Labour. Thus, the Conservatives won 321 seats to Labour's 295, and the overall majority of 17 was enough to sustain the new government for the next parliament.

Now an opposition backbencher, it was the Bevanite group that dominated Wilson's political activity. He became its chair, and set up specialist policy groups. On Saturday, 15 December 1951, the Bevanites organised a weekend conference. It was hosted by Gavin Faringdon – the Second Lord Faringdon, then an executive member of the Fabian Society – at his eighteenth-century country house, Buscot Park, in Oxfordshire. There was tension between Thomas Balogh and Wilson over the 'bonfire' of controls which was indicative of the fault-line in the gathering. Wilson wanted to defend his actions as a minister; Balogh was concerned that ending wartime restrictions meant a loss of state direction in the economy. This friction was not, however, indicative of how the relationship between Wilson and Balogh was to develop. Balogh, a Hungarian Jew from Budapest, had attended the Minta Gymnasium, the 'Winchester of Hungary' before going on to Budapest University in the 1920s where he produced a thesis on German inflation, a timely topic given the economy of the Weimar Republic, for which he was awarded a fellowship of the Royal Hungarian College that set him up for a career in academic research.[10] He moved on to the University of Berlin, then to America. By the age of twenty-six, Balogh had also worked for the Central Banks of Germany and

France. He came to Britain in 1930: Professor J.A. Schumpeter, a tutor of Balogh, gave him letters of introduction to John Maynard Keynes. By the late 1930s, Balogh was teaching at Balliol College, Oxford, and met Wilson for the first time in 1938. He was brilliant but eccentric – in tutorials he would say to his students, 'Poppet, you can't possibly believe that!' then fall silent with no further explanation.[11] Balogh had advised Hugh Gaitskell during the period of the Attlee government, though he was a regular visitor to the Wilsons at the Hampstead Garden Suburb, as he lived close by. Balogh produced papers for the Bevanites, attracted to the group by his own passion for economic planning. Wilson was comfortable with Balogh, who was highly intelligent, and never posed a political threat.

This was no ordinary meeting of like-minded backbenchers. The former ministers had views shaped by their experience of power, and records in office to defend. Wilson opened the meeting with a paper on the financial situation facing the country. Crossman recorded in his diary that it led to 'another sterile argument about whether the £3,600 million arms programme accepted in September 1950 would have been tolerable . . . there was also a strong reluctance on the part of Nye to accept the thesis, on which Wilson and Balogh agreed, that merely cutting the arms programme would not remove our main difficulty, the dollar gap.'[12] Crossman's admiration for Wilson was growing: 'Harold Wilson was as neat and competent as ever. Whenever an idea is put forward, he remembers without fail an occasion on which he did it or set up a committee on it when he was at the Board of Trade. His complacency must be unique, but he has a good mind, is an excellent member of a group and is likeable into the bargain.'[13]

The Bevanite debates were stimulating, but the factional warfare was sapping. On the principal issue of the size of the rearmament programme Bevan found an unlikely ally in Churchill. Having taken civil service advice from Ian Bancroft, later head of the Home Civil Service, Churchill concluded that the amount of money allocated by Gaitskell – £1,250 million that year – could not all be spent in the time frame available. On 6 December 1951, in the Commons, Churchill told Bevan he was vindicated: 'it appears by accident, perhaps not for the best of motives [he] happened to be right'.[14] Wilson later reflected that: '. . . Nye would have been wise to leave things there.'[15] After all, it was a victory for Bevan. Instead, the battle with Gaitskell continued. Bevan veered between his dislike of Gaitskell and his innate understanding of power, in the knowledge that his small group of followers would never be enough to win the leadership. He was moody, and could lash out. Castle observed: 'It seemed to us that he wanted Bevanism without the Bevanites.'[16]

On 5 March 1952, there was a debate on the Churchill government's Defence White Paper that set out its proposed spending. The Bevanites opposed carrying out the rearmament programme. To seek to preserve unity, Attlee supported the policy of rearmament but expressed no confidence in the government to implement it. In parliamentary terms, this meant voting for an amendment to the motion to approve the White Paper and then abstaining on the proposition itself. The Labour amendment was defeated by 314 votes to 219, then 57 Labour MPs – including Wilson and Bevan – voted against the main motion, rather than follow the whip and abstain. The next day, to enforce discipline, the Standing Orders of the Parliamentary Labour Party (PLP), suspended as a gesture of goodwill in 1945, were reintroduced by 162 votes to 72.

The hostility continued into the 1952 party conference, which opened on 29 September at Morecambe. Dalton called it 'the worst Labour Party Conference for bad temper and general hatred, since 1926, the year of the general strike'.[17] Grassroots support was behind the Bevanites. For the constituency section of the National Executive Committee, elected by the party rank and file, Bevan topped the poll, with Wilson also elected alongside Castle, Crossman, Mikardo and Tom Driberg. Morrison, Dalton, Gaitskell and Callaghan had all failed to get elected.

On the Monday after conference, on 5 October, Gaitskell struck back with a speech at Stalybridge, citing the 'number of resolutions and speeches which were Communist-inspired' and said: 'It is time to end the attempt at mob rule by a group of frustrated journalists.'[18]

With Senator Joseph McCarthy listing and investigating alleged communist infiltrators in the American government, and a 'McCarthyite' witch-hunt against those in public life underway on the other side of the Atlantic, the words incensed the Bevanites. Speaking in Bebington, Wilson said he was 'surprised and a little shocked at the intemperate outburst of Hugh Gaitskell. Phrases such as "mob rule" are hardly worthy of him.'[19] Later that month, the parliamentary committee recommended to the parliamentary party that groups within the party be disbanded, which was passed by 188 votes to 51. In December 1952, the Bevanites complied and disbanded, though informal meetings continued, at Crossman's house in Vincent Square and, on a couple of occasions, hosted by Wilson in Hampstead Garden Suburb. An NEC sub-committee investigation in early 1953 did not result in a ban on the 'Brains Trusts' which continued, as did Bevanite popularity in the constituencies.

At the 1953 party conference in Margate that opened on 28 September, the election results for the constituency section of the NEC saw Wilson move up from fifth to third place, with 934,000 votes against the previous year's 632,000. Bevan and Castle headed the polls, and, noted Wilson with some glee: 'Hugh Gaitskell [was] runner-up as eighth man.'[20] In parliament, though, the story was very different: Bevan unsuccessfully challenged Morrison for the deputy leadership at the opening of two parliamentary sessions, losing by 194 votes to 82 on 11 November 1952, and by 181 votes to 76 on 29 October 1953.

In travel, Wilson not only found escapism but a way to continue to build his political profile. He visited North America in early 1953, and drew on his experience in a debate in the House of Commons on 3 February. He criticised government restrictions on capital expenditure which, he argued, meant that the British economy would be weaker in the face of competition from American industry. Wilson also emphasised the imperative of increasing trade with Canada.[21] It was also trade that dominated Wilson's first visit to Moscow representing Montague Meyer in May 1953. He extracted maximum publicity for it: the visit was pre-announced in *The Times* on 24 April 1953, and he agreed to write a series of articles in *Reynold's News* as 'the first leading British Socialist to visit Russia since the death of Stalin' that had occurred only weeks previously, on 5 March. Such a trip by an opposition backbencher could have infuriated the prime minister, but Wilson made sure that he spoke to Churchill about the trip before leaving. As a fellow member of the Privy Council, he was duty-bound to inform him in any event. Wilson sought out Churchill in Members' Bar, who was more than happy: 'Shertainly, my boy, shertainly you should go. You'll meet some of the top leaders. What you must look out for is what they are doing in the way of conshumer goods.'[22]

Wilson left London airport on 10 May. The next day, he stopped off in East Berlin to meet a Chinese communist trade mission to discuss the easing of restrictions to trade between communist and non-communist countries. He then travelled on to Moscow via Prague, arriving on 13 May. While Wilson was at pains to insist his visit was unofficial, and that its purpose was to explore the prospects for timber exports, he was, nonetheless, met at the airport by British embassy officials, in addition to V. Nichkov and A.G. Cholokhov, president and vice-president of the Soviets' timber exporting agency. Wilson was also careful to make clear he was discussing general East–West trade prospects, too, giving the visit the air of a summit between leaders. He stayed at the imposing Hotel National in the heart of Moscow, close to the Kremlin. He had two meetings with Mikoyan and was a guest at lunch at the British embassy with deputy Foreign Minister Gromyko on 19 May, later securing an hour's meeting with Molotov, with whom Wilson said he was able to talk 'freely and frankly . . . no questions were barred'. Accompanied by Sir Alvary Gascoigne, the British ambassador, Wilson even put Churchill's proposal of a 'big powers' conference to him, to which he replied 'Most interesting.' Wilson travelled back via Budapest, where the Hungarian foreign minister and minister for Trade both found time to meet him. Wilson, while making encouraging noises about trade, was clear that economic links could only resume once the Briton Edgar Sanders, who had been imprisoned in 1949 on espionage charges, was released by the Hungarian authorities. He touched down at Northolt on 24 May, his visit having generated widespread coverage in the national press.[23] Wilson wrote in *Reynold's News* on 7 June that he told Molotov and Mikoyan to 'join the human race' in helping the poorest around the world. He spoke of Soviet history since 1917 in developing industry and food production: 'Could not that experience be mobilized in mankind's war on human poverty, through the United Nations and its specialized agencies?'[24]

Wilson returned to Moscow some ten months later on another Montague Meyer trip, this time meeting Georgy Malenkov, who was Stalin's successor for a short period before the rise of Nikita Khrushchev. He called for a new trade pact with Russia.[25] He commented: '. . . we have not yet fully realized the possibilities of closer Anglo-Soviet understanding, with Britain restraining America on the one hand and Russia restraining China and other revolutionary forces in Asia on the other.'[26] This was in line with Bevan's idea of a 'Third Force' foreign policy. Bevan wanted to use his own links to 'non-aligned' countries such as India and Yugoslavia to change the pattern of Cold War diplomacy, with its division of the world into two rival camps with spending focused on arms at the expense of addressing poverty.

Wilson also visited China for the first time in his life. At the European economic conference in Geneva, the Chinese government's minister in Switzerland passed on an invitation from Zhou Enlai, then Chinese premier and foreign minister, to visit Beijing (then called Peking). Wilson accepted eagerly, flying to China via Hong Kong. He needed a sponsor, so drew on his expertise as an economist to attract the Bank of China, which became his host. On arrival, it was the cost of consumer goods that fascinated him. He bought Mary a silk dress at a reasonable price; in Moscow, the cost would have been ten or twelve times that of the London clothes shops: 'My interest in the price charged was to feature in any discussions with the Chinese financiers.' He spent seven hours with Zhou; the Chinese premier was interested in Wilson's assessment of the Soviet economy. Wilson remained convinced that Zhou's conviction that the Soviet Union was economically exploiting China contributed to the eventual Sino-Soviet split.[27] Wilson co-hosted a group of Chinese trade experts, led by Tsao Chung-shu, at the House of Commons on 6 July 1954.[28] In September, Wilson wrote to *The Times* arguing for the lifting of the trade embargo on China, imposed by United Nations resolution on 18 May 1951 after Chinese intervention in the Korean War.[29]

Wilson's focus on trade reflected his personal passion and interest, but he also saw the ultimate purpose of economic activity in addressing poverty. On 12 February 1951, the *Manchester Guardian* published a letter from the left-wing publisher Victor Gollancz, calling for the end of the Korean War and an international fund with its purpose summed up in the words of the Prophet Isaiah, to 'turn swords into ploughshares'. As a result, the Association for World Peace was created the following month; Wilson chaired a committee on world poverty that produced a report in February 1952, 'The Problem of World Poverty', that was published by Victor Gollancz as *War on Want* in May. In this period, Wilson produced a number of pieces on world poverty and international aid: *In Place of Dollars*, the title chosen with one eye on Bevan's book *In Place of Fear*, also published in 1952; then, the following year, *Today They Die: The Case for World Co-operation* and *Two Out of Three: The Problem of World Poverty*.[30] In August 1953, he published a full-length book, *The War on World Poverty*, which he subtitled: *An Appeal to the Conscience of Mankind*.[31] Wilson was ahead of his time, arguing for an International Development Authority, and a proportion of national income being allocated to it: 'This would involve a contribution by the advanced countries of, on the average, about 3 per cent of their national income . . .'[32] Set alongside his belief in an interventionist role for the state in industry and prices – he argued a free price mechanism was inadequate – Wilson was developing a coherent political argument for policy-making at home and abroad.

Wilson was always careful not to become limited by the Bevanite faction. In May 1954, when Malcolm Muggeridge asked him on TV if he was a Bevanite, he fudged the issue, saying the question was 'not quite as simple as it sounds. Certainly I have not changed any of my ideas about politics.'³³ He later reflected: 'The truth is that a bunch of us were in the wilderness together and, since Moses was there and overshadowed the rest of us, we should have been more conveniently dubbed "Moses-ites". I disliked the word Bevanite as much as Nye did. I was a co-belligerent, not a satellite.'³⁴ At the same time, Wilson was seeking peace terms: '. . . I was at pains to maintain a personal and political relationship with Hugh Gaitskell. I used to sit in the second row behind him in the House and we often used to meet behind the scenes or in Party gatherings upstairs to discuss matters, particularly our response to the Government's financial legislation. As early as 1952, Hugh Gaitskell and I were collaborating closely on fighting [Conservative Chancellor] Rab Bulter's budget.'³⁵ This contact with Gaitskell was to become significant for the future. None of this, though, is to suggest it was easy for Wilson personally with the ferocity of the factionalism: he saw the years from 1951 until his return to the frontbench in 1954 as 'the worst I . . . ever had to live through in nearly four decades in the House of Commons'.³⁶

Wilson's own return to the shadow cabinet was what caused the greatest rupture with his political and social circle. The shadow cabinet was then elected on an annual basis by the Parliamentary Labour Party.³⁷ Bevan had returned to the shadow cabinet in the final, twelfth place in November 1952. In the election of November 1953, Bevan had been elected in ninth place. Wilson had missed out on a place by a single vote; Glenvil Hall, a treasury minister under Attlee, had taken the final, twelfth place, with 106 votes to Wilson's 105. Wilson's thirteenth position was to prove highly significant. An issue of foreign policy caused a split. The 'Big Four' foreign ministers' conference in Berlin took place from 25 January to 18 February. The foreign secretary, Anthony Eden, joined Molotov, Georges Bidault of France, and American secretary of state John Foster Dulles. Reporting back to the Commons on 24 February, Eden was clear that he believed that 'the real question is not whether Germany will rearm, but how she will rearm, and we are quite convinced that E.D.C., within N.A.T.O. offers the surest method yet devised for the security of Germany, the security of

Europe, and even for the security of Soviet Russia. We therefore look forward to the early establishment of the European Defence Community.'[38] From the opposition benches, Morrison gave broad support but openly acknowledged 'sincere differences of opinion' within the Parliamentary Labour Party.[39] Eden and Dulles were seeking to achieve the incorporation of an independent West Germany into a Western defence structure. The European Defence Community had been a French idea to seek to water down German rearmament, but it was France that now became the problem: not only fearing the prospect of renewed German militarism but concerned that control of its own army would be ceded. After months of delay, Pierre Mendes-France, prime minister of France from June 1954, put the matter to the French National Assembly on 30 August 1954, where the vote was to postpone discussion of the issue indefinitely.[40] Barbara Castle later reflected that it was 'the growing nationalistic fervour in the [West German] Federal Republic under Chancellor Adenauer's leadership which alarmed most of us [Bevanites].'[41]

Bevan agreed with Crossman's suggestion that Wilson move the Bevanite resolution against German rearmament at the meeting of the Parliamentary Labour Party on 23 February 1954. That Wilson was regarded as the person 'who would lose us fewer votes' was indicative of his position across the party: a broad spectrum of MPs could work with him. Crossman recorded: 'After Attlee, Harold Wilson spoke with very great skill. It was a quiet, inoffensive speech, without any edge to it, such as I could never possibly deliver. I think it was calculated and, sitting beside Harold, as he had requested me to do, to brief him if things went wrong, I rated him even higher as a politician than I had before.'[42] Wilson later recalled that few PLP meetings since the war, if any, had ended in such uproar, principally because Attlee allowed Labour peers to vote. The Bevanite motion was defeated 111 to 109; the shadow cabinet position then carried 113 to 104.[43]

The tension was raised further in the next few weeks as it emerged that America had exploded a hydrogen bomb in the Pacific Ocean on 1 March. On 5 April in the House of Commons, Attlee sought to calm matters by 'asking for high-level talks between the Prime Minister, Mr. Eisenhower and Mr. Malenkov to discuss not just the question of the hydrogen bomb and of disarmament, but to discuss the problem that faces the world in the existence of the hydrogen bomb.'[44] Churchill then turned on Attlee, accusing him of abandoning the secret Quebec Agreement between America and Britain to share information; Attlee retorted that it was the US Atomic Energy Act of 1946 – the McMahon Act – that prevented the American administration sharing nuclear secrets. The exchange became so heated that James Callaghan accused Churchill of 'dragging us down to the gutter'.[45]

Just over a week later, Bevan exploded. Dulles, who, as far as Bevan was concerned, personified America's ideological crusade against communism, argued for the creation of a South-East Asia NATO as a counterweight to Chinese influence. The success of communist insurgents in French Indochina prompted particular concern. On 13 April, Eden argued for the Dulles proposition in the Commons. Attlee, mindful of containing Communism but maintaining party unity, trod carefully in response: '. . . in building up the strength of the free nations of Asia against aggression . . . this should be free to all the peoples of Asia and should not in any way be represented, as it may be misrepresented, as a defence of an obsolete colonialism.'[46] Eden thanked Attlee, before Bevan grasped the dispatch box and contradicted his party leader: '. . . the interpretation that may be placed upon his statement, unless he clarifies it further, is that we shall assist in establishing a N.A.T.O. in South-East Asia for the purpose of imposing European colonial rule upon certain people in that area, and will he realise that if that course is persisted in it will estrange the Commonwealth members in that part of the world?'[47] The next day, Bevan resigned.

This created a vacancy in the shadow cabinet. Under the standing orders of the Parliamentary Labour Party, the position was offered to the person with the highest vote in the parliamentary committee elections who had not been successful in securing a shadow cabinet place. It was not at this moment that Wilson's ambition to be party leader was crystallised, but it was revealed to colleagues in stark terms as he decided to take Bevan's place. Wilson tried to take refuge in the technical detail: as the thirteenth person in the elections he was *automatically* co-opted to the shadow cabinet. Therefore, he could not actually refuse; he would have to resign: 'Someone had to put in the Shadow Cabinet the views of nearly half the parliamentary party.' In his notes for his memoirs, Wilson initially wrote: 'Nye was, indeed, furious' before striking out the word 'furious' and replacing it with 'carried away by his anger at my seeming apostasy'. He told Wilson he would be 'chucked off the National Executive Committee' at the next conference. Mikardo, who did not think Wilson could take the place as he had supported Bevan's position, felt that from that moment on Bevan never fully trusted Crossman, who had privately discussed the matter with Wilson first.[48]

The episode confirmed Crossman's status as an *eminence grise* in Wilson's political life. The reality was that Wilson needed to emerge from Bevan's shadow and become a big player in his own right. Crossman had a fine academic mind with a grasp of detail. Unlike Wilson, who evolved from his academic life into a politician with a popular touch, Crossman retained his donnish air – arguably, he still looked like a university lecturer, with his black-rimmed spectacles. As late as 1972, he was still describing himself as a 'don turned politician' with 'an odd sense of detachment from my political activity.'[49] Crucially, he had no personal support base in the Parliamentary Labour Party, so allying himself to Wilson gave him influence. Crossman told Bevan that it was now more likely that Wilson would be prime minister rather than him.[50] The move was not without personal cost to Wilson. Arthur Irvine, MP for Liverpool Edge Hill, and later Wilson's solicitor-general from 1967 to 1970, pulled out of addressing a meeting in Huyton, declaring himself in agreement with Bevan on opposition to the Dulles South-East Asia policy and German rearmament: 'So it appears, is Mr. Wilson. But he has decided to join the Parliamentary Committee.'[51] When Crossman married his third wife, Anne McDougall, later in the year, Wilson did not attend to avoid Bevan and Jennie Lee who would be among the guests.[52]

The issue of German rearmament rumbled on. In July 1954, *Tribune* published *It Need Not Happen: The Alternative to German Rearmament*. With Wilson now in the shadow cabinet, it was Bevan who led in putting it together. It accepted that Germany could be reunited, but that would need the agreement of the Soviet Union. Arming West Germany not only had the potential to threaten the Soviet Union, which would not help in resolving the issue, but there was also a risk that, armed, West Germany could seek to unite itself with the east with a new war. The matter came to a head at the party conference in Scarborough later that year. On 28 September, the resolution from the Amalgamated Union of Foundry Workers, agreeing on the need for a democratic and united Germany, but opposing German rearmament, was defeated 3,281,000 to 2,910,000.[53] The next day, at a *Tribune* rally, in anger at Gaitskell's coldness, Bevan remarked that the right kind of leader for the Labour Party was a 'desiccated calculating machine'.[54]

Wilson grew in stature. With Bevan standing for the post of party treasurer, for which Gaitskell defeated him, Wilson was to top the constituency section of the NEC with over a million votes.[55] When he returned to Parliament after the party conference, he was re-elected to the shadow cabinet in twelfth place with 120 votes. It proved a springboard. In 1955, he rose to fifth with 147 votes; in 1956 he topped the poll with 185 votes and was top again in 1957 with 193. In 1958, he fell to second with 191 votes to Bevan's 206, but was again back on top in 1959 with 167 votes.[56]

Wilson also cultivated his links with the unions. The cotton trade unions had asked Wilson to produce a paper on the future of the industry, drawing on his experience as president of the Board of Trade. At the end of October 1954, Raymond Streat was given a copy and was horrified. The proposals included the setting up of a cotton industry reorganisation committee to provide fixed and working capital, to draw up schemes of amalgamation and for government acquiring a controlling interest with share purchases. Streat read the seventy-five neatly argued pages and lamented: 'It shows that Harold Wilson is an able draughtsman, even a brilliant one.' But it made 'one absolutely frightened about what Wilson would do if he became, shall we say, Chancellor of the Exchequer or Prime Minister. He has a fantastic belief in the power of the government and individual Ministers to supervise and decide things for the public good. He seems to have no conception of what is involved in totalitarianism of this sort.'[57] Streat's recoiling from such state direction of the industry reflected his personal views, but it was also notable that, far from seeing Wilson as someone who had set off on a political adventure in the wilderness as he had in 1951, he now saw him as a contender for the highest offices of state.

The dispute between Bevan and Gaitskell reached its height in March 1955. Gaitskell urged Attlee to move to expel Bevan from the party, knowing that would take him out of play as a leadership rival. Following the South-East Asia NATO episode, Bevan had put down a motion on the Commons order paper on 15 February urging talks with Russia about Germany despite there being no such agreement to do so from the parliamentary committee; in March he had confronted Attlee in a debate on nuclear weapons challenging him about their use in a conflict where the opponent was using conventional weapons.[58] Attlee, however, looking to preserve unity, wanted to keep Bevan in the party. On 7 March, the parliamentary committee voted to remove the whip from Bevan, though Wilson voted against, showing some residual loyalty. This decision was confirmed by the PLP on 16 March by 141 votes to 112. The matter moved to the NEC, which had to decide on Bevan's party membership. Here, Attlee intervened decisively in the meeting of 23 March 1955, carrying by the slimmest of margins, 14 votes to 13, the proposal that Bevan should submit a statement and be questioned on it by a sub-committee. Attlee met Bevan and agreed a statement. The sub-committee met on 29 March; the next day, the full NEC accepted Bevan's apology, and the PLP restored the party whip on 21 April.

With this turmoil in the Labour Party, the new prime minister, Anthony Eden, who had replaced Churchill on 7 April, had called a general election on 26 May 1955. Bevan was once again the bogeyman of the campaign, with 10 per cent of Tory candidates mentioning him in their election addresses.[59] The Tories won comfortably, taking 49.7 per cent of the vote to Labour's 46.4 per cent, securing 344 seats to Labour's 277. Internal strife and a failure to produce an alternative, forward-looking programme had cost Labour dear, with rising living standards helping the Conservatives. In Huyton, Wilson more than doubled his majority to 2,558, taking 24,858 votes with a single Tory opponent polling 22,300. Attlee visited the constituency to support Wilson, indicative of his return to the parliamentary frontline, and Wilson, with Edith Summerskill, even presented one of the party's three party political broadcasts on 16 May. Wilson caught the eye of the national press, who contrasted his dull parliamentary speeches with his style on the hustings: 'He twinkles with quips.'[60] The 1951–55 parliament had shown him as ambitious and decisive when he needed to be.

Chapter 7

Pots and pans

Working with Gaitskell, 1955–59

Given the factional strife of the early 1950s, the 1955 general election result should not have come as a surprise to the Labour Party. Nonetheless, the stark fact that the Conservatives had not only retained power, but increased their majority from 17 to 58, prompted recriminations. In the immediate aftermath of the election, the party general secretary, Morgan Phillips, produced a report highlighting the lack of desire among the electorate for change after 'four years of comparative prosperity' under the Conservatives. Phillips argued that, while the internal dispute had not moved voters in itself, it had seriously lowered the morale of volunteers, meaning the party machine was less effective than it had been in previous general elections. This was not enough for many in the party who wanted answers: Hugh Gaitskell warned Phillips that there was a call for a thorough investigation of party machinery.[1]

At the first post-election meeting of the National Executive, on 22 June, a sub-committee was set up to look at Labour organisation across the country, with a remit to produce an interim report by the party conference. Wilson was appointed its chair, and was joined by three allies: Arthur Skeffington, then MP for Hayes and Harlington, whose son was Wilson's godchild; Margaret Herbison, a former teacher and MP for North Lanarkshire; and the trade unionist Jack Cooper who had also, briefly, served as MP for Deptford.[2] A few days later, they lunched with Phillips at St Ermin's Hotel, but made no effort to contact him afterwards, or offer him the chance to feed in his views. Between 5 July and 24 September 1955 there were forty-nine meetings across the country with MPs, regional staff, the National Union of Labour Organisers, constituency agents, and groups of local parties. On 26 September, two days before the National Executive Committee was due to meet to consider the recommendations, the report was leaked to the *Daily Mirror.* Wilson makes no mention of the leak in his memoirs, but making the findings public in this way guaranteed that the party could not try to bury it and avoid taking action.

Wilson used the report to emphasise the importance of a healthy organisation and campaigning. He lamented constituency parties in safe Labour seats excluding people out of fear of changing the power dynamics within. Wilson's own view was characteristically pragmatic, preferring the Labour Party to be in power changing lives than wandering with uncompromising doctrine in the wilderness. He decried those whose argument amounted to saying that the party should 'issue a truly Socialist Manifesto, nationalising everything and nearly everybody, and the undeniable purity of our approach would lead to victory after victory and drive the Tories, Liberals and moderate Socialists into oblivion.'[3] Wilson thought the party should not advocate a mass extension of public ownership, which was unpopular: instead, it should consider individual cases, such as the chemicals industry.[4]

The headline sentence, though, was on party organisation: 'compared with our opponents we are still at the penny-farthing stage in a jet propelled era, and our machine, at that, is getting rusty and deteriorating with age.' Phillips was incensed: 'An organisation based on volunteers can always be said to be penny-farthing in a jet age.'[5] Wilson was no friend of Phillips who, for him, personified Morrison's control over Transport House, and represented at best inertia, at worst an out-of-date mode of running the party, with Phillips fixing party jobs and NEC votes for his patron. The report itself, though, had, ironically, built a bridge to the right of the PLP, not, as Wilson put it with delightful understatement, 'up to that point my natural allies.'[6] After party conference, the newly elected National Executive Committee reconstituted its sub-committees:

Wilson became the first chair of the organisation sub-committee, tasked with reforming the party. 'Org Sub' was to become one of the most powerful National Executive Committees in the post-war era, tasked with parliamentary selections.

Alongside his profile-building around the country, Wilson flourished on the frontbench in the House of Commons. His assessment of his prospects was perceptive. On 6 June, he lunched with Crossman, who told him that Gaitskell disliked him so much because he saw him as a rival. Wilson demurred: 'he was not a real rival to Gaitskell, but that Gaitskell realised that if he ever made a mess of things Harold was there to step into his shoes as a *tertium gaudens*.'[7] In the longer-term Wilson certainly did prove to be the third party who profited from the Bevan–Gaitskell dispute. The politics of the succession to Attlee were more complicated, with Morrison and Gaitskell still the leading contenders on the right of the PLP. On the left stood the giant figure of Bevan, still commanding the loyalty of a following that Wilson lacked. Wilson correctly identified the deputy leadership as a realistic option if Bevan remained out of the contest: 'He thought it was silly of Nye to stand for the deputy leadership but added that he would probably do so and that it wouldn't do much harm.'[8] With Bevan a rival in any election, Wilson's potential list of supporters was significantly shortened.

In July 1955, no doubt mindful of the impact of Bevan taking the dispatch box and criticising him in the previous parliament, Attlee moved to ensure that the shadow cabinet members each had their own portfolios and could speak outside it in the Commons. Previously, though the former cabinet ministers from the 1945–51 governments were generally expected to respond on matters that were the responsibility of their former departments, other speakers were chosen each week for different debates. Wilson was more than happy to be allocated the Board of Trade, supported by Arthur Bottomley, former secretary for overseas trade.

Attlee finally announced his retirement on 7 December. After twenty years with one leader, the successor was chosen within a week: forty-eight hours for nominations with a vote on 14

December. Morrison, by now sixty-seven, faced the two leaders of the next generation: Gaitskell, forty-nine, and Bevan, fifty-eight. Gaitskell won a majority in the first round, taking 157 votes to 70 for Bevan and 40 for Morrison. Attlee's holding on to the leadership for so long had reduced Morrison's chances of succeeding him. Electing Gaitskell settled the leadership for the longer-term; as the newly elected leader told Morrison: 'Herbert, there is nothing but the years between us.'[9] Bevan had been unable to expand his support far beyond the 57 whose rebellion in March 1952 had marked the start of the 'Bevanite' controversy. He had fared better when he had stood against Morrison for the deputy leadership in November 1951 when he had polled 82 votes. To add insult to injury, the moderate Jim Griffiths defeated Bevan for the deputy leadership by 141 votes to 111. Wilson had wisely stayed out of a contest he had no chance of winning.

In the leadership election itself, Wilson had promised Gaitskell his support as early as 14 October 1955. Gaitskell gave Wilson a lift back to Hampstead after they had broadcast together. In the insalubrious surroundings of a Soho side street, Wilson, saying Bevan had now ruled himself out with his erratic behaviour, offered his backing on the basis he would seek 'accommodation not constant confrontations'.[10] The payback he wanted in return was for Gaitskell to appoint him shadow chancellor. In February 1954, *The Economist* had coined the terms 'Butskellism' to point out the alignment of policy between the Conservative chancellor, R.A. Butler, and the then shadow chancellor Gaitskell. Anyone watching the Labour response to Butler's budget of October 1955 could be forgiven for doubting this. At the committee stage of the Finance Bill – when the Commons considers legislation line-by-line – Wilson working closely with Gaitskell to exploit Butler's decision to put individual tax measures on different items led to there being pages and pages in the bill from brooms and mops to rolling pins. Butler's 'Pots and Pans' budget, as it became known, led to a triumph for Wilson. At 8 a.m. on 17 November, after an all-night sitting with opposition members filibustering at every opportunity, Wilson intervened in a procedural row about ending the debate: 'I should like to ask whether you will accept as an alternative, the Motion, "That the Chairman do leave the Chair forthwith," it being understood that it would be moved in the spirit of Erskine May's [the book of rules of parliamentary procedure] suggestion that this is an alternative way of bringing a debate in Committee to a conclusion when there are reasons, or when there has been a refusal of the Motion, to report Progress.'[11] Sir Charles MacAndrew, Chairman of Ways and Means, in the chair, did not rule it out of order. Sydney Silverman MP, a procedural expert but a loose cannon on the Labour benches, saw what Wilson was doing and the consequence it had of killing off the Finance Bill, and tried to intervene, but MacAndrew was unperturbed and the bill fell. While the government had the majority to bring it back, it was a victory for Wilson.

At the start of January 1956, Gaitskell saw the elected members of the shadow cabinet one by one. He recognised that 'it is clear that Harold Wilson will have to have the Treasury' despite George Brown, an emerging force on the right of the PLP, dripping poison into Gaitskell's ear: '. . . he found it very hard to stomach Harold Wilson . . . He said that Harold Wilson had said far worse things about me than Nye ever had . . .'[12] As if to further demonstrate his credentials for a senior position on Gaitskell's frontbench, Wilson departed for Moscow for a three-day visit to the Soviet Ministry of Foreign Trade in his role at Montague Meyer, before leaving for home on 13 January. Wilson spoke to Mikoyan for 75 minutes and Nikita Khrushchev for 90 minutes. He was tight-lipped on what was discussed. When asked if the Soviet leaders' planned visit to London in April had been discussed, his language was tortuous: 'it can be deduced that this was not omitted'.[13] In the event, Khrushchev and Bulganin met leading Labour figures for a dinner at the House of Commons on 23 April. The event became chaotic as the Soviet leaders were confronted with the issue of repression of their political opponents at home. George Brown harangued Khrushchev and Bulganin during their speeches; Gaitskell presented Khrushchev with a list of social democrats who had been imprisoned in Soviet satellite states. When Khrushchev replied that they were 'enemies of our country', Bevan, back on the frontbench as shadow colonial secretary, supported Gaitskell: 'We have not the same interpretation of the enemies of the working class as Comrade Khrushchev has.'[14]

Also present at the dinner was a person who was to become a central part of Wilson's life. Marcia Williams, then aged twenty-four, one of Phillips' secretaries at Transport House, was taking notes in shorthand.[15] It is perhaps a reflection of the debate around Wilson's relationship with Williams, which has too often generated more heat than light, that there is not even agreement about when they first met. One suggestion is that he gave her a lift home that night. Joe Haines, later Wilson's press secretary, said: 'Something of significance must have happened that night. Discussions recalling that evening always made Marcia jumpy, so much so that it became a standing joke among a few of us that if I wanted to induce panic in her, I would simply send her a postcard with the numbers 23456 on it. She would have known that they stood for 23 April 1956.'[16] Williams herself said she actually met Wilson after that: he saw her at a bus stop, recognised her as a member of the party staff, and gave her a lift.[17] Wilson himself wrote that the first contact, at least, was earlier, and that he had been 'greatly assisted in all . . . [the] . . . work on Party organization by a young lady on the staff of Morgan Phillips . . .'[18] Such assistance, though, was in the form of anonymous notes sent to him, warning him about Phillips' machinations on the National Executive Committee.[19]

She was born Marcia Matilda Field at Long Buckby, Northamptonshire, on 10 March 1932. Her father, Harry, a Conservative, managed a brickworks. Her mother, Dorothy, was rumoured to be an unacknowledged daughter of Edward VII; the story ran that an aide-de-camp, Falkender, claimed her fatherhood to spare royal blushes, a name Williams herself was to take for her title – her mother's maiden name – when she was elevated to the House of Lords in 1974.[20] She went to Northampton High School, then Queen Mary's College, London, where she was awarded a second-class degree in history, then went on to secretarial college (there she achieved an impressive shorthand: 120 wpm; typing 50 wpm).[21]

It was at Queen Mary's College that she made her first political contact. James Callaghan met her when he spoke at the College Labour Club, of which she was secretary. He was so impressed he recommended her to Phillips for a job at Transport House. She started there as a secretary in early 1955. That same year, she married George Edmund Williams – known as Ed – a student of aerodynamics. He had been the chair of the Conservative Association at Queen Mary's College. 'We were both too young,' was her explanation as to why the marriage ended in divorce in 1960.[22] They certainly spent time apart. Ed Williams, then twenty-six, left to work at Boeing Aircraft Co. in Seattle on 1 September 1957. However, there was no intention to end the relationship at that point. Marcia contacted the then Minister of Pensions and National Insurance, Sir John Boyd-Carpenter, about making her husband's national insurance contributions while he was working away. It was only on advice that she decided to discontinue them while he was out of the country.[23] Ed eventually moved to America permanently and had three children by a second marriage.

Marcia Williams has polarised debate for decades. One political journalist, James Margach, wrote: 'I doubt very much whether Harold Wilson would ever have become Party leader and Prime Minister but for the ambitious thrust provided by Mrs Williams.'[24] Williams herself was more circumspect, telling Wilson's official biographer Philip Ziegler: 'I helped to encourage and build the enthusiasm that he already felt . . . I couldn't have put it there. But I did keep him going through difficult times.'[25] Haines reflected: 'She was, for a while, his driving force. But, ultimately, she damaged his life, his political career and his reputation.'[26]

At this stage, though, all of this was in the future. In 1956, Williams was at the beginning of a decades-long period working for Wilson, at his side in parliament until he stepped down from the House of Commons in 1983. Already, though, some features were apparent. First, she was a highly ambitious, capable person with sound political antennae. Her major judgement that was to prove a spectacular success was who she chose to work for. She wanted a job with a Labour MP, and already had options. She had done some temporary work for James Callaghan, but wanted something 'more stimulating' and had turned down a job with Hugh Gaitskell on the basis he was 'too autocratic and too right-wing'.[27] Then, the break came. Through Skeffington, she was offered a job with Wilson when his existing secretary became pregnant. She started in October 1956, working in the Montague Meyer office, walking down to the Commons in the evenings with the post. Her choice of Wilson was at one level a natural one. Working in the old-fashioned, stultifying atmosphere of Transport House, Wilson was the dynamic one seeking change and reform. At the same time, it was a canny choice. She had spotted Wilson's potential, seen him as a politician with whom she could rise to the top.

Wilson's great quality was adaptability. As a politician, he evolved. His Commons speeches, while marked by technical excellence, had been turgid. Now, he introduced humour and invective. Castle captures this: 'When he first got on to the front bench he was one of the dullest speakers in the House . . . I watched him deliberately turn himself into a witty debater whom the Opposition feared. In due course his command of the House became masterly.'[28] The journalist Alun Watkins wrote that Wilson 'acquired his parliamentary wit after years of hard endeavour. Gallons and gallons of midnight oil have been consumed in the enterprise.' He added: 'It is a type of wit which depends, not on a reaction to circumstances as they arise, but on a carefully prepared use of words.'[29]

With Harold Macmillan as chancellor, Wilson developed a fine political rivalry, marked by fierce clashes across the dispatch box, but with respect for each other's political skill. Macmillan observed the change in Wilson's approach. In April 1956, Macmillan introduced Premium Bonds for savers: rather than interest being earned with each individual investment, the interest is put together into a draw for a tax-free prize. Wilson's Congregationalist background coloured his response: 'what a commentary it is on the financial stewardship of the party opposite when the Chancellor of the Exchequer has to have recourse to such measures! In 1951, they promised us a "Britain Strong and Free." Now Britain's strength, freedom and solvency apparently depend on the proceeds of a squalid raffle.'[30] Another occasion arose when, in June 1956, the

Texas Oil Company offered £63m to buy the assets and rights of the Trinidad Oil Company, a price estimated to be around twice the market value. Under the terms of the 1947 Exchange Control Act, Macmillan had the power to block it. Conservative back-benchers urged Macmillan not to sell out the Empire to America and a wide cross-section of the press – a combination of the *Daily Worker*, the *Daily Herald* and the *Daily Express* – were opposed. However, the chancellor saw the economic gain to the Trinidad economy in allowing the transaction to go through. Wilson seized the opportunity to exploit the government's discomfort. Macmillan watched with quiet admiration as MPs were treated to the 'brilliant attack delivered by Wilson . . . I never heard him give such a display of virtuosity. Epigram followed epigram, and the continual flashes of wit were from time to time relieved by more serious arguments.'[31] Wilson focused on the unearned profit going into the pockets of the shareholders. These unmerited gains, Wilson said, made for a 'Windfall State'.[32] As shadow chancellor, he was flourishing.

Williams securing the role also meant that Wilson was never to have a right-hand man, but a right-hand *woman*. For this, Wilson does deserve credit: in contrast to the gentlemen's club atmosphere and attitudes of many of his contemporaries, he enjoyed the company of women, and promoted them when he had the chance to. That it was so unusual in this period inevitably led to gossip as to whether they were having a sexual relationship. Later, Macmillan is said to have quipped: 'Funny fellow, Wilson. Keeps his mistress at No 10. Always kept mine in St John's Wood.'[33] Rose Rosenberg had been Ramsay MacDonald's private secretary in the 1920s and 1930s, but that was in a different media age. The Move's record 'Flowers in the Rain' – the first played on the newly launched BBC Radio 1 in September 1967 – was promoted with a cartoon postcard featuring a naked Wilson in bed with Williams. Wilson sued and won, with the consequence that all the royalties went to charities of his choice.[34] These rumours would never have swirled had Williams been male. She was a woman in a very senior position in a political world dominated by men to such an extent that only a handful of women had even reached cabinet level. On the Labour side, only Margaret Bondfield (1929–31) and Ellen Wilkinson (1945–7) had sat around government's top table before Wilson himself promoted Castle, then Judith Hart and Shirley Williams. On the Conservative side, there was only Florence Horsburgh (1953–4) and Margaret Thatcher (1970–74). Indeed, until Thatcher herself became prime minister in 1979, there is an argument that Marcia Williams was closer to the centre of power in 10 Downing Street than any of them.

Marcia joined Wilson just as British and international politics were about to be overwhelmed by the Suez crisis, leading to the resignation of Prime Minister Anthony Eden in January 1957. On 26 July 1956, Egyptian President Nasser unilaterally nationalised the Suez Canal. Bevan criticised Nasser for putting Egyptian nationalism above other priorities, such as economic and political reform. What Bevan did not support was the use of force by the British and French governments to seize back control of the canal. On 30 October, Eden told the Commons that Israeli troops had invaded Egypt, and urged Israel and Egypt to cease conflict. He issued a twelve-hour ultimatum to Nasser to agree to British and French troops being stationed in Port Said, Ismailia and Suez. Since none was forthcoming, Britain and France took military action. Gaitskell broadcast to the country on 4 November that the government had violated the Charter of the United Nations. That same day, the Soviet Union invaded Hungary, to suppress the revolt that had started on 23 October when a rally in Budapest had turned into a demonstration on the reinstatement of the deposed prime minister, Imre Nagy, and an end to Soviet rule. Bevan quickly made the link with the British government vacating the moral high ground: 'I do not believe that it is possible to separate the events in Hungary from the events in Egypt.'[35] The United States reined Eden in. President Eisenhower could block a British drawing on the IMF, without which the serious run on the pound the crisis had caused seemed likely to drain the foreign-exchange reserves. Eden took the threat seriously and announced a ceasefire on 6 November.

Wilson did not have direct responsibility for Suez as a Labour spokesperson. He was restricted to one parliamentary speech on the issue, on 12 November 1956, on the economic consequences of the closure of the Canal: '. . . ships will be diverted round the Cape, but it will be obvious to hon. Members in all parts of the House that we can expect far less oil brought round the Cape in the same number of tankers than if the tankers had come straight through the Canal, and, certainly, we can expect increased prices.'[36]

While his own role was not central in Labour's response, Wilson understood the profound consequences of the Suez crisis. Firstly, the end of Anthony Eden's political career: though Wilson praised him for his opposition to Chamberlain's policy of appeasement. He saw the crisis as marking the 'ending of Britain's role as a world power which she had held since the days of the Younger Pitt'. Like France, Britain was now a 'significant influence' but not dominant. It also marked the 'consummation of a development created by World War II, the unchallenged role of the USA and the Soviet Union as world's two principal super-powers.' Wilson also saw Suez as 'the arrival at the centre of affairs of Harold Macmillan whose patrician skulduggery had made him virtually the inspiration of the attack on Suez, the failure of which led to him assuming the premiership.' Macmillan had been 'First In, First Out'. As for the Labour Party, its leader was transformed, with 'the emergence of Hugh Gaitskell from the role of a numerate Chancellor of the Exchequer to the rank of a world statesman as, day by day, he dissociated his party from the Government's actions, with a long series of orations combining statesmanship with a power of oratory few had associated with him.'[37]

The crisis united the Labour Party. In shadow cabinet, Wilson noted the 'remarkable co-operation of George Brown. George had been for years a passionate pro-Arab . . . Hugh informed the meeting that George had, after much discussion between them, come to accept the existence, even, of the Israeli state.'[38] Wilson reminded shadow cabinet colleagues of the dangers of being anti-war, and the incident when a young David Lloyd George had to be smuggled out after a speech in Birmingham during the Boer War.[39]

Even Wilson was close to Gaitskell: 'In no sense was I a member of the "Hampstead Set" apart from a brief weekend membership during the Suez crisis.'[40]

If Wilson's first twelve years in parliament had showcased his ability to find his way through political situations, he was by no means infallible. Later, he reflected: 'It was in the Autumn of 1957 that I made what I have believed ever since to have been the greatest error of my political career – the affair of the "Bank Rate Leak" . . .'[41] That he wrote this is an indication of the extent to which the episode stung him. On 19 September, the chancellor, Peter Thorneycroft, increased the bank rate from 5 per cent to 7 per cent, putting it at its highest level since 1920, in order to stem a run on the pound. On 24 September, Wilson, with the chancellor abroad, wrote a letter to Enoch Powell, financial secretary to the Treasury, alleging that the intention to raise the rate had been leaked in advance. Powell replied two days later saying an investigation had turned up no evidence. Wilson persisted. Writing on 4 October, from the Labour Party conference in Brighton, he said prima facie evidence had been brought to his attention indicating the 'leak emanated from a political source'. Macmillan challenged him to put the evidence to the lord chancellor, Lord Kilmuir. On 7 October, Wilson and Jim Griffiths met Macmillan and Kilmuir: Wilson produced no evidence as he said the information was based on the statements of others.[42] There was only a series of anonymous telephone calls to Morgan Phillips.[43] Thorneycroft was accused of confiding the news of the rate rise to Oliver Poole, deputy chairman of the Conservative Party organisation, the day before the announcement. With no firm evidence, on 22 October, Macmillan told Gaitskell and Wilson that there would not be an inquiry. Not to be deterred, Wilson put Deptford MP Dick Plummer up to asking a question of Thorneycroft in the Commons on 12 November. The chancellor failed to deny he had seen Poole and said it would 'be quite inappropriate for me to state whom I saw or for what purpose on this or any other day.'[44] The next day, Macmillan announced a tribunal of inquiry.

Wilson had gone a long way on unnamed sources. Crossman

confided to his diary: 'I haven't met anybody who really believes that anything can possibly be proved against Oliver Poole.'[45] Wilson submitted to the inquiry that, with financial interests himself, Poole told City contacts before the after-hours dealing of that evening ended. In January, the tribunal exonerated the government, and found no evidence of a leak. The debate, on 3 February, was the most difficult Wilson had faced in the Commons up to then. Not only was the government in the clear, it now looked as if Wilson had attacked the government with no solid evidential basis, prompting the appointment of an inquiry that had been a waste of time. He dreaded the prospect of the debate, but stuck to his usual method of detailed, meticulous preparation.[46] Butler, opening the debate for the government, accused Wilson of cowardice and low ethical standards for making unfounded allegations against Poole. Parliamentary privilege, protecting MPs from being sued for libel for what they say in the Commons chamber 'imposes on us an infinitely higher standard of responsibility for our privileged utterances than that which guided the right hon. Gentleman opposite. Meanwhile, let us be thankful that, massive as is the machinery of the Tribunal, it has broken the political weapon of the smear.'[47]

Wilson argued that, given the press reports, any responsible government had to act: '*The Times* referred to "inspired selling", the *Financial Times* referred to "an early whisper", while the *Manchester Guardian* said that it was a complete surprise to all but one or two people who seemed to have got wind that something was afoot.'[48] While accepting he had worked with Plummer on his questioning on 12 November, Wilson pointed out that it was Thorneycroft's failure to give a direct answer that was the issue that led to the appointment of the inquiry: 'If he had said that [a denial], the House would have accepted that assurance.'[49] He then moved to wider issues. The Attlee governments' bank nationalisation structure, whereby there could be part-time directors with other financial interests, had to be revisited. He lamented the 'essentially amateurish way in which vital decisions affecting our whole economic well-being are taken – the "old boy" network, the grouse moors . . .'[50] Fending off hostile interventions and heckling throughout, it was hardly a vintage performance, but it was a bat-tling display in the most difficult of circumstances.

The debate marked a turn in fortunes for the government, and revenge for Wilson. Thorneycroft himself was by now a back-bencher: his resignation on 6 January, together with his two junior Treasury ministers, Nigel Birch and Enoch Powell, had shaken the government. To put a stop to the recurring sterling crises, Thorneycroft proposed deflation and public spending cuts, and, in an argument that prefigured the emergence of Thatcherism over two decades later, argued that Britain should be living within its means. Macmillan was not willing to accept that the only way in-flation could be kept low was through high unemployment. In the economic debate on 23 January, facing the new chancellor, Derick Heathcoat-Amory, Wilson had attacked Butler, Macmillan and Thorneycroft for the money they had squandered on the foreign exchanges: '. . . over the three years the three chancellors between them lost 2,150 million dollars'.[51]

Labour, meanwhile, had been finessing its stance on nation-alisation. In 1956, Anthony Crosland had published *The Future of Socialism*. Dark-haired and dashing, Crosland was also a deep thinker with an intellectual elan that gave him the confidence to challenge orthodoxy. He argued that Morrisonian public own-ership – government purchase of private industries and running them via appointed boards – was not an end in itself. Rather, the 'objective is not wholly to destroy private ownership, but to alter its distribution . . .' and state ownership in itself was not necessary for this. Different models had to be considered, with the goal of creat-ing a more equal society.[52] Crosland put forward the idea of the state owning shares in the top 200 or so companies, thus sharing profits between private investors and the public. This found expres-sion in the policy document *Industry and Society*. The right mocked it; the *Spectator* commenting: 'After all these years they have dis-covered that the right thing to do is not to attack capitalism but to cash in on it.'[53] Nonetheless, *Industry and Society* was endorsed at the 1957 party conference. Wilson set out his own solutions for controlling inflation in three articles for the *Manchester Guardian*, which were published in a Labour Party pamphlet. In a precursor to what was to be his approach as prime minister, Wilson offered to 'secure an understanding with the unions which would make wage restraint possible'. A Labour government would introduce national planning and invest in industry, and also deal with inflation by keeping prices steady. Wilson's approach would be to introduce a 'socially just' budget, but one that would not frighten swing voters with the prospect of tax rises: 'what is needed is a widening of the tax-base by attacking fiscal privilege – business expenses and perks, covenants and other avoidance devices . . .'[54]

At the same time Bevan's rapprochement with Gaitskell continued. At the 1956 party conference, Gaitskell stood down as party treasurer, and Bevan defeated Brown for the post. Gaitskell promoted Bevan to shadow foreign secretary in place of Alf Robens, and Bevan denounced the case for unilateral nuclear disarmament at the 1957 party conference, declaring that it would be like sending the next foreign secretary 'naked into the conference chamber' in any multilateral disarmament negotiations.[55] Wilson was not a unilateralist, either, though he maintained his relationships with those MPs who were: the Campaign for Nuclear Disarmament was founded in February 1958, with Michael Foot a stalwart of its annual marches on the Atomic Weapons Research Establishment at Aldermaston.

It was characteristic of Wilson to be both a part of something and apart from it at the same time. This principle also extended to another of his lifelong attachments: the Isles of Scilly. The islands are British, yet they feel a distance away. Wilson could travel overseas for his holidays, but at the same time remain in the UK. The archipelago of 145 islands and rocks lies 28 miles south-west of Cornwall. Five of the islands are inhabited: St Mary's, by far the largest with the bulk of the population; St Martin's; Tresco; Bryher; and St Agnes.[56] Further south-west lies the Bishop Rock lighthouse, the point at which transatlantic ocean liners officially started the timing of their voyages to New York to compete for the Blue Riband, awarded to the ship that made the fastest crossing. Truly, this is the very edge of the UK. The mild climate, warmed by the Gulf Stream, allows a wide range of flowers and foliage to flourish.[57] Wilson could relax and be away from the pressures of everyday politics but at the same time feel at home. His island of choice was St Mary's. With an area of just over two and a half square miles, it consists of a small, garrisoned hill connected by a narrow isthmus, where the capital, Hugh Town, is situated, to the main body of the island. It has an airport, a road network, and a large harbour.

When he was at the top of British politics as Labour leader and prime minister, Wilson's choice of holiday destination gave the Scillies a real boost. As one resident put it: 'In the sixties and seventies Scilly was synonymous with the Wilsons and vice-versa. In those days a great advertisement for the special attraction of our islands.'[58] In 1965, dressed in a white polo shirt and shorts, pipe in hand, a relaxed-looking Wilson gave a press conference on tiny Samson island, uninhabited since 1855, journalists crowding around him in suits, camera shots featuring not only the prime minister but also the sand and defining twin hills of the island's landscape behind him.[59]

Wilson was the first prime minister to 'reveal his knees in public' on his summer break.[60] A saucy seaside postcard from him in the Scillies appeared on a *Private Eye* front cover, with Wilson's speech bubble stating: 'If the tide comes in it'll tickle my fancy.'[61] Yet he was no mere tourist. He bought a property and established a firm link with St Mary's. He purchased land from the Duchy of Cornwall and had a three-bedroom bungalow built in 1959. It was named 'Lowenva': an old Cornish word meaning 'house of happiness'. It was also a reminder of his mother Ethel, who had died from cancer in October 1958. Ethel and Herbert's home just outside St Austell had had the same name. Wilson had been at his mother's side with his father and sister when she passed away, and had immersed himself in his work to deal with her serious illness and his grief.

Establishing a property in the Scillies meant a permanent place of refuge from pressures was available. It was not ostentatious, but was, rather, a grey-stone, unobtrusive, ordinary property that fitted in with its surroundings: 'Many expressed surprise that it was so small, for there was still the idea in that decade that anyone prominent in public life was sure to live in an opulent dwelling, even apparently when on holiday.'[62] Situated on the brow of the hill above Hugh Town, with sea views from its garden, and shops within walking distance, only half a kilometre away, it was an ideal location for Wilson.[63]

Wilson first visited in 1952; his son Robin first joined his parents there in 1953. The Wilsons would travel to Penzance on the train or by car. They sometimes travelled on to St Mary's via the hazardous sea journey – Robin remembered being sick five times on one occasion – and sometimes flew to St Mary's from St Just, the De Havilland taking off over the cliff. The Wilsons usually went three times a year: in summer, at Easter, and in the winter. He threw himself into island life. He often wandered on the Hugh Town quayside speaking to people who approached him. A regular at the Mumford's shop in the centre of the town to collect a daily newspaper, Wilson was a familiar face to many Scillonians, though perhaps not all. On one occasion he was in the Mumford's queue when a man in front of him started criticising the Labour government and said if he saw that Harold Wilson he would give him a piece of his mind. The person serving at the counter pointed out Harold, and the man crumbled! Wilson played golf on the 9-hole course, making up foursomes with three local people. He managed to get his handicap down to twelve. Plotting his way around a golf course suited Wilson: when he lived in Hampstead Garden Suburb, he always made time to play a round on a Sunday afternoon.[64]

Wilson's walks, his approachability, and his willingness to engage with local people won him many friends. Wilson also used his considerable influence to help the islands in practical terms. The Isles of Scilly are linked to the mainland by a regular shipping service provided by the Isles of Scilly Steamship Company vessel *Scillonian*. The first *Scillonian* entered service in 1926 and was replaced by *Scillonian II* in 1956. This was, in turn, replaced by *Scillonian III* in 1977, and Wilson was 'instrumental in the Government giving an interest free loan' to construct it.[65] One Scillonian said Wilson had, quite simply, become one of them: 'The Wilsons have been considered Islanders by most of us for a long time now and their affection for Scilly has been mirrored by our acceptance of them.'[66] Wilson and Mary regularly saw in the New Year at the Scillonian Club in Hugh Town: with a wedding anniversary on New Year's Day, it was only fitting that they danced the Anniversary Waltz.[67]

Mary adored the Scillies. They were a haven for her from the pressures of public life. In the late 1950s, as her husband became more famous, Gladys Wilson became Mary Wilson. This was chiefly because Gladys was seen to be a rather provincial and old-fashioned name. Mary was a name for use in public life and political circles. Old friends and intimates still continued to call her Gladys: to her niece and nephew she remained Auntie Gladys. On her grave marker on the Isles of Scilly she is remembered as 'Gladys Mary'.[68] Both her poetry collections contain 'Scillonian Poems' inspired by her time there. One of her verses, 'St Agnes', captured her attachment to the beautiful isolation of the islands. The first stanza speaks of her love of escaping from the glare of the public eye: 'Could I but live here all alone/Alone with rocks and sea and sky/Hearing no footsteps but my own/And scream of wind, and curlew's cry'. What the Scillies gave her is summed up in the third stanza: 'So, when I come to die/May it be in these Isles I love—' and then in the final two lines: 'This will be immortality and all the heaven I shall desire.'[69]

As such a well-known public figure, Wilson's privacy was never, however, fully assured. Stories of his activities while on holiday did leak out. In early August 1973 he was rowing in a dinghy to a friend's launch with his dog, Paddy. As he moved to climb onto the launch, the dog pushed the dinghy away, leaving Wilson hanging on to the side of the launch. Wearing a life-jacket, he was in no danger of drowning but could not climb onto the boat because the side was too steep. He shouted for help, which eventually came after around 20–25 minutes when he noticed a family on the shore. At first the family went out to view the scene with a small paddle boat, then returned with a larger boat having seen it was Wilson who was in trouble. Wilson was then hauled out of the water by Simon Wolff, a sixteen-year-old public schoolboy at Rugby, whose father Paul was a lifelong Tory supporter. Haines, then his press secretary, told journalists, while Wilson was a fine swimmer, he just could not get into the boat: 'He didn't attempt to swim it because it was a fair distance and there were fairly strong currents.' Wilson addressed party workers in Redruth, back on the mainland in Cornwall, on 8 September. Pipe in hand, he quipped: '. . . there is one political lesson in this which I think all the commentators seem to have missed – floating Harold Wilson is better than a sinking Tory pound!'[70]

By the end of the summer of 1959, speculation about a general election was growing. On 8 September, Macmillan visited the queen at Balmoral to seek a dissolution, and, on his return, announced the poll for 8 October. As shadow chancellor, Wilson remained disciplined in his message, seeking to avoid suggestions Labour would raise taxes for working people. A scandal broke on 16 September when the share value of the Jasper group of property companies slumped with a takeover bid for a brewery running into trouble. Wilson jumped on the 'casino mentality of the City of London'.[71] On 22 September, in a BBC interview, Wilson said that a Labour government would not raise taxes to fund spending, but would increase production. The affairs of the Jasper group continued to unravel, and, on 25 September, a QC was appointed to look into its activities.

The Conservatives sought to exploit the fear of Labour raising taxes by turning the Jasper case against Wilson. On 26 September, the *Daily Herald* led with the banner headline, 'The Jasper Election' covering a Hailsham speech in which he shot back at the shadow chancellor: 'When the time comes I fear Mr. Harold Wilson will be like some other prominent financial experts who cannot find the cash they promised.'[72] Yet, up to this point, Wilson was more than holding his own. On 27 September, the *Daily Mail* observed: 'The Labour Party have undoubtedly had the best of the battle so far.'[73] Two events changed this.[74] The first was a speech from Gaitskell in Newcastle on 28 September during which he pledged: 'There will be no increase in the standard or other rates of income tax so long as normal peacetime conditions continue.' Macmillan dismissed it as electioneering. Then, on 1 October, at the daily Transport House news conference, a handout was distributed pledging that Labour would remove purchase tax from essential goods. While Labour pointed out this was nothing new – Wilson had said it in his 22 September broadcast – the problem was that Labour seemed to be making one promise after another without the underlying credibility on the economy to make them believable. 'A bribe a day keeps the Tories away,' mocked Butler. Macmillan pressed home the advantage in a speech in Nottingham later on 1 October: 'It was this addiction to figures, on which he [Mr. Gaitskell] built what seems now a false reputation, that led Mr. Bevan to describe him as a desiccated calculating machine. That is now only a half-truth. I think he is still rather desiccated but his reputation as a calculator has gone with the wind . . . Mr Gaitskell has brought himself down to the level of Mr. Harold Wilson.'[75]

The result of the general election came as a shock to Labour. The Conservatives took 49.4 per cent of the popular vote to Labour's 43.8 per cent, winning 365 seats to Labour's 258, resulting in an increased overall majority of 100. In Huyton, Wilson, building on his incumbency and the continuing demographic change, increased his majority to 5,927, winning 33,111 votes while his sole Conservative opponent took 27,184. The politics of Wilson's constituency was summed up by George Howarth, MP for the successor seat of Knowsley as follows: 'Huyton, following the Second World War, was an uneasy amalgam consisting of a Lancashire town which, in the inter-war years and thereafter was augmented by a new population of slum clearance residents from Liverpool, who occupied newly-built council property, mainly in the north of the town. Later, new council estates were built in the 1950s and 60s in south Huyton by the then Huyton Urban District Council.'[76]

Wilson's view was that those who moved into the Huyton constituency from Liverpool were mostly Catholics, and likely to be Labour voters. The Protestants, on the other hand, he saw as Conservatives. As the council estates of North Huyton and Kirkby evolved to become more Catholic, they developed a greater propensity to vote for the Labour Party. General elections meant campaigning all over the country, rather than the home patch receiving day-to-day personal attention, so the safer Huyton was, the better. Wilson also understood the Catholic vote: given his own religious upbringing, their instincts matched his own social conservatism.

Alongside his achievements on the national stage, Wilson was a hard-working local MP. The need for housing dominated his regular constituency surgeries, after which Wilson would then 'draft sixty or seventy letters to the Liverpool Corporation Housing Department, who ignored the lot'.[77] Having local industry also played to his strengths: 'His understanding of the grant system and extensive knowledge of Whitehall meant that he could play a critical role in attracting new industrial investment. One example of this was bringing the Ford Motor Company to Halewood, which, although not in his constituency, brought well-paid jobs for many of his constituents.'[78] Yet, for all the progress in Huyton, the national situation was dire.

Chapter 8

One of the ablest men in the Labour Party

To the Leadership, 1959–63

For the second general election in a row, the Conservatives had increased their majority while in office. This time, Labour did not have the excuse of internal division: in contrast to 1955, Bevan and Gaitskell had contested the election in harness. Gaitskell summoned his troops to Frognal Gardens in the aftermath of the defeat: Anthony Crosland, Gordon Walker, Jay, Roy and Jennifer Jenkins, Harris, Dalton and the chief whip Herbert Bowden concluded that the Labour Party needed radical change. That Wilson was not invited was an indication that Gaitskell did not see him as a trustworthy ally in the coming debate. Given that it was its approach to the economy that was seen to have cost Labour, the shadow chancellor was in a vulnerable position. In the days after the election the *Daily Mail* speculated that Wilson, 'one of the ablest men in the Labour Party, looks like becoming the scapegoat for the 1959 general election defeat just as Mr Morgan Phillips was blamed in 1955.' This time it was Wilson being blamed for an organisational failure in marginal seats, the promise to abolish purchase tax on essentials, and for failing to prevent Gaitskell making the income tax pledge in his Newcastle speech.[1] The third charge was clearly designed to deflect blame from the party leader onto Wilson, who later reflected: 'Although my relations with Hugh Gaitskell in the later 'fifties were much improved, a further crisis arose in 1959.'[2]

On 12 October, Roy Jenkins, Reg Prentice and Shirley Williams appeared on the BBC's *Panorama* with Jenkins attacking the

Labour position on nationalisation. It was obvious that Gaitskell himself was behind it, and, the next morning, his wife Dora rang Richard Crossman to ask if the party leader could spend the Tuesday night with him at Prescote, after a lunch with Bevan. With Jim Griffiths having stood aside as deputy leader, Bevan had confirmed he would like to take his place. Gaitskell, aware of Crossman's continuing behind-the-scenes influence, tried to charm him by taking him into his confidence, telling him that he wanted to re-write Clause IV of the party constitution, the commitment to nationalisation: 'to secure to the workers by hand and brain the full fruits of their labour through the common ownership of the means of production, distribution and exchange . . .' With an eye on the Bevanites' surge of the early 1950s, Gaitskell also wanted to take away the right of constituency parties to elect MPs to the National Executive Committee: they would have to elect rank-and-file members. He also confirmed his plan to move Wilson from his post. Crossman remained loyal to Wilson, and suggested he should be shadow leader of the House with a co-ordinating role, 'if he [Wilson] would regard that as a promotion.'[3] On 14 October, Crossman lunched with Wilson, and passed on the information. Wilson was so furious that Crossman was taken aback: 'He regarded this as a conspiracy to chase him out of the Shadow Chancellorship and stood pat, with the only expression of anger and passion I've ever heard him use.'[4] Wilson made clear he was not going to countenance Gaitskell's proposed reforms.

The atmosphere deteriorated as the party turned in on itself. On 16 October, Douglas Jay, in the Gaitskellite journal *Forward*, developed the internal debate, suggesting that the party change its name to 'Labour and Radical' or 'Labour and Reform' and drop its commitment to nationalisation. On 23 October, in a speech at the Cambridge University Labour Club, Wilson set out his position. He said that, had the election taken place before mid-1958, Labour would have won: 'It was only the windfall gain in import prices – worth £300 millions in 1958 – which enabled the Tories to claim stability of prices, to drop the credit squeeze, to embark on the election-winning hire purchase boom, to make big Budget hand-outs, and to reverse the policies which were leading to un-employment.' His message to Gaitskell was unmistakable: it was 'for conference to decide on any changes that may be considered necessary, whether in organization or policy'.[5] Meanwhile, the Commons chamber was 'utterly lifeless and bloodless' with MPs' attention focused elsewhere.[6] Wilson was deeply suspicious of all around him, including Crossman, whom he was convinced was part of the plot to move him from the shadow chancellorship. Balogh, who was close to Wilson, tried to mediate. He not only walked on Hampstead Heath with Wilson on a Sunday, he also met him on a weekly basis.[7] Bevan remained aloof from the machinations in parliament, but his position on Gaitskell's proposals would be key.

If Wilson's position was under threat, he nonetheless retained considerable strengths. Top of the shadow cabinet poll at the opening of the parliamentary session, Wilson also became chair of the Public Accounts Committee. There he remained, re-elected each year until 1962, only resigning on becoming Labour leader in February 1963. This was a significant role. First, the Public Ac-counts Committee gave Wilson an unrivalled perspective on how money was spent by government departments. Founded in 1866 as a guardian of the public purse, the Public Accounts Committee has a unique standing in parliament. His knowledge of the machinery of government was now matched by experience in scrutinising its operation. No other prime minister had ever served as its chair. As Meg Hillier, who became chair of the Public Accounts Committee in 2015 puts it: 'The benefit for Wilson, apart from access to a large meeting room, would have been a detailed understanding of how Whitehall worked and what effective delivery of policy looked like. He would have had unrivalled knowledge and understand-ing of the challenges of delivering large projects, the time it takes to plan for delivery and how to ensure outcomes from manifesto promises as well as getting to know Whitehall's senior manda-rins.' Hillier observed: 'On today's committee we often see over-optimistic and ill-thought out manifesto policies fail. No doubt Wilson saw and learned from these. This no doubt helped him focus on how to deliver some of the radical reforms of the Wilson governments.'[8]

The practical aspect should not be underestimated: the office in the Palace of Westminster gave a proximity to other MPs that was important in this period. It also allowed Wilson to give up his role with Montague Meyer, as there was no longer any need for an office on the Strand.

The party conference had been delayed because of the general election: it took place at Blackpool on 28 and 29 November. Bevan and Wilson arrived separately: Bevan on the train, Wilson by car. Bevan was, by now, raging. Wilson 'wasn't going to be disloyal but I was not going to back Gaitskell on a position where the party was split and I knew that Nye was liable to go into orbit at any moment . . . . Nye told all his friends on the way down by train . . . that he was going to move in on Gaitskell, and was going to take over the leadership. He never said that to me.'[9] That he did not say it to Wilson was an indication that he and Bevan were now rivals vying for the leadership.

Barbara Castle, in the chair, opened the conference defending the policy of nationalisation. Gaitskell argued that it had lost Labour votes: existing industries in public ownership were unpopular and inefficient. He said that public ownership was a means to greater equality, full employment and higher productivity, not an end in itself. Thus, Clause IV of the party constitution needed to be updated as in its current form it was misleading: Labour was not proposing to nationalise everything. Wilson recalled that 'all hell was let loose. Hugh was denounced not only by the left, but even by right-wing trade unionists.'[10] Bevan, with the conference in turmoil, responded with a speech of unity and common purpose. Since both Castle and Gaitskell had quoted Bevan on conquering the economy's commanding heights, Bevan recalled Euclid's deduction: if two things are equal to a third thing, they are equal to each other: 'Barbara and Hugh and both equal to me, and therefore must be equal to one another.' His peroration was a fine one: 'I have enough faith in my fellow creatures in Great Britain . . . when they realize that all the tides of history are flowing in our direction, that we are not beaten, that we represent the future: then, when we say it and mean it, then we shall lead our people to where they deserve to be led.'[11]

The brilliance of Bevan's oratory could not, however, mask the reality. The party was in a state of civil war. Gaitskell and Bevan had a row about the removal of standing orders in the shadow cabinet, which would have allowed its members to be freer to disagree in public. The shouting was of such intensity that Bevan was soon outside the room threatening to resign and campaign in the country. Wilson told him if he did he would put himself 'beyond the pale once again' and to stay and fight.[12] Wilson managed him skilfully: 'In the end I persuaded him that this was just what the Hampstead set were hoping for, and he cooled down.' Wilson's next claim, however, may have been over-optimistic: 'We agreed that I should make the challenge [to Gaitskell] when the time came.'[13] Whether Bevan would actually have accepted that will never be known.

Wilson's positioning in these internal party debates required a careful balance. On the one hand, he tried to avoid open conflict with Gaitskell, but, on the other, he sought to differentiate himself, showing that he was the person who could unite the party. On 7 December, the *Daily Express* summed up his approach: 'Harold the Peacemaker is sticking to his key position – on the fence . . .' He was 'curiously unloved' but he was 'indispensable' and one day Labour might find that 'quietly, cleverly, he has inherited the party leadership . . . [as a] . . . latter-day Attlee.' Wilson left for a lecture tour of America and Canada over Christmas in a position of some strength. Personally, he had had a good party conference. He had been re-elected to the NEC in second place, and become chair of its Home Policy Committee. He also became the NEC nominee to the TUC General Council.

By the time Wilson returned home, Bevan, ill with stomach cancer, could no longer play a part in active politics. On 27 December, Bevan had gone into the Royal Free Hospital for an operation, and remained at home at his farm, Asheridge in Buckinghamshire, until his death on 6 July 1960. His death was a profound shock to the whole Labour movement and his absence from politics was of great significance to Wilson. It would be totally unfair to suggest Wilson's association with Bevan was a mere marriage of convenience. Wilson and Bevan, in their different ways, could make a powerful moral case for socialism. They also became political rivals. Bevan's death not only took away the immediate debate as to whether he or Wilson would be the left challenger to Gaitskell in 1960, it also took away the one major competitor Wilson had to be the left's preferred candidate for the leadership for many years afterwards. Only when Tony Benn emerged with his proposals for an Alternative Economy Strategy in 1975 did another rival emerge. Bevan saw Wilson as a technocrat, as Wilson's story of one of their final conversations reveals: 'I recall one of my last smoke-room chats with him. Robin was by this time 16, and Nye asked me what I thought he was going to be. When I said that he looked like becoming a mathematician, Nye responded in a flash, "Just like his father. All bloody facts. No bloody vision."'[14] Considering Wilson's career up to 1960, this argument had force. Yet Wilson, as he so often did, was able to adapt in the years ahead.

On the Clause IV debate, Wilson took the middle way: 'I was in favour of neither outright nationalisation nor a complete ban on all further nationalisation. The question, I told my colleagues and such of the press as were listening, is "daft". It was a matter of degree and of proving a case.'[15] His approach was pragmatic: each industry should be judged individually. Gaitskell, meanwhile, was in retreat. With Morgan Phillips, who was himself to be incapacitated by a stroke that August, urging Gaitskell to re-think his approach with the party in the country in uproar, he compromised, deciding not to change Clause IV itself, but to supplement it with a Statement of Aims that reaffirmed the commitment to public ownership while stating it should take different forms. On 16 March, the NEC considered the matter. Wilson succeeded in amending the words linking Clause IV and the new Aims. Originally drafted as 'The following is the restatement and amplification of Party objects adopted in 1960 in the light of post-war developments and the historic achievements of the first majority Labour Government',

Wilson deleted all the words after 'is' up to and including 'objects', and Jennie Lee, passing on Bevan's views, managed to insert her husband's 'the commanding heights of the economy' phrase into the new Aims.[16] The Statement of Aims was, in reality, an attempt at face-saving by Gaitskell. Reliant on his small Hampstead set, unable to rely on the support of the trade union leaders, whom he should have lined up beforehand, Gaitskell had not built wide support for his approach and had been defeated.

Though this seemed to have settled the debate on reform of the party constitution, the issue of the nuclear bomb continued to divide the party. In April, the Union of Shop, Distributive and Allied Workers swung to unilateralism, as did the Amalgamated Engineering Union less than two weeks later. Driving all this was the passionate unilateralist, Frank Cousins, the leader of the largest union. The son of a miner, Cousins had become a lorry driver, and risen through the transport section of the Transport and General Workers' Union to become its general secretary, succeeding Jock Tiffin in 1956. Cousins represented a distinct shift to the left for the union since the days of Ernest Bevin. He was also, in the words of his biographer Geoffrey Goodman, an 'Awkward Warrior' who was unafraid to stand out from the crowd. As a young transport worker, when his fellow long-distance drivers had pilfered as an accepted practice, he made himself unpopular by standing against it.[17] He had one major preoccupation: to ban the bomb. At Easter 1959, Cousins had been at Trafalgar Square for the conclusion of the second Aldermaston march. Cousins had been in direct conflict with Bevan, who 'scorned Cousins's lack of understanding of what was possible in international affairs'.[18]

At the end of May 1960, the joint meeting of the TUC and the Labour Party executives appointed a 'Committee of Nine' to find a compromise on defence between Gaitskell, passionately committed to the NATO Alliance, with Britain contributing its nuclear weapons, and Cousins. It was a bitter fight between two stubborn men. Though Gaitskell had found a compromise on Clause IV, Cousins continued to argue in public against any attempt to dilute Labour's commitment to public ownership. On 3 June, the TGWU executive reaffirmed its unilateralist position against testing, manufacture or use of nuclear weapons. On 22 June, the NEC approved a new defence policy of a review of its approach to NATO to ensure no first use of nuclear weapons. This was, however, not enough for Cousins. In September 1960, the TUC annual conference was held on the Isle of Man. There, two resolutions were carried. The first was the official position drawn up by the council that supported membership of NATO and called for a new British disarmament plan, reducing NATO's dependence on nuclear weapons. The opportunity for compromise was again lost; the same TUC passed a motion moved by Cousins calling for a rejection of any defence policy based on nuclear weapons.

It was becoming clear that the matter would have to be resolved one way or the other at the Labour conference, scheduled to be held in Scarborough from 3–7 October 1960. Wilson maintained a position of being a non-unilateralist, but at the same time arguing that Gaitskell would have to accept the decision of the conference, whichever way it went. George Brown, meanwhile, came out against any further attempt by Britain to manufacture an independent nuclear deterrent, much to Gaitskell's annoyance. Wilson's rivalry with Brown intensified. Wilson had decided not to stand against Brown for the deputy leadership after Bevan's death because, he said, 'the PLP needed to consolidate its relationship with the unions'.[19]

Brown, born in Lambeth, had left school at fifteen. After a year as a ledger clerk in the City, he worked for the John Lewis Partnership as a fur salesman in its Oxford Street store. He never quite lost the sales patter: he could be a captivating, inspiring speaker, and, at twenty-two, joined the Transport and General Workers' Union, again as a ledger clerk before being elected to parliament for Belper in 1945. With governmental experience in the form of serving as the minister of Works for the last six months of the Attlee government, and strong trade union links, Brown was a formidable politician. Therein lies the reason why Wilson did not think it in his interests to stand against Brown at that time: it ran the risk of allowing Brown to demonstrate his political strength with a huge victory. Brown's distrust of intellectuals was one of his defining characteristics, and a reason he loathed Wilson: 'the little man' as he referred to him.[20] He was also a heavy drinker: this, with his skills of oratory and deep determination to succeed, made him a brilliant but highly unstable politician.

Brown's impulsiveness was on show in the days after Bevan died. One arena where Wilson was superior to him was the House of Commons. There, Wilson continued to develop his new, sparkling speaking style. On 11 July, five days after Bevan passed away, Brown decided to intervene in an economics debate, with Wilson opening it and him closing. Wilson contrasted what the Conservatives had said about economic prosperity at the election with what had happened since. They 'toasted themselves in champagne only a few months ago, and now we have the morning after . . . Within nine months of the election we have had in quick succession a tough Budget, hire-purchase restrictions, the reintroduction of the credit squeeze, an announcement about cuts in Government expenditure and now a crisis level Bank Rate of 6 per cent.'[21] Wilson started well but Brown finished poorly. Convinced that the speech had been written for him, it was, Wilson observed 'as he [Brown] was the first to confess, a disaster'.[22] It was a ranting, inexpert display. Reginald Maudling, then president of the Board of Trade, was gleeful as he closed the debate: '. . . in an incursion into an economic debate which we hope will be repeated, I felt that neither in loudness nor in length did he compensate for the absence of good argument. There was no pointed or effective criticism of Government policy and certainly no shred of any alternative policy.'[23]

As the party conference in Blackpool approached, Brown swayed one way then the other. He asked, as defence spokesperson, to attend the NEC sub-committee dealing with conference resolutions, but Sam Watson, the Durham area general secretary of the National Union of Mineworkers, vetoed it as Brown was not a member. Gaitskell gave Brown 'absolute hell' and Brown 'who wanted a shoulder to weep on rang . . . [Wilson] . . . and said he would never do anything for Hugh again.' At conference itself

Wilson saw Brown 'almost in tears: he withdrew to his room and stayed there for two days'.[24]

The sense of drama had been heightened as, on the pre-conference Sunday, Tony Benn resigned from the NEC as Gaitskell 'had refused to accept the vote for the TGWU resolution on disarmament'.[25] Wilson addressed the pre-conference rally and made the point that on German rearmament the Bevanites had accepted the decision of conference. His own speech, closing the morning's debate on Tuesday, 4 October, showed he could articulate a vision. His later speeches about the technological revolution have their roots in this speech: '. . . we say today that socialism must be harnessed to science and science to socialism.'[26] Wilson was drawing on his own knowledge, picked up by attending dinners run by the left-wing physicist Patrick Blackett in the 1950s.

At the time, though, the speech was little noticed, partly because it was overshadowed by the speech given the following day by Gaitskell. There was no compromise with Cousins, and, facing a defeat on unilateralism on the floor of the party conference, he produced the speech of his life. Had Bevan been alive to witness it, he would have had to reconsider his view of Gaitskell. On the platform was not a Labour leader who was a desiccated calculating machine, but a man who argued with conviction. His peroration was passionate and heartfelt: 'I say this to you: we may lose the vote today and the result may deal this Party a grave blow. It may not be possible to prevent it, but I think there are many of us who will not accept that this blow need be mortal, who will not believe that such an end is inevitable. There are some of us, Mr Chairman, who will fight and fight again to save the party we love.'[27] Tony Benn captured the mood: 'In the vote the platform was totally defeated but the Left was dejected and the right wing exultant at this "moral victory".'[28]

Magnificent though Gaitskell's performance was, it confirmed that he was taking on the party rather than bringing it together. Wilson, for whom unity was always one of the primary considerations, would never have made such a speech. As the applause died away, the reality of the politics came back into view. Another of the right-wing trade unionists, Welsh-born Ray Gunter, president of the Transport and Salaried Staffs Association (TSSA), thought it was all going Wilson's way.[29] With Bevan dead, Wilson was now the only possible successor to Gaitskell from the left. Gaitskell's remoteness was even emphasised by his choice of accommodation: he stayed in the Grand Hotel, while the NEC stayed at the Royal. Gaitskell was, however, shoring up his position in the shadow cabinet. First, he promised Callaghan the chancellorship if Labour won the next general election.

This was clever politics from Gaitskell. On the face of it, Callaghan was another trade unionist from the Labour right. Born into a working-class background in naval Portsmouth, Callaghan had joined the Inland Revenue Tax Office in 1929. There he met Douglas Houghton, who led the Association of Officers of Taxes. Houghton mentored Callaghan, who joined its National Executive Committee and became its full-time assistant secretary at twenty-four. After naval service in the Second World War, Callaghan had been elected to parliament for Cardiff South in 1945. Houghton shortly followed him, winning the Sowerby by-election in 1949. 'Big Jim' stood at over six feet tall and, in contrast to the irascible George Brown, he had an even temperament, fine political judgement, and a strategic mind. Gaitskell was wise to placate him.[30] Meanwhile, Brown was told: 'if you get up on the rostrum and denounce Frank Cousins "you're in and you'll be Deputy Leader." Brown took the hint.'[31] In November 1960, Brown was duly elected deputy leader, defeating the left candidate, Newton MP Frederick Lee, and Callaghan, who was eliminated in the first round. Meanwhile, Wilson thought he was once again in trouble, convinced that Gaitskell would try and oust him from the shadow cabinet.

Back in London after the party conference, Tony Greenwood, Dick Crossman, Castle and Jennie Lee tried to persuade Wilson to run for leader. Wilson worried it 'would be a deliberately divisive act . . . I would be to a considerable extent dependent on the unilateralist votes, though I resented Hugh's attacks on them as irresponsible neutralists.' Gaitskell's intimates were putting it about he would expel fifty or sixty unilateralist MPs and said

CND was 'a conspiracy to take over the Labour Party and had to be destroyed'.[32] On the matter of substance, Wilson agreed with Gaitskell: he was not a unilateralist either. His disagreement was that Gaitskell should respect the vote of conference, but as a justification for a leadership challenge it was, to say the least, thin. But it was also clear that Tony Greenwood would contest the leadership if Wilson did not. Crossman recorded in his diary on 13 October: 'They all bullied Harold and threatened him and pushed at him and tugged at him and this little spherical thing kept twirling round in dismay . . .'[33]

Wilson later recalled that he decided to stand 'for the unhappy reason that if Hugh were unopposed he could claim an undeniable mandate to act against a substantial number of loyal members of the Parliamentary Party. On the other hand, if Tony stood, the votes would be a straight division between Bevanites and others further to the left, on the one hand, while middle-of-the-roaders would be driven into the Gaitskell camp.' Wilson called it 'the most miserable decision I ever had to take.'[34] Wilson would have preferred not to have stood. He was certainly correct that he had wider appeal to the centre-ground Labour MPs than Greenwood. What is missing from this analysis is the point that, had he not stood, and Greenwood done so, the left would have had a new standard-bearer, which would be a real problem in a future contest. That possibility Wilson could not have allowed. Greenwood had read politics, philosophy and economics at Balliol College, Oxford, and served as president of the Oxford Union, the debating society where so many future politicians have honed their skills. After service both as a wartime civil servant, including at the Ministry of Information, and in the military itself, when he joined the Royal Air Force, Greenwood entered Parliament in 1946. Neatly presented, never a hair out of place, and highly ambitious, he rose to the shadow cabinet and, like Wilson, he had served on the National Executive Committee.[35] Greenwood knew his way around the Labour Party's structures – his father Arthur Greenwood had spent a decade as Labour's deputy leader after 1935 – and he could have emerged as a threat.

Wilson therefore stood and made a plea for the party to come together: '. . . the issue facing us today is not defence. It is the unity, indeed the survival, of this party. I want to see party unity given a much higher priority than it has enjoyed in the past year.'[36] The reason Wilson was so depressed about the whole business was because he knew he would lose by a substantial margin. Whatever longer-term interests there may be in a political decision, inevitable short-term defeats lower the mood. In the event, on 3 November, he lost 166–81. A year later, in November 1961, Greenwood did stand against Gaitskell. His defeat, 171–59, served to illustrate that Wilson had the broader appeal as a left candidate.

While Wilson's strategy throughout 1960 was pitching him as a candidate for the leadership, it would be unfair to suggest he was motivated only by political calculation. Wilson thought Gaitskell's strategy of taking on the party was wrong. Gaitskell 'wanted the party to recant. I once expressed it as being as heartless as saying to a Salvation Army Officer, or priest or minister, "There is no God. Everything you have preached is wrong. There is no after-world. No heaven, no hell."' This, Wilson, thought, came from a lack of understanding on Gaitskell's part: 'Hugh's background and introduction to politics, despite his noble work when young, in slum settlements, denied him any knowledge of how ordinary people thought. He undoubtedly learned far more from Leeds then he ever learned from Winchester, but even there it was from the right-wingers that he chose his tutors.'[37] Wilson, in contrast, had a feel for how those involved in Labour politics thought. He understood the rank and file and had a natural affinity with them, understood their desire to be led by a guiding mission.

This sense of purpose was clear in Wilson's speeches, and he continued to excel in parliamentary debate. On 2 November 1960, Wilson spoke in the debate on the queen's speech, and was outstanding. Norman Shrapnel, the *Guardian*'s parliamentary sketch writer, wrote: 'Wilson decided it was an occasion to shine, and he shone. I always remember his speech as one of the most compelling performances I ever heard in Parliament . . . We were projecting what he regarded as an appallingly materialistic image.'[38]

Wilson contrasted the shallowness of Macmillan's Britain of spivs with the moral dignity of Clement Attlee, who, in 1950, was '. . . saving the peace of the world and doing it with far less publicity than the Prime Minister gets when he goes grouse shooting; a Bevin building a strong foreign policy out of the ruins of the war; or a Cripps giving a sense of moral purpose to our social and economic life.'[39]

In 1961, he reached his peak as shadow chancellor, producing a damning indictment of the decade of Conservative rule and the whole Tory approach to economics. Wilson told the Commons on 18 July: 'This debate is the moment of truth, not only for the Tory Party but for the nation . . . This is a secular crisis and a long-term trend, the payoff for ten years of Conservative policy.' Wilson tore into the Conservatives: 'We have had the lowest rate of expansion in Europe . . . This represents an utter failure to increase exports, which have gone up by only 23 per cent. since 1951. Not another country in the world has done as badly.'[40] Wilson told the current incumbent, Selwyn Lloyd: 'I appeal to him not to follow other Tory Chancellors by thinking that the right way to fight the crisis is by placing burdens on those least able to bear them – the old, the sick, the disabled, the children who take school meals, and the rest.'[41]

Shrapnel sketched it as Wilson taking on five Tory chancellors: 'Thorneycroft with a smile frozen on his face, Macmillan busily scribbling, Butler looking ever more enigmatical than usual. Selwyn Lloyd nervously recalling that the existing Chancellor was none other than himself. But then their mocker came to the fifth of his victims . . .' It was none other than Winston Churchill: 'Did he remember he was once Chancellor too?'[42]

It was a fitting finale to Wilson's six years in the brief. He had firmly established himself as a contender for the leadership of the party and had shown a remarkable ability to evolve. His speeches retained their firm grasp of detail, but were now entertaining, spectacles that attracted attention across parliament and in the press. His political strength was a reason Gaitskell – though mistrustful of him and furious that he had stood against him – could never have sacked him. Instead Wilson was moved sideways. On 30 November 1961, Wilson was appointed shadow foreign secretary. The explanation given to the press was that 'the chief reason for this and the accompanying moves is the belief among Labour leaders that the time has come to broaden the range of the party's top people and create a team of all-rounders'.[43] This had some force: Brown became shadow home secretary and Callaghan shadow chancellor. In reality, though, it was an assertion of authority by Gaitskell. Callaghan was rewarded for loyalty. Brown was kept in a prominent position. The Foreign Affairs brief kept Wilson in a very senior role but took him away from the most central role on the domestic economy. Meanwhile, Christopher Mayhew was made Wilson's deputy with a firm instruction from Gaitskell: 'I want you to keep an eye on Harold.'[44] Wilson himself was philosophical about it: 'I was more than ready to accept. I had become too specialised on financial and industrial questions, in any case I had a feeling that Hugh Gaitskell's friends in the City and in the right wing of the Party had for some time been putting pressure on him to move me elsewhere. In any case a change of "scenery" could do me no harm.'[45] That final point proved prescient.

As it happened, Wilson was the Labour Party National Executive Committee chair for the year 1961–2. The holder of the role rotated each year – Buggins' turn as it was called – and it left Wilson in a prominent position within the party as he settled into his new role in Foreign Affairs. In addition, the central issue Wilson was to deal with in his fifteen months in the brief was one which was not only to dominate politics in 1962, but was to become a recurrent, divisive issue at the top of British politics for years ahead. On 31 July 1961, Macmillan had confirmed to the House of Commons that the government would apply for UK membership of the EEC. Within ten weeks, negotiations opened in Brussels, with Edward Heath in charge.

The Labour leadership was divided. A united front was preserved by the party agreeing not to take a firm position on entry until the negotiated terms were known. The different attitudes, though, were clear. At the 1962 party conference, in Brighton in the first days of October, Gaitskell's words were memorable. If, he argued, the goal of the European project was a federation it would mean 'the end of Britain as an independent European state. I make no apology for repeating it. It means the end of a thousand years of history.'[46] Gaitskell's position distanced him from his natural supporters. Dora worried that 'all the wrong people are cheering'.[47] In contrast, Brown's speech was passionately pro-European, wanting Britain to be 'able and willing to play our part in the world; not as one little island, not as a member of a group of little islands, not even as a member of a tight group of our own choosing, but in a bigger and outward-looking European Community.'[48]

Wilson's own position was more nuanced. He opened the debate for the opposition in the House of Commons on the second day of the EEC entry debate on 7 June 1962, and stuck to party policy: '. . . it really is senseless to decide our attitude to Britain's entry until the terms are known . . .'[49] Wilson worried about the Common Market ending the possibility of the economic policy he was most passionate about – government planning: 'The plain fact is that the whole conception of the Treaty of Rome is anti-planning, at any rate anti-national planning in the sense that either hon. Members on this side of the House or the Government understand it . . . What planning is contemplated – a tremendous amount of planning is involved in the Common Market – is supranational, not national, but it is planning for the one purpose of enhancing free competition.'[50] He was also concerned that it would affect the plans of a future Labour Government to expand public ownership, which 'might well fall foul of the provisions about subsidies and State intervention'.[51] The position of the Commonwealth was also an issue close to Wilson's heart, and he emphasised opposition to the development of the EEC as a United States of Europe with a common foreign policy for 'perhaps for one [reason] above all, namely, Britain's position in the world, due to our special relation with the Commonwealth . . .'[52] Wilson did not, however, present a wholly negative case: 'I think there is more general agreement that, in the long term, while on balance Britain's industry may gain, *which is the view I take* [author's emphasis], we also face a serious risk that our industrial cost structure will be raised through dearer food and the effect of dearer food on wages, and that in the short-term we are virtually certain to face rather serious financial consequences . . .'[53]

Thus, Wilson was sceptical but not against entry in principle. Wilson's view can be contrasted to that of Clement Attlee, whose opposition to the idea of integration was on the basis that he would never submit the authority of the UK parliament to a supra-national body. When presented with the Schuman proposal for British participation in the negotiations for the European Coal and Steel Community in 1950, Attlee rejected it out of hand, telling the Commons that the government could not 'accept at the outset the principles of the pooling of resources and of a high authority whose decisions would be binding on Governments'.[54] Wilson did, however, argue that Macmillan would need to put the idea of entry to the people in a general election, penning an article entitled 'Let the People Decide' in the *Daily Express* on 16 September 1962.[55]

In the end, Labour were spared having to make any choice at all. Negotiations between Macmillan's government and the EEC broke down in January 1963. The British dependence on American nuclear weapons after the Nassau agreement was an issue. The terms of the deal, concluded on 21 December 1962, were that President Kennedy agreed to sell Polaris missiles to Britain, on condition that Britain take part in his proposed multilateral force (MLF), a fleet of surface ships carrying nuclear missiles with control shared between all NATO members: even those states without nuclear weapons would provide crews. There would be at least three nationalities on each ship. Kennedy made the same offer to de Gaulle. On 14 January 1963, de Gaulle held a press conference at which he effectively ended the prospects of Britain joining the Common Market and France accepting Kennedy's offer: 'he could hardly have come nearer to giving a flat "no" to both enterprises; and in each instance his personal distrust of the United States was clearly at the core of the arguments. With Britain as a member, he saw the Common Market extending into a colossal Atlantic community.'[56] Wilson thought de Gaulle was 'obdurate. He did not want Britain in . . . Britain was a world power, and he resented it.' The threat to French farmers also played a part, in Wilson's view, as his hopes for a 'tightly-knit, protectionist economic Western Europe would be greatly at risk if we were in a position to lower continental tariff barriers'.[57]

Wilson was not wholly immersed in foreign affairs, as his role as chair of the Home Policy Sub-Committee of the NEC allowed him to retain a central role in the shaping of domestic policy. Meanwhile, Macmillan's government had run into trouble. In July 1961, a 'pay pause' had been introduced to allow production to catch up with wages. The creation of a National Economic Development Council was announced, bringing together unions, management and government for a measure of economic planning. It first met in February 1962, but did not improve the government's fortunes. That same month, the government published a White Paper on Incomes Policy,[58] indicating that a 2.5 per cent 'guiding light' should be followed, but this did not prevent a by-election defeat to the Liberals at Orpington on 14 March. It was a sensation: the victorious candidate, Eric Lubbock, toasted the possibility of 'the next [Liberal] government' with the result 'universally regarded as being of quite unprecedented significance'.[59] The 'pay pause' eventually ended on 1 April and in late July the government created a National Incomes Commission to examine and pronounce upon wage claims. Macmillan refreshed the cabinet with his 'Night of the Long Knives' reshuffle on 13 July as he sacked seven – a third – of its members, including chancellor Selwyn Lloyd. Wilson later quipped that the prime minister had sacked 'half his Cabinet – the wrong half, as it turned out.'[60] Labour led the Conservatives in that month's Gallup opinion poll by 37 per cent to 29.5 per cent, with the Liberals surging to 19 per cent after the by-election success.[61]

It was in this context that Wilson oversaw the drafting of the policy document *Signposts for the Sixties* that was published in July 1962 for presentation to the annual conference. It focused on reforming social security, extending public ownership of building land, expanding higher education and – of crucial importance for Wilson – planning economic expansion.[62] In his chairman's address, opening the conference on 1 October, he spoke movingly about Labour representing the whole country: '. . . in our debates this week – and television will not fail to record this – in our rich and varied accents (and I make no apology for my Yorkshire accent), we shall be voicing the aspirations, the hopes and visions of all our people.' Labour was on the threshold of government, seeking power for a purpose: 'For no Socialist Party can be satisfied with an electoral victory based on a mere swing against the Government. This Party is a moral crusade or it is nothing. That is why we have rejected timorous and defeatist proposals for a Lib.-Lab. alliance. We are not going to sail into power under any flags of convenience.'[63] Herbert Wilson proposed the vote of thanks, saying that fifty-six years had passed since he had voted Labour for the first time in a parliamentary election in 1906: 'Let all of us be worthy of the great heritage that has been handed down to us.'[64] Having his father do this may seem overly sentimental, but Wilson understood the Labour rank and file. It was a nice touch.

With the threat to Gaitskell's position having passed, Wilson set his sights on the deputy leadership. Brown's pro-European stance had opened up an opportunity. On 30 October, there was already bad blood: 'Mr. Brown's friends were already saying . . . with bitterness, that there was not only a strong argument but almost a tradition for balancing a middle-class intellectual leader, with a working-class and preferably trade union deputy leader.' Wilson could 'now expect to attract the votes of anti-marketeers, including some trade union MPs who would normally be loyal to Mr. Brown, and also the votes of the Labour MPs who have disapproved of Mr. Brown's connection with the *Daily Mirror* as an adviser on industrial affairs.'[65] Incumbency is, however, a big advantage. On 8 November Brown defeated Wilson by 133 votes to 103. It did, however, show, as with unilateralism, that Wilson was relying on supporters – in this case anti-Marketeers – whose views he did not entirely share. This stored up problems for the future, but mattered little at the time. As *The Times* put: 'Mr. Wilson, who is 46, had much to gain and nothing to lose in the contest. His status in the Labour movement, inside and outside Westminster, is always assured not only by his exceptional abilities.' Wilson was now an established contender for the party leadership.

Chapter 9

The new Britain

Leader of the Opposition, 1963–64

In late 1962, Harold Wilson was looking forward to his regular winter lecture tour in the United States, but it was events at home that were to prove much more significant. Hugh Gaitskell was admitted to the Manor House Hospital on 15 December, with a viral infection, and was not discharged until 23 December to go home for Christmas. On 4 January, he was taken into the Middlesex Hospital with what was thought to be a recurrence.[1] This gave Wilson a dilemma about whether he should still travel to the United States. In the end he judged that it would be distasteful to cancel, but made sure he would be updated by Marcia every day.

Wilson left for Chicago on 13 January, speaking at the university, before moving on to speak at the Foreign Affairs Institute in New York. That evening, Wilson took seven or eight calls during dinner, including from Dick Plummer, as Gaitskell's condition worsened: he developed abdominal and renal complications. Meanwhile, George Brown was with the journalist Geoffrey Goodman in a hotel in Burnley when the news about Gaitskell being in mortal danger came through. He and Douglas Jay, whom, like Wilson, he loathed as another intellectual, were on a speaking tour of areas of high unemployment. Brown was given a whisky to calm him, and he told Goodman: 'Yes, of course I want to lead the party and I must stop that little man [Harold Wilson].'[2] He flew back to London in an RAF plane from Manchester, arriving at Northolt in the early hours of 17 January. That same day, Williams urged

Wilson to come home, but he procrastinated. Blood transfusions and an artificial kidney could not save Gaitskell. At 9.12 p.m. on 18 January, with Dora at his bedside, he died at the age of fifty-six.[3] He had the rare immunological disease lupus erythematosus, about which little was known at the time.[4]

His death was shocking and devastating. His ally Roy Jenkins was also in America, in Connecticut, and was telephoned by the *Daily Express* in New York, minutes after Gaitskell's death had been announced, for a comment. Jenkins, who revered Gaitskell, was so upset that he declined to give one, only to be told that 'Harold Wilson, who is in New York, was able to give us a very moving one without difficulty'. Jenkins snapped back, with heavy sarcasm: '. . . you have to remember that he was very fond of Gaitskell' and rang off.[5] This incident illustrated two problems for Wilson: first, that he had to be careful not to publicly throw himself into a leadership campaign with unseemly haste, thereby disrespecting Gaitskell; and, second, that the Hampstead set were implacably opposed to him: 'they considered him an opportunist, preoccupied with tactics, conservative. Even had they judged his character less harshly, they could not have voted for him: he had challenged Hugh.'[6]

Wilson was actually in a strong position. Though the party had lost 19 seats in the 1959 general election, the political make-up of the parliamentary party was remarkably similar. The Labour right remained dominant, and a credible candidate from that part of the party could have expected to win, as Gaitskell had done in 1955. Yet three factors favoured Wilson. The first was that the leading figure of the right, Brown, was widely regarded to be too impulsive, and too dependent on drink, to be leader. It was why Wilson's defeat in the deputy leadership contest was not a pointer to how a leadership battle between the same protagonists would play out. That is not to say that Wilson was universally preferred to Brown, and his perceived opportunism led to MPs referring to a drunk Brown being better than a sober Wilson.[7] But Brown as Number Two to Gaitskell was a very different proposition to Brown as Number One. Benn, who at this time was an MP in the centre of the parliamentary party, captured this: '. . . his [Gaitskell's] death seems a disaster because it looks as if George Brown will succeed him and for a number of reasons he is totally unsuited to be Leader of the Party.'[8] When the Gaitskellites met at Anthony Crosland's flat, they actually considered supporting Callaghan and only pulled back because they thought he could not get through the first round.[9] This pointed to the second factor favouring Wilson: that having more than one candidate from the right of the party meant he could establish a lead on the first ballot, and gather momentum. Other MPs *thinking* he would win at that stage would be useful for the second ballot. Early in the contest, Wilson left Brown to make the moves to try to secure his position on the right, and the deputy leader failed in seeking a guarantee from Callaghan not to stand against him. Thirdly, the death of Bevan meant that Wilson had no rival to be the left's favoured candidate. One MP from the right tried to encourage Tony Greenwood to stand, but Greenwood saw through it as an attempt to split the left vote.[10] Not only could Wilson rely on a core of loyal support, he could also appeal to more centrist MPs without losing votes. Wilson was an excellent candidate: he had served in the Attlee government, in senior shadow cabinet roles, was a master of the House of Commons, effective on television, and was ferociously intelligent. Benn, who also voted for Wilson in November 1960, thought he was 'an excellent chairman, gets on well with people and has some radical instincts where Hugh had none'.[11]

Brown had one major advantage that Wilson sought to neutralise. As deputy leader, Brown became the acting leader: he was the incumbent and could use that to show he could do the job permanently. On 21 January, Brown chaired the shadow cabinet and spoke to Wilson at the end of the meeting. Brown thought he had secured a gentleman's agreement for a clean fight; Wilson, meanwhile, had it put into three newspapers that each would serve under the other. The headline was an obvious one: 'Labour Rivals In Unity Pact'. This was a clever Wilson tactic, because it left Brown giving the impression he would be happy to continue as deputy leader, lessening the significance of him being acting leader; the only other option was for Brown to deny such an agreement existed, which would make him appear divisive in comparison to Wilson's attempt to unify the party after the leadership contest. Brown took the latter course, in an interview with a local newspaper in his Belper constituency, the *Derby Evening Telegraph*, saying there was no such pact. Wilson thought it a major blunder from Brown.[12] Though Wilson himself had set the trap, Brown's campaign had walked into it: after shadow cabinet, Charles Pannell, who was working on Brown's campaign, had suggested such an agreement to Crossman before they both appeared on that night's *Panorama*.[13]

Dick Crossman was labelled Wilson's 'Kingmaker' but it was George Wigg whom Wilson relied upon most to run his campaign. The eldest of six children, Wigg was a Hampshire grammar school boy whose education was brought to an abrupt end at fourteen after the dairy business of his alcoholic father failed. Forced to find work, he joined the army just before his seventeenth birthday in 1917. There he remained until 1937, then he left to work for the Workers' Educational Service, before re-joining the army at the start of the Second World War, becoming a lieutenant-colonel in the Royal Army Education Corps. In 1945, he was elected MP for Dudley, serving as parliamentary private secretary to Emanuel Shinwell before returning to the backbenches when Labour lost power in 1951, and becoming close to Wilson. It was to Wigg that Wilson turned for advice when he re-joined the shadow cabinet in 1954, when he stood against Gaitskell in 1960, and against Brown for the deputy leadership. Jenkins dismissed Wigg as 'half-comic, half-sinister',[14] but Wigg offered Wilson one commodity that is very precious in politics: information. This did not endear him to his colleagues, but it made him invaluable to Wilson: the former army officer who picked up intelligence around Westminster and fed it back to him on a regular basis.

Wigg agreed with Wilson that he would help with the campaign on the basis that Crossman be excluded from the confidential plans as he could not be trusted and would gossip. Instead Wigg relied on a tightly-knit group of MPs: Judith Hart, who had entered parliament for the Lanark constituency in 1959; Harold Davies, a

Wilson friend from Bevanite days; and Ben Parkin, also on the left. The plan was not to canvass aggressively, but to ascertain voting intentions, and to ensure that Wilson himself spoke to those who were doubtful. In addition to the small team, Wigg also relied on a wider group to gather information that included George Thomas and Dick Plummer.[15] Wigg also tried to shift votes from Brown to Callaghan, to reduce the deputy leader's vote on the first round. Playing on Brown's drinking, he would say to waverers: 'Put your nose in the smoke room, Brown is at it again!'[16] Unlike in 1955, the TGWU did not line up behind the candidate of the right. Cousins met Wilson for a two-hour chat in his Austin saloon outside parliament. Wilson convinced him he would lead a radical Labour government. Cousins informed his TGWU-sponsored MPs that he was supporting Wilson.[17]

The three candidates were also given a parliamentary test on 31 January. After attending Gaitskell's memorial service in Westminster Abbey at midday, they all spoke in a defence debate in the House of Commons. Wilson shone with an intervention from the prime minister. Macmillan, sensing the chance to make mischief, challenged Wilson on whether he agreed with a Gaitskell quote on Britain always having its own nuclear weapons rather than sharing capability with NATO and the United States. With his prodigious memory, Wilson recognised the speech, from 1 March 1960, and knew Gaitskell had said nothing of the kind: 'He should point out that at that time Hugh Gaitskell was putting the arguments on both sides, for and against the nuclear case. This was part of his fair, balanced argument as he saw it for an independent deterrent. He also put the case against. I must say that the Prime Minister's choice of a quotation is very repugnant to some of us.'[18] Dora Gaitskell wrote to Macmillan to say how deeply hurt she had been by his playing politics in this way.

Wigg estimated that Wilson would receive 118 votes on the first ballot, and hoped Wilson might scrape an overall majority.[19] In the event, on 7 February, Wilson took 115 votes, with 88 for Brown and 41 for Callaghan, who now dropped out. Wilson was agonisingly close, and needed only eight additional votes to win. Wigg set to work immediately and, that night, at Dick Crossman's house, with Plummer and Tony Greenwood, confirmed to Wilson that he had secured a dozen pledges of support from Callaghan's supporters. Wilson, with a nice touch, raised a glass and proposed a toast to the memory of Nye Bevan, in the very room he had so often sat in during the Bevanite years.[20] In the second ballot a week later, Wilson won comfortably, taking 144 votes to Brown's 103. The results were announced in the House of Commons Committee Room 14, where meetings of the Parliamentary Labour Party are still held. Brown was in the chair, and struggled to accept his defeat.

The plain fact, though, was that, at forty-six, Wilson was the party leader. The press reaction, from right to left, was positive. The *Daily Telegraph* called him a man 'genuinely on the side of "plain living and high thinking"'.[21] An *Observer* profile praised him for his speeches that 'cascade with wit . . . Vain but not conceited, with a hard inner assurance, dependable and industrious' and labelled him 'a contemporary, classless figure'.[22] As leader, Wilson's speech-making again evolved. Marcia Williams, who had helped to bring out his humour, now corrected this.[23] While Wilson never lost his ability to make his audience laugh or employ a biting one-liner on his political opponents, his tone became more serious. This was in response to him being compared by the media to the Canadian-born American stand-up comedian and satirist Mort Sahl.[24] Like him, Wilson could speak in a conversational style and then deliver a devastating punchline. Yet his appearance contrasted unfavourably with the dark-haired, thin Sahl. Wilson was described as a 'chubby pipe smoker with a round face that has been called "cherry-stone smooth"'.[25] He could not afford to be seen as a comic figure. Williams' influence grew and grew. She moved into a private office at the House of Commons that Beryl Skelly had occupied as private secretary to Attlee and Gaitskell. At first Skelly stayed but soon left as she and Williams 'proved incompatible'. Marcia Williams would never have tolerated such a threat to her influence.[26]

Wilson's immediate task was to appoint his shadow cabinet. Brown, in a rage at how the leadership had been taken from him, left to go to Scotland. Managing the deputy leader was to become a key challenge for Wilson in the years ahead. The triumvirate that contested the leadership election became the dominant force in Labour politics in the mid-1960s, certainly until the devaluation crisis of November 1967. Wilson's treatment of his two rivals was, therefore, key. It was easy enough to leave Callaghan as shadow chancellor, and Wilson appointed his ally Douglas Houghton to support him, shadowing the chief secretary to the Treasury. Houghton also succeeded Wilson as chair of the Public Accounts Committee. Brown was more difficult: he yearned to be shadow foreign secretary. Wilson, however, knew how troublesome he could be, so instead appointed Patrick Gordon Walker, an able, cerebral, arch-Gaitskellite who had helped run Brown's leadership campaign.[27] This made sense, as Gordon Walker was the only other shadow cabinet member to have been an actual cabinet member aside from Wilson – he had been secretary of state for Commonwealth relations under Attlee. To placate Brown, who remained as deputy leader, Wilson had to supplement him remaining in the role of shadow home secretary with an 'overlordship' role allowing him to intervene as he saw fit in domestic policy areas. Richard Crossman, who had resigned from the frontbench after an argument with Gaitskell over pensions policy, was rewarded with the science portfolio.[28] Later that year, Wilson also persuaded Jenkins to turn down the editorship of the *Economist* and remain in politics. Jenkins accepted Wilson's assurance about forming a broad-based cabinet, and observed that Wilson delivered on this: fifteen of the nineteen MPs in his first cabinet had voted for Gaitskell over him in 1960.[29]

With his team in place, Wilson set about creating a dynamism and momentum as leader of the opposition that would drive Labour to power. His major advantage was timing: he would not face the long slog of a four or five-year parliament. It was over three years since the last general election, and he knew there would be another within twenty months. In his first party political broadcast as leader on 27 February, he took on the issue of nationalisation. He confirmed that a Labour government would take steel into public ownership but said that was to focus on production; he rubbished Tories who claimed Labour would nationalise the local chemist's shop: 'Why can't they be their age?' The next day, *The Times* noted, admiringly: 'He was telling his party workers that clause four still means what it used to mean, but he was remembering that the floating voter was also in earshot.'[30] On the Common Market, he did not rule out another application to join: 'We do not turn our backs on the idea of ultimate negotiations even with the Six themselves.' On nuclear weapons, Britain would not immediately divest itself of its nuclear weapons: 'If Labour came to power it would "phase out" Britain's nuclear deterrent.'[31] As he sought to hone his appeal to the mainstream electorate, he needed to manage the left. On Sunday, 10 March 1963, Castle hosted Wilson, Judith Hart, Michael Foot, George Wigg, Tony Greenwood and Dick Crossman for supper. Wilson said he was boxed in: 'You must understand that I am running a Bolshevik Revolution with a Tsarist Shadow Cabinet.'[32] Though this was true in the sense that he had so many senior Gaitskellites at the top table, it was also how Wilson managed the party. At no point in his premierships were former Bevanites appointed to the great offices of state. Wilson, as the saying goes, liked to keep his friends close, but his enemies closer.[33] That is not to say he did not support his allies. The solicitor Arnold Goodman had been instructed by Gaitskell to run a claim for breach of copyright over leaks from the National Executive Committee to the *Manchester Guardian* for which Crossman was prime suspect. Wilson discontinued the claim as soon as he became leader, and became close to Goodman, who was a larger-than-life character. One obituary captured him as follows: 'Goodman's wit, his shape "like a polar bear", his orotundity, his monumental tact, his energy, his omniscience and august common sense made him the living legend of which he was aware.'[34] *Private Eye* put it in a more cruel way, labelling him 'Lord Two Dinners'.[35] Wilson saw him on a regular basis over the next thirteen years, with Goodman at his side to offer legal advice and – increasingly – issue libel writs against various newspapers. Initially, Goodman called in to see Wilson at 8 p.m. in the evening, but then asked the Labour

Leader if he could come at 9 p.m. instead so that he could have dinner first: 'Accordingly the time was changed: I went in at 9 p.m. and often stayed until midnight or past.' In these sessions, Wilson would ruminate on the issues of the day, with Goodman happy to be used as 'the wall of a fives court against which he banged the ball'.[36] On 29 May, the Labour whip was restored to left-wing MPs Michael Foot, Sydney Silverman, Emrys Hughes, S.O. Davies and William Baxter. Two years previously, Gaitskell had removed the whip from the quintet for voting against the service estimates. Foot repaid the loyalty with an admiring biography of Wilson in 1964: 'His instinctive responses to a situation are likely to be those of rank-and-file members of the Labour Party. For all his sophisticated abilities, he is not at loggerheads or out of sympathy with those he aspires to lead.'[37]

Wilson also established himself on the international stage. On 29 April, he arrived in Washington for a five-day visit. He neatly sidestepped the convention of not criticising the British government while abroad by declaring the chances of a change of administration at home were 'very very high.' and, after meeting President John F. Kennedy, said he 'felt he could work well' with him.[38] In Moscow with Gordon Walker in June, he had a three-hour meeting with Khrushchev in which he 'exchanged compliments' and showed a fine grasp of the issue of the nuclear arms race between the superpowers, as he told a press conference that the 'immediate prospects of a full test-ban agreement based on inspection are not very hopeful. On the other hand, the possibility of a test-ban confined to atmospheric tests, space and underwater tests, which we put to him, seems to offer more hope of an agreement'.[39]

On his return, two of Wilson's key priorities emerged. First, his abhorrence of race discrimination and the need for measures to address it. On 29 April, in Bristol, a youth worker called Paul Stephenson and an action group, West Indian Development Council, protested against the 'colour bar' operated by the Bristol Omnibus Company meaning that it did not employ black or Asian workers. Inspired by Rosa Parks' action against segregation in 1955 in Montgomery, Alabama, they announced a 'bus boycott'. The bus company was blaming the local Transport and General Workers' Union for the racist policy. A local Labour alderman, Heny Hennessy, accused the union of colluding with management.[40] Wilson, however, gave no support to the local union branch and unequivocally condemned the 'colour bar' at a meeting in London arranged by the Campaign for Freedom in South Africa on 2 May.[41] After four months, 28 August, the same day as Martin Luther King gave his 'I Have a Dream' speech at the Lincoln Memorial in Washington, the bus company and the local TGWU branch issued a joint statement ending the discrimination.[42]

Second, work on a policy to introduce economic planning was moving forward, with Balogh, now advising Wilson on economics, having produced a paper by 25 May.[43] Balogh believed passionately in planning, and believed it was a failure of the Attlee governments not to have introduced it. In fairness, had the government sought to fix wage levels in advance across industry or introduced a formal incomes policy, there would have been strong trade union opposition. Another option was the model developed in France, with the 'Commissariat general du Plan' setting targets, the identification of likely constraints in their achievement, and then encouragement of both private enterprise and nationalised industry to meet them. This involved providing a degree of certainty that what was being planned would actually come about, and by providing access to capital. Yet Balogh thought that the civil service was 'an administrative personnel for a Nightwatchman State presiding over the breathtaking expansion of private industrial capitalism'.[44] Balogh cited Wilson's own words: 'Whoever is in office, the Whigs are in power.'[45] For any form of economic planning to become a reality, it had to be prised away from the Treasury: '. . . whose traditional role . . . is to oppose any increase in expenditure.'[46]

It was not, however, the penny-pinching of the mandarins that preoccupied Wilson in mid-1963. His focus was on what became one of the great political scandals of the twentieth century, involving the secretary of state for war, John Profumo. In his handling of the affair, Wilson was once again assisted by Wigg. Ian Aitken, the political editor of the *Daily Express* at the time, wrote many years later that Wigg 'believed that Jack Profumo had committed a grave sin by sending unprepared British troops to Kuwait, where they became disabled by the desert heat, and that he had then committed an even graver crime by lying to him (Wigg) about the episode.' Wigg told Aitken he would 'get Profumo'.[47] Profumo had been having an affair with model Christine Keeler, who was simultaneously having a relationship with Yevgeni Ivanov, senior naval attaché at the Soviet Embassy. Wigg had been told to 'look at Profumo' by an anonymous telephone caller in November 1962. Then, a former Labour MP, John Lewis, attended a pre-Christmas party at which Keeler was also present. Keeler asked if she could telephone Lewis and asked for his help, telling him about her friendships with Ivanov and Profumo. A man called Stephen Ward, an osteopath, had asked her to find out about the supply of atomic weapons to Germany from Profumo, but she had not done so. Lewis told Keeler to speak to a solicitor and passed the information on to Wigg. At Castle's supper party of 10 March, Wigg recalled that he spoke to Wilson privately, setting out what he knew, including that, on 14 December, a man called John Edgecombe had, in a jealous rage, attended Ward's flat with a gun, convinced Keeler was there with another man, shooting at a front door lock and a window. Keeler was there, though not with another man, and was now a key witness in Edgecombe's forthcoming trial. Ivanov had left the country to return to Moscow on 29 January.[48] Crossman's account of the Castle supper differs: 'George Wigg blurted it all out and we told him to stay quiet.'[49]

Either way, Wilson's instincts were the same. He abhorred the idea of an attack on moral grounds. This was a political and personal judgement: he knew Profumo and his wife, the actress Valerie Hobson, from his time as president of the Board of Trade. Thus, he would leave Wigg to raise the matter. Wilson himself would only raise the matter in terms of the national security risk, and would consider a demand for an inquiry at the appropriate moment.

The Profumo scandal marked a step-change in the relationship between press and politicians. Prior to it, the private lives of politicians remained off-limits. One reason for this was the risk of libel actions – but no such problem exists for politicians speaking in the Commons, who can plead parliamentary privilege, protecting them from any such legal proceedings. As rumours swirled, Aitken wrote a story that Profumo had offered his resignation to Macmillan 'for personal reasons' at the same time as Keeler herself failed to attend Edgecombe's trial on 17 March. Wigg used the *Daily Express* story to put the government on the spot in parliament on the issue. On 21 March 1963, he laid down his challenge: '. . . I rightly use the Privilege of the House of Commons – that is what it is given to me for – to ask the Home Secretary, who is the senior member of the Government on the Treasury Bench now, to go to the Dispatch Box – he knows the rumour to which I refer relates to Miss Christine Keeler and Miss Davies and a shooting by a West Indian – and, on behalf of the Government, categorically deny the truth of these rumours.'[50] The next day, Profumo made a fateful personal statement, misleading the House of Commons: 'I understand my name has been connected with the rumours about the disappearance of Miss Keeler . . . I last saw Miss Keeler in December, 1961, and I have not seen her since . . . I shall not hesitate to issue writs for libel and slander if these scandalous allegations are made or repeated outside this House.'[51]

The following Monday, 25 March, Wigg appeared on *Panorama*, declaring Ward and Ivanov security risks. Ward saw Wigg's remarks about him, and contacted him at the Commons the next day. Wigg invited Ward to parliament that evening, and had a three-hour conversation with him. Ward said he had met Ivanov at the Garrick Club in 1961, and that the security services knew about the association. He said he had acted as an intermediary between Ivanov and members of the government which he said was of value to Britain. After the conversation, Wigg sought out Wilson and said Ward had mentioned a letter to him sent at the end of the Cuban Missile Crisis the previous year. Wilson fished it out, remembering the 'I was the intermediary' phrase being used to describe Ward's role between Ivanov and the Foreign Office. Wilson was calm, methodical and strategic. First, he asked Wigg to prepare a note of his conversation with Ward and, on 9 April, provided that, together

with the letter, and a covering letter addressed to the prime minister, to the Tory chief whip, Martin Redmayne. Macmillan replied
with an acknowledgement only, so – after waiting for a month – on
13 May, Wilson wrote again, pressing for a substantive response.
This time the prime minister responded that he intended to take no
further action. Ward then demanded an audience with Macmillan;
the prime minister directed that his principal private secretary,
Timothy Bligh, should see Ward with a member of the security
services. Ward said Profumo had lied to the Commons about his
relationship with Keeler. Then, on 19 May, Ward wrote to his local
MP, Sir Wavell Wakefield, the home secretary, the prime minister
and Wilson, together with issuing a statement to the press that he
had placed 'certain facts' about the Profumo–Keeler relationship
before the home secretary. On receipt of the letter, Wilson sought
a meeting with Macmillan that was fixed for 27 May with their
respective chief whips, Redmayne, and Herbert Bowden. Macmillan still did not act, suspicious of Wilson seeking to exploit
the situation for party advantage. A note of the conversation was
provided to the director of MI5, Sir Roger Hollis. Hollis then told
Macmillan on 29 May that Keeler had suggested in January that
Ward had encouraged her to ask Profumo about West Germany's
economic secrets. Macmillan finally conceded an inquiry into the
security issues led by the lord chancellor, Dilhorne, and informed
Wilson the next day. Dilhorne sought an interview with Profumo,
who was in Venice, and, on 4 June, the day before he was due to
meet the lord chancellor, Profumo resigned, writing to Macmillan:
'In my statement I said that there had been no impropriety . . . To
my very deep regret I have to admit this was not true, and that I
misled you and my colleagues and the House.'[52] Wilson's approach,
of using Wigg to keep an arm's length from Ward, of scrupulously
handing over information to the prime minister, while also increasing pressure with letters, had paid off.[53]

In the Commons debate on 17 June, Wilson was forensic and
effective. He handled the personal aspect of the matter sensitively:
'There is the personal and family tragedy of a man lately our colleague here . . . We are not here as a court of morals.' Instead, there

were two key issues: that 'the former Secretary of State for War, faced with rumours and innuendoes that could not be ignored, chose deliberately to lie to this House' and, secondly, 'whether a man in a position of high trust, privy to the most secret information available to a Government, through a continuing association with this squalid network, imperilled our national security . . .'[54] There was now a strong argument for an independent judicial inquiry. Wilson pressed the case, pointing out that, if the security services knew of Profumo's relationship with Keeler in 1961, and if they did not tell the prime minister, there was 'a clear case for a ruthless inquiry into those responsible'.[55] In the same debate, Nigel Birch, five years after his departure from the Treasury, twisted the knife into Macmillan, quoting Robert Browning's poem, 'The Lost Leader' and urging him to move on: '"Never glad confident morning again!" – so I hope that the change will not be too long delayed.'[56] On 21 June, Macmillan announced that the government would set up an inquiry to examine the security aspects of the affair. The next day, at a constituency garden party, as he posed for a photograph with the daughter of a constituent, a passer-by said: 'Don't you wish it was Christine Keeler?'[57]

The prime minister was badly shaken. In July 1963, Arthur Koestler edited a series of essays under the title *Suicide of a Nation?* In his introduction, he pointed to Britain's economic decline: 'within the last ten years our percentual share in world trade has shrunk by as much as in the course of the whole previous half-century.' To blame for this was a sense of complacency, the cult of the amateur, and distrust of expertise. This was exemplified in Macmillan himself. As Malcolm Muggeridge put it in his contribution, 'England, Whose England?': '. . . Macmillan seemed, in his very person, to embody the national decay he supposed himself to be confuting. He exuded a flavour of moth balls.'[58]

Wilson was having his own problems. That same July, Dick Crossman urged him to make a speech at conference on 'Labour in the Science Age' but found the leader despairing with the continued behaviour of Brown: 'He's been drunk constantly and he's been raving around.' Wilson recounted an incident where an inebriated

Brown had left a piece of paper with the name of the director general of MI6 – then never made public – hanging out of a car.[59] Outwardly, though, Wilson continued to exude modernity. On 8 September, in a speech in Glasgow, he confirmed that Labour was working on plans for a 'University of the Air' for which broadcast time would be found on either the existing TV channels or a new, fourth channel. Wilson's vision of education was lifelong and inclusive, from the technicians who left school at sixteen or seventeen but who, after two or three years in industry, felt they could qualify as graduates; there were those in other occupations who might want to acquire new skills, and housewives who might like to secure qualifications.[60] The 'Open University', as it became known, was to become Wilson's proudest achievement. On his American lecture tours, Wilson studied the University of Chicago's 'extra-mural system' that was based in part on television. The idea was gaining traction. Wilson himself also credited Geoffrey Crowther, editor of *The Economist*, with setting out detailed plans. Meanwhile, in 1962, Michael, later Lord, Young had argued for an 'open university' for adults to be able to learn at home.[61]

Wilson accelerated the momentum he had built up as Labour leader with his 'white heat' speech at the 1963 Labour Party conference a month later. His oration was forward-looking and hopeful. He combined a compelling vision of the future with the promise of practical action to make it a reality. This, he said, was a seminal moment: 'It is, of course, a cliché that we are living at a time of such rapid scientific change that our children are accepting as part of their everyday life things which would have been dismissed as science fiction a year ago. We are living perhaps in a more rapid revolution than some of us realise.' Wilson's rivalry with Gaitskell when the party conference had been at the same venue three years previously seemed a distant memory as he nodded back to it: 'The period of 15 years from the last time we were in Scarborough, in 1960, to the middle of the 1970s will embrace a period of technical change, particularly in industrial methods, greater than in the whole industrial revolution of the last 250 years.' Using a broad historical sweep, Wilson went even further back for his next comparison, to the ancient world: 'When you reckon, as it is calculated, that 97 per cent of all the scientists who have ever lived in the history of the world since the days of Euclid, Pythagoras and Archimedes, are alive and at work today, you get some idea of the rate of progress we have to face.'[62]

A motor car in America could already be produced 'without a single worker touching it'. The only reason jobs were not being lost yet was because the automated process was not yet cost-effective. Technology, Wilson argued, would replace 'the hitherto unique human functions of memory and of judgment'. Thus, a 'modern computer in a fraction of a second can make calculations and can make decisions of judgment which all the mathematicians in Britain and America combined could by ordinary methods in the space of a year.'[63]

The choice was between another Conservative administration under which a free market approach would destroy jobs, and a Labour government led by Wilson that would ensure the benefits were shared widely: 'Since technological progress left to the mechanism of private industry and private property can lead only to high profits for a few, a high rate of employment for a few, and to mass redundancies for the many, if there had never been a case for Socialism before, automation would have created it.' National planning was crucial: 'It is the choice between the blind imposition of technological advance, with all that means in terms of unemployment, and the conscious, planned, purposive use of scientific progress to provide undreamed of living standards and the possibility of leisure ultimately on an unbelievable scale.'[64] The status quo was not an option, since Britain would be left behind unless people embraced change. The international challenge was coming from Russia, which was 'at the present time training ten to eleven as many scientists and technologists.'[65] Wilson would create a Ministry of Science, and Britain would produce more scientists, retain them in the country, make better use of them, and organise industry to apply their research to production. 'Mr Wilson's Four Points for Harnessing Science' was the next day's *The Times* headline.[66]

In contrast to Wilson's great performance, Macmillan did not even attend the Conservative party conference, as he went into hospital on 8 October for an operation to cure a 'prostatic obstruction'.[67] Two days later, from his hospital bed, he announced his resignation.[68] Wilson was genuinely moved: '. . . I had a warm affection for him, both as a Conservative leader of high gifts and a political operator of extraordinary skill.'[69] After a bitter behind-closed-doors battle in Macmillan's cabinet about the succession, Macmillan telephoned Alec Douglas-Home on 17 October to indicate he would be recommending him to the queen as his successor. The next day, the queen arrived at King Edward VII Hospital in Beaumont Street to formally receive Macmillan's resignation, and then invited Home to form a government. This fed Wilson's narrative about him representing modernity, while the Tories were out-of-date patrician Edwardians. For a start, Home had not even been elected by Tory MPs: he had been chosen by informal soundings. Second, he was an aristocrat who had to disclaim his peerage, and enter the Commons via the Kinross and Western Perthshire by-election on 7 November. The fourteenth Earl of Home, rather than Butler, was Wilson's opponent of choice. That is not to say Home did not have some fine qualities. He was a man of great courtesy, was reassuringly calm and had a lightness of touch. He had been a first-class cricketer and retained his passion for the game and for cricketing metaphors. His background was, however, an issue. Interviewed on the BBC on 21 October, Home had to protest that he did know how the other half lived.[70] Remarkably, it was a Labour MP who tried to cause problems for Wilson. Desmond Donnelly, having first allied himself to Bevan before falling out with him over German rearmament, which he thought was needed, and becoming a supporter of Gaitskell, was smarting having not been offered a frontbench role under Wilson.[71] He wrote to *The Times* on 23 October that Home 'cannot help his antecedents any more than the rest of us'. But Wilson had judged the public mood well. When Gallup asked the public whether Home's privileged background was a strength as prime minister, only 24 per cent thought it was, with 44 per cent viewing it as a weakness.[72]

Having quickly defined Home, Wilson's task was to set out

Labour's alternative vision for the country. He made seven major speeches between January and April 1964, that were published as a small book in June 1964, *The New Britain: Labour's Plan Outlined by Harold Wilson*.[73] Starting at the Town Hall in Birmingham on 19 January, he argued that 1964 was a time for change and that Labour would replace the elitist, 'closed, exclusive society by an open society'.[74] At Swansea six days later, Wilson argued for sustained economic expansion and the appointment of a minister of Economic Planning. On 6 February, in the House of Commons, though he did not rule out ever joining the Common Market, he made the case for trade with the Commonwealth.[75] Two days later in Leeds, he promised a dynamic programme of house-building by a National Development Corporation. He crossed the Atlantic for his speech on Britain's role in the world, which he gave at Bridgeport University, Connecticut, on 3 March. On 2 March, he called at the White House to meet President Johnson: and said that, as a Yorkshireman, he had got on 'all right' with the Texan. 'Yorkshiremen have a reputation for always speaking frankly and I think the President has the same reputation.'[76] The bone of contention was still the MLF, and whether a future Labour government would participate in it. If other NATO members wanted a greater degree of control over when America used its nuclear force, then the burden on America had to be reduced. There was also the issue of West Germany, a NATO member since 1955. Though Chancellor Konrad Adenauer had promised that West Germany would not develop nuclear weapons of its own, there was unease, particularly as its economic success made such a project feasible. Kennedy's solution was to integrate West Germany and other European allies into a nuclear force, the MLF. Wilson decided the best approach was to be direct, and told Johnson that 'the only circumstances in which the Labor [sic] government would support the MLF would be if this were the only way to prevent Germany from acquiring a national nuclear force'.[77]

The next day, in his lecture, Wilson reflected on the legacy of John F. Kennedy after his assassination in Dallas on 22 November 1963, noting it was his first visit to the United States since the funeral. Wilson argued that Kennedy had not seen NATO as inward-looking, but as a means of contributing to peace across the world. Wilson again said that Britain giving up its nuclear weapons was not an immediate possibility and cited Gaitskell's compromise of only the United States and the Soviet Union having nuclear weapons as that would make proliferation easier to control. He built on his theme of planning to argue for it on an international level, with the United Nations the first step towards a world government. On 8 March, in Liverpool, Wilson turned Benjamin Disraeli's 'Two Nations' analysis on the Conservatives: '. . . Tory freedom has produced the two nations, an over-congested southeast and the starved north' and promised full employment.[78] On 21 March, in Edinburgh, he promised the creation of a Ministry of Technology to apply the developments in science to industry. This would build on the National Research Development Corporation (NRDC) Wilson had set up at the Board of Trade in 1948. Based on an idea from Cripps, its purpose was to take inventions by UK scientists and university research laboratories and develop them to the production stage. At the Royal Albert Hall on 5 April, he defined Labour's social purpose, laying bare the extent of poverty in the Tories' so-called 'affluent society': 'much of it is hidden behind lace curtains in back streets'.[79] Speaking to the Society of Labour Lawyers on 20 April in London, he promised legislation against race discrimination.

The speaking tour had been intended to create pre-election momentum, but Home did not oblige by calling a poll before the summer. Wilson once again showed his credentials on the world stage, meeting Khrushchev in Moscow for two hours on 2 June, and declaring afterwards 'that east-west agreement on halting the spread of nuclear weapons now seemed to offer one of the best hopes for a disarmament breakthrough.'[80] Keen to find a new way of generating energy, Wilson settled on the idea of adopting Kennedy's '100 days' mantra. On 15 July, he declared, in a television broadcast that, after years of stagnation in the United States, Kennedy had had a hundred days of dynamic action. In Britain, Wilson's Labour government would do the same.[81] In saying that, Wilson also had an eye on party management. He compared the Labour Party to an old stagecoach: '. . . if it is rattling along at a rare old speed most of the passengers are so exhilarated – perhaps sea sick – they don't start arguing or quarrelling. As soon as it stops they start arguing about which way to go. The whole thing is to keep it at an exhilarating speed.'[82] He continued to prepare for a possible Labour government at pace. With one eye on Bevin's relationship with Attlee, as a former trade union leader, he invited Cousins to join him in the Scillies on his annual holiday, and offered him a role in his cabinet. Wilson also started to manage expectations. He told Benn, whom he saw regularly, that he would appoint him postmastergeneral. Since it was a job outside the cabinet, Wilson reassured him that it was only for eighteen months: 'My real Cabinet will be made in 1966 – just as Clem's was made in 1947.'[83] Benn, Crossman, Marcia and Peter Shore, an ally of Wilson's within party headquarters, who was shortly to enter Parliament for Stepney, made up a trusted inner circle. Shore was a fine speaker who emphasised points with movement, from his gesticulating hands, to his flying hair and swirling tie. He had read history at Cambridge, served in the Royal Air Force from 1943 to 1946 before joining the Labour Party's research department, of which he became the head in 1959. He admired Wilson's belief in the power of state intervention to reduce inequality in society.[84]

The polls were tightening. In July 1964, Labour led by 46.5 per cent to 37 per cent; by the following month, it was 44.5 per cent to 39 per cent, though Wilson's ratings remained very high, with him thought a good leader by 67 per cent to 17 per cent.[85] With an autumn election now a certainty, Wilson spoke at the TUC Conference on 7 September, and promised to restore trade union rights after the *Rookes v Barnard*[86] case had threatened the existence of the closed shop. Douglas Rookes, an employee of BOAC, had resigned from his union but tried to continue in his job. The union, the Association of Engineering and Shipbuilding Draughtsmen, had threatened strike action unless he was dismissed, which he then was. This threat had been held to be unlawful. Wilson pledged to pass a piece of legislation and dismissed the idea of kicking the issue into the long grass with a memorable phrase: 'I see no need for a royal commission into this, that will take minutes and waste years.'[87] This was not to prevent Wilson setting up other royal commissions when he thought a delay was advantageous, but he did keep his promise on this and reversed the *Rookes* decision with the Trade Disputes Act of 1965. On 11 September, Labour launched its manifesto, *The New Britain* promising: 'mobilising the resources of technology under a national plan' thereby 'reversing the decline of the thirteen wasted years.'[88] The next day, Wilson addressed a rally at the Empire Pool, Wembley, arguing for a 'dynamic, expanding, confident, and, above all, purposive New Britain.'[89] On 14 September, just as Macmillan had done in 1959, Home visited the queen at Balmoral to seek a dissolution on 25 September, with the general election set for 15 October.

Wilson, mindful of the issues surrounding Gaitskell's Newcastle speech in 1959, kept a tight personal control on the campaign. He appeared fresh throughout. Speaking in Cardiff on 27 September, alluding to the BBC hit comedy series *Steptoe and Son*, he labelled Home and Selwyn Lloyd 'Stop-Go and Son'.[90] He shone on the media. The Conservative vice-chair, Lord Poole said, admiringly: 'He's the only really competent political TV performer this country has produced.'[91] The ride to victory was not, however, an entirely smooth one. On Wednesday 30 September, the National Opinion Poll in the *Daily Mail* showed a 2.9 per cent Tory lead. Wilson was rattled, causing his 'only serious lapse in the campaign'. Referring to an unofficial strike at the component firm Hardy Spicer, which could precipitate a stoppage across the motor industry, and recalling British Oxygen strikes in 1955 and 1959, Wilson said at his press conference that a case could be made for an inquiry into the Conservatives fomenting strikes at election time. Wilson was ridiculed, and NOP found that only 15 per cent of voters thought the strike had been fomented for political reasons.[92] Nonetheless, he bounced back quickly. The same day, the balance of payments figures for the second quarter of 1964 were published, showing a £73m deficit. Speaking at Norwich that evening, Wilson likened Macmillan to John Bloom, the entrepreneur whose aggressive attempts to compete in cutting prices in household durables during the 'Washing Machine Wars' of 1962–4 had ended in voluntary liquidation.

Wilson was to have a further rocky moment, as the Conservatives speculated on his relationship with Marcia. On 6 October, Hailsham, in a speech at Plymouth, was heckled about Profumo, and shot back: 'If you can tell me there are no adulterers on the front bench of the Labour Party you can talk to me about Profumo.'[93] The news soon reached Wilson, who was speaking in Birmingham that night for Labour candidates Roy Hattersley and Brian Walden. Geoffrey Goodman was told by Alf Richman, one of Wilson's aides, that 'Harold is sucking his pipe, Marcia is in a state of hysteria, Mary is in tears in a corner'.[94] The next day, Wilson chose not to respond, and asked Attlee, aged eighty-one, but campaigning vigorously, to comment. The last Labour prime minister responded magisterially to Hailsham: 'It is time he grew up.'[95]

On 12 October, with Attlee appearing first, Wilson made his final TV appeal to the electorate, to 'make this a country which cares, and in which the prosperity of the nation is shared by every family.' He said: 'If you want to see Britain moving ahead and getting ahead, if you want to sweep away outmoded ideas, the old boy network that has condemned so many of our ablest young people to frustration, then you feel with us the sense of challenge, of excitement and adventure. For if the past belongs to the Tories the future belongs to us, all of us.'[96] NOP's final prediction saw Labour's lead move from 0.1 per cent to 3.1 per cent.[97]

The result was a true cliff-hanger. The scale of the task should not be underestimated. After all, Wilson was trying to turn a three-figure Conservative majority into a Labour one within a single parliament. Wilson's eve-of-poll speech was at the St George's Hall, Liverpool, after which he and Mary went back to the Adelphi Hotel. Marcia's brother, Tony Field, drove Wilson, Mary and his press officer John Harris to Huyton where Wilson won a huge vote of 42,213 and a majority of 19,273 over his Tory opponent, with a 'Communist anti-revisionist' polling just 899 votes. Other results

– just about – kept Wilson on course for Downing Street. The only negative was Gordon Walker's loss at Smethwick in the Midlands to an anti-immigration Tory opponent that prompted Poole, in shame, to walk out of the results party he was attending at the Savoy Hotel. After little more than a couple of hours' sleep back at the Adelphi Hotel, Wilson, with Mary, his father, Marcia, Harris and John Allen, a researcher from Transport House, boarded the train from Liverpool to London. Wilson, in what was to become his trademark Gannex macintosh, ate sausages, bacon and sauté potatoes en route; Harris briefed that it was enjoyed with another Wilson favourite, HP Sauce. Finally, at 2.48 p.m., Labour held the Brecon and Radnor constituency, reaching 315 seats, and an overall majority.[98] Once counting was complete, Labour won 317 seats, the Conservatives 304 (including the speaker), and the Liberals 9, giving Labour an overall majority of four. Home went to Buckingham Palace at 3.20 p.m. to resign. The thirteen years of Conservative rule were over.

Chapter 10

A week is a long time in politics

Into Office: Prime Minister, 1964–65

At precisely 3.50 p.m. on 16 October 1964, Sir Michael Adeane, the queen's private secretary, telephoned Harold Wilson. Ten minutes later, Wilson arrived at Buckingham Palace with his father, Mary, his sons Robin and Giles, and Marcia Williams. The Labour leader was taken to the queen's private apartment: 'She simply asked me if I could form an Administration. Despite the narrowness of my majority, I was in no doubt that a Government could be formed and I was made Prime Minister on the spot.'[1] Martin Charteris, then the queen's assistant private secretary, recalled: 'There was no feeling of a problem, though when he came to the Palace with his family it was a bit of a culture shock.'[2]

This was unsurprising. The queen's first four prime ministers were from very different backgrounds. Winston Churchill was the grandson of the Seventh Duke of Marlborough; Eden, Macmillan and Home were all old Etonians. The transition from the four-teenth Earl of Home to the fourteenth Mr Wilson was signifi-cant not only for the queen but for the country, showing that the premiership was not restricted to an elite group. Wilson was the first post-war prime minister not to have been privately educated, a grammar school boy with a different outlook and attitude.

Wilson's first priority was to appoint his cabinet. Waiting for the call and watching the telephone is an agonising process for potential candidates for senior frontbench positions, so Wilson put people out of their misery quickly, starting to make appointments that evening. He chose Brown as first secretary of state, reflecting his status as deputy leader, and secretary of state for economic affairs, with Callaghan as chancellor. These were obvious choices. The only other realistic option was to have appointed them the other way around, but having Brown next door in 11 Downing Street would have made managing him even harder. Gordon Walker was appointed as foreign secretary despite losing his seat; Denis Healey became defence secretary; and the hard-working Bowden became lord president and leader of the House of Commons.[3] Sir Frank Soskice, a close friend of Gaitskell, a barrister who had served as solicitor-general – and attorney-general – under Attlee, brought his lawyer's expertise to the role of home secretary. Jay took the Board of Trade. Crossman became secretary of state for housing and local government. James Griffiths, another veteran of the Attlee governments, became the first secretary of state for Wales.

Wilson drew on his own knowledge of the machinery of White-hall to make other innovations. Frank Cousins was appointed minister of technology.[4] The NRCD would become part of the new ministry, but its remit would widen. Its two central tasks would be to increase efficiency within existing industries and, secondly, to apply new scientific methods to production. Patrick Blackett was to become the deputy chair of the new department's advisory council. Wilson also asked Cousins to deal with a more immediate priority: the British computer industry had to be rescued – within a month. Future generations can be grateful that Cousins succeeded. Also appointed to cabinet was another trade unionist, Ray Gunter, president of the Transport Salaried Staffs' Association, as Minister of Labour.

Another new ministry, Overseas Development, was also created. Wilson had been impressed by the Food and Agriculture Organisation of the United Nations, and saw the need for a British government department working with such specialist UN agencies. Barbara Castle was appointed to head the new department with a seat in cabinet. Wilson quickly prised responsibility for the Arts from the grasp of the Treasury, and gave it a formidable advocate in Jennie Lee. After placing her in the Ministry of Building and

Public Works, Wilson then moved her to the Department of Education and Science at the turn of the year.

George Wigg, as paymaster general, was given a wide-ranging responsibility for keeping Wilson informed on security matters while not interfering in departmental responsibilities. Wilson at first sought to transfer security responsibilities from the home secretary to Wigg. This provoked uproar from the permanent secretary at the Home Office, Sir Charles Cunningham, and the then MI5 director general, Sir Roger Hollis, on the basis that their whole system of signing warrants would be thrown into chaos, since Wigg would not be a secretary of state, and therefore did not have the authority to sign them off. The cabinet secretary, Sir Burke Trend, smoothed things over and found a solution. While the responsibility for the security services would remain with the home secretary, '. . . the Prime Minister did intend to give Wigg a charge to assist him from time to time on questions of security. Apparently what he had in mind was that Wigg should safeguard the Prime Minister against scandals taking him unaware and he did not want to be caught in the position of Macmillan at the time of the Profumo case.'[5] In reality, Wigg was Wilson's eyes and ears in Westminster and Whitehall, and the wider security community.

It was, however, the economic position that was to dominate Wilson's early days in office as prime minister. On the Saturday after the election, 17 October, Wilson, Callaghan and Brown met at 10 Downing Street to discuss a Treasury Memorandum prepared for the incoming government confirming that Britain was facing a deficit of £800 million on its overseas payments for 1964. Wilson reflected: 'It was this inheritance which was to dominate almost every action of the Government for the five years, eight months we were in office.'[6] Since 1949, sterling had been pegged to the dollar at $2.80. The memorandum offered three policy options: devaluation from $2.80; import quotas; and a temporary additional tariff on imports. An obvious political option here would have been to have devalued and blamed it entirely on the previous government. On 1 October, two weeks before the election, Wilson had accused the government of running a deficit of £1 million per day.

This, which would have yielded an annual figure of £365 million, was dismissed by the Conservatives as scaremongering. Wilson could have argued that, having opened the books, the situation was worse than expected, and that the most responsible thing was to act immediately. He could have blamed the last chancellor, Reginald Maudling, for cutting taxes in a 'dash for growth' in his budget of April 1963, then refusing to raise them in his budget a year later, despite balance of payments issues. Maudling, Wilson could have argued, put party before country. Wilson wrote: 'we were not unaware of the temptation. But I was convinced, and my colleagues agreed, that to devalue could have the most dangerous consequences.'[7] Quotas, which Wilson had administered two decades previously, were rejected: he thought they protected inefficient firms and damaged industrial production. The decision was, therefore, to impose a 15 per cent tariff on all imports with the exception of food, tobacco and basic raw materials, which was announced on 26 October. This was followed by an autumn budget from Callaghan on 11 November, when 6d per gallon was added to the road fuel tax, and a rise in income tax announced for the spring, though the chancellor also made good on manifesto promises to raise pensions and – symbolically for Wilson given his resignation thirteen years earlier – announced the abolition of prescription charges, which took effect from February 1965.

The head of the government economic service, Sir Alec Cairncross, bemoaned that the 'decisions taken in October 1964 and on all subsequent occasions when devaluation was mooted, owed little or nothing to official advice'.[8] The incoming Labour government distrusted the civil service, convinced that mandarins were imbued with the Conservative approach after thirteen years of single-party government. Yet the civil service advice to incoming ministers was not strongly in favour of devaluation in any event: 'When the Labour Government took office, ministers were presented with extensive briefs prepared in the Treasury and the Bank of England stating the case for and against devaluation. The Treasury, while less strongly opposed to devaluation than the Bank, saw it as having no compelling advantages and some considerable disadvantages.'[9]

There were, however, differing views. Sir Donald MacDougall, a government economic adviser since the days of Churchill, and then director general at the Department for Economic Affairs under Brown, favoured immediate devaluation.

At weekends, the economists Wilson had brought in as advisers met in private at Tony Crosland's house on Hobury Street. There was Balogh, now based at 10 Downing Street, but about whom the civil servants were very wary. He was allocated a room on the first floor of the Cabinet Office, overlooking Whitehall: a fine prospect in itself but, crucially, the connecting door to Number Ten was kept locked. If he wanted access to the prime minister he had to apply to William Reid, cabinet secretary Burke Trend's principal private secretary.[10] From the Treasury there was the Hungarian Nicky Kaldor, an economist at King's College, Cambridge, like Balogh from Budapest. Two and a half years Balogh's junior, Kaldor had attended the same school, Minta Gymnasium, the same University, Berlin, and come to Britain a couple of years before Balogh, in the late 1920s. Macmillan had sneered that 'the Budapest group . . . Balogh and Kaldor are not valuable immigrants'.[11] Another Cambridge economist, Robert Neild, also at the Treasury, attended.

Kaldor and Nield favoured devaluation. Balogh had been against devaluation on coming to office: his view was unchanged from 1949: 'It will obviously redistribute the National Income in favour of profits, and, internationally, it will make the rich, i.e. the Americans, richer, and the poor, i.e. the rest of us, poorer.'[12] Within three weeks, Balogh had changed his mind, but realised it was too late: 'I thought it shouldn't be done until we had an incomes policy . . . I thought an adviser could influence timing: I realised too late that he could only influence the next seven days; beyond that it's too complicated . . .'[13]

Ultimately, though, it was Wilson's decision. He was the prime minister; Brown and Callaghan had not even held cabinet rank before. The reality is that Wilson *did* see the political opportunity to devalue immediately, but he felt other considerations outweighed it. Wilson was concerned that the Labour government would look like it had taken the easy option, and that this would have an impact every time a future economic difficulty came along, since speculation would be created that the government would devalue again. Wilson thought an early devaluation, taken without having sought to defend the currency, meant that central banks and other governments would not see it as a necessity but as an expediency; it could even have set off 1930s-style 'beggar-my-neighbour currency devaluations' which would have impacted the world economy. Wilson also thought, based on his 1949 experience, that the general principle of making exports cheaper and imports dearer meant a transfer of resources from consumption at home to overseas markets, and tough restraints on public and private expenditure.[14]

The argument that Wilson should have devalued immediately also ignores the parliamentary context. He had a tiny majority and could by no means have been certain that the measures accompanying it would have cleared the Commons. He was to be given a sharp reminder of the power of individual MPs when, in May 1965, he had to retreat on steel renationalisation as just two Labour MPs – the troublesome Donnelly and Woodrow Wyatt – would not budge in their demand that outright public ownership be abandoned in favour of the government taking controlling interests in existing companies. Castle called it: 'the worst blow yet for the Government'.[15]

Wilson also knew that he would have to have another general election in the foreseeable future, and he was only too aware that the 1949 devaluation had contributed to the demise of the Attlee government. It was during this initial crisis, in a briefing of the parliamentary lobby, that Wilson uttered a phrase that defined him: 'A week is a long time in politics.' It is memorable in part because it is so obviously true. The attention of the national media on a particular issue is invariably short-lived, and the agenda moves on, even more quickly in the twenty-four-hour media of the twenty-first century. But it also became a form of insult to Wilson, that his approach was so short-termist it neglected any sense of long-term strategy. Yet it did not mean Wilson lived day-to-day; rather, it was, as he put it: 'a prescription for long-term strategic thinking and planning, ignoring the day-to-day issues and pressures which may hit the headlines but which must not be allowed to get out of focus while longer-term policies are taking effect.'[16]

The crisis had not, however, passed. Sterling continued to come under heavy pressure with doubts about the government's ability to keep dollar parity. On 22 November it was reported: 'European bankers are now talking openly about a possible devaluation of the pound; gold and foreign exchange is flowing out of London faster even than during the election . . .'[17] The bank rate was increased from 5 per cent to 7 per cent the next day but losses continued; it was the governor of the Bank of England, Lord Cromer, who saved the day by raising $3,000 million from central banks on 25 November. The crisis was averted – for now. Britain was, however, reliant on the assistance of others to prop up sterling: in particular, the Federal Reserve Bank of New York, which Wilson had to be conscious of in his dealings with the United States. The measures introduced by the Wilson government in its early days did work, at least temporarily: in the event, the balance of payments deficit was £428 million.[18]

A more reasonable criticism from Cairncross was that Wilson making 'devaluation' an unmentionable word in cabinet made it difficult for civil servants to discern direction. The rival recommendations from the advisers, on devaluation, and the Treasury, on deflation, were destroyed. From then on: 'it was difficult for officials and advisers to know how to proceed'.[19] Callaghan was clear he could not continue as chancellor if the pound was devalued so did not want to dwell on the topic. For Brown, his policy of expansion under a National Plan was undermined by rounds of cuts: speaking of devaluation was a reminder of the alternative course that could have been pursued. Wilson did not want to reopen the debate for fear he might lose control of the decision-making if Brown and Callaghan combined against him.

While the economic situation hung over the new government, Wilson wasted no time in condemning the Tory campaign at Smethwick. Gordon Walker had lost his majority of 3,554 votes, against the national swing, with the Conservative, Peter Griffiths, winning by 1,774. The small West Midlands town became a focus of national attention as Griffiths ran a vile, racist campaign, whipping up prejudice and hatred. As the campaign progressed, stickers appeared with the slogan ' If you want a n****r neighbour vote Liberal or Labour.'[20] They were not official Conservative posters: Griffiths took the coward's route of not putting his own name on them, but not disowning them either, saying they were a 'manifestation of popular feeling'.[21] His 10-point plan included 'assisted passages back home' for migrants who could not find work.[22] The words 'N****r lover' were daubed on Gordon Walker's own posters. At a Conservative campaign meeting, there was a disturbance when someone – apparently a supporter of Griffiths – said: 'If you black your face and go into a pub Gordon Walker will buy you a drink.'[23] Smethwick had become so notorious that on 12 February 1965, the American civil rights activist Malcolm X visited, nine days before his assassination. People shouted at him: 'We don't want any more black people here!' and 'What is your business here?'[24] Opening the debate on the queen's speech debate on 3 November, Wilson cited the 'the utterly squalid campaign of the Smethwick Conservatives.'[25] With the Tory benches heckling and interrupting, Wilson ploughed on, challenging Home to deny Griffiths the Conservative whip. If he did: 'the Smethwick Conservatives can have the satisfaction of having topped the poll, and of having sent here as their Member one who, until a further general election restores him to oblivion, will serve his term here as a Parliamentary leper.'[26] Griffiths was defeated by the Labour candidate, Andrew Faulds, in 1966.

Wilson's condemnation was a precursor to wider measures. The following year, his government passed the very first piece of legislation addressing discrimination on grounds of race. The Race Relations Act 1965 outlawed race discrimination in public places such as hotels, pubs and theatres, and created a new criminal offence of incitement to racial hatred, together with a Race Relations Board. Less impressive was the Immigration White Paper published on 2 August that year: vouchers issued for those coming from the Commonwealth to work on an annual basis were reduced from 20,800 to 8,500; and the home secretary was to be given the power to deport anyone who evaded the rules. It was badly received. *The Times'* view was that it was 'bound to do some harm to Commonwealth relations . . . The Government have not handled it well.'[27] Though the paper was the work of a cabinet committee chaired by Bowden, Soskice was blamed for it, and it contributed to his replacement by Jenkins as home secretary on 23 December.[28]

The ending of capital punishment, after many years of campaigning by Sidney Silverman, through the Murder (Abolition of Death Penalty) Act 1965, was, however, another major achievement of Soskice's time at the Home Office.[29] Wilson was very proud of abolishing hanging. Like all matters of conscience it was a free vote for MPs but the government had to provide sufficient parliamentary time for it: 'We had made it clear throughout . . . that we would provide Government time for getting such a bill through if it were the free will of the House.' Every member of the cabinet was in favour of abolition.[30]

Wilson and his family were settling in to life in Downing Street. On 18 November, Mary entertained thirty female journalists for tea.[31] She spoke openly about missing what she called the 'cosy suburban life' of Hampstead Garden Suburb. Number Ten had its advantages, though: she was seeing more of her husband due to the proximity of Downing Street to the Commons. She respected the building, liking the decorations and the 'historic association'. She spoke of its impact on her daily life: she had no requirement for a cook, since she only prepared breakfast and an evening meal for her husband and sons; she lunched alone. By this time, Robin was in his third year at Balliol College, Oxford; Giles was still at school. She did the washing-up and had brought in a washing machine, as there had previously been only a spin-dryer. That Mary spoke of these apparently mundane matters was satirised by *Private Eye* in 'Mrs Wilson's Diary'. Take the entry for 3 September 1965: 'I had gone to great trouble to get some Birds Eye Frozen Cod-fingers with Broccoli . . . but Harold pushed them moodily away and would have nothing but a piece of Krispiwheet and a portion of Dairylea Processed Cheese.'[32] Wilson himself also had occasion to bemoan Mary's habit of giving out such details: 'When he attended the

HP Company's centenary dinner in 1975 he said that he consumed more Worcester sauce than its "thicker sister product". He blamed his wife for creating the myth [of him loving HP Sauce] by telling a newspaperman in 1962 that her main criticism of him was that he always seemed to cover her cooking with lots of HP.'[33] That said, he encouraged the myth, and HP Sauce being known as 'Wilson's Gravy' did his image no harm at all. That Mary's bookcase had been brought over from Hampstead, containing the novels of Jane Austen and poetry, was actually a surer guide to her future: she was to become a published poet.

If Mary had given details of activities in the Downing Street kitchen, it was the creation of the Kitchen Cabinet that was to prove critical for the years ahead. Marcia Williams was appointed personal and political secretary to the prime minister. She was paid for out of the prime minister's allowance, so was not a civil servant. She was assisted by the reliable Brenda Dew, whose wages were funded by the Labour Party. Alf Richman, formerly a *Daily Herald* journalist, helped with political events. There was an opening battle between Williams and the civil service over control of Wilson's correspondence. Initially told she could only deal with letters from Huyton constituents and local Labour parties, Williams protested, and also secured the power to deal with correspondence from Labour MPs, party members across the country and affiliated trade unions.[34] Her instincts were sound: to understand the politics of the wider Labour movement, she could not allow such matters to be dealt with via mandarins. Williams also took control of Wilson's political and personal engagements. Wigg thought '... the influence exerted by Mrs Williams inside No. 10 was great and pervasive, for there was no doubt the Prime Minister rated her opinions as important and on many issues her reaction markedly influenced his thinking.'[35] This was an accurate observation. It was a position of status in Wilson's life that Williams guarded with all she had. When Wigg tried to discuss confidential matters with Wilson and Williams was asked to leave his side, she reacted in a temper and stormed out.

Yet, as with all Wilson's associates, Williams outlasted them all. Wigg was to leave the House of Commons in November 1967, appointed as chair of the Horseracing Betting Levy Board, by then having lost his closeness to the prime minister.[36] Balogh became a temporary civil servant in his role as economic adviser and had a small staff, a forerunner of the Downing Street Policy Unit created in 1974. He was joined by Balliol economist Andrew Graham and John Allen. John Harris went to the Foreign Office with Gordon Walker. Trevor Lloyd-Hughes, like Wilson, a Yorkshireman and a Methodist who had attended Jesus College, Oxford, was recruited from Wilson's constituency newspaper, the *Liverpool Daily Post* to become press officer. However, he was a neutral civil servant, so, in August 1965, Gerald Kaufman, then a journalist at the *New Statesman*, joined as a political press officer, and became another source of advice for Wilson, becoming an MP in 1970. Ernest Fernyhough, a former union official, and [Peter] Shore became Wilson's parliamentary private secretaries, his eyes and ears among MPs.

But the centre of the Downing Street political operation was Williams' office, which had previously been a waiting room for visitors next to the cabinet room, where Wilson worked in the mornings with his papers. Crossman, Castle, Benn, Hart and Jennie Lee regularly called in. Dick Crossman, with breathtaking arrogance, thought that Wilson, though '. . . enormously intelligent, he was certainly not an intellectual. He would also say cheerfully that one of Wilson's great merits was that he was not afraid of his [Crossman's] brutal brain power.'[37] Wilson certainly did turn to him for advice. Crossman remained in cabinet throughout Wilson's first period in government. In August 1966, he moved to the role of leader of the House of Commons, before becoming secretary of state for health and social security in November 1968.

Though they had their ups and downs, Castle and Wilson also remained close. Castle moved to become a reforming minister for transport in December 1965, shaping road safety laws: she introduced speed limits, compulsory seat belts and breathalyser tests. Moving her there was not without political cost: Wilson had sacked Tom Fraser, the previous incumbent, a move certain to cause bad feeling. Brown threatened to resign and join Fraser on the backbenches. Wilson did not back down. In April 1968 Castle became first secretary of state and secretary of state for employment and productivity. She said that Wilson often interrupted and then went off at a tangent but: 'I am in the sort of relaxed relationship with him that enables me to chip in, tapping him on the knee to stop him firmly in mid-course, and say doggedly, "Harold, listen to me."' Castle had a genuine warmth for Wilson: 'I think he knows I have considerable affection for him, even while I despair sometimes over his ideological limitations and am ready to resign, if necessary, if his tactical subtleties ever betray my beliefs. He knows, too, that I will always be honest with him . . .'[38]

There were immediate tensions between Wilson's political staff and the civil service. Though Macmillan had had a self-financing private secretary, John Wyndham, Wilson's staff were a new phenomenon, resented in Whitehall. Wilson's principal private secretary was Derek Mitchell, who chided Williams for Wilson's irresponsible use of the term 'parliamentary leper': Williams shot back that she could hardly have changed it in the speech since she had not seen it in advance. Mitchell pointed out that the speech had been put on Williams' desk on the day of the speech. Williams replied that it was while she had been out at lunch. In any event, she would not have removed the words.[39] Until 1966, when Mitchell moved on, Williams found it difficult to have an input into speeches as Wilson dictated them to the 'Garden Girls' – the civil service typists – and only saw them after they were completed. Laurence Helsby, head of the Home Civil Service, was not giving Balogh economic papers until it was too late to change them.[40] Helsby left in 1968. Meanwhile, Williams was locked in battle with the cabinet secretary, Burke Trend, for access to cabinet papers. Eventually, a compromise was agreed whereby she could see all papers save for those marked 'Top Secret', those relating to foreign policy and defence, and cabinet conclusions.[41]

Wilson was convinced of the need for change. On 8 February 1966, he appointed a committee chaired by John Fulton, whom he had known in the wartime civil service, to look at the workings of the civil service. When it reported in June 1968, Wilson accepted the recommendation that the chance of progression needed to be opened up, rather than it being restricted to only one of the four 'classes' that then existed: the Administrative Class. As he put it: 'all in future, the school-leaver, the graduate, the accountant, the engineer, the scientist, the lawyer – for all of them there will be an open road to the top.'[42]

Yet, when he travelled to the United States on 6 December 1964, the civil service secured a victory over Marcia Williams, who was excluded from the trip on the ground that a political member of staff had never been on a prime ministerial visit abroad, though Mitchell – patronisingly – told her that, on a future trip she could go if Mary did, in the capacity of a maid.[43] Wilson had already decided to press ahead with building the Polaris submarines, with a decision-making process that was to become typical of his time in office. He started in a difficult position, the 1964 manifesto being heavily critical of the proposal: 'Its possession will impress neither friend nor potential foe.'[44] He then used several sub-committees, allowing cabinet members significant time to speak on the subject, and also had a quiet word with Healey to make sure the case was put as favourably as possible, asking his defence secretary to justify the project on the basis it was past the point of no return. This was not quite right: though two hulls had been laid down, they could still have been converted to non-nuclear submarines.[45] On 11 November, a tiny cabinet sub-committee, 'MISC 16', made up of Wilson, Gordon Walker and Healey made the decision to build at least three submarines, which was regarded as the minimum the UK needed for a continuous deterrent should NATO ever be dissolved. Wilson then held a defence conference at Chequers over the weekend of 21 and 22 November, with ten other ministers making up another sub-committee, 'MISC 17'. Full cabinet then considered the matter on 26 November, with the decision in principle taken to proceed.[46] The logic for this was exactly as Bevan had set out at Brighton in 1957. As Healey put it: 'there was little chance of influencing [American Secretary of Defence] McNamara's nuclear strategy if we had renounced nuclear weapons ourselves . . .'[47] There was opposition from Wigg, who deplored the downgrading of the conventional army by relying on nuclear weapons, and Brown, who first wanted to cancel Polaris altogether, then reduce the proposed five submarines to three. While the final decision to build four submarines, the minimum required if one was to be permanently kept east of Suez, was made in January 1965 by the Defence and Overseas Policy Committee of the cabinet,[48] Wilson had steered the cabinet to accept the principle of building Polaris before he crossed the Atlantic. The task in Washington was to retreat from Macmillan's commitment to the MLF. Putting crews of at least three nationalities on ships achieved nothing in terms of influencing American control of NATO's nuclear weapons and was hated by the British defence chiefs.

Wilson knew he faced a challenge. At the meeting in February, Johnson told him he would never trust a British prime minister again, after Home had made a casual reference to the objections America had raised to the British supply of buses to Cuba,* before giving the impression in public that he had expressed himself in unyielding terms. Wilson said he would be consistent in what he said inside and outside the meetings. Johnson was seeking support for American policy in Vietnam and a guarantee that Britain would maintain commitments east of Suez, to share the burden of peace-keeping. Reducing UK military expenditure overseas to assist with its balance of payments position was one thing, but it should not be at the expense of additional costs to America, thereby affecting its own balance of payments.[49] Wilson wanted American backing for sterling and support for British policy in South Rhodesia. Johnson raised the issue of 'co-operating with him in South Vietnam, even if only on a limited – even a token – basis'. Wilson was clear that he could not promise this. Johnson's secretary of state, Dean Rusk, later said: 'All we needed was one regiment. The Black Watch would have done. Just one regiment, but you wouldn't. Well, don't expect

---

* In January 1964, Britain agreed to supply 450 buses to Fidel Castro's government. The Leyland Motor Corporation would deliver the buses and the spare parts. This undermined America's policy of isolating the Cuban regime with an economic blockade and was immediately criticised by the US State Department (see *New York Times*, 7 January 1964).

us to save you again. They can invade Sussex and we wouldn't do a damn thing about it.'[50] However, Wilson emphasised the 'East of Suez' commitment, including the 54,000 British troops stationed in Malaysia, which seemed to come as news to Johnson.[51] Johnson took this commitment at face value, and said he would continue to back sterling and British policy in southern Africa. However, this was in the context of an explicit commitment Wilson had given to Johnson not to devalue the pound. The meeting during which the pledge was given was minuted, but it took place on the basis that 'It was agreed . . . this was a meeting which never occurred.' Wilson concluded his remarks by 'committing himself and his government with complete firmness against any possibility of a devaluation of the pound.'[52] This was an expression of Wilson's own desire to avoid devaluation, but giving such a personal pledge to Johnson in this way no doubt reinforced him in that determination.

This left the problematic issue of the MLF. The American side saw British participation in the surface fleet as a '*sine qua non* for the successful outcome of these talks'.[53] Rather than simply refusing to take part in the MLF and allowing a vacuum, into which America could come to a bilateral agreement with West Germany, Wilson instead made a counter-proposal: an Atlantic Nuclear Force (ANF).[54] Britain would commit all its strategic nuclear weapons to the ANF, but it would also retain the right to employ the aircraft for conventional use. America would commit an equal number of Polaris submarines, and possibly some Minuteman missiles in the United States. Non-nuclear powers could contribute to some sort of mixed-crew element, and it was open to France to join. The compromise was enough for Johnson to accept, which was a great triumph for Wilson. Within a year the ANF idea was dropped altogether, but it had served its purpose. In a situation where a firm British commitment to the MLF had been a central American negotiating goal, Wilson avoided it.

Wilson travelled home, after meeting with Canadian prime minister Lester Pearson in Ottawa, heading straight for the Labour Party conference in Brighton. The next day, with Herbert Wilson, on his eighty-second birthday, looking on in great pride, Wilson's speech was a mixture of harsh reality and soaring oratory. He set out the central issue of the dire situation the Tories had left: 'No one will now underestimate our economic inheritance, the worst that in its gravity was denied and denied again for political purposes before the election.'[55] But he also captured the significance of the moment, referring to those who founded the Labour movement, the defeat of 1931, and the power of the political volunteer: 'Now, as a result of the faith which they bequeathed to us, as a result of the courage of men and women in this room today, who have kept the flag flying – 33 years ago when our enemies thought this movement of ours was destroyed – as a result of the efforts of everyone in this hall and countless others in these past few months, the day for which we and those that went before us waited is here. It is our task to be worthy of the torch they have handed on to us.'[56]

There was an air of optimism as Christmas approached. On 16 December, at Lancaster House, Brown took the first steps towards preparing a National Plan. Flanked by George Woodcock, general secretary of the TUC, Jay, Callaghan and Gunter, Brown presented a 'Statement of Intent on Productivity, Prices and Incomes' signed by the government, the TUC and employers' organisations. A week later, the Wilson family caught the overnight train from Paddington to Penzance and flew by helicopter to the Scillies for Christmas and New Year. It was his first break since coming to office, and a very important one: it was the Wilsons' silver wedding anniversary on 1 January 1965. Wilson's wonderful day was capped with his first New Year's Honours list featuring a knighthood for Stanley Matthews, the first that was explicitly for services to football.[57]

If this was a high point for Wilson, a low point came a few weeks later with Gordon Walker resigning from the Foreign Office after his attempt to return to the Commons ended in defeat in the Leyton by-election on 21 January. The next day, Wilson chose Michael Stewart as his successor. This left the Education and Science portfolio vacant. Stewart, a former teacher and a passionate educationalist, had been an ideal fit. Yet he was also a capable and dependable minister who could have occupied most cabinet posts with distinction. In appointing him, Wilson also showed he understood the value of loyalty. Burke Trend advised Wilson that Roy Jenkins, outside the cabinet as minister of aviation, was the best minister in the government. Wilson therefore offered him the education portfolio. Jenkins demurred, using the excuse that his three children were at fee-paying schools. This was not a unique situation among Labour politicians at the time. Wilson replied that his two sons were privately educated, too. Nonetheless, Jenkins turned the job down, hoping for a promotion to the Home Office to replace the ailing Soskice.[58]

Wilson turned instead to Anthony Crosland, then Brown's number two at the Ministry of Economic Affairs. Crosland accepted, and led the push to abolish academic selection at the age of eleven, via his Circular 10/65, of 12 July 1965, issued to local education authorities and governors of direct grant, voluntary aided and special agreement schools, to move to a system of comprehensives. In *The Future of Socialism*, Crosland had argued that the tripartite educational system introduced in the Education Act of 1944, with prestigious grammar schools based on academic selection at the age of eleven – with secondary moderns and technical schools for the rest – was not providing equality of opportunity for all. Crosland thought the 'school system in Britain remains the most divisive, unjust and wasteful of all the aspects of social inequality'.[59] On fee-paying schools, Crosland did not think they could be forcibly closed since 'the interference with private liberty would be intolerable' but he thought the 'most sensible approach is to work for a gradual integration of these schools into the State system of education.'[60] Thus, the immediate priority was to end the segregation of children on the basis of their performance in the 'eleven-plus' examination that was so crucial to their life chances, and was, in Crosland's view, discriminating against those from working-class backgrounds and favouring the middle classes. As he put it: 'The class distribution of the grammar school is still markedly askew.'[61] This was not only morally wrong, it wasted talent. His remark to his wife Susan captured his determination to change the secondary school system, though not in elegant terms: 'If it is the last thing

I do, I'm going to destroy every fucking grammar school . . .'[62] Crosland's reliance on a policy of persuading local authorities to change to a comprehensive system, rather than mandating them, has been criticised on the basis it led to reform being 'implemented in an uneven way'.[63] Some local authorities were able to retain grammar schools. Yet, while Crosland did not close all of them, he did set off a systemic change: from a peak of 1,298 grammar schools in 1964, only 163 remained in 2021.[64]

The appointment of Crosland was of great significance, but the news of the mini-reshuffle was quickly overtaken. On 24 January, Winston Churchill died at the age of ninety. As it happened, it was Wilson's hundredth day in office. The *Sunday Mirror* lobby correspondent Anthony Shrimsley published *The First Hundred Days of Harold Wilson* soon after, praising the prime minister's sure-footed performances in parliament.[65] The next day, in the Commons, Wilson paid a fulsome tribute to the wartime leader: '. . . it will be for those war years that his name will be remembered for as long as history is written and history is read . . . His record of leadership in those five years speaks for itself beyond the power of any words of any of us to enhance or even to assess. This was his finest hour, Britain's finest hour.'[66] Wilson himself had risen to the occasion, proving his own ability to capture the significance of the moment of national mourning. He was establishing himself as prime minister.

Chapter 11

Weeks rather than months

Staying in Office, 1965–66

Harold Wilson had a deep attachment to the Crown. He told the *Daily Express* that he had 'great respect for tradition . . . the real ceremonies of the Monarchy . . .'[1] This was authentic: he had a sentimental view of the Commonwealth and took an almost boyish pleasure in its pomp and circumstance. Stephen P. Barry, who served as a valet to Prince Charles, said it was known that 'a great respect had grown up between the Queen and . . . Wilson.' Barry recalled that Wilson saw the queen on Tuesdays at 6.30 p.m. when parliament was in session and 'spent a good deal of . . . [the] . . . evening keeping her up to date with all that was going on.' Palace staff said that Wilson 'had weighed up his monarch's character very cleverly.' He sometimes paid a second weekly visit: '. . . the Prime Minister would often have something to impart on a Friday, something of which she simply must be informed.'[2]

Wilson saw his relationship with the queen in a meritocratic sense: his audiences with her were a symbol of where he had risen to by dint of his own talents. He also had a genuine warmth towards her: she was another strong female figure in his life whom he respected. Mary also liked the queen, sympathising with the way the monarch sought to keep a private life alongside her public role. One of Mary's poems captured this, describing the queen on her country estates: 'She notes a crumbling wall, an open gate/With countrywoman's eyes she views the scene/Yet, walking free upon her own estate/Still, in her solitude, she is the Queen.'[3]

Wilson was steadfast in his loyalty, not least when royal issues became controversial, such as the investiture of Prince Charles as Prince of Wales at Caernarfon Castle on 1 July 1969. After the victory of the Plaid Cymru candidate, Gwynfor Evans, in the Carmarthen by-election of July 1966, Welsh Nationalist feeling seemed to be running high. Wilson appointed George Thomas, a virulent opponent of Welsh Nationalism, as secretary of state for Wales in April 1968 with a brief to arrange the investiture. There was criticism from within the Labour Party about the £200,000 cost of the ceremony and with concerns about extremists in some parts of Wales there were deep concerns about Prince Charles's safety. Wilson kept the queen advised throughout and never deviated from the plan.[4] After Wilson resigned as prime minister for the second time, the queen showed her high regard for him by attending a farewell dinner for him with Prince Philip at 10 Downing Street on 23 March 1976. Only Winston Churchill, in 1955, had previously been accorded a similar retirement party. In his speech, Wilson said that the monarchy was 'more firmly based on popular support and affection than at any time in the century'.[5] Wilson's affection for the queen was genuine, but it was also politically advantageous for him to be close to her. The investiture, for example, allowed Wilson and Thomas to harness the enduring popularity of the queen with the wider Welsh public against the hardline Welsh Nationalists. Within weeks of taking office, newspapers were briefed that the queen and Wilson were getting on well.[6] Prime minister and monarch even featured together on a *Private Eye* front cover, with the queen saying 'We can't go on meeting like this.'[7]

Wilson also sought to employ the monarch to his advantage in Rhodesia, which was to become a headache for him in the years ahead. On 3 February 1960, Macmillan spoke in Cape Town, and declared that the 'wind of change' was blowing through Africa in the form of a growth of national consciousness. However, a leader emerged who was determined to build a shelter over his white-minority government in Southern Rhodesia while the gales swept everything else away. Until his fall in 1979, Ian Smith's actions presented a challenge to successive British governments, but it was to Harold Wilson that he was most provocative, with his illegal Unilateral Declaration of Independence in November 1965.

Smith embodied British colonialism. His father Jock had emigrated from Scotland in 1898, running a farm and a mine. Smith himself was born in 1919, and was a child when Rhodesia had become a self-governing colony in 1923. He served as a fighter pilot in the Second World War before entering politics, then purchased a farm and stood for the Rhodesian parliament in 1948. Between 1953 and 1961, Rhodesia was part of the Central African Federation of Nyasaland (today's Malawi), Northern Rhodesia (now Zambia), and Southern Rhodesia (now Zimbabwe). This, under the force of a desire for self-government, started to break up. A 1961 constitution established a parliamentary system of government for Southern Rhodesia, but also a deeply unfair, racist voting franchise, arranged on a system of voter rolls (A and B), with property and educational qualifications designed to maintain white minority rule in parliament, as the land was predominantly owned by white farmers, and the black population had not had the same educational opportunities. In March 1962, Smith had co-founded the Rhodesian Front, seeking to preserve white minority rule, and it won power in the general election that December. Smith replaced Winston Field as its leader, and prime minister, in April 1964, after the Federation of Nyasaland and Rhodesia had formally dissolved at the end of 1963. On 24 October 1964, Northern Rhodesia became Zambia, and the Southern Rhodesian government referred to itself as the government of Rhodesia.

Wilson set out a firm position in a statement published on 27 October: 'The only way Southern Rhodesia can become a sovereign independent state is by an Act of the British Parliament. A declaration of independence would be an open act of defiance and rebellion and it would be treasonable to take steps to give effect to it.'[8] On 5 November, Smith held a referendum of the highly restricted, mostly white electorate, that resulted in landslide support for independence.

Thus, the stage was set for Smith's clash with Wilson. The

practical issue for the white settlers, though they owned substantial land, was one of numbers. The white population was around 230,000 in comparison to the four million black men and women who lived there. The coming of mass democracy would replace white minority rule with a black majority government. Every solution Wilson offered was to be delayed or rejected because Smith was determined to preserve that white minority rule. Wilson would never have tolerated that.

As early as December 1964, Wilson mentioned to the queen that Smith and other ministers should be dismissed if they declared independence illegally.[9] There was an extraordinarily bad-tempered exchange between Smith and Wilson a few weeks later. On 12 January, Smith accused Wilson of seeking to interfere with the internal affairs of Rhodesia. He claimed his government had 'the overwhelming support of the electorate and the three million Africans in the tribal trust areas to guide the development of our country . . .'[10] Smith's rant extended to Wilson's proposal to send a small all-party group of senior MPs to Rhodesia to see the situation at first-hand: 'As the Secretary of State for Commonwealth Relations has refused to proceed to Rhodesia to consult at a Government level, I see no purpose in a mission being sent out by you.'[11] Smith was not finished. On 13 January he followed this up with another attack, claiming that 'the Government of Rhodesia was persuaded to attend the Victoria Falls Conference [in 1963] on the clear understanding that the question of Rhodesia's independence would be settled as soon as the Conference had been concluded. Obviously the Government of Rhodesia was deceived over this vital issue.'[12]

Wilson responded via personal telegram on 15 January. He was far more restrained than Smith, but was firm: 'I am bound to express the deep disappointment at the messages which your High Commissioner has delivered to me. So long as you and I cannot meet for frank and objective talks, and cannot agree upon other possible ways forward, I do not see how we can hope to dispel the climate of mistrust which presently confronts us and prevents all progress.' He added: 'In the meantime, I would only reiterate our own determination to find a means of constructive discussion and negotiation towards a peaceable solution.'[13]

It was Churchill's funeral on 30 January that provided the opportunity for Smith and Wilson to meet at Downing Street. Smith later claimed that he and Wilson 'did not discuss politics'.[14] This is nonsense. Smith told Wilson that day that 'the issue was one of life or death, so that he was bound to take a tough line . . . He would wait for an opportunity and then use it. He was quite clear that negotiations would take us no further and that it was a matter simply of waiting for the moment.' Wilson pounced and asked 'whether this meant waiting for some provocative act on the part of H.M.G.' Mr Smith said that it did. Wilson asked what the urgency was with a Unilateral Declaration of Independence; Smith claimed the economy was suffering and immigration was being slowed down. Loftily, he claimed the majority of the population was 'too inarticulate' to express a view. Wilson replied in disgust: 'it was difficult to explain to Parliament that, while other countries in Africa had moved to independence, yet in Rhodesia alone the native population were too inarticulate and too backward to express a view.' Smith was intransigent: 'The Prime Minister asked what would lead to progress, and Mr Smith indicated that independence was the only thing that would.'[15] Wilson thought Smith 'almost obsessional': he told Keith Holyoake, the prime minister of New Zealand, that 'Mr Smith had indicated to him that he hoped to maintain the present system of white supremacy in Southern Rhodesia for 70 years or more.'[16]

Eventually, on 5 February, Smith agreed to a visit from the Commonwealth secretary, Arthur Bottomley, and the lord chancellor, Gerald Gardiner, on the basis he was 'kept in the forefront throughout' and that negotiations would remain exclusively between the two governments and that the Rhodesian government would arrange the itinerary.[17] The 10-day cabinet mission duly arrived in Salisbury on 21 February. It made little progress. After meeting Bottomley, Lord Malvern, the former prime minister of Rhodesia, commented: 'We just had a waffle.'[18] Bottomley was taken in by Smith. This contribution to a Commons debate later in the year is telling: 'Mr. Smith himself stood out as a man of character and integrity . . . we had, sadly, to recognise that the broad masses of the people supported the Rhodesia Front Government and the policy of a unilateral declaration of independence. [HON. MEMBERS: 'The white people.'] Yes, the white people.'[19] Wilson was treading more carefully. On 14 April, in a private discussion with UN secretary-general U Thant, he emphasised it was 'essential . . . not to give Mr. Smith any excuse for seizing U.D.I. before all chance of reaching a negotiated settlement had been lost.'[20]

Things were getting worse. In the Rhodesian general election of 7 May, Smith's Rhodesia Front party won all fifty seats on the A-roll. Since there were only 15 seats elected on the B-roll, it was a landslide victory. In the UK, Wilson formulated five principles upon which negotiations with Smith would be based: unimpeded progress to majority rule; guarantees against retrospective amendment of the 1961 constitution; immediate improvement in the political status of the African population; progress towards ending racial discrimination; and the British government being assured that any proposal for independence was acceptable 'to the people of Rhodesia as a whole.'[21]

This did not produce an uncontroversial way forward. When Wilson hosted the Commonwealth prime ministers' conference at Marlborough House in June, without Smith, he managed to keep his options open. Yet the pressure was mounting for the British government to impose a solution and use force if necessary. A form of words was agreed but no explicit commitment given: 'the British Government . . . undertook to take full account, in relation to these discussions, of all the views which had been expressed during the meeting.'[22]

Wilson now sought to do all he could, short of military action, to avoid a unilateral declaration of independence by Rhodesia. Smith arrived in London on 4 October for talks, but these broke down four days later without Smith even accepting the five principles that the British government had set out for the negotiations. Wilson was careful to manage the domestic audience. On 12 October, he made a television broadcast: 'After 40 years of limited self-government, the control lay in the hands of 230,000 Europeans, while nearly four million Africans remained effectively without the vote.'[23] Smith's position on this indefensible position was risible. He claimed: '. . . there was no racial connotation to the franchise, and from that date there have been people of every race, colour and creed on the voters' roll.'[24] He knew perfectly well that the qualifications themselves ensured that most Africans could not vote. He made no effort to hide his white supremacist views.

It was at this point that Wilson turned to the queen for help, asking for a letter to deliver to Smith urging him to find a solution. The queen duly obliged and Wilson left for Rhodesia on 24 October, in a last-ditch attempt to prevent a unilateral declaration of independence.[25] However, the wily Smith sought to turn the letter to his advantage by reading it out at the banquet he held for Wilson, claiming it was 'the sort of thing we live for in Rhodesia' and wrote back to the queen assuring her of engagement in the discussions with the 'utmost sincerity, frankness and goodwill'.[26] Wilson ensured that he met African nationalist leaders Joshua Nkomo, of the Zimbabwe African People's Union (ZAPU) and Reverend Ndabaningi Sithole, of the Zimbabwe African National Union (ZANU), both being detained by Smith's regime. Wilson was incensed by their treatment, having a 'blazing row' with the Rhodesian authorities when he discovered Nkomo had no food provided, and, when he realised the same had happened to Sithole, he recalled 'for the first time in my life, I totally lost my temper to the point where I was out of control'.[27]

Zambia kept up the pressure on the negotiations from outside. On 28 October, Simon Kapwepwe, the foreign minister said that his country might secede from the Commonwealth and withdraw its sterling balance from London if Wilson conceded independence to Smith without one man, one vote.[28] Wilson continued to counsel against an invasion. On 31 October, in Accra, following a meeting with President Nkrumah of Ghana, Wilson 'told the press that Britain does not believe in the use of military force to settle constitutional disputes' though he added that 'a unilateral declaration of independence was a revolt against the Crown'.[29]

On 1 November, back in the Commons, with no progress to report, Wilson explained the two propositions he had put to Smith. First, he would put Smith's claim of independence without universal suffrage to a referendum of the Rhodesian people, and would hold it on the basis of a restricted franchise of the white settlers and those Africans who were paying taxes. The second proposition was the setting up of a royal commission, under the chairmanship of Rhodesia's Chief Justice, Sir Hugh Beadle, to recommend how the British government's five principles could be put into effect in a way that was acceptable to the people.[30] Wilson had to be careful not to concede too much in order to reach a solution. Nkrumah wrote to Wilson the next day: 'What you are suggesting is that there shall be a Royal Commission of three Europeans with a built-in settler majority to determine under what Constitution the four million Africans of Southern Rhodesia should be governed . . . It was for this reason that my Government described this scheme as a betrayal of the four million Africans of the Colony.'[31]

A day later a weary Wilson was back at the dispatch box, with a final offer: 'We should still be willing, as an alternative to the Royal Commission, to agree that the Rhodesian Government's Constitutional proposals should be submitted to the test of a referendum of the whole Rhodesian people.'[32] Beadle himself was cabling Wilson with an insight into Smith's thinking. He painted the Rhodesian premier as under pressure from his extreme right wing, determined to get the idea of a commission rejected to clear the way for a unilateral declaration of independence.[33] On 7 November, Wilson messaged Smith: 'The purpose of our present exchanges is to try to get a Royal Commission set up. No doors are being closed by me.'[34]

It was to no avail. Smith chose Armistice Day, 11 November, for his declaration. The morning began with news that Smith had messaged the queen to offer loyalty. Her Majesty's response was that she was confident 'all her Rhodesian people will demonstrate their loyalty by continuing to act in a constitutional manner.' Castle noted that 'Harold has certainly got her superbly organised.'[35] Wilson was presiding over a cabinet meeting when a note was brought to him confirming that, in a broadcast, Smith had made his announcement.[36] Wilson immediately termed it an 'IDI': an illegal declaration of independence. The next day, United Nations Security Council Resolution 216 condemned the declaration by a 'racist minority'.

It was a moment of profound failure: the British government could not find a solution that offered a viable future to an area of the world dealing with the consequences of empire, and had a government in open defiance of the UK parliament. Wilson had spent the time trying to find a way forward, but had he done enough? That Wilson removed even the threat of using force has been seen as a fundamental mistake as it was argued that maintaining it would have held Smith back. Castle thought Wilson was genuine in his support for the African cause but that he was worried about the reaction at home among those who saw the white Rhodesian settlers as 'kith and kin'. She thought: 'Harold sold the pass by making it clear he would not use force to bring the illegal regime to heel. All Ian Smith had to do was to sweat it out.'[37]

This analysis is not fair. For a start, the firm civil service advice given to Wilson was that the use of force was practically impossible: 'It is obvious when looking at the land-locked nature of Southern Rhodesia and the geographical dispersal of its airfields that military intervention by our Armed Forces is out of the question.'[38] But there were deeper considerations at stake. The prime minister was strongly opposed to military action on principled grounds, as he set out in a telegram to the Commonwealth prime ministers: '. . . I do not believe it would be right to intervene in this manner . . . It is the one thing that would unite all the white Rhodesians.' He found the idea of a war on grounds of race abhorrent:

> Apart from the destruction, I am appalled by the prospect of the racial war between African and European into which a military intervention might develop. I doubt whether we could set bounds on such a war if it began; the results would be incalculable in terms of death and destruction. It would also put an end to any prospect of building up the sort of equal societies in which all

races can live in harmony, and which are already coming about in the newly independent Commonwealth countries in Africa. And it would go directly counter to our declared object of restoring the rule of law in Rhodesia.[39]

There is an argument that Wilson could have threatened force, even if he did not intend to use it, but that would have been to risk Smith calling the bluff and then a humiliation if he had not followed through.

This meant that Wilson had to put his faith in sanctions to bring down the Smith regime. He told the Commonwealth prime ministers: 'It is my belief that there is a good possibility of bringing down the regime and making a new start in Rhodesia without bloodshed and destruction . . . Given the appalling consequences of any likely alternative policy, I hope I can count on your support . . .'[40] Wilson acted swiftly to announce measures on the day of Smith's declaration. Smith and his ministers were told they no longer held office. Tobacco and sugar purchases, which constituted 70 per cent of Rhodesia's exports to Britain, were banned.[41] Arms exports were ended, as was all British aid. Rhodesia was expelled from the sterling area, and exchange controls introduced, with access to the London capital market stopped. British capital could no longer be exported to Rhodesia. Commonwealth preference for Rhodesian goods ceased. The British high commissioner in Salisbury was to be withdrawn and the Southern Rhodesia high commissioner in London asked to leave. Passports issued or renewed by the illegal regime would not be recognised. This left one major issue outstanding: oil. Wilson waited until he had gained American support for international oil sanctions. On 17 December, Britain duly declared an oil embargo on Rhodesia, with Wilson confirming a plan to airlift oil to Zambia in the Commons on 20 December.[42]

In cabinet, Callaghan argued for immediate, strong measures to achieve a 'quick kill'.[43] This became a plan for Zambia to sever its economic relationship with Rhodesia, with Britain providing support to ensure that Zambia itself was not affected adversely. This, however, came to nothing as, on 14 February 1966, President

Kaunda said in a BBC interview that he thought only military intervention could take down Smith's regime, particularly given the support Rhodesia was receiving from South Africa. Zambia was economically dependent on Southern Rhodesia; and Smith's regime was militarily stronger: it had far more aircraft, and more infantry battalions on the ground.[44] Rhodesia could cut off coal and power to Zambia, losing 40 per cent of the world's copper supplies.[45] Wilson was also acutely aware that Britain was dependent on Zambian copper, without which he thought there would be two million unemployed within months.[46] Wilson was willing to send troops to Zambia to man the northern bank of the Zambezi River to offer protection in the event of a pre-emptive strike by Smith, but Kaunda would only accept them if they had orders to cross the border into Rhodesia and occupy Kariba.[47] This Wilson could not accept. Kaunda urged Wilson to do more, including the arrest of Smith. Wilson reiterated his position against the use of force, and emphasised his confidence that 'the economic measures and steps which we are taking will have a steady cumulative effect'.[48] Indeed, United Nations Security Council Resolution 217 of 20 November 1965 had urged states to 'do their utmost to break all economic relations with Southern Rhodesia'.

The failure of 'Quick Kill' was another blow after Smith's unilateral declaration. Yet Wilson's personal efforts on the issue of Rhodesia had retained support at home. In December 1965, Labour had an opinion poll lead of 44.5 per cent to 38.5 per cent over the Conservatives, and its handling of Rhodesia had a 55 per cent approval rating with 25 per cent disapproving.[49] One criticism of Wilson – made by Marcia Williams – was that on Rhodesia, he had 'completely taken off and got out of touch with the real problems at home'. Benn thought Williams felt cut off from Wilson, and the comment may reflect this frustration.[50] Prime ministers rarely have the luxury of focusing on one issue for a sustained period of time; mostly, they have to move swiftly between different policy areas and make quick decisions. Focusing on Rhodesia in late 1965 had been a reasonable thing to do. Yet other issues were never far away.

After the economic troubles of Wilson's early weeks in office, there was relief at the start of 1965. When the Defence White Paper was published on 23 February, it reaffirmed Britain's global ambitions.[51] It was sensible to reduce the number of British troops stationed in Western Europe given that any conventional warfare would be short-lived in the nuclear age. Yet, in light of China's nuclear weapons test the previous October, Britain would commit to remaining as a nuclear power in the Far East. That month, the balance of payments showed a surplus of £11m. But, by March, this had become a deficit. On 6 April, Callaghan delivered his budget, stating that his aim was to balance imports and exports: he would 'decrease the pressure on our resources, through lower public expenditure and higher taxation, by £250 million'.[52] The cuts included the cancellation of the costly TSR2 British military aircraft and their replacement by the cheaper American alternative, the F-111. The measures were insufficient. When the May trade figures were published on 15 June, there was a £49m deficit.[53] Imports were rising and exports were static.

The unstable parliamentary situation was not helping. After the death of sitting MP Llywelyn Williams on 4 February, Labour had held the Abertillery seat in a by-election on 1 April, but election speculation continued. Wilson ruled out a dissolution of parliament for the rest of the year in a speech in Glasgow on 26 June, but it was to no avail. Confidence in sterling remained weak and pressure increased. Once again, the option of devaluation loomed. Yet, this summer, Wilson, Callaghan and Brown were united in wanting to avoid it. Dick Crossman recorded in his diary: 'All the economists were urging that the pound should float, while the three politicians, strongly backed by George Wigg, were fighting for the pound on the ground that no Labour government could survive devaluation in 1965 after the devaluations of 1931 and 1949.'[54] With sterling selling heavily, Callaghan announced stringent measures on 27 July, to reduce demand at home and tighten exchange control. Starting dates for most capital projects were delayed by six months. Repayment periods on hire purchase were shortened.

Wilson left for three weeks in the Scillies on 6 August with the economic situation still precarious. There was a scrambler telephone installed in Lowenva, and a teleprinter line to Number Ten in Customs House, operated by the 'Garden Room Girls'. On 5 August, the day before Wilson had left, the NEDC, with Brown in the chair, had approved his National Plan, to be published in mid-September, aiming for a growth in national product of 25 per cent between 1964 and 1970. It was Brown's voluntary prices and incomes policy that caused concern in Wilson's evening calls from the Scillies: was this strong enough to withstand the pressures for higher wages? Wilson arrived back at Penzance on 27 August and, on 1 September, cabinet decided to make the National Board for Prices and Incomes a statutory body: the secretary of state could refer prices or wage disputes to it and had the power to enforce its decisions.[55]

The next day, the House of Commons Speaker, who had been a Conservative MP, Sir Harry Hylton-Foster, collapsed and died. Wilson and Gunter were hosting a conference on the motor industry at Downing Street, to address the issue of unofficial strikes and the damage they were causing to the national economy. Sterling came under renewed pressure; the next day, the *Daily Mail* declared: 'Wilson on the edge of the precipice.' The problem was that the deputy speaker, Labour's Horace King, replaced Hylton-Foster, with the Conservative Sir Samuel Storey, the second deputy speaker, taking King's place. By not offering a replacement for Storey, the Conservatives now provided only one of the three full-time occupants of the chair, rather than two. By not providing the third MP, they hoped to force Labour into having to do it, thereby reducing the number of votes the government could rely on. Labour was already without an MP for Erith and Crayford, as the incumbent Norman Dodds had died on 22 August. Wilson managed to find a solution by persuading a Liberal, the lawyer Roderic Bowen, to accept the role. James Wellbeloved then held Erith and Crayford for Labour in a by-election on 11 November.

The National Plan appeared on 16 September: its 25 per cent increase in national output would be achieved with expanded productive capacity, and improved efficiency, with British goods becoming more competitive in world markets. There would need to be an annual average growth of 3.8 per cent. Its optimistic ambition stood in stark contrast to the sombre tone of Wilson's party conference speech on 28 September at Blackpool. The prime minister used Nye Bevan's words to justify the government's actions in the face of its 'entry into office . . . [being] . . . dominated by a deep-lying industrial and trade crisis.' He was downbeat: 'We said it would not be easy. We said, in the spirit of the imperishable philosophy of Nye Bevan, first proclaimed here in Blackpool, that our actions would be governed by the language of priorities.'[56] As prime minister, he was learning on the job. The following month, he gave an interview to the *Observer* to mark a year in office, and remarked: 'The more things you take an interest in, the more information comes back to you. A Prime Minister governs by curiosity and range of interest.'[57]

Yet public opinion was turning. A consequence of Wilson's announcement to rule out a general election in 1965 was that the Conservatives took the opportunity to change leader. Home did not enjoy life as leader of the opposition in the Commons: 'the slick knockabout was something at which Mr Wilson excelled.'[58] He announced his resignation on 22 July. Five days later, Edward Heath faced Reginald Maudling and Enoch Powell in the first round of the leadership contest. It was the first time a Conservative Party leader had been chosen by a ballot of MPs, rather than informal soundings. Heath took 150 votes with Maudling on 133 and Powell on 15. Though Heath had won an overall majority of votes cast, the rules stated he also needed a lead of 15 per cent, so a second ballot was required, but Maudling pulled out. Heath was therefore elected Conservative Party leader and leader of the opposition.

He was to spend a decade opposite Wilson, the man whose election unquestionably influenced his own capture of the leadership of his party. The choice of Heath, a forty-nine-year-old grammar school boy, was a moment of change in those chosen to lead the Conservatives. Not for another forty years was a candidate educated at a fee-paying school selected as party leader, when David Cameron, an old Etonian, defeated David Davis. The Conservatives had been forced to respond to Wilson's popularity and his jibes about Macmillan and Home representing the Edwardian era. Heath had been an organ scholar at Balliol College, Oxford with a significant hinterland including being an international yachts-man who was to go on to captain the British team to victory in the Admiral's Cup in 1971. But he lacked Wilson's relaxed charm and easy popular appeal. Heath could be awkward and rude, and was intensely private. Though it was unfair, his status as a life-long bachelor contrasted with Wilson's appeal as a family man. Wilson's personal ratings were far superior: by February 1966 60 per cent were satisfied with the job Wilson was doing, with 32 per cent dissatisfied; Heath was thought to be doing a good job as Conservative leader by only 40 per cent, with 36 per cent having a negative view.[59] Wilson had a feel for public opinion. On 12 June 1965, it was announced that the queen, on Wilson's recommenda-tion, had awarded MBEs to Violet Carson, the actress who played Ena Sharples in *Coronation Street*, and to the four members of The Beatles, in the Birthday honours. The furore afterwards suggested this was highly controversial: a former RAF squadron leader, Paul Pearson, posted his MBE back to the queen, accusing Wilson of having 'debased and cheapened' the honours system. A retired army officer, Colonel Wagg, resigned his Labour membership, and cancelled a £12,000 bequest to the party in his will.[60] Yet it did Wilson's ratings with the wider public no damage.

If Wilson was popular at home, there were still challenges abroad. The two major foreign policy challenges he faced came to-gether during his trip to America at the end of the year. On 16 De-cember, twenty African delegates walked out of Wilson's speech at the United Nations General Assembly in protest at him not taking a stronger stance on Rhodesia. That afternoon, Wilson moved on to Washington for a meeting with Johnson. Wilson once again used a plain-speaking approach. It had been a turbulent twelve months in their relationship. On 7 February, an attack by the Viet Cong–North Vietnamese forces on the American airfield and base at Pleiku had led Johnson to respond with heavy bombing. The Soviet premier, Alexei Kosygin, was in Hanoi, and condemned it, as did fifty Labour backbenchers who signed a motion in parliament. Late on 10 February the Viet Cong destroyed a club in the Saigon area used by American servicemen. Remembering Attlee's flight to speak to President Truman in 1950 to try to prevent America using nuclear weapons in the Korean War, Wilson called Johnson – at 3.30 a.m. British time – on the transatlantic 'hotline' connecting Number Ten and the White House. Wilson, thinking he could fly to Washington to prevent Johnson escalating the conflict, offered to visit America for talks. Johnson was furious: '. . . If you want to help us some in Vietnam [sic] send us some men and send us some folks to deal with these guerrillas. And announce to the press that you are going to help us . . .'[61] Wilson managed to calm him, and the next day Johnson sent a friendly telegram suggesting a visit in a few weeks' time.

On 14 April, Wilson left for the United States, but in chaotic circumstances. Brown had offered his resignation – the first of many such offers he was to make – over a decision to call up stand-by civilian reservists for military service in Aden, where the communist National Liberation Front was seeking to end British colonial rule, and wanted Wilson to cancel the trip altogether. Wilson crossed the Atlantic anyway, and, on arrival in New York he received a telegram from Brown demanding a call. He decided to ignore it and continued with his itinerary. After a speech to the Economic Club at the Waldorf Astoria, Wilson flew to Washington the next day, where he lunched with Johnson at the White House. The Australian government had committed a battalion to Vietnam. Wilson welcomed this, though pointed out that this added to Britain's 'Malaysian burdens since although the Australians were partners in Malaysia their contribution was much smaller than ours . . .' Johnson did not press the matter of Britain sending troops.[62] Wilson left the next day having achieved a workable position: 'The American Government would not be deflected from its military task; but, equally, he [Johnson] would give full backing to any British initiative which had any chance of getting peace-talks on the move.'[63]

Getting an initiative off the ground proved easier said than done. A Commonwealth mission suggested at the Marlborough House conference in June was turned down by North Vietnam in a broadcast from Hanoi on 1 July. Wilson tried a different approach: Harold Davies, then parliamentary secretary at the Ministry of Pensions and National Insurance, had previously visited Hanoi, and had written about Ho Chi Minh, independence movement leader and North Vietnamese president. Wilson instructed Davies to ask two North Vietnamese journalists in London, who were a *de facto* diplomatic presence for the regime, if he could visit. This was welcomed, but a leak while Davies was en route undermined his secret mission and he was only allowed to see party officials on arrival in North Vietnam, not Ho Chi Minh, making no progress. There was more positive news later in the year. Soviet foreign minister Andrei Gromyko agreed to Michael Stewart's proposal 'that we should re-activate the long-standing but often dormant Disarmament Conference' founded to foster dialogue between the superpowers and avoid nuclear war.[64]

Again, Wilson used a direct approach in the meeting with Johnson. He told him directly that the bombing should be suspended to see if there could be negotiations, and made clear that if American aircraft bombed Hanoi or Haiphong, he would dissociate Britain from it. Wilson also told Johnson, bluntly, that, while Britain remained committed to a limited East of Suez presence, there would be substantial cuts to defence expenditure. Johnson not only supported Wilson on Rhodesia, he also said he regarded Britain's role as trying to bring the parties to the conference table. Wilson, happy with progress, flew to Philadelphia to see Robin, who was then a post-graduate at Pennsylvania before going on to Canada to meet Lester Pearson, who offered support for the oil airlift to Zambia. The good news kept coming. Johnson announced a bombing pause over Christmas.

Wilson could relax, and address other matters. He made his first visit to Stoke Mandeville Hospital on Boxing Day: he and Mary spent several hours speaking to the disabled children; Wilson was to become a strong supporter of the work done there. The Wilson family left for their Christmas trip to the Scillies in good spirits.

One issue above all others now dominated: the date of the general election.

His first task was to navigate the Commonwealth prime ministers' conference held in Lagos, Nigeria, from 10 to 12 January 1966, called for the sole purpose of discussion about dealing with Smith. Wilson once again sought to stave off pressure to use force. With one eye on an imminent general election, he offered a judgement that was going to come back to haunt him as the Smith regime remained in place in the years afterwards: 'the cumulative effects of the economic and financial sanctions might well bring the rebellion to an end within a matter of weeks rather than months.'[65]

Wilson flew to Zambia and then to Kenya to inspect the RAF airlift before, on his return to Britain, his attention turned to the Hull North by-election, called after the death of the sitting MP Henry Solomons on 7 November. On 21 January, Wilson announced a plan to build the Humber Bridge, hoping to capture voters with his vision of Hull as a link between the north and the Midlands, and western Europe. Though Wilson was reaching a position of having to go to the country in any event, the result of the by-election on 27 January, with a 4.5 per cent swing to Labour, increasing the majority from 1,181 to 5,351, meant there would never be a better time to call a general election.

The announcement had to wait as Wilson was visiting Moscow from 21 to 24 February. His initial challenge was who accompanied him. He had made the retired army colonel Alun Gwynne-Jones a peer, as Lord Chalfont, and appointed him minister of disarmament, so he joined the trip, as did Cousins, who had threatened to resign the previous September over incomes policy.[66] An attempt by Wilson to keep him in the government by making the Ministry of Technology a 'super-ministry' of Industry and Production was vetoed by a very angry Brown, who saw it as an attack on his bailiwick.[67] Cousins' presence on the visit was Wilson's latest attempt to prevent his resignation, and Cousins did remain in the government – for now. Chalfont, meanwhile, was afforded a six-hour talk at the North Vietnamese embassy. But Wilson was downbeat about

Vietnam: 'We did not make much progress . . . For the present we do not see any early moves.'[68] Yet the visit was well-received at home. It was noted that Wilson 'wore his Gannex [raincoat] with bulldog determination'.[69] Mary also accompanied him, and enjoyed a tea party with Mrs Brezhnev and Mrs Kosygin. It was the apparently cordial nature of the visit that created a positive impression. Wilson also confirmed he would not support West Germany having control of a nuclear weapon, a view he knew went down favourably in Moscow. The *Daily Express* reported: 'The Russians want to talk . . . they are anxious to keep open the line to London – and through London, to Washington . . .'[70]

While Wilson was away, on 22 February, Healey presented his latest Defence White Paper to parliament.[71] This was to generate controversy. The Polaris submarines would take over the UK nuclear commitment to NATO from 1969–70; indeed, the use of submarines to host the nuclear deterrent has endured to the present day. A commitment to a British military presence in the Far East was confirmed but with reductions. The withdrawal of British forces from Aden was announced for 1968; in the event, it was achieved in 1967. Further reductions were confirmed for Cyprus, Malta, Guyana and South-East Asia after the conflict with Indonesia was at an end. The decision to phase out aircraft carriers in the 1970s with none on order to replace them caused the resignations of the first sea lord, Sir David Lucen and the minister of defence for the Navy, Christopher Mayhew.

This did not, however, deflect Wilson from his intention to call an election. To prepare for this, he had also published *Purpose in Power*, a selection of his speeches as prime minister, as a follow-up to *Purpose in Politics*. In its introduction, Wilson emphasised the National Plan: the drive for exports would fund welfare, pensions, health and education: 'Purposeful planning, based on priorities . . . is not an act of Government imposed upon a people. It is a great and historic exercise of Government by consent.'[72] What Wilson was seeking was a parliamentary majority to put the plan into full effect. He announced the general election on 28 February, with polling day set for 31 March. He told BBC's *Panorama* that evening:

'I think the country wants a Government, a Government able to do the job of a government.'[73]

Wilson planned the campaign down to the last detail. He approved the appointment of an election business committee within government, chaired by him, making sure the election was run from 10 Downing Street: Callaghan, Stewart, Crossman, Bowden and Gunter were the other members.[74] The idea was to seek a mandate for Labour to complete its programme: a combination of reassurance and ambition captured in the slogan 'You know Labour government works'.[75] The next day, Callaghan announced an improving balance of payments position in the Commons.[76] On 18 March, Heath challenged Wilson to stop agriculture minister Fred Peart and Jay from making speeches around the country saying that it was impossible for Britain to enter the Common Market. Jenkins later said of Peart, an understated former school teacher who had risen to the rank of captain in the Royal Artillery during the Second World War, that he 'held great offices without flamboyance'.[77] At this time, though, Peart was attracting too much attention for Wilson's liking. Heath said it had 'always been known that Mr Wilson has been anti-European'. Wilson replied: 'Given a fair wind we will negotiate our way into the Common Market, head held high, not crawl in.' He mocked Heath for 'rolling on his back like a spaniel at any kind gesture from the French.' Heath called this 'poisonous' and 'filthy' and 'too sordid for words.'[78] Two days later, Wilson suggested that Smith's regime in Rhodesia was holding out for a Tory victory; Heath replied the next day accusing Wilson of breaking any residual national unity. Heath reiterated the need for talks; Wilson reiterated that force would not be used. But there was no sense the issue changed any people's minds.[79]

In his final appeal to the country, Wilson contrasted the thirteen wasted years from 1951–64 with Labour's achievements in office so far, including the National Plan, the rise in pensions, and the Rent Act of 1965 that had introduced security of tenure and independent officers to deal with disputes over rent. He was realistic, and said 'a hard road still lies ahead of us' but spoke of British history showing 'deep reserves of strength and power which are brought out to the full when Britain has a government prepared to tell people the facts.' He finished with a rhetorical flourish: 'This is your country – now let us join together to work for it.'[80]

Throughout the campaign, Wilson had celebrity status with the public. Marcia Williams recalled the personal ups and downs: she had shingles, and a schoolboy threw a stink bomb that hit Wilson in the eye. But it was the crowds that caught her eye: 'All the visits we made from the Adelphi Hotel in Liverpool to the constituency with Harold were an absolute joy.'[81] On election night, people gathered outside Wilson's count in Huyton to clap and cheer as local people delivered him a majority of 20,940, as the prime minister took 41,122 votes against 20,182 for his Conservative opponent.[82] The election produced a landslide victory across the country with Labour winning 364 seats, taking 13.1 million votes to the Conservatives' 253 seats and 11.4 million votes. Labour now had a majority of 97: Wilson's handling of the 1964–66 parliament had proved a triumph.

Chapter 12

The pound in your pocket

Landslide to Devaluation

Labour's general election victory in 1966 gave the party what was, at the time, the second-largest parliamentary majority in its history, second only to 1945. What was all the more remarkable was that the Conservatives had won a majority of 100 less than seven years before. Wilson had turned national opinion around in a short time frame, and secured 48 per cent of the popular vote. The spring and summer of 1966 should have seen the prime minister ascendant over the country and his party. Wilson had offered personal leadership throughout. Callaghan summed this up, praised the timing of the poll as 'flawless, as was Harold Wilson's conduct of the campaign . . .'[1]

While the general election secured the government in office, Wilson did not take the opportunity it offered to make decisive decisions on major issues. Remarkably, he received criticism for his campaign despite winning a landslide. Castle wrote: 'I felt the campaign was merely an unavoidable hiatus in our work and I think this is what the country felt: they had made up their minds at the start and they remained unchanged. I was disappointed in Harold's performances. I know he was tired before he started but he failed to strike any new notes – not even the old one about modernization.'[2] This was partly Wilson's own fault. He did not seek to capitalise on the result. That he did not do so was a matter of temperament and approach. On 1 April, in the Number Ten lift, he told Williams: 'Now we can have a rest from politics'.[3] Momentarily,

Wilson clearly hoped the election would mean a quieter life, and he had no intention of acting so as to create conflict. Wilson had disagreed with Gaitskell's approach of confronting his own party, preferring to put the cause of party unity first. This meant that Wilson often managed people and sought to give them what they wanted to keep them happy. Far from seeing the swelled numbers on the government benches as providing the perfect moment to stamp his personal authority on the government, Wilson saw the newly elected Labour MPs as yet another set of problems to deal with. The prime minister met Ayub Khan, the president of Pakistan, after the election, and spent a weekend with him at Chequers. They were practising their putting on the drawing-room carpet. 'How is your handicap, Harold?' asked Khan. 'Up from 3 to 97,' replied Wilson.[4]

There were no major cabinet changes. Cledwyn Hughes replaced the seventy-five-year-old Griffiths as secretary of state for Wales. Fred Lee was moved from the Ministry of Power to the Colonial Office, keeping him in cabinet as a solid vote in support of Wilson but at a department declining in importance. Wilson replaced him with a Gaitskellite, Richard Marsh. Aged thirty-eight, dark-haired and charismatic, Marsh was seen as a possible leader in the future.[5] George Thomson, an ally of Callaghan, became chancellor of the Duchy of Lancaster, replacing Houghton, who was kept on as minister without portfolio. Houghton was to be replaced by Gordon Walker in January 1967, and, three months later, Houghton became chair of the liaison committee between Labour backbenchers and the cabinet, and chaired the Parliamentary Labour Party, a position of great influence. Also significant for the future were the talented newcomers that were promoted to junior ministerial level. Shirley Williams was appointed to the Ministry of Labour. The daughter of the political scientist George Catlin and the feminist author Vera Brittain, Williams had been brought up in an intellectual household, yet she was not a remote character. Her clear, personable way of speaking was to give her a great popular appeal as a politician in the years ahead. Wilson told her she could be party leader.[6] The energetic David Ennals and the hard-working Merlyn Rees joined the Ministry of Defence; Peter Shore was put in at Technology and the highly able supporter of Roy Jenkins, Dick Taverne, went to the Home Office.

One person who did assert herself in this period was Marcia Williams. Mitchell left to join the Department for Economic Affairs having completed a standard two-year spell as principal private secretary at Downing Street. Wilson then took the opportunity to appoint a principal private secretary whom he thought Marcia could work with constructively, and chose Michael Halls, who had been his private secretary at the Board of Trade. Sir Laurence Helsby, permanent secretary to the Treasury and head of the Home Civil Service, told Wilson it was improper for him to choose a candidate in this way. Wilson overruled him: 'If I am told that this is a question of patronage and challenged to choose between Prime Ministerial patronage and patronage exercised by a small, self-perpetuating oligarchy of Permanent Secretaries, I have no alternative but to say that patronage, if patronage it be, must be exercised by me.'[7] Williams immediately spoke to Halls about changes. The 'Garden Girls' were all from wealthy backgrounds; Marcia sought to open up the system of recruitment: 'By 1970 the girls with the twin-set and pearls had largely gone.' She also agreed a system for dealing with the vast quantities of letters received by the prime minister: colour-coding would identify letters sent to departments for civil servants to draft replies using the information at their disposal which would be edited by the political office. Balogh moved into an office on the second floor, no longer cut off from the centre of power. Williams put in place a timetable for Wilson to meet all the newly elected MPs on a Wednesday evening. Yet she later recalled: 'I hated that summer. It all seemed so disillusioning after such a terrific election victory. We had won, yet we didn't seem to have won.'[8]

On 16 May, the National Union of Seamen (NUS) launched a national strike – the first since 1911. The issue was that a conventional five-day working week was not possible at sea. In April 1965, in order to compensate for the additional hours being worked on Saturdays and Sundays, a wage increase had been agreed that the shipowners claimed represented an increase of 13 per cent. In 1966, with some shipowners having forced seamen to work extra hours on weekends, breaking the spirit of the settlement, the union argued for the seven-day-a-week wage becoming the five-day-a-week wage, with overtime for weekends. As Wilson said in a television broadcast on the night the strike was declared: 'This would mean an increase of 17 per cent over and above the 13 per cent or so increase agreed last year.'[9] Wilson and Gunter had offered an immediate 3 per cent increase with a court of inquiry into working conditions at sea, which had been rejected by the union. Wilson denounced the strike as unnecessary and warned about its stark consequences. First, a 17 per cent increase would wreck the government's prices and incomes policy: on 8 April 1965, in advance of the Prices and Incomes Board starting work the following month, a government White Paper had set a 'pay norm' of 3 per cent to 3.5 per cent. Breaking this would cause unemployment. Second, confining the whole merchant shipping fleet to harbour, ceasing trade across the seas, would have dire consequences for the balance of payments.

If it was a chess game, Wilson at least had the advantage of seeing his opponent's thinking before the next move. For MI5 was regularly updating him on the communist activity in the NUS that he was convinced was at the core of the dispute. At the same time, while the evidence from MI5 strengthened Wilson's resolve, it also meant that there was a substantial part of the material he could not make available even to colleagues, meaning that his public statements could appear ill-judged. On 19 May, Sir Charles Cunningham, permanent secretary at the Home Office, forwarded the first of many reports from Martin Furnival Jones, director general of MI5. Furnival Jones's briefings sat alongside the civil service notes on Wilson's desk, with the NUS headquarters having been bugged. Furnival Jones thought the problem lay not in communist dominance of the wider union, but in the way the party had secured positions of influence within its leadership. Of the four members of the negotiating committee elected from the floor at the Union AGM, the chair, Gordon Norris, was a Communist Party member, and two others were said to be sympathisers. The chair of the Victoria and Albert Docks committee, Jack Coward, and the chair of the Liverpool strike committee, Roger Woods, were also party members. Furnival Jones felt that the communist influence was sufficient to extend the stoppage.[10]

On 23 May, Wilson made a statement in the Commons on the proclamation of a State of Emergency the next day. In the event, the additional government powers were not used. As Wilson later reported to the Commons on 14 June, that was because there had 'been little interference with the main flow of essential supplies for this country.'[11] In order to find a way to end the dispute, Wilson appointed a court of inquiry under Lord Pearson on 26 May. The scale of the problem was enormous. On 3 June Wilson was told that, on 16 May, there were 6,500 strikers; by 2 June it was 20,750, and was projected to rise to 30,000 on 13 June.[12] Wilson, as a statistician, pressed the civil service to collect different figures. He asked for numbers on British ocean-going ships compared with foreign, and a comparison with a normal month. He was initially told 'normal month' figures would be a 'big task'. But the prime minister did have some success, as the information he was provided with became more detailed. He was given figures on the number of ships delayed every day, distinguishing between crews on home trade agreements, and those on foreign trade agreements.[13]

When Pearson reported on 8 June, he suggested an immediate 48-hour week, reducing to 40 in a year's time with an increase in annual leave. The estimated cost of settlement amounted to just under 5 per cent in the first year and 4.5 per cent in the second year. The next day, Furnival Jones reported to Wilson that the report of the court of inquiry was rejected as a basis for negotiation by the NUS political committee on the basis of press summaries without the members even viewing the document.[14] Wilson's concerns about communist influence were fed by the Americans; when he discussed the seamen's strike with Dean Rusk, the US secretary of state 'commented that he had been disturbed by the extent of Communist Party activity in the United States over Vietnam'.[15]

Wilson hosted both sides for talks at Downing Street on Friday,

17 June, the first significant example of what became known as his 'beer and sandwiches' approach to solving industrial disputes. When the NUS chose to continue the strike action, Wilson's patience snapped. On Monday, 20 June, he told the Commons: 'It is difficult for us to appreciate the pressures which are being put on men I know to be realistic and reasonable . . . by this *tightly knit group of politically motivated men* [author's emphasis] who . . . are now determined to exercise backstage pressures, forcing great hardship on the members of the union and their families, and endangering the security of the industry and the economic welfare of the nation.'[16] An incensed Shore rang Benn to say it was 'completely bonkers' and Benn agreed: 'I think I share that view.'[17]

Castle wrote that she 'couldn't find anyone in the Cabinet who thought it very clever'. In cabinet the next day, she asked for details. Wilson said, 'there were some things that were better not revealed'. Cousins said 'such a statement was hardly calculated to help end the strike.'[18] The problem was that Wilson was speaking on the basis of evidence only he was seeing.

The news from Furnival Jones was more positive: 'The Communist Party's reaction to the Prime Minister's statement is predictably to regard it as a smear.' John Gollan, the Communist Party's general secretary, was, however, defeatist: 'he would be surprised if the strike lasted another week.'[19] Emboldened, Wilson did not back down, telling the Commons on 28 June: 'Time and again in this dispute the Communist Party's objectives have rapidly become the policy of the executive.'[20] Wilson said the objective of the Communists was to destroy his prices and incomes policy. He named the people he thought were responsible, including Bert Ramelson, the Communist Party's national industrial organiser and Dennis Goodwin, another official who was his effective deputy. Others included Gordon Norris, on the negotiating committee, and chairs of strike committees like Jack Coward in London and Roger Woods in Liverpool.

That debate was also significant in souring the relationship between Wilson and Heath. The leader of the opposition posed the question: 'When the Prime Minister says that he doubts whether the members of the executive were their own masters, is his conclusion justified?'[21] Wilson was incensed. He had seen the Conservative leader with MI5 officers privately, and given him the information he had. These meetings between senior politicians – known as happening 'on Privy Council terms' – are important for sharing information on national security. They are based on mutual trust, without which the system would break down. Wilson complained afterwards that Heath 'exploited my weakness': having had such a confidential briefing, Heath was demanding information that he knew Wilson could never make public as he could not disclose the source of it: the security services. Wilson thought it was contemptible behaviour and, while there was never a complaint around him not behaving entirely properly towards Heath with sharing sensitive information in the years afterwards, it left him with a profoundly negative view that did not change.[22] The feeling was mutual: Heath did 'tend to strongly dislike his political opponents' and 'hated' Wilson.[23] At Prime Minister's Questions, Wilson usually bested Heath. As Patrick Cosgrave, a speech-writer for Heath and Thatcher put it, it was a 'game which never interested Mr Heath very much, and at which he was, to put it mildly, not very good'.[24] Wilson, in contrast, was a master, well-prepared, quick-thinking, and able to use the arena for party management, treating his backbenchers with great respect: 'he recalled their special interests and referred to them in his almost invariably lengthy replies; and he always looked over his shoulder at them.'[25] This all said, Heath did treat Wilson and his family with a personal respect and dignity.[26]

In any event, the strike was coming to an end. On 29 June, the NUS executive voted 29–16 to settle on the basis of 48 days' annual leave rather than 39 as Pearson had proposed. The 56-hour week would be immediately reduced to 48, with a further reduction to 40 within a year. The victory for Wilson was that the NUS made concessions – fewer men on navigation watch and giving up overtime pay for bank holidays spent at sea – to ensure that the cost was the same as the original Pearson framework. Wilson had used MI5 extensively, though – within months MPs were convinced that they themselves were also having their telephones tapped.

Wilson assured parliamentarians that this was not the case, and the 'Wilson Doctrine' was born: MPs could not have their communications intercepted by the security services.[27] In any event, on 1 July, the 47-day strike was over.

That same day, Wilson spoke with Brown and Callaghan at what became known as the 'blue skies' meeting as Callaghan advised that the ending of the seamen's strike had stabilised the situation, meaning no special action by the government was necessary. The positive atmosphere did not last. On 3 July, Cousins resigned, the day before the publication of the Prices and Incomes Bill. Cousins could have accepted price control but thought incomes control penalised trade unions.[28] This gave Benn his big chance, as Wilson appointed him to the Ministry of Technology in Cousins' place. Benn later recalled that his 'brief from Wilson was to try to improve industrial performance by micro-economic measures such as mergers . . .' Benn became frustrated as time went on, believing '(a) that it would not work, (b) that it was corporatist, and (c) that it was anti-trade union and undemocratic.' From 1968, he saw himself as in conflict with Wilson, who prevented Benn from making speeches on a more radical agenda around the future of socialism.[29]

Benn had a deeply political family background. Both his grandfathers had been Liberal MPs. His father, William Wedgwood Benn had also been a Liberal MP, but he left the Liberal Party to join Labour, serving as secretary of state for India in the Labour government of 1929–31.[30] The Second World War was to have a profound impact on the family. In 1942, William Wedgwood Benn was appointed to the House of Lords. This meant a hereditary peerage, and he became the First Viscount Stansgate. This seemed of little concern to Tony Benn, his second son, who himself served in the Royal Air Force from 1943. Yet, the following year, Michael, his older brother, also in the Royal Air Force, died in an aviation accident. This meant Tony Benn would inherit the peerage on his father's death and would enter the House of Lords. Benn's distinctive, cultivated accent was evidence of his aristocratic background, but he fought against inheriting his father's title after his death in

1960, since it meant him having to give up his seat in the House of Commons. Initially, Benn was disqualified from being an MP as he automatically inherited the title, resulting in a by-election in his Bristol South East constituency in 1961. A defiant Benn stood and won the most votes but was barred from taking his seat. The situation forced a change in the law, the Peerage Act 1963, that allowed him to disclaim the peerage, stand in a further by-election, and win his seat back.[31] It confirmed Benn as a determined, ambitious man, unafraid of taking on the establishment to which his background had given him great access. His education was a privileged one, from Westminster School to New College Oxford, where he read Philosophy, Politics and Economics and was president of the Oxford Union. In short, Benn had all the credentials to emerge as a political threat to Wilson in the longer term.

For now, there were far more immediate issues. On 4 July, a £49m fall in the gold reserves showed a further drain on sterling. A visit from Georges Pompidou on 6 July added to the problems, as it was briefed that the French prime minister thought devaluation unavoidable prior to British entry into the Common Market. Wilson thought the French were seeking to weaken the dollar–sterling axis by encouraging attacks on the pound: 'Politically motivated men were not confined to the seamen's executive,' he noted wryly.[32] Leslie O'Brien, who had succeeded Cromer as governor of the Bank of England after the general election, found himself using the reserves to stabilise the pound as short-selling intensified again. O'Brien – a Wandsworth Grammar School boy whom Wilson liked – had a significant influence. He was against a unilateral devaluation, though he thought it might be necessary if Britain joined the Common Market. He urged Wilson to increase the bank rate, given rising interest rates abroad.

When cabinet met on 12 July, there was an air of hopelessness about it. Brown was in favour of immediate devaluation in order to pursue a policy of industrial expansion, without which he thought the National Plan was doomed. Wilson did not think devaluation would save the National Plan since it would need tough, accompanying measures to divert resources from the domestic market to exports in any event: 'when we did devalue, with a much less strained economy, this was shown to be the case.'[33] Tony Crosland complained that he did not want to repeat what he saw as the mistakes of July 1965: 'He didn't want us once again combating inflation by cutting public expenditure.' Dick Crossman agreed and told Callaghan: 'the essence of a socialist policy is a shift from private to public expenditure . . . There can be no question of a cut-back.' Callaghan told the cabinet 'frankly that he didn't know how we were going to get out of the mess.'[34]

The next day, returning from Sussex University where he had been awarded an honorary degree, Wilson 'heard a suggestion that under George Brown's pressure Jim Callaghan was weakening.' But the prime minister was strong: 'It was the first time this had been suggested, and I made it plain that there would be no devaluation. We were going to fight. If, in the end, we lost, then the world would know we had done everything to avoid it, and would know that we had not chosen devaluation as an easy way out.' As he put it himself: 'That settled it . . .'[35] Sir William Armstrong, permanent secretary at the Treasury, thought that 'Harold browbeat Jim. Jim retreated.'[36] Callaghan recalled: 'I was strongly against devaluation, and believed it could be avoided, but I reluctantly concluded that our lack of action was making it inevitable.'[37]

Since there was still no agreement on what measures to take, Wilson gave what amounted to a holding, non-specific statement in the House of Commons on 14 July: 'I have repeatedly made it clear that the Government will not hesitate to take whatever measures we regard as necessary to ensure the balance of the economy, to strengthen our balance of payments and to maintain the strength of sterling.'[38] The bank rate was raised to 7 per cent. Later, in the Commons tea room, Wilson told Castle, who disliked the idea of British entry into the Common Market, that Brown and Callaghan were plotting to overthrow him: 'You know what the game is: devalue and get into Europe. We've got to scotch it.'[39] That same day, Labour was defeated in a by-election in Carmarthen caused by the death of Megan Lloyd George. Her 9,233 majority in 1966 became a 2,436 majority for Plaid Cymru's Gwynfor Evans.

It hardly mattered in terms of the size of the government majority, but it certainly added to the sense of crisis.

Wilson departed for Moscow on Saturday, 16 July to view the British Trade Fair as Kosygin's guest, and to press for peace in Vietnam. 'Government urged to act quickly as pound takes a hammering' was the headline in the *Guardian*. Several months later, in October, rumours surfaced that, at this moment, there was a significant move to replace Wilson with Callaghan as head of a coalition government.[40] A coalition was never a possibility, and there was no organised plot. Indeed, Wilson himself gave inconsistent accounts. He told Benn: 'Roy Jenkins and his gang decided to get rid of George Brown and to make Jim Callaghan No. 2, with a view to getting Roy in as No. 1.'[41] The 'plot' was based on Wilson's belief that a meeting to discuss deposing him had taken place that July weekend at Ann Fleming's country house at Sevenhampton in Wiltshire. Wigg had passed on information from Fleming's friend Lady Pamela Berry, the wife of Baron Hartwell, proprietor of the *Daily Telegraph*. Jenkins was staying there; Brown was at the Durham Miners' Gala and Callaghan was in Sussex.[42] Jenkins spoke separately to Brown, who threatened to resign if Wilson pursued deflation, and Callaghan, who sent Neild to discuss a 3–6 month delay in devaluation with the chancellor. The Jenkins–Callaghan plot against Brown *and* Wilson was not a realistic possibility. The actual danger to Wilson was if Brown and Callaghan had combined against him.

On the Sunday, Wilson duly received a cable from Brown threatening resignation. The next day, Castle found Brown 'brooding ominously in his vast room. He had drunk enough to be voluble, though not offensive.'[43] The first secretary was adamant he was not going to let Wilson get away with imposing a policy of deflation and austerity and wanted to have it out in cabinet. He said he knew he would lose, and then would resign. Castle told him she thought he would win. Brown said, 'No, I can't win because a Cabinet can't sack the Prime Minister. You wouldn't have me for Leader, would you?' Castle told him no. 'There you are then . . . But I'm not going to wear this. And you will side with him.'[44] Castle records

Benn joining the conversation at this point; according to Benn, Brown was 'in a state of high excitement'.[45] But in his diary Benn also records Castle firmly telling Brown she did not want him as Leader. The two diarists' accounts are, therefore, not identical, but there can be no doubting Castle's loyalty to Wilson. Meanwhile, Wigg kept Wilson up to date with matters at home, though he only reported 'idle chatter' and no major move in cabinet.[46]

Wilson returned to London on Tuesday, 19 July on a 7 a.m. flight. The cabinet then met at 5 p.m. for a marathon session, not finishing until 9.45 p.m., and even then the gathering only broke up due to senior ministers having to attend Buckingham Palace for the state visit of King Hussein of Jordan. The formal decision was made not to devalue. Rather, the government would use a strategy of deflation and austerity. Wilson dominated the discussion, opening with a strong statement of opinion. He set out the disadvantages to an immediate devaluation. Should this be to a lower, fixed rate, other countries might well follow suit, meaning any advantage would be short-lived. Should the government decide to move to a floating pound, this could encourage other countries to act in a similar way when facing economic problems. Stability of export prices was in any event an argument against a floating currency. Wilson was dextrous in playing for time: 'If the choice lay simply between devaluation and the maintenance of full employment, he would prefer to devalue. In fact, however, it did not appear that we had reached the point at which devaluation was inevitable.'[47] Crossman and Jenkins put the case for devaluation. Jay spoke against, on the basis that the 1949 devaluation had solved nothing. Brown made his case for devaluation, as did Castle, who felt that freeing Britain from monetary obligations to the United States would lessen political obligations. Benn closed the discussion with an argument in favour of devaluation.[48] Wilson won the vote by 17 votes to 6 but, ominously, Brown, who was in the minority, repeated his view that an immediate devaluation was the wiser course and reserved his position.[49] Wilson said, calmly, that this was not for discussion in cabinet and indicated had the decision gone the other way he would have considered his position. Later, over a drink, he chided

Castle for disagreeing with him, saying those who wanted to devalue to enter the Common Market had pulled the wool over her eyes. She worried that Wilson would not trust her again: 'Behind that blandness he never forgets'.[50]

Cabinet resumed the next day at 9 a.m. to sign off the details of the measures Wilson proposed to announce.[51] Wilson then addressed the House of Commons that afternoon. To reduce private demand, the government restricted the availability of hire purchase: increasing the down payments required to secure credit, and reducing the period for repayment. There were increases in alcohol and fuel duties, and Purchase Tax, the forerunner of VAT.[52] Supertax on high incomes – then called surtax – was increased. Public investment was cut by £55 million in 1967–8. Government overseas expenditure was reduced by £100 million. Private overseas expenditure was also restricted, with a £50 allowance for travel outside the sterling area. To encourage overseas visitors to Britain, the government introduced a one-year scheme of loan assistance to build or modernise hotels.[53]

Wilson declared the end of voluntary wage restraint, pointing out that, since the Declaration of Intent of December 1964, incomes had been rising faster than production: in 1965, of the £1,300 million increase in wages, only £600 million had been earned through increased production. Wage increases had often been above the 3.5 per cent norm: 'The Government are now calling for a six-month standstill on wages, salaries and other types of income, followed by a further six months of severe restraint, and for a similar standstill on prices.'[54] In response, Heath attacked Wilson directly: 'Does the Prime Minister recognise that it is fundamentally a crisis of confidence in himself and his Administration?'[55]

Brown's future was in the balance. He was absent from the frontbench while Wilson spoke, and, later that evening, *Coronation Street* was interrupted with a news flash on his departure from the government. Wilson had the roughest of evenings. With Brown refusing to speak to the CBI and TUC to discuss the measures, Wilson had to conduct the meetings himself, as well as make a live TV broadcast. All the while the leader of the House and the whips were relaying tales about the efforts from MPs – letters and pleadings – going to Brown to urge him to stay in the government. Later that evening, at 10.30 p.m., he returned to Number Ten to speak to Wilson. Wilson cleverly boxed him in. First, Wilson told him that if his mind was made up on resignation, he would not talk him out of it. Second, when Brown asked to be made lord privy seal – a non-economic portfolio in which he could escape full responsibility for the tough measures – Wilson wisely refused. Brown desultorily consulted with Bowden and Wigg before caving in to Wilson. He left Number Ten and announced that he had changed his mind: 'We've decided at the end of the day that my duty is to stay . . . and to bring the country to a point where we can once again resume our policies of expansion.'[56] The immediate crisis had been averted: Wilson had at least provided some economic certainty and, by keeping Brown in the government, staved off political instability. There was, however, a portent of trouble ahead. That same evening, Cousins, back as general secretary of the TGWU, appeared on television to announce that the union would not accept the pay freeze.[57]

Nonetheless, a relieved Wilson boarded an RAF Comet to Washington on 28 July: he 'suddenly felt once again like a schoolboy going on holiday. I had some ten hours free of meetings, telephones and colleagues . . .'[58] After reading his briefing notes and refuelling at Gander in Newfoundland, he slept before having a quick drink with Dean Rusk on arrival at Blair House, opposite the White House. The previous weeks had taken their toll on him, but he bounced back: 'For the first time since going to No. 10 I asked for a sleeping pill, in case I came to at English waking-time.' Wilson managed 'eleven and half hours' sleep, and was fully recovered'.[59] The next day, when he met Johnson, Wilson was surprised at the warmth of the reception, given events in Vietnam and the sterling crisis. Johnson showered him with compliments: '. . . I must say that England is blessed now, as it was then, with gallant and hardy leadership. In you, sir, she has a man of mettle . . .'[60]

Wilson then left for Ottawa to meet Lester Pearson before dashing back to London just in time for the month's main event:

the football World Cup Final at Wembley on 30 July. Pearson bet Wilson five dollars that England would lose. This was at least one piece of currency that was coming into the sterling area. Wilson touched down at 1.10 p.m. in time for the kick-off at 3 p.m. England's famous 4–2 victory after extra time gave him one record that has still not been broken: that England only win the World Cup under a Labour government. At the celebration at the Royal Garden Hotel that night, Wilson and Brown were back in harness. Wilson was proposing toasts in Russian to the Soviet team that had reached the semi-finals, and Brown led his table singing West Ham United's anthem in honour of captain Bobby Moore: 'I'm forever blowing bubbles'. Thus, the month ended in a rare moment of shared celebration.[61] On 2 August, Wilson even managed to reference the victory at Prime Minister's Question Time. Conservative MP, Ian Lloyd, said that the idea of 'sides of industry' was as obsolete as the debunked phlogiston theory that flammable objects contained a substance called phlogiston that was released during the process of burning. Wilson was playful: 'I do not think that I want at this point the make a pronouncement about the phlogiston theory. I would rather make one about the World Cup.'[62]

When cabinet met on 4 August, Wilson was keen to emphasise the support of the bankers for the decision not to devalue. He, Brown and Callaghan had met representatives of the financial sector who 'had been unanimous in rejecting a devaluation of sterling'.[63] Callaghan was firm that it 'was now essential that the Cabinet should dismiss devaluation from consideration . . .'[64] Yet, in reality, the crisis marked the end of Wilson's ascendancy over the British political scene. A brutal *Private Eye* front cover on 5 August featured an inebriated-looking Brown saying 'Brothers, we're on our way out.'[65] The prime minister was now mortgaging the future on the deflationary measures being effective. As he told the party conference later in the year: 'The July measures, in fact, must now provide us with a once-for-all opportunity to break the whole miserable cycle we inherited.'[66] Instead of devaluing while he had a large parliamentary majority, with Brown in favour, and

Callaghan persuadable, Wilson now left himself at the mercy of events.

What remained within his control was the shape of his cabinet. Before he left for the Isles of Scilly on 11 August, the prime minister conducted a major reshuffle. First, he gave Brown the job he craved, as foreign secretary, to drive the process of entry into the EEC. For Wilson, he was 'the appropriate leader for the task . . .'[67] Brown swapped jobs with Stewart, who took his move with good grace. With the ongoing situation in Rhodesia, Wilson thought Bowden, who had shown patient temperament and sound judgement as leader of the House of Commons, would be the ideal candidate to deal with Smith, so moved him to Commonwealth Relations. Crossman, who loved the minutiae of parliamentary procedure, replaced Bowden. Wilson also created a new ministerial committee on economic policy, the 'Steering Committee on Economic Policy' which he would chair himself; Attlee had created a similar economic policy committee after the currency crisis in 1947.

The problem was that the moves were four months too late. By August, the National Plan was effectively finished, with the proposed 25 per cent increase in output little more than a pipe-dream. Yet Brown's yearning for the foreign affairs post was longstanding. Rather than offer it to him to manage him after a crisis, Brown could have been given the job after the 1966 general election. After all, in the queen's speech on 21 April, the government made clear its readiness to enter the EEC if national and Commonwealth interests could be protected.

The summer of 1966 also marked a step-change in Wilson's relationship with the press. As Margach wrote, when he 'became leader . . . and indeed in the first eighteen months of his Premiership, he had the sunniest honeymoon, in my experience, of any national leader.'[68] Now he became increasingly preoccupied with what cabinet members were whispering in the ears of journalists and what was written about him. He operated a 'leak procedure' whereby civil servants would establish which ministers had access to particular information then issue questionnaires to the cabinet to find out who had been talking to which journalist.

In June 1966, Wilson, furious with an account in *The Times* of the cabinet decision on 25 May to contract out of the European Space Vehicle Launcher Development Organisation on grounds of cost, demanded all ministers fill in a questionnaire, though he had little success in finding the culprit. He pored over the newspapers and what certain reporters were interested in. He had a particular issue with Nora Beloff of the *Observer* and her interest in Marcia Williams and the 'Kitchen Cabinet': 'She is a dedicated enemy of this Government – takes everything straight to Heath.'[69] When the Thomson Organisation was looking to take over *The Times*, Roy Thomson asked the prime minister his advice. Wilson said the first thing he would do was sack the political correspondent, David Wood, whom he was convinced was biased against him. Wilson also sought the sacking of Harold Hutchinson, political correspondent on the *Daily Herald* (later the *Sun*), on the basis he was a Gaitskellite who treated him unfairly.[70] Friends became concerned about the depth of his obsession: 'I think Harold is getting quite pathological about the press' wrote a worried Castle.[71]

It was in early 1967 that open hostility broke out after a major issue arose over the D-Notice system: the voluntary arrangement whereby notices were issued to newspaper editors, the BBC and other outlets giving guidance as to what should not be published in the interests of national security. The Services, Press and Broadcasting Committee issuing them was chaired by the permanent under-secretary of state at the Ministry of Defence, and the press nominated representatives to sit around the table with officials.[72] Notices were observed with little controversy. It was in this context that Wilson, by his own admission, made 'one of my costliest mistakes of our near six years in office'.[73]

On 21 February 1967, Chapman Pincher, an investigative journalist, who found fame in unearthing state secrets and conspiracies, had a front-page story in the *Daily Express* claiming that telegraph cables being sent by members of the public 'were regularly made available to the security services for scrutiny'.[74] Wilson, answering a parliamentary question later that day, waded in, calling it 'a sensationalised and inaccurate story purporting to describe a situation in which in fact the powers and practice have not changed for well over 40 years.'[75] He added that the *Daily Express* had breached two D-Notices, after it had been repeatedly warned publication of the article would contravene them.

The next day, the *Daily Express* published a statement insisting that the secretary of the D-Notice Committee, Colonel Sammy Lohan, had confirmed it was not in breach of a D-Notice, though he had urged the newspaper not to publish the story. Heath pressured Wilson to appoint a committee of privy counsellors to look into it. Wilson thought he had a way out by asking the Services, Press and Broadcasting Committee itself to investigate, but its press representatives refused to sit in judgement on the *Daily Express*. Wilson therefore conceded, with Lord Radcliffe chairing a committee of privy counsellors with Selwyn Lloyd and Manny Shinwell as the other members. When it reported on 13 June, it was disastrous for Wilson. It found that the *Daily Express* had not been warned that publication breached a D-Notice, and that, in going ahead with its front-page splash, it had done nothing wrong.[76] Wilson was incensed. He decided to publish a government White Paper in response disputing the findings on the issues around publication of the article. This centred on a lunch between Lohan and Pincher: Lohan had been under instructions from the Foreign Office to seek to block publication on D-Notice grounds. Wilson's case was that what he had said in the Commons in February was based on official advice; Lohan had not done what he was asked to do.[77] On 20 June, Lohan resigned on the basis that, given the government's view, his impartiality was undermined. That same day, Castle wrote that blame for Wilson's misjudgement lay with the 'evil genius . . . George Wigg – "Harold's Rasputin."' Brown and Burke Trend had begged Wilson not to take the line he did.[78]

Two days later, in a heated Commons debate, Wilson attacked Lohan's 'over-close association with journalists and especially with Mr Chapman Pincher' and said Lohan had not even been given 'full positive vetting clearance'.[79] Wilson had had suspicions of Lohan since a cocktail party at Pincher's house on 20 December 1966. He was a gossip and had passed on to Conservative MP Henry Kerby that a Labour minister was having an affair with a married woman with Communist connections. Kerby was a spy in the Conservative camp who provided information to Wigg. When he passed this on, Wigg immediately satisfied himself that there was no truth in the rumour, though he passed on details of the incident to Wilson. Wigg also secured information from MI5 about Lohan's links to journalists, including Pincher himself.[80]

Wilson secured Lohan's demise but it was at an enormous cost. One casualty was his relationship with Wigg, who had even ignored the Labour whip to vote in favour of the Common Market on 10 May. There was 'Coolness 'twixt Wigg and Wilson' as *The Times* reported.[81] Marcia Williams called the D-Notice affair the 'real watershed' in Wilson's relations with the press, coming after what the prime minister felt was hostile reporting on the seamen's strike and leadership plot.[82] Wilson ended his regular meetings with the parliamentary lobby journalists; and he grew evermore angry with them. When Wilson and Pincher met in 1978 to bury the hatchet, Wilson apologised and said, 'It was that dreadful fellow Lohan, that I was after, you know.'[83] His dealings with the press would never be the same again. Margach thought that Wilson's 'relations with Fleet Street might never have become as embittered as they did' had he not chosen to embroil himself in the D-Notice affair.[84]

While Wilson's relationship with Fleet Street deteriorated, sterling staged something of a recovery between September 1966 and April 1967. In this lull, Wilson decided to press ahead with the application for EEC membership. In October 1966, Johnson came out in favour of British membership. Wilson's case for joining was pragmatic and based on hard-headed economics. The proportion of exports from Commonwealth countries to the UK was falling, from 29 per cent in 1948 to 15 per cent by 1967; and the proportion of imports was on a downward trend, too: from 26 per cent in 1948 to 13 per cent in 1967.[85] Britain needed a new export market. Thus, Wilson and Brown began a charm offensive, touring the capitals of the six members states between December 1966 and March 1967.

Wilson then used the tactic of holding lengthy cabinet discussions, allowing everyone the chance to have their say, to decide on the application. He held seven cabinet meetings between 18 April and 2 May 1967, including two in one day on Sunday 30 April.[86] Castle wrote: 'I am more than ever convinced that Harold is now a dedicated European and that all this is shadow boxing.'[87] She scribbled a note to Benn: 'We shall go into Europe on a wave of exhaustion.' Benn replied, 'Just boring our way in.'[88] Wilson was, as ever, ingenious, leaving those opposed with the option of a further argument on the conditions for entry, once known. He concluded the discussions with a proposal for an 'unconditional application for negotiations about the conditions for entry.'[89] Seventy-four Labour MPs signed a statement published in *Tribune* on 5 May arguing, as Wilson had previously done, that the Treaty of Rome was about free competition within the Community rather than socialist planning. On 10 May, Wilson sent the formal application to Renaat van Elslande, chair of the Council of Ministers. It took only six days for de Gaulle to express his opposition. At a press conference on 16 May, while he did not formally exercise the veto, he argued that the entry of Britain into the Common Market would transform it into an entirely new entity.

Meanwhile, the bank rate was reduced to 5.5 per cent by early May. Callaghan was still working on the basis that the July 1966 measures were working and pursuing a policy of cautious reflation. In his budget of 11 April, he had started to ease hire purchase restrictions: first on motorcycles (much to Castle's annoyance, who thought them highly dangerous); then in June on cars and goods vehicles and then a wider easing including household durables on 30 August. In early September, pension increases were rolled out. However, events started to crowd in on Wilson. While trade figures for May, published on 13 June, showed a £41m balance of payments surplus, there was a trend of rising imports, exports had fallen, and unemployment was rising.[90]

The gamble on the July 1966 measures was not paying off. First, oil supplies were disrupted by the Nigerian Civil War. Emeka Ojukwu, the military governor of the Eastern Region of Nigeria, declared independence as the Republic of Biafra on 30 May 1967, with Yakubu Gowan's federal government troops attacking soon afterwards to put down the rebellion. There was a scramble to secure the revenues from the lucrative oil-producing Niger Delta. In cabinet on 25 July, Richard Marsh, minister of power, said that petrol rationing might have to be considered. Two days later, it was confirmed at cabinet that, with federal troops only thirty-five miles from Biafra's main oil refinery, it looked likely that the federal government would triumph, so it was in Britain's interests that the Shell oil company 'make payment of oil revenues to the Federal Government and none to Biafra.'[91] Many Labour backbenchers were outraged at the government supplying arms to the federal government. Wilson's argument for not imposing an embargo was thin: 'The problem is to get both sides to agree to a cease-fire. A limitation of arms would not, of itself, achieve that.'[92] Though Wilson visited Lagos in March 1969 to press for peace negotiations before Biafra surrendered in January 1970, this was a case of brutal *realpolitik*: to preserve oil supplies, Britain backed the likely winner in the civil war, while nearly two million Biafrans – including many children – starved to death. It was a discreditable episode; within Wilson's inner circle, Arnold Goodman took him to task, backing the Biafran cause. Goodman recalled that he 'made various futile efforts during the war to persuade Harold Wilson to a like view'.[93]

The oil supply situation was exacerbated by events in the Middle East. On 23 May 1967, Nasser declared the Straits of Tiran closed to Israeli shipping, meaning that access to and from Eilat, Israel's only port on the Red Sea, was blocked. Wilson had a deep, lifelong affiliation to Israel. Later, he wrote: 'In Britain, as in the United States, there has been and is very strong support for Israel and her people, from politicians and communities extending far beyond the relatively small numbers of Jews who are our citizens.' Wilson numbered himself among these politicians, and he reflected: 'How far this [support] is due to admiration for the courage and tenacity of the Israelis, how far – as is certainly true in my own case – it is in part a response to the teaching of religious history in our day schools and Sunday schools, chapels, churches, kirks and conventicles, I would find it hard to say.'[94] Learning about the history of the Jewish people had had a profound impact on Wilson, who abhorred the persecution and anti-Semitism suffered by the Jewish people over centuries. He was a passionate defender of Israel that he saw as a 'beleaguered . . . state' with its existence under threat.[95] The *Daily Mail* even suggested the prime minister's reaction to the Egyptian president's action was so angry that it was 'The Day Wilson Almost Went to War.'[96] Wilson denied this.[97] But he did tell Abba Eban, Israel's foreign minister, that '. . . Britain would join with others in an effort to open the Straits.'[98] Eban later reflected: 'Among European statesmen whom I have known, some have stood out in the special preoccupation that Israel evoked in their hearts. Harold Wilson is pre-eminent among these.'[99] Wilson had indeed secured cabinet backing for the use of force provided proposals 'were sufficiently international in character and that an acceptable military plan for this purpose could be devised.'[100] Wilson crossed the Atlantic to seek Canadian and American support for a declaration from maritime nations to support free passage for Israel. However, fighting broke out on 5 June in what became known as the Six Days War. The conflict between Israel, Syria, Jordan and Egypt, led to the closure of the Suez Canal, putting further pressures on trade. Until September Britain was also subject to a total Arab oil embargo.

Problems piled up. An unofficial docks strike involving 16,000 men also interfered with trade, particularly exports: by 18 September, almost all workers in Liverpool and Birkenhead were out, with some docks in London affected as well.[101] In August, the trade deficit was £27m; by September it was £52m, the largest for 15 months. Exports fell to £404m, the lowest since the measures of July 1966.[102] To seek to recapture momentum, in August 1967, Wilson made changes to the economic portfolios in cabinet. He decided to supervise the Department for Economic Affairs himself, with Shore as secretary of state; Stewart remained as first secretary of state with oversight of social policy. The anti-Market Jay was dismissed and replaced at the Board of Trade by Crosland, with Gordon Walker taking his former role at education. But, by 21 October, it was predicted that the government faced an end-of-year balance of payments deficit approaching £300m.[103]

Sterling was now under severe pressure. An increase in the bank rate to 6 per cent on 19 October was to no avail. With reserves falling fast, the limits of borrowing to maintain the parity had been reached. Alec Cairncross wrote to Callaghan on 2 November that all the measures taken to avoid devaluation had not worked. The next day he saw Callaghan in his room: he 'agreed that the government had been out of luck' but warned that credit lines could run out by the end of the month.[104] On 8 November, the Steering Committee on Economic Policy was in favour of devaluation.[105] Callaghan told Wilson sterling could not be held and that they should devalue ten days later. Another increase in the bank rate, to 6.5 per cent, on 9 November, was to no avail.

Such was the strain Wilson was under he was drinking whisky at the cabinet table, rather than water.[106] He continued to search for alternatives. Given his promise to Johnson on devaluation in 1964, and the fact that it would mean cuts in public expenditure and the end of the 'East of Suez' commitment, was it worth a trip to Washington to appeal to the American president for a package to support sterling? The idea was dismissed as it was thought such generosity would not pass Congress even if Johnson agreed, and despite telegrams across the Atlantic, no help was forthcoming.

On Saturday, 11 November, he met with Brown and Callaghan. There was no disagreement about devaluation, and Wilson floated the idea of creating an inner cabinet, an offer of more power for them to keep them loyal. Politically, they were not combining against him and remained rivals. They had a discussion on who might succeed Wilson if he fell under a bus. Callaghan claimed he had reached the limits of his ambition but would stand if Wilson was out of the way. Brown said he would not stand against him in that scenario; Callaghan said he thought Jenkins would. After Callaghan left, Brown said he was after Wilson's job and not to trust him. 'I had learnt a great deal about human nature,' noted Wilson.[107]

The reality was that the prime minister had no choice left. At a grim meeting on 16 November, cabinet agreed to a devaluation. Wilson put aside the formal agenda to ask Callaghan to speak first.

The chancellor said that on Saturday, 18 November, sterling should move 'to a new fixed parity of $2.40 to the pound . . . it marked the end of the economic strategy he had been pursuing hitherto; and he was prepared to draw the necessary conclusion as regards his personal position.' Callaghan added: 'If we attempted to hold the present parity, therefore, we should be liable to exhaust the reserves still available and should then be unable to defend even a reduced parity.'[108]

The date agreed, the formal announcement was made at 9.30 p.m., in order to avoid negative coverage in the Sunday newspapers. The bank rate was also raised to 8 per cent, and hire purchase regulations tightened back up; £100m was cut from defence expenditure, another £100m from capital expenditure on the nationalised industries, and the export rebate abolished, saving another £100m. Corporation tax was raised from 40 per cent to 42.5 per cent. On the Sunday, Wilson held a lunch with friendly journalists. He was, perhaps surprisingly, in buoyant mood. He felt a sense of release: '. . . devaluation has made me the most powerful Prime Minister since Walpole. I can do whatever I like now, my power is absolute in economic and financial policies.'[109]

What was now left was the prime ministerial TV broadcast to take place that evening. He recalled the impact of the 1949 devaluation when frightened people queued at bank counters convinced that their deposited pounds were now only worth seventeen shillings each. He wanted to counter this, and distinguish between the impact of devaluation at home and abroad. He was provided with a Treasury draft on the impact of devaluation: 'It does not mean that the money in our pockets is worth 14 per cent less to us now . . .' Wilson changed this to use the more alliterative 'pound' rather than 'money'.[110] He delivered the statement in sombre mood: 'From now on, the pound abroad is worth 14 per cent or so less in terms of other currencies. That doesn't mean, of course, that the pound here in Britain, in your pocket or purse or in your bank, has been devalued.'

This framing provoked a furore. Benn recorded in his diary: '. . . a great defeat for Harold. The following day he did his absurd broadcast on television saying, "The pound in your pocket won't be devalued.'"[111] Wilson was right in the sense that anyone with a hundred pounds in savings still had a hundred pounds in savings after devaluation. But its *value* in terms of purchasing goods and currency from abroad had been diminished. Two days later, in the Commons, Heath attacked him: 'It will be remembered as the most dishonest statement ever made, even by the Prime Minister.'[112] A letter from a member of the public in Bournemouth summed up the problem. In the process of emigrating to Australia, her family had lost £673 in currency exchange. This meant her sons, age 14 and 11, who had been saving, had lost money: 'I hold you personally responsible for our loss . . .'[113] On 23 November, Peter Jay, then economic editor of *The Times*, and who had been a Treasury civil servant until a few months before, wrote an article pinning blame on Macmillan for not taking full advantage of the 1949 devaluation and Wilson, for 'refusing to admit the basic facts of the economic situation' and pursuing policies such as hire purchase relaxations and the Common Market application that made devaluation inevitable. He accused Wilson of deliberately suppressing a report from his economic advisers demanding devaluation, and said that he ordered to be destroyed all but one of the copies of a report from civil servants in 1966.

The immediate political task was to replace Callaghan, though another setback was not far away. On 27 November, at his half-yearly news conference at the Elysée Palace, de Gaulle set out trenchant opposition to UK membership of the EEC, and confirmed he would – again – veto the application to join. He observed that the Common Market was incompatible with the British economy, citing working practices and agriculture as particular problems, and said that if the other five members sought to force France into having the UK as a member then it would break up the EEC. Wilson waited a couple of days to respond and, in the midst of it all, rather enjoyed taking on de Gaulle's arguments. His mind was never far away from economic statistics: 'If the General was referring to strikes in Britain then, in 1966, Britain lost, through industrial disputes for every 1000 persons employed, 180 man-days against 240 in France.'[114] It did at least mean that the government's bad news all came at once.

Jenkins had seen Callaghan on 23 November, when the chancellor had said that he thought Tony Crosland was likely to succeed him, though Healey was a possibility. Jenkins, however, thought he and Wilson could get on in a way the more distant Crosland and the prime minister could not. While he would become a leadership rival, Wilson was better off binding him in so that they had a mutual interest in the survival of the government.[115] There is something in this, though there is another crucial point. The danger to Wilson's personal position since 1964 was if Brown and Callaghan had ever combined against him. Wilson needed holders of the great offices of state who were themselves leadership rivals. If he was to move Callaghan but keep him in a senior position to avoid him going to the backbenches and becoming a threat from there, promoting Crosland alongside him would not work: Tony Crosland had supported Callaghan for the leadership in 1963 and could easily have joined forces with him. Wilson came up with the straight swap: Callaghan to the Home Office, Jenkins to the Treasury.

The sense of crisis was heightened by some loose talk from Callaghan. Returning from a week's holiday to recover from the strain of the devaluation, he attended a dinner of the 'under-forties' club of Labour MPs, where he questioned the ban on the sale of arms to South Africa. His defence was that he was trying to provoke debate across the dinner table, but in the febrile atmosphere, it created a further headache for Wilson, who wrote that it produced 'strains more serious than any other in our six years of Government . . .'[116] Callaghan was unaware of a decision made at the cabinet's review of defence and overseas policy the previous Friday, 8 December, after Jenkins, as the new chancellor, had undertaken his full review of post-devaluation departmental spending. So dire was the government's financial position that this was being considered: arms sales would boost exports. There was a potential £100m on the table for an order for what was principally naval equipment. But South Africa's apartheid regime was an abhorrence. The news leaked into the press; on 12 December *The Times* reported 'increasing signs that the Government intend to rescind the present ban on arms sales to South Africa'. That same day, a parliamentary motion tabled by two Labour MPs, Kevin McNamara, who had been at the under-forties dinner, and John Ellis, was published, calling for the retention of the arms embargo. It attracted 140 signatures. Sensing the opportunity to exploit a Labour split, the Conservative opposition, which was in favour of resuming arms sales, put in a Private Notice Question to the speaker, which was not granted on the basis that Wilson would answer a question from Sir Dingle Foot in the Commons on the matter. Wilson called a cabinet meeting for the morning of 14 December, but, since Brown was delayed in his return from a Western European Union meeting, stuck in a fogbound Brussels airport, he postponed the discussion, leaving him reaffirming the embargo but having to promise a 'fuller statement' on the issue in answer to Foot.[117]

This merely heightened suspicion. The pragmatists, including Brown, thought that, if the UK did not supply the arms, another country would. On the other side were the moralists, including Wilson, who would not countenance providing arms to a racist government. The next day, Wilson addressed the group of Northern Labour MPs and confirmed his position that the arms embargo should remain in place.[118] At cabinet on Monday, 18 December, with Brown now present, Wilson opened with a stinging attack on the leaking over the weekend that had suggested there was a majority against him in cabinet. Convinced Brown was responsible in order to threaten his position as prime minister, he secured agreement that he would put an end to the speculation.[119] Later that day, he confirmed in the Commons: '. . . policy on this matter . . . remains unchanged.'[120] Brown's complaint was on process: that Wilson had pre-empted the Monday decision with his speech to the Northern MPs. Wilson, though, was right on the substance of the issue.

It was an unseemly end to the year, and showed the extent to which Wilson's stock had fallen. Politically, he was in trouble. The pound was a great symbol of national pride. Wilson was uniquely associated with defending the currency in the crises of 1964, 1965 and 1966, and the strategy had failed. The measures of the summer of 1966 had represented the last chance to change direction. It was Wilson's choice to go on. He could have altered the policy and did not. The devaluation left him personally exposed, and his approval ratings plunged. In December, only 34 per cent were satisfied with his performance as prime minister, with 57 per cent dissatisfied, the worst that had been recorded for him.[121] There were to be the most difficult times ahead.

Chapter 13

A moral crusade

Reform

The record of Wilson's 1964–70 Labour governments on progressive reform is impressive. The lives of millions of people were changed for the better by legislation that transformed society. Wilson unquestionably left Britain a fairer place, and the changes were achieved against a backdrop of continuous economic uncertainty. Wilson had a particular anger about racism, and was determined to create a society where people could live free of prejudice. It was the most noble of aims, and Wilson sought to give it practical effect.

A second Race Relations Act came into force in November 1968, outlawing discrimination in housing, employment and access to public services, building on the provisions of the 1965 Act. The powers of the Race Relations Board were extended, so that it not only dealt with complaints, but could institute its own investigations. Enoch Powell had spoken against the measures in his infamous speech in Birmingham on 20 April 1968. Quoting the epic poem *Aeneid*, and the prophecy of wars, he predicted a race conflict: 'As I look ahead, I am filled with foreboding. Like the Roman, I seem to see "the River Tiber foaming with much blood".' The 'Rivers of Blood' speech, as it was to become known, was a speech of hatred and division. Heath sacked Powell from the shadow cabinet. Wilson, horrified at the racism, responded with a set-piece speech of his own in Birmingham on 5 May: '. . . I am not prepared to stand aside and see this country engulfed by the racial conflict which calculated orators or ignorant prejudice can create.' He appealed to a very different history to that of Powell, citing British values of 'tolerance, of kindliness, and of fair play, qualities for which the British people are admired throughout the world'. He referred to Will Dyson's *Daily Herald* cartoon of 1919 accusing the politicians of the Versailles conference of endangering the peace that millions had fought for in the First World War: 'They must not be able to say what Will Dyson said of the men of Versailles, that we did not heed the weeping of that child. And be it in terms of the survival of this nation, or be it in terms of a world divided by race and colour, I ask not whether that child is black or brown or white . . .' The next day, the *Guardian* said Wilson had reminded people that the Labour movement 'is a moral crusade or it is nothing.' Peter Jenkins, who had heard the speech live, called it 'the practical down-to-earth north-country moral force of the historic Labour movement – not by reciting the moral imperatives of metropolitan liberalism.'[1] It was, in short, authentically Wilson.

If this was a high point, the Commonwealth Immigrants Act of 1968 was a low. Rushed through parliament in a matter of days, the legislation was designed to stop Asians from Kenya and Uganda, who had a right to settle in the UK, coming in large numbers to escape discrimination as their governments pursued 'Africaniza- tion' policies. The right to settle in the UK would be limited to those born here, or who had parents or grandparents here. Wilson saw it as part of an overall immigration policy that provided a balance be- tween tough controls and fairness through the anti-discrimination legislation. Yet, not offering a safe haven for those fleeing persecu- tion was wrong in itself, but, worse still, as the *Guardian* put it at the time, it was 'a concession to racialism. The exception for people "with substantial connections with this country, as for example by birth or parentage," clearly refers to white emigrants to Kenya who might want to return. No previous British immigration legislation has ever been quite so plainly discriminatory as this.'[2]

The Act was a far cry from the liberalism of Jenkins' tenure at the Home Office. The 1967 Criminal Justice Act outlawed cor- poral punishment in prisons; Jenkins was careful to ensure that he kept a credibility as tough on crime by introducing majority verdicts in jury trials to increase conviction rates and reduced the number of territorial police forces from 117 to 43, to make them better able to investigate serious and organised crime. This stance also allowed Jenkins to weather adverse storms, as when the spy and double-agent George Blake escaped from prison at Wormwood Scrubs in October 1966. On moral issues, the government stuck to the convention of remaining neutral, but Jenkins argued successfully in cabinet that parliamentary time be made available to ensure that backbench-sponsored Private Members' Bills on abortion and homosexuality reached the statute book. The cabinet would have free votes on such matters of conscience, but Jenkins could use his authority as home secretary to drive them through, speaking in favour of them at the dispatch box, while relying upon the attention to detail of his minister of state, Alice Bacon. As her biographer Rachel Reeves puts it, though she was criticised as '. . . an administrator and not an innovator, this was precisely what was required after 1964'.[3]

On abortion, Jenkins argued as many as 100,000 backstreet terminations were taking place every year.[4] The Liberal MP David Steel introduced the bill, which legalised abortion up to 24 weeks provided it was signed off by two doctors. The Family Planning Act of 1967 – another Private Member's Bill, sponsored by Edwin Brooks MP – allowed local health authorities to give contraceptive advice, regardless of marital status and on social, as well as medical, grounds. Leo Abse, the flamboyant, campaigning MP for Pontypool, brought forward the Sexual Offences Bill, which aimed to 'dismantle our barbaric homosexual laws'.[5] With over a thousand men a year imprisoned for their sexuality, the Wolfenden Report had, in 1957, recommended that homosexual acts that took place in private should not be subject to the criminal law. Yet this change had not been implemented. Now, it would be: homosexual acts that took place in private between consenting adults over the age of twenty-one were decriminalised. The opponents of reform tried to filibuster them, and there were three all-night sittings in 1967: the Abortion Bill from 29 to 30 June and 13 to 14 July; and the Sexual Offences Bill from 3 to 4 July.

These pieces of legislation changed everyday experience. The Sexual Offences Act ended the persecution of people for who they were. No longer would gay people have to live their lives partly in public, partly in the shadows, vulnerable to blackmail and prosecution. That people could now love who they wanted to was one of the great social changes of the century. The Abortion Act ended the awful, dangerous practice of pregnancies being ended without any proper medical supervision and gave women control over their own bodies.

That both pieces of legislation were ground-breaking is not in dispute. What is debated is the extent to which Wilson can take credit for them. Jenkins enabled their passage through parliament, building different coalitions of support: Abse himself, for example, was not in favour of the changes on abortion. Jenkins also made the case in cabinet for them to be given priority in the government timetable. Abse also credited John Silkin, the chief whip, who told him: 'by hook or by crook, [he] would find the parliamentary time . . .'[6] On 27 October 1966, as Jenkins made the case for time to be found for homosexual law reform, Crossman records the cabinet reaction as follows: 'Callaghan, the Prime Minister, George Brown and others asked why time should be given at all to such a Bill and why we should abandon the neutrality which the Labour Cabinet had always shown to such controversial issues as homosexuality, abortion, divorce and Sunday opening of cinemas.'[7] A key argument was that, since the campaigns would continue, it was thought that an early debate was better: that is, further away from the next general election. Wilson insisted the government would be neutral.[8] He took advantage of one of the laws his government later changed. Prior to the abolition of the theatre censorship powers of the lord chamberlain in September 1968, it was Wilson himself who had exercised his right to remove parts of the script of the play *Mrs Wilson's Diary*, including a spoof poem and references to the drunkenness of Brown.[9]

In his account of the 1964–70 Labour governments, Wilson references the abolition of capital punishment, but makes no mention of either the Sexual Offences Act or the Abortion Act. He did not vote in any of the 45 divisions during the passage of the two pieces of legislation through parliament; in contrast, Jenkins voted in them all. Crossman was convinced Wilson was personally opposed to the reforms on religious grounds: 'He has a number of moral convictions: he's a perfectly sincere Sunday Methodist; he's against the legal reforms to deal with homosexuality or abortion.'[10] Wilson's press secretary Joe Haines said: 'Harold thought the measures were right, necessary and would support them, but took the view that did not mean he had to like them.'[11]

There is no doubt that Wilson was socially conservative. Yet he could have stopped these reforms and chose not to do so. After all, Brown and Callaghan shared his concerns about time being given to the Bills: so, had Wilson overruled Jenkins, the position would have been supported by the entire triumvirate which, at this point, still represented the ultimate power in cabinet. Wilson appointed Jenkins as home secretary knowing he had an agenda for liberal reform which had been set out in a short book, *The Labour Case*, published back in 1959.[12] There was also a concern that traditional Labour support would be lost as a result of support for the changes. Some Labour whips 'objected fiercely that it was turning our own working-class support against us'.[13] Had this happened, it would have damaged the cause of further progressive change being put forward by Labour. That it did not happen was in large part due to Wilson himself, who always had a popularity with Labour voters that balanced Jenkins' liberalism. As prime minister, Wilson does, therefore, take a significant amount of credit for these social reforms.

He must also accept blame for failing to do the right thing. On 21 October 1966, after three weeks of heavy rain, fifty thousand lorry-loads of waste from a spoil tip above the South Wales mining village of Aberfan slid down onto Pantglas Junior School and a row of houses, killing 116 children and 28 adults. The disaster happened at 9.13 a.m. and, to his credit, Wilson was on the scene that evening. The unimaginable scale of the tragedy, with it happening only minutes after the start of the school day; the arrival of help from all over the country to dig through the sludge in the

His childhood political hero was a resident of Number Eleven, Philip Snowden, but the famous image of the young Harold is on the steps of Number Ten.

Harold was the youngest Cabinet Minister of the twentieth century – here he is as the 'Baby of the Attlee Cabinet' with William Jowitt, the Lord Chancellor, and Nye Bevan.

Harold Wilson arriving at Downing Street with two of his great political rivals, George Brown and Hugh Gaitskell, for a meeting with Harold Macmillan during the 1962 Cuban Missile Crisis.

Harold moving the Labour Party forward 'fifty years in fifty minutes' with his 'White Heat' speech in October 1963.

'Wilson, Yeah Yeah Yeah!' – Harold with The Beatles in March 1964.

The first post-war Prime Minister not to have been privately educated – Harold at 10 Downing Street in October 1964.

The first Prime Minister to reveal his knees in public –
Harold on holiday in the Scillies with wife Mary and son Giles in
August 1965, paying a visit to the uninhabited island of Samson.

Harold with son Robin, daughter-in-law Joy and wife Mary out walking
whilst at Chequers. Harold loved it at the old country house;
Mary preferred to stay elsewhere.

'From now on, the pound abroad is worth 14 per cent or so less in terms of other currencies. That doesn't mean, of course, that the pound here in Britain, in your pocket or purse or in your bank, has been devalued.' Harold delivering the words that came to haunt him in November 1967.

Would he ever trust a British Prime Minister again? Harold with President Lyndon B. Johnson at the White House in July 1966.

The rebellion was not brought to an end 'within a matter of weeks rather than months' – Harold negotiating with Ian Smith on HMS *Fearless* in October 1968.

Harold was a consummate party manager: one of his chosen Labour frontbenches in the House of Commons.

'She will undoubtedly follow him into the wilderness when the time comes.' She did. Harold and Marcia in October 1972.

Harold's inner circle evolved over the course of his leadership, but two of its most influential members were unquestionably Bernard Donoughue and Joe Haines.

Leaders who could secure the result they wanted in a European referendum.
Harold with James Callaghan in Paris.

The Queen showed her
high regard for Harold
by attending a farewell
dinner for him at
10 Downing Street.

hope of finding victims alive; and the quiet dignity of the grieving Aberfan community, touched a chord with people all around the world. Within less than a year, over £1.7m was sent in donations to the Aberfan Disaster Fund.[14] Lord Justice Edmund Davies chaired the inquiry, the findings of which were published on 3 August 1967, placing blame squarely on the National Coal Board, and the failure to have any formal tipping policy. In response, Wilson's government passed the Mines and Quarries (Tips) Act of 1969, placing a legal obligation on mine owners and managers to keep such tips secure. Yet no individual within the National Coal Board was ever held to account. The other issue was the removal of the spoil tips themselves, still towering above the village. The National Coal Board took sixty feet of material away from the two tips and argued that they were now made safe. In an unseemly episode, the Treasury would not release the money for their full removal. George Thomas approached Wilson, who brokered a compromise whereby the Aberfan Disaster Fund contributed 25 per cent, the Coal Board 25 per cent and the government 50 per cent, and this solution was announced in July 1968.[15] The money, £150,000, should never have been taken from the Disaster Fund. In 1997, the Labour government returned the £150,000, but without interest, and, in 2007, the Welsh government donated £2m in recognition of the injustice. Thomas deserves criticism for not making a stronger case to Wilson, but, ultimately, the prime minister should not have allowed it to happen.

In other areas of reform, Wilson was personally involved. One of his great passions, flagged in his Glasgow speech of September 1963, was for a University of the Air. Money was the perennial issue. In advance of a cabinet discussion on the matter to finalise a White Paper, the cabinet secretary, Burke Trend, suggested the option of a pilot scheme if the full project could not be financed through advertising or the Exchequer.[16] The next day, 8 February 1966, Jennie Lee attended cabinet where those present reached 'unanimous agreement that an open university should be launched, if it could be made financially possible. The questions which remain are cost, and the television channel to be used.'[17] The key word here was 'if': with the economic crises that were to follow, the allocation of resources to the project was what mattered above all. A planning committee was set up to turn the idea into a reality, chaired by Sir Peter Venables, vice-chancellor of the University of Aston. Crucially, Wilson ensured that the project did not fall victim to spending cuts.

Wilson's second problem was managing Tony Crosland, then secretary of state for education and science, who was not happy about being overshadowed by Lee, and grumbled to the prime minister that she was 'something of a lone wolf . . . he obviously feels that if he tries to assert the normal authority of a Minister over a Parliamentary Secretary Miss Lee may take umbrage on the ground that whatever the theory, in practice she reports to you.'[18] Ultimately, though, Crosland had little option but to accept the situation: Lee's status as Bevan's widow gave her a special standing within the Labour movement and with Wilson himself.

Yet Crosland continued to be troublesome. In May 1967, *The Times Educational Supplement* reported that the plan for an Open University by 1969 would 'depend largely on the amount of support Mr Crosland gives it.'[19] Wilson, though, was always one step ahead. When the planning committee completed its work in early 1969, the new secretary of state for education and science, Ted Short, was concerned his proposed statement upon it had not been cleared with cabinet. Short, with his neat, swept-back hair, was a northerner, originally from Cumbria. He had served as a captain in the Durham Light Infantry during the Second World War, a councillor on Newcastle-upon-Tyne council, and had been a headteacher. Indeed, in the House of Commons, he was seen as a safe pair of hands who 'could [still] resemble the more serious sort of headteacher'.[20] Crucially, he was not someone who involved himself in intrigue and was always loyal to Wilson, who was firm in allowing Short to avoid cabinet – and Tony Crosland – altogether: 'It is a technical report which we obviously endorse. The Secretary of State should feel perfectly free to make a statement endorsing the report and speaking as warmly as he likes on it.'[21]

The planning committee report was published on 27 January

1969. Short announced in the Commons that student enrolments would begin in the autumn of 1970 'and that courses, including broadcasts on radio and BBC 2, correspondence tuition, and tutorials at local study centres, will start in January, 1971.' The BBC were to be 'educational partners' of the university.[22] Even after that, there were disagreements. Jenkins and Short differed on the size of the first year intake. Jenkins insisted on 10,000 students; Short on 25,000.[23] Short triumphed and, on 18 May 1970, the Open University buildings were declared open by Lord Mountbatten. He wrote to Wilson: 'the whole concept of this University is entirely yours. I felt I ought to write and tell you how very well the ceremony went off and how deeply impressed we were with what we all saw.'[24] Wilson was rightly proud of the Open University. It provided opportunities for those who had not thrived in their formal education, or had not been able to access higher education, and addressed the need to skill and re-skill people throughout their adult lives. It has stood the test of time, and has had over two million students, and is one of the largest universities in Europe.[25] None of these opportunities would have been available without Wilson's passion to see the policy through.

Another of his interests was history: the Public Records Act of 1967 reduced the period for the release of official documents from fifty years to thirty, thereby helping future historians. Meanwhile, the Welsh Language Act of the same year allowed the Welsh language to be used in court proceedings and gave Ministers the power to order that public documents be produced in Welsh. The Representation of the People Act of 1969 reduced the voting age from 21 to 18.

Reform of the House of Lords was, however, unsuccessful. Cross-party talks began in November 1967 but Wilson ended them on 20 June 1968, two days after the House of Lords rejected the order that gave effect to the United Nations extending mandatory sanctions on Smith's regime. A White Paper was published on 1 November: new life peers would continue to be created by the queen on the advice of the prime minister. The current Lords would be composed of two tiers: life peers would continue to vote but current hereditary peers would be stripped of their voting rights, though some would be appointed life peers to soften the blow. Future hereditary peers would have titles but no right to sit in the Lords.[26] The proposals alienated both the Tory traditionalists such as Enoch Powell and those on the Labour side such as Michael Foot who thought the Upper House should be abolished. On 20 November, despite a three-line whip, only 231 Labour MPs voted in favour of the proposals. Many abstained and 45 Labour MPs rebelled; indeed, across the Commons, only 270 MPs, less than half, voted in favour, despite both frontbenches being in favour of change. The proposals were dropped.

There were other important social changes. The Divorce Law Reform Act of 1969, following another Leo Abse campaign, introduced 'No Fault' divorce so that people were no longer trapped in loveless marriages. The Matrimonial Proceedings and Property Act 1970 allowed courts to order financial support for children from either spouse when marriages broke down, and also sought to correct the gender bias whereby both parties kept their earnings and inheritances post-divorce, which meant, at the time, that women, who often did not work, lost out. Instead, the intention was to place parties in the position they would have been had the divorce not happened.

In the wider fields of housing, social services and health, despite the doses of deflation and the rounds of spending cuts, the Wilson governments' overall record is impressive. In the full years Labour was in office from 1965 to 1969, over 2 million permanent dwellings were constructed, more than was managed in the Conservatives' final six years. Of these, 964,000 were Local Authority properties built for rent.[27] Later criticism of high rise, on grounds of architecture and crime, has to be balanced against the new generation of 'New Towns' including Milton Keynes, which was designated in January 1967. At the 1967 Party Conference, Wilson said that the government had 'put in hand a dramatic deployment of resources in favour of those in greatest need, in favour of the under-privileged, on all fronts of social action . . . the most massive ever carried through'. He spoke about over £2,300 million extra spending on social services, a 47 per cent increase, with more schools and hospitals being built.[28]

The significant increase in spending on the welfare state was designed to help the poorest. The National Assistance Board was replaced with a Supplementary Benefits Commission by the Ministry of Social Security Act 1966. Since it contained an earnings-related element, this meant higher unemployment, sickness and widows' benefits. As David Ennals, then minister at the Department of Health and Social Security put it in 1969: 'even after taking account of the rise in prices since 1964, family allowances are still worth 72 per cent. more in real terms to a low income family with three children than they were when the Government took office, an achievement of which we have reason to be proud.'[29] In addition to this higher provision, Wilson could claim two other achievements. First, seeking to end the stigma attached to relying on state handouts. Hence the language was changed to one of rights that people could expect. The 'test of need' was replaced with a 'test of requirements'. Practically, this meant ending the 'two-book system' whereby pensioners had to queue up with one book for the insurance-based pension, and another for means-tested assistance, ending the shame people felt whereby their neighbours knew they were 'on assistance'. As a consequence of this, the second achievement was to increase the take-up of benefits: the number of those claiming supplementary benefit rose by 365,000 in the first year.[30]

In the workplace, the government sought to address the huge unfairness to women. On 7 June 1968, the sewing machinists who made car seat covers at Ford's Dagenham plant had stopped work after a pay regrading favouring male workers. Employees in other Ford plants withdrew their labour too, and, while a compromise was found within three weeks, the pay of the women remained 8 per cent below that of the men. Castle responded with the Equal Pay Act of 1970, which came into force five years later, outlawing discrimination between men and women in terms and conditions of employment.

This legislation was a fitting end to Wilson's first period in office, which had improved the status of women in the workplace, taken away the need for backstreet abortions, and allowed couples to escape unhappy relationships without an unfair penalty on the female spouse. Taken together, Wilson's governments' reforms had a profound impact on society and the freedom with which people were able to live their lives without persecution by the authorities for who they were. Wilson's Britain moved beyond the judgemental, stultifying society of the 1950s. His was a country of tolerance, respect and second chances. The Open University opened up the prospect of education at any point in life for millions of people. In *The Labour Case*, Jenkins had asked if Britain was a civilised place. By the time Wilson left office in 1970, great progress had been made in making it so.

Chapter 14

A new and much more hopeful phase

International Diplomat

Harold Wilson had been a presence on the international stage since his Montague Meyer trips of the 1950s. He enjoyed travel, and found it easy to build a rapport with people he met around the world. As prime minister, he drew on his extensive knowledge and experience, and focused on the two issues that were to dominate his first period in office: Vietnam and Rhodesia. On the former, he continued to give formal support to the American approach without committing British troops. His strategy with Ian Smith was to seek to find an agreement that granted independence but with majority rule, not the racist white minority rule that the rebel regime was seeking to perpetuate.

Wilson hoped that Bowden would bring a more streetwise approach to dealing with the wily Smith. His first problem arose with the Commonwealth. Ghana and Tanzania suspended diplomatic relations over Britain's failure to oust Smith by military force. At the meeting of the Commonwealth prime ministers in September 1966, once again held at Marlborough House in London, Wilson agreed to abide by the pledge of 'No Independence Before Majority Rule' – NIBMAR as it became known – which was a key Commonwealth demand. Smith would never agree to this voluntarily, and the sanctions regime remained crucial.

At the same time, Wilson continued with talks. In December 1966, he met Smith for further negotiations. Wilson had considered three locations away from the UK and Rhodesia: the British military base at Akrotiri in Cyprus; Malta; or a naval vessel off Gibraltar. Since the Royal Navy Cruiser HMS *Hermes* was at Casablanca, it could reach Gibraltar quickly, so it provided a physically secure location, away from interruptions.[1] Wilson continued to use the five principles he had set out as the basis for talks, to which he had added another, earlier in the year: 'To these [the existing five] must now be added a sixth principle, namely, the need to ensure that, regardless of race, there is no oppression of majority by minority or of minority by majority.'[2] The discussion began on Friday, 2 December and went on into the early hours of Sunday. At times it was heated. Take this example of a discussion on whether or not the views of the Rhodesian people on the future could be ascertained within four weeks. Wilson said 'he doubted whether it would be possible adequately to sound Rhodesian opinion in one month. He reminded Mr Smith that the world was not interested in the niceties of the Rhodesian constitution . . .' He told Smith that patience at the United Nations was becoming exhausted and if a solution was not found 'they would certainly act in the United Nations and it would not be possible for Britain to plead for yet another month in which to seek a peaceful settlement.' Smith retorted: 'Mr Wilson had great powers of persuasion . . . he had no doubt that Mr Wilson could tell a fantastically convincing story to the United Nations that Britain could let the test [of public opinion] take place . . .' Wilson shot back: 'The Prime Minister agreed that it would make a fantastic story but not a convincing one. The United Nations would say that Britain was not in *de facto* control and would urge us to send troops into Rhodesia in order to take control.'[3]

On the final day, Wilson thought he had a settlement that satisfied the six principles and that he could have recommended to parliament: 'This was the position at 5 o'clock last Saturday.'[4]

Smith avoided final agreement by saying he had to go back to cabinet colleagues and that he did not have the authority to accept the terms himself. Wilson – with no other choice if he wanted to keep the possibility of an agreement alive – allowed this: 'It was, therefore, agreed that both documents should be considered by the

British Government, and by Mr. Smith and his colleagues, on the clear understanding that it must be accepted or rejected as a whole, and a straight answer given, "Yes" or "No" by this Monday.'[5] This was, however, to no avail: 'They have confirmed that they insist on maintaining their illegality until, in conditions in which no free expression of Rhodesian opinion would be possible, a Royal Commission has reported and independence has been granted.'[6]

Smith's rejection left Wilson very pessimistic about ever finding a solution. On 13 December, Wilson told the South African ambassador, Dr Carel de Wet, that he 'had tried to persuade Smith that he had the option of becoming a great multi-racial leader. But Smith was in evil company.' For Wilson, the door to a settlement was now 'almost closed. If there were a dramatic change in the situation in Rhodesia and Smith got rid of his extremists and indicated his willingness to accept the TIGER document, the Government would naturally examine this. But there could be no question in present circumstances of further visits to Salisbury by the Commonwealth Secretary or of continuing talks of the kind we had in recent months.'[7]

This left sanctions as the only tool available. Castle – who always feared a sell-out to Smith – criticised Wilson on the basis that he resisted oil sanctions and that it took until March 1968 for him to support mandatory United Nations sanctions, when international anger at Smith forced his hand.[8] On 6 March, Smith's regime prompted an outcry, executing three African nationalist leaders: James Dhlamini, Victor Mlambo and Duly Shadrack, despite them all being granted a reprieve by the queen. From the Labour backbenches, Dingle Foot summed up the mood: 'there can be no valid or honourable settlement with this gang of criminals in Salisbury'.[9] Castle's analysis is not quite correct. A British-sponsored resolution was passed by the United Nations Security Council on 16 December 1966 for a compulsory boycott, including oil, which was added by the African countries. Only coal and manufactured goods were exempted, on the basis that Britain said this would greatly damage Zambia. Britain did resist the call to 'prevent by all means the transport to Southern Rhodesia of oil or oil products' since this would have required Wilson's government to impose a naval blockade on the whole of Southern Africa. Nonetheless, this was the first time in its then twenty-one-year history that the United Nations had imposed mandatory sanctions.

It is true, though, that, on 29 May 1968, United Nations Security Council Resolution 253, condemning the executions, made the boycott mandatory, by removing the exemptions, and called on member states to assist Zambia. However, Wilson had to deal with the political reality. Having Zambia as a constructive partner was crucial given its proximity to Rhodesia. While he abhorred its apartheid system, South Africa was not only one of Britain's largest export markets, Britain also depended on its gold supplies. Indeed, Wilson saw 'the world monetary system as fed by gold from three large gold mines, South Africa, the Soviet Union and Fort Knox'.[10] It was not as if this led Wilson to do nothing. He had announced an arms embargo on South Africa on 17 November 1964.[11] However, he saw the likely impact on the domestic economy of a full confrontation.

There is an argument that Wilson should have handed over the matter to the United Nations. Indeed, in February 1964, Evan Campbell, Southern Rhodesia's high commissioner in London, stated his concern that Labour would 'throw Southern Rhodesia to the United Nations wolves'.[12] There was a precedent: the Attlee government had handed over the Palestine Mandate in 1948. That, however, had not enhanced Britain's international prestige and was a sign of failure. Wilson himself was deeply ashamed by it, and saw Ernest Bevin as having abandoned Britain's commitment to a national home for the Jewish people, established in the 1917 Balfour Declaration. Bevin treated such promises as 'tiresome undertakings to be got round or, if he was provoked, challenged head on.'[13] Even if Wilson had chosen this path, it would have meant handing over control, and any influence he had on the economic impact on Britain would have been severely reduced. There was also a Cold War element at play: that the Soviet Union could have become involved in any United Nations-led action taken in Rhodesia.

Wilson tried again with Smith in October 1968, this time on

the amphibious assault ship HMS *Fearless*. *Fearless* later appeared in the James Bond movie *The Spy Who Loved Me*, but there was little in the way of glamour or excitement in the talks. Wilson had once again changed his secretary of state: George Thomson replaced Bowden who had been appointed chair of the Independent Television Authority. There was a sense of optimism at the outset. Sir Humphrey Gibbs told Wilson that he thought Smith wanted a settlement. Wilson thought the presence of Desmond Lardner-Burke, one of Smith's hardliners, might assist in reaching an agreement that the rest of the Rhodesian cabinet could accept.[14] However, Smith's uncompromising, racist views made the situation impossible: 'So long as Africans were happy to go on living quietly, he did not favour forcing the vote on them.' Thomson responded calmly and said a royal commission would have to find evidence of this desire of Africans not wanting the vote.[15] Smith's latest problem was a suggestion by the British government that amendments to the Rhodesian constitution could be struck down by the UK judicial committee of the Privy Council if, for example, they discriminated against the black population: this would give a post-independence 'external guarantee' for the British government. Smith said: '. . . since no concessions whatever were made to him about the Privy Council, he might as well fly home.' The situation seemed hopeless. Smith flaunted his racism, telling Wilson that 'when he had been interviewed recently by Mr. David Frost for British television, he had been asked what he would do if his son wished to marry a black girl. He had replied that he would advise him against it. But he would not try to overrule it.'[16] In the Commons on 22 October, Wilson defended his unwillingness to compromise as he saw the government as 'trustees for improvements in the constitutional position of the Africans and trustees on their behalf so far as discrimination is concerned – the third and the fourth [of the negotiation] principles.'[17] Thomson captured why no solution had been found: 'Britain has responsibility for Rhodesia without power inside Rhodesia . . . In Rhodesia, Britain has always been, not a toothless bulldog, as the famous gibe had it, but an absentee bulldog.'[18]

Smith declared Rhodesia a republic in 1970. In December 1971, Alec Douglas-Home, by now foreign secretary, eventually reached a settlement, but it was without Smith committing to abide by the recommendations of a royal commission, a position he defended on the basis that no 'Government anywhere could be asked to accept all the recommendations of a Commission blind.'[19] In parliament, Labour opposed it, citing the fact that the well-established negotiation principles had not been met, and expressing alarm at Smith's racist regime. Smith could afford to accept Home's proposals because they delayed majority rule: the addition of seats for the black population to the Rhodesian parliament would take place at such a slow pace that equality would take decades. Unsurprisingly, the commission under Lord Pearce found huge opposition to this among the majority black population so that killed it off. Meanwhile, the Rhodesian bush war intensified. Eventually, in March 1978, Smith agreed to the creation of a government including Africans via the 'Internal Settlement'. On 21 February 1979, at Lancaster House in London, the new foreign secretary Peter Carrington, brokered an agreement that led to a general election in February 1980, and Robert Mugabe returned from exile to become the country's first black prime minister, over fourteen years after the UDI. Wilson took a rational approach to dealing with Smith but was unable to topple him. His avoidance of using force has remained controversial. As Stewart later reflected: 'In the light of the events of the last fifteen years, I still believe our decision was right . . . Yet I do not reach this conclusion easily . . .'[20]

On the issue of British involvement in the war in Vietnam, however, there is far less debate. Wilson's decision not to commit British ground troops has looked even more impressive as the years have passed. Thanks to him, no British lives were lost in the conflict, and he also sought to find a peace settlement to end the bloodshed for all those involved. While his position undoubtedly irritated Johnson, he preserved the transatlantic relationship in circumstances where the president was asking for something Wilson would not provide.

Wilson balanced his support for the United States' position in Vietnam with attempts to offer himself as a go-between with the Soviet Union to secure peace. His efforts also bought him political space with his internal opponents in the Labour Party. Ultimately, Britain did not have the clout on the world stage to bring about peace in Vietnam on its own. Wilson did all he could between the two Cold War superpowers, maintaining influence while ensuring that his own country never formally entered the war. If at times he looked as if he was relying on pragmatism over principle, that is because he was.

The extent to which the Vietnam War dominated political debate is now difficult to imagine. While student protest did not reach the level of say, France, with the riots in Paris of May 1968, it provoked demonstrations and disorder on the street. The Vietnam Solidarity Campaign was founded in June 1966, with support from the philosopher Bertrand Russell. It condemned American aggression and demanded the withdrawal of its armed forces and military bases, giving the Vietnamese people the right to self-determination. At protests, marchers flew the flag of the National Liberation Front of South Vietnam, the Viet Cong. There was a protest in London in July 1967, and another in October: thousands marched from Trafalgar Square to the US Embassy in Grosvenor Square. The campaign gathered momentum, and, in March 1968, the speakers at Trafalgar Square included Tariq Ali, a leader of the campaign, before thousands marched to the US embassy, where another of the speakers, the actress Vanessa Redgrave, handed in a petition. The event was marred by violent clashes between protesters and mounted horses. There were a number of arrests; by the time of the next – and final – major anti-war protest in London in October 1968, security was tighter.

For the protesters, Wilson was a guilty man, complicit in the American action by virtue of his support for war. Peter Hain, anti-apartheid campaigner, later a Labour MP and cabinet minister, was at the demonstrations. Protesters, he said, 'saw Harold as a sell-out. That he didn't send troops simply passed by the Vietnam Solidarity Campaign protesters. They were not conscious of

Harold's dilemma between maintaining the support of anti-war Labour MPs and the transatlantic relationship.'[21]

Vietnam is situated on the eastern edge of the Indochina peninsula in South-East Asia. A French colony from the nineteenth century, Japanese forces invaded in 1940, during the Second World War. In 1941, the communist Ho Chi Minh formed the Viet Minh, a coalition of groups seeking independence; when the Japanese withdrew in 1945, Ho's forces revolted against French rule in what became known as the August General Uprising, declaring a Democratic Republic of Vietnam. From December 1946, France sought to re-establish its control, leading to the first Indochina War between French forces and the Viet Minh, concluding with French defeat at the Battle of Dien Bien Phu in May 1954. That July, the Geneva Agreements effectively partitioned Vietnam: the North above the 17th parallel controlled by the Viet Minh and the South under Emperor Bao Dai, though he was swiftly replaced by the anti-communist Ngo Dinh Diem. President Harry S. Truman's 1947 doctrine of containing the spread of Soviet Communism, which became the bedrock of America's Cold War policy, meant supporting South Vietnam. John F. Kennedy, on taking office in January 1961, chose 'a middle course, rejecting (for the time being) direct military participation, but increasing aid and providing South Vietnam with training, helicopter transport and "combat advisers"'.[22] The basis of the Geneva settlement was the holding of elections in 1956 on reunification, though Diem – and the United States – refused to countenance this. Diem was deposed in a military coup on the first day of November 1963, after which he was executed, the Buddhist majority rising against his Roman Catholic government. The United States recognised the new South Vietnamese government.

Kennedy's middle way was abandoned in favour of direct military involvement by Johnson. An incident in the Gulf of Tonkin, the sea east of the Vietnamese coast, gave the new president the opportunity to take action as he saw fit. On 2 August 1964, the US Navy destroyer USS *Maddox*, while patrolling close to the North Vietnamese coast, was attacked by the torpedo squadron of the North Vietnamese Navy. There was another alleged attack two days later, but no evidence it ever took place. On 7 August, both Houses of Congress approved what became known as the 'Gulf of Tonkin Resolution'. Later, the 1973 War Powers Act was to check the president's power in relation to war, but, at this time, Johnson interpreted the Gulf of Tonkin Resolution as giving him the authority to ramp up military involvement in support of South Vietnam against the Communist North. The Soviet Union 'did not reciprocate, but (with China) it poured in, albeit surprisingly inconspicuously, the weapons and supplies without which North Vietnam's ultimate victory would have been impossible' and the 'Vietnam War' developed a hold on international public opinion.[23]

It also developed a hold on the Parliamentary Labour Party. Edward Short, chief whip for Wilson's first twenty-one months in office, faced a significant problem with discipline when the American government launched 'Operation Rolling Thunder', the bombing of the supply lines and military bases in North Vietnam, in March 1965. For Short, it was 'by far the most troublesome political problem I had to contend with among our backbenchers . . .' Sydney Silverman tabled an anti-American motion in the House of Commons. Before the end of March five parliamentary private secretaries, led by David Ennals, sent their own statement on Vietnam to the press, breaching collective responsibility. Short 'had to send for David, and dressed him down in the most severe headmasterly manner' he could muster.[24] Short put his finger on the real issue. It was not only the support for America; it was that 'the left of the Party still saw the war in Vietnam as a patriotic national uprising by the Viet Cong'.[25] By May 1965, Wilson had received around 170 resolutions from trade unions.[26]

Short was concerned that, because of Wilson's desire not to inflame Johnson, his efforts to stop the spread of the war were not being made public.[27] Thus, Wilson openly told the 1965 party conference that he had turned down a request from the United States government to commit troops to Vietnam.[28] Wilson needed all his guile. Once, Manny Shinwell showed Short a Vietnam motion he intended to table. Co-signed by Philip Noel-Baker, a winner of a

Nobel Peace Prize, and Arthur Henderson (son of a former party leader who had also won a Nobel Peace Prize), and Sidney Silverman, Short noted: 'My already considerable opinion of Harold's skill and cunning went even higher when I saw this, for the motion not only encompassed the party establishment but also a pillar of the left wing. Although he did not tell me he was behind it, and I was careful not to ask him, it had Harold's fingerprints all over it.'[29] Knowing that a condemnation was going to be tabled by MPs, this ensured that the criticism that appeared was softened.

Even Wilson could not stave off a defeat on Vietnam at the 1966 party conference, which left him looking for a new peace initiative.[30] The opportunity arose when Kosygin and Gromyko, both of whom Wilson had known from his trips to Moscow, visited Britain in early 1967, arriving at Gatwick airport on 6 February. Two days later, the four-day 'Tet' truce for the Vietnamese New Year began, seeming to offer a window for peace negotiations. On 8 February, Kosygin spoke at a lunch held in his honour at the Guildhall by the City of London, and held out the possibility of a peace settlement: '. . . The first step in this direction should be the unconditional termination of the American bombing and of all their other acts of aggression against the democratic republic of Vietnam.'[31]

The failure to reach a settlement was a sorry tale of miscommunication that led to a furious row between Brown and Wilson. The working arrangement was that Wilson would deal with Washington and Kosygin would deal with Hanoi. Brown recalled: 'Never before or since has the "hot line" from No.10 to the White House been so hot as it was over that period.'[32] Chet Cooper, a former CIA officer, was speaking for Johnson, and advising Wilson. Wilson gave Kosygin what he thought was an agreed British–American proposal in two parts: Phase 'A' was the cessation of American bombing; Phase 'B' would be the reduction of military activity by both America and North Vietnam. This was not signed off by Johnson, who had already sent Ho Chi Minh a message to say that if North Vietnam stopped its infiltration of the South, he would cease the bombing. In other words, his plan was that the cessation of bombing would be the second step, not the first. The situation then became farcical. Late on the Friday evening, 10 February, a Downing Street private secretary was sent to King's Cross station to find Kosygin and Gromyko, who were on their way to Glasgow. The new piece of paper with the Johnson proposal reached Kosygin in time, who agreed to relay the new terms to Hanoi, but there was no response. The opportunity had slipped away.

Johnson's patience with Wilson was wearing thin. Vice-president Hubert Humphrey visited Downing Street on 4 April 1967, to warn Wilson 'most earnestly against saying or doing anything which could imply a shift in the British position away from Washington and towards Hanoi.' He said: 'If he [Johnson] was given cause to think that, as he would see it, he was being "betrayed" by the Prime Minister his reaction would be very violent indeed.'[33] Wilson spoke to Johnson on the telephone on 2 June. Johnson made clear that he was thinking of changing policy on Vietnam: 'He had reached the conclusion that the present policy was not achieving results and was incurring increasing costs, particularly in terms of the number of planes he was losing.' Johnson wanted to judge the reaction, and to see, if he stopped the bombing, the North Vietnamese would reciprocate with de-escalation and come to the negotiating table. Wilson told Johnson that he had to plan the diplomatic side more carefully: 'If the President thought this was a dying horse – as a Texan he would know more about these things than the Prime Minister – should he not try to get the best possible price for it before morbidity set in.'[34]

Wilson's internal problems within the Labour Party contin-ued. In September 1967, four Labour MPs, Frank Allaun, John Mendelson, Stan Orme and Russell Kerr, visited Washington, and called a press conference after an 'argumentative' breakfast with an apparently intransigent Dean Rusk, the atmosphere at which was presumably not assisted by the fact that the four had turned up late. The visit by the party of MPs turned into a vehicle for a wide-ranging attack on Wilson by Allaun as spokesperson for the group. He said that Wilson's stance on Vietnam ran 'counter to the views of the British people or the Labor [sic] party rank and file'. To add to this, Wilson was made to look weak as Allaun boasted that he thought the prime minister would be 'nudged toward their way of thinking'.[35] Allaun and Orme then left for home; Kerr and Mendelson stayed behind to attend the British embassy that evening where Mendelson openly accused Wilson of duplicity between what he said in private and in public. Wilson was assured by the British embassy that it had all 'made very little impact locally' and that something which could have been damaging, ultimately was not, because so little attention was paid to it.[36]

On 29 September, Johnson made a significant intervention with a speech at San Antonio, Texas. What became known as the 'San Antonio Formula' was Johnson's offer to pause bombing of North Vietnam when it would lead promptly to productive discussions, during which he would expect North Vietnam not to take advantage of such a cessation. Wilson and Johnson, both in Australia for the memorial service of Harold Holt, who had disappeared at sea and whose body was never discovered, spoke in Melbourne on 22 December. Johnson told Wilson that he was holding the ring between extreme positions. Seventeen per cent of the American public wanted withdrawal from Vietnam or to limit the aim to stability at the present position. Too much attention was paid to them when 45–47 per cent wanted to step up efforts to achieve victory. Balancing different points of view was something Wilson sympathised with. He said there was 'in Britain now a wide-based opposition to the Vietnam war . . . [but] . . . he could hold the position on the basis of President Johnson's San Antonio speech . . .' Johnson urged Wilson to 'impress upon Kosygin the real dangers presented by the pressures in the United States for an escalation of the war effort.'[37]

Wilson visited Moscow in January 1968 with these words in mind. There was, however, a tragi-comic element to Wilson's discussion with Kosygin on 23 January, which took place during the second act of the opera *Carmen*. Kosygin had little trust in Johnson, doubting whether he really wanted a peace settlement, and questioning whether he was playing politics with one eye on his re-election. Wilson used Johnson's argument of many people in America wanting a stronger line on Vietnam, so he said it was a risk for the American president to go for peace. Kosygin said 'he could not understand this because everybody he met in America wanted peace and denounced Johnson'. After applauding the Toreador Song, Kosygin moved ground and said he thought achieving peace in Vietnam would probably win the election. In fairness to Wilson, he did try to pin Kosygin down, and asked him directly: 'was he really saying to me that when we had said there were significant talks going on, this was not true?' Kosygin eventually conceded that there were 'probings' though the performance again got in the way: 'by this time he felt that the Opera demanded some attention'. Eventually, Kosygin told Wilson that a concrete American peace proposal could be passed to him or Wilson to hand on to Hanoi. It was, Wilson recorded, a 'very colourful Second Act'.[38]

In Vietnam, things became much worse. In the early hours of 31 January, the Viet Cong launched the 'Tet Offensive' attacking cities, towns and military installations across South Vietnam, managing to take temporary control of part of the American embassy in Saigon. It was in this new context that Wilson's next visit to Washington took place. On 8 February, proposing a toast to Johnson at a White House state banquet, Wilson said: 'he was frequently urged to dissociate the British Government from American action – and in particular to call for the unconditional ending of all bombing. He had not done so because he knew a good deal of the negotiations . . . aimed at getting away from the battlefield.'[39]

Twelve days later, Johnson granted an interview to Louis Heren, Washington correspondent of *The Times*. Two articles then appeared. On 22 February, Heren wrote that the Tet Offensive had made Johnson determined to 'do everything necessary to defeat North Vietnam and the Vietcong, except use nuclear weapons'.[40] The next day, Heren penned a piece that worried Wilson. Under the heading 'Anglo-U.S. relationship comes under strain' it was reported that Wilson had offered 'gratuitous advice on the need for restraint in Vietnam, but Mr Johnson is well aware of the need to placate party factions.' Wilson's insistence that a peace deal on Vietnam was close attracted derision: 'It was the Prime Minister's insistence that only a narrow gap had to be bridged to bring peace to Vietnam that apparently reduces him to the homely expletives of the Texas hill country.' Wilson's speech had not placated the American president: 'Whatever audience he was addressing that night in the White House, for . . . Johnson it was just as bad as sending buses to Cuba.' Wilson 'now seems to be bunched with Mr. Lester Pearson, sometimes known here as "that feller up in Ottawa" and other "peaceniks" in striped trousers.'[41] As far as Johnson was concerned, 'Hanoi's only response during the Tet truce was a massive re-supply effort for its troops in the South.'[42] As for the supply of buses to Cuba, it continued to be a source of tension, and it was linked to continuing support for Britain on the issue of Rhodesia. The extension of credit to Castro's government would 'cause difficulties in terms of US–UK relations and particularly Congressional and public attitudes on Rhodesia.'[43] Wilson, in an unusually long handwritten annotation to a civil service briefing on 26 February 1968, accepted the recommendation that the articles be placed before Johnson so that he could see how his interview had been presented. He added, though, that it should be stressed that he did not give interviews to American newspapers embarrassing the president, and that, secondly the attitude of *The Times* to Wilson was paralleled by the attitude of the *New York Times* to Johnson. He said he had made clear at parliamentary questions last week that it was Hanoi failing to close the gap, and that he would take the opportunity to stress that the gap being bridged was a very wide one.[44]

It was, however, to no avail. Johnson felt betrayed by Wilson over Vietnam and was bitter towards him. The president thought that Wilson played politics while denying the United States any military support there.[45] Throughout this, Wilson knew that the way to repair the relationship with Johnson was to commit troops to Vietnam. He also knew that he only needed to offer token support – the single battalion that would have made the difference. It is to his credit that he did not succumb to the temptation, risk lives, and involve Britain in the escalating situation. Yet, at the same time, Wilson had his admirers within the American administration: Benjamin H. Read, executive secretary at the State Department, wrote: 'Prime Minister Wilson has demonstrated great political skill in keeping the vociferous critics of American policy under control without making basic alterations in his policy of support for the United States.'[46] Even when Wilson's leadership seemed under threat in early 1968, Johnson's administration never thought he would be replaced: 'Wilson has proved himself highly skilful and resilient in the past, and he probably still has time to convince the party and the public that he and his administration are in control of events and thereby to regain their confidence.'[47]

Johnson's own problems at home were mounting. The Tet Offensive had a huge impact on American public opinion. Murray MacLehose the British ambassador in Saigon, reported on 6 March to the Foreign Office that the Tet Offensive had demoralised the Americans: '. . . many of them have lost this faith.'[48] On 31 March 1968, with Senator Eugene McCarthy running for the Democratic party presidential nomination on a platform of ending the Vietnam War, and Robert Kennedy also challenging the incumbent president, Johnson gave a televised address on Vietnam. He outlined the reduction in military activity by the US, and called on Britain and the Soviet Union as co-chairmen of the Geneva Conference to build on his act of de-escalation to secure peace.[49] Towards the end of the speech, in a *coup de théâtre*, Johnson announced that he would not seek another term as president. There would be a different Democratic nominee for the November presidential election.

That same day, Wilson and Michael Stewart met at Chequers. Stewart thought Johnson's announcement to cut back on the bombing was shrewd, but Wilson thought Hanoi might try to hang on until the presidential election to see if there was a change in policy.[50] Wilson sent Johnson his personal assessment of the speech that praised it as wise and generous, but was pessimistic about its impact: 'I must confess that I doubt whether Hanoi will in fact respond to it.'[51] Johnson replied that any further steps would be dependent on the response in Hanoi.'[52] The North Vietnam response was broadcast by Hanoi Radio on 3 April 1968 confirming 'its readiness to send its representatives to make contact with US representatives to decide with the US side the unconditional cessation of bombing and all other war acts by the USA . . . so that talks could be begun.'[53]

The problem was worsening. As of 13 April 1968, the American forces had lost 5,395 killed since the turn of the year, with 33,989 wounded; 78,767 Viet Cong fighters had died.[54] Johnson held a press conference on 3 May 1968 announcing that Hanoi was willing to meet for talks in Paris on 10 May, or just afterwards.[55] Wilson's assessment that North Vietnam would wait to see who Johnson's successor was proved shrewd. The Soviet ambassador to France, Valerian Zorin, said 'if the Americans did not soon agree to halt bombing without conditions, they would wait to make a deal with the next American administration'.[56] On 24 May, Johnson said there had been 'no visible lessening of Hanoi's aggressive efforts'.[57]

On a brighter note, on 1 July 1968, the Nuclear Non-Proliferation Treaty was signed by Moscow, London and Washington: progress, Johnson said, 'toward stable peace on this threatened planet'. It was followed up by the establishment of a new commercial air link between the two superpowers, and a new cultural exchange agreement for 1968–69, 'under which the two nations will exchange performing groups, cultural exhibits and language and graduate students.' There would be further talks on restrictions on offensive and defensive strategic weapons.[58]

In Vietnam, things still seemed bleak. There was no movement in the Paris talks: Hanoi was still seeking unconditional cessation of bombing from the United States.[59] Finally, Johnson addressed the nation on Friday, 1 November 1968 to confirm the end of the bombing on the basis that the talks had entered a 'new and much more hopeful phase.'[60] There were to be further peace initiatives, and a resumption of American bombing in December 1972 when negotiations broke down, before the fall of Saigon came on 30 April 1975, and Vietnam was reunified.

The pressure on Wilson was never the same after 1968. In Britain, the position on the streets eased. Peter Hain recalled: 'The high noon of the Vietnam Solidarity Campaign was 1968. Momentum ebbed, and there was no clear strategy to take the movement anywhere.'[61] Dick Taverne, who viewed Vietnam from the vantage point of being, at one point, Healey's parliamentary private secretary, said that the prime minister '. . . showed a considerable degree of statesmanship in keeping the UK out of the Vietnam War but maintaining the Anglo-American Alliance. This took considerable strength . . . a strong person was needed in standing up to the Americans.'[62] Taverne's judgement is prescient, and it is all the more credible for coming from someone who was no ally of Wilson at the time. Similarly, David Owen, who had been elected as MP for Plymouth Devonport in 1966, believes Wilson held the Labour Party together on Vietnam in a way that nobody else could have done.[63]

It was to Wilson's credit that Johnson's successor, Richard Nixon, when he stepped off Air Force One in London on 24 February 1969, spoke positively about Anglo-American relations and used the term 'special relationship'. Wilson reassured Nixon, as he had Johnson, that he would not repeat things in public outside private meetings unless by formal statement. On 3 August, Wilson was there to greet Nixon, then at the end of a world tour, when he touched down at the United States Air Force base in Suffolk. The *Daily Mail* was scathing the next day, accusing the prime minister of having 'scurried to Mildenhall to make obeisance on "Anglo-American" soil'. Yet, when Wilson visited the White House in January 1970, Nixon used the term 'special relationship' again.[64] It seemed that Wilson was a better judge of his relationship with the president than his critics.

Wilson avoided committing British troops to Vietnam or to Rhodesia. He had negotiated with Smith; he had tried to broker a deal on Vietnam. Wilson had saved the lives of British troops that would have undoubtedly been lost, and tried to find diplomatic solutions to stop others dying too. His efforts, and his fine achievements, should be accorded the credit they deserve.

Chapter 15

Tanks off my lawn

Sterling and Strife

As Harold Wilson spent the Christmas of 1967 at Chequers, he could take little satisfaction in the fact that, as he had always predicted, devaluation was not a panacea. Instead, he now had to face working with Jenkins to carry a substantial round of spending cuts through cabinet. To achieve this, Wilson's first instinct was to create an 'inner cabinet' of eleven senior ministers who met on 27 December. However, Callaghan, having implemented many cuts himself, changed tack and proved difficult, so Wilson abandoned the idea.[1] Therefore, he saw in the New Year, as usual, in the Isles of Scilly, and returned to his tried-and-tested method of marathon cabinet meetings, holding eight sessions over thirty-two hours from 4 to 15 January.[2]

The cuts fell into four broad categories: the withdrawal from East of Suez brought forward to 1970–71; in a personal blow to Wilson, the restoration of prescription charges; spending on roads and housing; and postponing the raising of the school leaving age to sixteen, which proved the most controversial. The minutes of the final cabinet meeting capture the strength of feeling, with Brown and Callaghan particularly outraged. Lord Longford, the lord privy seal, said he could not defend the decision, and resigned from the government the next day.[3] The withdrawal of forces from 'East of Suez' marked the end of Empire. After all, the term was more than a geographical reality: it came from Rudyard Kipling's poem 'Mandalay': 'Ship me somewheres [sic] east of Suez . . .'[4] Heath accused the government of diminishing Britain's role in the world, both by the withdrawal of forces and going back on the reassurances Wilson had previously given to allies around the world: 'Some are angry and say that they cannot trust Britain's word again. Worst of all, most of them are beginning to ignore us, simply because they do not believe that Britain's power or influence matter any more.'[5] As Wilson himself had put it: 'East of Suez lies our ability to help other Commonwealth nations when they call upon us to meet aggression . . . East of Suez lies our ability to contribute to United Nations peace-keeping . . .'[6] The removal of forces certainly took away Britain's ability to launch operations around the world. In South-East Asia, there was a major base in Singapore together with a smaller facility in Borneo, a garrison in Hong Kong and an Indian Ocean air base at Gan. In the Middle East, there was the large base at Aden, from which forces had already withdrawn in November 1967, with a more minor facility in Bahrain. Johnson's administration thought 'premature British departure from certain areas . . . presents real problems for us.'[7] It was less problematic in the Labour Party; indeed, Healey's Defence White Paper of February 1967 provoked a rebellion in the parliamentary party on the basis that the withdrawal was not fast enough.[8] It was only a visit by Lee Kuan Yew, prime minister of Singapore, to Downing Street, for a dinner on 14 January, that led to the withdrawal date being put back from March 1971 to the end of the year.

On 17 January, Jenkins told the Commons to expect a 'hard Budget' and that there were 'two years of hard slog ahead'.[9] There was, however, further pressure on sterling before Jenkins had the chance to finalise his proposals. In early March, the reserves started to fall once again, in a pattern horribly familiar to Wilson. The cost of the Vietnam War put pressure on the dollar, and there was a serious question as to whether the convertibility rate between the dollar and gold could hold. Dollars were being converted into gold, and sterling, in turn, was being converted into dollars to buy gold. It is difficult to see how Wilson could have survived another devaluation.

On the evening of 14 March, at 6 p.m. at the House of Commons,

Jenkins told Wilson that the US Treasury wanted to solve the problem by introducing a two-tier system whereby countries agreed to sell gold used as reserves to each other at a fixed price, separate from the gold commodity market. Wilson summoned Michael Halls to parliament to set up an emergency office for the evening. Wilson then attended the archbishop of Canterbury's Immigration Committee, where there was deep concern over the proposed Commonwealth Immigrants Bill, and where he discussed the gold situation with Callaghan. Wilson's account is he then sent a 'high-powered Foreign Office search party' to find Brown, and waited an hour with no result. Wilson returned to Number Ten and asked for the search to continue, but it was to no avail. At 10.40 p.m. American Treasury secretary Henry Fowler called Jenkins to ask that, to end the immediate demand for gold, the London gold market be closed the next day. That meant declaring a bank holiday, for which a meeting of the Privy Council would be required to pass an Order in Council. Halls was dispatched to the Commons to inform Crossman as lord president of the Council. Wilson's condition for acceding to the request was that the American Treasury would support sterling on the New York markets, which were remaining open. Eventually, the guarantee to support sterling came through at 12.05 a.m. A meeting of the Privy Council was held at 12.15 a.m., with Shore called in to provide a quorum with Jenkins and Wilson.[10]

Brown's account was that, with the Transport Bill being debated in the Commons, he went back to his official residence at Carlton Gardens at 8 p.m., which had a telephone link to the Foreign Office: if you telephoned and asked for the foreign secretary, you would be put through to the flat. Brown says he was not contacted, and returned to the House to vote at 10 p.m., after which he sat in the chamber where he was passed a note by Halls who said the prime minister had asked him to pass on a message. Brown then spoke to the secretary and was told Wilson was on the way to the palace for a Privy Council meeting to declare the next day a bank holiday. Another account has Halls in a dinner jacket leading a furious Brown to call him a 'popinjay' and a 'stooge messenger' for

Wilson.[11] Brown rang Number Ten and this was confirmed, but after a pause which raised his suspicion that Wilson was still there. This would have been around 12.10 a.m.

There was another vote, and as MPs trooped through the division lobbies, Brown started asking any cabinet ministers he could see if they knew about this meeting; only Crossman did. He exploded at this and called an immediate meeting in a room at the Commons that included Benn, Crosland, Marsh, Stewart and Thomas and others. Brown telephoned Wilson who clearly thought his deputy was drunk. This sent Brown into an even greater rage, who kept repeating back: '*Don't say in my condition.*' Wilson demanded to know who was with Brown and the conversation descended into a row as the prime minister told him he had no right to call an irregular meeting of the cabinet. Brown demanded Wilson come to the meeting; an infuriated Wilson refused, before Stewart took the phone and Wilson agreed to the ministers coming to Number Ten. At that meeting, Brown told Wilson he did not believe he had tried to contact him. Wilson said he would not be called a liar. Brown demanded to know from Michael Palliser how long Wilson had been trying to contact him. Palliser, a professional civil servant to his fingertips, would not answer. Brown got up, shouting, and stormed out.[12]

Jenkins made his statement to the Commons at 3.20 a.m. announcing the bank holiday. The next morning there was a formal meeting of the cabinet at 10.30 a.m. Brown did not attend and sent his private secretary to see Wilson at lunchtime. Wilson said he had no comment to make. Nor did Wilson respond to a message via Brown's PPS Ernest Davies or another visit by the secretary later in the day. Brown eventually sent a letter that Wilson received at 6 p.m. saying: 'I think it better we should part company.' Brown had written: 'It is, in short, the way this Government is run, and the manner in which we reach our decisions.' Wilson treated it as a resignation, though he did pause momentarily to see if Brown retracted. He replied, defending his own conduct: '. . . unsuccessful attempts were made to get in touch with you at a critical phase . . .'[13]

Wilson had run out of patience. The cabinet meeting Brown had called had spooked him: he feared a coup was on the cards. The truth of the previous night and whether Brown was actually drunk in his flat is a moot point. Castle saw Brown at the 10 p.m. vote, when he had been 'unbuttoning the back of my blouse. When I had chided him he had grinned like a schoolboy and would have given anyone who didn't know him an impression almost of euphoria.'[14] However, she did not think he was inebriated. He may well not have been on this particular occasion; the reality is that in calling the impromptu meeting of the cabinet he had crossed a line with the prime minister.

Brown was a rumbling volcano throughout his time in Wilson's cabinet. Wilson showed great patience in managing him, even acting as a de facto marriage guidance counsellor. Brown's relationship with his wife Sophie was tempestuous, with frequent rows and reconciliations. Wilson often played peacemaker with Sophie contacting him to ask for help with her husband, and the prime minister inviting Brown to 10 Downing Street to give him advice on his personal life.[15] As it happened, his departure did not destabilise Wilson. On 17 March, *The Sunday Times* called Brown and Wilson the 'hot potato and the cold fish'.[16] There is something in this. Their temperaments were very different: Brown lacked Wilson's ability to put emotion aside and think through a situation coolly. The tragedy for Brown is that if he could have turned his own temperature down during his own political career he could have achieved a great deal more. He could be a compelling speaker, and a strong cabinet minister who could knock heads together and get things done. His resignation speech on 18 March pledged loyalty and had little impact. What could have caused great damage was if he had resigned as deputy leader, as it would have precipitated a contest that would have been seen as a proxy for the succession to Wilson himself. Brown chose not to resign and then lost his seat at Belper in 1970. Wilson then sent him to the Lords, where, in typically idiosyncratic fashion, he chose to hyphenate his first name and surname to create his title, 'Lord George-Brown'.

Attention moved swiftly to Jenkins's budget, delivered to the Commons on 19 March. Its purpose was a 'major reduction in public and private consumption.'[17] Thus, the budget was austere on a scale then unprecedented in the post-war era, increasing taxes by an eye-watering £923m.[18] Yet, for its principal political aim, to send a signal to the markets that the government had the strength to turn around the balance of payments post-devaluation, it received a positive reaction from the press. With Wilson at a low ebb, Jenkins' positive press rankled. Peter Jay's glowing assessment in *The Times* was typical: 'Roy Jenkins has risen fully and magnificently to the occasion. Yesterday's Budget was really everything that was economically needed.'[19]

Jenkins was unhappy with Wilson's proposed cabinet changes after Brown's departure. First, he objected – unsuccessfully – to Stewart's return as foreign secretary as he would have preferred Healey, whom he thought would be a more colourful character. The authoritative, assertive Healey, with his distinctive bushy eyebrows, was certainly more memorable than the steady Stewart, who exuded a quiet competence. However, Stewart's reliability mattered to Wilson, and he was actually given an expanded department as the Commonwealth Office was joined to it: the Foreign and Commonwealth Office was born. This left the title of first secretary that Wilson wanted to give to Castle along with the Department for Economic Affairs. Jenkins blocked this, telling Castle at Number Eleven that he thought she was 'one of the three outstanding Ministers in the Government' and could not tolerate such a strong presence reviving the department and making it a rival to the Treasury.[20] Wilson relented, and Shore remained at the Department for Economic Affairs until it was wound up in October 1969. Wilson instead made Castle first secretary of state and added the Department for Employment and Productivity, an expanded Ministry of Labour. This displaced Gunter, who, while he was moved to become minister of power, resigned on 29 June, attacking Wilson personally: 'I no longer desire to be a member of *your* [author's emphasis] Government and am therefore tendering my resignation.'[21]

Wilson's authority was damaged. He sought to concentrate power in a permanent inner cabinet: known as the parliamentary committee in its first year and the management committee in its second. In April 1968, it had a membership of eight: Wilson himself, Stewart, Gardiner, Healey, Castle, Jenkins, Crossman and Peart. However, others were often added for particular agenda items, making it large and unwieldy. In May 1969, it was restricted to seven: Wilson, Stewart, Jenkins, Crossman, Castle, Healey and Callaghan.[22]

When Jenkins made a speech in Birmingham on 15 June on Lords reform, Wilson reacted with fury. He was convinced the chancellor was undermining him and using the memory of the chancellor before the First World War David Lloyd George attacking the Lords, to seek radical left support to replace him. He told Dick Crossman the speech was 'deliberately intended to put me in my place'.[23] Wilson's anger boiled over on 25 June, after a leak about government plans to reform the House of Lords. Wilson opened cabinet with yet another warning about leaking, and a personal attack on Jenkins: 'I know where a great part of the leaking and the backbiting comes from. It arises from the ambitions of one member of this Cabinet to sit in my place.' When it emerged that what had actually happened was that Crossman had, perfectly reasonably, discussed the issue with Peter Carrington on the Conservative side, Wilson had to apologise.[24]

Wilson had every reason to feel insecure. The previous month, the *Daily Mirror* had called for him to go. Cecil King, chair of the International Publishing Corporation, of which the *Daily Mirror* was a part, was a newspaperman in the mould of his uncle, Lord Northcliffe, whose titles included the *Daily Mail* and *The Times*, who had exerted significant pressure for the replacement of Asquith by Lloyd George in December 1916.

In the summer of 1967, King's then deputy, Hugh Cudlipp, spoke to Lord Mountbatten at dinner, who confirmed that it had been suggested that he could play a part in a new regime that replaced Wilson's government, but thought himself too old.[25] Cudlipp himself recalled: 'The scenario for "The Fall of Harold Wilson" was perfected in King's mind during 1967.' In the first four months of 1968 his principal concern was who would be in the replacement administration and what it would be called, mooting 'Emergency Government'.[26] It is certainly the case that those interested in politics discuss who might feature in their fantasy government. Few do so as part of a plan to create one. King told Cudlipp that Wilson would be out of power within three months: 'A financial crash and another devaluation, leading to the swift collapse of Labour in power, was inevitable . . .'[27]

Cudlipp arranged a meeting between Mountbatten, King, and himself for 8 May 1968. They gathered at Kinnerton Street, Mountbatten's mews residence in London. The host had telephoned ahead to confirm that he would be joined by Solly Zuckerman, then the government's chief scientific adviser. According to Cudlipp, King 'awaited the arrival of Sir Solly and then at once expounded his views on the national situation, the urgency for action, and then embarked upon a shopping-list of the Prime Minister's shortcomings.' King 'explained that in the crisis he foresaw as just being around the corner the government would disintegrate, there would be bloodshed in the streets, the armed forces would be involved.' He then put his point directly: 'The public would be looking to somebody like Lord Mountbatten as the titular head of a new administration, somebody renowned as a leader of men . . . He ended with a question to Mountbatten – would he agree to be the titular head of a new administration in such circumstances?'[28] Mountbatten was canny in a way King was not. He turned to Zuckerman and asked his view. He was uncompromising: 'This is rank treachery. All this talk of machine-guns at street corners is appalling. I am a public servant and have nothing to do with it. Nor should you, Dickie.' Mountbatten agreed and Zuckerman departed. He was '. . . courteous but firm: he explained explicitly but briefly that he entirely agreed with Solly and that that sort of role, so far as he was concerned, was "simply not on".' His private secretary, John Barratt, showed Cudlipp and King to their car.[29]

On 9 May, the local elections brought the predictable anti-government result, with the Tory opposition making substantial gains, not least in London, where they gained control of nineteen additional councils. King used this to launch his attack on Wilson.

On the Friday, 10 May, the *Daily Mirror* led with 'ENOUGH IS ENOUGH' and called for a new Labour leader and prime minister. King wrote that the local elections were a confirmation of the opinion polls and the by-election defeat in Dudley on 28 March, when Labour had also been defeated in by-elections in Warwick and Leamington, Meriden and Acton on the same day. King characterised the situation as the 'greatest financial crisis in our history' needing a change of leadership.[30] King, who had overridden the *Daily Mirror*'s editorial independence to write the front page himself, was dismissed by the board on 30 May, with Cudlipp taking his place.

Supporters of Jenkins, including Gordon Walker, Mayhew and Dick Taverne, were also pressing for the chancellor to move against Wilson by organising a mass of letters from MPs to Douglas Houghton. Gordon Walker confided to his diary on 17 June: 'The Conspiracy is now in full swing.' But Jenkins hesitated, uncertain that he could land a knockout blow. He told Gordon Walker: '. . . better not move now. He did not want to say, at any time, that we should move . . . He clearly did not want to be implicated in actually launching an action.' By 19 July, Jenkins' supporters thought the moment had gone, ironically with improving trade figures – for which Jenkins himself could claim credit – being one factor in shifting PLP opinion back in support of Wilson.[31] Wilson had been making his own moves, too. David Owen was dining with Bob Maclennan, then also a Labour MP, when an urgent message arrived from Wilson to go to Number Ten. The sole purpose of the dinner was to discuss the prime minister's removal. Owen went to Downing Street to find Wilson alone in the cabinet room puffing on his pipe. 'I want to offer you Under-Secretary for the Royal Navy,' he said to Owen. Owen blurted back, 'Harold, I am one of your biggest critics!' He smiled and puffed. 'Well, you can't be now!'[32] Owen duly took up the post in early July.

Arguably, Jenkins' best opportunity of becoming prime minister had passed. At first glance, Jenkins had unarguable credentials to be Labour leader. Born in the Eastern Valley of the South Wales coalfield, Jenkins's background lay in the mining heritage of the

Labour movement. His father, Arthur, was a miner who had been a local councillor and MP for Pontypool. Imprisoned during the General Strike of 1926, Arthur Jenkins bore the scars of the industrial struggles of the inter-war period. Jenkins, by dint of his own efforts, won a place at Balliol College, Oxford, and served with the Bletchley Park codebreakers during the Second World War, before entering parliament. Yet nobody would guess this was Jenkins' Labour pedigree. Unlike Wilson, who always spoke in a Yorkshire accent, Jenkins spoke as if he had been educated at an English private school. Added to that was the taste for fine food and expensive claret, and the finishing of work every evening at 6–7 p.m. to go for dinner. Jenkins could have used his background to build a formidable case to be Labour leader; instead he became defined by his love of high-society company. Wilson, who worked until past 11 p.m., referred to him contemptuously as 'Old Beaujolais'.[33]

A further threat to Wilson's position was to emerge from the issue of trade union reform that initially landed on Castle's desk with the publication of the Donovan Report on 14 June 1968.[34] In its final months the Conservative government had suggested a royal commission to avoid a firm commitment to legislating to overturn the *Rookes v Barnard* decision. Gunter, rather than drop the idea altogether, decided to appoint a commission in April 1965, with the support of George Woodcock, general secretary of the TUC, who could see the case for proposing moderate reform and avoiding the government imposing a legal framework. Woodcock had fine judgement. He was later described as the 'outstanding trade union leader of his time' and became a recognisable figure on the television screen, with his wild, bushy eyebrows and silver hair.[35] He was duly appointed to the commission, which was chaired by Lord Donovan. Donovan's principal finding was that, the voluntary system of collective bargaining should be preserved but changed. The report identified that the 'formal' system relied on trade unions being able to persuade their members to accept negotiated settlements while an 'informal' system existed on the factory floor. What was needed was not legal enforcement of settlements and a crackdown on unofficial strikes but reform to introduce formal machinery for negotiation at local level to replace custom and practice. The shadow chancellor, Iain McLeod, called it a 'blueprint for inaction'.[36] The Conservative position was to make collective agreements enforceable in law.

Castle was clear that something had to be done about unofficial strikes, an issue that was worsening. Outside the coal industry, in 1956 there were 572 strikes; in 1967, it was 1,694, most of which were unofficial.[37] Matters were coming to a head in late 1968. A strike at the Girling brake factory in Cheshire on 11 November 1968 was the fifty-seventh dispute there in eighteen months. When 22 machine setters struck, more than 5,000 car workers were laid off at other plants.[38] The factory did not reopen until 9 December, by which time there had been yet another sterling crisis. Jenkins had travelled to Bonn for a meeting of the Group of 10 – G10 – after speculation against the deutschmark and the franc had put pressure on sterling. Neither currency had been devalued, but, on his return, the chancellor made a statement raising another £250m in taxes to reduce demand for imports.[39] On 6 December, what Wilson was to call 'stupid rumours' about another devaluation led to a panic and a selling of sterling on what became known as 'Black Friday'.[40] That month, an opinion poll showed that Labour had fallen 23 per cent behind the Conservatives, who led 49 per cent to 26 per cent.[41]

There were, therefore, strong incentives for Wilson to address the issue of unofficial strikes, not only to continue to address Britain's productivity and economic performance, but also to regain the political initiative. Castle produced her White Paper with an eye on the title of Bevan's book *In Place of Fear*. She named it 'In Place of Strife'. The furore it generated was about the fundamental issue of whether trade unions could continue to engage in free collective bargaining or if the government could impose a formal legal framework on industrial relations: in short, was wage regulation voluntary or compulsory?

Castle saw the issue in terms of rights and responsibilities. Trade unions should have formal recognition and their positive role recognised, but with that should come wider responsibilities to society as a whole. The White Paper proposed to strengthen workers' rights: 'There is need for legislation to establish statutory machinery to safeguard both unionists and non-unionists against unfair dismissal.' It also proposed to increase longstanding employees' entitlement to notice before dismissal.[42] With this, however, came increased power for government: 'The state should recognise the right to strike and the right to bargain collectively to improve wages and conditions.' But the state should also act 'to contain the disruptive consequences of the struggle for those not immediately affected . . .'[43]

To achieve this, there were three highly contentious proposals. First, the twenty-eight-day 'conciliation pause' when workers could be ordered back to work pending negotiations. Second, a minister could impose a settlement where there was an inter-union dispute. Third, there was the power for a minister to order a strike ballot. Any legal framework to be enforced, and the penalties for failing to comply only added to the controversy. As early as 8 January, Judith Hart, then paymaster general, circulated her own memorandum to cabinet, setting out her deep concern about employees who continued to participate in unconstitutional strikes being fined.[44]

In terms of political competition with the Conservatives, 'In Place of Strife' made sense. It was in the middle ground between the Donovan defence of the status quo and the Conservative move to legal enforcement with no measures to strengthen workers' rights. Where it did not make sense was in an area where Wilson had so often been so shrewd: the views of the Labour rank and file. As Neil Kinnock, who was at that time teaching industrial relations for the Workers' Educational Association, said: 'shop stewards in steel, chemical, engineering and manufacturing, all loyal to Labour, were alienated. Labour seemed to be saying they could not be trusted and could be pushed around.'[45] Wilson allowed his instincts in high politics to trump the likely reaction within his own party. Marcia Williams thought it the 'most unpleasant, disastrous and dramatic' period of the 1964–70 governments.[46]

Opposition to the measures grew in every part of the Labour movement. Wilson was in a very different situation with the trade unions from either of his predecessors as Labour leader. Attlee relied on Ernest Bevin who still had enormous influence over the largest union, the TGWU. Gaitskell could rely on Arthur Deakin, Will Lawther and Tom Williamson to support the leadership line. In 1969, the leaders of the two largest unions were Jack Jones, general secretary of the TGWU, and Hugh Scanlon, general secretary of the Amalgamated Engineering Union (AEU), who, far from supporting Wilson, confronted his proposals head-on. On 8 January, the TUC gave short shrift to the proposals, rejecting them within an hour.[47]

Wilson used his tried-and-tested method of multiple cabinet meetings, holding four in just under two weeks prior to the publication of 'In Place of Strife' on 17 January 1969.[48] The leading opponent of the proposals was Callaghan, who was to test Wilson's authority to the limit. Yet, even those closer to Wilson were deeply worried. At cabinet on 14 January, Crossman 'remained doubtful that the compulsory conciliation pause was practical or desirable' and urged Wilson to remain open to the suggestion of an alternative voluntary scheme from the TUC. Castle, however, argued that her proposals meant 'trade unions would accept they were directed to strengthening the trade unions and not weakening them'.[49] As Kinnock put it, Castle was a 'bull at a gate. The only politics she and [her husband] Ted knew was to fix bayonets and charge'.[50]

Callaghan's influence was also significant in two other arenas. First, in the Parliamentary Labour Party, where his ally and friend Houghton was now the chair. On 3 March, after the debate in the White Paper in the Commons, 55 Labour MPs voted against the proposals, and around 40 abstained. Second, on the NEC, of which he was a member. At the meeting on 26 March, the attitude was so hostile that resolutions were carried stating that it could not support the White Paper, and against even welcoming the fact that Castle was going to be speaking to the trade unions about it, with Callaghan voting in the majority and against the government position on both.[51] It was a canny move from the home secretary. He signalled to the trade unions, and their sponsored MPs, that he was on their side. Despite the egregious breach of cabinet collective discipline, Wilson was too weak to sack him, and left with issuing an 'open reprimand' to observe discipline.

Meanwhile, Wilson agreed with Castle and Jenkins to introduce a short, interim, Industrial Relations Bill while offering the unions a softer approach on prices and incomes. This had the advantage of closing the matter before the TUC Congress and party conference in the autumn. On 14 April, at cabinet, with only Callaghan and Marsh dissenting, this was agreed.[52] The next day, Jenkins announced the bargain in his budget, and confirmed that the main proposals in 'In Place of Strife' would be brought forward.[53]

Wilson, anxious for a more disciplinarian approach to the rebellious parliamentary party, replaced Silkin with Bob Mellish as chief whip on 29 April. Mellish, the thirteenth of fourteen children of a London docker, had gone straight from school to a job at the office of the Transport and General Workers' Union in Stratford, and had served as a sapper in the Second World War, rising to the rank of major in the Royal Engineers. He has been described as 'the authentic voice of working-class Dockland London'.[54] He proved an adroit chief whip, confounding expectations that he would be a bully. At the time of his appointment, though, Castle was enraged. She saw Silkin as someone who would always have defended Wilson and the Bevanite left, while Mellish would start a crackdown. She told Crossman over dinner: 'I'm through with Harold now . . . Henceforth I dedicate myself to his destruction. I'm going to send him the sort of letter on which he ought to ask for my resignation.' Wilson saw Castle the next day, and assured her that Mellish had not been brought in to 'clobber the left' but to bring the 'middle-of-the-roaders' on board. Though Castle was still angry, it was enough to patch things up. She was 'really frightened at Harold's state'.[55] The prime minister had stomach trouble: evidence of the physical toll the pressure was exacting on him.

At this point, Wilson's leadership became vulnerable. On 2 May, *The Times* reported that a coup 'might have been plotted, and that it might break into the open in the next few days' with the purpose of installing Callaghan in Number Ten. Houghton's requirement to open up the issue of the leadership at the meeting of the parliamentary party was a request from 120 MPs. This bar was set high because, if it were met, it was doubtful Wilson could survive. Houghton was ensuring that an attack would not simply wound Wilson; at that level it would be a fatal political strike. The number was already too large for Wilson's liking. Sixty were willing to request such a meeting, and another forty would be prepared to vote against the prime minister in a secret ballot once the meeting was called.[56]

Wilson, worried that even the 'Praetorian Guard were deserting', was speaking at the May Day rally at the Festival Hall on 4 May. Here, he showed not only his extraordinary resilience but his lightness of touch in a grave situation. It was the start of him regaining the initiative, and securing his position as party leader. He turned the speculation about his future to his advantage by drawing laughter from the crowd: 'I know what is going on,' he began, and added: 'I am going on.'[57] Wilson's advantage was that Jenkins and Callaghan both wanted the top job, so did not combine against him. Jenkins could hardly mount a challenge against Wilson on the basis of 'In Place of Strife' since he was bound in to supporting it with the prime minister and Castle. Jenkins needed another challenger to Wilson to emerge and to come into a leadership contest at a later stage. Wilson also had the advantage of having no threat from the left, who still saw him as preferable to Callaghan.

Houghton told the Parliamentary Labour Party on 7 May that 'Our unity and political purpose matters more to the country than the marginal damage done by unconstitutional strikes.' He made the comments public, leading to Wilson being taunted in the Commons the next day that he needed Houghton's permission to introduce legislation. Wilson was quick in response, and said the Tories should not assume that Houghton 'exercises in relation to this Front Bench what the right hon. Gentleman the Member for Wolverhampton, South-West (Mr. Powell) exercises in relation to that [Conservative] Front Bench'.[58] However, Callaghan's problem was the increasing tension between opposing the government's major policy in public and not resigning as home secretary. At cabinet on 8 May, Dick Crossman lost his temper and shouted: 'Get out, Jim, get out'. Callaghan was taken aback; Crossman recorded that he 'had been punctured. He hadn't responded, he had crawled, and it was quite a moment.'[59] The next day, at a joint meeting of the cabinet and the NEC, Callaghan again criticised the government, but it was clear, without the 120 signatures or a resignation, the moment had passed. As the Motherwell MP George Lawson put it: 'our thing broke down'.[60] Wilson's position was strengthening. He removed Callaghan from the inner cabinet on 13 May.

Wilson had consolidated his personal position, but he had not secured agreement with the trade unions on the bill, despite he and Castle seeking a solution. On 5 June, the TUC held a special congress at Croydon to consider its position on 'In Place of Strife'. Vic Feather, the general secretary, was both a flamboyant character with a quick wit and an effective broker of deals. He proclaimed 'not a step forward but a great leap forward' but the TUC remained implacably opposed to 'statutory financial penalties on work people or on trade unions' and only said some of the other proposals 'could in principle help to improve industrial relations'.[61] Wilson's patience with the union leaders had already snapped. The previous weekend, at Chequers, the prime minister and Castle had met Feather with Jones and Scanlon. Scanlon told Wilson: 'Prime Minister, we don't want you to become another Ramsay Macdonald.' Wilson retorted: 'Get your tanks off my lawn, Hughie!'[62]

The final episodes in the drama started with cabinet meetings on 17 June. It ended inconclusively, though with a typical piece of Wilsonian flexibility to give him and Castle wriggle room. He said they would try to avoid committing the government to 'any precise form of statutory disciplinary procedures since the Cabinet were not in agreement on this matter' but said it would not be possible 'to avoid indicating the advice which they themselves would feel compelled to give their Cabinet colleagues if the negotiations reached a final deadlock.'[63] In other words, the stick Wilson would use in negotiation with the TUC would not be the likely position of the cabinet, but the view of him and Castle.

The next day, the meeting between the cabinet and the TUC

took place. Cabinet ministers sat together with the TUC delegation upstairs, including Feather, Scanlon and Jones. Wilson shuttled between the two rooms. Both sides were keen to settle the dispute, and the tenacious, shrewd Joe Haines, a journalist at the *Sun* who had joined Wilson's Downing Street operation as deputy press secretary on 1 January 1969, sat with the union leaders.[64] Len Murray, a quiet pragmatist with sound judgement, then assistant general secretary of the TUC, whispered to him: 'Doesn't Harold understand that the TUC are paper tigers?'[65] The solution, which did not require legislation, was for the TUC to give a 'solemn and binding' undertaking about intervening in illegal strikes. Rather than be compelled to act, the TUC would give a binding promise to act: it was not government control, but the TUC offering to control. The press were merciless in their treatment of Wilson, inventing a new character: Mr Solomon Binding. 'The popular old gentleman's last-minute appearance at the talks between the Labour Government and the TUC enabled Mr Wilson to run away from his own proposed industrial legislation.'[66] It was another low moment for Wilson and the government. Wilson and Castle's plan to curb unconstitutional strikes was completely destroyed, with Wilson having put his leadership at great risk. The best thing that could be said is that he met one of politics' most important objectives: he had survived.

Chapter 16

Why did he take Charlton off?

Recovery and Defeat in 1970

Harold Wilson's retreat on 'In Place of Strife' marked the end of a period when his government, and his leadership, felt under siege. The final year of his first period in office, though it was to end in disappointment with a general election defeat, was a period when Labour not only closed the gap in the opinion polls with the Conservatives, but surged ahead. This recovery was as a consequences of two issues. The first, ironically, was yet another crisis, this time in Northern Ireland, though the government's handling of it proved popular with the public. The second was the improving state of the economy, as Jenkins' tough measures started to produce results.

Wilson had no desire to be drawn into the politics of Northern Ireland. In May 1966, Gerry Fitt, then a Republican Labour MP, told Wilson that democracy did not exist in the statelet. Wilson's answer expressed his gut instinct: '. . . I am not taking sides in this because there are allegations and counter-allegations by one side or another within Northern Ireland.'[1] Fitt was, however, giving voice to serious grievances on the part of the Catholic community. Since the partition of Ireland, and formation of the parliament of Northern Ireland in 1921, it had been, in the words of its first prime minister, James Craig, 'a Protestant Parliament and a Protestant State'.[2]

In Derry, a majority Catholic population lived under a majority Unionist county borough council due to gerrymandered electoral boundaries. The Unionist Stormont government was accused of favouring Protestant areas for investment, and of anti-Catholic discrimination in areas such as the allocation of public housing and public sector jobs. The Stormont parliament relied on the Royal Ulster Constabulary to maintain order. Founded on 1 June 1922, on the disbandment of the Royal Irish Constabulary, the RUC was supported by a reserve police force, the Special Constabulary, of which one section, the part-time 'B Specials' not only survived for decades afterwards, but was wholly Protestant, and came to be seen by Catholics not as an auxiliary police force but as a Protestant army. Worse still, the Civil Authorities (Special Powers) Act 1922 had handed the Stormont government wide-ranging powers to suspend civil liberties, including the use of arrest and detainment, without due process, in the name of keeping order. The Flags and Emblems (Display) Act 1954, also passed by Stormont, put a duty on police to remove flags and emblems likely to cause a breach of the peace, with the exception of the union flag, meaning displays of the Irish tricolour were vulnerable to law enforcement. These pieces of legislation were used against the Catholic community, and were highly discriminatory.

Terence O'Neill, who was elected Northern Ireland prime minister in 1963, sought friendly association with the South and economic co-operation, meeting Taoiseach Sean Lemass and his successor Jack Lynch. In some ways, conditions were better for Catholics in the North than the South, not least on welfare and healthcare. It was, however, on the issue of providing housing on grounds of religion that matters came to a head, with the Derry Housing Action Committee, formed in early 1968, challenging housing allocation and accommodation conditions. On 5 October 1968, a civil rights march in Derry was baton-charged by the RUC, leading to widespread violence and rioting in subsequent days.

The disorder continued. On 4 January 1969, a People's Democracy March from Belfast to Derry was ambushed by loyalists while passing through Burntollet. The stability of the Northern Ireland statelet was now under threat. O'Neill resigned, to be replaced by James Chichester-Clark on 1 May 1969. Initially, the situation seemed promising for the new prime minister. The Civil Rights

Association announced that it would suspend its demonstrations for six weeks to give the new administration time to show its intent. Chichester-Clark looked to be continuing with reform, sending a model scheme for public housing allocation to local authorities on 12 June; Sir Edmund Compton was appointed parliamentary commissioner for administration on 1 July; and the next day a White Paper on local government reorganisation was published. But it proved a temporary respite. On 28 June, the Civil Rights Association resumed its demonstrations on the basis that there was no firm timetable for delivering reform. Initial Civil Rights rallies in Strabane and Newry were peaceful; a march in Armagh led to scuffles but nothing more. Then, the Orange Order processions on 12 July led to three days of violence centred in Londonderry and Dungiven, with incidents in Belfast, Lurgan and Limavady. In all, 154 police officers were injured, including 116 in Londonderry; 54 civilians were injured, of which 46 were in Londonderry.[3]

On 28 July Callaghan circulated a memorandum to cabinet warning of potential consequences of the Apprentice Boys of Londonderry's Annual Parade on 12 August. Commemorating the relief of the city in 1689, and named after the thirteen young men who locked the city gates against the Earl of Antrim, leading the forces of the Catholic king, James II, in 1688, it was feared that the Protestant march could lead to disturbances and rioting. The Catholic population was said to have lost respect for law and order and for the Royal Ulster Constabulary and Special Constabulary. Callaghan set out that the police might lose control, and that the Northern Ireland government would ask for military help to restore order. He asked that he, Healey and Wilson be given authority to decide urgent matters without reference to cabinet, which was agreed at the formal cabinet meeting two days later.[4]

The warnings proved prescient. On the nights of 2 and 3 August, there was rioting in Belfast and petrol bombs thrown. Callaghan, fearing the worst, urged Chichester-Clark to ban the proposed mid-August marches: of the Civil Rights Association on Monday, 11 August, the Apprentice Boys on 12 August, and the meeting of the (Catholic) Order of Hibernians on 15 August. Chichester-Clark would not do this, emphasising that he could not ban one without banning them all; in any event he did not accept the risk of violence. There was disorder at the Civil Rights March; the next day violence broke out in Londonderry, with the residents of the Bogside trying to keep the RUC out of the Catholic areas. These days became known as the 'Battle of the Bogside': on the Thursday, with rioting worsening, and tension in Belfast, Callaghan met Wilson at St Mawgan, the RAF Station in Cornwall, the prime minister breaking off his holiday in the Scillies for the crucial decision to send in the military. It was just after 3 p.m. that day when three hundred troops from the 1st Battalion, Prince of Wales's Own Regiment of Yorkshire, occupied the centre of Londonderry. Initially, they were welcomed, not least by the Catholics, who sang from behind the barricades that they had brought the Stormont government down.[5]

Wilson was keen to stress that this was not a permanent arrangement. On 19 August, he, Stewart, Callaghan, Healey, and Lord Stonham, the minister of state at the Home Office responsible for Northern Ireland, met senior ministers from the Northern Ireland government for a marathon six-hour meeting at Number Ten, and issued a declaration that was unambiguous: 'troops will be withdrawn when law and order has been restored'.[6]

Wilson had not wanted to become embroiled in Northern Irish politics, but found himself sending in troops that did not leave for decades. It is, however, difficult to see what else he could have done in the face of continuing disorder. When the public were asked, 62 per cent thought the government had been right to send in the troops, with only 22 per cent against.[7] Callaghan was also recovering his reputation. In early September, Wilson restored him to the inner cabinet.

Jenkins' two years' hard slog also paid off. The monthly figures for August 1969 showed a £40m balance of payments surplus and this continued to increase, reaching £387m by the end of the year. It was a remarkable turnaround in two years. It had been a bitter irony that the monthly trade figures that Wilson could recite had, on so many occasions, caused economic and political turmoil for the government. Now they were evidence of a great success, and it paid political dividends. By December, Labour had closed the gap on the Conservatives in the opinion polls to 9 per cent, with 35 per cent to 44 per cent for the Conservatives. Attitudes towards the government were changing. A further poll conducted in April and May 1970 showed a 7 per cent Labour lead, 45 per cent to 38 per cent.[8]

While the transformation of the balance of payments position was crucial, it is important not to neglect other economic changes. Wilson's aim was to encourage industrial restructuring. The Ministry of Technology, 'MinTech' as it was known, was crucial in this, whatever Benn's doubts about the policies might have been. In January 1968, Benn encouraged the merger of Leyland Motors and British Motor Holdings into British Leyland. Later that year, the Industrial Expansion Act gave powers to the government to intervene directly and swiftly, with Benn complaining that the arm's-length Industrial Reorganisation Corporation, created in 1966, had led to delay, which 'meant that action within the time scale which, after all, in all these cases, is dictated by industrial realities, has been almost impossible'.[9] Benn then moved quickly to merge International Computers and Tabulators Ltd and English Electric Computers Ltd, creating International Computers Ltd (ICL), the largest computer firm outside the United States. The same approach, of creating larger concerns to take advantage of economies of scale, was taken in other sectors. The General Electric Company took over the English Electric Company, developing electronics and engineering. Sir Reay Geddes, Managing Director at Dunlop, chaired a committee looking at the shipbuilding industry. Its recommendation that the twenty-seven main British shipbuilders be consolidated into five, was implemented in the 1967 Shipbuilding Industry Act, with these based in the North-East of England, on the River Clyde, and in Belfast.[10] The Iron and Steel Act 1967, renationalising the industry, brought fourteen private companies together as the British Steel Corporation.

In October 1969, Wilson merged the Ministry of Power into the Ministry of Technology, expanding Benn's Whitehall empire.

Harold Lever, who had made a fortune as a barrister and stock market investor, and was well-respected in the City, became Benn's deputy, as paymaster general, with Judith Hart moving to become minister for overseas development. Marsh, who had opposed Wilson over 'In Place of Strife', was dropped. The Department for Economic Affairs was wound up, with Shore made minister without portfolio. Wilson also made changes with one eye to the future, and he promoted women. Joan Lestor became a junior minister at Education, where she joined Jennie Lee and Alice Bacon, who had moved there in 1967. Shirley Williams left the department to move to the Home Office. In an effort to promote unity before a general election, Wilson had even offered Brown a return to government, but he would accept nothing less than deputy prime minister, so it did not happen.[11]

Wilson was also reshaping his own office at Number Ten. Marcia Williams' influence had not diminished, but Wilson's heavy commitments meant her time with him was more limited. Marcia's own life was changing, too. On the one hand, with Mitchell having moved on, she could accompany Wilson on trips abroad. In December 1966, she was on board HMS *Tiger* with Wilson for the talks with Ian Smith; and she sat at the same table with him in the Kremlin.[12] On the other, there were additional pressures on her time. She gave birth to two sons, one in August 1968 and another in June 1969. The father was Walter Terry, political editor of the *Daily Mail*, who was himself married with children. This was, however, kept away from the newspapers until 1974. Marcia, with the help of a nanny and her sister Peggy, was able to keep working for Wilson, but the days of her at the prime minister's side until late into the evening were over.

There is no evidence that Wilson begrudged Marcia her time with her sons, but their arrival did worry him in terms of the potential rumours that might be set off. The prime minister's new recruit in this period, Haines, had joined on the basis that he would move from deputy to chief press officer as soon as he had settled in, and took on the full role when Lloyd-Hughes left in June 1969.[13] Wilson soon tasked Haines with ensuring Jenkins' closest adviser

John Harris (and, thereby, the chancellor himself) knew about Marcia's children. This, at least, would put a stop to Jenkins being tempted to try to use the issue to bring Wilson down; the obvious line of attack was to suggest the children were his.

Initially, Haines was impressed by Marcia Williams. She was, on the whole, charming to those she did not know well, and dominated in social settings without being domineering: 'For a time, when I first worked with her, my admiration for her sheer brain-power was considerable, almost unquestioning. Had she gone into the House of Commons she would have forced her way into the Cabinet at an age when most single women were still hoping to get married. That, eventually, no Cabinet beyond one in size would have been big enough to hold her, is irrelevant.'[14] A profile of Williams appeared in *Punch* in April 1969 with this anecdote: 'The story goes that an important visitor called at Number 10 and asked if he could speak to Mr Wilson's secretary. "I'm sorry," was the reply, "Mrs Williams is very busy, but the Prime Minister can see you now."' She was then thirty-six. 'She pays his bills, types his speeches, hands round drinks at his parties, and keeps confidential files for him. She is a natural organiser, a gifted political hostess, and a close friend of the Wilson family (her sister Peggy is now working for Mrs Wilson).'[15] She was, however, far more influential than this. Politically, her skill lay in sharpening Wilson's communications, making them accessible to the general public. Haines observed that 'she could transform a pedestrian political speech by the Prime Minister into a highly effective one with a few simple but vivid thoughts, plus a general restructuring of its order . . .' Her stock phrase meant part of a speech would be removed: 'Forgive me, fellers, for being a poor, ignorant woman, but I do not understand what this paragraph means.'[16] Later, reflecting on her role, she summed it up as being a link between Wilson and the Labour Party: the party knowing what he was thinking, and he knowing what the party was thinking. She was, she said, his 'eyes and ears'.[17]

Even this, though, fails to capture the essence of her relationship with Wilson. Her words to those who worked for Wilson were indicative: 'Remember, fellers, that our loyalty is to Harold

Wilson. No one else. Never forget that.'[18] As the *Punch* profile put it: 'She will undoubtedly follow him into the wilderness when the time comes.'[19] That final prediction was to prove entirely accurate. Whatever the criticisms of Marcia, nobody could accuse her of dropping Wilson when it was inconvenient. She remained with him until the end.

Williams had a presence. She had a strong personality and could erupt with a huge, destructive force. Asked in an interview in 1984 about government ministers being in awe of her, she remarked that it would equally be the case if a man was in her role, and that the coverage about her influence was exaggerated 'simply because I was a woman'.[20] This is undoubtedly true. Haines observed: 'It is a tiresome fact that women holding down senior posts are still treated by Fleet Street as sex objects if they are young or good-looking and Marcia was still both.'[21] At the same time, the price of Williams' proximity to Wilson was her desire for control. Losing her temper was actually a way of emphasising her status. At the 1969 party conference in Brighton, with Wilson and Benn discussing his speech with Haines and others, all with pipes and cigars, she claimed the smoke was getting into her throat, stormed out and went back to London. As Haines put it: 'By such scenes it was certainly demonstrated that she was more important than anyone else.'[22] Later, there were claims that her influence was so destructive that it led to serious consequences for those around her. Michael Halls died, prematurely, on 3 April 1970. In March 1973, his widow, Marjorie, sued the government. Halls said her husband had enjoyed his job until 1968, when Marcia Williams had become pregnant. Wilson was said to have become obsessed with the personal lives of his staff to such an extent that Halls' ability to do his work was impeded. The stress of existing within Wilson's inner circle was said to have worn him down and caused his death.[23] In early 1970, Williams moved house, and Halls was expected to help with the arrangements. The allegations even included Williams telephoning Marjorie Halls, threatening to bring down the prime minister if Halls did not establish a telephone connection at her new home. Williams' and Wilson's quarrels were said to be causing problems. In March 1970, Wilson called Halls after another quarrel with Williams to update him: 'She has gone off at last, screaming her bloody head off.'[24] It was in Wilson's second period as prime minister that Williams' intensity was to increase even further, but, with a general election imminent, he had a Kitchen Cabinet he could rely on.

The prime minister continued to value his time with his family. The close proximity between private and public life was neatly summed up by Robin playing the harmonium and the tune of 'Onward Christian Soldiers' being heard in the cabinet room.[25] Robin, who was studying in America from 1965 to 1968, used to return to Number Ten in the summer, where he had a twenty-first birthday party, and an engagement party with his future wife, Joy, in 1967. Mary's first collection of poetry was published in 1970. Elegant and accessible, her *Selected Poems* was a sensation. That September, it was the fastest-selling book in Britain.[26] The poem 'Oxford' is in the voice of a former student but reflected her own longing for that period in her life: 'The music of those three short years/He will not know again'. 'Aberfan' was an expression of her emotional reaction to the disaster, and the visit she and Wilson paid to the village to open the new school in June 1969: 'Where grief and bitter anger lay their burden/On those whose lives are broken' but now 'The stream runs on by the memorial garden/The murd'rous tip of slag is disappearing.' She also reflected on special moments from Downing Street, including the visit of the Apollo astronauts for dinner in October 1969 in 'The Lunarnaut': "'What did the earth look like," I asked him/"As you stood there on the moon?"'[27]

That evening, Wilson, who loved puns, had insisted that Eric Moonman MP be invited as a guest.[28] A drunk George Brown was less amusing, rising to his feet to offer a toast to 'the real Michael Collins'. What the astronaut thought of this mention of the Irish Nationalist leader is unknown, but the response around the table was an awkward silence.[29] Wilson, as in his days at the Board of Trade, loved to meet famous people, with the sculptor Henry Moore, the pop star Cliff Richard and the television personality Harry Secombe all finding their way to parties at Downing Street.[30] Yet he was not somebody who, in social situations, spoke only to those whom he thought could be of use to him. David Lipsey, an adviser in the 1970s, remembered being with Tony Crosland at party conference when Wilson made a point of asking both of them to dinner, not only his senior Labour colleague.[31]

Mary's devotion and sense of duty are not in question. Yet she did not enjoy the public glare of life in Downing Street. In May 1969, she appeared on *Desert Island Discs*. She was convinced she would enjoy the loneliness of the desert island, at least initially. She chose Henry Smart's hymn 'Hark Hark My Soul' as it reminded her of her childhood years. Her favourite song was the final chorus from Charles Gounod's opera *Faust*. Her luxury item was a mirror, make-up set and comb; her favourite book Emily Brontë's *Wuthering Heights*.[32] Wilson himself never did appear, though he did prepare a note for what he would have chosen had he done so. There were no surprises: Gilbert and Sullivan's *Pirates of Penzance*; the comic singer Stanley Holloway's monologue 'Yorkshire Pudden' and Johann Strauss' *Radetzky March*: as played on the Last Night of the Proms or by the Black Dyke Mills Brass Band. Alas, his favourite song, luxury item and book are not recorded.[33]

By early 1970, Wilson had recharged himself. At the end of January, Heath and his shadow cabinet gathered at the Selsdon Park Hotel in Surrey to give publicity to the Conservatives' proposed policy programme. Wilson seized on two issues: the Tory attitude to trade union reform that he said would take Britain back to pre-war days; and the toughening of laws to deal with trespass to curb street protest and squatting. Heath, Wilson said, would take Britain backwards to the Stone Age: the Tory leader may not be 'Neanderthal Man' but he was certainly 'Selsdon Man' – a label he kept repeating.[34] On 14 April, Jenkins delivered his final budget, and refused to depart from his disciplined approach and deliver a pre-election giveaway. Wilson asked him to take sixpence off income tax, but he would not.[35] His tone remained sober, declaring that his objective was 'to maintain the strength of the position we have won, and, at the same time, to guide the economy into steadily increasing growth'.[36]

Wilson was left with choosing the date of the general election. Though the parliament could have lasted for five years, the proposed introduction of decimalisation in February 1971 was expected to be unpopular, so it meant the only choices were the early summer or autumn of 1970. Shore was brought in to the discussions, and favoured June, as did Kaufman and, though he had doubts, Haines. Haines' concern was not so much with June as with the exact date. Since the trade figures were published on 15 June, Haines thought it best not to take the risk they might be adverse and go for 11 June. Marcia Williams 'favoured June, provided Labour was not going to lose; otherwise she preferred to go on until the "bitter end".' What tipped the balance for June was that the Conservatives' planned £1m advertising campaign for the summer would then not go ahead.[37]

On 13 May, Wilson spoke to Jenkins, confident of victory. He told the chancellor he would be appointed foreign secretary after the election.[38] His brief would be to secure UK entry into the EEC. Anglo-French relations, poor after the second de Gaulle veto, had become worse after L'affaire Soames. Wilson had appointed Churchill's son-in-law Christopher Soames as UK ambassador to France in order to press for British entry into the EEC, but it had started badly, with De Gaulle accusing Soames of breaking the confidence of a private lunch at the Elysée Palace held on 4 February 1969.[39] However, De Gaulle then lost a referendum on constitutional change and he stepped down at the end of April. With him gone, the path to British entry was clear. Wilson also told Jenkins of his intention to stand down as prime minister in 1972 or 1973.

On 18 May, Wilson called the general election for 18 June. The campaign was run from Williams' sister Peggy's office at Number Ten, rather than Transport House, giving Wilson tight personal control, focusing on him as prime minister. The manifesto had his photograph on the front page with a simple message: 'Now

Britain's strong let's make it great to live in.'[40] Another election address, that of Enoch Powell, published on 30 May, called to 'halt immigration now' and caused great controversy. However, it was thought unlikely that the issue of immigration swayed many voters, though the defeat of David Pitt, a black man, on a large swing in the Wandsworth Clapham constituency, was put down to racism.[41]

It was a month of beautiful weather and Wilson went out to 'meet the people' events. While this brought problems – on 4 June, Wilson was hit by boiled eggs in two separate incidents in Battersea and Putney, where Mary was also hit by talcum powder[42] – the presidential style was a far cry from the low points he had experienced since the summer of 1966. In the *Observer* on 7 June, even his bête noire Nora Beloff wrote: 'Both party leaders are now recognising that only a bolt from the blue . . . can save Harold Wilson from becoming the first Prime Minister in British history to win three general elections in a row.'[43] On the Friday before the poll, the Labour lead in NOP was 12.4 per cent, but the Sunday Gallup poll did show cause for concern with the lead at 2.5 per cent.[44]

Things began to turn. That same Sunday, the England football team were knocked out of the World Cup in Mexico, surrendering a 2–0 lead to go down 3–2 to West Germany. At 2–1, manager Sir Alf Ramsey had substituted the great Bobby Charlton; West Germany then equalised in normal time, before winning the match in extra time. Questions were asked of goalkeeper Peter Bonetti, playing after Gordon Banks had gone down with food poisoning. Wilson had a theory there was 'mystical symbiosis between the fortunes of the Labour Party and the English football eleven'.[45] He was convinced that the negative mood it generated affected the general election result.[46] The next day, football issues dominated. 'Why did he take Charlton off, Denis?' was the shout to Denis Howell, who recorded having doubts about Labour's prospects for the first time, detecting a changing mood.[47]

It is, however, difficult to isolate the game as a factor on its own. That final Monday of the campaign, the trade figures were announced, and showed a £31m deficit for May, after nine months of positive figures. The problem was that the government's recovery had been based on the turnaround in the balance of payments and this meant doubts about economic competence resurfaced. Heath pounced: '. . . It is becoming increasingly clear that we are over the best.' Wilson countered that Heath was trying to make a 'jumbo-sized scare' since the one-off purchase of two jumbo-jets costing £18m was contributing to the figure.[48] Yet Labour candidates – including Albert Murray at Gravesend – reported back to Haines that this had a negative impact on the doorsteps: 'It was all going swimmingly until then.'[49] Thus, economics, rather than football, was cutting through.

Yet Wilson's mood remained buoyant. He was in sparkling form on the hustings once again. At his eve-of-poll rally in Huyton, he spoke and took questions with his local party chair, George Rodgers, later an MP himself, chairing. First, an angry man turned on Wilson: 'you said in 1966 that they would abolish the grammar schools over your dead body and now it is in your manifesto – what have you got to say about that?' Wilson initially answered two further questions, then turned back to his inquisitor on education: 'As regards you, my friend, you're showing a morbid curiosity with my corpse.'[50]

The hot sun of polling day gave way to gloom for Wilson and his inner circle. Early results showed a swing to the Conservatives, and there was even a small swing in Huyton, though Wilson took 45,583 votes, a 21,074 majority over the Conservative challenger on 24,509, with a Democratic candidate on 1,202 and a Communist on 890. Nationally, the Conservatives won 46.4 per cent of the vote and 330 seats; Labour trailed with 43.1 per cent and 288 seats. Wilson returned to Downing Street by car this time, arriving back at 7 a.m. He faced the cameras and was almost wistful about how he had wanted to use the strong economic position had Labour won: 'as we have never been able to, in the past five or six years . . . in the social services, health and education and social security and housing – to accelerate what we have been doing . . .'[51]

Wilson was no stranger to setbacks, and he had had to work his way back before, not least in the early 1950s. But this was a defeat on a different scale. His six-year premiership had been ended by the electorate in circumstances where he had not only endured a lengthy battle to keep his grip on the top job, but had been convinced he would be re-elected. Herbert Wilson, aged eighty-seven, had been at Number Ten, ready to celebrate victory with his son, of whom he was deeply proud. Instead, he had to go, mournfully, back to Cornwall, and was to die the following year. Marcia Williams later recalled the psychological trauma of the election defeat: '. . . we had expected to win – more, at the beginning of the campaign we were *sure* that we would win. We were quite unprepared for defeat.'[52] For the one and only time in his four general election contests with Heath, he had lost.

Chapter 17

Is Harold really necessary?

Bouncing Back, 1970–74

In June 1970, Harold Wilson was fifty-four, younger than either of the previous two Labour prime ministers when they first took office. He had age on his side. What was not on his side was the history. Since 1945, no party had ever returned to office after only one term in opposition. For Wilson to be elected prime minister again was going to be a tough task. His first judgement was that, even if he had had the stomach for an immediate battle with the new prime minister, such a course was unwise. He told Haines that there was no point attacking Edward Heath for the rest of the year because he would look like a sore loser. It was better to allow Heath time to bed in then wait until the turn of the year to fight back.[1]

Wilson needed an outlet for his prodigious energy, and his quick mind settled on writing a book on his period in government as early as the drive back to London from Huyton in the early hours of the morning after his constituency count. Sitting in the car, he started to sketch its outline, and Haines wrote the first chapter soon afterwards. It was over the book that the tension between Marcia Williams and Joe Haines intensified. Haines had already witnessed Williams' temper during the 1970 general election campaign when, with everyone under strain, a typist was seeking to retrieve a file from under Williams' armchair with Williams herself saying it was not there. The typist was crying, and asked Haines to pick up the file. This Haines sought to do; as he tried to retrieve the file, Williams flew into a rage, with shouting and tears.

Haines shouted back that he would not be bullied. Peggy played peacemaker, and told Haines that Williams did not want to argue with him and could not stop crying. Haines apologised and the crying ended.

After the defeat Wilson praised Williams for her judgement in being a 'bitter ender' and not calling an early general election. Haines, recalling Williams' advice, thought it was easy to be right if you backed both horses in a race![2] Williams said Haines should have no part in the writing of the book, ostensibly as revenge for Haines having attended a secretary's leaving party to which she had not been invited. However, partly because the book was printed in Tonbridge close to his home, Haines remained involved. While Peggy typed the manuscript, Haines edited it: he collected the proofs and removed over 50,000 words.

The book also had another purpose: raising money to fund Wilson's own office. Wilson, who was paid around £240,000 for the serialisation rights by the *Sunday Times*, had left office £14,000 in debt.[3] Moving his Kitchen Cabinet from government to opposition was difficult. At this time, opposition parties in the House of Commons did not have access to public money to carry out their crucial scrutiny functions. The situation was only dealt with on Labour's return to government in 1974. Short, then leader of the House of Commons, introduced a scheme in 1975 whereby funds would be made available from the public purse, known as 'Short Money'. This meant that, to have the effective leader of the opposition's office he wanted, Wilson needed to raise cash. Part of this meant digging into his own pocket. One estimate is that, by November 1971, he had poured in £40,000 of his own money.[4] Officials at Transport House were not helpful, offering him only £6,000 for the cost of his extensive travel as party leader, and refusing to pay for Mary to accompany him until he said he would refuse to go as she was more popular with the public than him. They then conceded. Haines was, for nearly two years, paid his salary in £50 notes out of an £8,000 cash donation from the retired army officer and businessman, Desmond Brayley, later a peer and government minister.[5] The nine secretaries Wilson employed were reduced due to the lack of money. Office managers came and went. First, there was Tony Field, but, after his marriage in 1973, he was replaced by a former official at Transport House, Ken Peay, who, after demanding Wilson choose between him and Marcia Williams, left within months. In late 1973, the role was taken on by Albert Murray, who had lost his seat in 1970.[6]

Joe Haines and Marcia Williams were the two dominant figures. On the Friday before polling day in 1970, Haines had reminded Wilson of a promise he had made to remain for two years and asked to be released from it so that he could return to journalism. Wilson refused, and Haines remained with him until his resignation as prime minister.[7] Haines was deeply committed to Wilson, and promoted his boss's interests fearlessly. A determined man, Haines had risen from a slum terrace to become a journalist. He later recalled: 'I had my hiccups on the way to Fleet Street but I never deviated from my ambition to escape the drudgery and poverty which was Rotherhithe . . .'[8] In their drive to succeed, and their loyalty to Wilson, Williams and Haines were similar. Yet their relationship soured, with Haines citing Williams' 'Greed, jealousy and uncontrolled rages [that] had for some time been eating into her previously acute political perception.' A single incident on 12 January 1972 'demonstrated how startling that change was'. It was Mary's birthday, and Wilson had taken her for a meal to the L'Epicure restaurant in Soho. Williams, who ran Wilson's diary with an iron discipline, had not been told in advance about the lunch. She had only found out from a secretary who had seen a notice Haines had put up on the lobby correspondents' notice board in the Commons press gallery. Haines, who usually put up a few sentences on Wilson's engagements for the day, had included it as an item for the gossip columns.

Haines' account of what happened next is what he says Wilson himself told him. Williams was furious, demanding to see Mary, who went to Williams' home in Wyndham Mews. When Mary arrived, Williams told her: 'I have only one thing to say to you. I went to bed with your husband six times in 1956 and it wasn't satisfactory.' Wilson denied the allegation, and Haines said: 'At the time, I found his rejection of Marcia's story convincing. It had force and apparent sincerity. He said that Mary believed him rather than Marcia and, on the whole, so did I.' Haines' account is that Wilson's final remark to him that evening was: 'Well, she has dropped her atomic bomb at last. She can't hurt me any more.' He banned Williams from coming into the office for six weeks.[9] This situation, as described by Haines, could never have arisen had Wilson not entered politics. Had he remained an Oxford don, Mary would still have been a fine poet, no doubt with an eye on the life and scenery of the city. As it was, Mary could only contemplate the life of the Oxford college wistfully while the intense personal politics in Wilson's inner circle at the top of British public life swirled around him.

Marcia Williams was not mentioned at all in Wilson's book, which had been completed at speed, with the manuscript delivered by 1 February 1971. One day he wrote twelve thousand words by hand. Haines was convinced it had a bad effect on Wilson, draining him of energy, and that there were early signs in this period of his mental decline.[10] The 800-page tome is a detailed narrative account of the 1964–70 period, and allowed Wilson to present a defence of his premiership, and its achievement of the 'transformation of many of Britain's political and social institutions, including the modernisation of the law and the mobilisation of our people in our policies at home and abroad against racialism and discrimination.'[11]

It was a persuasive case, but the book was limited by the fact that Wilson produced it mid-career. Even putting aside the necessity of maintaining secrecy on sensitive policy areas, the reality was that Wilson could not criticise too many political colleagues as he was still working with them. His comments would have an impact on existing relationships. Thus, he hid behind the shield of confidentiality: 'Throughout this book with one justifiable exception – that relating to South Africa – I have maintained the secrecy and collective responsibility of Cabinet.' Wilson made a further exception for the critical meeting on the fate of 'In Place of Strife' on 17 June 1969, when he made clear he would not have accepted a mere 'Letter of Intent' from the TUC, despite cabinet colleagues urging him to do so. However, these exceptions made little difference to the overall approach.[12] The book is very useful: it is detailed, thoughtful and shows the day-to-day pressures Wilson was subjected to as prime minister. What it lacks is a sustained analysis of the impact of different factors – and people – on Wilson's decision-making.

In opposition, Wilson faced two immediate challenges. First, he needed to retain the leadership. The advantage was that there was no automatic assumption that he would resign following the election result. Neither Attlee, after 1951, nor Gaitskell, after 1959, had quit after general election defeats. Back in London on Friday, 19 June, Wilson convened a 4 p.m. meeting of his inner cabinet. Tony Benn recorded a 'shell-shocked feeling' as a small number of ministers gathered at Number Ten: Castle could not be found; Peart, Mellish and Crosland did not attend; Healey wandered in late.[13] There was no sign of a threat to his leadership. Wilson said he thought Bob Mellish should continue as chief whip and, as Crossman recorded: 'it was also agreed that we hoped Harold himself would be automatically re-elected to the leadership but that there should be a re-election for the Deputy Leader.'[14] That there was a vacancy for that post was uncontroversial as George Brown had lost his seat.

The contest itself presented another challenge for Wilson. At a time when the election of party leaders was purely on the votes of MPs, the deputy leadership contest could become an indication of where the strength of numbers was for a candidate to succeed him. As Benn himself put it: '. . . the PLP is a right-wing body . . . It is extremely difficult for anyone who has any left-wing instincts ever to be elected to anything.'[15] With the two leading candidates of the right of the PLP, Callaghan and Jenkins, both in the room, eyeing the deputy leadership, everyone else was 'far too discreet to ask whether this would be a contested election'.[16] There was no question of either man acting in the unstable way Brown had, but Wilson knew that he would be having to manage someone from the right of the PLP in the leadership team to maintain balance.

In the awkward silence, the sound of packing cases closing and moving went on around the building; British democracy is brutal in its swift dispatch of defeated incumbents. Mary wanted to 'live in the centre of London rather than going back to Hampstead'.[17] Williams arranged a three-month let on 14 Vincent Square for the Wilsons, only a short walk from parliament. Wilson was trying to recreate the pattern of his life as prime minister, with one base in London and another in the countryside. He soon purchased 5 Lord North Street on a twenty-year lease. The Georgian terrace is so close to the House of Commons that the walking time is regarded as within the eight-minute limit MPs are permitted after division bells ring to go through the lobbies and cast their votes. Before the end of the year, the Wilsons also purchased Grange Farm, at Kingshill, close to Great Missenden in Buckinghamshire, allowing them to leave London when parliament was not sitting.

On the Tuesday after the general election, 23 June, Wilson asked Jenkins to come to see him in parliament for an urgent meeting. Jenkins recalled that Wilson 'offered to make one small room available to me (he eventually made two), but not he implied to anyone else. This, it elliptically emerged, was a sort of grudging mating offering, for it appeared to carry with it his support for the deputy leadership. This offer, if not the small box-room, was generous.'[18] As in 1968, Wilson wanted to bind Jenkins in; far worse to have the right of the PLP, in a show of strength, elect someone against his wishes. Callaghan, meanwhile, did not enter the contest. A defeat to Jenkins would have been damaging for him and in any event, it was not worth the risk. Since Attlee's move to the leadership in 1935, a string of deputy leaders – Greenwood, Morrison, Griffiths, Bevan and Brown – had all, admittedly for differing reasons, failed to become leader. It was hardly a necessary election to win for Callaghan to succeed Wilson. Instead, in Jenkins' words, he 'lurked like a big pike in the shadows, powerful, perhaps menacing, but restrained'.[19]

Wilson's plans for the deputy leadership were, however, thrown into disarray as Castle informed him she wanted to stand. He was incandescent, and threatened her with his own resignation if she stood: 'The great thing I have done is to unite this party and I don't intend to preside over a party that is splitting again. If you want it that way you must find another leader.'[20] Marcia Williams told Castle that Wilson needed to 'keep the right under control'. As gossip spread about her intention to stand, Wilson told Rupert Murdoch that if she stood, she 'would not get more than twenty votes'.[21] Castle bowed to the pressure not to put her name forward, but she resented Wilson's reaction: 'Harold's behaviour crystallised for me once again my always latent anxieties about his attitudes. I now believe that he is disastrous as leader. The only thing that keeps him there is the lack of a less disastrous alternative.'[22] The election took place on 8 July 1970: Jenkins took 133 votes, Foot 67 and Peart trailed in with 48. The same month, shadow cabinet elections, once again required annually with Labour back in opposition, were held, and Wilson moved quickly to assemble a balanced team. Michael Foot was elected for the first time, and appointed as spokesperson for fuel and power. Shirley Williams became shadow secretary of state for health and social services and the pro-Market Harold Lever became shadow minister for Europe. The one major casualty was Stewart, who failed to win election, so Wilson promoted Healey to shadow foreign secretary, leaving Callaghan shadowing the Home Office and Jenkins as shadow chancellor.

With Jenkins now bound in, Wilson focused on his writing. Castle recalled: 'What worried me during this period was Harold's mood. Following his election defeat he seemed deflated and detached. The only thing that seemed to keep him going was the brandy and water he sipped incessantly, even presiding over the Shadow Cabinet with glass in hand . . .' However, 'it was the issue of the Common Market, as we called it in those days, which stirred Harold into a show of life again, though in his own devious and convoluted form.'[23] Castle's comment sums up what has become the widely accepted account of Wilson's handling of the European issue: he was opportunist and short-termist, lacking in principle, in contrast with the philosophical pro-Europeanism of Jenkins, who put the issue above that of party interest. The Jenkinsite Bill Rodgers, while recognising the argument about keeping the party together, thought Wilson's position, 'from the application to join to turning and being against in the 1970s, was Harold at his worst. It was "typical Harold" – switching backwards and forwards.'[24]

This analysis is unfair. The issue of UK entry into the EEC caused a schism in the Labour Party. For many on the left, their opposition to the whole European project was economic, political and constitutional: not only was the purpose of the Market to promote competition, its rules would prevent socialism being implemented at home even if a Labour government were elected by a landslide. Worse still, the EEC's external tariff barriers would make rich countries richer at the expense of poorer countries around the world. For those passionately in favour of entry, like Jenkins, there was a philosophical belief in the cause of European unity, a new international role for Britain as part of the EEC, and a recognition that many political problems could not be solved by countries working alone.[25] In the years of opposition, Wilson fought valiantly to prevent Labour becoming an explicit anti-Market party. While he sought to keep the party together, it was not at any cost. He would not have accepted a position where the party opposed entry into the Common Market on principle.

The Labour Party divide went deeper than the issue itself. With the party swinging to the left in opposition, there arose a critical question on the relationship between the views of the party rank and file, expressed through constituency parties and the annual conference, and the freedom of MPs to vote as they saw fit: were they representatives able to exercise discretion or were they mandated delegates from the Labour Party? What were the reasonable grounds on which a local Labour party could decide it no longer wanted its sitting MP as its chosen candidate? Was it simply that the person's views were not reflective of theirs or did it have to be personal conduct that was deemed unacceptable? This issue came to a head when the pro-Market Dick Taverne was deselected by the management committee of his local Lincoln Labour party in June 1972. Taverne resigned as MP, forcing a by-election on 1 March 1973, which he won as a 'Democratic Labour' candidate with a majority of 13,191 votes. The issue was crystallised in Taverne's leaflet: 'Who do you want as your MP, a man or a mouse?'[26] That same year, on the other side of the argument, the Campaign for Labour Party Democracy was founded, with mandatory re-selection for MPs and widening the voting franchise in leadership elections beyond the parliamentary party among its demands.

Wilson was to make two significant political moves to deal with all this. The first was to oppose entry to the EEC *on the Tory terms negotiated*. The very day after the general election defeat, Wilson had mused to Castle that it was 'not inconceivable that the terms they get . . . will not be acceptable to us.' She marvelled at him: 'So that's what the wily old devil is plotting!'[27] The second, once it was clear that the government legislation was going to pass through parliament, was to offer to renegotiate the terms and hold a referendum on the issue of membership, rather than make a straight promise that a future Labour government would withdraw Britain from the Common Market.

Wilson's two great rivals for the leadership, Callaghan and Jenkins, took very different positions. On 25 May 1971, Callaghan gave a speech in Southampton. President Pompidou had commented about having French as the language of Europe. Callaghan leapt on this, responding with robust nationalism: 'Millions of people in Britain have been surprised to hear that the language of Chaucer, Shakespeare and Milton must in future be regarded as an American import from which we must protect ourselves if we are to build a new Europe.' He added: '. . . if we are to prove our Europeanism by accepting that French is the dominant language in the Community, then the answer is quite clear and I will say it in French to prevent any misunderstanding: "Non, merci beaucoup."' Callaghan did not look back on the speech with any pride; he did not even mention it in his autobiography and commented, with understatement, that the 'years of Opposition from 1970 to 1974 pulled me in different directions'.[28] On 9 June, Jenkins offered to support Wilson to hold the line of supporting EEC entry against Callaghan.[29] Wilson was far too wise to place the future of his leadership in the hands of the Jenkinsites, who had no loyalty to him, and wanted him replaced with their own patron. Jenkins then made a speech in Birmingham on 18 June, explicitly challenging

Wilson on a change in position: 'I can see now the basis on which it was right to seek entry in 1967, and to persist in this enterprise . . . but to oppose it in principle in 1971 . . . unless we believe that a party should take a different attitude to the nation's interests and say different things in Government than in opposition.'[30] Six days later, Wilson confided to Castle that he was about to go through the worst three months of his political career: 'The press will crucify me. But I will bring the party out of this united and then I am seriously giving up the leadership.'[31] Wilson's own view remained that Britain was better off in the Market. Writing in the *Daily Mail* on 2 July, Walter Terry – who, through his relationship with Marcia Williams, knew more than most – wrote that Wilson was privately in favour of entry and 'a far better Marketeer than Ted Heath'.[32]

The government published its White Paper setting out the negotiated terms of entry into the EEC on 7 July.[33] On 23 June, the NEC had voted 13–11 to hold a special conference on the party's position, with Shirley Williams' vote in favour being crucial: despite being pro-Market, she was in favour of having the discussion. When the special conference took place on 17 July, Hugh Scanlon's contribution summed up the essence of the problem with party unity that Wilson faced when he said what was most important: 'Perhaps above everything else, [that] there is a definite decision that decisions of Party Conference are binding on us all, and that includes every MP of this party.'[34] Wilson ended the day promising to 'respect and honour the views of all members of the Party' and gave the assurance that, even in the midst of this debate: 'our main objective is, and must continue to be the defeat of this Tory Government . . .'[35]

This final point was crucial. Heath could not rely on the votes of all his MPs to enter the EEC. Therefore, the vote would also provide an opportunity to vote down the Conservative government on a central plank of its policy. This was a major issue for Jenkins, since the consequence of Labour votes outnumbering Tory rebels, and giving the prime minister a majority, was to give greater importance to entry into the EEC than to that of having a Labour government. Placing the European issue above the interests of the party was damaging to Jenkins' prospects of becoming Labour leader.

There followed seven meetings of the Parliamentary Labour Party, including one on 19 July, at which Jenkins argued that the last Labour government would have accepted the terms of entry.[36] This did highlight Wilson's major difficulty: as prime minister, he had applied to join the EEC, and was now opposing this. When he spoke in the Commons on 21 July, the Labour leader tried to justify this. Wilson set out that his position had been consistent since 1962: he saw advantages in membership provided that 'British and Commonwealth interests are safeguarded'.[37] He expressed concerns around British governments being fettered in regional policy, unable to use incentives to attract industry to poorer areas; and over barriers to food imports from the Commonwealth, particularly from New Zealand, that relied upon its exports of agricultural products to Britain. For the Liberals, David Steel accused Wilson of a 'circus performance' and Chalfont, who had been responsible for Common Market affairs in 1967–8, said he would have been 'very surprised' if Wilson's Labour government had not accepted the terms.[38] Wilson had, however, succeeded in moving the party's position. On 28 July, the National Executive Committee voted by 16 votes to 6 to oppose entry on the terms negotiated by the Conservatives. As he himself suspected, though, Wilson's own change in position brought him stinging personal criticism. On 30 July, a *New Statesman* editorial asked 'Is Harold really necessary?' accusing him of 'Walter Mitty tendencies' and an inability to plan ahead.[39]

That summer was a difficult one for Wilson. On 17 June, the BBC broadcast an edition of its current affairs show *24 Hours* subtitled 'Yesterday's Men'. It sparked a heated exchange between Labour and the BBC, and Wilson avoided future interviews with its presenter, David Dimbleby. News of the dispute appeared in *The Times* the next day: 'Only 11 hours before a film about the Shadow Cabinet was due to be shown on the BBC Television programme *24 Hours* last night extra staff were called in to make an alternative programme. But the original film, subtitled "Yesterday's Men", was shown.'[40] In the face of threat of legal proceedings from Wilson, the BBC had decided to go ahead with the broadcast, but with a section omitted. Given the interference in the content of the programme, Dimbleby's name, and that of the producer, Angela Pope, did not appear on the credits: 'The uncut part of the programme that was screened examined with an inquisitorial eye, a cool commentary and a background gloss sung by The Scaffold, what happens to British politicians when they fall suddenly from the top of the castle'.[41]

At first, it had all seemed innocuous. The idea of a programme examining the impact on politicians' lives when they lose high office did not seem problematic. Wilson thought he had an assurance that his private earnings would not be raised. He spotted trouble as soon as he saw the transcript in advance of the broadcast. He objected to the subtitle, 'Yesterday's Men', and saw that he was being singled out from colleagues: 'Only Harold Wilson became richer in opposition by using his privileged access to Government records to write his memoirs'.[42] The subtitle was not changed and, in the event, the section cut from the programme was leaked, in which David Dimbleby pressed Wilson on the serialisation rights. Wilson shot back: 'I do not think it is a matter of interest to the BBC or anybody else.'[43]

For Wilson, the programme was politically dangerous for two reasons. Turning a slogan, 'Yesterday's Men', that Wilson had used on the Conservatives back on him was a clever ruse for the BBC, but the last thing Wilson wanted was to be seen as part of the past, not the future. His folksy image was also at risk if he was to be seen as wealthy, especially in circumstances where he'd garnered such riches by taking unfair advantage of his time as prime minister. Hence his ferocious response. Senior colleagues rallied round. Callaghan was ultra-loyal: 'I think that Harold Wilson is the most skilled leader the country has seen for many years. In my view he would be the best leader of the party at the next election. He is a young man still, with all the tenacity and grit of a Yorkshireman.' Jenkins added: 'Mr Wilson is a very young man to be an ex-Prime Minister.'[44]

Charles Hill, chair of the BBC Board of Governors, ordered an inquiry. In the event, the governors went no further than to say 'the BBC regrets certain aspects of the programme'. No official apology was offered, and the issue of the leak was sidestepped: 'The BBC condemned the leaks but said they were difficult to trace.'[45] Haines wanted to keep Wilson off the TV in any event: 'people were turning on the TV, seeing politicians, then turning it off'.[46]

At the party conference in Brighton in October, the position of opposing entry on the Tory terms and calling for them to be tested in a general election was passed. The only question that remained was whether MPs would be whipped to vote in the House of Commons. Matters came to a head in shadow cabinet on 18 October. At the meeting that morning, Jenkins had proposed having a free vote, but the view around the table was for a vote against, on a strong three-line whip. Immediately after the meeting, it was announced that Heath had given Conservative MPs a free vote. Momentarily, Wilson saw a way out. Another shadow cabinet meeting was called for 7.15 p.m. Wilson said: 'If Heath gives a free vote, we shall have to have a free vote.' Benn, who happened to be chair of the Labour Party for 1971–2, lost his temper in response: 'I don't know what game you are playing but we cannot have a free vote when the Party has decided its view.' Wilson could not press the matter further, so the initial shadow cabinet decision was left unchanged. Jenkins had gone for dinner, and was not present, so there was another meeting the next morning. There, to no avail, Jenkins argued for a compromise whereby the shadow cabinet recognised their differences on the principle of entry into the Common Market, but agreed they had no confidence in the government to deal with the post-entry situation. The majority view remained unchanged. That evening, at the meeting of the PLP, a motion for a free vote was defeated 140–111.[47]

Sir Alec Douglas-Home, as foreign secretary, opened the great debate on 21 October, and immediately attacked Wilson's chicanery: '. . . had the Socialist Party been elected, it would have resumed the negotiations with the European Community where it had left off.'[48] Home teased Wilson: 'What is more, according to those Ministers in the Socialist Government who were closest to the negotiation, these terms bear a marked resemblance to what the Socialist Government would have accepted.' On cue, Tory backbenchers shouted, 'Ask and find out.' It brought Wilson to his feet: 'The right hon. Gentleman has gratuitously referred to me. In the last debate I quoted, in accordance with the right one has in this matter, exactly what was put to the Cabinet by my noble Friend, Lord George-Brown, and myself on the terms which we would require as a Cabinet to satisfy the Cabinet.' The Tory backbenchers continued to bait him: 'Wriggling,' they chimed. Home was mildly patronising in response: 'I do not think that the right hon. Gentleman need get so heated . . . Lord George-Brown does not agree . . .'[49] Brown, ever-unhelpful as far as Wilson was concerned, told the House of Lords five days later: 'This is the final call for the aeroplane leaving for Europe' and declared himself despondent at the state of the Labour Party: 'I am sad for them now: sad that they will not be catching the plane with us.'[50]

Wilson's speech on the final day of the debate, a week later, will never feature in the lists of great parliamentary speeches: the adversarial nature of the Commons does not lend itself easily to nuanced arguments. It was a binary question: to be in Europe, or out. Wilson's position of opposition on the basis of the terms of entry satisfied no purist, but he did enough to hold the bulk of the party together. If your position is causing problems on your own side, the most effective strategy in the Commons is to focus criticism on the opposing party. Thus, Wilson deployed a combination of attack lines on the government together with a pointer towards the policy of a future Labour government in putting the issue back to the people. His criticism of the Tory terms of entry centred on the treatment of the Commonwealth. He accused Geoffrey Rippon, the government's negotiator, of having 'caved in in the small hours at the coffee and cognac stage'.[51] He raised two principal issues: first, he declared: 'I regard the Government's deal over sugar as a betrayal . . . [as it] . . . failed to maintain the privileged access to the British market accorded by the Commonwealth Sugar Agreement or the equivalent access to a wider European market.'[52] He then turned to New Zealand, and hit back at Brown: 'I repeat that in the recommendations from the Foreign Secretary and myself, on what the then Cabinet made application, it was laid down, and was accepted by the Cabinet, that either by a permanent derogation or a period of transition lasting "for a generation" the British consumer would have a guaranteed right to buy cheap New Zealand butter.'[53] He finished by questioning the government's democratic mandate, and seized on the words in the Tory manifesto: 'Our sole commitment is to negotiate; no more, no less.'[54] Thus, Heath had 'no mandate, for he sought none and obtained none, to take Britain into the Common Market except with the full-hearted consent of the British people. That is not at his command, and no vote of this House can of itself redeem his personal pledge to the British people . . . Let him now seek from those people the mandate he spuriously claims by submitting this, and all his policies, to the free vote of a free British people.'[55]

That day, 28 October, was Bill Rodgers' birthday. His evening was spent as de facto whip for the group who were to become known as the 'Labour Europeans'.[56] The rebellion held firm, as Jenkins was one of sixty-nine rebel Labour MPs who walked into the government lobbies. Another twenty abstained, including Tony Crosland. Thirty-three anti-Market Conservatives voted against, including Enoch Powell. Yet it was the Labour MPs who had tipped the balance. The government won by 356 to 244 votes: the majority of 112 would have been wiped out had all Labour MPs followed the whip. The following month, Jenkins was challenged for the deputy leadership. On 10 November, Jenkins won 140 votes to 96 for Foot and 46 for Benn. This meant a second ballot was required; Jenkins narrowly defeated Foot 140–126 a week later. Labour MPs then worked with the government throughout the committee stage of the legislation, as it was considered line by line. Ken Clarke, elected MP for Rushcliffe in 1970, and then in the Conservative whips' office, said the government 'relied totally on the support of the Jenkinsites'.[57] John Roper acted as their informal whip, and Clarke negotiated with him on behalf of the government, ensuring that sufficient numbers of Labour MPs were always absent to secure Conservative majorities in the votes. Finally, the bill cleared its Commons third reading on 3 July 1972 by 301 votes to 284.

By then, Wilson had moved to support a referendum. As long ago as the shadow cabinet meeting of 20 July 1970, Benn, then in favour of EEC entry, had told Wilson he would 'think aloud' on the possibility of a referendum. He then penned a letter to his constituents, 'Britain and the Common Market – The Case for a Referendum'. At a further shadow cabinet on 11 November 1970, with Wilson away at De Gaulle's funeral, the document was merely noted, though Callaghan's comment proved prescient: 'Tony may be launching a little rubber life-raft which we will all be glad of in a year's time.'[58] When it came, Wilson's decision to board was executed in a matter of days, ironically. On 15 March, Benn had once again presented his referendum proposal to the NEC but only attracted four supporters. The next day, though, the situation completely changed with what Benn labelled 'an absolute bombshell': Pompidou announced a referendum on whether the French people wanted the EEC enlarged.[59] Things then moved quickly, as, on 22 March, the NEC voted 13–11 in favour of a referendum.

Wilson's absence from this meeting was not, however, an indication of his lack of influence. In fact, he worked behind the scenes throughout the period in opposition to prevent the NEC adopting a position of outright opposition to the Market. He told Joe Haines that he thought Britain should join the Common Market and stay in it but that he would have to 'duck and weave' politically to achieve this. His modus operandi was to instruct Haines to speak to his 'girl friends' (a label he applied to any female MP Haines knew) on the NEC: Judith Hart and Joan Lestor, both on the left and loyal to Wilson.[60] After the TUC passed a motion committing the trade union movement to EEC withdrawal in September 1973, there was another attempt to shift the NEC to that position. Wilson told Haines: 'You had better go and see your girl friends . . . tell them that I'm going to resign if I lose this vote.' Much to Wilson's relief, the NEC stood firm, and defeated the proposed change by 14 votes to 11.[61]

On 29 March 1972, at shadow cabinet, Wilson said the situation had been changed by Pompidou's decision, and supported a referendum. Immediately, Labour MPs would be whipped to support a rebel Conservative backbench amendment to secure one. His view carried by 8 votes to 6.[62] This seemed like a sound judgement in terms of party unity. Neil Kinnock thought the referendum proposal represented an 'honours even' outcome for the party's warring factions.[63] However, it now threw into question the position of Jenkins as deputy leader. Eventually, on 10 April, Jenkins resigned, echoing the opinion of Attlee on plebiscites, calling the referendum a 'splendid weapon for demagogues and dictators'.[64] Harold Lever and George Thomson also resigned from the shadow cabinet; David Owen, Dick Taverne, Dickson Mabon and Chalfont resigned from junior positions. Rodgers would have been expected to resign, but had already been dismissed by Wilson in January. Quickly, Wilson moved to secure his position. Shirley Williams, a Jenkins supporter who had not resigned, was appointed shadow home secretary; Healey became shadow chancellor, and Callaghan shadow foreign secretary. Short, a unity candidate loyal to Wilson, won the deputy leadership vacated by Jenkins, defeating Foot 145–116 in the final round, after Crosland had dropped out.

The episode had, however, damaged Wilson personally. On 26 May 1972, the *New Statesman* called for the end of his tenure as Labour leader: 'his very presence in Labour's leadership pollutes the atmosphere of politics'.[65] Yet the events were to prove more significant for Jenkins' prospects than Wilson's. The principled stand on the EEC had won Jenkins the prestigious Charlemagne Prize for promoting European unity on 7 March 1972, but it also confirmed the suspicion, already fuelled by his taste for high living, that he lacked tribal loyalty to the party. Kinnock told the story of an elderly Yorkshire MP sitting in the House of Commons tea room who was asked by one of Jenkins' acolytes if he would be supporting him in the leadership contest in 1976. The reply said it all: 'No, lad, we're all Labour here.'[66]

Wilson had at least reached a settled position on the EEC for

Labour going into the next general election, whenever it came. Other problems, however, crowded in. In November 1971, Wilson visited Northern Ireland before moving on to Dublin to meet the Irish taoiseach Jack Lynch. He had not visited Ireland – North or South – as prime minister, so the visit attracted a lot of attention, with speculation as to whether Wilson's visit would prompt a new peace initiative. Wilson's intervention, when it came, was dramatic. In an editorial, *The Times* captured its significance: 'Not since the early demise of the unity provisions of the 1920 Government of Ireland Act had a leader of a governing party in Britain or of an alternative governing party publicly broached the question of the unification of Ireland. Now Mr Harold Wilson has done so.'[67] Wilson made clear that violence had to cease first of all, and that troops would remain as long as they were needed to maintain order. Wilson's view was that if the violence had stopped for a period of five years he would then consider a united Ireland, back in the Commonwealth with Dominion status.[68] He ruled out direct rule from Westminster as a policy choice, though accepted it might turn out to be a necessity. This qualification proved prescient as the situation in Northern Ireland deteriorated still further. On 30 January 1972, the day that became known as 'Bloody Sunday', thirteen people died and fifteen were wounded when the British Army opened fire on a civil rights march in Derry. When Heath reimposed direct rule on Northern Ireland on 24 March 1972, it was with Wilson's support.

It was, however, the issue of the economy, the constant problem throughout Wilson's 1964–70 premiership, that unexpectedly provided the opportunity for his return to office. Picking up where 'In Place of Strife' had left off, Heath had passed the Industrial Relations Act in 1971, imposing a legal framework on disputes. The National Industrial Relations Court came into being at the end of the year, with a power to grant injunctions. In parliament, Labour opposed the bill, with the TUC holding 'Days of Action' to march against it. Soon, however, economic pressures caused Heath to change course towards government intervention. Unemployment rose to over a million in January 1972. The following month, the government announced a financial rescue package for the ailing Upper Clyde Shipbuilders, which was itself a Benn creation in his Ministry of Technology days. At the same time, Heath was forced to award a substantial wage rise to the miners. The National Union of Mineworkers had demanded a 45 per cent pay increase in July 1971, while lowering the majority needed to call a strike from 66 per cent to 55 per cent. After a proposed 8 per cent increase from the National Coal Board, the NUM called a national strike on 9 January 1972. With coal stocks mostly at the pithead, Heath could not hold out, so appointed Lord Wilberforce to chair an inquiry into miners' wages. Picketing of the Saltley Coke Works, the last remaining open fuel depot, led to its closure on 10 February, meaning the miners had cut off the country's fuel supplies. On 18 February, Wilberforce recommended a pay increase worth more than 20 per cent. Heath conceded. In a broadcast to the country on 27 February the prime minister claimed this was not a victory for the miners and that 'everyone has lost'.[69] However, it was a stark demonstration of the power of the miners.

It was a time of economic instability. In August 1971, the United States suspended dollar convertibility into gold, thereby removing the foundation of the Bretton Woods agreement. In June 1972, the pound started floating against the dollar; by March 1973 the system of fixed exchange rates had totally collapsed, leaving a general system of floating currencies. At home, inflation became a major problem: in January 1972 it stood at 8.16 per cent; though it fell to 5.80 per cent in July, it was back at 7.86 per cent in October.[70]

With tripartite talks between government, TUC and CBI having broken down, Heath introduced a Prices and Incomes policy. Wilson mocked the prime minister's reversal of position when he announced it in the Commons on 6 November: 'This is not the time to remind the right hon. Gentleman of all the many strongly worded statements, since he became Leader of the Conservative Party, in every debate in this House, on every proposal of the Labour Government, and during the general election . . .'[71] Heath's plan was in three stages. Stage I was a freeze in prices and incomes until 31 March 1973[72]; Stage II would impose limits on pay increases until 6 November 1973.[73] Stage III included the idea of 'threshold' payments triggering automatic pay rises if inflation rose by more than 7 per cent. Wilson thought the first two stages 'achieved a remarkable degree of success and apparent acceptability' with strike losses falling, but knew the test would come at the third stage.[74]

So it proved. On 6 October 1973, just as Yom Kippur ended, Egypt and Syria attacked Israel. Over two weeks of bloody fighting followed, before a ceasefire eventually became effective on 24 October. As soon as he could, Wilson sought a briefing from the Israeli ambassador to the Court of St James's, Michael Conay, and learned that the Conservative government had placed an embargo on the shipment of ammunition and spare parts to Israel required for the Centurion tanks the Labour government had previously supplied. Wilson, aware that the Soviet Union was airlifting military supplies to Egypt and Syria, and that there was an almighty tank battle along the front with Egypt, pressed Heath to change this. When he refused, Wilson took up the cause in public. While Callaghan supported him, Jenkins, who had by now returned to the shadow cabinet, and had been made shadow home secretary, did not, and argued that the government arms embargo should be supported.[75] Wilson's patience with him snapped: 'Look, Roy, I've accommodated your [expletive deleted] conscience for years. Now you're going to have to take account of mine: I feel as strongly about the Middle East as you do about the Common Market.' Wilson was also conscious that the view of the Labour left had changed away from the pro-Israel stance of Ernest Bevin and Richard Crossman to a 'marked adherence to the Palestinian cause'.[76] When Wilson spoke in the Commons on 16 October, his passion showed in his words: '. . . I believe that something is owed by some of us to the only democratic social State in that vast region . . . We must not be blackmailed by oil sanctions . . . I am grateful to the House for its forbearance in what has been for me a very difficult speech to make . . .'[77] In the event, fifteen Labour MPs voted with the government that night.

The impact of the oil embargo imposed by the Organization of the Petroleum Exporting Countries (OPEC) was, however, profound. This was the major tool available to the Arab countries to force a settlement on their terms in the Middle East. That same day, in Kuwait, the Arab leaders met and announced that oil supplies would be cut by 5 per cent a month until Israel withdrew from the territories it had gained in 1967, alongside a complete ban on supplies to the two countries regarded as Israel's closest allies in the West: the United States and Holland. The cost of a barrel of crude oil, $2.40 at the start of the year, rose to over $5. This would inevitably have wide economic consequences. By January 1974, inflation in Britain had reached 11.94 per cent.

Heath was, once again, locked in dispute with the National Union of Mineworkers. In July, the miners had demanded a pay settlement that the prime minister claimed amounted to as much as 50 per cent for some colliers.[78] On 10 October, as the Yom Kippur War raged, the National Coal Board had offered around 13 per cent. Though the miners' leader, Joe Gormley, wanted to avoid another national strike, this proposal was rejected by the union, and, on 12 November, miners started an overtime ban. The next day, Heath proclaimed a State of Emergency: in just over three years as prime minister, he declared five. The overtime ban caused a sharp fall in coal supplies, and when, on 12 December, the train drivers also started industrial action, restricting the transportation of coal to power stations, Heath responded with severe measures to conserve energy. The following day, in the Commons, he announced the shut-down of television at 10.30 p.m. each evening from 17 December, and, from midnight on 31 December, a three-day working week. Wilson seized on Heath's waning authority: 'The Prime Minister has shown that he is no longer in charge of the situation.'[79]

Now, Labour's own economic plans came into focus. The party's initial response to the 1970 defeat had been to move to the left, as it tends to do after losing power. As Wilson put it, the NEC, and its home policy sub-committee 'were obsessed with a determination to use our period in Opposition to commit the party to a wide-ranging policy of nationalising major companies.'[80] Thus,

Wilson attempted to moderate the policies proposed. At the 1973 party conference in Blackpool, he warned: 'If our words here are to become the reality of life in Britain for the next generation, what we can accept here must be acceptable to the British people . . .' Otherwise, he feared: 'this Party will be reduced for years to the frustrations of Parliamentary Opposition . . .'[81] The two major policy documents produced by the NEC were *Labour's Programme for Britain* in 1972 and *Labour's Programme 1973*. Wilson was especially concerned over a proposal for a future Labour government to nationalise 25 of the 100 biggest companies, passed by the NEC by 7 votes to 6 at an all-day meeting in the Whitsun recess late in the day when many members had left. Wilson thought it was an 'outlandish proposal'.[82] It would frighten middle-of-the-road voters, and also cause a further division in the party. Jenkins said it was 'no good pretending a transfer of ownership in itself solves our problems'.[83] Wilson found a compromise. First, he emphasised that the Labour Party constitution meant that the shadow cabinet had to agree to the proposal for it to be put into the next manifesto, and that such agreement would not be forthcoming. Then, he offered a more general extension of public ownership for which the next Labour government would '. . . create a powerful National Enterprise Board with the structure and functions set out in *Labour's Programme 1973*'. It was regional *planning* as set out in *Labour's Programme 1973* – still a residual Wilson interest – that the next general election manifesto emphasised.[84]

The centrepiece of Wilson's economic offering to the country was what became known as the Social Contract. His approach, based on co-operation, rather than confrontation, had been set out at the International Symposium on Public Employment Labour Relations in New York, called by its then governor, Nelson Rockefeller, on 4 May 1971. A Labour government would repeal Heath's Industrial Relations Act and replace it with what the *Guardian* the following day labelled a 'voluntary compact between the Government and the two sides of industry.' After the rancour caused by 'In Place of Strife', regular meetings had been set up between the TUC, NEC and Parliamentary Labour Party. A document was agreed,

Economic Policy and the Cost of Living, and published on 28 February 1973, that became the Social Contract. Unions would accept pay restraint but in exchange for comprehensive social reform, going much wider than the focus on price controls offered in the 1960s. This could include 'food subsidies . . . housing and rents, transport and a redistribution of income and wealth, combined with a policy for increasing investment in industry'.[85] Not only was this distinct from the previous Labour government's approach, it meant Wilson could steer a pragmatic, middle course on the dispute with the miners.

The NUM's case was that miners were leaving the industry because their pay had fallen relative to other industries. Since this was still happening, the 1972 settlement had not dealt with this issue. Miners were, therefore a special case. Heath accepted the principle of a 'relativities procedure' to pay the miners more, though he pointed out that the Pay Board had ruled out its use during a crisis.[86] With no agreement forthcoming, the NUM balloted its members, who, on 4 February, voted by over 80 per cent for an all-out strike. Two days later, Heath requested a dissolution of parliament with a snap general election on 28 February, asking the question: 'Who Governs Britain?'

Wilson anticipated a difficult first week for Labour, knowing the Conservatives would emphasise the party's link to strikes and the miners, before he could later respond on prices and Europe. He used the historical analogy of the Battle of Marston Moor: 'like Cromwell, he was keeping his disciplined cavalry under control until the Royalists had spent themselves.'[87] On 15 February, when the price index was published, Wilson went on the attack. With a perfect photo opportunity speaking to customers and staff in a supermarket in Kirby, Liverpool, Wilson could point to the highest annual rise in food prices since the 1950s: a 2.9 per cent rise in January 1974 meant a 20p increase over 12 months. Overall, prices were rising faster than at any time since the retail price index was started in its current form in 1947.[88]

The 1970 Labour campaign was seen to have focused too heavily on Wilson himself, and the absence of socialist policies led to voters staying at home. This led to a division in the campaign: Wilson, who used a consensual style to reassure floating voters, and those who wanted a radical, socialist offer to fire up its working-class support: 'I want to see the Labour Party mobilise its vote whence it came' said the general secretary, Ron Hayward.[89] There was an NEC-appointed campaign committee, and also Wilson and his advisers. This could have led to a split, particularly as Wilson planned to run the campaign from the leader of the opposition's office in Westminster, rather than at Transport House. Hayward approached Haines and asked him to persuade Wilson to use offices at Transport House: this Haines successfully did, meaning that the staff at Transport House worked smoothly with Wilson's team.[90]

A new face in that team was Bernard Donoughue, a journalist and academic at the London School of Economics. Donoughue, though a Gaitskellite who had often been frustrated by what he termed Wilson's 'fudge' style of leadership, had started working for the Labour leader the previous autumn in his opinion polling team. Donoughue thought Marcia Williams had recruited him as a counterweight to Haines's influence, and perhaps even with an eye on replacing him. Now, Donoughue became a part of Wilson's campaign team alongside Haines and Williams.[91]

This time, the manifesto did not feature Wilson on its front page; rather it showed photographs of fifteen people from different walks of life on a map of Britain with the message: 'Let us *work* together: Labour's way out of the crisis.'[92] However, the manifesto was still radical, promising 'a fundamental and irreversible shift in the balance of power and wealth in favour of working people and their families.'[93] Healey had already promised to increase income tax on the wealthy from whom he said there would be 'howls of anguish'.[94] On 18 February, in a speech at Lincoln, Healey went even further and promised to 'squeeze property speculators until the pips squeak'.[95] With Wilson trying to emphasise the importance of the consensual approach of the Social Contract, that same day, Scanlon unhelpfully told Robin Day in a BBC interview that 'We are not agreed on any specific policy as of now.' Wilson had to call on Len Murray, the TUC general secretary, to confirm the reality of the agreement.[96]

It was the chancellor, Tony Barber, who inadvertently assisted with an ill-judged party political broadcast the next day decrying the idea 'that militants should be able to create so much chaos that they could make the Government, and so the British people, do just what they wanted.' With Labour politicians shown on the screen, it looked like irresponsible mud-slinging.[97] Meanwhile, Pay Board hearings on the relative position of miners' pay had begun on 18 February. On Thursday, 21 February, the Press Association reported a 'sensational slip' whereby, rather than miners' pay being above the national average for manual workers in manufacturing industries, it was 8 per cent below. However, it emerged this was not a slip: at the 5 p.m. briefing by the deputy chair, Derek Robinson, it had been set out that the Pay Board had just taken into account the miners' concessionary coal and other workers' holiday pay. Haines rang Wilson, who was about to speak in Ilford that evening, and he added in some comments to his script: 'Something funny is going on.' 'The Great Pit Blunder' was the next day's *Daily Mail* headline. Thus, the whole reason for Heath calling the election was thrown into doubt. The surname of Sir Frank Figgures, chair of the Pay Board, formed the label given to the whole episode: the 'Figgures Figures' benefited Labour.

In the final week of the campaign came a maverick intervention from Enoch Powell on the issue of Common Market membership. Powell had declined to stand as a Conservative candidate in the election, and denounced not only Heath's prices and incomes policy, but the prime minister's decision to call a snap election.[98] But it was the issue of British sovereignty on which he spoke out. On Saturday 23 February, in Birmingham, Powell called the coming poll 'the first and last election at which the British people will be given to decide whether their country is to remain a democratic nation . . . or whether it will become one province in a new European super-state . . .' Two days later, on the Monday, Powell spoke at Shipley, encouraging anti-Market Tories to vote Labour, and confirmed the next day on Thames Television he had voted Labour by post in Wolverhampton South-West. By speaking out more than once, Powell generated five days of front-page newspaper coverage.[99] He had tipped off Labour in advance through a friendly journalist, Andrew Alexander, and Joe Haines, with Wilson himself – wisely, given Powell's views on immigration – avoiding direct contact: 'Wilson and Haines did their best to present me with a clear run for my speeches on the Saturday and the Monday,' Powell recalled.[100] As it happened, that same Monday, another story helped Labour. The monthly trade figures were published, showing a £383m deficit for January, the largest on record. Wilson immediately pointed out that the miners' strike was not the cause. Just as the timing of the announcement of trade figures had worked against him in 1970, now it worked to his advantage.

The poll three days later represented a reversal of the situation in 1951: this time it was Labour that lost the popular vote to the Conservatives, by 37.9 per cent to 37.2 per cent, but won the most seats: 301 to 297. Throughout the campaign, Labour had never polled above 40 per cent, and the London Weekend Television poll on the final weekend had Labour on 31.5 per cent. The opinion polls on polling day itself showed Conservative leads over Labour ranging from 2 per cent to 5 per cent.[101] It seemed that, as in 1970, when the polls had also been wrong, there had been a late swing between the main parties.[102] Powell was convinced his intervention had caused the Conservative defeat, a view Heath himself apparently shared. The two men had the same doctor, Brian Warren, who said: 'Ted's got this idea that, were it not for Enoch, he might just have won that election.'[103] Yet the public sent a message to the Conservative and Labour parties, both of which had lower shares of the vote than in 1970, as the Liberal vote surged from 7.5 per cent in 1970 to 19.3 per cent, thereby winning 14 seats.

In Huyton, a Liberal stood against Wilson and won 13.5 per cent of the vote, cutting his majority over his Conservative opponent to 15,305. The SNP also won seven Scottish seats. Butler and Kavanagh's study of the election concluded that the very short three-week campaign was decisive and that: 'Mr Wilson's quickness helped . . . to exploit the lucky breaks that came its way

– the retail price index, the Barber broadcasts, the trade figures and, above all, the Figgures' figures.'[104] Even with a deeply divided party, Wilson had won a general election after only one term in opposition: no other post-war party leader has achieved that. For that he deserves great credit.

Chapter 18

Herbie Roberts of the Arsenal team

Prime Minister Again, 1974

After his usual election-night stay at the Adelphi Hotel in Liverpool, Wilson returned to London on an early train. The shadow cabinet met that afternoon and issued a statement indicating it was 'prepared to form a government and to submit its programme for the endorsement of Parliament'. During the campaign, Wilson had ruled out a coalition with the Liberals.[1] Heath did enter into negotiations with the Liberal leader, Jeremy Thorpe, to try to put together a deal to remain in Number Ten. Here, Callaghan was canny, containing Wilson's enthusiasm to return to Downing Street, arguing that Heath should be left to 'swing in the wind' as he thought the talks with Thorpe would fail. When Wilson telephoned him on the Sunday to say the press were 'bombarding him for a statement' and whether he should respond, Callaghan said: 'Emphatically not.'[2]

Instead, that weekend, Wilson turned his mind to possible cabinet appointments, and how he would achieve political balance. Managing Jenkins was crucial. Wilson contemplated sending him back to the Treasury, by shifting Healey to the Foreign Office and giving Callaghan a role in charge of industrial relations. However, Callaghan was immoveable. Having served as chancellor and home secretary, he wanted to hold the only one of the three great offices of state he had not then held. Donoughue passed on this bad news to Jenkins on Monday, 4 March. After sitting through shadow cabinet at 2.30 p.m. with 'an unusually jumpy' Healey,

Jenkins was given another message from Wilson via Donoughue: 'Would *I* let him *him* know when I wanted to see him.' Jenkins' patience snapped and he told Donoughue: 'if he [Wilson] goes on messing about like this I won't be in his bloody Government at all . . .' Wilson ended up having to visit Jenkins in his attic room in the parliament. In an attempt to persuade him, he offered him the Home Office and Northern Ireland together. Jenkins declined the latter, and eventually accepted to return as home secretary the next morning.[3] That evening, just before 7 p.m., as Shirley Williams and Benn were preparing a press statement for the shadow cabinet, the message came through that the government ministers were packing up. Wilson quickly returned home to Lord North Street to get changed. Heath resigned and Wilson, for the second time, was summoned to Buckingham Palace to be appointed prime minister. Back at Number Ten that evening, Donoughue captured the mood: 'everybody feels marvellous. Means a great deal to Marcia and Joe because of the horrible circumstances in which they were booted out last time. This is rubbing out the past, paying off old scores.'[4]

Wilson set to work immediately, arranging urgent meetings with the TUC and CBI for the next day to settle the miners' dispute and starting to appoint his cabinet. His position was very different from that of 1964, when only he, Gordon Walker and Griffiths had held office of cabinet rank previously. Now, fourteen of his appointees had been members of the outgoing Labour cabinet in 1970. Wilson spoke to Donoughue on polling day, and turned to a footballing metaphor to describe his new style. He would not be, as he was in his first government, the striker scoring all the goals. He would not have a first 'hundred days', he would not have beer and sandwiches at 10 Downing Street to solve trade union disputes. He would allow his experienced cabinet members to take the lead, and he would be the deep-lying centre-half, sweeping up after them.[5] Wilson developed this analysis further at a post-election meeting of the Parliamentary Labour Party, telling his MPs: 'I would be no more than what used to be called a deep-lying centre-half – I instanced [Herbie] Roberts of the pre-war Arsenal team – concentrating on defence, initiating attacks, distributing the ball and moving up-field only for set-piece occasions (witness, as I had done, Roberts's famous winning goal in the sixth round of the FA Cup against Huddersfield in 1927).'[6]

Once Jenkins had been placated, other appointments fell into place easily: Healey became chancellor and Callaghan was appointed foreign secretary, with an instruction that Wilson 'would not want a meticulous account of . . . handling of . . . policy with the exception of two areas – Israel and South Africa.'[7] With the Conservative government having lifted the arms embargo on the apartheid regime, Wilson quickly reimposed it, and told Heath his policy towards South Africa had been 'contemptible'.[8] On the issue of dealing with the trade unions, as he had done with Frank Cousins in 1964, Wilson would have liked to have brought Jack Jones into cabinet. While Jones said he was happy to help, he was uninterested in a position in government.[9] As it was, Michael Foot took his first cabinet position as secretary of state for employment with a brief to oversee the Social Contract. Benn was appointed to Industry, Shore to Trade, Crosland to Environment. Shirley Williams became secretary of state for prices and consumer protection with Castle appointed to Social Services. Mellish remained chief whip, his five years' experience in post vital in navigating the hung parliament. Ted Short, with the authority of deputy leader, became leader of the House of Commons.

A change of approach was required for the territorial secretaries of state. After the Plaid Cymru by-election victory in 1966 had been followed by an SNP by-election success at Hamilton in 1967, Wilson had set up a royal commission on the constitution: first chaired by Lord Crowther, it had been taken over by Lord Kilbrandon and reported in 1973, putting the issue of devolution on the agenda. With the SNP gains and two Plaid Cymru MPs elected in Wales, the issue was an immediate priority. Wilson stuck with the experienced William Ross as Scottish secretary, who had held the role throughout his first period as prime minister. Ross was to change his mind to become in favour of devolution.[10] However, the virulently anti-devolutionist George Thomas was not re-appointed as secretary of state for Wales. Rather, Wilson supported him in becoming Commons speaker, which was to happen in February 1976, and appointed the Aberavon MP and barrister John Morris as secretary of state for Wales, telling him: 'I know you are a devolutionist, so I expect to hear your proposals.'[11] Merlyn Rees, who had held the Northern Ireland portfolio in opposition, became its secretary of state: his knowledge would be vital in dealing with the Troubles.

Wilson also authorised his cabinet ministers to appoint political advisers. While the idea of outside advisers was not wholly new, this was a systemic change, with thirty such advisers around fifteen departments.[12] This built on the position in opposition, when the Joseph Rowntree Social Service Trust had funded a pilot project of paid research assistants for the shadow cabinet: given the source of their salaries, they became known as the 'Chocolate Soldiers'.[13]

In his own Kitchen Cabinet, there were now three distinct sections: Marcia Williams as head of the political office, Joe Haines as press secretary, and Bernard Donoughue appointed to head a new prime minister's policy unit. There was an early sign of the tension around Wilson that would become a feature of the next couple of years when, on 7 March, Williams spoke to Donoughue on the telephone, attacking him, Haines and Albert Murray, who had maintained his position from opposition in government: 'Says we are all out for ourselves. Ganging up against her. And that I am out to replace her.'[14]

Wilson's immediate priority was to settle the miners' dispute. This he achieved with remarkable speed. On 6 March, the strike ended, with a one-year wage settlement that represented a 35 per cent pay increase. On 7 March, it was announced that the three-day week restrictions were lifted. On 8 March, Tony Crosland froze public and private sector housing rents, helping millions of people. The following day, a Saturday, Wilson spoke at High Wycombe, warning Heath that the public wanted to see the Labour government given a chance to get the country on the road to recovery, and that he would vote down Labour's queen's speech 'at his electoral peril'.[15] On 11 March, the State of Emergency formally ended, and, in the vote on the queen's speech a week later, the Conservatives abstained, with the government winning the vote 294 to 7. While the OPEC oil embargo ended that month, its result was to quadruple the value of a barrel of oil, so Healey prioritised reducing the cost of essentials in his budget on 26 March, allocating £500m to food subsidies: 'nothing less will suffice to give ordinary families the help they need to cope with the alarming increase in their cost of living'.[16] The chancellor also increased pensions to £10 for single people and £16 for couples, after pressure from Castle.[17] Foot introduced the Trade Union and Labour Relations Bill on 30 April, to repeal most of the Industrial Relations Act, save for its protections against unfair dismissal, which the unions wanted to see retained. Thus, within weeks, working at pace, Wilson had delivered on the Social Contract, settling the major industrial dispute of the day, while taking action on rents and prices.

This all pointed to holding a general election in June, but what became known as the 'Land Deals Affair' destroyed any possibility of that. A reporter from the *Guardian*, Gareth Parry, had called on Joe Haines at Transport House a few days before the election about a story the paper had about the prime minister's involvement in land speculation. Wilson telephoned the paper's editor, Alastair Hetherington, with a denial.[18] Then, on 18 March, the *Daily Mail* published an article: 'The case of Ronald Milhench and his £950,000 land deal.'[19] Tony Field, who was a trained geologist, had been working with the Iraq Petroleum Company in the Middle East. He then returned home and, after a brief period with the Bath and Portland Cement Company, had decided to set up his own business. He purchased land at Ince-in-Makerfield, close to Wigan, on which there was a large amount of slag, and also a nearby stone quarry. The idea was to sell the slag and the stone: Field ran this business while working on a voluntary basis for Wilson. Marcia Williams had a share in the company – first 25 per cent, then 20 per cent – to give her long-term financial security since no pension was attached to her job with Wilson. She played no active part in the business. In 1973, with the supplies of slag and stone reaching exhaustion, and land values having risen, Field moved to sell the land. He was introduced to a Wolverhampton insurance broker, Ronald Milhench. Milhench bought some of the land, though not all of it, and a Birmingham businessman, Victor Harper, acted as Field's agent. Selling the land was Field's right and he had done nothing illegal.

The controversy focused on two letters. The first, apparently signed by Wilson, was shown by Milhench to a *Daily Mail* reporter. Dated 16 March 1973, it stated: 'Tony and I feel sure you are quite capable of carrying our Ince-in-Makerfield through with efficiency and discretion.' On the face of it, the purpose of the letter was to provide evidence of Milhench's reliability and, thereby, creditworthiness, to raise money for the deal. However, Wilson's signature was a fake. On 3 April, the *Daily Mail* asked: 'Who forged Wilson's signature?'

That same day, the *Daily Express* splashed its front page with a story by Chapman Pincher: 'Wilson Man in Land Deal Row'. The *Daily Express* had obtained another letter, written on Wilson's headed notepaper in August 1972 to Warwickshire County Council signed 'H.A. Field' in the capacity of 'private secretary' seeking advice or comments on behalf of Harper regarding the prospects of obtaining planning permission for the development of Jerrings Hall Farm in Solihull. It also emerged that Harper was an undischarged bankrupt. The explanation for the existence of the letter was that, while Field had been on holiday with the Wilson family in the Scillies, a Downing Street secretary had followed the standard procedure that if a member of the public wrote to the prime minister with an issue with a public authority, the matter would be taken up with the relevant body: in this case, the county council.[20] As with the first letter, Wilson had done nothing wrong. Field had not secured any special treatment for Harper. Had any other person written in, the same thing would have happened.

Given that there was no impropriety on Wilson's part at all, it was the charge of hypocrisy that the Conservatives sought to press home in the Commons the next day, baiting the prime minister with his previous condemnation of excessive profits made by property speculators. Wilson the meritocrat stood for making money through hard work, not risky financial deals. Only two years previously, he had called rising land values 'a cancer of our Tory society' and argued for public ownership of development land.[21] In his defence, he relied on an uncomfortable distinction that brought him derision: the 'difference between property speculation and land reclamation. [Laughter.] This is not a laughing matter. My hon. Friends know that if one buys land on which there is a slag heap 120 ft. high and it costs £100,000 to remove that slag, that is not land speculation in the sense that we condemn it. It is land reclamation.'[22] It was not a tenable position. On 5 April, Field disclosed that he had made profits of £85,000, £4,000 and £21,000 in three transactions relating to the land at Ince-in-Makerfield.[23] Castle thought, correctly, that Wilson 'could have been loyal to Marcia (and rightly so) without going overboard for Tony Field . . .'[24]

These were two weeks of unremitting intensity. Haines wrote that they were 'hellish': from 3 to 11 April more than six thousand column inches were devoted to the story.[25] The significance of the episode had nothing to do with Wilson's probity; rather, it laid bare two other issues. The first was the hostility of a significant section of the press to Wilson. The second was the instability that now existed within his private office, about which Donoughue and Haines have written extensively. Both aspects came together in those early days of April.

On the Thursday, 4 April, Marcia Williams, holed up at Wyndham Mews with her sister Peggy, rang Wilson in tears, asking for help in moving the press pack camped outside her front door. Donoughue and Murray took a taxi to Marylebone, where 'journalists were constantly ringing the doorbell, beating on the door, shouting and pushing written demands for interviews through the letterbox, climbing on the window sills and trying to take photographs through Marcia's curtained windows, including her bathroom.' Donoughue and Murray battled their way through, but, on arrival, found Williams blaming Wilson for her plight, saying he had abandoned her.[26]

Wilson was totally distracted by it all. The next day, Irish taoiseach Liam Cosgrave arrived at Downing Street for a lunch to discuss the situation in Northern Ireland, but Wilson's mind was never far from the land deals saga. As always in a crisis, he called on Arnold Goodman who, on the prime minister's behalf, issued libel writs against the *Daily Mail* and *Daily Express*, while Williams issued them against the *Daily Mail*, *Evening News*, *Evening Standard* and the *Sun*. However, on Friday evening, things took a turn for the worse as the *Daily Express* threatened to make public the existence of Williams' two children with Terry. Joe Haines, with Goodman's help, tried desperately to track down the newspaper's proprietor, Sir Max Aitken.[27] Eventually, Aitken, who was in the Bahamas, and had been told by his office about attempts to contact him, called Goodman, and agreed to direct the editor not to publish the story.[28]

That night, Wilson was speaking at the Oxford University Labour Club. Donoughue was due at a dinner party with friends. As he sat down to eat, the telephone rang. It was the prime minister, who told Donoughue that Williams was threatening 'to reveal all' and asked him to return to Wyndham Mews and 'pull the telephone out of the wall to stop her speaking to the press'. Donoughue dutifully went back to the scene, but concluded that, given the state of 'near nervous collapse' of Williams and her sister Peggy, there was no danger of her communicating anything of sense to the press and wisely left the telephone lines alone.[29]

On Monday, 8 April, Wilson gave a statement to the Commons. He said that many MPs 'know her [Williams] and would pay tribute to her loyalty to our party and her contribution to the political life of this present generation. For several days now she has been subject to an intolerable degree of newspaper harassment on her doorstep, including an unauthorised entry into her car, and the incitement of children to hammer upon her door.' The prime minister said it was 'a cowardly way of attacking me, which is the purpose, and, through me, the Government.'[30]

This did not placate Williams, who, when Donoughue visited her two days later, was still 'attacking all who try to help her' and castigating Wilson as the 'King Rat'.[31] The political editor of the *Daily Mirror*, Terry Lancaster, who was close to Wilson's inner circle, had been trying to persuade Williams to give a statement to the paper. Williams had another outburst, with Lancaster knocking on her bedroom door to try to persuade her to come out, but she did issue the statement later that day.[32] She said that her conscience was clear and that she was not resigning. The statement was well received. Williams said she 'can only hope that now some measure of privacy and peace will be accorded to us after the so-called "exposure" of our family finances has been concluded.' Williams, writing nine years later, said the period was 'still horribly painful to recall.'[33] Haines, who had re-drafted the statement, was to be shocked when the *Guardian*'s leader-writer declared that 'Mrs Williams was the only person to emerge with dignity from the whole affair but that the Prime Minister would be well-advised to get rid of his Press Secretary, Joe Haines.' Haines wrote that he 'was never more hurt by anything written about me'.[34]

In cabinet that day, Wilson warned that there were two colleagues who would be in a race to succeed him that the press were tailing. Benn recorded: 'This was Harold telling us that if any of us made a move against him, he might take action against them. It was an extraordinary thing and showed him in his cheapest light . . .'[35] As it happened, the only member of the cabinet to suffer public embarrassment was Short, whom Wilson stood by. T. Dan Smith, former leader of Newcastle City Council, had been found guilty of corruption, accepting bribes from the architect John Poulson to secure building contracts. Short accepted receiving £250 in unsolicited expenses from Smith, which he said were 'reimbursement for a substantial number of expenses which I had incurred on his behalf'. However, he denied that he was 'paid by Mr Smith to use my influence to ensure that a contract with a firm in which he had an interest was awarded to that firm'.[36] An allegation that Short had a Swiss bank account into which £22,800 had been deposited was based on forged documents.[37]

They were heady days, though there was some light relief. Nixon, on a state visit to Britain, was in Number Ten on 7 April, and saw Haines' deputy Janet Hewlett-Davies, thinking she was Marcia Williams: 'Is that the one we've been reading about?'[38] In quieter moments, Wilson mused that it was like one of his beloved Agatha

Christie novels: 'We are still at the last but one chapter. It could be any of five who did the forgery.'[39] The denouement was not far away. By 18 April, Milhench had been detained by the police on suspicion of forging Wilson's signature.[40] The arrest meant that the immediate pressure eased. On 8 November, he was to be sentenced to three years in prison. The libel writs were settled. In the case of the *Daily Express*, it was by a joint statement in open court: 'The Defendants only intend to state, as was the fact, that a member of the Plaintiff's staff, Mr. H.A. Field, was engaged in land dealings; and that he had on occasions used the facilities of the Plaintiff's office for this purpose.'[41]

Wilson was not, however, finished with the press. After his usual Easter break in the Scillies, he returned to announce a wide-ranging royal commission on 2 May to look into the practices of the press that was still completing its work when he left office. Heath asked: 'What is the real purpose of a Royal Commission at this time on these matters?'[42] Then, on 23 May, Wilson had a private dinner with Wigg, whom he was convinced was behind the press attacks on Marcia Williams.[43] Haines records that Wilson had hired a private detective to follow Wigg, who had discovered that he had a second, secret family. Wilson would threaten to expose Wigg unless Williams was left alone.[44]

Then, Wilson made his most audacious move of all. On 24 May, it was announced that Williams was to be given a seat in the House of Lords. This would have happened anyway, but the timing was designed to send a message to the press. It was a public vote of confidence in Williams, a stark demonstration that Wilson was exercising power as prime minister, whatever the views of Fleet Street. Wilson looked on as, on 23 July, she took her place in the House of Lords as Baroness Falkender, flanked by Lord Shepherd, leader of the Lords, and Baroness Llewelyn-Davies, the Lords chief whip. The press did not, however, take this lying down, and in a profile in *The Times* that day, it was finally revealed in public that Williams had had two children with Terry. 'Mrs Wilson's Diary' in *Private Eye* had the prime minister's wife preparing flowers: 'Mr Haines had requested my assistance in preparing a floral gladioli corsage for Lady Forkbender's First Night at the House of Lords . . .'[45]

The extent of the turmoil in Wilson's private office was shown by what happened after the land deals controversy had died down. That the suggestion was even made that Williams should be *murdered*, is extraordinary. Haines recalled that Wilson's personal doctor, Joe Stone, 'said that he could "dispose" of her in such a way that it would seem to be from natural causes.' Haines made clear there was no way he would 'go down that road'; when he raised the incident with Donoughue, he confirmed that Stone had approached him with the same suggestion and he had given the same answer.[46] Donoughue recalled Stone offering 'a shocking solution . . . referring puzzlingly (possibly, though not clearly, humorously) to "putting her down"' and, on another occasion, to 'the "need to dispose" of her'.[47] Rivalry between the close circle of advisers around political leaders is hardly novel. Having to deal with crises is commonplace. But this was at a different level.

It also points to another aspect of the Wilson–Williams relationship. Stone was concerned about Marcia's impact on Wilson and there is a question as to whether she disturbed him so much because she had a specific 'hold' over him. When she spoke about ruining him, and tapping her handbag where the secrets were kept, what did she know? Haines, writing in 2019, offered this reflection: 'There was nothing in the handbag at all. It was a gigantic bluff, successfully carried out over the years. We were all fooled . . . the "hold" was not sexual impropriety, financial malpractice or treachery [the baseless allegation that Wilson was a Soviet spy] but psychological.'[48] Haines' assessment is difficult to fault. There is no evidence of sex, money or anything else from Wilson's past being held over him by Marcia Williams. Rather, Williams was at his side in the good times and the bad. She knew the times when he said things privately that he contradicted in public, she knew the options he had seriously considered and then rejected, she knew his real opinions of his colleagues and political rivals. Wilson drew emotional support from her in a way he did not from any other friend or staff member.

Williams' *modus operandi* was control. She could insist Wilson did things and he would listen. If she wanted her correspondence dealt with, it had to be a priority for the prime minister: 'He was pleading for food, for sandwiches, but Marcia insisted that he sign her letters before he got his sandwiches. So he sat there signing and grumbling, but chuckling away . . .'[49] Her losses of temper were themselves a mechanism of control on others. She survived on a day-to-day basis on her 'Purple Hearts': a combination of amphetamine and barbiturate that kept her going. Her outbursts at people, including Wilson himself, showed that she had a status that others should not threaten. She could also show her importance to the outside world. On 15 May 1975, Wilson was hosting an official dinner for the prime minister of Fiji, Kamisese Mara. Williams arrived twenty minutes late, keeping the guests waiting. Then, as Mara spoke, she left the room, only to return to the reception afterwards with her friend the financier Eric Miller and Frank Sinatra.[50] It was breathtaking chutzpah, sending out a clear signal of her own status and importance: she was not deferential to world leaders, and the world's most famous singer was at her beck and call. There is no doubt that civil servants saw her as having Wilson's ear. One official told *The Times* on 23 July 1974: '. . . to save time I used to debate with her an issue I wanted to raise with the Prime Minister. I knew if I couldn't convince her I should never convince him.' Williams, as Robin Butler, then one of Wilson's private secretaries, observed, could 'shout at Wilson; she could argue with him and get her own way. She was often right and had great political intelligence. She was never deferential to Wilson.'[51] Butler struck up a friendship with Donoughue and Haines, whom he described as enemies of Williams, and said the office was 'bedlam'. Donoughue described the situation as 'periodic mayhem'.[52]

Yet none of this should be taken to mean that all those who worked for Wilson were unhappy. Sue Utting, who started working as a secretary for Wilson in September 1973, never heard Wilson raise his voice. She found him easy to work for, and always calm. He was very appreciative and encouraging; he was caring, and always said to make sure she had her lunch. Utting also said she rarely heard Marcia Williams raise her voice, but added: 'I was always a bit nervous of her. It was almost as if she liked to have tension around her.'[53] Williams was, however, mostly working from home then, with Wilson's driver Bill Housden driving her, and dictation tapes, back and forth as required.

Wilson himself was, however, becoming weary. He needed a couple of brandies before Prime Minister's Questions. Even a party political broadcast, at which Wilson had been a past master, could only be done with a very large brandy.[54] He was suffering episodes of 'racing heart' and, at a summit in Rome in November 1975 he 'felt almost too ill to attend the meetings'.[55] John Warwicker, Wilson's Special Branch protection officer, said Wilson was also suffering from recurrent stomach problems. All this made him less able to cope with the tension around him. Wilson described January 1975 as Williams' 'worst black period' when she was 'going through the roof about everything'. The month began badly when he had not telephoned her on New Year's Eve as she expected him to, and failed to visit her on New Year's Day as he was travelling back from the Scillies.[56] He took refuge in Haines' room and, as Warwicker put it: 'conspired to spend more time with . . . Janet Hewlett-Davies . . . She . . . provided sympathetic female company and the warm understanding he had once enjoyed with Marcia Williams. However, this relationship did not please . . . [Williams] . . .'[57]

There was no respite from the economic divide in the government that was showing in major policy initiatives. Benn produced a draft White Paper in July setting out the proposal for a National Enterprise Board but, alongside it, interpreted 'planning agreements' to mean no limits on the compulsory acquisition of controlling shares in private companies, in addition to existing manifesto promises to nationalise shipbuilding and aerospace. Wilson was horrified, and, nodding to Benn's position on the National Executive Committee, wrote that it was 'polemical, indeed menacing, in tone, redolent more of an NEC Home Policy Committee document than a Command Paper . . . it appeared to place more emphasis on the somewhat amorphous proposals for planning agreements than on the NEB.'[58] With the NEC also having decided on 24 July to have a special conference on the party's position in the promised European referendum, Jenkins responded with a speech in Haverfordwest two days later in favour of remaining in the Common Market, and warning about a lurch to the left damaging the prospect of electing a majority Labour government: 'it cannot be done upon the basis of ignoring middle opinion and telling everyone who does not agree with you to go to hell'.[59] Lever, who, as chancellor of the Duchy of Lancaster, had a roving economic brief reporting directly back to Wilson, thought Benn's proposals would be a 'ruinous blow to industry'. What Benn, who had also been marching with the miners during the strike, while Wilson pursued a more pragmatic line, represented, was something the Labour leader had not previously encountered: a threat to his leadership from the left. Thus, the prime minister sought to reassert his authority. Asked by Robin Day on television on 1 August whether Benn or Lever spoke for the Labour Party, Wilson's answer was firm: 'I'm in charge. I'm in control.'[60] Wilson took over the drafting of the White Paper himself, chairing a small cabinet sub-committee that included Healey, Foot and Shirley Williams alongside Benn. When *The Regeneration of British Industry* was published on 15 August the proposals on planning were made voluntary.[61]

Wilson concentrated on changes he could make with such a small majority. He asked ministers to come up with initiatives which, though 'they may not be of major importance in the total context of Government policy, arouse strong feelings in the country and among our supporters . . . [and do] . . . not pre-empt any significant amounts of public expenditure.'[62] Proposals ranged from a May Day bank holiday (which eventually happened in 1978), concessionary rail fares (the British Rail Board were asked to carry out a review), providing information to taxpayers about how the government budget is spent (Wilson said he was 'not excited' about this one), preserving the pint and abolishing hare-coursing.[63] Lever put forward the idea of regional investment banks lending on an interest-free or low-interest basis.[64] This was rejected as too ambitious to feature in the '"little things" category'. Morris was more successful, pitching for £50,000 for the Welsh National Eisteddfod, and so began the annual grant.[65]

There were also major reforms that had a lasting impact. Ben Pimlott dismissed the party manifesto's policy prospectus as 'at best, a shopping list, at worst a collection of slogans . . .'[66] His biography fails to grasp the significance of the legislation Wilson's later governments passed, the achievement made greater by the fact they were secured with difficult parliamentary arithmetic. On 31 July 1974, the Health and Safety at Work etc. Bill, having completed its passage through parliament, was given its Royal Assent. Fatalities at work were rising, and given sharp focus by the James Watt Street fire in Glasgow in November 1968 when twenty-two workers died in a factory fire from which the building design meant there was little chance of escape. In the final days of the previous Labour government, on 29 May 1970, Castle appointed a 'Safety and Health at Work' committee to be chaired by Alf Robens, to consider whether changes were required for the provision of health and safety in the workplace.[67] The 'Robens Report' criticised existing law as haphazard.[68] What was needed was a comprehensive framework. Foot, opening the debate in the Commons, said that anyone who wished to understand the bill, which was of 'major significance', only had to read the opening sentences of the Robens Report, setting out that, every year, industrial injuries and accidents killed 'nearly 1,000 people . . . 500,000 workers are injured, and 23 million working days are lost'.[69] The philosophy behind the legislation was that it would not be unduly prescriptive. Instead, it created a general legal duty on 'every employer to ensure, so far as is reasonably practicable, the health, safety and welfare at work of all his employees'.[70] This was to replace the piecemeal approach of the past, and ensure that the risk of danger in the workplace was reduced to the lowest possible level. The bill created the Health and Safety Commission (HSC), to provide information and advice and the Health and Safety Executive (HSE), still the enforcement body for health and safety at work in the 2020s.[71] Willie Whitelaw, employment secretary in the final months of the Heath government, was quick to point out that a bill in his name had been produced in the last parliament.[72] While that is correct, the Robens Report had appeared in July 1972, and the Conservatives had hardly rushed to drive through legislative changes afterwards: the credit should be given to Wilson's government. In the first four decades of the operation of the Act, employee fatalities fell by 85 per cent and non-fatal injuries by 77 per cent.[73] That is, of course, also due to the changing nature of work itself, with a decline in dangerous manual jobs, but it is incontestable that the Health and Safety at Work etc. Act created a durable, lasting framework that saved lives.

Michael Foot's proposal to bring back the closed shop, abolished by the Industrial Relations Act 1971, caused deep controversy, especially among newspaper editors who claimed it threatened journalistic freedom, and, awkwardly for Wilson, the Editors' Guild brought in Arnold Goodman as their spokesperson. In the end, a 'Charter on freedom of the press' was agreed.[74] Yet the Trade Union and Labour Relations (Amendment) Bill did not finally complete its passage through parliament and receive royal Assent until 27 March 1976. This episode should not, however, obscure that the Health and Safety at Work etc. Act was one of a group that brought about profound change. The Employment Protection Act 1975 introduced the UK's first maternity leave legislation, introducing six weeks of paid leave after having a baby and a right to return to the same or similar job for up to twenty-nine weeks. It also introduced the Advisory, Conciliation and Arbitration Service (ACAS), a body that could be called upon to facilitate the finding of solutions in industrial disagreements that proved so effective it is still a central aspect of dispute resolution in the 2020s. The Sex Discrimination Act of the same year, which came into force along with Castle's Equal Pay Act on 29 December 1975 created an Equal Opportunities Commission to promote equality between men and women, and formally outlawed sex discrimination in the workplace: from job applications to progression opportunities and employment practices. The Act was limited to married people – men and women – but it still broke new ground. As Lindsay Mackie observed in the *Guardian*, it made 'illegal what has been until today legal and respectable (for instance 'women's appointments' columns in national newspapers).' It also meant there would be profound change in the provision of services: 'No more will hotel managers be able to refuse to serve drinks to unaccompanied women. No more will banks, hire purchase companies or the taxman be able to require a man's signature in addition to the woman's.'[75] The Race Relations Act 1976, though it completed its passage through parliament after Wilson had left office, modified laws on race in response to the Sex Discrimination Act, outlawing indirect, as well as direct, discrimination. A worker who was subject to discrimination on grounds of race now had a right to enforce this in law. These changes, achieved in a House of Commons without a substantial majority, are a considerable achievement.

Wilson wanted to make sure the issue of the referendum on the Common Market was, as far as possible, left until after the next general election that he knew was imminent. He met German chancellor Helmut Schmidt in June 1974. *The Times*' bureau chief in Bonn, Dan van der Vat, described the meeting as a 'goalless draw' – after all, it was watching the scoreless World Cup football match between Scotland and Brazil in Frankfurt that had brought Wilson to West Germany, allowing him to call in on Schmidt. The meeting was good-natured but avoided divisive issues.[76] Wilson spoke to Nicholas Henderson, then British ambassador to West Germany: 'He was quite frank about his main objective, which was to keep all the clashing balls of the Labour Party in the air at the same time.' He said he remained Labour leader because there was no alternative: '"They keep me there . . . not because they love me but because there is no one else who can keep the party together."'[77] Wilson had one more meeting on the EEC to navigate, as, on 14 September, the prime minister attended the first of the quarterly heads of government meetings the new French president, Valéry Giscard d'Estaing, had instituted. Wilson spoke to him directly over lunch about the renegotiation, stressing the importance of how the EEC budget was put together and that Britain would oppose moves towards political union.[78] There was, however, no progress as a further poll was imminent. In August 1974, Labour had a narrow opinion poll lead, with 35.5 per cent to the Conservatives' 32 per cent, though the Liberal vote remained high, at 19 per cent.[79] On 18 September, Wilson called a general election for 10 October.

The manifesto featured Labour's new branding, with rosettes on its front page, each carrying the same message: 'Britain will *win* with Labour.'[80] Wilson showed his resilience and dominance of his party, as he once again took personal control. He took the morning press conferences in London, before spending the rest of the day travelling, attending evening rallies. Butler and Kavanagh concluded: 'In his fifth election as Labour leader his continued "feel" for the management of a campaign was much admired in Labour's camp.'[81] Heath's absences from the Conservative morning press conferences led Wilson to joke that he would issue a writ of *habeas corpus* to locate the 'missing' Tory leader. Wilson stressed Labour's achievements in office: 'We ended the state of emergency. The lights went on again. We brought the heating back. We did what we said we would . . .' As the campaign wore on he started to lighten up, referencing the 'Dark Age' of February, and joking about the Social Contract: 'The Tories say Harold Wilson's got a social contract. We'll have a social contract – [pause] – All God's chillun want a social contract.'[82] Wilson was showing that he could bring the country together in a way Heath could not. Enoch Powell, out of the Conservative Party and entering Northern Ireland politics as Ulster Unionist candidate for South Down, once again pledged his vote to Labour, but 'the audience that he commanded had diminished . . .'[83]

On 10 October, *The Times* declared that the 'election is concerned with the survival of the present social and political system of Britain . . .'[84] In the event, combined support for the two major parties fell to 75 per cent; from 1931 to 1970 it had never fallen below 87 per cent. The SNP vote in Scotland rose from 11 per cent in June 1970 to 22 per cent in February 1974 to 30 per cent, as they won 11 seats north of the border. Plaid Cymru gained a third seat in Wales. The swing from the Conservatives to Labour in England and Wales was 2.2 per cent. Labour had won a small overall majority of three, with 319 seats from 635. The number of MPs from smaller parties elected also meant there was a strong possibility of the parliament lasting a number of years, as negotiations with them for government support was always a possibility: this proved to be the case in practice. In Huyton, Wilson was returned with a slightly larger majority of 16,233. Labour's MORI surveys showed that, for all the apparent upheaval in the party system, two-thirds of voters identified the cost of living as the most urgent problem. Wilson's strategy of spending the election attacking the Conservatives and largely ignoring the smaller parties succeeded.[85] It was yet another historic achievement: Wilson had matched the great Victorian Liberal prime minister William Gladstone with four general election victories to his name.

Chapter 19

Mary would never allow that

Referendum to Resignation

By the end of October 1974, Wilson had settled back into the office of prime minister, if not back into 10 Downing Street. *Private Eye* seized on Mary's desire to remain at Lord North Street. 'Mrs Wilson's Diary' had Wilson telling her: '"A Prime Minister has to live at Number Ten. It is part of history. Just as the Queen has to live at Balmoral, whether she likes it or not." "But Her Majesty is not likely to be thrown out on her neck next week," I replied.'[1] Mary 'had found it uncomfortable before, chiefly because of the lack of privacy: many of the staff have access to the private flat.' However, neither Wilson nor Mary wanted to move back in. The one effect this had was to lengthen Wilson's working day, as he now had to get a car every morning and evening, though the distance was a short one: only around half a mile.[2] On Chequers, Wilson and Mary did disagree. Wilson loved the place and its history; Mary was far less keen. The compromise was that, on Fridays, they would both travel to Grange Farm at Great Missenden. Mary liked to sleep there, in her own bed with her own possessions around her. If Wilson had a meeting at Chequers the next day, he would drive on to there, and stay the night.[3] Wilson did, however, have less time to enjoy the facilities. He no longer swam in the pool, and did not have time for his weekly round of golf at the nearby Ellesborough Golf Course. That said, when Robin and his wife Joy welcomed twin baby girls, Wilson not only held their christenings at Chequers, he also celebrated their first birthday in the White Parlour.[4]

The Scillies remained a constant place of retreat, though Wilson's journey there was somewhat different now. To ensure the security of the prime ministerial red boxes, the RAF would fly him to Culdrose on the Lizard Peninsula, and a Sea King helicopter would fly him to St Mary from there. Lowenva was now known on the local tourist tours as 'Number Ten and a Half, Downing Street'.[5]

The haven of the Scillies seemed very distant when, on 21 November, the worst terrorist atrocity since 1945 was perpetrated in Birmingham by the IRA: bombs exploded in two pubs killing twenty-one people and injuring 182 others. It was a grim reminder that Britain was not separated from the issue of Northern Ireland by the Irish Sea. The previous year, there had seemed to be hope when Heath reached an agreement at Sunningdale Park in December. There would be a devolved power-sharing executive in Northern Ireland and an advisory Council of Ireland which would consist of seven ministers from that executive and seven from the government of the Republic of Ireland. It was this latter body that caused controversy on the Unionist side. On New Year's Day, the executive had been set up with Ulster Unionist Party leader Brian Faulkner as its Chief. On 14 May, a hardline unionist motion condemning the arrangements agreed under Sunningdale was defeated. The next day, the Ulster workers' strike began, with Protestants not attending work, loyalist paramilitaries manning road blocks, and power cuts. On 17 May, loyalist paramilitary bombings killed 33 people in Dublin and Monaghan. Wilson was incensed. Bearing in mind the £70 million assistance for Harland and Wolff shipbuilders which benefited the very workers now out on the streets, he broadcast on 25 May: 'The people on this side of the water – British parents – have seen their sons vilified and spat upon and murdered . . . They see property destroyed by evil violence and are asked to pick up the bill for rebuilding it. Yet people who benefit from all this . . . spend their lives sponging on Westminster and British democracy and then systematically assault democratic methods.'[6] However, Faulkner's resignation on 28 May effectively finished power-sharing. The strike ended and a Northern Ireland Bill reintroducing direct rule received its Royal Assent on 17 July 1974.

Merlyn Rees put his faith in a 78-member elected Constitutional Convention to find a solution. Chaired by Lord Chief Justice Robert Lowry, it was elected on 1 May 1975. There was a short-lived IRA ceasefire announced on 10 February and there was a reduction in violence in Northern Ireland: in the six months from 1 February 1975, shooting incidents involving the security forces numbered 198, as compared to 1,021 in the same period in 1974.[7] However, the year ended with little hope of settlement. On 20 November, the Constitutional Convention Report recommended a return to the past in the form of majority Unionist rule.[8] The draconian policy of internment without trial, introduced by the Northern Ireland Executive in 1971, continued until December 1975. In March 1976, the Convention was wound up.

Wilson's visit to Northern Ireland just before Christmas 1975 brought home to him the human cost of the Troubles. He left on 18 December, flying by helicopter from Aldergrove airport to Londonderry. He visited Ebrington barracks and chatted to infantrymen about to go out on a routine patrol. By the time he reached Belfast an hour later the final two he had spoken to had been killed by a booby-trap bomb in a car of which they were suspicious. It was a painful reminder of the 'mindless violence and the vulnerability of our troops'. Wilson had lunch at Stormont with the secretary of state, then went on to Ballykinker where he met the Queen's Lancashire Regiment and the part-time Ulster Defence Regiment 'whose members have faced murderous attacks in their homes and elsewhere'. He recalled: 'It had been a grim day – the worst of all my Ulster visits.'[9] Haines, who attended most of Wilson's Northern Ireland visits, commented, presciently: 'Pacification, which by 1976 was all that was left to hope for in Northern Ireland, is not policy enough.'[10]

Wilson's visit to Northern Ireland came at the end of a year that had been dominated by the problem of inflation. By March, it was over 21 per cent.[11] Introducing his budget on 15 April 1975, Healey said: 'I hope that I do not need to stress the domestic damage which would be caused if inflation continued at this rate. Such inflation redistributes the nation's wealth and income in an arbitrary and anti-social way. It engenders a deep sense of insecurity in all sections of society.'[12] Healey raised income tax, cut food subsidies and extended the higher 25 per cent VAT rate he had introduced the previous November to domestic appliances, a large increase from the existing 8 per cent. This was putting the Social Contract under threat. In May, inflation hit 25 per cent.[13] On 22 May, Healey, surveying the economic future up to 1978–9, told cabinet that officials needed to identify £3,000 million of potential savings. Wilson deftly avoided committing to anything in particular at that stage, insisting this would be a series of options to consider.[14]

The position was unsustainable, and matters came to a head the next month. The rail workers were threatening to strike on 23 June unless wage rises of 30–35 per cent were agreed. In the Commons on 17 June, Wilson said the government 'cannot possibly go along with the union's claim or with negotiations related to getting anything like that'.[15] The next day, Wilson called in Donoughue and asked him to submit policy proposals for a solution. The day after, the Policy Unit considered the options, with Haines called in to ensure the political realities were factored in.[16] The rail strike was averted; on 23 June, Foot announced that rail workers had been given a pay settlement amounting to a 29.8 per cent rise.[17] The inflationary spiral was continuing. The policy that emerged was evidence of the power of the Policy Unit under Donoughue. It was not that it provided a different source of advice and direction that had not been available in the same way in the 1960s; rather, it was that the Policy Unit had the authority to be a counterweight to Treasury orthodoxy. Wilson's remark that 'Whichever party is in office, the Treasury is in power' reflected his many dealings with its mandarins, but, as prime minister, he could also face them down.[18]

There were several options available for Wilson to consider. On the right, Keith Joseph was arguing for monetarism: restricting the money supply to curb inflation. Wilson rejected this because of the inevitable impact on jobs: 'he could not face in his final year the prospect of retiring and bequeathing record post-war unemployment'.[19] On the left, there was Benn's 'Alternative Economic Strategy' set out in January 1975, that he described as follows: 'Strategy A . . . is the Government of national unity, the Tory strategy of a pay policy, higher taxes all round and deflation, with Britain staying in the Common Market. The Strategy B which is the real Labour policy of saving jobs, a vigorous micro-investment programme, import control, control of the banks and insurance companies, control of export, of capital, higher taxation of the rich, and Britain leaving the Common Market.'[20] By now, Benn had reversed his position of being in favour of Common Market membership.

The reference to a cross-party government aside, Benn's 'Strategy A' was a barely concealed attack on Wilson's approach. Yet Wilson *was* willing to extend public ownership. Benn had announced the nationalisation of the aerospace industry on 15 January 1975.[21] The nationalisation of shipbuilding was agreed the next day by the cabinet's Industrial Development Committee in less than a minute.[22] The bill, however, had a tortuous passage through parliament and the Aircraft and Shipbuilding Industries Act did not reach the statute book until 1977, but Wilson was committed to it. The National Enterprise Board was established, though it was on a state intervention model, supporting industries falling into difficulty. In June 1975, it was announced that the government shares in the ailing British Leyland would come under the control of the National Enterprise Board, once the Industry Bill creating it had completed its passage through parliament. It was a long way from the state controller of private industry as Benn had envisaged it. Wilson firmly rejected Benn's 'Strategy B' in favour of his own pragmatism, and determination that Britain was better off in the Common Market. The choice left was an incomes policy, but there was a division between Treasury officials who argued for a statutory policy and the Policy Unit that wanted it to be on a sanctions-based voluntary basis. Haines proposed an easily understood flat-rate increase that would also have the advantage of being progressive, giving a higher percentage to the lowest paid.[23]

The former approach would have taken Wilson back to the whole argument over 'In Place of Strife' with the freedom of trade unions curtailed by the law, and would also force him to admit that his consensual approach embodied in the Social Contract had failed.

In addition to the cabinet's Economic Strategy Sub-Committee, and a committee of officials, Wilson had created a secret cabinet sub-committee to consider pay policy, 'MISC 91', on which he included Healey and Callaghan, in order to keep personal control. On 26 June, before a meeting of MISC 91, Donoughue gave Wilson the Policy Unit's proposals: a sanctions-backed voluntary policy. Though MISC 91 agreed this, the Treasury was determined to push for a statutory policy.

The prime minister could have been forgiven for a sense of déjà vu as sterling was coming under pressure. He remarked to Donoughue that it was 'at this point in the play when the Governor of the Bank of England enters from stage right'.[24] The right-wing Gordon Richardson duly arrived at Downing Street and declared that 'We must end this nonsense of getting the co-operation and consent of others, the trade unions, the Labour Party.'[25] Only a statutory incomes policy would do. Wilson wavered. With the key cabinet meeting due imminently on 1 July, Donoughue and Haines countered with a joint memorandum to the prime minister: 'We believe the Treasury are trying to bounce the Government along the same old path they have trodden before, with incalculable consequences for the Government and the party.' Wilson went to bed on 30 June intending to impose a statutory policy, but telephoned Haines in the night to confirm he had changed his mind and to say he accepted a statutory policy would split the government. He would speak to Healey before cabinet.[26]

At cabinet the next morning, the chancellor set out that sterling's rate of exchange against a basket of other currencies had been falling since the last quarter of 1974, but that decline had now accelerated. There had been a 4 per cent fall in April and May, a further 4 per cent fall in June and a 1 per cent fall the previous day. Healey set out the Treasury view: 'He doubted whether a voluntary policy, coupled with sanctions . . . would carry the conviction needed to stop further loss of confidence in sterling.' This met with strong opposition: 'Making any norm into a legal limit was something which would be strongly opposed by the whole trade union movement.'[27] That afternoon, Healey gave a statement to parliament leaving room for a voluntary policy to be negotiated: 'We are determined to bring the rate of domestic inflation down to 10 per cent. by the end of the next pay round and to single figures by the end of 1976. This means the increase in wages and salaries during the next pay round cannot exceed 10 per cent . . . a voluntary policy will not be acceptable to the Government unless it satisfies the targets they have set for reducing inflation and includes convincing arrangements for ensuring compliance.'[28]

Wilson now turned to Jack Jones, who negotiated a limit of £6. As the general secretary of the Transport and General Workers' Union put it, echoing Haines: the advantage of the flat-rate schemes was that the 'lower the income, the smaller the sacrifice'. They would be simple to apply and straightforward in effect. No one could get round them by plausible interpretation. They would be seen as fair.[29] Jones, however, had a deeper concern: the survival of the government. He urged Foot and Benn not to resign: 'Were I to be responsible for bringing down the Government and, as I saw it, doing a disservice to trade unionists and the nation? I decided to see it through.'[30] On 3 July, the TUC agreed to a voluntary policy. The Policy Unit then worked for hours on a White Paper with the '£6 norm' that was launched by Wilson on 11 July. It worked. Within a year, inflation had halved.[31] In August 1975, Labour still led in the opinion polls, with 38.5 per cent to the Conservatives' 37.5 per cent.[32]

That summer also saw the culmination of the European issue that had dominated Wilson's leadership for so long. There was laughter in cabinet when, on 21 January 1975, the prime minister said, in self-deprecation: 'You talk about a messy middle-of-the-road muddle, but if the Cabinet understands what I mean, I'm at my best in a messy middle-of-the-road muddle.'[33] This statement did contain a key truth about Wilson, and his ability to devise positions that kept the party together. Yet his position on membership of the EEC was about far more than that.

On returning to office in 1974, Wilson was determined that the UK would remain in Europe. By instinct, Wilson remained a Commonwealth man. This was hardly a secret, as he set out in public, not least in an interview with Thames Television during the referendum campaign itself.[34] His view that the UK's interests were best served by remaining in the Common Market was rational, free of any grand principle. He did not tour the country with the official campaign to stay in the Common Market. Instead, he put the government position, using his unquestioned influence with Labour voters, and shaped the whole referendum debate.

Wilson set out his strategy in his first full day back at Downing Street in March 1974. Robert Armstrong, who had served Heath as principal private secretary from July 1970, was publicly associated with the negotiations for joining in the first place. Armstrong had heard that Marcia Williams wanted him out, so sought Wilson for a discussion on his future. If Wilson wanted to take a different approach to the Common Market, then Armstrong assumed his days would be numbered. But Wilson was firm: 'You stay around'. Armstrong remained in that post until April 1975, when he was succeeded by Stowe. He had no doubt Wilson always intended to stay in the Common Market and 'greatly admired the skill with which Harold kept his real views concealed from party colleagues'.[35] To keep the party together, Wilson at times appeared agnostic. He told the cabinet on 21 January 1975: '. . . as far as my constituency agent is concerned, when the Referendum campaign begins, he's going to lock up the canvassing records and go on holiday.'[36] Robin Butler, later cabinet secretary, was a private secretary at Number Ten from February 1974 to December 1975, when he returned to the Treasury. He, too, concurs with Armstrong's view, and saw great significance in Wilson not changing any of the civil service team that had worked for Heath on the negotiations for entry into the EEC. Butler thought that Wilson wanted to keep the Labour Party together, achieve better terms of entry, and keep the UK in the Common Market.[37]

In order to hold the referendum, Wilson had first to negotiate renegotiate the terms of entry. For this purpose, he created two cabinet committees: a European Strategy Committee (ES), which he chaired; and another, EQS, on the detail of the negotiations, chaired by Callaghan. On 20 December 1974, Wilson, Callaghan,

Jenkins and Short met at 10 Downing Street to agree a provisional timetable.[38] With the European Council in Dublin in mid-March, the plan was to have the cabinet decide by the end of March whether to recommend continued membership of the Community on the renegotiated terms. The referendum campaign itself would start in May, with the poll held in June. There was to be no higher threshold in terms of the majority for the result ('It may be difficult to justify departing from the simple proposition of a bare majority, whatever the size of the poll').[39] The cabinet secretary, Sir John Hunt, thought there was an argument for having a central UK-wide count to avoid an overt distinction between how different nations voted, thus fuelling separatism.[40] This was, however, rejected by the House of Commons, which voted for separate counts in each county of England and Wales, each region and island area of Scotland, and one for the whole province of Northern Ireland.

The Labour manifesto of February 1974 contained the renegotiation objectives. These would include renegotiating the Common Agricultural Policy, to allow low-cost food from around the world to access the UK market and contributing to the Community Budget 'only such sums as were fair in relation to what is paid and what is received by other member countries'. For the future, Labour would reject any international agreement that 'compelled us to accept increased unemployment for the sake of maintaining a fixed parity' – as current proposals for Economic and Monetary Union would – and opposed harmonisation of VAT. Parliament would retain the economic levers to pursue 'regional, industrial and fiscal policies' at home and the freedom in foreign policy to safeguard the Commonwealth both by securing continued access to UK markets, and for Community aid and trade to benefit 'developing countries throughout the world'.[41] The immediate aims were opaque and limited to give Wilson a realistic chance of achieving them. The further points about sovereignty were, more than anything, a marker for the future.

West German chancellor Schmidt addressed the Labour Party conference on 30 November 1974, after which he stayed with Wilson at Chequers. Butler believes that it was there that an agreement as to what could be successfully renegotiated on the UK terms of entry was thrashed out. In public, Wilson's line was that if he could not achieve the improvements he wanted, then he would recommend withdrawal in the referendum. The next European Council was to be held in Paris on 9 and 10 December 1974. There, Wilson was to set out the UK priorities for the renegotiation. The night before he was due to leave for France, Wilson spoke at the assembled gathering of London Labour mayors, and shifted his language, saying that if the terms were improved, he would recommend staying in the Common Market. That evening, Robin Butler was on duty at Number Ten, and fielded telephone calls from anti-Marketeers Tony Benn, Michael Foot, Peter Shore and Eric Varley, all querying Wilson's choice of words. Butler thought they could 'see the trap opening up' and gave them the agreed line: 'the one is the corollary of the other'.[42] But it was a definite and deliberate shift from Wilson.

Wilson completed the negotiation at the meeting of the European heads of government at Dublin Castle. Once the seat of British government in Ireland, it was now the taoiseach, Cosgrave, who hosted this crucial gathering for the UK's future relationship with its neighbours. The two key problems were the budget and continuing UK imports of New Zealand cheese. On the budgetary contribution, the first issue was eligibility: a member state would not be able to claim a refund at all if it ran, on average, a balance of payments surplus over three years. The second was the limit on any refund, the 'two-thirds limitation' whereby any repayment was limited to two-thirds of the figure by which a member state's contribution was in excess of its share of the whole EEC's Gross National Product. The French were insisting on the balance of payments qualification; the Germans wanted a £125m ceiling on refunds. On cheese, the 1971 entry terms agreed to by Heath would have ended imports in 1977; the aim was to find a way around this. The Heads of Government dinner on 10 March did not bring satisfactory progress; Wilson, on his way to the lounge to start coffee and brandy just before midnight, took Callaghan and his entourage into the less than elegant location of a large lavatory for an update, agreeing to push further the next day. By 5.30 p.m. on 11 March, there was still no breakthrough, but, with Schmidt due to leave at 6.30 p.m., and time running out, a formula had been found for the budget, and the New Zealand cheese issue had been solved alongside it.[43]

Wilson had hardly forced the European Economic Community in a different direction, but he had achieved concessions. When he addressed the House of Commons the next day, he had concrete progress to report. Here, the advantage of not setting the bar for the renegotiations too high was clear. On the importance of aid for developing countries, Wilson told MPs he had set this out at the summit. He referenced the Lome Convention – signed in Lome, Togo, between the EEC and 71 African, Caribbean and Pacific nations – and speaking further to the Commonwealth. He would build on his work with the United States and the work of the World Food Council, which had been established by the United Nations at the end of the previous year. On food, the UK would be a bridge between the EEC and the rest of the world.[44]

Wilson then moved to the detail of what had been achieved: 'On renegotiation, we reached agreement on the budget correcting mechanism and on access and pricing provision for New Zealand dairy produce.'[45] On the budget refund, Wilson summed up the effect of a complicated formula: 'The arrangements which the Community has now agreed would, if Britain remains a member of the EEC, give us an assurance of a repayment of hard cash if we found ourselves in the future paying an unfair share of the Community budget.'[46] On New Zealand cheese, while there would be reviews of prices, the central aim had been achieved: 'we have now kept the option for some continuing imports of New Zealand cheese after 1977 when they were due to cease under the 1971 terms.'[47] In the event, imports were to significantly reduce, but a transition for New Zealand had been achieved.

Attention now turned to the cabinet, with meetings on 17 and 18 March. By leaving the vote to the second day, Wilson could get through the regular Monday meeting of the Parliamentary Labour Party on 17 March without having to defend a decision either way.

He used the opportunity instead to emphasise that guidelines on the 'agreement to differ' would be issued and cautioned against Labour MPs attacking each other. This suspension of collective responsibility allowed the cabinet to take different positions in public, but Wilson knew he had to put the party back together afterwards.

Callaghan produced a memorandum for cabinet, 'EEC: Renegotiation Stocktaking' dated 14 March: '. . . it will be a matter for judgment by the Cabinet as to the extent to which we have fulfilled our Manifesto objectives, and as to whether Britain's interests will be best served inside or outside the community.'[48] The foreign secretary took the cabinet through the renegotiation in detail. He accepted that the fundamentals of the Common Agricultural Policy were unchanged: preference for countries in the EU, import levies, and support buying. However, he felt that the setting of prices was on a more soundly based economic footing and the system of compensation to producers would keep down costs to consumers. He lauded the concession achieved on continuing imports of New Zealand dairy products. A 'stocktaking' would now take place within the Community giving an opportunity to argue for further changes, including the general ban on beef imports. Callaghan argued that EEC membership did not include the acceptance of higher unemployment to achieve a fixed parity. The aim of achieving economic and monetary union by 1980 had been tacitly abandoned. On regional policy, there was an acceptance that national parliaments were the 'best judges' of spending. Callaghan did not believe there was a major issue with the EEC fettering industry policy since the government had taken office in 1974. Wilson intervened in the discussion on the issue of steel. The issue was that EEC membership would prevent full public ownership and the government taking over private steel firms if it chose to do so. He said he had indicated in Dublin that he would seek to find a solution within the existing Treaty arrangements but would seek Treaty amendment if necessary, though it was not practicable to deal with this before the referendum. On fiscal policies, Callaghan was confident that any proposals on VAT that the UK government did not like could be blocked.[49]

The key vote in cabinet took place the next day, on 18 March 1975. That morning, with the meeting starting at 9.30 a.m., Bernard Donoughue walked with Tony Benn to Number Ten from Horse Guards Parade. Donoughue put to Benn that it was a shame the referendum campaign was so far away; Benn 'disagreed and said that it was too soon: such an issue required a really long campaign!'[50] Cabinet opened with a discussion on sovereignty. Benn opened his remarks with a rhetorical flourish, arguing that membership would mean 'a reversal of hundreds of years of history which have progressively widened the power of the people over their governors. Now great chunks are to be handed to the Commission. I can think of no body of men outside the Kremlin who have so much power without a shred of accountability.' Foot joined in and said the cabinet was 'conniving at the dismemberment of Parliament'.[51] In this heavy discussion followed one light moment. Foot pointed out that the phrase 'draconian curtailment of the power of the British Parliament' was in the manifesto. Wilson pointed out – correctly – that that was in the February 1974 manifesto.[52] Foot countered that the October 1974 manifesto contained a phrase about Labour not agreeing to support membership of the Common Market if it would 'destroy the authority of Parliament' – which was also correct.[53] Wilson quipped: 'these are the differences between the Old and the New Testaments'.[54] The discussion on sovereignty included two rival interpretations. The first was on parliament ceding control over the laws that governed day-to-day life in the United Kingdom. Benn expressed this eloquently: '. . . one of the reasons we have a small Communist Party, why the ultra-Left is so unimportant, because we can say to people "Change your MP and you can change the law". That's where the attack on democracy is coming from.' Set against that was the idea of sovereignty as an ultimate recourse. Short, in responding to the discussion, captured this: 'it was clear that Parliament could not divest itself ultimately of its sovereignty and was in a position to bring the United Kingdom out of the Community at any time by repealing the European Communities Act 1972.'[55]

That discussion concluded, Wilson moved directly to the question of accepting the newly negotiated terms. He opened strongly with his own view: 'I recommend that we should stay in and that is the view of the Foreign Secretary, though he will speak for himself. We have substantially achieved our objectives, the Community has changed *de facto* and *de jure*.' He pointed out that the attitude of the Commonwealth had changed and added: 'I am only persuaded 51 per cent to 49, indeed I had anxieties right up to the last few days, but I now recommend that we stay in.'[56] This was a concealment of Wilson's real view, but it was important in one crucial respect: he would not alienate those arguing to withdraw.

As he took views around the cabinet table, the majority view that emerged was one of pragmatism. Wilson, while he did not claim all of the renegotiation aims had been met, said they had 'substantially been met'. There was no treaty change, but the EEC was 'now operating much more under the political direction of the Governments of Member States'.[57] That is not to say that ideology was not an issue. The European Economic Community was seen as a 'capitalist club' by many on the left, promoting free markets and competition above all else. Barbara Castle captured this: 'we were asking the British people to remain in an organisation in whose principles we said we did not believe . . .'[58] The vote was 16–7, with Ross, Varley, Silkin, Foot, Castle, Shore and Benn the dissenters. Wilson asked who wanted to take advantage of the agreement to differ, and only Ross, of the seven, did not. Donoughue told Wilson: 'Ted Heath took the British Establishment into the Market. You will take in the British people.'[59] The anti-marketeer cabinet members held a 'Cabinet Against the Market' lobby conference before all anti-market Labour MPs – around 80 – attended a meeting called by Douglas Jay in the Grand Committee Room. An Early Day motion urging MPs to support withdrawal was quickly tabled.[60]

Wilson's statement in the House of Commons opened in a downbeat fashion, but it marked his respect for parliament and his command of detail: 'I regret that this will inevitably be somewhat lengthy, but this is one of the most important parliamentary occasions in our history . . .'[61] The characterisation of the renegotiation is that what Wilson achieved was 'largely cosmetic' but it was more than that.[62] Wilson went through the negotiating objectives one by one. On the Common Agricultural Policy, Wilson pointed to greater flexibility, emphasising that member states would no longer be required to stockpile beef to maintain high prices; rather, it could be sold at reasonable prices and the loss to producers partly financed by the EEC. He said there would be guaranteed access for up to 1.4 million tonnes of sugar from developing countries, and highlighted his negotiated concession on New Zealand dairy produce. On the budget, Wilson pointed to the rebate of up to £125 million per year; on the prospect of economic and monetary union, Wilson said there was no chance of pressure to agree to something which would adversely affect UK employment levels. On regional aid, he confirmed the Commission's acceptance that national parliaments were the best judges of what was required. He believed that, within the Treaty of Rome, there was enough flexibility to protect the balance of payments. On aid being used to assist a wider range of developing countries, he pointed to the Lome Convention.

Finally, on VAT, Wilson said the UK could resist proposals it did not agree with. He did not oversell the renegotiation: 'To sum up, therefore, I believe that our renegotiation objectives have been substantially, though not completely, achieved.'[63] The wider Commonwealth was in support: 'We have to face the fact that practically all the members of the Commonwealth . . . want Britain to stay in the Community.'[64] Wilson also claimed a change in how the EEC operated: 'A fundamental change not in the Treaty but in the practice has been brought about by the new system of Heads of Government summits of a regular, routine character, started with that convened by President Giscard d'Estaing in Paris last September . . . as compared with even a year ago, vital interests of individual nations are now getting much more of a fair hearing.'[65] However, the deep split in the party remained. In the Commons vote on the government's White Paper supporting continued membership on the basis of the renegotiation on 9 April 1975, 145 Labour MPs voted in favour, with 137 against, with ministers voting 45 to 38 in favour.[66]

At least Wilson could now take his case to the country in advance of the referendum on 5 June. On 11 April, the campaign's co-ordinating committee was set up within government, and by 23 April, there was already a confidence in victory for the government: 'The opinion polls, for what they are worth, give the impression that the Government is going to win a majority for its recommendation . . . The *Evening Standard* poll on Friday showed 60 per cent for continued membership and 28 per cent against, with 12 per cent don't knows.'[67] On 29 May, Wilson and Callaghan met Schmidt at the NATO summit. They were still optimistic. Callaghan 'said he was prepared to chance his arm and forecast a 17 million to 8 million vote in favour of the pro-marketeers.'[68] The foreign secretary circulated a note to all ministers and backbenchers supportive of government going into the final week: 'All the indications are that there is strong support for the Government's recommendation and that if anything this support is hardening.'[69]

The small booklet sent to every household was entitled 'Britain's New Deal in Europe', with a quote from the prime minister on the front page: 'Her Majesty's Government have decided to recommend to the British people to vote for staying in the Community'. Including both covers, it ran to 16 pages and was an impressive piece of work, distilling the government's case down into simple, easily communicated propositions. Wilson emphasised the importance of his negotiations but was careful to show a realism in the way he portrayed the changes to the UK terms of entry: 'We do not pretend, and have never pretended, that we got everything we wanted in those negotiations. But we did get big and significant improvements on the previous terms.'[70]

The booklet presented the terms in a way that was relevant to everyday life. Under the heading 'Food' it was set out that 'Britain had to ensure that shoppers could get secure supplies of food at fair prices'. The Common Agricultural Policy 'now works more flexibly to the benefit of both housewives and farmers in Britain. The special arrangements made for sugar and beef are a good example.' It was added: 'At the same time many food prices in the rest of the world have shot up, and our food prices are now no higher because Britain is in the Common Market than if we were outside.' Further, the 'Government also won a better deal on food imports from countries outside the Common Market, particularly Commonwealth sugar and for New Zealand dairy products. These will continue to be on sale in our shops.' Under a separate heading of 'Money and Jobs' the booklet emphasised that, under the Dublin agreement, the UK could 'get back from Market funds up to £125 million a year', seeking to allay concerns on the level of contribution to the Common Market budget. It was added: 'Britain will not have to put VAT on necessities like food'. Finally, with a nod to the nations and regions of the UK: 'We have also maintained our freedom to pursue our own policies on taxation and on industry, and to develop Scotland and Wales and the regions where unemployment is high.'

There was a reassurance that 'Market aid for the poorer areas of the world must go to those in most need' and the support of the Commonwealth for the UK remaining in the EEC was confirmed with supportive quotes from Gough Whitlam, prime minister of Australia; Wallace Rowling, prime minister of New Zealand; and Donald Owen Mills, Jamaican ambassador to the United Nations. On sovereignty: 'Membership of the Common Market imposes new rights and duties on Britain, but does not deprive us of our national identity. To say that membership could force Britain to eat Euro-bread or drink Euro-beer is nonsense'. On trade rules, if the UK left: 'We would just be outsiders looking in'.[71]

In a half-hour television interview on 15 May, Wilson looked fidgety and tired. But, pipe in hand, he gave a flawless performance. He defended the decision to hold the referendum on the basis that the Heath government had not sought the consent of the British people, and that, in the event of a vote to stay in, people would get behind the decision. It was a choice for a generation; membership in itself would not solve Britain's economic problems, but he judged that it was best for the country to be in the Common Market. He distinguished between those who were committed to staying in or leaving whatever the consequences, and those – like him – working out the best thing to do for their families. When required, he attacked the question. The interviewer Llew Gardner questioned him on his low profile in the campaign, and his apparent lack of commitment to the UK remaining in the Common Market. Wilson pointed out that he had been to the Commonwealth Heads of Government Conference (held in Jamaica from 29 April to 6 May) and that he had made a number of speeches. The reference to the Commonwealth conference was a smart political move: not attending and concentrating on the referendum could have been portrayed as abandoning the Commonwealth for the sake of Europe. He said he did not stand on the south coast, look towards the continent and see a New Jerusalem; he declared himself an 'emotional Commonwealth Man' and accepted his approach to the European question was a practical one. He spoke of the problem of buying sugar at scarcity prices due to being in the Common Market on Heath's terms of entry. This said, he insisted that he was recommending remaining in the Common Market 'and in strong terms'.

He was asked if it was his position as prime minister or the importance of party unity that led him to the low profile he was taking. Neither, he said. Wilson made the valid point that people would become fed up of the 'screaming and cacophony' on both sides and that the approach of being the calm voice of reason – he said Callaghan took the same view – was more likely to get a hearing with the public. He attacked the media, saying that he was only allowed two television interviews – one with the BBC, and one with independent television – in pursuit of the 'mysterious concept of balance'. How, therefore, could the interviewer credibly criticise him for the number of TV interviews? He said there were allies in the Common Market – not least West Germany – in reducing European bureaucracy. When challenged as to how people could be expected to make up their minds when the cabinet was so divided, he said he relied on the intelligence of the British people. He was coy on what would happen in the event of a vote to leave. Too strong an answer might have led to headlines that he expected to lose. He said there would need to be an Act of Parliament to repeal the Accession Treaty and that 'contingency plans wouldn't take long to work out'.[72]

Having cabinet ministers on different sides inevitably brought tensions. Jenkins joined Heath and Thorpe in campaigning for 'Yes' on a cross-party basis, with Benn a powerful advocate for 'No'. As early as 20 March, Wilson had issued guidelines to be adhered to, including those of differing views avoiding staged confrontations with each other.[73] These were formalised in a paper on 3 April. There was trouble the following month: on 27 May, Jenkins attacked Benn's assertion that EEC membership had already cost jobs: 'I find it increasingly difficult to take Mr Benn seriously as an economic minister.' Wilson was irritated at Jenkins: 'If your remarks about the Secretary of State for Industry were correctly reported by the BBC and all today's papers, they cannot be regarded as other than a breach of the guidelines. The interpretation put on them in different papers is inevitably either that you are putting irresistible pressure on me and limiting the options in a reshuffle, or that you are already privy to my intentions about Tony Benn, which of course is not the case.' Wilson, who intended to demote Benn after the referendum, said the controversy caused had upstaged his own speech on employment and industrial policy in Dewsbury: 'When you and I discussed arrangements for the campaign, many weeks ago, you rightly said that each of us would be appealing to a different audience. My speech was carefully crafted to appeal to our own people, particularly those worried about jobs. But it did not get a chance.'[74] The following Monday, 2 June, Benn and Jenkins debated on *Panorama*, but stuck to the issues.

Three days later, the British people gave a resounding 'Yes' to the EEC, with nearly 17.4 million people, 67 per cent, voting to stay in. It was a two-to-one majority. The next morning, Wilson sat with his new principal private secretary, Ken Stowe. He told Stowe the result had taken him ten years to achieve: 'People say I have no strategy, cannot think strategically.' Stowe wrote: 'There was – and is – no doubt in my mind how much this meant to him; which is why it stands out so clearly in my memory.'[75] That same day, he told Donoughue: 'pulling out of Europe would put the wrong people in power in Britain, like Benn and Enoch Powell.'[76] On Monday, 9 June, the prime minister addressed the Commons:

The debate is now over. The two tests set out in our manifesto of successful renegotiation and the expressed approval of the majority of the British people have been met. The historic decision has been made. I hope that this House and the country as a whole will follow the lead which the Government intend to give in placing past divisions behind us, and in working together to play a full and constructive part in all Community policies and activities.[77]

Wilson also made clear that opening the door to the Common Market did not mean closing the door on the Commonwealth or the wider world: 'I would also wish to say to our friends and allies in the Commonwealth who made clear their hope that we would remain within the Community – and to all the developing countries – that we shall hope to bring even more to our relationship with them following the clear decision of the British electorate last Thursday.'[78]

He concluded his statement by closing the debate on the issue, but also looking to the future. Established membership of the EEC was not a panacea, but it gave a platform to build upon.

We now have that settled position, and we are determined to make a success of it. But our future will continue to depend on what we are prepared to do by our own efforts, our skill, our technology – and our restraint, a restraint which demonstrates our concern for the interests of those members of our national community least able to help themselves.[79]

It was a fine statement, skilfully seeking to end the debate on EEC membership while setting out the Labour Party's internationalist values in the context of the wider world. The leader of the opposition, Margaret Thatcher, who had replaced Heath as Conservative leader in February, rose to join the prime minister in celebrating the result: 'We are particularly pleased with the number of people who came out to vote for Britain's staying in the EEC and also with the strong "Yes" from each of the four parts of the United Kingdom, which confirmed the strength of the British ties which unite us.'[80]

Wilson's judgement that Britain was economically better off in the EEC was supported by the evidence. In 1960, the UK was the richest country of the Nine; by 1973 it was the third poorest after Italy and Ireland. National income per head was 1159 for the UK, 2055 for Germany, 1769 for France and 1742 for Belgium. Looking at average rates of growth from 1960–73, the UK's was the lowest, at 3.3 per cent; the EEC(9) average was 5.0 per cent, with France the highest at 5.9 per cent.[81] Being outside the European Economic Community was not in the UK's interests.

Ironically, the highest praise came from the right-wing press. On 7 June, the day after the referendum, the *Daily Telegraph* could not have been clearer: 'The result is quite frankly a triumph for Mr Wilson.' So it was, though Wilson himself was careful to spread the credit around. He told Callaghan: '. . . basically it was the success of your renegotiations and the way in which you masterminded them that brought about the result.'[82] He also credited Short for his 'careful planning and . . . success in defending decisions which you had taken, with our colleagues' support, to Parliament.'[83] He even wrote to Jenkins that it was a 'stroke of genius to think of appointing Sir Philip Allen to the principal post in the conduct of electoral arrangements.'[84]

Wilson had set out to keep the UK in the Common Market and he had achieved the aim. Yet he has not been given the credit he deserves. Ben Pimlott's judgement, for example, was circumspect: 'By one measure, Wilson succeeded. He remained Leader, and Labour stayed together, even forming another administration, though some would argue that the seeds of the Party's later division were sown by his handling of it at this time.'[85] By 'another measure – the issue of principle about Britain's future and continued membership of the EEC, and the appropriate stand for Labour in Opposition to take on it – the verdict depends to a large extent on the commitment and outlook of the judge.'[86]

However, Wilson's handling of this issue can now be considered from the vantage point of the UK having left the European project altogether. Until the rise of Euroscepticism in the UK well over thirty years after the 1975 referendum, the UK position in the

EEC, and, as it became, the EU, was secure. It is correct that the dispute over Europe rumbled on in the Labour Party, and that the party manifesto of 1983 advocated withdrawal from the European institutions. Yet that position was to prove the exception, not the rule: in every other election manifesto between 1975 and 2017, neither of the two main political parties advocated withdrawal: after all, in 2015, Prime Minister David Cameron's position was to offer an 'in/out' referendum, not a position of outright withdrawal. It was only in the general election of 2017, after the referendum had taken place on 23 June 2016, that the political parties had to grapple with delivering withdrawal.

The result of the 1975 Common Market referendum was actually a triumph of strategy. Wilson showed that prime ministers do not always need to lead from the front. Directing from the back, Wilson secured the result he sought, for which he deserves great credit. He ranks among those few politicians who successfully dealt with the European issue in British politics. Any assessment of it should change Wilson's reputation for short-termism. The prime minister did not put himself at the front and centre of the public debates. Yet he determined the date and circumstances of the referendum, and he still dominated the activities of the government. He made the case to the public with a leaflet to every household in the country that focused on the terms he had negotiated. As he told Jenkins, he could speak to Labour voters in a way that his home secretary could not. He was not the Herbie Roberts of the campaign, only coming up the pitch for set pieces. Rather, he was a continental-style deeplying playmaker: towards the back, definitely, but controlling the pace of the game. Naturally, though, Wilson would prefer the comparison with Roberts. That collective responsibility had been suspended is on one level a sign of weakness: that the government could not enforce its own position. At the same time, there was no threat to Wilson's position as prime minister.

The post-referendum reshuffle was less successful, but still achieved one key aim. On the Monday evening after the referendum, Wilson told Benn that he wanted to move him to Energy. Benn took it badly, and Wilson was concerned he would go to the backbenches: 'the last place I wanted to see him'. Foot intervened on Benn's behalf but Wilson was adamant. The next day Benn accepted. Wilson noted, wryly, that closer contact with the miners was 'a potential power-base for any future ambitions . . .' and that Benn would be in control of North Sea oil.[87] In November, the queen inaugurated the flow from the Forties Oil Field at British Petroleum's control centre in Dyce, near Aberdeen. The up-and-coming Eric Varley took Benn's place. Having demoted a prominent left-winger, Wilson sought to balance it with demoting Reg Prentice from the Labour right to Overseas Aid from Education, placing him outside the cabinet. Jenkins interceded and confronted Wilson, saying 'some ultimately unforgivable things about the general triviality of his mind and his incapacity to rise to the level of events.'[88] Wilson, even under such provocation, found a solution, with Prentice moving to Overseas Aid but remaining in the cabinet. Hart did not appreciate being displaced from Overseas Aid, turned down Wilson's offer of the Transport job and left the government. This time it was Castle and Foot who intervened together. Foot bemoaned 'poor Judith's blood on the carpet'.[89] Next, Mellish turned down the Transport job as well and remained as chief whip. It was a sorry state of affairs, but Wilson had successfully demoted Benn.

Wilson was starting to slow up. Haines believes that Wilson at times lacked the will to force things through cabinet. In 1975, Haines put to Wilson that there should be a Labour policy on the sale of council houses. Wilson commented that 'This could be historic'. It was different from Thatcher's later policy in that all the money received would have been reinvested into building new council houses. Donoughue's Policy Unit produced a package of schemes for tenants to own their own homes in October 1975.[90] The proposal went to a cabinet committee (MISC 127) on 24 March 1976 where it was blocked by Crosland who said 'our people wouldn't put up with it': that is, local councillors. Ross and paymaster general Edmund Dell joined with Crosland in opposition. Haines felt that Wilson handed it to a cabinet committee and accepted the conclusion.[91]

Wilson had told Donoughue in March 1974 only to get leave from the London School of Economics until Easter 1976 because

'I will then retire.'[92] He also mentioned that he was only staying two more years on the weekend after the general election of February 1974 to Haines, Lancaster, and Williams, who were all together with Donoughue.[93] In that summer of 1975 he told Donoughue: 'Bernard, I have been around this course so often that I am too bored to face jumping any more hurdles.' Another time he said: 'The trouble with me now is that I only have the same old solutions for the same old problems.'[94] His brilliant memory was also starting to fade. In December 1975, Wilson invited the government whips to Lord North Street for Christmas drinks. Tom Pendry, then one of the whips, noticed some very good paintings on the stairs and asked for a closer look. Wilson started 'pointing out who painted one after another of the paintings, until he came to one when he froze, and the anguish on his face was something that I recognise must have been particularly painful as he had one of the best memories that anyone in Parliament at the time could not match . . .'[95] After Healey had been rude to him at cabinet on 3 December, Wilson told Donoughue in the privacy of the bathroom: 'Bernard, oh I am so exhausted!' On doctor's orders, Wilson was trying to reduce his workload: Stowe had been told to clear the diary, and the cabinet secretary, Sir John Hunt, was asked to reduce the prime minister's burden of chairing committees. Donoughue mused: 'I wondered if the wild dogs of the Opposition would smell that the old lion was finally weakening; but apparently not.'[96] John Tomlinson, Wilson's PPS from late 1975, used to try to shield Wilson from backbenchers immediately after Prime Minister's Questions. Tomlinson made sure Wilson and Mary had until 3.45 p.m. for a cup of tea while he spoke to the MPs, then he would arrange for some to come in to see the prime minister.[97]

For all this, Wilson's political instincts remained untouched. Ken Clarke, who saw Wilson at close quarters in parliament during this period, said that he was 'good in the House of Commons but not a brilliant charismatic speaker. He had an earnest voice and could be monotonous. But he had an air of authority about him. He was a man of intellectual and political ability.' Clarke said: 'Harold was not disliked but was not much loved. But he was held in perfectly high regard. He was a wheeler-dealer, a pragmatist. He loved the political game and was good at it.'[98] Dennis Skinner, elected as MP in 1970, thought Wilson was the best prime minister he had seen in the Commons; Margaret Beckett, who had defeated Taverne at Lincoln in October 1974, said Wilson 'was so impressive because he always had the facts at his fingertips. He was witty, great at one-line put-downs.'[99]

He continued to demonstrate his political skills. In November 1975, the American parent company of the motor car manufacturer, Chrysler, was looking to close its British operations, causing 30,000 job losses. At first Wilson thought it was a clear case of the American management being to blame. However, Ross and the Scottish minister Bruce Millan threatened to resign: the closure of the Chrysler plant in Linwood would hit Scotland hard. Wilson then decided to save the plant; by 8 December Lever had £140m on the table. Donoughue thought bailing it out was a 'bad deal for the British taxpayer and probably bad for British industry' but Wilson had, for now at least, prevented the closure, saved the jobs, and kept Ross and Millan in the cabinet.[100]

Wilson's final months in office were legislation-heavy. The 1975-6 session of parliament, Wilson's last as a party leader and prime minister, opened on 19 November: 'Devolution apart, it was not an ambitious programme, reflecting as it did the difficulties we were facing with our majority position in Parliament.'[101] While this was correct in comparison to Wilson's 1960s government, there were still a number of significant Bills that started their passage through parliament in the spring of 1976. All received Royal Assent and passed into law by the end of the year. Having moved from grammars and secondary moderns to comprehensives via the device of issuing Circulars and offering money, the government legislated for the principle of school reorganisation on comprehensive lines through the Education Bill, with its Second Reading on 4 February. There was the Dock Work Regulation Bill, debated on 10 February, increasing employment safeguards for dock workers. On 4 March, it was the Race Relations Bill. Jenkins opened the debate: 'members of Britain's racial minorities are entitled to full and equal treatment, regardless of their colour, race or national origins. Racial discrimination and the disadvantages experienced by sections of the community are morally repugnant to a civilised and democratic society.'[102] Fittingly, on 23 March, as Wilson's premiership drew to a close, the New Towns (Amendment) Bill was moved at its Second Reading by Lewis Silkin's son, John. Wilson had started his ministerial career over three decades before, house-building at the Ministry of Works. The principle of houses being built by the New Town Corporations transferring to the local authorities had been broken in 1959 with the creation of the Commission for the New Towns. Now, the principle of housing transfer from the corporations to councils was re-established with the commission taking over the industrial and commercial assets. Such a tidying-up exercise was a fitting tribute to Wilson's orderly mind.

Wilson's positions in cabinet remained decisive. Healey was proposing cuts in public expenditure of £3.5bn. Secretary of state for Defence Roy Mason was holding out against defence cuts on the basis of Britain not being able to maintain its NATO commitment. On 15 January 1976, at cabinet, Wilson intervened: with Mason offering £175 million of cuts, and the general view of cabinet that it should be kept under £200 million, he settled on £193 million.[103] In fact, it was Healey's position on cutting public expenditure that Wilson used to damage his chances of succeeding him as prime minister. Knowing he was going to resign within days, Wilson left Healey to debate his White Paper containing his proposed expenditure cuts to the Commons on 9 and 10 March 1976. Labour rebels combined with the opposition to defeat it by 284 votes to 256. Wilson had 'mischievously left the unsuspecting Healey with the task of bullying his own rebellious backbenchers . . .'[104] Wilson had to introduce a vote the next day to reverse the defeat: 'the House must understand that this is a vote of confidence in the Government and the Government's financial and economic policies.'[105] This time, the government won by 297 votes to 280. This all had the effect of delaying Wilson's resignation by a few days.

That Wilson had the option to change the day of the announcement was an indication of his power at the point of departure. He is the only post-war prime minister to have left at a time of his own choosing. He was not cast out of Number Ten by an angry electorate, nor was he forced out by plotting parliamentarians. The only other prime minister who even set a date of his own departure was Tony Blair, and that was under extreme pressure having already promised to step down prior to the 2005 general election. David Cameron chose to walk away, but it was after the defeat of the Remain side that he led in the EU referendum of 23 June 2016 forced his hand. At the same time his decision has given rise to a range of theories. This was Wilson's decision, after all: surely there had to be an ulterior motive? In her diary, Castle captured this sentiment: 'What exactly *was* Harold up to? More than had met the eye, I have no doubt.'[106]

The reality is more straightforward. Wilson had promised his family at the time of the 1970 general election that he would stay around eighteen months to two years, then step down. After Labour was defeated, he wanted to try to return to Downing Street. His son, Robin, in line with the earlier plan, now only expected his father to remain in office for the same period, and, most likely to retire on his sixtieth birthday.[107] Wilson's resignation was effected with an elan that befitted his skill as a politician. In 1975, Wilson had asked Haines to draw up plans for his resignation. The original plan was for him to resign on 28 February. He wanted to resign in the afternoon due to the NEC meeting that morning ('Didn't want the buggers interfering!'). Haines wrote a programme and gave it to Wilson. He consulted the prime minister's principal private secretary, Ken Stowe, for the governmental side of things. A resignation timetable was constructed, with an initial plan for Callaghan and Healey to be informed just before a cabinet meeting at which Wilson's announcement would be made.[108] Haines is sure Wilson told Callaghan much earlier, most likely on a train to Brighton; Wilson also told his foreign secretary on 11 March, in the back of a car on the way from his sixtieth birthday dinner to a Commons vote. Jenkins had been tipped off by Goodman at a Christmas Party in December 1975.[109]

On 16 March 1976, as soon as cabinet members had sat down,

Wilson told them he had been to the palace and had a statement to make. As he spoke, in a fine touch, a signed copy was circulated to every one of his colleagues. He set out that he had told the queen of his intention to resign as prime minister as soon as a successor could be elected by the Parliamentary Labour Party; in doing so, he was confirming a decision he had already told her about in December 1975. He had decided in March 1974 that he would serve no more than two years: he had not changed his mind and that decision was 'irrevocable'. Though he insisted he would play no part in the election of his successor, he did discount his own age as a reason for leaving: 'The fact that I am leaving shortly after my sixtieth birthday has no bearing on the choice to be made.' This was helpful to Callaghan, four years his senior. Wilson had once seen Jenkins as his successor, but no longer. The foreign secretary was the natural successor now.[110]

The reasons Wilson gave were, firstly, his length of tenure: 'My period as Prime Minister has been longer than any of my peacetime predecessors in this century.' Second, he did not think he should remain so long in office as to deny other talented colleagues the opportunity to lead: 'This is the most experienced and talented team in this century, in my view transcending that of Campbell-Bannerman 70 years ago.' Third, he believed his successor needed time to make their own mark, but sounded a note of continuity as well as change, setting out his expectation that his successor would continue with a strategy of counter-inflation. Finally, he set out his belief that because he had faced similar decisions so many times over his period in office, he had to avoid 'a tendency to say you have [already] been into that, so that you do not give the fresh consideration the circumstances require'.

He insisted these reasons offered a complete explanation for his decision, and that there were no coming circumstances the country would face, hidden in some way from colleagues, that played a part. In fact he said that 'For two years we have had to face the consequence of world inflation and world unemployment. But now the economy is beginning to revive.' He believed that the argument that Britain was ungovernable had now been defeated. Industrial problems were being tackled by 'relevant micro-economic action in place of an over-reliance on clumsy and often ineffective macro-economic lurches'; the economy was being modernised through the NEDC. The housing programme had been restored to over 300,000 new homes annually. There had been the 'greatest ever improvements in the standards of pensioners and others dependent on the social services, particularly the disabled, previously so neglected'. In foreign affairs, membership of the European Community had been settled; American president Gerald Ford had described relations across the Atlantic as 'as good as they have ever been'. On his own future, he said he would remain in Parliament: 'I am above all a Parliamentarian. I love Parliament and want to go on serving it and serving in it.' He added that he had considered resigning before the 1975 party conference and again at Christmas but had 'felt it necessary to remain in order to lead the campaign for acceptance of the pay policy set for the year from the end of July 1975.' In typical style, Wilson also peppered his remarks with statistics: he had chaired 472 cabinets and answered more than 12,000 parliamentary questions. He had worked seven days a week for at least 12 to 14 hours a day, and, after a hectic week considered an average of at least 500 different documents and submissions on a weekend. Prime ministers, though, needed to know all that was going on, and there was great breadth and fascination in this reading. Wilson said that it was 'an office to cherish' and offered one firm piece of advice to his successor and their soon-to-be-formed cabinet, which was to 'get out into the country, meet the people, tell them, explain to them, listen to them; and above all remember the Party is the Party in the country – not the Palace of Westminster, not Smith Square.' Wilson himself said he had averaged over 100 political and other meetings around the country each year.[111]

The news came as no surprise to the queen. The artist Michael Noakes was painting her portrait when the news came through, and she said: 'I expected he'd go at about this point.'[112] In August 1975, he had raised the possibility of leaving at the party conference in the autumn, but Marcia said that would create an 'unseemly battle for the succession' and she managed to talk him out of resigning at Christmas on the basis that seeking to resign during a public holiday with 'a dearth of newspapers, would be a messy way of doing it.'[113] What was more difficult – even for Williams, with her influence – was to argue that Wilson should go beyond his sixtieth birthday. At the prime minister's annual Balmoral visit in September 1975, Wilson had informed Martin Charteris, by then the queen's private secretary, that he intended to resign within six months. He had also told the queen herself informally. Mary Wilson, approvingly, entered 'D-Day' into her diary for Tuesday 16 March 1976, which would be the first meeting of the cabinet after Wilson's birthday.[114] On 9 December, he confirmed to the queen at his weekly audience that he would resign around his birthday on 11 March 1976.[115]

The reaction to Wilson's resignation, even from his tormentors, was sympathetic. In *The Times*, Bernard Levin wrote: 'Harold Wilson's sense of the politically dramatic was always acute, and never more so than in the manner of his departure from the office for which he had so long striven and in which his mastery of the political arts was so unceasingly displayed, to the confounding of the prophets, the discomfiture of his critics and the helpless rage of his political opponents.' This was from a self-confessed Wilson critic: 'It is probable that none of his critics ever said more things intended to wound him, or anything intended to wound him more deeply, than did I.'[116] Patrick Cosgrave, a speech-writer for Heath and Thatcher, wrote that 'his final epitaph is likely to suggest he was a palliator of crisis, not a man who could solve great problems. He is Labour's Baldwin . . .'[117] The comparison with Conservative prime minister Stanley Baldwin, seen on the right as a leader who sought industrial peace, was not uncomplimentary.

Fittingly, one of Wilson's final public engagements as prime minister was on Tuesday, 30 March 1976, addressing the annual conference of the Association of Independent Cinemas on 'The Future of the British Film Industry'. As David Robinson put it in *The Times*: 'Twenty-nine years earlier, as the thirty-one-year-old whiz-kid president of the Board of Trade, he was responsible for measures which probably saved British films from total extinction.'[118]

The election to succeed Wilson was conducted swiftly. As with 1963, the PLP was still skewed to the right. Though there were six candidates from across the political spectrum, the contest was between Callaghan and Jenkins to be the leading candidate on the right. In the first round on 25 March, Foot led with 90 votes, Callaghan was second on 84, Jenkins secured 56, Benn 37, Healey 30, and Crosland 17. Healey ploughed on into the next round, held on 30 March, with Callaghan taking the lead on 141 votes, Foot on 133 and Healey himself on 38. On 5 April, in the third round, Callaghan defeated Foot by 176 votes to 137. That day, Benn dropped in at Number Ten and was speaking to the victorious Callaghan and Williams. Benn teased Callaghan, asking what would happen if Wilson, at that point not the Labour leader, but still prime minister, did not formally resign? 'Mary would never allow that,' replied Callaghan.[119]

Chapter 20

The Wilson Plot?

Later Years

In Wilson's absence, the government entered its most severe economic crisis. Healey, re-appointed as chancellor by Callaghan, announced on 28 September 1976 that he would be making an application to the International Monetary Fund for a loan of nearly $4bn. For Britain to be apparently unable to pay its own way and to have to seek such a bail-out was to become a symbol of Labour's alleged inability to manage the British economy in later years. It also seemed to be further evidence that Wilson had left before the going got even tougher. Michael Heseltine, then in the shadow cabinet, later observed: 'Harold Wilson had done Jim Callaghan no favours in handing the reins to him when he did.'[1] Negative attitudes to Wilson became more and more commonplace, and three issues in particular damaged his reputation: honours; an apparent obsession with the activities of the security services; and, perhaps most surprisingly, given his passionate anti-apartheid views, revelations about his policy towards South Africa while in office.

In the weeks after he left office, Wilson was given his own fine accolade. On 23 April, the queen announced that Wilson would be appointed a knight of the garter. At Windsor Castle on 14 June, Wilson would be given the most eminent of honours: becoming a member of an elite club limited to the sovereign, the Prince of Wales, and twenty-four others.[2] Sir Harold Wilson would be part of the highest order of chivalry. Yet the positivity around this was not to last. It was the publication of Wilson's own resignation honours on 27 May 1976 that provoked fury, ending the generally positive coverage he had received since leaving office. Firstly, the delay in making the list public raised questions and there were leaks to the *Sunday Times*. On 2 May 1976, Wilson had issued a flat denial that anything was amiss: 'The statement in today's *Sunday Times* that names proposed for life peerages have been "stalled" by Whitehall and by the Political Honours Scrutiny Committee are totally untrue.'[3] However, Edith Summerskill, the committee's chair, said they had made clear that they did not approve of at least half of the list.[4]

Some of the names on the list were to be expected from a retiring prime minister, rewarding those who had served and assisted him. Ted Short became a Companion of Honour. Albert Murray was made a peer, as was Joe Stone and Wilson's publisher, George Weidenfeld. Terry Boston, a Labour MP who had lost his Faversham seat in 1970, and had assisted Wilson during the two 1974 election campaigns, joined them on the red benches. Wilson's constituency agent, Arthur Smith, was awarded a CBE. Peggy, in her capacity as personal secretary to Mary, was awarded an MBE. The controversy arose because of the inclusion of a number of businessmen who had provided no 'political service' for the purpose of the honours list, had no apparent link to the Labour Party, and who subsequently became involved in scandals themselves.

The common theme appeared to be that they were friends of Marcia Williams. This applied to James Goldsmith, then a financier and industrialist, who was knighted, and Professor John Vaizey of Brunel University, who was made a peer. According to Haines, Vaizey had been 'helping Lady Falkender in her search for a suitable public school for her two children'.[5] There was the property developer Max Rayne, who also went to the House of Lords; Eric Miller, another Williams friend, who was knighted, committed suicide in 1977 while the subject of a fraud investigation.

Left-wing MPs expressed anger and disgust. Sydney Bidwell, Labour MP for Ealing Southall, and a former chair of the Tribune Group, said the 'names on the list have nothing to do with the promotion of socialism which is what the Labour Party and the

Labour Government mission is supposed to be about'. Jeff Rooker, Labour MP for Birmingham Perry Barr, said: 'I have 50 people in my local party who have done more individually than this lot put together.' On the Tory side, Edward Taylor, MP for Glasgow Cathcart, thought the list would 'cheapen the whole system of honours', while Neil Macfarlane, MP for Sutton and Cheam, said it illustrated the way the country had been 'demeaned and debased' by Wilson's leadership.[6] Ian Hildreth, director general of the Institute of Directors, could not contain his glee: 'As an organisation devoted to the support of free enterprise and the business leader we have naturally observed with lively interest the conversion to our beliefs of Sir Harold Wilson, as evidenced by the names of those appearing in his Honours list.'[7]

On 29 May 1976, the political journalist, and biographer of Edward Heath, George Hutchinson, penned a coruscating opinion piece in *The Times*: 'By his last act of patronage Sir Harold has succeeded in reducing himself, and not only himself. He has demeaned the office of Prime Minister and embarrassed his successor. He has likewise embarrassed the Crown. He has injured the Labour Party, and thereby the Government.' Hutchinson did not spare Williams, either: 'While it is right that principals should accept the blame when things go wrong, Sir Harold's amanuensis and advisor (one might almost say accomplice) can hardly be exonerated. Lady Falkender has claimed too much influence and responsibility in the past to escape comment and attention now.'[8]

Williams wrote to *The Times* on 30 May 1976 in aggressive terms: 'The Resignation List was Sir Harold Wilson's list and his alone'. She added: 'The comment on the list itself has been sickening . . . It has been sanctimonious protest by the unimaginative half of the Establishment on their own behalf; it has been unadulterated snobbery; and, much more serious, it has often been covert anti-Semitism [referring to the fact that a number of those awarded honours were Jewish].' She defended Wilson: 'Perhaps behind this whole affair lies some other story, some other motive for it, where frustration, malice and envy are being expressed in a final attack upon a man who has contributed so much to our national life, to the lives of ordinary people; though not necessarily to the lives of those living within certain small select circles in Metropolitan London.'

Within a year of Wilson leaving office, Haines published *The Politics of Power*, in which he set out that: 'the list from which Sir Harold Wilson prepared his own list was Lady Falkender's written out in her own hand on the lavender-coloured notepaper she often used'.[9] On 7 February 1977, the week before the book's publication, Terry Lancaster's *Daily Mirror* front-page splash was that Williams 'drew up Sir Harold Wilson's main resignation honours list on her own lavender notepaper'.

Williams, however, continued to defend herself. In 2006, the BBC broadcast a docudrama *The Lavender List*: it was 'loosely – very loosely' based on Joe Haines' book, *Glimmers of Twilight*, though Haines himself identified fifty-six errors in the production.[10] Williams sued, and, in 2007, it was confirmed that an out-of-court settlement had been reached: 'The BBC is to pay Lady Falkender £75,000 in damages over a drama documentary claiming she conducted an adulterous affair with Harold Wilson and exercised undue influence over the compilation of his resignation honours list.' Williams herself issued a statement: 'As Lord Wilson always made clear throughout the period after he left office, and as I myself have always made clear, the 1976 list was his own work and included only those individuals he himself believed ought to be honoured.'[11]

Yet the controversy continued. In 2018, Williams confirmed that the eight pieces of notepaper making up the 'Lavender List' were to be sold at auction by Sotheby's, as would the government documents accompanying it. These confirmed the warnings Wilson was given about the names on the list. Gordon Richardson advised that 'on no account' should a knighthood be given to Goldsmith. Joseph Kagan was refusing to co-operate with a 'major tax investigation'. Kagan, made a peer, was eventually sentenced to ten months' imprisonment in 1980 for theft from his own company and false accounting. Even Sigmund Sternberg, a Labour Party donor, had been deemed unsuitable, with Stowe expressing concern that there was an 'unfavourable' report on him from the Department of Trade. Williams' son, Tim, called the Lavender List an 'accursed object' and said of his mother: 'She drew it up but the idea that she imposed it upon him [Wilson] against his will is not true.'[12] However, it seemed that the list remained cursed, as the Cabinet Office prevented it from being sold on the basis that it needed to establish the category the documents fell into, and whether they 'belonged to the nation'.[13]

The Lavender List was not the only issue that could not be shaken off, either. Wilson's deeply held concerns about the activities of the security services towards him, his close circle, and his government led to him being accused of unfounded allegations and paranoia. However, debate on the 'Wilson Plot' and subsequent events have proved that Wilson's suspicions about a group in the security services plotting to bring about his downfall, and that he was under surveillance, were far from groundless. While there is no evidence of a deliberate plan from MI5, headed from the top, to bring down Wilson, there is confirmation of activity against Wilson that points to a problem with the lack of accountability and supervision by parliament of the activities of the deep state during Wilson's period in office. The 1989 Security Service Act finally put the security service on a statutory basis. Parliament's Intelligence and Security Committee, established by the Intelligence Services Act 1994, now provides the scrutiny that in Wilson's time was so badly lacking.

Separating facts from conspiracies in this area is notoriously difficult. However, there is published evidence available, and witness accounts. In his authorised history of MI5, Christopher Andrew devoted a chapter to the 'Wilson Plot'.[14] In order to put Wilson's allegations in context, it is first necessary to consider the charges against him. The suggestion that Wilson was a Soviet agent is nonsense. Yet it was believed by some people. In the pages of *Private Eye*, Auberon Waugh attacked Wilson relentlessly. Take this example from 19 September 1975: 'I have never attempted to disguise my belief that Wilson is one [a Soviet agent], recruited in Moscow and London in 1956–8.' *Private Eye* also managed to come into possession of a Christmas card Mikoyan sent to Wilson in 1961, and Patrick Marnham, a *Private Eye* staffer, claimed to have been passed a dossier of information on Wilson by a reporter on *The Times* that had originated with MI5, referring back to the sale of jet engines to the Soviet Union in 1947.[15] The concern was that Wilson's decision to sell such technology would have allowed Soviet agents, under the guise of people needing training to use it, to establish a greater spying capacity in Britain.[16]

The former MI5 officer Peter Wright also believed it. He published a notorious autobiography, *Spycatcher*, breaking the lifelong duty of secret service confidentiality by detailing his activities over decades. The British government sought to prevent publication of the book, but Wright published it in America and Australia in 1987.[17] Eventually, in 1988, publication was permitted in the UK, as the government lost in court. Wright also appeared on BBC's *Panorama*.[18] However, Wright's only evidence was the number of trips Wilson had made to the Soviet Union: that did not even amount to an argument about there being no smoke without fire, as this was not even smoke. Yet Wright asserts: 'It was inevitable that Wilson would come to the attention of MI5. Before he became prime minister he worked for an East–West trading organisation and paid many visits to Russia. MI5, well aware that the KGB will stop at nothing to entrap or frame visitors, were concerned that he should be well aware of the risk of being compromised by the Russians.'[19]

Awareness of risk is quite a long way from being a spy. Nonetheless, the CIA became aware of the suspicions against Wilson held by parts of MI5.[20] Just after Wilson became prime minister, James Angleton, the CIA chief of counterintelligence, came to England to pass an allegation from a source (one that he would not name) that Wilson was a Soviet agent. MI5, no doubt influenced by the fact the information was passed on by such a senior source, recorded the information under the code name *Oatsheaf*.[21] But when Wright later pressed Angleton on this, it came to nothing: 'when he was pushed for details, there were none, and I knew from bitter experience Angleton was more than capable of manufacturing evidence when none existed'.[22]

Wilson was convinced that the CIA were seeking to infiltrate British trade unions and that the South African security service BOSS were 'up to no good in London'. The MI5 director general, Sir Michael Hanley, submitted two reports indicating that the 'reports of alleged CIA activities in trade unions are unsubstantiated' and that MI5 'had no liaison with South African intelligence' but kept a close eye on them.[23] Wilson wrote to George Bush, who became director of the Central Intelligence Agency (CIA) in January 1976, via Weidenfeld and Senator Hubert Humphrey, asking if the CIA was attempting to infiltrate his office. Bush flew to London to reassure him.[24] Wilson had, however, also sought the help of the CIA in examining the plot against him, which was embarrassing to MI5.[25]

Wright even examined the possibility that Gaitskell had been poisoned to make way for Wilson as party leader and prime minister. After Gaitskell's death, his doctor had apparently contacted MI5 on the basis that lupus, to which he had succumbed, 'was rare in temperate climates and there was no evidence that Gaitskell had been anywhere recently where he could have contracted the disease'. The KGB defector Anatoli Golitsin told MI5 that 'just before he left he knew that the KGB were planning a high-level political assassination in Europe in order to get their man into the top place'.[26] A Russian scientific paper 'described the use of a special chemical which the Russians had found would induce lupus in experimental rats'.[27] But repeated, significant doses would be required over a significant period: Gaitskell could not have been assassinated by dropping something into his coffee.[28] To the extent that Wilson had a secret relationship with the Soviet Union, it was for the laudable reason that he persuaded the Kremlin to release up to eighty Russian Jews to go to Israel to live their lives free from persecution. He did not seek publicity for this.[29]

In the weeks after he left office, on 12 May 1976, Wilson summoned the BBC journalists Barrie Penrose and Roger Courtiour to Lord North Street for early evening drinks. According to Penrose and Courtiour, as he lit a cigar, he told them: 'I think you as journalists should investigate the forces that are threatening democratic countries like Britain.' He spoke of 'South African interference . . . [and] . . . his distrust of a section of the British Secret Service.' Over the last eight months of his premiership, he said he did not fully know what was happening in security. Wilson said: 'I see myself as the big fat spider in the corner of the room. Sometimes I speak when I'm asleep. You should both listen. Occasionally when we meet I might tell you to go to the Charing Cross Road and kick a blind man standing on the corner. That blind man may tell you something, lead you somewhere.'[30] Williams told Wilson's official biographer Philip Ziegler that she supposed 'this Buchanesque fantasy must have been intended as an obscure joke'; Ziegler points to a letter from Wilson himself to *The Times* on 2 February 1977 bemoaning the stories written by journalists of limited experience and 'little sense of humour'.[31] In the United States, Bob Woodward and Carl Bernstein's reporting of the burglary at the Watergate complex, the headquarters of the Democratic National Committee in June 1972, led to the crime being linked to President Richard Nixon and his resignation from office in August 1974. The pair of *Washington Post* journalists were dubbed 'Woodstein'; in the UK, *Private Eye* nicknamed Penrose and Courtiour 'Pencourt'. The journalists embraced it and started writing their book, *The Pencourt File*.

Wilson also made specific allegations against MI5. The first was of a group within the security service that was plotting his downfall. This is an account of one conversation with Chapman Pincher: 'He [Wilson] has told me recently how one of his close friends, whose identity I know, told him that he had heard that certain officers of MI5 considered the Prime Minister himself to be a security risk.' As to what he did in response to this, Wilson said he '. . . took steps to ask the director general, Sir Michael Hanley, personally if this was true . . . He replied that he believed it was true but that only a small number of right-wing officers were concerned.'[32] This was disputed by Hanley, who claims that he did not confirm this to be true. Rather, Wilson had said that 'because there were a number of former army officers in the Service, there was likely to be some sort of bias against Labour Ministers'.

Hanley 'acknowledged that there were a number of retired [army] officers in the Security Service, but did not accept that that meant that their loyalty and integrity as public servants was in question.'[33] Another account, though, supports the Wilson version that he was told there was a dissident group in MI5, but the conversation is with the head of MI6, Sir Maurice Oldfield, rather than Hanley. Anthony Cavendish, an MI6 officer, stated: 'Maurice [Oldfield] did tell me . . . he had to admit to the Prime Minister that there was "a section of MI5 which was unreliable".'[34] In a further account, it was also Oldfield who made this admission to Wilson. David Leigh, author of *The Wilson Plot*, confirms it is from Pincher who, along with Cavendish, received it from Oldfield, and Penrose who heard it from Wilson.

Wilson had called in Oldfield after a lunch on 7 August 1975 with Weidenfeld, who had told the prime minister that 'the whole of London was now awash with talk about the "Communist cell" in Downing Street'. The finger was being pointed at Marcia Williams as leading it. Wilson had already been informed of this allegation being made at a lunch-party attended by the historian Martin Gilbert in 1974, so this was a confirmation. He was furious.[35] Williams had, however, fuelled some rumours by refusing to undergo security vetting in order to view government papers classified as 'secret' and 'top secret'. News of this reached Douglas Hurd, now an MP having been Edward Heath's political secretary from 1970 to 1974, and he questioned Robert Sheldon, minister for the Civil Service, on 6 May 1974, about political advisers undergoing security vetting procedures, and was told the 'procedure which has prevailed in the past is being carried out now'.[36] Wilson had, in fact settled on a compromise whereby Williams' role was said to be concerned only with the party political side of Number Ten and so would not need access to official government papers and did not to require security clearance.

The story of Oldfield's admission continued to be told. Several years later, on 26 March 1981, Prime Minister Margaret Thatcher made a statement to the House of Commons dismissing the suggestion that Sir Roger Hollis, head of MI5 from 1956 to 1965, had been a KGB agent, and rumours around Wilson's treatment by the security services again surfaced in the *Sunday Times*: '. . . officials with MI5 connections openly discussed the "fact" that Wilson and Lady Falkender had Communist links . . . Wilson's basic concern was that British Intelligence – or a section of it – had been quoted by reliable witnesses as being the actual source for such rumours. His first action was to call in the late Sir Maurice Oldfield, then Head of MI6. Before he went on holiday to the Scillies in August, 1975, Wilson learned from the MI6 chief that a group of security service officials was vehemently anti-Labour and anti-Wilson.'[37]

Then there were the burglaries. In 1974, Wilson had asked the police to investigate the stealing of his tax records from Lord North Street, convinced that the Secret Service were responsible. Haines remarked that 'The plumbers have been in', referring to the Watergate scandal in which the group that had broken into the headquarters of the Democratic National Committee were known as 'the plumbers'. Haines' worry was that Wilson had sold his memoirs to the *Sunday Times* for a large amount of capital to reduce tax on income.[38] Geoffrey Goodman, who started work at Number Ten as head of the Counter-Inflation Publicity Unit in July 1975, was also burgled, along with, he wrote, a dozen other members of Wilson's inner circle. When Goodman told Williams the next day, she responded: 'So why should you expect any different treatment from the rest of us here?'[39] Wright claimed that these burglaries were not carried out by MI5 as, if they had been, nobody would have noticed.[40] This would leave BOSS in the frame for responsibility but there is no proof.

The South African dimension is an important aspect of the story. As anti-Apartheid campaigner Peter Hain put it: 'there was a commonality of interest between the South African Bureau of State Security (BOSS), and right-wing elements of the British Security Services regarding the attitude of Labour Governments to South Africa'. Thus, there was an attempt to smear Labour and Liberal politicians so as to make a Tory government more likely.[41] In *A Putney Plot?* Hain told the story of how 'in 1975–76: I was arrested and later tried at the Old Bailey for a bank theft I had not committed.' Hain concluded: 'If there was such a plot to frame me, it would have to have been what is known as a "deniable operation" – which is precisely why it is so difficult to prove. What can be proved, however, was that I was on MI5's psy ops [to influence Hain's state of mind] target list . . . that the hard right were anxious to neutralise me, that the South Africans were especially keen to damage me . . .'[42]

Wilson became convinced that BOSS were behind allegations against Jeremy Thorpe. At first, though, he had a different view. In March 1974, with rumours swirling that Thorpe's price for a coalition to keep Heath in power was the post of home secretary, Joe Haines claimed Wilson had a plan to stop him: George Thomas and Ted Short would 'come forward and disclose his homosexual relationship with a man called Norman Scott, who was obsessed by the belief that Thorpe had his National Insurance records which prevented him from getting work. It was not intended to destroy Thorpe for being a homosexual but from being a politician.'[43] Wilson also deputed Jack Straw, then special adviser to Castle, to look through the files at the Department of Social Security.[44] Yet, within two years, Wilson was convinced Thorpe was the victim of a secret plot to destroy him. In answer to a planted question on 9 March 1976, the prime minister said: 'I have no doubt at all that there is strong South African participation in recent activities relating to the right hon. Gentleman the Leader of the Liberal Party, based on massive reserves of business money and private agents of various kinds and various qualities.'[45] Though Scott had a friendship with Gordon Winter, a South African journalist who also worked part-time for BOSS, there was 'no hard evidence of any South African involvement'.[46] Thorpe was to be acquitted of a conspiracy to murder to Scott in 1979, and, two years later, Wilson was still calling for an inquiry into allegations of BOSS activity against him.[47]

This should all be seen in the context of the time. The fall of the Heath government, precipitated by a clash with organised labour in the form of the miners, and its replacement by Wilson's Labour administration, prompted private right-wing 'action groups' to form, ready to act if society broke down. David Stirling, the founder of the SAS, created 'GB75' to thwart the perceived far left threat, ready to challenge a general strike. General Sir Walter Walker, who had retired as commander of allied forces in Northern Europe, supported the Unison Committee for Action that claimed it could intervene to save the rule of law and run essential services in the event of a breakdown of order in society. Formed in 1973 by a former deputy director of MI6, George Kennedy Young, Unison saw itself as preventing a communist coup in Britain. The historian Dominic Sandbrook – who described Walker as 'Britain's [General] Pinochet' after Chile's military dictator – noted: 'Ludicrous as it might sound, not everybody dismissed Unison as a joke.'[48] This was also in circumstances where there had already been a plan to remove Wilson in 1968. In 1981, *The Sunday Times* reported: 'Sir Martin Furnival Jones, the former head of MI5, has revealed that an alleged plot to remove the Wilson government in 1968 was the subject of a secret service investigation.' Marcia Williams said that the details of the proposed military coup were not known until a former cabinet adviser told them in 1975: it 'was horrible – like a Michael Caine movie. Harold was worried about the business when the troops did an anti-terrorist exercise at London Airport. He said to me: "Have you thought that they could be used in a different way? They could turn that lot against the government – totally." It was very scary. Like *1984*.'[49]

The very making of the allegations, and them being denied, was damaging Wilson's reputation. Christopher Andrew put it like this: 'Wilson's mental and physical decline was accompanied by, and may partly explain, his increasing tendency (long present in more muted form) to conspiracy theory.'[50] On 17 July 1977, there was an *Observer* front-page splash from Wilson: 'Why I Lost My Faith in MI5' accompanying the publication of *The Pencourt File*. Callaghan was at pains to close the matter down: '. . . there is very little hard fact, as far as I can see. If anyone who has any information about what has taken place cares to place it before the appropriate authority – who in this case would be the Home Secretary – then, of course, the matter will be looked into. As to the present situation, I am quite satisfied with the arrangements at No.

10 and with what is going on in the security services.'[51] On 29 July, Chapman Pincher wrote in the *Daily Express* that Wilson had been bugged at 10 Downing Street; Wilson issued a press statement to the Press Association the next day: 'Mr Chapman Pincher has long been known to have had close contact with certain of the officers of the Security Service, and I have known him long enough to be sure that whatever his sources – right or wrong – he would not print such a story if he did not believe it.'[52] On 23 August, Callaghan issued a terse statement confirming that the security services had not undertaken electronic surveillance at Downing Street or in the prime minister's room at the Commons.

Unsurprisingly, Wilson distanced himself from the book. A Tory MP, Peter Blaker, wrote to him on 8 November 1977 to seek answers about what information he had given to Penrose and Courtiour. Wilson responded on 16 November, indicating that Albert Murray had been approached by the BBC with a request to meet two young researchers to discuss South Africa. The director general, Sir Charles Curran, had come to see Wilson to ask for all the help he could give. However, Curran had subsequently come to see Wilson to indicate that the BBC was dissociating itself from their research as Penrose and Courtiour were insisting on publication as individuals in their own names despite being 'on the BBC pay-roll . . . [with] . . . research undertaken in BBC time and at BBC expense.' Then, Wilson 'gave them no further assistance but saw them thereafter, when they informed me that they had gone independent, and also produced a story about an intended military take-over of the British Government.' Wilson went on: 'I later learnt that their book, supposedly on the "South Africa connection" had switched to sensational stories about murder plots. I refused to read the book, when the publishers offered to make it available, and I do not know what it contains.' Wilson confirmed that, at the time of Callaghan's statement in August, he was in the Scillies, where he was telephoned by the *Observer*: 'I confirmed that my anxieties referred to a small group, now mainly, probably wholly retired. I also asked that *The Observer* put on the record, "as a final benediction on this story", my view that any activities were by people who had gone, and to express my total agreement with the Prime Minister's statement.'[53]

The question now is what the available evidence actually points to? First, MI5 did have a file on Wilson, and it was hidden. On Labour's return to power in 1974, the director general of MI5, Sir Michael Hanley, ordered that the Wilson file should no longer show up on the Registry Central Index: 'A look-up on Harold Wilson would therefore be No Trace.' Access was permitted only with the permission of the director general. Andrew concludes: 'Though the file was never used to undermine Harold Wilson, Hanley's decision to preserve it, approved by [Bernard] Sheldon [Legal Adviser], would doubtless not have been approved by either the Home Secretary or the Prime Minister.'[54] It can be safely assumed that Wilson would not have approved of a decision to retain a file on himself, and that Jenkins would not have allowed it, either.

Second, Number Ten *was* bugged. When Wilson appointed Shirley Williams to the cabinet in 1974, he took her into the cabinet room 'and pointed to a small object in the corner of the ceiling. It was, he told me, for bugging Cabinet discussions. I remember thinking that my boss was getting a bit paranoid.'[55] This was, however, more than paranoia. Bugging devices *were* installed in the cabinet room, the waiting room and the prime minister's study in July 1963, on the orders of Macmillan. Though they were removed when he left office in the October, Alec Douglas-Home had them reinstated. They were not finally taken away until 1977, on Callaghan's instructions. MI5's official historian, Christopher Andrew, was, apparently, unhappy that, on the orders of the Cabinet Office, he was unable to include this in his authorised history. Whether the listening devices were active throughout this period is a moot point, but they were there.[56]

Third, MI5 interest in Wilson's friends was pursued with vigour. The focus was on the contacts Wilson had made during his years working for Montague Meyer in the 1950s. Andrew identifies a number of Wilson acquaintances who attracted unfavourable attention from MI5. The first of these was Joseph Kagan. Born in 1915 in Lithuania, Kagan had initially come to the UK in 1933 to study at Leeds University but, on his return home, was interned – as a Jew – in Kaunas Ghetto in 1941 by the invading Nazis. He married his wife, Margarita, in the ghetto, and, after a spell hidden in an attic, they eventually made it back to the UK in 1946. In 1951, Kagan invented the waterproof textile Gannex, worn by Wilson, and founded Kagan Textiles Limited.

Wilson had recommended Kagan for a knighthood in his 1970 resignation honours. Attending the ceremony at Buckingham Palace was a Lithuanian officer in the KGB, Richardas Vaygauskas: 'possibly the first ever [investiture of a knight] attended by a KGB officer'.[57] Vaygauskas was one of the Soviet intelligence agents expelled by Britain in September 1971, and, two months later, Kagan was interviewed by Tony Brooks, part of K5 (the security services' counter-espionage operation). Brooks recorded that Kagan admitted, on Vaygauskas' request, seeking to influence Jewish community leaders in Britain to tone down their activities in opposition to trials of Russian Jews in Leningrad on the spurious basis that this would lead to better treatment for them. He also let slip to Brooks that if Vaygauskas had been collecting gossip and scandal on public figures, he could have provided him with a substantial amount, including the allegation that Harold Wilson was having an affair with a female member of his staff (no doubt the gossip about Marcia had reached Kagan). According to Wright, MI5 had Kagan 'under intensive surveillance and attempted to recruit agents inside his factory'.[58]

Kagan was close to Wilson and contributed to the running of his political office. By November 1971, Kagan had already donated £10,000.[59] Haines wrote that Kagan was also close to Williams: 'Kagan and [Eric] Miller helped her [Williams] to live a lifestyle that means she owned two expensive houses in a West End mews.'[60] In October 1972, Wilson had requested a meeting with MI5 to discuss information Kagan had passed to him. Wilson was told that Kagan 'was being used consciously or unconsciously by Vaygauskas to supply items of news or scandal as a medium for obtaining access to the famous' and that Kagan himself admitted this. Wilson offered to speak to Kagan and 'warn him about talking to the Russians'. He was, according to the security service records, 'startled' when told that there was a case around '. . . a Lithuanian employed in the Electrical Dept. in the House of Commons who had been introduced to Vaygauskas by Kagan.'[61] John Allen, an MI5 officer in section KX (responsible for investigative operations) took the view that Kagan was 'clearly a target of the highest importance for the KGB because of his close association with Mr Wilson and other Labour Party leaders. I do not believe Kagan has been, or is now likely to become, a conscious Soviet agent but I am sure he has been a valuable source of intelligence.'[62]

Then there was Rudy Sternberg, born in Austria in 1917, who had also been recommended by Wilson for a knighthood in 1970. Sternberg had arrived in the UK in 1937 to study at London University, and remained in England after the outbreak of war as a refugee from Hitler's persecution of the Jews. He had founded the Sterling Group in 1948, manufacturing Bakelite, and Dominion Exports. It was this international trade with the Soviet bloc, and his ostentatious links with communist East Germany, that aroused concern at MI5. Like Kagan, Sternberg contributed financially to Wilson's private office. In May 1974, Armstrong had contacted the director general of MI5 to ask if there was 'anything we ought to know' about Sternberg, and was told: 'It is a measure of the interest taken in him by the Soviet bloc intelligence services that of the many Soviet bloc officials with whom he has been in contact over the years, at least thirty-two are intelligence officers or suspected intelligence officers. With some of these he has been on first-name terms and remained in touch after they have left the UK.'[63] In the 1975 New Year's Honours, Wilson gave Sternberg a peerage.

The third Wilson contact that the security services were concerned about, according to Andrew, was Harry Kissin, another wealthy donor to the private office. Born in 1912 in Danzig, he had moved to the UK in 1933. He made his money in finance, becoming executive chairman of Guinness Peat Group Limited, an investment holding company. The son of Russian-Jewish parents, Kissin was another who profited from trade with the communist bloc. MI5 advice was that he was 'obviously not a man to be trusted with confidences,' though it seems this was due to his involvement with call-girls, rather than espionage. He also appears to have told one prostitute in September 1973 that he was 'contributing money in support of Wilson's mounting campaign to boost the Liberal Party and so alienate wavering Tories [from voting Conservative] before the next election' and added that 'Wilson is not the man he was. He is ill.'[64] Wilson recommended Kissin for a peerage in June 1974.

Andrew's evidence is from the security services archive, and there is no reason to doubt the accuracy of the views he sets out. Wilson did seek money for his office when leader of the opposition. The fund was chaired by a former junior minister, Wilfred Brown, then Arnold Goodman, then Sir Samuel Fisher, a Wilson friend and former Labour councillor. However, there was a limit to what he was accepting money for. Days after Wilson returned from a visit to Moscow to discuss trade, *Private Eye* claimed, on 24 September 1971: 'This is Wilson's 18th trip to the Soviet Union. Only four of these . . . have been paid for by the poor British taxpayer. Some have been paid for by Wilson's good friend Sir Joseph Kagan, the manufacturer of waterproof garments who has employed Wilson as commercial traveller and male model for the last seven years at an annual salary of £5,000 to £10,000.'[65] Arnold Goodman instructed Oswald Hickson, Collier & Co. who told *Private Eye*'s solicitors that 'the words complained [of] went far beyond the bounds of even the most abrasive satire as it imputed corruption'.[66] *Private Eye* agreed to publish an apology and cover a large proportion of Wilson's legal costs.[67]

Finally, what of the Wilson plot itself? There is no shortage of suggestions of an attempt to force Wilson to resign emanating from the security services. Writing in the *Guardian* on 15 March 2006, under a headline 'Enough of this cover-up: the Wilson plot was our Watergate' the journalist Jonathan Freedland wrote that Wilson's 'resignation has never been fully explained'. Cavendish wrote: 'It was always clear to me from things he said that Maurice was somehow involved in the sudden departure of Harold Wilson from the premiership.'[68] Cavendish, who was close to Oldfield, thought that his old boss had been circulating the evidence he had against Wilson. Cavendish's account lacks solid proof. For example, he states: 'if something came into Maurice's hands relating to the Prime Minister of the day, his duty would be clear. He would show it to one of three people: the Prime Minister himself, the Cabinet Secretary or his immediate boss, the Foreign Secretary. I believe from things Maurice said that *something may have come into his hands* [author's emphasis] and that he showed it to the Foreign Secretary, James Callaghan.'[69] This is hardly conclusive.

In 1987, the then director general of MI5, Sir Antony Duff, conducted a four-month investigation. The prime minister, Margaret Thatcher, reported to the Commons: 'He has given me his personal assurance that the stories are false. In particular, he has advised me that all the security service officers who have been interviewed have categorically denied that they were involved in, or were aware of, any activities or plans to undermine or discredit Lord Wilson and his Government when he was Prime Minister.'[70] The key words here are '*officers who have been interviewed*': Wright claimed that he and another officer had not been asked.[71]

Indeed, it is the evidence of Wright that needs to be considered carefully. However, the account of the 'Wilson Plot' in his autobiography differs from what he said in a *Panorama* interview on 13 October 1988. In *Spycatcher*, Wright set out a plan to force Wilson from office: 'MI5 would arrange for selective details of the intelligence about leading Labor [sic] figures, but especially Wilson, to be leaked to sympathetic pressmen.' Wright's position was that 'Soundings in the office had been taken, and up to thirty officers had given their approval to the scheme.'[72] Wright was asked to get the files from the director general's safe, but, in the end, decided not to, after talking to Victor Rothschild, then a former MI5 agent who advised Thatcher on security: 'I had little more than a year to go. Why destroy everything in a moment of madness?'[73] Wright was called in by Oldfield, who had been called in by Wilson: 'Apparently he's heard that your boys have been going around town stirring things up about him and Marcia Falkender, and Communists at No. 10.' Oldfield asked Wright if Hanley knew; when Wright said he did not, he was told to go and tell him.

This, according to Wright, he did; Hanley 'went white as a sheet'.[74]

The account given by Wright on *Panorama* varied. First, the method being used to force Wilson to stand down was different. Leaking would have been a last resort; instead, the plan was to confront Wilson with the 'Henry Worthington' file. Wright thought that 'Wilson would have folded up – he wasn't a very gutsy man, you know.' Second, the number of people involved differed. Wright now claimed the number 'thirty' meant those who were aware of the plan, and that a maximum of eight or nine were ever involved, and only one other than him was serious about carrying it through. Hanley, meanwhile, is said to have denied having a conversation with Wright about the plot. When challenged on the inconsistencies, Wright first blamed his ghostwriter, Paul Greengrass. When it was shown Wright had checked the offending section of the book before publication, he said he thought inaccuracies would not matter since the plot had not been executed.

Such discrepancies should not be dismissed, and do cast doubt on Wright's reliability. They show, at least, that the *Spycatcher* account exaggerated who was actively involved in the plot. It should also be remembered that Wright had no evidence that the 'Henry Worthington' file showed Wilson had been compromised by Eastern Bloc intelligence services. Wright was disenchanted with MI5, whom he believed had not paid him the pension to which he was entitled, so he had an axe to grind. At the same time, Wright was a senior MI5 operative, the 'Spycatcher' deputed to root out moles, and an assistant director. He is on the record as having wanted to bring Wilson down, and conceived of how he might do it. Even if it was only him who was involved, that is an extraordinarily serious matter.

Looking back, therefore, Wilson's fears about the activities of the security services were far from groundless. In addition, despite his suspicions, there is no suggestion that, as prime minister, he dismissed information from MI5 or that he failed to take national security threats seriously. Judith Hart was positively vetted for raising the issue of communists imprisoned by the new regime in Chile. On 17 October 1974, Castle, who was with Hart at a dinner when it emerged, was dismissive of MI5: 'Didn't the fools realize that there were even more non-Communists in gaol there than Communists.'[75] Nonetheless, that night, Wilson called Hart in to Number Ten and sought reassurance from her. A month later, on 20 November, John Stonehouse left clothes on Miami beach in an – ultimately unsuccessful – attempt to fake his own death. Stonehouse was actually a Czech spy, turned after being caught in a 'honeytrap' in 1959, when a casual sex encounter was filmed. Wilson was told in 1969, but thought Stonehouse a crook rather than a spy.[76] Stonehouse remained in the government as minister of posts and telecommunications until Labour was defeated in 1970, but was then not reappointed to the frontbench.[77]

None of this, though, helped Wilson at the time. His reputation continued to fall, and it was the situation in Rhodesia that caused even more damage. David Owen, newly installed as foreign secretary, was determined to press for majority rule in Zimbabwe. He wanted to visit Africa, but immediately hit upon a problem. 'Tiny' Rowland, chief executive of Lonrho, a giant company with interests and investments in a range of sectors in Africa, had shown evidence of British oil companies breaking the Rhodesia oil sanctions to President Kaunda of Zambia. Kaunda was refusing to meet Owen when he visited Lusaka unless he ordered an investigation. This Owen did, setting up an inquiry under Thomas Bingham QC in May 1977, which reported in September 1978.

Under Wilson's first Labour government, no oil reached Rhodesia's sole refinery after 31 December 1965, and it remained closed. For the oil sanctions to work, tankers had to be stopped from supplying oil through the port of Beira in Mozambique, from where a pipeline ran to Rhodesia. Pirate tankers were intercepted pursuant to United Nations Resolution 221 of 9 April 1966. The Royal Navy's 'Beira Patrol' operated from 1966 until 1975, when the Portuguese left Mozambique. The problem was that this was not the only route to supply oil. There was another route overland via South Africa, and oil could be delivered via another Mozambique port, Maputo (then called Lourenco Marques), or South African ports. Closing this route was much more difficult.

In 1967, Total, a French oil company, had come to a 'swap' arrangement with Shell and BP. Total would supply the oil to Rhodesia, and Shell and BP would pay them compensation. Hence there would be no British company in breach of the sanctions, as they would not be supplying the oil. This continued until 1971, when the agreement lapsed.[78] The impact of this was to undermine the whole oil sanctions policy, save to the extent that the government was closing off the easiest and cheapest route. The question was the extent to which the senior members of the 1960s Labour government knew about it and turned a blind eye. Heath claimed that his incoming government had not been told of the swap arrangement in 1970. Michael Stewart and George Thomson accepted that they knew about the swap arrangement.

The question that remained was the then prime minister's own knowledge. On 7 November 1978, Wilson put his side of events in the House of Commons. Anticipating the publication of the Bingham report, he had looked at all the relevant documents, to which he had a right of access as a former prime minister. Thomson, now in the House of Lords, had 'said in a Granada Television programme that he had apprised me of the fact that British oil was getting through to Rhodesia'.[79] Whether the accusation is proven depends upon two documents. The first is a letter dated 15 March 1968, from Thomson's secretary to Wilson's, in reply to a request from the prime minister for an investigation into Zambian President Kaunda's allegations of British breaches of oil sanctions: 'I had ticked it in the usual way.' Wilson noted that Thomson's letter actually said that British, French and American oil was getting through to Rhodesia.[80] As prime minister, he had checked what this meant. French, American and Portuguese companies were the main culprits. In terms of Britain, Wilson's checks, he said, revealed that the supplies were coming from 'spivs, the unreliable secondary dealers, whom the Government and the oil companies agreed should be investigated and dealt with by denying supplies case by case'.[81] The second document was the Foreign Office note of the meeting held on 6 February 1969, between Thomson, Foreign Office officials and the chairmen of Shell and BP. Wilson was clear that: 'It was not marked to me. There is no record of my seeing it.'[82]

Owen himself exonerated Wilson on this point: 'In fairness he would only read such minutes if put before him by his Private Office.' Owen did, however, accuse Wilson's government of evading the choice before it, which was to impose sanctions on South Africa as well, to make the blockade fully effective, or to continue with Rhodesia-only sanctions while accepting that oil would continue to be supplied through South Africa: 'Characteristically, George Brown wanted to confront the South Africans. Equally characteristically, Harold Wilson wanted to duck out of the real choice.'[83]

The argument Wilson made in the Commons was compelling. It is certainly enough to give him the benefit of the doubt. The document he had seen would have been one among many he had ticked that day, and, in any event, he had questioned its contents. There is no evidence he had seen the second document. Joe Haines believes that Thomson, an ally of Brown, tried to ensure that Wilson shared the blame, when all that a tired and exhausted Wilson had done was tick a box to indicate the document had been noted.[84] Crossman's diary is also consistent with Wilson's account. On 22 March 1968, a week after the date of the first document, Wilson was at a meeting of the cabinet's Overseas Policy and Defence Committee, arguing to 'turn the heat on the French oil company which was putting oil into Rhodesia through Mozambique . . .' When Crossman, among others, argued that this would antagonise South Africa, Wilson did not back down entirely, and a special study of the issue at the Commonwealth conference was agreed.[85] If Wilson was hiding something, it made no sense to shine a light on the situation in this way. Wilson's argument on the blockade on South Africa was also sound: he said it was not practical and, in any event, would be doomed to failure: 'The Beira patrol took five frigates. A study of a possible Lourenco Marques patrol suggested that a further 17 would be needed . . . Even if it had been possible . . . Rhodesia's [oil] consumption was 8 per cent. of South Africa's. In an old phrase, the South Africans could have put aside the supplies needed for Rhodesia in their eye corner and seen no worse.'[86]

Yet the damage to Wilson's reputation continued. In November 1977, Andrew Roth's biography, *Sir Harold Wilson: Yorkshire Walter Mitty* was published. Wilson took legal action against the publishers MacDonald and Janes Publishers Limited and Richard Clay (The Chaucer Press) Limited: 'Comparison was made between the First Plaintiff and James Thurber's fictitious character Walter Mitty, the nobody who dreamed of achieving fame and fortune but never did.' Wilson achieved 'startling stature' in real life. Mary also defended herself against accusations, including that she saw 'every advance for her bright and ambitious husband as a set back for herself.' Rather, she attended 26 party conferences from 1945, save for one when her mother was dying, meetings with party members and tea parties at Number Ten for ministers' wives. There was also an accusation of Mary having an affair. That claim was also made in her obituary in the *Guardian* on 7 June 2018, by Julia Langdon, though the only evidence is Mary's poem, 'The Train', apparently covering when she confessed to Wilson: 'And still you stood there, silent and unbending/God! What an ending!'[87] However, in 1977, Mary flatly denied having been unfaithful to Wilson when he was in Washington as a junior minister in 1946. Roth's publishers accepted there was no foundation for any of this, apologised, paid damages and covered legal costs.[88]

Joe Haines' book, *The Politics of Power* was also published that year, revealing Williams' behaviour within Wilson's private office. Wilson himself said he 'never suspected . . . Haines of saving "titbits" while he was his press secretary.'[89] Meanwhile, Mary wrote to *The Times* on 21 February 1977: 'I was like a rather unwilling recruit to a group of professional soldiers when I first went to Number 10, and Lady Falkender's help and advice were invaluable to me in all the work I tried to do there. Of course there were tears and tensions, particularly at election times – there must be clashes of temperament in all large organisations, but there was plenty of laughter and enjoyment too. And I should like to add that Lady Falkender's family also were extremely helpful to me over many years.' When Wilson's account of his final period in office, *Final Term: The Labour Government 1974–1976*, appeared in

1979, he made no mention of the internal politics of his private office.

Wilson's own book, *The Governance of Britain*, had appeared in 1976. It is best read as his response to Crossman's argument that the long-accepted notion of cabinet government, with the prime minister as *primus inter pares*, had given way to a system of prime ministerial government. In his introduction to Walter Bagehot's Victorian classic, *The English Constitution*, penned in 1963, Crossman's contention was that cabinet had become a rubber-stamp on prime ministerial decisions, with every minister dependent on the leader for their political futures. The power of cabinet was limited to protest; decisions could not be changed. When he gave the Godkin lectures at Harvard University in 1970, reflecting on his own experiences, Crossman bemoaned the 'Myths of Cabinet Government'.[90] His diaries of his time in Wilson's cabinet began to be published posthumously, from 1975. Serialised in *The Sunday Times*, they caused a sensation, as the attorney-general, Sam Silkin, led unsuccessful government efforts in the courts to prevent publication. In the Commons, Wilson said 'there were many statements in those diaries which I know to have been not only not true but not even possibly true . . .'[91] No less a figure than Lord Widgery, the Lord Chief Justice, called the diaries a 'flat out attack' on the rules of ministerial confidentiality.[92]

The Governance of Britain can be read as a direct response, based on the reality of his own experience in office: 'My own conclusion is that the predominantly academic verdict of overriding prime ministerial power is wrong. It ignores the system of democratic checks and balances, in Parliament, in the cabinet, and not least in the party machine and the party in the country.' These constraints, Wilson wrote, operated all the time: 'The checks and balances operate not only as a long-term safeguard, but also, in one way or another (often unpredictable), almost every day.'[93] Though respectful of Crossman, and expressing gratitude for his loyalty during the attempt to oust him in 1969, Wilson sought to dismantle his argument: 'For me, the classical refutation . . . was Richard Crossman as a minister, and his unfailing, frequently argumentative, role from 1964 to 1970 in ruthlessly examining every proposal, policy or projection put before Cabinet by departmental ministers – or by the prime minister.'[94] Wilson wrote that the 'alleged freedom of a prime minister in Cabinet appointments, except perhaps on first coming into office, bears little relation to reality'. He not only had to balance left and right; in the 1970s he had to balance those who were in favour of entry into the Common Market and those that were against.[95] Wilson acknowledged that his account was written in hindsight, but pointed out, gently, that he could never have kept contemporaneous records in the way Crossman did: '. . . I must make it clear that not a word of this book was written until 7 April 1976, two days after I left No. 10. No prime minister in the 1970s would have the time either to do that or to keep a diary.'[96]

Alongside his writing, Wilson was kept busy with his chairmanship of two significant committees. The struggles of the manufacturing sector were blamed, in part, on financial institutions not providing the funds required. Callaghan therefore appointed an eighteen-member committee to review the functioning of financial institutions on 7 October 1976, under Wilson. Its final report, of a quarter of a million words, was published on 26 June 1980, after fifty-five meetings of the main committee. One of its staffers was future Conservative prime minister Theresa May. May said that Wilson 'was very much the Chair, not involved in day-to-day functioning of the Committee' but 'came alive when there was a dispute to be settled. He was keen to find solutions and was effective in doing so.'[97] The report he signed off bears a number of his hallmarks. First, it was pragmatic: the lack of availability of funds was not the sole reason for a lack of investment in industry, but, at the same time, there were criticisms to be made, not least in relation to the finance available to small firms. Extending public ownership in the banking and insurance sectors was not considered as an effective option; instead, regulation should be toughened.[98] Second, it was prescient, given the financial crises to follow in future decades: the report lamented the fact that there was no single body keeping regulation of the financial sector under review and making recommendation to parliament for changes. Third, it drew on Wilson's experience: it was no surprise that one of the ways the report suggested the financial sector could improve was through its collection of statistics. May recalls Wilson quoting trade figures from memory at one of the committee's dinners: 'Nobody could know if they were right or wrong but he quoted them in detail!'[99]

The second committee Wilson chaired was also related to his time as president of the Board of Trade. As prime minister, in August 1975, he had set up a working party, chaired by the managing director of the National Film Finance Corporation, to report on what was required for a successful British industry over the next decade. In January 1976, the report considered the creation of a British Film Authority. After Wilson's resignation, Callaghan appointed an interim action committee on the film industry. With Wilson as chair, a firm proposal for a British Film Authority was made in 1978.[100] This was not taken forward as Labour was soon out of office, but Wilson continued in the role. In 1984, the Conservative government published a White Paper on film policy. As a consequence, the Eady Levy was abolished in 1985, on the basis that, since money was going to distributors rather than producers, and cinema attendance was falling, it was no longer fulfilling its initial purpose.[101] However, the British Screen Advisory Council was established. In January 2020 it became the British Screen Forum 'where the best informed and most influential people in the UK screen sectors convene to interrogate issues of importance and influence policy and the thinking around policy.'[102]

This important work represents what Wilson's retirement might have been, drawing on his expertise in public roles. The same can be said of his work on television. Working with David Frost, he presented an ITV series, *A Prime Minister on Prime Ministers*, broadcast from November 1977 to February 1978, with an accompanying coffee-table book. There were some acute observations. Of Attlee, Wilson wrote: 'crispness in Cabinet reflected his greatest quality, courage'.[103] Of Macmillan, he wrote that 'behind that public nonchalance was the real professional.'[104] Wilson's quiet admiration for both Macmillan and Churchill shone through. Wilson used his humour when he appeared in a sketch on the *Morecambe and Wise Christmas Show* in 1978, poking gentle fun at Eric Morecambe being a Luton Town football fan, joking that the club had paid £250,000 for two extra supporters![105] He also tried his hand as a chat-show host on *Friday Night, Saturday Morning*. On 12 October 1979, he interviewed *Coronation Street* star Pat Phoenix, discussing how a northern soap opera had become a part of the national fabric. Wilson said, as a northerner himself, he had been concerned that 'the south won't wear it'.[106] Over a number of shows, there was the odd awkward pause, where Wilson was not entirely au fait with the use of autocue, but, on the whole, his interviews showed him as knowledgeable, with an easy-going manner, persuading his guests to open up, and able to make audiences laugh.

One of Wilson's guests on *Friday Night, Saturday Morning* was Mary, reading from her new poetry collection, *New Poems*, published in 1979. Her reputation as a poet was burgeoning. In 1983, Mary published an anthology of ninety poems that she chose as her favourites. The book's jacket cover billed her as 'one of our best loved women poets'. She chose two from her close friend, the Poet Laureate, John Betjeman: 'Station Syren' and 'Sunday Morning, King's Cambridge'. Reading of the 'white of windy Cambridge courts, the cobbles brown and dry' no doubt captured Mary's wistfulness about the life she could have had as a don's wife.[107] The two of her own poems that Mary chose were indicative, too. The first, 'St Cross', referenced the grave of Charles Williams. Mary had selected Williams's poem, 'A Dream', in the collection, and 'St Cross' describes Oxford: 'In old St Cross, all through the day/The floating chimes of Merton clock/Signal the hours and years away.' The second, 'Summer', described Mary's grandchildren paddling around the Isles of Scilly: 'summer is only a memory/Of little girls at the edge of the sea'.[108]

In politics, developments in both major parties were moving against Wilson. Callaghan had decided not to call a general election in the autumn of 1978, and soldiered on. The strikes in the months that followed became known as the 'Winter of Discontent' after the opening line of Shakespeare's *Richard III*. After the Labour government lost a confidence motion by a single vote on 28 March 1979, the Conservatives won the resulting general election on 3 May. As the new prime minister, Thatcher defined herself against the prevailing consensus of the 1960s and 1970s of which Wilson was such a central part. According to her, democratic socialism in Britain had been 'a miserable failure in every respect' and 'by 1979 we [Britain] were widely dismissed as "the sick man of Europe".'[109] Ironically, Thatcher herself, though no fan of Wilson's governments, thought Wilson himself a very tough opponent: 'He was a master of Commons repartee, and I usually scored nothing better than a draw against him in the House.'[110]

In the Labour Party, now in opposition, Tony Benn had decided not to stand for shadow cabinet, and was focusing on a campaign for internal party reforms, including a change in the leadership election rules. No longer would the choice be restricted to MPs but would be the subject of an electoral college comprised of MPs, unions and affiliates, and party members. Before the change could be made, Callaghan resigned as party leader to ensure that the next leadership contest took place under the old rules. In the final round on 10 November 1980, Foot defeated Healey by 139 votes to 129. Wilson voted for Healey on the first round, and Foot on the second. He later reflected: 'I was probably wrong'. He called Healey a 'thug' but insisted it was a term of praise. Foot, Wilson thought, could have held his own against 'a bigot such as Edward Heath'.[111] However, opposing Thatcher required toughness and Foot was 'a decent man, an idealist'.[112] It was certainly an odd choice. Perhaps, in Foot, he saw a more consensual style of leadership akin to his own, in contrast to Healey's abrasiveness. Healey, when Wilson told him what he had done, thought it 'an existentialist *acte gratuit* – he did not explain'.[113]

Wilson was vehemently opposed to the reform of Labour's leadership election rules. For him, 'the first pre-requisite is the assertion of the central position of the Parliamentary Labour Party'. He condemned the 'egregious "33,33,33" formula which a seven-year old could have told them did not add up to 100'.[114] Nonetheless, the new electoral college was adopted at a special conference at Wembley on 24 January 1981. The next day, Roy Jenkins, Shirley Williams, David Owen and Bill Rodgers issued the Limehouse Declaration, the precursor to the setting up of a breakaway Social Democratic Party (SDP). The outcome Wilson had tried so hard to avoid when he had been leader had come to pass: the Labour Party had finally split. Benn then stood – unsuccessfully – against Healey for the deputy leadership. Wilson did not approve: 'I have always said about Tony [Benn] that he immatures with age.'[115]

Wilson did not approve of the SDP. When Jenkins stood against the Labour candidate in a by-election at Warrington on 16 July 1981, Wilson campaigned against him. It was his social pretensions that Wilson chided. Asked if Jenkins had been a good chancellor, Wilson quipped: 'up to seven p.m.'[116] Wilson damned his former colleague with faint praise: 'Roy is an impressive figure, very impressive, has a lot of friends . . . developed them by his social contacts and all the rest of it . . . I never thought the Labour Party could be run on the basis of dinner parties. I hardly had any, actually . . . [a] sandwich occasionally . . .'[117] Jenkins came within 1,759 votes of taking a safe Labour seat, and returned to parliament the following year.

Wilson had confirmed that he would stand down from parliament at the next general election on 27 February 1981.[118] He despaired of Labour's leftward drift under Michael Foot: in the 1983 general election, the party would pledge to withdraw from the Common Market without even a further referendum. On 17 September 1982, he spoke in Huyton: 'Eight years ago in Party Conference, I was able to claim, with four general election victories out of five contests, that Labour had become the Natural Party of Government. Today we hardly present the image of a Natural Party of Opposition.'[119] He was excoriating about Labour's 'pantomime performance' in recent years and talked of the party 'infiltrated by the self-styled Militant Tendency, which even in our most difficult days in opposition and in Government would never have been given political house-room.'[120]

Wilson also published *The Chariot of Israel: Britain, America and*

the State of Israel, in 1981, a sizeable 381-page, professionally referenced tome on the history of the Jewish people, the establishment
of the State of Israel in 1948, and Anglo-Israeli relations. As he put
it, the book 'inevitably deals with the varying motives, from fear or
a racialist desire for conquest, which have forced her [Israel] almost
continuously to regard herself as a small embattled community, not
however lacking powerful friends from Jewish groups and statesmen of almost every religious persuasion in the Western world.'[121]
As such a statesman, Wilson's support for the Jewish people had
been recognised in Israel itself: he had been awarded an honorary
Doctorate of Philosophy by the Weizmann Institute of Science in
Rehovot in 1977. *The Chariot of Israel* is a fitting summary of Wilson's views. Writing the postscript in June 1980, he commented on
his visit to Israel in the April to 'make the principal speech in the
commemoration of the life and achievements of Yigal Allon, my
closest friend among all the Israelis'.[122] Allon had been a military
commander before becoming an Israeli Labour politician, and
served as minister of labour in the 1960s. He was one of many
Jewish friends of Wilson.

It was in this period that Wilson wrote the manuscript for the
final volume of his memoirs that was to be published as *Memoirs 1916–64: The Making of a Prime Minister* in 1986. Sue Utting
continued to help with typing constituency letters and the notes
for his books. Yet Wilson's mind was deteriorating. In 1980, he
was diagnosed with bowel cancer. He had three operations and a
temporary colostomy. He was in hospital – St Mark's – for a few
months where Utting used to visit him. In a sad lament, he used to
say: 'I wish the surgeon could give me my memory back.'[123]

Wilson finally retired as an MP in 1983, after thirty-eight years
on the green benches. He did have some last-minute doubts,
confiding to Utting: 'I don't quite know why I'm going'.[124] Nonetheless, he was soon elevated to the House of Lords, choosing as
his title the place in Yorkshire where his family had originated
from: the Abbey at Rievaulx. Thus, he was introduced as Baron
Wilson of Rievaulx, of Kirklees in the County of West Yorkshire,
by Pakenham, the Earl of Longford, and Lord Shackleton, on 15

November 1983. However, his mental deterioration prevented him from making a full contribution to the Upper House, and deprived British politics of a remarkable voice of experience and expertise in the later 1980s and early 1990s. John Tomlinson, who stood for Labour in the 1984 European elections, contacted Wilson as his former PPS, to ask if he could come and speak for him during the campaign. He spoke to Marcia Williams, who said he 'could ask Harold but she doubted he would know who John was. He didn't, sadly.'[125] Robin Wilson says that it was 'in the mid-1980s when the dementia was beginning to show'.[126] In 1985, Harold gave up his much cherished role as Chancellor of Bradford University, a role he had held since the foundation of the institution in 1966, and in which he had conferred thousands of degrees. There was a slow deterioration. When Wilson's successor in Huyton, Sean Hughes, died suddenly in 1990, Wilson did not recognise Utting at the memorial service: 'his gaze was as if he should know her but he did not know her name.'[127]

Thus, the Wilson contributions to the Lords are scarce. There was, however, a delightful symmetry to his maiden speech, given on 14 March 1984. Thirty-nine years since he had first entered parliament, Wilson found himself – physically at least – in the same place: 'My first parliamentary speech in 1945, in the role of the then lowest form of ministerial life – Parliamentary Secretary to the Ministry of Public Building and Works – was made from the Front Bench in here because, owing to the bombing of another part of the Palace of Westminster, their then Lordships graciously made this Chamber available.'[128] He spoke with pride of the Open University: 'I had conceived the idea of the Open University well before anyone ever thought of making me Leader of Her Majesty's Opposition. I think that I called it the University of the Air.'[129] A week later, he returned to the European issue, and the budget, supporting Thatcher's position that the UK was willing to accept an increase in the Community budget on the basis of all member states paying fair shares and effective controls on spending, particularly agriculture. Wilson said: '. . . is this not a coup which is even more unacceptable than anything that even President de

Gaulle aimed at, and is not the whole thing due to the grasping habits of the French Government, whose agriculture is almost the worst organised in Europe?'[130]

On 9 May 1984, Wilson led a debate on unemployment, still a key issue for him: 'As one who learned his way about the realities of unemployment, and the statistics thereof, as a researcher for three years working with William Beveridge in the late 1930s, and also as a former head of the government manpower statistics branch under the Churchill Administration in wartime, I have to put on record today that the official figures of adult unemployment grossly understate the true position.'[131] Wilson argued for a focus on youth unemployment and a 'fuller use of Government, and joint Government–City and Government–industry ventures', urging ministers to 'sit down patiently with the trade unions'.[132]

It was to be over two years before he spoke again, and it was to be for the final time. It was on the apparently obscure issue of the government failing to consult Trinity House about marine pilotage. The government had published a Green Paper in December 1985 on ports deciding their own needs for such pilotage and then implementing them. Wilson and others argued that there should not be a need for legislation and that the government should have found a solution. Wilson was proud of his association with Trinity House, and wore his red ensign badge when travelling on the *Scillonian* to the Isles of Scilly: 'My Lords, as an elder brother of Trinity House of some 18 years' standing . . . I find it difficult to understand how pilotage affairs have been allowed to deteriorate to such an extent that a Green Paper became necessary, and why, in preparing it, the Minister's predecessors and their officials did not see fit to consult Trinity House as the pilotage authority responsible for half the pilotage in this country and with experience going back literally for several centuries.'[133]

Without a script, Wilson could no longer speak at length. In 1986, he spoke at a party hosted by the then owner of the *Daily Mirror*, where Haines was political editor: 'Wilson had begun his speech brightly enough, but then clearly forgot who he was supposed to be talking about.'[134]

In 1987, Wilson's business career ended. He had been involved with the ICE Group that had been founded in 1980 by Roger Shashoua, a larger-than-life entrepreneur, to run international trade exhibitions and conferences. With characteristic chutzpah, Shashoua recruited Wilson by parading outside his house with the Union Jack flag and a placard that read: 'England Needs You'.[135] He later recalled: 'I got arrested. The police came and moved me on.'[136] However, the stunt was effective: Wilson became a non-executive director of ICE and Marcia Williams a consultant. One of Wilson's first tasks was to visit Beijing to seek backing for Shashoua's proposal of a China Trade Centre as part of the re-generation of East London under the auspices of the London Docklands Development Corporation (LDDC). In a memoir, Shashoua wrote: 'From the moment of his arrival at Beijing airport in April 1985, Lord Wilson's visit was a major success. His meeting with Premier Zhao Ziyang gained official blessing for our project.'[137] Yet, the literary adviser for Shashoua's book, Ian Waitt, points out that there was more to it than that. In 1987, a visit to Malaysia for Wilson was being considered, with Shashoua keen to enter the lucrative overseas student market with an education show in Kuala Lumpur, where the authorities were interested to receive the former prime minister. Waitt then received a telephone call from a UK Foreign Office civil servant who told him that the trip should not happen, as, on the China visit: 'Harold had made a rambling, incoherent speech, speaking about having breakfast that morning with Zhou Enlai.' It had prompted laughter.[138] There was a sadness about this: Wilson had met Zhou, who had died in 1976, on his visit to China in 1954. The official was firm: 'We can't have our former Prime Minister subjected to ridicule.'[139] Waitt then confronted Shashoua and offered an ultimatum. Waitt, who had considerable connections in the Far East himself, would have no further involvement with Shashoua if he risked Wilson's reputation for commercial gain.[140] Shashoua therefore decided against sending Wilson back to the Far East and his role with ICE came to an end. Shashoua's plans were derailed in any event, as China made a deci-sion to deal with the LDDC directly, cutting ICE out. With ICE in financial difficulty, Shashoua invited Williams to become its chair in March 1987, to stabilise the situation, and her involvement continued.[141]

Wilson had been a popular figure at ICE social gatherings. He had the status of a former prime minister, and still had use of a government car, though he was always circumspect in his comments about Margaret Thatcher, concerned she might take the vehicle away. There were also flashes of his customary wit. Waitt, present at one ICE event, was approached by Wilson who said: 'My father smoked cigarettes – he died at 87. My grandfather smoked a pipe – he died at 97. Smoke a pipe, lad, smoke a pipe!'[142]

His public appearances thinned out. In April 1988, when he was asked to contribute to a programme about Bessie Braddock MP, he refused: 'No, very long ago' he wrote back, though he did appear at the Garter ceremony that year. On 22 September 1990, he unveiled the plaque on the Wilson Building at the Open University site in Milton Keynes, commemorating the institution's twenty-first anniversary.[143] In hospital for a hernia operation in 1991, he was confused: 'I don't really think I should be here,' he said. Callaghan, in a nice touch, rang the hospital to see how he was.[144] His final years were spent with Mary, dementia robbing him of the active retirement that he should have had, contributing to the national conversation.

On 24 May 1995, Mary announced that Harold had 'died peacefully in his sleep around midnight' and tributes were paid in the House of Commons that afternoon. Tony Blair, by then Labour leader, said: 'To many, he is defined as a clever politician – and he was. Yet it would be most unfair to let that eclipse his real character and his deep commitment. He had, in the end, a very simple belief in the virtues of social justice and equality . . .'[145] From the backbenches, Benn added a lighter note about Wilson's obsession with people manoeuvring to succeed him: 'I asked him once, when the plot stories were thickening, "Harold, what shall we do if you are knocked down by a bus?" and Harold said, "Find out who was driving the bus."'[146] In the same spirit, Kaufman, also on the backbenches, told the story of Wilson's speech at the Labour

Party conference in 1968, when he arrived on stage to a rapturous ovation: '. . . after waiting carefully for every last vestige of applause to die down, he said, "I suppose the BBC news tonight will describe that as a cool reception." He then got another ovation.'[47]

Wilson was buried on his beloved Scillies. Blair was among the mourners at the funeral on 6 June at the Parish Church of St Mary the Virgin. Mary composed the eulogy:

> My love you have stumbled slowly
> On the quiet way to death
> And you lie where the wind blows strongly
> With a salty spray on its breath . . .[48]

Conclusion

Harold's den

The *sine qua non* of a successful leader is to win elections. By this standard, Wilson has to be ranked towards the top of the list of those who have led the Labour Party. No other Labour leader has won four general elections. After the only general election Wilson lost, in 1970, Reginald Maudling remarked that Britain was 'now a Conservative country that sometimes voted Labour'.[1] In Wilson's thirteen years as party leader, this was not the case. Britain was a Labour country that once voted Conservative. Yet periods of Labour dominance are rare in British politics.

Attlee, who won two general elections, must still be at the very top of the pantheon, because of the great achievements of his post-war Labour governments: comprehensive welfare provision, the creation of the National Health Service and the nationalisation of vast swathes of the British economy. Decolonisation – most notably in India – and the Atlanticism of the government's foreign policy became established in British politics. His governments set the framework of policy for decades to come: the so-called 'post-war consensus' shared by party leaders when in office of a mixed economy and the maintenance of high employment lasted until the Conservative general election victory of 1979.

Since Attlee lost power in 1951, only two Labour leaders have won general elections: Wilson and Blair. They must surely rank just behind Attlee. Had Wilson achieved his ambition of introducing economic planning, he could have stood alongside Attlee. Richard

Toye has argued that 'the leadership group [of the Attlee government] had largely abandoned Labour's pre-1945 conception of the planned economy.'[2] There was more than one option available. The first was the model France developed: the setting of targets by the 'Commissariat general du Plan', the identification of the likely constraints on meeting them, then the encouragement of private enterprise and public industries actually to meet them. Government could not only provide a level of certainty that targets would be met; it would also provide access to capital. An alternative was to fix wage levels in advance across industry. The Attlee government backed away, no doubt conscious of trade union opposition to interference in free collective bargaining. Therefore, had Wilson introduced planning, he would have been taking the Labour Party into territory that not even the 1945–51 government had occupied, while building on their achievements. In the National Plan, Wilson had a potentially viable way to do this. That he did not is the central criticism of his governments.

Wilson's time in office serves as a reminder that prime ministers' room for manoeuvre is determined by circumstances. His 1964–70 governments were shaped by the economic inheritance: not only the significant balance of payments deficit but the structural problem of an overvalued pound within the Bretton Woods system. There was a window of opportunity in the weeks after he took office to devalue, but his judgement that this would have wrecked the new ministers' credibility before they had even begun work is a sound one. Even had he decided to take the politically expedient option of blaming the previous government for the measure, its impact, and the strenuous economic measures that followed it, would have been difficult to carry through parliament with such a tiny majority. The same logic applies with the decision to avoid devaluation in July 1965. However, it is difficult to avoid the conclusion that Wilson should have abandoned the existing parity of sterling in the summer of 1966.

At the same time, the fact that the debate is about the *timing* of the devaluation is also an indication of the economic straitjacket his governments were in. In adopting a policy of deflation, the

National Plan became impossible to implement. Wilson knew the pound was a symbol of national pride, and he had seen the Attlee government thrown from office two years after the devaluation of 1949. He had promised Lyndon Johnson that he would not devalue, and he also knew that the measure was not a panacea. In November 1967, his television broadcast was ill-judged; Jenkins' harsh measures at the Treasury, implemented with Wilson's backing did, however, produce a turnaround in the balance of payments.

By the time Wilson returned to office in 1974, the Bretton Woods system had broken down, and it was the problem of inflation that defined economic policy. Balancing fair wage increases with the cost of living had led Wilson to a prices and incomes policy in the 1960s and an attempt at statutory regulation in 'In Place of Strife'. Yet it is difficult to see how he could ever have forced the proposals through the Parliamentary Labour Party. As it was, he put his leadership at risk. In his second period in office, he turned to the Social Contract, which offered wider reforms to improve the conditions of working people in return for wage discipline. It is easy to criticise Wilson for his consensual approach to industrial relations in view of what came next: the strikes in the winter of 1978 and early 1979 that led to the fall of the Callaghan government. Yet Wilson always knew the alternative was a confrontational approach and high unemployment: that is precisely what happened under Margaret Thatcher's governments in the 1980s. Mass joblessness was not a price Wilson was willing to pay.

'Blame me for his politics,' said his father Herbert Wilson. As Michael Foot put it: 'The horror and despair induced by continued mass unemployment cut too deep among those with eyes to see.'[3] When Wilson spoke at the 1967 party conference on this, it was heartfelt:

> For us unemployment is not a matter of social, still less economic, statistics. It is a human problem, and for very many people in this hall it has human – and bitter – memories.
>
> No-one who was brought up in one of our older industrial areas in the years of the Depression – as I was in the West

Riding . . . could ever erase those memories from his mind: what unemployment meant for his neighbours, his friends – one's own family – not in terms of living standards only, but the deeper psychological effects that loss of work, loss of status, loss of dignity, loss of security and, perhaps above all, loss of hope brought to a family.

For many of us here, certainly for most of us who remember those days, this was the issue which brought us into politics . . .[4]

Avoiding unemployment was central to Wilson's politics, and he believed in extensive government intervention in the economy to achieve this. Wilson's resignation in 1951 was – partly – based on shrewd political calculation, as it gave him a credibility with the left of the Parliamentary Labour Party. But he was also far closer politically to Bevan than to Gaitskell, not least on economic planning.

Wilson's politics were, however, about much more than economics. He was a man of apparent contradictions: the cerebral academic who developed a popular touch; the social conservative who presided over a period of profound societal change. As his critics saw it, he regularly sacrificed principle for short-term pragmatism. For a more considered analysis of Wilson, understanding his background and influences is critical, as is the scrutiny of what he said and did, not only in the case of individual decisions, but throughout his lengthy period in politics. Looking at all the evidence over time is what allows the most penetrating analysis and, as it is nearly half a century since he left office as prime minister, the longer-term impact of his judgements can now be examined.

The Labour Party as the ethical inspiration of the churches and chapels, rather than inspired by the communism of Karl Marx, was embodied in Harold Wilson. It was Morgan Phillips who argued that the Labour Party owed more to Methodism than to Marx, in a speech to the International Socialist Conference in Copenhagen in June 1950. The 'British labour movement, both on its trade union and on its political side, drew heavily upon the religious communities.' In contrast: '. . . Marxism as a philosophy of materialism, as an economic theory and as a form of political organisation with revolutionary intention and aim is historically an aberrant tendency in the development of British socialism.'[5] Wilson's Congregationalist background was evident in his remark, made in 1962, that the Labour Party was a moral crusade or it was nothing.

He always retained a Scout's sense of duty, and a reverence for Britain's constitutional settlement, particularly the monarchy. He was a social conservative: he recognised the necessity of the radical social changes his governments made in the 1960s, and he did not put a stop to them, but he retained a traditionalist instinct. His words to Donoughue in 1974 on the content of his speeches are revealing: 'Remember that I don't want too many of those Guardianisms, Environmentalism, Genderism etc. . . . "I want my speeches always to include what working people are concerned with: Jobs, pay, prices, pensions, homes, kids, schools, health."'[6] Therein lies his contribution to the success of the 1960s reforms. He believed passionately in protecting, and enhancing, the rights of minorities, but he knew that, to win general elections, he had to focus on issues that affected the everyday lives of millions. The Open University, of which he was – rightly – very proud, improved opportunity for generations of people.

Wilson's outlook on the world was quintessentially British. Though he was well travelled, his holiday destination of choice was the English Isles of Scilly. Not for him the weeks in France or Italy sampling different cultures and cuisines. He loved the crime novels of Agatha Christie and the musicals of Gilbert and Sullivan. He had an attachment to the Commonwealth, and a pragmatic view of Britain's place in the new European Economic Community.

Yet he did have a strategy for British entry, even if he was not a philosophical pro-European. It was Dean Acheson, then the former American secretary of state, who commented in December 1962 that Britain had lost an empire and not yet found a role.[7] At that moment, Macmillan's application to join the EEC had not been rejected. When Britain did eventually enter the EEC, it was not Harold Wilson who signed the Treaty of Accession at the Palais d'Egmont in Brussels on 22 January 1972, but Edward

Heath. Wilson did oppose entry on the Tory terms, to keep his party together, but he ensured that Labour never committed to outright withdrawal from the Common Market. By holding, and winning, the 1975 referendum, Wilson secured Britain's place in Europe for decades afterwards. It was not until the growth of Euroscepticism in the early part of the next century that Britain's exit from what had by then become the European Union became a serious prospect. In his own lifetime, Wilson settled the European Question in British politics.

In doing so, he found a role for Britain. For this he deserves great credit. His attitude was based on his belief that Britain was better off in, and that being outside would put the wrong people in charge of the country. Wilson is not the only prime minister to take a more pragmatic view towards the European debate. When put to her that Wilson had said that on one side of the debate there was a group of people who wanted to stay in come-what-may and, on the other, anti-Marketeers who wanted to leave come-what-may and that Wilson felt he was with many people in the middle: pragmatic and wanting to do what was in the national interest, Theresa May said: 'I have more in common with Harold Wilson than I realised.'[8]

His achievement in keeping Britain out of the Vietnam War should not be underestimated. He not only avoided the deaths of British soldiers, he also sought to find a solution to the conflict to save the lives of all combatants. Wilson was no isolationist Little Englander. Tackling world poverty was a lifelong passion of his, as was standing up for those who were oppressed around the world. His support for the Jewish people was a consistent feature of his whole political career. Wilson also abhorred racism, and the apartheid regime in South Africa. While Ian Smith's continuance in office in Rhodesia until after Wilson had himself left the premiership was an embarrassment, Wilson's argument that the use of force could lead to awful, unpredictable consequences is a perfectly rational one. Wilson's ethical approach was blended with realpolitik, not least in his approach to the Nigerian Civil War, which is not creditable. On immigration, he pursued a strategy of controls allied to anti-discrimination legislation. The Commonwealth

Immigrants Act is not to his credit, but placing laws on the statute book to outlaw racism most definitely is.

Like all successful politicians, Wilson needed good fortune to reach the top. Often, that luck is another politician's tragedy. The only two Labour leaders who have – so far – won general elections since Attlee lost power in 1951 both benefited from the sudden deaths of leaders: for Wilson, it was the loss of Gaitskell in January 1963; for Tony Blair it was the loss of John Smith in May 1994. At the same time, politicians have to be in a position to capitalise on the chances that come their way. Wilson was not born into privilege. He made his own way in life and reached the top on his own abilities. As Norman Shrapnel put it: 'From all appearances, Wilson was the most ordinary man ever to become a great parliamentarian. At least, he managed to seem ordinary, which his enemies no doubt regarded as part of his diabolical cleverness.'[9] Marcia Williams, reflecting on Wilson's achievements, captured this as well as anyone: 'I think they will see him as a man who actually did liberate a vast area of national life and gave a special role to the ordinary man. I mean . . . he expressed what ordinary people had suddenly been able to achieve in their lives . . . the working man had actually broken through into top jobs . . . and he had got there on his own merits not by being born into a well-to-do family.'[10]

Williams herself was central to Wilson's success in politics. Arnold Goodman said that Wilson 'will not go down in history as one of the great prime ministers, but if it had not been for that woman he would have gone down as the greatest'.[11] This is unfair. Williams did not have an all-pervading influence on the political direction of Wilson's governments. It says a great deal that, on the issue of the Common Market, which Wilson dealt with for over a decade, her view was the opposing one to what Wilson achieved: she wanted Britain to remain outside the EEC. Yet Williams made three significant contributions to Wilson's political career – two highly positive, and one negative.

First, she was the person who reinforced what was arguably his greatest quality: adaptability. In asking the question as to how

Wilson evolved from the very formal, technocratic president of the Board of Trade, whose speeches were detailed but leaden, to the witty master of invective that he became from the late 1950s, Williams is a large part of the answer. Though Macmillan had observed change a few months before Williams started to work for the then shadow chancellor, it was she who reinforced the development. She was the one who could read his speeches, and advise on how the Labour movement would receive them. She was also the one who could make harsh criticisms, and offer herself as an example: if she could not understand what Wilson was saying, then, she would say, the general public could not. Second, Williams contributed to Wilson's resilience. She was the one who was always there, at his side, both as a political support in the loneliness of leadership, and also someone who could provide him with emotional support and affirmation. Marcia Williams was not a member of staff who would come and go, and the value of this to a politician is incalculable. Peter Shore observed: 'Harold derived from her a particular kind of stimulus . . . She disturbed him, made him see things in a different way, more than anybody else I can recall.'[12]

Yet the corollary of this was that her very closeness to Wilson meant she could be highly disruptive, particularly during his second period as prime minister. As Haines put it: '. . . if by 1974 she was a wasting asset, there was no doubt that she had contributed much to Harold Wilson's success. If she had retired in 1970 when she said she was going to, then the historical verdict on her role as the party's leader and Prime Minister's closest adviser and confidante would have found much to her credit. But during the two years of Harold Wilson's last administrations the entries on the debit side multiplied.'[13] Those turbulent two years unquestionably distracted Wilson, but it would be a mistake to dismiss his 1974–6 governments as lacking in constructive achievement: aside from the EEC referendum, the legislation delivered, both within the Social Contract, and outside it, made a lasting difference, not least to workplace rights.

The very fact that Wilson won two general elections in 1974

was significant. The accepted rule that divided parties do not win general elections was broken by him. Nobody could credibly argue that the Labour Party of 1974 was united, either in its approach to the economy or the major issue of the day, the UK entry into the Common Market. Yet he led the party back to power, after only one term in opposition. Labour's internal struggles in the 1970s were as wearing on its participants as at any other of its periods in opposition. That no other Labour leader has achieved this is unsurprising, and it is a testament to him that he did. Yet the resignation honours – the 'Lavender List' – was a misjudgement from Wilson. His reputation, and that of Williams, has been soiled by it. He should have heeded the advice he was given regarding some individuals on the list. The responsibility was his. The list was not given to the palace in secret by Williams and it was not as if he did not have the option to remove some of the names. At the same time, while acknowledging the error – and it was a serious error – it cannot be allowed to define his whole career.

What Williams did not show was the same loyalty to the Labour Party she showed to Wilson personally. In the general election of May 1979, she told Alistair McAlpine, the Conservative Party treasurer, a friend of hers, 'that she admired Mrs Thatcher and would like to help her.' McAlpine introduced her to TV producer Gordon Reece who was advising Thatcher, and an aide to Lord Thorneycroft, whom she worked with: 'The purpose of the meetings was for Lady Falkender to convey to the Tory campaigners her assessment of what the Labour Party was thinking.'[14] At the same time, she was not feted by the Labour Party. While Wilson left office at the age of sixty, she was only forty-four when she left Number Ten for the last time. As the Labour Party embraced all-women shortlists in the 1990s, and pressed for gender equality, Marcia Williams was nowhere to be seen. It was hardly as if this was because of a desire to move on from the Wilson years. In 2000, Barbara Castle was on the stage at the Labour Party conference to make the case for a fair deal for Britain's pensioners. Until her death in 2019, Williams remained a forgotten figure. There is, surely, a need for biographies of her.

While Marcia Williams represented Wilson's political family, Wilson adored his actual family. Mary Wilson was not the dour, suburban housewife that *Private Eye* defined her as. Rather, she was a highly accomplished poet with a profound sense of public duty. She would not have chosen a life as a prime minister's spouse, and undoubtedly pined for the idyllic life at Oxford that would undoubtedly have been hers had Wilson decided to remain as an academic. Yet she was a constant support, not least in his dark, final years as dementia took hold of his magnificent brain. What she did, throughout his time in public life, was maintain a guarded private sphere. It allowed Wilson to dote on his sons Robin and Giles, and then his grandchildren. Whether it was at Lowenva, Lord North Street, or Great Missenden, Mary Wilson offered love and solace to her husband: hers was a benign but critical influence in his life. After his death, she continued to represent him at public functions before becoming unable to do so herself, dying at the age of 102 in 2018.

Wilson deserves to be remembered for his achievements: the lasting changes that made Britain a fairer place, but also as one of the twentieth century's great political personalities. As *The Times* put it, Wilson was 'the memory man of the music hall who will answer random challenges from the audience, beginning, where possible, with the phrase: "It was at the Blackpool Conference in 1959." His memory is one of the best known aspects of his personality.' It added, tellingly: 'The intimacies of Sir Harold's life are better known than those of any individual outside the Royal Family. His pipe, his wife Mary, his dry Yorkshire wit played on a flat accent, his dog Paddy, his secret preference for brandy and cigars, his bungalow in the Scillies, all contribute to the Wilson image.'[15] He did smoke a pipe in private as well as in public but he also enjoyed cigars. Cigars were not part of the Wilson image. If he attended a dinner and was sure journalists were not present, he would pull a cigar from his pocket instead of a pipe. Yet he did not do this surreptitiously. He did it openly, and made sure that people in the room knew what he was doing.[16] It raised smiles on the faces of fellow guests, and made him likeable. As the novelist Kingsley

Amis put it, he knew him 'just enough to guess that he would be fun to have a couple of drinks with . . .'[17]

Wilson was a kind and generous man who had a connection to people; and they had a great affection for him. Perhaps this was best illustrated in the workingmen's clubs up and down the country, particularly during bingo. The author's grandmother, Olwyn Thomas, used to recount a story of Wilson himself walking in during a game. The caller paused, and the room fell silent. Heads turned to the entrance where Wilson was stood still. He allowed a moment to pass, and then he smiled. 'Number Ten!' he shouted, and pointed across the room. 'Harold's den!' they chorused back. So it was, not just once, but twice.

Bibliography

Primary Sources

Unpublished Wilson Autobiography held at the Bodleian Library, Oxford in boxes CMD 16194/1–5. The text of part of this is from Wilson's interviews with Leslie Smith, which he sold to him (CMD 16194/3). He also wrote his own notes, which Wilson's typist Ella typed in 1982 (CMD 16194/3).

Labour Party Annual Conference Reports

Labour Party Papers

National Council of Labour

Lyndon Johnson Presidential Library

National Archives:

  Board of Trade Papers: BT

  The Cabinet Papers: CAB

  Foreign Office Papers: FO

  Foreign and Commonwealth Office Papers: FCO

  Ministry of Labour Papers: LAB

  Ministry of Power Papers: POWE

  Prime Minister's Office Papers: PREM

  Treasury Papers: T

  Ministry of Works Papers: WORKS

The Attlee Papers: Bodleian Library, Oxford.

The Castle Papers: Bodleian Library, Oxford.

The Gaitskell Papers: University College, London.

The Wilson Papers: Bodleian Library, Oxford.

Hansard:

  House of Commons

  House of Lords

  Northern Ireland House of Commons

HMSO:

  Financial Agreement between the Governments of the United States and the United Kingdom, Cmnd 6708.

  Incomes Policy: The Next Step, Cmnd 1676.

  D-Notice Matters, Cmnd 3309.

D-Notice System, Cmnd 3312.
Royal Commission on Trade Unions and Employers' Associations, Cmnd 3623.
House of Lords Reform, Cmnd 3799.
'In Place of Strife: A Policy for Industrial Relations', Cmnd 3888.
Statement on the Defence Estimates 1965, Cmnd 2592.
Statement on the Defence Estimates 1966, Cmnd 2901.
The Regeneration of British Industry, Cmnd 5710.
The United Kingdom and the European Communities, Cmnd 4715.
Proposals for the setting up of a British Film Authority, Cmnd 7071.
Committee to Review the Functioning of Financial Institutions: Report, Cmnd 7937.
Film Policy, Cmnd 9319.
Today in Parliament script for 9 October 1945 supplied by Mark D'Arcy, parliamentary correspondent for *Today in Parliament*.

Newspapers, Periodicals and Journals

Birmingham Mail
Daily Express
Daily Mail and *Sunday Mail*
Daily Telegraph
Evening Standard
Independent
Liverpool Daily Post
Los Angeles Times
Manchester Guardian and *Guardian*
National News-Letter
New York Times
Ormskirk Advertiser
Reynolds News
The Times and *The Sunday Times*
Encounter
Family History, Journal of the Institute of Heraldic and Genealogical Studies
New Statesman
Occupational Medicine
Private Eye
Public Administration
Punch
Scilly Up To Date, Isles of Scilly Museum
Scillonian magazine, Isles of Scilly Museum
Spectator
Where 10

Television

A Prime Minister on Prime Ministers, original transmission on ITV, 5 November 1977 to 22 February 1978: David Paradine Histories Ltd, 1977, available on Network DVD.

Panorama, original transmission on BBC, 13 October 1988: copy kindly provided on DVD to the author by the BBC.

Interviews

Lord (Robert) Armstrong, 14 September 2018
Dame Margaret Beckett, 15 September 2020
Lord (Robin) Butler, 10 September 2018
Lord (Kenneth) Clarke, 11 July 2018
Sir David Garrard, 2 February 2021
Lord (Peter) Hain, 19 August 2020
Joe Haines: 23 April 2018; 3 September 2018; 2 September 2019; 22 December 2020
Lord (Neil) Kinnock, 2 April 2020
Lord (David) Lipsey, 26 March 2019
Rt Hon Theresa May MP, 18 March 2020
Lord (Kenneth O.) Morgan, 8 July 2019
Lord (John) Morris, 17 April 2018
Lord (David) Owen, 27 September 2018
Lord (Tom) Pendry, 6 February 2018
Lord (William) Rodgers, 22 October 2018
Dennis Skinner, 19 June 2018
Lord (Dick) Taverne, 8 July 2019
Lord (John) Tomlinson, 14 May 2019
Sue Utting, 3 July 2019
Ian Waitt, 31 December 2021
Baroness (Shirley) Williams, 13 January 2020
Professor Robin Wilson, 2 October 2018

I am also grateful to Professor Robin Wilson and Joy Crispin-Wilson for email correspondence, and for the privilege of being invited to Lady Wilson's Service of Thanksgiving on Monday, 26 November 2018 at St-Martin's-within-Ludgate Church.

Thank you to Meg Hillier MP for her email, to John Cox, Lord (Bernard) Donoughue, Lord (Peter) Hennessy, Lord (Paul) Murphy and Lord (Don) Touhig for discussions, and to George Howarth MP for the permission to quote from his piece on the constituency work of Harold Wilson.

Books and Articles by Harold Wilson

'Industrial Activity in the Eighteenth Century', *Economica*, Vol. VII, No. 26 (May 1940).

New Deal for Coal (London: Contact, 1945).

In Place of Dollars (London: Tribune Publications, 1952).

Today They Die: The Case for World Co-operation (London: National Peace Council, 1953; Peace Aims Pamphlet No. 54).

The War on World Poverty (London: Victor Gollancz, 1953).

Two out of Three: The Problem of World Poverty (London: National Peace Council, 1953; Peace Aims Pamphlet No. 57).

The War on World Poverty (London: Victor Gollancz, 1953).

Remedies for Inflation (London: The Labour Party, 1957).

The New Britain (London: Middlesex, 1964).

Purpose in Politics (London: Weidenfeld & Nicolson, 1964).

The Relevance of British Socialism (London: Weidenfeld & Nicolson, 1964).

Purpose in Power (London: Weidenfeld & Nicolson, 1966).

The Labour Government 1964–1970 (Weidenfeld & Nicolson, and Michael Joseph Ltd, 1971).

The Governance of Britain (London: Weidenfeld & Nicolson, and Michael Joseph Ltd, 1976).

A Prime Minister on Prime Ministers (London: Weidenfeld & Nicolson, and Michael Joseph Ltd, David Paradine Histories Ltd, 1977).

Final Term: The Labour Government 1974–1976 (London: Weidenfeld & Nicolson, and Michael Joseph Ltd, 1979).

The Chariot of Israel (London: Weidenfeld & Nicolson, 1981).

Memoirs: The Making of a Prime Minister 1916–1964 (London: Weidenfeld & Nicolson, and Michael Joseph Ltd, 1986).

Secondary Sources

www.bankofengland.co.uk
www.barnebys.co.uk
www.bbc.co.uk
www.birminghammail.co.uk
www.britishscreenforum.co.uk
www.cain.ulster.ac.uk
www.ec.europa.eu
www.goodschoolsguide.co.uk
www.gov.uk
www.guardian.com
www.inflation.eu
www.latimes.com
www.open.ac.uk
www.private-eye.co.uk
www.quotationspage.com
www.parliament.uk
www.erskinemay.parliament.uk
www.sibleysonscilly.co.uk
www.youtube.com

Leo Abse, *Private Member* (London: Macdonald, 1973).

Chris Cook and John Ramsden (eds), *By-elections in British politics* (London: UCL Press Ltd, 1997).

Kingsley Amis (ed.), *Harold's Years: Impressions from the New Statesman and the Spectator* (London: Quarter Books, 1977).

Christopher Andrew, *The Defence of the Realm: The Authorized History of MI5* (London: Penguin Books, 2010 edition).

Norman Angell, *The Great Illusion* (Jungle Land Publishing, 2015: printed in Great Britain by Amazon).

Leonard Woolsey Bacon, *The Congregationalists* (New York: The Baker and Taylor Co., 1904; reproduced: Charleston, South Carolina: BibloBazaar, 2010).

Walter Bagehot, *The English Constitution* with an Introduction by R.H.S. Crossman (London: Collins, 1963).

Thomas Balogh, 'The Apotheosis of the Dilettante', in Hugh Thomas (ed.), *The Establishment* (London: First Ace Books, 1962).

Stephen P. Barry, *Royal Service* (New York: Macmillan, 1983).

Tony Benn, *Out of the Wilderness: Diaries 1963–7* (London: Hutchinson, 1987).

Tony Benn, *Office Without Power: Diaries 1968–72* (London: Hutchinson, 1988).

Tony Benn, *Against the Tide: Diaries 1973–76* (London: Hutchinson, 1989).

Tony Benn and New Left Review, *Parliament, People & Power: Agenda For a Free Society: Interviews with New Left Review* (London: Verso, 1982).

Aneurin Bevan, *In Place of Fear* (London: Quartet Books Ltd, 1990 edition).

Lord Beveridge, *Power and Influence* (London: Hodder & Stoughton, 1953).

R.L. Bowley, *The Fortunate Islands: The story of the Isles of Scilly* (St Mary's, Isles of Scilly: Bowley Publications Limited, 2004).

Christopher Bray, *1965: The Year Modern Britain Was Born* (London: Simon & Schuster UK Ltd, paperback edition, 2015).

Brian Brivati, *Lord Goodman* (London: Richard Cohen Books, 1999).

George Brown, *In My Way* (London: Victor Gollancz, 1971).

Chris Bryant, *Stafford Cripps: The First Modern Chancellor* (London: Hodder & Stoughton, 1997).

D.E. Butler, *The British General Election of 1955* (London: Macmillan & Co. Ltd, 1955).

D.E. Butler and Richard Rose, *The General Election of 1959* (London: Macmillan & Co. Ltd, 1960).

D.E. Butler and Anthony King, *The British General Election of 1964* (London: Macmillan & Co. Ltd, 1965).

D.E. Butler and Anthony King, *The British General Election of 1966* (London: Macmillan & Co. Ltd, 1966).

David Butler and Michael Pinto-Duschinsky, *The British General Election of 1970* (London: The Macmillan Press Ltd, 1971).

David Butler and Dennis Kavanagh, *The British General Election of February 1974* (London: Macmillan Press Ltd, 1974).

David Butler and Dennis Kavanagh, *The British General Election of October 1974* (London: Macmillan Press Ltd, 1974).

David Butler and Gareth Butler, *British Political Facts 1900–2000* (London: Macmillan, 8th edition, 2000).

Alec Cairncross, *Living with the Century* (Fife: inyx, Countess of Moray's, 1998).

Alec Cairncross (ed.), *The Robert Hall Diaries 1947–1953* (Abingdon: Routledge, 2015 edition).

Alec Cairncross and Barry Eichengreen, *Sterling in Decline: The Devaluations of 1931, 1949 and 1967* (Oxford: Basil Blackwell Publisher Ltd, 1983).

James Callaghan, *Time and Chance* (London: Politico's Publishing, 2006).

John Campbell, *Roy Jenkins: A Well-Rounded Life* (London: Jonathan Cape, 2014).

Barbara Castle, *The Castle Diaries 1964–70* (London: Weidenfeld & Nicolson, 1984).

Barbara Castle, *The Castle Diaries 1974–76* (London: Weidenfeld & Nicolson, 1980).

Barbara Castle, *Fighting All the Way* (London: Pan Books Ltd, 1994 edition).

Peter Catterall, *The Macmillan Diaries Vol. II: Prime Minister and After, 1957–66* (London: Macmillan, 2011).

Anthony Cavendish, *Inside Intelligence: The Revelations of an MI6 Officer* (London: HarperCollins; 2nd revised edition, 1997).

Paul Chrystal, *Huddersfield Through Time* (Gloucestershire: Amberley Publishing, 2016).

Peter Clarke, *The Cripps Version: The Life of Sir Stafford Cripps* (London: Penguin Group, 2002).

G.D.H. Cole, *Guild Socialism Re-Stated* (London: Leonard Parsons Ltd, 1920; reproduced London: Forgotten Books, 2012).

Michael Cockerell, *Unmasking Our Leaders: Confessions of a Political Documentary-Maker* (London: Biteback Publishing Ltd, 2021).

Andrew S. Crines and Kevin Hickson (eds), *Harold Wilson: The Unprincipled Prime Minister? Reappraising Harold Wilson* (London: Biteback, 2016).

Susan Crosland, *Tony Crosland* (London: Jonathan Cape Ltd, 1982).

Tony Crosland, *The Future of Socialism* (London: Constable & Robinson Ltd, 2006 edition).

Richard Crossman, *Myths of Cabinet Government* (Harvard: Harvard University Press, 1972).

Richard Crossman, *Three Lectures on Prime Ministerial Government* (London: Jonathan Cape, 1972).

Richard Crossman, *The Diaries of a Cabinet Minister: Volume One* (London: Hamish Hamilton and Jonathan Cape, 1975).

Richard Crossman, *The Diaries of a Cabinet Minister: Volume Two* (London: Hamish Hamilton, 1976).

Richard Crossman, *The Diaries of a Cabinet Minister: Volume Three* (London: Hamish Hamilton, 1977).

Hugh Cudlipp, *Walking on the Water* (London: The Bodley Head Ltd, 1976).

Iain Dale (ed.), *Labour Party General Election Manifestos 1900–1997* (London: Routledge, 2000).

R.W. Dale and W.B. Selbie, *Mansfield College, Oxford: Its Origin and Opening, October 14–16, 1889* (London: James Clarke & Co., 1890; reproduced Victoria, Australia: Leopold Classic Library, 2016).

Hugh Dalton, *The Fateful Years: Memoirs 1931–1945* (London: Frederick Muller Ltd, 1957).

Hugh Dalton, *High Tide and After: Memoirs 1945–1960* (London: Frederick Muller Ltd, 1962).

Tam Dalyell, *Dick Crossman: A Portrait* (London: Weidenfeld & Nicolson, 1989).

Richard Davenport-Hines, *An English Affair* (London: William Collins, 2013 paperback edition).

Bernard Donoughue, *Downing Street Diary: With Harold Wilson in No. 10* (London: Pimlico edition, 2006).

Bernard Donoughue, *Prime Minister: Conduct of Policy Under Harold Wilson and James Callaghan, 1974–79* (London: Jonathan Cape Ltd, 1987).

Bernard Donoughue and George Jones, *Herbert Morrison: Portrait of a Politician* (London: Weidenfeld & Nicolson, 2001 paperback edition).

Bernard Donoughue, *The Heat of the Kitchen* (London: Politico's, 2003).

Stephen Dorrill and Robin Ramsay, *Smear! Wilson and the Secret State* (London: Fourth Estate Ltd, 1991).

Alec Douglas-Home, *The Way the Wind Blows* (London: William Collins, 1976).

J.P.D. Dunbabin, *The Cold War: The Great Powers and their Allies* (Harlow: Pearson Education Ltd, 2008 edition).

Marguerite Dupree (ed.), *Lancashire and Whitehall: The Diary of Sir Raymond Streat: Volume Two: 1939–57* (Manchester: Manchester University Press, 1987).

Abba Eban, *An Autobiography* (Worthing: Littlehampton Book Services Ltd, 1978).

Steven Fielding, *The Labour Governments 1964–1970: Labour and cultural change: Volume I* (Manchester: Manchester University Press, 2003).

Paul Foot, *The Politics of Harold Wilson* (Harmondsworth: Penguin Books Ltd, 1968).

Hywel Francis and Dai Smith, *The Fed: A History of the South Wales Miners in the Twentieth Century* (Cardiff: University of Wales Press, 1998 edition).

Michael Foot, *Harold Wilson: A Pictorial Biography* (Oxford: Pergamon Press Ltd, 1964).

Michael Foot, *Aneurin Bevan, Volume Two 1945–1960* (London: Granada Publishing Ltd, 1975).

George H. Gallup, *The Gallup Public Opinion Polls: Great Britain 1937–1975: Volume One 1937–1964* (Random House: New York).

George H. Gallup, *The Gallup Public Opinion Polls: Great Britain 1937–1975: Volume Two 1965–1975* (Random House: New York).

Arnold Goodman, *Tell Them I'm On My Way* (London: Chapmans, 1993).

Geoffrey Goodman, *The Awkward Warrior: Frank Cousins: His Life and Times* (London: Davis-Poynter Ltd, 1979).

Geoffrey Goodman, *From Bevan to Blair* (Brighton: Revel Barker Publishing, 2010 edition).

D.R. Grenfell, *Coal* (London: Victor Gollancz Ltd, 1947).

Brian Haigh and Sue Gillooley, *A Century of Huddersfield* (Gloucestershire: The History Press, 2012 reprint).

Peter Hain, *A Putney Plot?* (Nottingham: Spokesman, 1987).

Joe Haines, *The Politics of Power* (London: Jonathan Cape, 1977).

Joe Haines, *Glimmers of Twilight* (London: Politico's, 2003).

Joe Haines, *Kick 'Em Back: Wilson, Maxwell and Me* (London: Grosvenor House Publishing, 2019).

E.G. Hardy, *University of Oxford. College Histories. Jesus College* (Victoria, Australia: Leopold Classic Library edition, Leopold Publishing, 2016).

Hart-Davis, Duff (ed.), *King's Counsellor: Abdication and War – The Diaries of Sir Alan Lascelles* (London: Phoenix, 2007).

Julian Hayes, *Stonehouse: Cabinet Minister, Fraudster, Spy* (London: Robinson, an imprint of Little, Brown Book Group).

Denis Healey, *The Time of My Life* (London: Penguin Books, 1990).

Edward Heath, *The Autobiography of Edward Heath: The Course of My Life* (London: Hodder & Stoughton, 1998).

Peter Hennessy, *Having It So Good: Britain in the Fifties* (London: Allen Lane, 2006).

Peter Hennessy, *Winds of Change: Britain in the Early Sixties* (London: Allen Lane, 2019).

Peter Hennessy, *Cabinets and the Bomb* (Oxford: Oxford University Press, published for the British Academy, 2007).

Peter Hennessy, *Whitehall* (London: Fontana Press, 1990).

Peter Hennessy, *The Prime Minister* (London: Penguin Books, 2000).

Simon Heffer, *Like the Roman: The Life of Enoch Powell* (London: Weidenfeld & Nicolson, 1998).

Michael Heseltine, *Life in the Jungle* (London: Hodder & Stoughton, 2000).

Kevin Hickson, Jasper Miles and Harry Taylor, *Peter Shore: Labour's Forgotten Patriot* (London: Biteback Publishing, 2020).

Patricia Hollis, *Jennie Lee* (Oxford: Oxford University Press, 1997).

Victoria Honeyman, *Richard Crossman: A Reforming Radical of the Labour Party* (London: I.B. Tauris, 2007).

Anthony Howard (ed.), *The Crossman Diaries* (London: Mandarin Paperbacks edition, 1991).

Anthony Howard and Richard West, *The Making of the Prime Minister* (London: Jonathan Cape, 1965).

George Howarth, 'Harold Wilson: A Constituency MP', November 2016, a 47-page document published on his website.

Denis Howell, *Made in Birmingham* (London: Macdonald & Co., 1990).

George Hutchinson, *Edward Heath: A Personal and Political Biography* (New Jersey: Prentice Hall Press, 1970).

George Hutchinson, *The Last Edwardian at No.10: An Impression of Harold Macmillan* (London: Quartet Books, 1980).

Richard Ingrams and John Wells, *Mrs Wilson's 2nd Diary* (London: Private Eye Productions Ltd, 1966).

Richard Ingrams and John Wells, *Mrs Wilson's Diary* (London: Harper Collins, 1975).

Douglas Jay, *Change and Fortune: A Political Record* (London: Hutchinson & Co. (Publishers) Ltd, 1980).

Mark Jenkins, *Bevanism: Labour's High Tide, the Cold War and the Democratic Mass Movement* (London: Spokesman Books, 1977).

Roy Jenkins, *Portraits and Miniatures* (London: Macmillan, 1993).

Roy Jenkins, *A Life at the Centre* (London and Basingstoke: Papermac, an imprint of Macmillan General Books, 1994).

Roy Jenkins, *Gladstone* (London: Pan Books, an imprint of Pan Macmillan Ltd, 2002 edition).

Peter Jenkins, *The Battle of Downing Street* (London: Charles Knight & Co. Ltd, 1970).

Jack Jones, *Union Man* (London: William Collins, 1986).

Ken Jones, *Education in Britain: 1944 to the Present* (Cambridge: Polity Press, second edition, 2016).

Ernest Kay, *Pragmatic Premier: An Intimate Portrait of Harold Wilson* (London: Leslie Frewin, 1967).

Peter Keating (ed.), *Rudyard Kipling: Selected Poems* (London: Penguin Books, 1993).

Anthony King and Ivor Crewe, *The Blunders of Our Governments* (London: Oneworld Publications, paperback edition 2014).

Cecil King, *The Cecil King Diary* (London: Jonathan Cape Ltd, 1972).

Uwe Kitzinger, *The Second Try: Labour and the EEC* (Oxford: Pergamon Press, 1968).

David Leigh, *The Wilson Plot: The Intelligence Services and the Discrediting of a Prime Minister 1945–76* (London: William Heinemann, 1988).

Brian MacArthur (ed.), *The Penguin Book of Twentieth-Century Speeches* (London: Penguin Books, 1993).

Harold Macmillan, *Riding the Storm: 1956–59* (London: Macmillan, 1971).

James Margach, *The Abuse of Power* (London: W.H. Allen/Virgin Books, 1978).

Patrick Marnham, *Trail of Havoc: In the Steps of Lord Lucan* (London: Penguin Books, 1987).

Ian Mikardo, *Back-bencher* (London: Weidenfeld & Nicolson, 1988).

B.R. Mitchell, *British Historical Statistics* (Cambridge: Cambridge University Press, 1988).

Charles Moore, *Margaret Thatcher: The Authorized Biography: Volume One: Not for Turning* (London: Penguin Books, 2014 edition).

Austen Morgan, *Harold Wilson* (London: Pluto Press, 1992).

Janet Morgan (ed.), *The Backbench Diaries of Richard Crossman* (London: Book Club Associates, 1981).

K.O. Morgan, *Callaghan: A Life* (Oxford: Oxford University Press, 1997).

K.O. Morgan, *Labour in Power 1945–1951* (Oxford: Oxford University Press, 2002 reprint).

K.O. Morgan, *Michael Foot* (London: Harper Perennial edition, 2008).

Lord Morris of Aberavon, *Fifty Years in Politics and the Law* (Cardiff, University of Wales Press, 2011).

June Morris, *The Life and Times of Thomas Balogh: A Macaw Among Mandarins* (Sussex Academic Press: Eastbourne, 2007).

Lord Morrison of Lambeth, *Herbert Morrison: An Autobiography* (London: Odhams Press Ltd, 1960).

Gerard Eyre Noel, *Harold Wilson and the New Britain* (London: Victor Gollancz Ltd, 1964).

David Owen, *Time to Declare* (London: Michael Joseph Ltd, 1991).

Peter Patterson, *Tired and Emotional: The Life of George Brown* (London: Chatto & Windus, 1993).

Robert Pearce (ed.), *Patrick Gordon Walker: Political Diaries 1932–1971* (Historians' Press, 1991).

Henry Pelling, *The Labour Governments, 1945–51* (London: Macmillan, 1984).

Barry Penrose and Roger Courtiour, *The Pencourt File* (London: Martin Secker & Warburg Ltd, 1978).

Anne Perkins, *Red Queen: The Authorised Biography of Barbara Castle* (London: Pan Books, 2004).

Morgan Phillips, *Labour Party Secretary* (Nottingham: Spokesman Books, 2017).

Ben Pimlott (ed.), *The Political Diary of Hugh Dalton 1918–40, 1945–60* (London: Jonathan Cape Ltd, 1986).

Ben Pimlott (ed.), *The Second World War Diary of Hugh Dalton 1940–45* (London: Jonathan Cape in association with the London School of Economics and Political Science, 1986).

Ben Pimlott, *The Queen* (London: HarperCollins, 2012 edition).

Ben Pimlott, *Harold Wilson* (London: HarperCollins, 1992); re-issued with an introduction by Peter Hennessy to commemorate the centenary of Wilson's birth (London: William Collins, 2016).

Chapman Pincher, *Inside Story: A Documentary of the Pursuit of Power* (London: Sidgwick and Jackson, 1978).

Chapman Pincher, *The Truth About Dirty Tricks* (London: Sidgwick and Jackson, 1991).

Clive Ponting, *Breach of Promise: Labour in Power 1964–70* (London: Hamish Hamilton Ltd, 1989).

Oliver Postgate, *Seeing Things: An Autobiography* (London: Sidgwick and Jackson, an imprint of Macmillan Publishers Ltd, 2000).

John Preston, *A Very English Scandal* (London: Penguin Books edition, 2017).

John Preston, *Fall: The Mystery of Robert Maxwell* (London: Penguin, 2020).

Nigel Rees, *Sayings of the Century* (London: Unwin Paperback edition, 1987).

Nigel Rees, *Brewer's Quotations* (London: Cassell, 1997 reprint).

John Ramsden, *The Winds of Change: Macmillan to Heath, 1957–1975* (London: Longman, 1996).

Rachel Reeves with Richard Carr, *Alice in Westminster: The Political Life of Alice Bacon* (London: I.B. Tauris, 2017).

Geoffrey Robertson, *Stephen Ward Was Innocent, OK* (London: Biteback Publishing, 2013).

A. Roth, *Harold Wilson: A Yorkshire Walter Mitty* (London: Macdonald, 1977).

Paul Routledge, *Wilson* (London: Haus Publishing, 2006).

Anthony Sampson, *The Changing Anatomy of Britain* (London: Hodder & Stoughton Ltd, 1982).

Dominic Sandbrook, *Never Had It So Good: A History of Britain from Suez to the Beatles: 1956–63* (London: Abacus edition, 2006).

Dominic Sandbrook, *White Heat: A History of Britain in the Swinging Sixties: 1964–70* (London: Abacus edition, 2006).

Dominic Sandbrook, *State of Emergency: The Way We Were: Britain 1970–1974* (London: Penguin Books edition, 2006).

Dominic Sandbrook, *Seasons in the Sun: The Battle for Britain: 1974–1979* (London: Penguin Books edition, 2013).

The Scout Association, *An Official History of Scouting* (London: Octopus Publishing Group Ltd, 2006). Introduction by Peter Duncan, Chief Scout of the United Kingdom.

Anthony Seldon, with Peter Snowdon and Daniel Collings, *Blair Unbound* (London: Simon & Schuster, 2007).

Anthony Seldon, with Jonathan Meakin and Illias Thoms, *The Impossible Office?* (Cambridge, Cambridge University Press, 2021).

Roger Shashoua, *The Paper Millionaire* (London: Duckworth, 1988).

Robert Shepherd, *Enoch Powell* (London: Pimlico edition, 1997).

Edward Short, *Whip to Wilson* (London: Macdonald & Co. (Publishers) Ltd, 1989).

Norman Shrapnel, *The Performers* (London: Constable & Co. Ltd, 1978).

Anthony Shrimsley, *The First Hundred Days of Harold Wilson* (London: Weidenfeld & Nicolson, 1965).

Dudley Smith, *Harold Wilson: A Critical Biography* (London: Robert Hale Ltd, 1964).

Ian Douglas Smith, *The Great Betrayal: The Memoirs of Ian Douglas Smith* (London: Blake Publishing Ltd, 1997).

Leslie Smith, *Harold Wilson* (London: Collins: Fontana edition, 1964).

Michael Stewart, *Life & Labour: An Autobiography* (London: Sidgwick and Jackson, 1980).

Dick Taverne, *Against the Tide* (London: Biteback Publishing, 2014).

Margaret Thatcher, *The Downing Street Years* (London: HarperCollins, 1993 paperback edition).

Margaret Thatcher, *The Path to Power* (London: HarperCollins, 1995).

George Thomas, *Mr Speaker* (London: Century Publishing, 1985).

Hugh Thomas, *John Strachey* (New York: Harper & Row, 1973).

Nicklaus Thomas-Symonds, *Attlee: A Life in Politics* (I.B. Tauris, paperback edition, 2012).

Nicklaus Thomas-Symonds, *Nye: The Political Life of Aneurin Bevan* (I.B. Tauris, paperback edition, 2016).

Nicholas Timmins, *The Five Giants: A Biography of the Welfare State* (London: Collins, 2017 edition).

Richard Toye, *The Labour Party and the Planned Economy* (Woodbridge, Suffolk: Boydell Press, 2003).

Stephen Wall, *The Official History of Britain and the European Community: Volume II: From Rejection to Referendum, 1963–1975* (Abingdon, Oxfordshire: Routledge, 2013).

John Warwicker, *An Outsider Inside No. 10* (Gloucestershire: The History Press, 2015).

William Whitelaw, *The Whitelaw Memoirs* (London: Aurum Press Ltd, 1989).

Lord Wigg, *George Wigg* (London: Michael Joseph Ltd, 1972).

Marcia Williams, *Inside Number 10* (London: New English Library edition, 1975).

Marcia Falkender, *Downing Street in Perspective* (London: George Weidenfeld & Nicolson Ltd, 1983).

Philip M. Williams, *Hugh Gaitskell* (Oxford: Oxford University Press, 1982 edition).

Philip M. Williams (ed.), *The Diary of Hugh Gaitskell 1945–56* (London: Jonathan Cape Ltd, 1983).

Shirley Williams, *Climbing the Bookshelves* (London: Virago Press, 2009).

Mary Wilson, *Selected Poems* (London: Hutchinson, 1970).

Mary Wilson, *New Poems* (London: Hutchinson, 1979).

Mary Wilson, *Poems I Like* (London: Hutchinson, 1983).

Ben Wright, *Order, Order! The Rise and Fall of Political Drinking* (London: Duckworth Overlook, 2016).

Peter Wright with Paul Greengrass, *Spycatcher: The Candid Autobiography of a Senior Intelligence Officer* (New York: Viking Penguin Inc., fifth printing, August 1987).

Philip Ziegler, *Wilson: The Authorised Life* (London: Weidenfeld & Nicolson, 1993).

Notes

Introduction: Forged in white heat

1 Unpublished Harold Wilson Autobiography CMD 16194/3: this is in five boxes (CMD 16194/1–16194/5) in the Bodleian Library, Oxford. The text formed the basis of Harold Wilson, *Memoirs: The Making of a Prime Minister 1916–1964* (London: Weidenfeld & Nicolson Ltd, and Michael Joseph Ltd, 1986). *Memoirs* is also based on Wilson's interviews with an early biographer, Leslie Smith, which he sold back to his subject (CMD 16194/3). Wilson's typist Ella was typing up Wilson's notes in 1982 (CMD 16194/3). Hereafter, references to the unpublished autobiography will be to the box in which the relevant text is found.

2 Before the speech, Wilson had started writing an article for *Encyclopaedia Britannica* on the modern idea of socialism. He completed it afterwards. See Harold Wilson, *The Relevance of British Socialism* (London: Weidenfeld & Nicolson, 1964), p. vii.

3 Ibid., pp. 42–3.

4 *Report of the 62nd Annual Conference, September 30 to October 4, 1963* (London: Labour Party, 1963), pp. 139–40. Hereafter, references are to the reports and pages only.

5 CMD 16194/3.

6 Ibid., p. 140.

7 Ibid., p. 134.

8 Christopher Bray, *1965: The Year Modern Britain Was Born* (London: Simon & Schuster UK Ltd, paperback edition, 2015), Introduction, pp. xiii–xiv.

9 Anthony Howard and Richard West, *The Making of the Prime Minister* (London: Jonathan Cape, 1965), p. 223.

10 Anthony King and Ivor Crewe, *The Blunders of Our Governments* (London: Oneworld Publications, paperback edition, 2014), pp. 27–8.

11 Peter Catterall, *The Macmillan Diaries Vol II: Prime Minister and After, 1957–66* (London: Macmillan), p. 541.

12 Philip Ziegler, *Edward Heath* (London: HarperPress paperback edition, 2011), p. 161.

13 CMD 16194/3.

14 See Chapter 10, note 16.

15 Edward Heath, *The Autobiography of Edward Heath: The Course of My Life* (London: Hodder & Stoughton, 1998), p. 557.

16 Clive Ponting, *Breach of Promise: Labour in Power 1964–70* (London: Hamish Hamilton Ltd, 1989), p. 408.

17 Roy Jenkins, *Portraits and Miniatures* (London: Macmillan, 1993), p. 322.

18 *Daily Mail*, 25 January 2013. http://www.dailymail.co.uk/news/article-2268426/Beware-ghost-slippery-Harold-David-Camerons-European-referendum-speech-hailed-masterstroke-weve-before.html#ixzz5BVbqQGkt

19 Anthony Seldon, *Blair Unbound* (London: Simon & Schuster, 2007), p. 559.

20 Statement by Sir John Chilcot, 6 July 2016, available at: http://www.gov.uk/government/publications/the-report-of-the-iraq-inquiry

21 Iraq Inquiry Report, Section 17: Civilian Casualties: paragraphs 256 and 257, available at www.webarchive.nationalarchives.gov.uk/20171123123237/http://www.iraqinquiry.org.uk/

22 Andrew S. Crines and Kevin Hickson (eds), *Harold Wilson: The Unprincipled Prime Minister? Reappraising Harold Wilson* (London: Biteback, 2016), p. xvii.

23 Ibid., p. xxiii.

24 Ibid., p. 287.

25 *The Times*, 20 May 2021.

26 http://www.bbc.co.uk/news/av/uk-politics-26664030/former-bbc-political-editor-david-holmes-interviews-harold-wilson

27 Harold Wilson, *The Labour Government 1964–1970* (Weidenfeld & Nicolson, and Michael Joseph Ltd, 1971).

28 Harold Wilson, *Final Term: The Labour Government 1974–1976* (London: Weidenfeld & Nicolson, and Michael Joseph Ltd, 1979), p. 234.

29 Ben Pimlott, *Harold Wilson* (London: HarperCollins, 1992); re-issued with an introduction by Peter Hennessy to commemorate the centenary of Wilson's birth (London: William Collins, 2016).

30 Philip Ziegler, *Wilson: The Authorised Life* (London: Weidenfeld & Nicolson, 1993).

31 Pimlott, *Wilson*, p. 601.

32 Ibid., p. 516.

33 Ibid., p. 517.

34 Ibid., p. 515.

35 See note 1.

36 There was a month-long radio broadcasting experiment in June 1975, and in 1983, it was the Lords, rather than the Commons, that first accepted cameras.

37 CAB 128/58/10: CC (76) 10th Conclusions: Conclusions of a Meeting of the Cabinet held at 10 Downing Street on Tuesday, 16 March 1976 at 11 a.m.

38 *The Times*, 31 March 1976.

39 Hansard, House of Commons, 30 March 1976, vol. 908, col. 1103.

Chapter 1: The fourteenth Mr Wilson

1   He was prime minister first in 1924, then from 1929 to 1935, though from 1931 to 1935 it was of a National Government, MacDonald having left the Labour Party in 1931.

2   Attlee was prime minister 1945–51.

3   For reference to the 'squeezed middle' see https://www.bbc.co.uk/news/uk-politics-11848303

4   *The Times*, 21 October 1963.

5   Television interview with Kenneth Harris, 21 October 1963: see Lord Home, *The Way the Wind Blows* (London: William Collins, 1976), p. 186.

6   C.R. Humphrey-Smith and Michael G. Heenan, 'The Ancestry of Mr Harold Wilson', in *Family History, Journal of the Institute of Heraldic and Genealogical Studies*, Vol. 3, No. 17/18 (Nov. 1965), pp. 135–55, p. 135.

7   Ibid., p. 137.

8   CMD 16194/1.

9   Ibid; the Liberal–Labour arrangement was under the terms of the Gladstone–MacDonald pact of 1903.

10 The institution was under the jurisdiction of the 'Technical Instruction Committee' of Manchester City Council and is now the University of Manchester Institute of Science and Technology. [MS.Wilson.c.1612, 'Manchester Technical School 1897–1899', by J. Herbert Wilson (Summer 1969)].

11 CMD 16194/1.

12 Ibid.

13 Paul Chrystal, *Huddersfield Through Time* (Gloucestershire: Amberley Publishing, 2016), p. 20.

14 Brian Haigh and Sue Gillooley, *A Century of Huddersfield* (Gloucestershire: The History Press, 2012 reprint), p. 14.

15 Leslie Smith, *Harold Wilson* (London: Collins: Fontana edition, 1964), p. 12: Smith's biography was based on interviews with Wilson. See note 1.

16 Ibid., p. 16.

17 Ibid.

18 CMD 16194/1.

19 Smith, *Wilson*, p. 22.

20 CMD 16194/1.

21 Ibid.

22 Ibid.

23 Ibid.

24 Interview with Robin Butler, 30 September 2018.

25 Leonard Woolsey Bacon, *The Congregationalists* (New York: The Baker and Taylor Co., 1904; reproduced: Charleston, South Carolina: BibloBazaar, 2010), p. 9.

26 Ibid., p. 266.

27 The Scout Association, *An Official History of Scouting* (London: Octopus Publishing Group Ltd, 2006), Introduction by Peter Duncan, Chief Scout of the United Kingdom, p. 9.

28 Smith, *Wilson*, pp. 33–4.

29   Smith, *Wilson*, pp. 38–9.

30   *The Times*, 2 October 1962.

31   CMD 16194/1.

32   Smith, *Wilson*, p. 27.

33   Smith, *Wilson*, p. 46.

34   Smith, *Wilson*, pp. 47–8: Smith quotes a review from *The Roydsian* written by girls from a nearby school who watched the play: 'He was very amusing in his relations with his mother and Miss Neville.'

35   Harold Wilson, *A Prime Minister on Prime Ministers* (London: Weidenfeld & Nicolson and Michael Joseph, David Paradine Histories Ltd, 1977), pp. 132–3. Arthur Balfour had resigned as prime minister in December 1905 hoping that the Liberals were too disunited to form a government.

36   Smith, *Wilson*, pp. 42–3.

37   CMD 16194/1.

38   A. Roth, *Harold Wilson: A Yorkshire Walter Mitty* (London: Macdonald, 1977), p. 58.

39   Oxford, Bodleian Library [MS.Wilson.c.1612].

40   CMD 16194/1.

41   CMD 16194/1.

42   Smith, *Wilson*, p. 17.

43   CMD 16194/1.

44   Ibid.

45   Ibid.

46   Norman Angell, *The Great Illusion* (Jungle Land Publishing, 2015: printed in Great Britain by Amazon; first published in 1910 by G.P. Putnam's Sons, New York and London, the Knickerbocker Press). A new edition was produced in 1933.

47   CMD 16194/1.

48   Sadly, Allen was killed at the age of only 26, slipping on a Cumberland mountain, a year after Wilson left for Oxford.

49   CMD 16194/1.

50   Smith, *Wilson*, p. 63: at the age of 21, Wilson still weighed less than 9½ stone.

51   Ernest Kay, *Pragmatic Premier: An Intimate Portrait of Harold Wilson* (London: Leslie Frewin, 1967), p. 18.

52   E.G. Hardy, *University of Oxford. College Histories. Jesus College* (London: F.E. Robinson and Co., 1899: Leopold Classic Library edition, published by Leopold Publishing, Victoria, Australia, 2016), pp. 151–162.

53   CMD 16194/1.

54   Ibid.

55   Ibid.

56   Kay, *Pragmatic Premier*, p. 18.

57   She will be referred to as 'Mary' throughout the book, though the change from Gladys to Mary is discussed in Chapter 7.

58   CMD 16194/1.

Chapter 2: Owed it to his family to be a success

1   CMD 16194/1.

2   Gerard Eyre Noel, *Harold Wilson and the New Britain* (London: Victor Gollancz Ltd, 1964), p. 37.

3   Smith, *Wilson*, p. 71.

4   Albert Goodwin, Obituary, *Independent*, 27 September 1995: https://www.independent.co.uk/news/obituaries/obituary-professor-albert-goodwin-1603120.html

5   Roy Jenkins, *Gladstone* (London: Pan Books, an imprint of Pan Macmillan Ltd, 2002 edition), p. 68.

6   CMD 16194/1.

7   Oxford, Bodleian Library [MS.Wilson.b.4 (Wilson personal and family papers 1909–64), 'The State and the Railways in Great Britain 1823–63', by Harold Wilson].

8   Smith, *Wilson*, pp. 71–2.

9   CMD 16194/1.

10 Ibid.

11 Pimlott, *Wilson*, p. 51: this is a quote from a letter Sharpe wrote to Pimlott for the purposes of the biography.

12 CMD 16194/1.

13 Frank Byers (1915–84) sat for North Dorset 1945–50, and was made a life peer in 1964. His granddaughter, Lisa Nandy, was elected Labour MP for Wigan in 2010.

14 Paul Foot, *The Politics of Harold Wilson* (Harmondsworth: Penguin Books Ltd, 1968), pp. 31–2.

15 Letter from R.B. McCallum to the author dated 19 April 1967, quoted and footnoted in Paul Foot, *The Politics of Harold Wilson* (Harmondsworth: Penguin Books Ltd, 1968), p. 31.

16 Dudley Smith, *Harold Wilson: A Critical Biography* (London: Robert Hale Ltd, 1964), p. 22.

17 CMD 16194/1.

18 'I saw him as being a mixture of Professor Bertrand Russell and my uncle, G.D.H. Cole. That was it! A bookish bird, a bird bookend, a wooden woodpecker called, naturally, Professor Yaffle.' Oliver Postgate, *Seeing Things: An Autobiography* (London: Sidgwick & Jackson, an imprint of Macmillan Publishers Ltd, 2000), p. 296.

19 G.D.H. Cole, *Guild Socialism Re-Stated* (London: Leonard Parsons Ltd, 1920; reproduced London: Forgotten Books, 2012), p. 10.

20 Ziegler, *Wilson*, p. 22.

21 Pimlott, *Wilson*, p. 59: this is based on an interview between Alec Cairncross and Pimlott.

22 Beveridge, *Power and Influence*, p. 259.

23 Ibid.

24 Ibid.

25 Pimlott, *Wilson*, p. 61: this is based on a telephone interview between Professor Arthur Brown and Pimlott.

26 CMD 16194/1.

27 CMD 16194/1.

28 Kingsley Martin's obituary of William Beveridge, *New Statesman*, 22 March 1963. https://www.newstatesman.com/politics/2013/04/kingsley-martins-obituary-william-beveridge-1879–1963

29 Ibid.

30 Ibid.

31 The author also began teaching at Oxford at age 21.

32 CMD 16194/1.

33 Ibid.

34 Ibid.

35 Ibid. Wilson has the by-election in 1939, caused by Arthur Salter's elevation to the Lords (which was actually in 1953), for the combined English universities seat (it was for the Oxford seat), Labour's Frank Pakenham being pressed to step aside and Hogg losing.

36 CMD 16194/1.

37 Ibid.

38 R.W. Dale and W.B. Selbie, *Mansfield College, Oxford: Its Origin and Opening, October 14–16, 1889* (London: James Clarke & Co., 1890; reproduced Victoria, Australia: Leopold Classic Library, 2016), p. 42.

39 Oxford, Bodleian Library [MS.Wilson.b.4 (Wilson personal and family papers 1909–64), letter dated Thursday, 17 December 1964 and enclosed article from Hunter Davies Atticus to Mary Wilson].

40 Harold Wilson, 'Industrial Activity in the Eighteenth Century', *Economica*, Vol. VII, No. 26 (May 1940), pp. 150–60.

41 Smith, *Wilson*, pp. 84–5.

42 Alec Cairncross, *Living with the Century* (Fife: iynx, Countess of Moray's, 1998), p. 136.

43 Peter Hennessy, *Whitehall* (London: Fontana Press, 1990), p. 88.

44 CMD 16194/1.

45 CMD 16194/1.

46 Douglas Jay, *Change and Fortune: A Political Record* (London: Hutchinson & Co. (Publishers) Ltd, 1980), p. 86.

47 Beveridge, *Power and Influence*, p. 278.

48 Ibid., p. 281. Conscription of women was introduced in December 1941, though the vast majority remained employed in essential work at home in any event.

49 CMD 16194/1.

Chapter 3: New deal for coal

1 Hugh Dalton, *The Fateful Years: Memoirs 1931–1945* (London: Frederick Muller Ltd, 1957), p. 389.

2 Ibid.

3 Hywel Francis and Dai Smith, *The Fed: A History of the South Wales Miners in the Twentieth Century* (Cardiff: University of Wales Press, 1998 edition), p. 396.

4 Essential Work (Coal Mining Industry) Order.

5 CMD 16194/1.

6   Ben Pimlott (ed.), *The Second World War Diary of Hugh Dalton 1940–45* (London: Jonathan Cape in association with the London School of Economics and Political Science, 1986), entry for 31 March 1942, p. 407.

7   D.R. Grenfell, *Coal* (London: Victor Gollancz Ltd, 1947), p. 6.

8   Pimlott, *Second World War Diary of Hugh Dalton*, p. 423.

9   CMD 16194/1.

10 Dalton, *Fateful Years*, p. 415.

11 Hansard, House of Commons, 11 June 1942, vol. 380, col. 1298.

12 Oxford, Bodleian Library [MS.Wilson.c.1609, Wilson Minute to Sir Frank Tribe, 18 January 1944].

13 Hansard, House of Commons, 13 October 1943, vol. 392, col. 921.

14 C.I. (43) 1st Meeting. War Cabinet: Committee on the Organisation of the Coalmining Industry: Record of the Minutes of a Meeting held on Friday, 8th October, 1943 at 4 p.m., T230/29.

15 Oxford, Bodleian Library [MS.Wilson.c.1605, Summary of 'The case against nationalisation of the Coal Mines', by A.K. McCosh].

16 Oxford, Bodleian Library [MS.Wilson.c.1606, 'A Plan for Coal', draft by H.W. 12.5.44].

17 N.C.L. Coal Sub-Committee, The Position of the Coal-Mining Industry, Labour Party Research, 5 January 1942, T 230/29.

18 Oxford, Bodleian Library [MS.Wilson.c.1605, 'The Finance of Railway Nationalisation: a Report to the Executive of the Railway Clerks' Association', by Harold Wilson OBE, March 1945].

19 CMD 16194/1.

20 CMD 16194/1.

21 Mary Wilson, *Selected Poems* (London: Hutchinson, 1970), p. 24.

22 CMD 16194/1.

23 Pimlott, *Wilson*, p. 83, note 17, based on Pimlott's interview with Mary Wilson.

24 CMD 16194/1.

25 Cairncross, *Living with the Century*, p. 136.

26 CMD 16194/1.

27 POWE 20/55.

28 9 February 1944.

29 *Ormskirk Advertiser*, 14 September 1944.

30 Ibid., 20 March 1947.

31 *Daily Telegraph*, 14 October 1944.

32 CMD 16194/1.

33 Harold Wilson, *New Deal for Coal* (London: Contact, 1945), p. 246.

34 *Oxford Mail*, 20 June 1945.

35 Hella Pick, Lord Weidenfeld Obituary, *Guardian*, 20 January 2016.

36 Labour Party, Report of the 44th Annual Conference. Churchill and Attlee's letters are at pp. 86–8.

37 Paul Addison, 'By-elections of the Second World War', in Chris Cook and John Ramsden (eds), *By-elections in British Politics* (London: UCL Press Ltd, 1997), pp. 130–150, p. 141.

38 'National News-Letter', No. 471, 19 July 1945.

39 Ibid., 2 August 1945.

40 CMD 16194/1.

41 Andrew Roth, *Sir Harold Wilson: Yorkshire Walter Mitty* (London: Macdonald and Jane's Publishers Ltd, 1977), p. 89.

Chapter 4: Said you tried to kill him

1 CMD 16194/1.

2 Bernard Donoughue and George Jones, *Herbert Morrison: Portrait of a Politician* (London: Weidenfeld & Nicolson, 2001 paperback edition), p. 3.

3 Lord Morrison of Lambeth, *Herbert Morrison: An Autobiography* (London: Odhams Press Ltd, 1960), p. 19.

4 Ibid.

5 Ibid.

6 Philip M. Williams (ed.), *The Diary of Hugh Gaitskell 1945–56* (London: Jonathan Cape Ltd, 1983), p. 7.

7 Ibid., p. 15.

8 Roth, *Wilson*, p. 92.

9 Ibid., p. 93.

10 CMD 16194/1.

11 Ibid.

12 *Sunday Times*, 9 February 1964.

13 Harold Wilson, *A Prime Minister on Prime Ministers* (London: Orion, 1977), p. 297.

14 Ben Pimlott (ed.), *The Political Diary of Hugh Dalton 1918–40, 1945–60* (London: Jonathan Cape Ltd, 1986), p. 466.

15 CMD 16194/1.

16 Circular 118/45: Ministry of Health: Permanent House Programme, 20 June 1945, LAB 8/1163.

17 W.L. Buxton to Mr Veysey, E.M.B. 287/1945, 15 November 1945, LAB 8/1163.

18 Short Note on Building Materials and Housing Bill, by E.F. Muir, 7 August 1945, WORKS 45/81.

19 CMD 16194/1.

20 Ibid.

21 Hansard, House of Commons, 26 November 1945, vol. 416, col. 902.

22 Hansard, House of Commons, 9 October 1945, vol. 414, col. 188.

23 Ibid., col. 189.

24 Ibid., col. 190.

25 Script supplied to the author by Mark D'Arcy, parliamentary correspondent at *Today in Parliament*.

26 Hansard, House of Commons, 25 March 1946, vol. 421, col. 151.

27 CMD 16194/2.

28 Williams (ed.), *Diary of Hugh Gaitskell*, p. 23.

29 Roth, *Wilson*, p. 101.

30 Dalton to Attlee, 4 September 1946, dep. 41, Attlee Papers.

31 Roth, *Wilson*, pp. 102–3.

32 Hansard, House of Commons, 6 February 1947, vol. 432, col. 2002.

33 Ibid., col. 1986.

34 Ibid., col. 1992.

35 CMD 16194/4.

36 Record of Meeting at 6 p.m. on 22 April 1947 at Ministry of Foreign Trade, BT 11/3417.

37 Record of Meeting at 3 p.m. on 24 April 1947 at Ministry of Foreign Trade, BT 11/3417.

38 'Timber from Russia, 1947', April 1947, signed 'R.F.B.', BT 11/3417.

39 Note of Meeting held at the Board of Trade at 11 a.m. on Monday, 12 May 1947, BT 11/3417.

40 Cypher/OTP from Board of Trade to Moscow, No. 22 Askew, 28 April 1947, BT 11/3417.

41 Cypher/OTP from Moscow to Board of Trade, No. 49 Askew, 4 May 1947, BT 11/3417.

42 Cypher/OTP from Moscow to Board of Trade, No. 60 Askew, 6 May 1947, BT 11/3417.

43 Hansard, House of Commons, 12 May 1947, vol. 437, c117W.

44 David Leigh, *The Wilson Plot: The Intelligence Services and the Discrediting of a Prime Minister 1945–76* (London: William Heinemann, 1988), p. 41.

45 Stephen Dorrill and Robin Ramsay, *Smear! Wilson and the Secret State* (London: Fourth Estate Ltd, 1991), p. 7.

46 Ibid., pp. 7–8.

47 Copy of document in Patrick Marnham, *Trail of Havoc: In the Steps of Lord Lucan* (London: Penguin Books Ltd, 1987), pp. 96–7.

48 Hansard, House of Commons, 28 July 1947, vol. 441, cols 36–7.

49 Ibid., col. 37.

50 CAB 128/10/21, CM (47) 70th Conclusions, 7 August 1947.

51 CAB 128/10/23, CM (47) 72nd Conclusions, 19 August 1947.

52 PREM 8/729, Note to Prime Minister, 5 February 1947.

53 PREM 8/489, Part I, BP WP (47) 1 (Revise), 25 April 1947.

54 Financial Agreement between the Governments of the United States and the United Kingdom dated 6 December 1945, CMD 6708 (London: His Majesty's Stationery Office, 1945).

55 PREM 8/489, Part I, BP WP (47) 1 (Revise), 25 April 1947.

56 CAB 195/5/51, CM 71(47), 17 August 1947.

57 *The Times*, 21 August 1947.

58 Hugh Dalton, *High Tide and After: Memoirs 1945–1960* (London: Frederick Muller Ltd, 1962), p. 240.

59 Ibid., p. 242.

60 *Sunday Times*, 9 February 1964.

61 Paul Foot, *The Politics of Harold Wilson* (Harmondsworth: Penguin Books Ltd, 1968), pp. 55–6.

62 Hansard, House of Commons, 7 August 1947, vol. 441, col. 1766.

63   Pimlott, *Second World War Diary of Hugh Dalton*, p. 595.

64   CMD 16194/2.

65   Roth, *Wilson*, pp. 110–11.

66   Wilson, *A Prime Minister on Prime Ministers*, p. 95.

Chapter 5: Aircraft engines revved up

1   Dupree (ed.), *Diary of Sir Raymond Street: Volume Two*, p. 414.

2   Hansard, House of Commons, 15 April 1947, vol. 436, col. 87.

3   CMD 16194/2.

4   Barbara Castle, *Fighting All the Way* (London: Pan Books Ltd, 1994 edition), pp. 163–4.

5   Ibid., p. 164.

6   *The Times*, 3 December 1947.

7   CMD 16194/2.

8   Hansard, House of Commons, 11 December 1947, vol. 445, col. 1203.

9   Report of the 62nd Annual Conference of the Labour Party, p. 140.

10   Interview between Neil Kinnock and the author, 2 April 2020.

11   CMD 16194/2.

12   Hampstead Garden Suburb Act.

13   *Evening Standard*, 4 December 1956.

14   Interview with Robin Wilson, 2 October 2018.

15   Alec Cairncross (ed.), *The Robert Hall Diaries 1947–1953* (Abingdon: Routledge, 2015 edition), p. 68, entry for 21 July 1949.

16   In Pimlott, *Wilson*, p. 110, note 11.

17   Alec Cairncross, *Living with the Century* (Fife: iynx, Countess of Moray's, 1998), p. 137. Diary entry of 12 October 1949.

18   Sir John Henry Woods, 'Administrative Problems of the Board of Trade' in *Public Administration*, Volume 26, Issue 2, pp. 65–136, June 1948.

19   CAB 129/21/28 CP (47) 278, 'Trade Negotiations in Geneva: Tariff Discussions with the U.S.A.', 6 October 1947.

20   CMD 16194/2.

21   *The Times*, 7 October 1948.

22   *New Statesman*, March 1951, as quoted in K.O. Morgan, *Labour in Power 1945–1951* (Oxford: Oxford University Press), p. 368.

23   CAB 128/15, CM 41 (49), meeting of 20 June 1949.

24   Hansard, House of Commons, 4 November 1948, vol. 457, cc113–9W.

25   *Reynolds' News*, 4 July 1948.

26   *Daily Telegraph*, 8 July 1948.

27   Norman Shrapnel, *The Performers* (London: Constable and Company Ltd, 1978), p. 42.

28   CMD 16194/1.

29   Hansard, House of Commons, 4 November 1948, vol. 457, cc113–9W.

30   David Renton, Hansard, House of Commons, 5 November 1948, vol. 457, col. 1215.

31   Ibid., col. 1217 and Wilson at col. 1224.

32 Hansard, House of Commons, 10 November 1948, vol. 457, col. 1686.

33 Henry Pelling, *The Labour Governments, 1945–51* (London: Macmillan, 1984), p. 223.

34 https://www.youtube.com/watch?v=IKqzLwyzWHI

35 Dupree (ed.), *Diary of Sir Raymond Streat: Volume Two*, p. 476.

36 Wilson confirmed this on *Friday Night, Saturday Morning* on 19 October 1979: available at https://www.youtube.com/watch?v=_4kS15y5MDE

37 Barbara Castle, *Fighting All the Way* (London: Pan Books Ltd, 1994 edition), p. 164.

38 Hansard, House of Commons, 14 December 1949, vol. 470, col. 2684.

39 Hansard, House of Commons, 11 March 1948, vol. 448, col. 1436.

40 Hansard, House of Commons, 14 June 1948, vol. 452, col. 41.

41 Hansard, House of Commons, 30 March 1949, vol. 463, col. 120W.

42 Hansard, House of Commons, 30 March 1950, vol. 473, col. 572.

43 Ibid., 473 col 575.

44 Hansard, House of Commons, 2 December 1948, vol. 458, col. 2189–90.

45 CMD 16194/3.

46 Hansard, House of Commons, 27 October 1948, vol. 457, col. 87–8.

47 Hugh Thomas, *John Strachey* (New York: Harper & Row, 1973), p. 247.

48 Hansard, House of Commons, 14 March 1949, vol. 462, col. 1761.

49 Gaitskell Papers, C26, 'Note by HG, January 1949'.

50 Ibid.

51 Hansard, House of Commons, 6 July 1949, vol. 466, col. 2160.

52 Douglas Jay, *Change and Fortune: A Political Record* (London: Hutchinson & Co. (Publishers) Ltd, 1980), p. 187.

53 Cairncross, *Living with the Century*, p. 136.

54 Cairncross (ed.), *Robert Hall Diaries*, p. 68.

55 Ibid., p. 67.

56 Ibid.

57 CMD 16194/2.

58 Ben Pimlott (ed.), *The Political Diary of Hugh Dalton 1918–40, 1945–60* (London: Jonathan Cape Ltd, 1986), p. 455.

59 Ibid., p. 456.

60 Ibid., p. 454.

61 CAB 128/16/8, Conclusions of a Meeting of the Cabinet, 29 July 1949, 10 a.m.

62 Philip M. Williams (ed.), *The Diary of Hugh Gaitskell 1945–1956* (London: Jonathan Cape, 1983), entry for 3 August 1949, p. 132.

63 CMD 16194/2.

64 PREM 8/973, CM (49) 53rd Conclusions, Monday, 29 August, at 11 a.m.

65 E.P.C. (50) 4, 30 December 1949, Cabinet: Economic Policy Committee, Exports to the United States of America, Memorandum by the President of the Board of Trade, BT 11/3417.

66 Ibid.

67 Morrison of Lambeth, *An Autobiography*, p. 267.

68 Hansard, House of Commons, 9 December 1949, vol. 470, col. 2247.

69 CMD 16194/3.

70 Nicklaus Thomas-Symonds, *Attlee: A Life in Politics* (London: I.B. Tauris, 2010), pp. 220–21.

71 *Sunday Express*, 28 November 1948.

72 The Conservatives took the new Ormskirk seat with a majority of over 14,000 over Labour.

73 Dupree (ed.), *Diary of Sir Raymond Street: Volume Two*, pp. 534–5; and, on the swing among Catholic voters see also Pimlott (ed.), *Political Diary of Hugh Dalton 1918–40, 1945–60*, p. 471.

74 CMD 16194/2.

75 Ibid.

76 Ibid.

77 Ibid.

78 Ibid.

79 Ibid.

80 PREM 8/1560, 'Top Secret – Record of Washington Talks – Atomic Weapon'.

81 See Nicklaus Thomas-Symonds, *Nye: The Political Life of Aneurin Bevan* (I.B. Tauris, paperback edition 2016), pp. 177–201.

82 CMD 16194/2.

83 CAB 128/19, CM (51) 25–6, 9 April 1951; it was £23 million in a full year.

84 CMD 16194/2.

85 Ibid.

86 Aneurin Bevan, *In Place of Fear* (London: Quartet Books Ltd, 1990 edition), p. 199.

87 Labour Party, *Report of the 44th Annual Conference*, p. 132.

88 'The State and Private Industry', by Harold Wilson, PREM 8/1183.

89 Labour Party, *Report of the 48th Annual Conference*, p. 134.

90 Ibid.

91 'The State and Private Industry', by Harold Wilson, PREM 8/1183.

92 Attlee to Wilson, 7 May 1950, PREM 8/1183.

93 Note of a Meeting at the House of Commons on 17 May 1950 at 7.30 p.m. to Discuss the Memorandum on the State and Private Industry, PREM 8/1183.

94 Ibid.

95 Morrison, *An Autobiography*, p. 325.

96 Hansard, House of Commons, 24 April 1951, vol. 287, col. 228.

97 Ibid., col. 231.

98 Ibid.

99 Dalton, *High Tide and After*, p. 358.

100 Dupree (ed.), *Diary of Sir Raymond Street: Volume Two*, p. 579.

Chapter 6: Keep left

1 The gathering on 26 April 1951 was completed by Hugh Delargy, Will Griffiths, and Tim Mackay. See Mark Jenkins, *Bevanism: Labour's High Tide, the Cold War and the Democratic Mass Movement* (London: Spokesman Books, 1977), pp. 152–3, drawing on the original Keep Left minutes; see p. 286 and associated appendix for the list of memberships given to Jenkins by Jo Richardson.

2   *The Times*, 7 May 1951.

3   *The Times*, 14 May 1951.

4   *The Times*, 10 July 1951.

5   *The Times*, 21 September 1951.

6   Michael Foot, *Aneurin Bevan 1945–1950* (London: Granada Publishing Ltd, 1975), p. 350.

7   CMD 16194/3.

8   Jenkins, *Bevanism*, p. 155.

9   CMD 16194/3.

10 June Morris, *The Life and Times of Thomas Balogh: A Macaw Among Mandarins* (Sussex Academic Press: Eastbourne, 2007), pp. 9–10.

11 Ibid., p. 37.

12 Janet Morgan (ed.), *The Backbench Diaries of Richard Crossman* (London: Book Club Associates, 1981), p. 52.

13 Ibid., pp. 53–4.

14 Hansard, House of Commons, 6 December 1951, vol. 494, col. 2602.

15 CMD 16194/5.

16 Castle, *Fighting All the Way*, p. 202.

17 Pimlott (ed.), *Political Diary of Hugh Dalton 1918–40, 1945–60*, p. 598.

18 *The Times*, 6 October 1952.

19 CMD 16194/3.

20 CMD 16194/3.

21 Hansard, House of Commons, 3 February 1953, vol. 510, cols 1781–2.

22 CMD 16194/3.

23 *The Times*: 12 May, 14 May, 20 May, 22 May, 23 May, 24 May 1953.

24 Harold Wilson, *The War on World Poverty* (London: Victor Gollancz, 1953), p. 207.

25 *The Times*, 8 March 1954.

26 *Manchester Guardian*, 5 July 1954.

27 CMD 16194/2.

28 *The Times*, 7 July 1954.

29 *The Times*, 17 September 1954; letter dated 15 September.

30 *In Place of Dollars* (London: Tribune Publications, 1952); *Today They Die: The Case for World Co-operation* (London: National Peace Council, 1953; Peace Aims Pamphlet No. 54); *Two out of Three: The Problem of World Poverty* (London: National Peace Council, 1953; Peace Aims Pamphlet No. 57).

31 Wilson, *War on World Poverty*,

32 Ibid., p. 175.

33 *Daily Telegraph*, 8 May 1954.

34 CMD 16194/2.

35 CMD 16194/2.

36 CMD 16194/2.

37 When in office, the Labour prime minister chose the cabinet. Ed Miliband abolished shadow cabinet elections in 2011.

38 Hansard, House of Commons, 24 February 1954, vol. 524, col. 413.

39 Ibid, col. 417.

40 J.P.D. Dunbabin, *The Cold War* (Harlow: Pearson Education, second edition, 2008), pp. 217–8.

41 Castle, *Fighting All the Way*, p. 222.

42 Morgan, *Backbench Diaries of Crossman*, p. 291.

43 CMD 16194/3.

44 Hansard, House of Commons, 5 April 1954, vol. 526, cols 40–41.

45 Ibid., col. 54.

46 Hansard, House of Commons, 13 April 1954, vol. 526, col. 970.

47 Ibid., col. 971.

48 Ian Mikardo, *Back-Bencher* (London: Weidenfeld & Nicolson, 1988), p. 154.

49 *The Times*, 11 May 1972.

50 Morgan, *Backbench Diaries of Crossman*, pp. 314–15.

51 *The Times*, 30 April 1954.

52 Victoria Honeyman, *Richard Crossman: A Reforming Radical of the Labour Party* (London: I.B. Tauris, 2007), p. 26.

53 Labour Party, *Report of the 53rd Annual Conference*, p. 101.

54 Thomas-Symonds, *Bevan*, p. 216.

55 CMD 16194/3.

56 It was only during his dispute with Gaitskell in 1960 (see Chapter 8) that he fell to ninth place with 124 votes.

57 Dupree (ed.), *Diary of Sir Raymond Streat: Volume Two*, pp. 733–4.

58 Williams (ed.), *Diary of Hugh Gaitskell*, pp. 375–82.

59 D.E. Butler, *The British General Election of 1955* (London: Macmillan, 1955), p. 33.

60 *Sunday Express*, 6 February 1955.

Chapter 7: Pots and pans

1   Morgan Phillips, *Labour Party Secretary* (Nottingham: Spokesman Books, 2017), pp. 59–60.

2   Skeffington had previously served as MP for Lewisham West.

3   CMD 16194/3.

4   Morgan, *Backbench Diaries of Crossman*, p. 423.

5   Phillips, *Labour Party Secretary*, p. 62.

6   CMD 16194/3.

7   Morgan, *Backbench Diaries of Crossman*, p. 423.

8   Ibid.

9   Donoghue and Jones, *Herbert Morrison: Portrait of a Politician*, p. 541.

10 Smith, *Wilson*, pp. 174–6.

11 HC Deb, 16 November 1955, vol. 546, col. 743. Thomas Erskine May's first edition of the *Treatise on the Law, Privileges, Proceedings and Usage of Parliament* was published in 1844 and its latest edition is now available online: https://erskinemay.parliament.uk

12 Williams (ed.), *Diary of Hugh Gaitskell*, 9 January 1956, pp. 409, 410.

13 *The Times*, 12 January 1956.

14 Barbara Castle Papers, MS Castle 174, folder 1, 'NEC April 1951–July 1960'. Castle took shorthand notes at the dinner from which a report was compiled.

15 Ziegler, *Wilson*, p. 120.

16 As quoted in Andy McSmith, 'Baroness Falkender: The lavender lady', *Independent*, 22 October 2011.

17 Julia Langon, Lady Falkender Obituary, *Guardian*, 16 February 2019.

18 CMD 16194/3.

19 Julia Langdon, Lady Falkender Obituary, *Guardian*, 16 February 2019.

20 Ibid.

21 *Punch*, 23 April 1969, pp. 601–2, Oxford, Bodleian Library [MS.Wilson.c.1612].

22 Ibid.

23 Oxford, Bodleian Library [MS.Wilson.b.4 (Wilson personal and family papers 1909–64), letter from Marcia Williams to The Manager, Ministry of Pensions & National Insurance, 1 May 1958].

24 James Margach, *The Abuse of Power* (London: W.H. Allen/Virgin Books, 1978), p. 141.

25 Ziegler, *Wilson*, p. 120.

26 Joe Haines, *Daily Mail*, 16 February 2019.

27 Ziegler, *Wilson*, p. 121.

28 Castle, *Fighting All the Way*, p. 164.

29 *Spectator*, 6 November 1964: article reproduced in Kingsley Amis (ed.), *Harold's Years: Impressions from the New Statesman and the Spectator* (London: Quarter Books, 1977), p. 22.

30 Hansard, House of Commons, 18 April 1956, vol. 551, col. 1026.

31 Harold Macmillan, *Riding the Storm: 1956–59* (London: Macmillan, 1971), p. 48.

32 Hansard, House of Commons, 20 June 1956, vol. 554, col. 1450.

33 As quoted in 'When Harold Met Marcia' by Ben Pimlott, *Independent*, 17 October 1992.

34 The first two were what was then called the Spastics Society, now Scope, and Stoke Mandeville Hospital, to help paraplegic patients.

35 Hansard, House of Commons, 8 November 1956, vol. 563, col. 392.

36 Hansard, House of Commons, 12 November 1956, vol. 560, cols 584–5.

37 CMD 16194/3.

38 Ibid.

39 Ibid.

40 Ibid.

41 Ibid.

42 *The Times*, 9 October 1957.

43 Harold Wilson file, 16 October 1957, 19 November 1957, G5/HW/12–14 (Labour Party papers).

44 Hansard, House of Commons, 12 November 1957, vol. 577, cols 755–6.

45 Morgan, *Backbench Diaries of Crossman*, p. 627.

46 Ibid., p. 663.

47 Hansard, House of Commons, 3 February 1958, vol. 581, col. 830.

48 Ibid., col. 832.

49 Ibid., col. 844.

50 Ibid., col. 857.

51 Ibid., col. 1365.

52 Tony Crosland, *The Future of Socialism* (London: Constable & Robinson Ltd, 2006 edition), pp. 384–5.

53 *The Spectator*, 19 July 1957.

54 Harold Wilson, *Remedies for Inflation* (London: The Labour Party), p. 14.

55 Thomas-Symonds, *Bevan*, pp. 232–3.

56 1,723 of the 2,203 total on St Mary's at the time of the 2011 census; the island of Gugh is also inhabited, but taken here as part of St Agnes, since it is linked to it at low tide by a sandy tombolo.

57 R.L. Bowley, *The Fortunate Islands: The story of the Isles of Scilly* (St Mary's, Isles of Scilly: Bowley Publications Ltd, 2004), pp. 94–5.

58 *Scilly Up to Date*, June 1995, No. 89, p. 3, recollection from John Nicholls.

59 *Scilly Up to Date*, July 1991, No. 57, pp. 22–3.

60 *Guardian*, 27 May 2016: 'Scilly, where Harold Wilson, the first PM to show his knees, found peace', by Ian Jack.

61 *Private Eye*, Issue 96, 20 August 1965.

62 R.L. Bowley, *The Fortunate Islands: The story of the Isles of Scilly* (St Mary's, Isles of Scilly: Bowley Publications Ltd, 2004), p. 162.

63 See www.sibleysonscilly.co.uk where the bungalow was advertised for sale in 2019.

64 Interview with Robin Wilson, 2 October 2018.

65 *Scilly Up to Date*, June 1995, No. 89, p. 3, recollection from B.C. Ward.

66 Ibid.

67 Ibid., recollection from Doris Guy.

68 Email from Joy Crispin-Wilson to the author, 8 April 2021.

69 Mary Wilson, *Selected Poems* (London: Hutchinson, 1970), p. 31.

70 *Scillonian Magazine*, Autumn 1973, No. 195, pp. 172–3.

71 D.E. Butler and Richard Rose, *The General Election of 1959* (London: Macmillan & Co., 1960), p. 51.

72 Ibid., p. 57.

73 As quoted in Butler and Rose, *General Election of 1959*, p. 58.

74 'In retrospect the two tax pledges appear as the turning point of the campaign itself' – Butler and Rose, *General Election of 1959*, p. 61.

75 Butler and Rose, *General Election of 1959*, p. 62.

76 'Harold Wilson: A Constituency MP' by Rt. Hon. George Howarth, November 2016, a 47-page document published on his website, p. 26. The successor seats were: Knowsley North (1986–97), Knowsley North and Sefton East (1997–2010), Knowsley (2010—).

77 CMD 16194/4.

78 'Wilson: A Constituency MP', by Rt. Hon. George Howarth, p. 29.

Chapter 8: One of the ablest men in the Labour Party

1 *Daily Mail*, 18 October 1959.

2   CMD 16194/3.

3   Morgan, *Backbench Diaries of Crossman*, p. 790.

4   Morgan, *Backbench Diaries of Crossman*, p. 791.

5   *The Times*, 24 October 1959.

6   Morgan (ed.), *Backbench Diaries of Crossman*, p. 798.

7   Morris, *Life and Times of Thomas Balogh*, p. 95.

8   Letter from Dame Meg Hillier MP to the author, 7 June 2021.

9   CMD 16194/3.

10 Ibid.

11 *Report of the 58th Annual Conference*, p. 155.

12 CMD 16194/3.

13 Ibid.

14 Ibid.

15 Ibid.

16 Geoffrey Goodman, *The Awkward Warrior: Frank Cousins: His Life and Times* (London: Davis-Poynter Ltd, 1979), p. 248.

17 Ibid., p. 35.

18 Ibid., p. 213.

19 CMD 16194/3.

20 Peter Patterson, *Tired and Emotional: The Life of George Brown* (London: Chatto & Windus, 1993), p. 2.

21 Hansard, House of Commons, 11 July 1960, vol. 626, cols 987–8.

22 CMD 16194/3.

23 Hansard, House of Commons, 11 July 1960, vol. 626, col. 1106.

24 CMD 16194/3.

25 Ibid.

26 *Report of the 59th Annual Conference*, p. 151.

27 Ibid., p. 201.

28 Ruth Winstone (ed.), *The Benn Diaries: Selected, Abridged and Introduced by Ruth Winstone* (London: Arrow Books, 1996 edition), p. 82.

29 CMD 16194/3.

30 'Statesmen and Stature: How Tall Are Our World Leaders?' *Guardian Datablog*, 15 May 2012: https://www.theguardian.com/news/datablog/2011/oct/18/world-leader-heights-tall. Wilson is listed as five feet eight inches tall.

31 Ibid.

32 Ibid.

33 Morgan, *Backbench Diaries of Crossman*, p. 881.

34 CMD 16194/3.

35 Greenwood won the Heywood and Radcliffe by-election in February 1946; after boundary changes he represented Rossendale.

36 *Manchester Guardian*, 21 October 1960.

37 CMD 16194/3.

38 Norman Shrapnel, *The Performers* (London: Constable and Company Ltd, 1978), pp. 42–3.

39 Hansard, House of Commons, 2 November 1960, vol. 629, col. 200.

40 Hansard, House of Commons, 18 July 1961, vol. 644, cols 1177–8.

41 Ibid., col. 1185

42 Shrapnel, *Performers*, p. 44.

43 *The Times*, 1 December 1961.

44 Pimlott interview with Christopher Mayhew in Pimlott, *Wilson*, p. 247.

45 CMD 16194/3.

46 *Report of the 61st Annual Conference*, p. 159.

47 Philip M. Williams, *Hugh Gaitskell* (Oxford: Oxford University Press, 1982 edition), p. 409.

48 *Report of the 61st Annual Conference*, p. 192.

49 Hansard, House of Commons, 7 June 1962, vol. 661, col. 676.

50 Ibid., col. 679.

51 Ibid., col. 681

52 Ibid., col. 695.

53 Ibid., cols 677–8.

54 Hansard, House of Commons, 13 June 1950, vol. 476, col. 37.

55 Harold Wilson, *Purpose in Politics* (London: Weidenfeld & Nicolson, 1964), p. 116.

56 *The Times*, 15 January 1963.

57 CMD 16194/3.

58 Incomes Policy: The Next Step (Cmnd 1676).

59 Ken Young, 'Orpington and the "Liberal revival"' in Chris Cook and John Ramsden (eds), *By-elections in British politics* (London: UCL Press Ltd, 1997), pp. 157–79, pp. 165–6.

60 Hansard, House of Commons 4 July 1968, vol. 767, col. 1688.

61 George H. Gallup, *The Gallup Public Opinion Polls Great Britain 1937–1975: Volume One 1937–1964* (New York: Random House), pp. 640, 646.

62 *Report of the 61st Annual Conference*, p. 29.

63 Ibid., p. 89.

64 Ibid., p. 240.

65 *The Times*, 30 October 1962.

Chapter 9: The new Britain

1 *The Times*, 5 January 1963.

2 Geoffrey Goodman, *From Bevan to Blair* (Brighton: Revel Barker Publishing, 2010 edition), p. 92.

3 *The Times*, 19 January 1963.

4 Williams, *Gaitskell*, p. 427.

5 Roy Jenkins, *A Life at the Centre* (London: Random House Inc., 1993), p. 147.

6 Susan Crosland, *Tony Crosland* (London: Jonathan Cape Ltd, 1982), p. 115.

7 'Lord George-Brown drunk is a better man than the Prime Minister sober' was actually published in *The Times* on 4 March 1976 after his resignation from the Labour Party over legislation to strengthen the closed shop.

8 Winstone, *Benn Diaries*, p. 95

9 Susan Crosland, *Tony Crosland*, p. 115

10 Geoffrey Goodman, *The Awkward Warrior: Frank Cousins: His Life and Times* (London: Davis-Poynter Ltd, 1979), pp. 45–6.

11 Winstone, *Benn Diaries*, p. 95.

12 Anthony Howard and Richard West, *The Making of the Prime Minister* (London: Jonathan Cape, 1965), pp. 18–19.

13 Morgan, *Backbench Diaries of Crossman*, p. 970.

14 Jenkins, *Life at the Centre*, p. 383.

15 The others were Stephen Swingler, Walter Monslow, Jack Mendelson, Tom Swain and Laurie Pavitt. See Lord Wigg, *George Wigg* (London: Michael Joseph Ltd, 1972), p. 256.

16 Denis Howell, *Made in Birmingham* (London: Macdonald & Co., 1990), pp. 110–11.

17 Goodman, *Awkward Warrior*, p. 346.

18 Hansard, House of Commons, 31 January 1963, vol. 670, col. 1253.

19 Morgan, *Backbench Diaries of Crossman*, pp. 970–71.

20 Howard and West, *Making of the Prime Minister*, p. 30.

21 *Daily Telegraph*, 15 February 1963.

22 *Observer*, 17 February 1963.

23 Interview with Joe Haines, 22 December 2020.

24 *New York Times*, 17 October 1964: 'He has been called the Mort Sahl of the House of Commons'.

25 Ibid. For an account of Sahl's life see his obituary in the *Los Angeles Times*, 26 October 2021.

26 *Punch*, 23 April 1969, pp. 601–2, Oxford, Bodleian Library [MS.Wilson.c.1612].

27 Howell, *Made in Birmingham*, p. 110.

28 *The Times*, 22 February 1963.

29 Jenkins spoke to Wilson on 12 September 1963. Jenkins, *Life at the Centre*, p. 150.

30 *The Times*, 28 February 1963.

31 *The Times*, 7 March 1963.

32 Morgan, *Backbench Diaries of Crossman*, p. 987.

33 The saying is often attributed to the Chinese military strategist Sun Tzu: see, for example, www.quotationspage.com

34 Anthony Blond, obituary of Arnold Goodman, *Independent*, 14 May 1995.

35 Brian Brivati, *Lord Goodman* (London: Richard Cohen Books, 1999), p. 266.

36 Arnold Goodman, *Tell Them I'm On My Way* (London: Chapmans, 1993), p. 210.

37 Michael Foot, *Harold Wilson: A Pictorial Biography* (Oxford: Pergamon Press Ltd, 1964), p. 11.

38 *The Times*, 3 April 1963.

39 *The Times*, 11 June 1963.

40 Unite, the successor union to the TGWU, issued an apology for the union's attitude at the time in 2013; also see blackhistorymonth.org.uk for an account of the boycott.

41 Tony Benn, *Out of the Wilderness: Diaries 1963–7* (London: Hutchinson, 1987), p. 13.

42 *The Times*, 29 August 1963.

43 Benn, *Out of the Wilderness*, p. 25.

44 Thomas Balogh, 'The Apotheosis of the Dilettante', in Hugh Thomas (ed.), *The Establishment* (London: First Ace Books edition, 1962), pp. 98–9.

45 Ibid., p. 101.

46 Ibid., p. 92.

47 *Guardian*, 11 March 2006.

48 Wigg, *George Wigg*, pp. 263–5.

49 Morgan, *Backbench Diaries of Crossman*, p. 989.

50 Hansard, House of Commons 21 March 1963, vol. 674, col. 725.

51 Hansard, House of Commons 22 March 1963, vol. 674, col. 809.

52 Wigg, *George Wigg*, p. 277.

53 On 31 July, Ward was convicted of two counts of living off immoral earnings; he was not at the Old Bailey to hear the verdict as, the previous day, he had taken an overdose. He died on 3 August. There has been an effort to overturn the convictions: see Geoffrey Robertson, *Stephen Ward Was Innocent, OK* (London: Biteback Publishing, 2013). However, in 2017, the Criminal Case Review Commission did not refer the case formally to the Court of Appeal to be reviewed: the transcript of the judge's summing up was missing, and, as it was 54 years after Ward's death it was deemed there could be no benefit to him in quashing the convictions. Had Ward been alive, they would have been 'minded to refer the case to the Court of Appeal': see Ruth Quinn, *Guardian*, 8 September 2017.

54 Hansard, House of Commons 17 June 1963, vol. 679, col. 35.

55 Ibid., col. 49.

56 Ibid., col. 99.

57 Richard Davenport-Hines, *An English Affair* (London: William Collins, 2013 paperback edition), p. 306.

58 *Encounter*, July 1963, Number 118 (London and Beccles: William Clowes and Sons, Ltd), p. 14.

59 Morgan, *Backbench Diaries of Richard Crossman*, pp. 1020, 1022.

60 *The Times*, 9 September 1963.

61 'Is Your Child in the Unlucky Generation?', *Where 10* (Autumn 1962), pp. 3–5.

62 *Report of the 62nd Annual Conference of the Labour Party*, p. 134.

63 Ibid.

64 Ibid., p. 135.

65 Ibid.

66 *The Times*, 2 October 1963.

67 *The Times*, 9 October 1963.

68 *The Times*, 11 October 1963.

69 CMD 16194/3.

70 *The Times*, 22 October 1963.

71 Donnelly resigned the Labour whip in 1968.

72 Gallup, *Volume One*, p. 745: poll held in July 1964.

73 Harold Wilson, *The New Britain: Labour's Plan Outlined by Harold Wilson* (London: Middlesex, 1964).

74 Ibid., p. 9.

75 Hansard, House of Commons, 6 February 1964, vol. 688, col. 1373.

NOTES

76 *The Times*, 3 March 1964.

77 Memo, Benjamin H. Read to the President, 'Tour d'Horizon with Harold Wilson, Leader of the British Labor Party', 2/3/64, #19a, 'United Kingdom, Meetings with Wilson, 3/2/64', Country File, NSF, Box 213, LBJ Library.

78 Wilson, *New Britain*, p. 74.

79 Ibid., p. 127.

80 *The Times*, 3 June 1964.

81 Benn, *Out of the Wilderness*, p. 131. Though Kennedy had said in his inaugural address that 'All this will not be finished in the first one hundred days' (see Brian MacArthur (ed.), *The Penguin Book of Twentieth-Century Speeches* (London: Penguin Books, 1993), p. 30), it was actually President Franklin D. Roosevelt who had coined the term. But it was the comparison with Kennedy, fresh in people's minds, that Wilson needed.

82 D.E. Butler and Anthony King, *The British General Election of 1966* (London: Macmillan & Co. Ltd, 1966), p. 6: interview before 1964 general election.

83 Benn, *Out of the Wilderness*, p. 131.

84 Kevin Hickson, Jasper Miles and Harry Taylor, *Peter Shore: Labour's Forgotten Patriot* (London: Biteback Publishing, 2020), p. 22.

85 Gallup, *Volume One*, pp. 745, 753, 761.

86 [1964] AC 1129.

87 *The Times*, 8 September 1964.

88 Iain Dale (ed.), *Labour Party General Election Manifestos 1900–1997* (London: Routledge, 2000), p. 105.

89 D.E. Butler and Anthony King, *The British General Election of 1964* (London: Macmillan & Co. Ltd, 1965), p. 110.

90 Ibid., p. 114.

91 Ibid., p. 198.

92 D.E. Butler and Anthony King, *The British General Election of 1964* (London: Macmillan & Co. Ltd, 1965), p. 115. The strike was settled on 5 October.

93 Howard and West, *Making of the Prime Minister*, p. 189.

94 Interview with Geoffrey Goodman as quoted in Ben Pimlott, *The Queen* (London: HarperCollins, 2012 edition), p. 316.

95 Butler and King, *General Election of 1964*, p. 120.

96 Ibid., p. 126.

97 Ibid., p. 127.

98 Howard and West, *Making of the Prime Minister*, p. 226.

Chapter 10: A week is a long time in politics

1 Harold Wilson, *The Labour Government 1964–1970* (Weidenfeld & Nicolson, and Michael Joseph Ltd, 1971), p. 2.

2 Interview with Ben Pimlott as quoted in Pimlott, *Queen*, p. 342.

3 Brown, Callaghan, Gordon Walker, Healey, Bowden and Lord Gardiner, as Lord Chancellor, were the first six appointments on the night of 16 October (Wilson, *Labour Government 1964–1970*, p. 4).

4   Cousins entered parliament via the Nuneaton by-election on 21 January 1965, with the incumbent, Frank Bowles, accepting a peerage to create the vacancy.

5   Christopher Andrew, *The Defence of the Realm: The Authorized History of MI5* (London: Penguin Books, 2010 edition), p. 523.

6   Harold Wilson, *The Labour Government 1964–1970* (Weidenfeld & Nicolson, and Michael Joseph Ltd, 1971), p. 5.

7   Ibid., p. 6.

8   Alec Cairncross and Barry Eichengreen, *Sterling in Decline: The Devaluations of 1931, 1949 and 1967* (Oxford: Basil Blackwell Publisher Ltd 1983), p. 166.

9   Ibid.

10 Morris, *Life and Times of Balogh*, p. 111.

11 Ibid., p. ix.

12 Ibid., pp. 66–7.

13 Susan Crosland, *Tony Crosland*, p. 135.

14 Wilson, *Labour Government 1964–1970*, pp. 6–7.

15 Barbara Castle, *The Castle Diaries 1964–70* (London: Weidenfeld & Nicolson, 1984), p. 30.

16 Nigel Rees, *Sayings of the Century* (London: Unwin Paperback edition, 1987), p. 149: Rees interviewed Wilson about the phrase in 1977. He could not recall when he first said it; Rees therefore made enquiries among political journalists.

17 *The Sunday Times* Business News, 22 November 1964, reported by Anthony Vice.

18 Bank of England Report for the Year Ended 28th February 1965, Issued by Order of the Court of Directors, 1st July 1965, available on https://www.bankofengland.co.uk

19 Cairncross and Eichengreen, *Sterling in Decline*, p. 167.

20 *The Times*, 7 October 1964.

21 *The Times*, 13 October 1964.

22 *The Times*, 1 October 1964.

23 *The Times*, 13 October 1964.

24 *Birmingham Mail*, 4 October 2021.

25 Hansard, House of Commons, 3 November 1964, vol. 701, col. 71.

26 Ibid.

27 *The Times*, 3 August 1965.

28 *The Times*, 6 October 1965.

29 The death penalty remained on the statute book for treason until 1998.

30 Wilson, *Labour Government 1964–1970*, p. 57.

31 *The Times*, 19 November 1964.

32 Richard Ingrams and John Wells, *Mrs Wilson's 2nd Diary* (London: Private Eye Productions Ltd, 1966), p. 3.

33 *The Times*, 24 September 1975.

34 Marcia Williams, *Inside Number 10* (London: New English Library Ltd edition, 1975), pp. 29–30.

35 Wigg, *George Wigg*, p. 316.

36 Wigg, *George Wigg*, p. 360.

37 Tam Dalyell, *Dick Crossman: A Portrait* (London: Weidenfeld & Nicolson, 1989), p. 82.

38 Castle, *Castle Diaries 1964–70*, p. 243.

39 Williams, *Inside Number 10*, p. 34.

40 Confidential interview with Ben Pimlott as quoted in Pimlott, *Wilson*, p. 344.

41 PREM 13/236: Wilson to Mitchell, undated.

42 Hansard, House of Commons, 26 June 1968, vol. 767, col. 456.

43 Williams, *Inside Number 10*, p. 38.

44 Dale, *Labour Party General Election Manifestos*, p. 123.

45 Denis Healey, *The Time of My Life* (London: Penguin Books edition, 1990), p. 302.

46 CAB 130/212, MISC 16, 1st Meeting, 11 November 1964; CAB 130/213, MISC 17, 4th Meeting, 22 November 1964; CAB 128/39, CC(64), 11th Conclusions.

47 Healey, *Time of My Life*, p. 307.

48 CAB 148/19, ODP(65), 5th Meeting, 29 January 1965.

49 Background Paper, Benjamin H. Read to Mr McGeorge Bundy, 'Visit of Prime Minister Harold Wilson December 7–8 1964', #56, 'United Kingdom, PM Wilson Visit Briefing Book, 12/64', Country File, NSF, Box 213, LBJ Library.

50 *The Times*, 5 August 1970, publishing from American edition of *The Times* Louis Heren's new book, *No Hail, No Farewell*, published by Harper & Row, New York.

51 Wilson, *Labour Government 1964–1970*, p. 48.

52 Notes of Off-the-record meeting of the President with Prime Minister Wilson, 4.45–6.00 p.m., December 7, 1964, prepared by Gardner Ackley, and checked for accuracy by Secretary Dillon and Mr Bundy, #1Q, 'United Kingdom, Off Record Meeting With PM Wilson, 12/7/64', Country File, NSF, Box 213, LBJ Library.

53 Memo, George W. Ball to the President, 'The Wilson Visit', 5/12/64', #5 'United Kingdom, PM Wilson Briefing Pack, 12/64', Country File, NSF, Box 213, LBJ Library.

54 C (65) 48, 26 March 1965: Atlantic Nuclear Force: Memorandum by the Secretary of State for Foreign Affairs.

55 *Report of the 63rd Annual Conference*, p. 110.

56 Ibid., p. 117.

57 John Charles Clegg had been knighted in 1927 but the citation did not mention football.

58 Jenkins, *Life at the Centre*, pp. 169–70.

59 Crosland, *Future of Socialism*, p. 216.

60 Ibid., pp. 220–21.

61 Ibid., pp. 216–17.

62 Susan Crosland, *Tony Crosland*, p. 148.

63 Ken Jones, *Education in Britain: 1944 to the Present* (Cambridge: Polity Press, second edition, 2016), p. 83, and, more generally, for the wider debate on the impact of the change to comprehensives.

64 B.R. Mitchell, *British Historical Statistics* (Cambridge: Cambridge University Press, 1988), Miscellaneous Statistics 11, Table A, pp. 805–6: in 1964, there were 1,298 in England and Wales; the 'around 163' that remain are all in England: www.goodschoolsguide.co.uk

65 Anthony Shrimsley, *The First Hundred Days of Harold Wilson* (London: Weidenfeld & Nicolson, 1965), pp. 147–8.

66 Hansard, House of Commons, 25 January 1965, vol. 705, col. 670–1.

Chapter 11: Weeks rather than months

1 *Daily Express*, 5 November 1965.

2 Stephen P. Barry, *Royal Service* (New York: Macmillan, 1983), p. 88.

3 Mary Wilson, *New Poems* (London: Hutchinson, 1979), 'The Opening of Parliament', p. 49.

4 George Thomas, *Mr Speaker* (London: Century Publishing, 1985), p. 119.

5 *The Times*, 24 March 1976.

6 *Daily Express*, 5 November 1965.

7 *Private Eye*, Issue 102, 12 November 1965.

8 *The Times*, 28 October 1964.

9 J.J. Saville Garner at Commonwealth Relations Office to Buckingham Palace, CAO 519/2/05, 24 December 1964, PREM 13/534.

10 High Commissioner for Southern Rhodesia to Wilson, 13 January 1965 (containing Smith's message of 12 January 1965), PREM 13/534.

11 Ibid.

12 Ibid., containing Smith's message of 13 January 1965.

13 Cypher/OTP No. 5, 15 January 1965, Prime Minister's Personal Telegram Serial No. T23/65, PREM 13/534.

14 Ian Douglas Smith, *The Great Betrayal: The Memoirs of Ian Douglas Smith* (London: Blake Publishing Ltd, 1997), p. 87.

15 Note of a Meeting at 10 Downing Street at 3.10 p.m. on Saturday, January 30, 1965, PREM 13/534.

16 Record of a Conversation between the Prime Minister and the Prime Minister of New Zealand, Mr Keith Holyoake, at No. 10 Downing Street at 10.00 a.m. on Monday, February 1, PREM 13/534.

17 High Commissioner for Southern Rhodesia to Wilson, 5 February 1965 (containing Smith's message of 5 February 1965), PREM 13/534.

18 *The Times*, 23 February 1965.

19 Hansard, House of Commons, 12 November 1965, vol. 720, cols 524–5.

20 Note for the Record, April 14, 1965, PREM 13/532.

21 Set out, for example, by Wilson in Hansard, House of Commons, 1 November 1965, vol. 718, cols 631–2.

22 *The Times*, 26 June 1965.

23 *The Times*, 13 October 1965.

24 Smith, *Great Betrayal*, p. 102.

25 PREM 13/556.

26 *Daily Telegraph*, 27 October 1965.

27 Wilson, *Labour Government 1964–1970*, pp. 158–9.

28 *The Times*, 29 October 1965.

29 *The Times*, 1 November 1965.

30 Hansard, House of Commons, 1 November 1965, vol. 718, cols 636–7.

31 Message from Osagyefo Dr Kwame Nkrumah to Wilson, 2 November 1965, PREM 13/544.

32 Hansard, House of Commons, 3 November 1965, vol. 718, cols 1025–8.

33 Cypher/OTP No. 1620 from Salisbury to Commonwealth Relations Office, personal for Prime Minister from Sir Hugh Beadle, 4 November 1965.

34 En Clair, No. 2170, T. 455/65: Message from the Prime Minister, Mr Harold Wilson, to Mr Ian Smith, Prime Minister of Rhodesia, 7 November 1965, PREM 13/544.

35 Barbara Castle, *The Castle Diaries 1964–70* (London: Weidenfeld & Nicolson, 1984), p. 67.

36 CAB 128/39/76, CC (65) 60th Conclusions, 11 November 1965.

37 Castle, *Fighting All the Way*, p. 385.

38 Note to Prime Minister, 'Military Situation – Southern Rhodesia', 4 November 1965, PREM 13/544.

39 Draft Telegram from Wilson to all Commonwealth Prime Ministers, T473/65, 16 November 1965, PREM 13/546.

40 Ibid.

41 *The Times*, 12 November 1965.

42 Hansard, House of Commons, 20 December 1965, vol. 722, cols 1690–92.

43 Richard Crossman, *The Diaries of a Cabinet Minister Volume One* (London: Hamish Hamilton and Jonathan Cape, 1975), p. 382.

44 Note to Prime Minister, 'Military Situation – Southern Rhodesia,' 4 November 1965, PREM 13/544.

45 Record of a Conversation between the Prime Minister and the Prime Minister of New Zealand, Mr Keith Holyoake, at No. 10 Downing Street at 10.00 a.m. on Monday, February 1, PREM 13/534.

46 Wilson, *Labour Government 1964–1970*, pp. 182–3.

47 Ibid., p. 182.

48 Cypher/OTP, Telegram Number 2185, Commonwealth Relations Office to Lusaka, 18 November 1965, PREM 13/546.

49 George H. Gallup, *The Gallup Public Opinion Polls Great Britain 1937–1975: Volume Two 1965–1975* (Random House: New York), pp. 842, 843.

50 Benn, *Out of the Wilderness*, p. 355: Entry of 23 November 1965.

51 Statement on the Defence Estimates 1965, Cmnd 2592.

52 Hansard, House of Commons, 6 April 1965, vol. 710, col. 244.

53 *The Times*, 16 June 1965.

54 Anthony Howard (ed.), *The Crossman Diaries* (London: Mandarin Paperbacks edition, 1991), p. 127.

55 CAB 128/39/62, CC (65) 46th Conclusions, Wednesday, 1 September 1965.

56 *Report of the 64th Annual Conference*, p. 155.

57 As quoted in Peter Hennessy, *The Prime Minister* (London: Penguin Books, 2000), p. 54, and see footnote 10.

58 Lord Home, *The Way the Wind Blows* (London: William Collins, 1976), p. 217.

59 Gallup, *Volume Two*, pp. 852, 854.

60 *The Times*, 12, 15 and 17 June 1965.

61 Wilson, *Labour Government 1964–1970*, p. 80.

62 Record of meeting on April 15, 1965 in PREM 13/532.

63 Wilson, *Labour Government 1964–1970*, p. 96.

64 Michael Stewart, *Life & Labour: An Autobiography* (London: Sidgwick & Jackson, 1980), p. 158.

65 *The Times*, 13 January 1966.

66 Crossman, *Diaries of a Cabinet Minister Volume One*, p. 321. Cousins had said at a Chequers meeting on 12 September to discuss the economic situation that he disagreed with the government's incomes policy: 'I think it's time I resigned.'

67 *The Times*, 6 October 1965.

68 *The Times*, 25 January 1966.

69 *The Times*, 8 December 1967.

70 *Daily Express*, 22 February 1966.

71 Statement on the Defence Estimates 1966, Cmnd 2901.

72 Harold Wilson, *Purpose in Power* (London: Weidenfeld & Nicolson, 1966),

73 *The Times*, 1 March 1966.

74 Minute from Sir Burke Trend to Wilson, 17 February 1966; Wilson's reply was on 21 February 1966, PREM 13/881.

75 David Butler and Anthony King, *The British General Election of 1966* (London: Macmillan & Co. Ltd, 1966), p. 87.

76 Hansard, House of Commons, 1 March 1966, vol. 725, col. 1106.

77 Hansard, House of Lords, 10 October 1988, vol. 500, col. 578.

78 Butler and King, *General Election of 1966*, pp. 111–12.

79 Ibid., p. 87.

80 Ibid., p. 124

81 Williams, *Inside Number 10*, p. 84.

82 A third candidate, David Sutch, later to found the Monster Raving Loony Party, took 585 votes as a 'National Teenage Party' candidate.

Chapter 12: The pound in your pocket

1 James Callaghan, *Time and Chance* (London: Politico's Publishing, 2006), p. 193.

2 Castle, *Diaries 1964–70*, p. 113.

3 Williams, *Inside Number 10*, p. 112.

4 Interview with Sir Oliver Wright in Pimlott, *Wilson*, pp. 400–401.

5 See Julia Langdon, Obituary of Lord Marsh, *Guardian*, 2 August 2011.

6 Williams confirmed this in an interview with Steve Richards, available here: https://www.youtube.com/watch?v=s9ULfKFthRU

7 Letter of 14 February 1966, as quoted in Ziegler, *Wilson*, pp. 213–14.

8 Williams, *Inside Number 10*, pp. 114, 119.

9 *The Times*, 17 May 1966.

10 'The Communist Party of Great Britain (C.P.G.B.) and the Seaman's Strike' by Martin Furnival Jones, 19 May 1966, CAB 301/233.

11 Hansard, House of Commons 14 June 1966, vol. 729, col. 1243.

12 Letter from K.R. Cooper, Private Secretary to the Minister of Labour, to Michael (Palliser?), 3 June 1966, PREM 13/883. It is, however, noted: 'The only figures available are those put out by the National Union of Seamen itself. For obvious reasons, these are likely to be somewhat exaggerated.'

13 'Number of Ships delayed as the result of the strike: Table 2'. PREM 13/883.

14 'The Communist Party of Great Britain (C.P.G.B.) and the Seaman's Strike' by Martin Furnival Jones, 9 June 1966, CAB 301/233.

15 Confidential Note by A.M. Palliser, 10 June 1966, CAB 301/233.

16 Hansard, House of Commons, 20 June 1966, vol. 730, cols 42–3.

17 Benn, *Out of the Wilderness*, p. 436.

18 Castle, *Diaries 1964–70*, p. 136.

19 'The Communist Party of Great Britain (C.P.G.B.) and the Seaman's Strike' by Martin Furnival Jones, 21 June 1966, CAB 301/233.

20 Hansard, House of Commons, 28 June 1966, vol. 730, col. 1619.

21 Ibid., col. 1638.

22 Joe Haines, *Glimmers of Twilight* (London: Politico's, 2003), p. 43.

23 Interview with Kenneth Clarke, 11 July 2018.

24 *Spectator*, 20 March 1976: article reproduced in Kingsley Amis (ed.), *Harold's Years: Impressions from the New Statesman and the Spectator* (London: Quarter Books, 1977), p. 172.

25 Ibid.

26 Wilson was dead by the time of Heath's eightieth birthday celebrations hosted at 10 Downing Street by John Major on 17 July 1996, but Heath made a point of inviting Mary in Harold's place.

27 Though he left it open as to whether previous Conservative governments had been doing this: 'I feel it right to inform the House that there is no tapping of the telephones of hon. Members, nor has there been since this Government came into office' Hansard, House of Commons, 17 November 1966, vol. 736, col. 634.

28 *The Times*, 4 July 1966.

29 Tony Benn and New Left Review, *Parliament, People & Power: Agenda For a Free Society: Interviews with New Left Review* (London: Verso, 1982), p. 10.

30 Benn's maternal grandfather, Daniel Holmes, was the Scottish Liberal MP for Govan 1910–18. His paternal grandfather, Sir John Benn, was the MP for Tower Hamlets, St George 1892–5 and for Devonport 1904–10. William Wedgwood Benn also became MP for Tower Hamlets, St George, in 1906, and held the seat until 1918, when he moved to Leith in Scotland. He resigned from the Liberal Party and from parliament in 1927, then joining the Labour Party. He was elected as Labour MP for Aberdeen North in a by-election in 1928, and held the seat until he was defeated in 1931. He then returned to parliament in 1937, winning the seat of Manchester Gorton.

31 In the first by-election, in 1961, Benn won the most votes but his defeated Conservative opponent, Malcolm St Clair, challenged the result in the courts and won, becoming the constituency's MP. Once the Peerage Act had been passed, St Clair resigned, and Benn won the subsequent by-election in 1963 with no Conservative opponent.

32 Wilson, *Labour Government 1964–1970*, p. 250.

33 Ibid., pp. 252–3.

34 Howard, *Crossman Diaries*, p. 219.

35 Wilson, *Labour Government 1964–1970*, p. 253.

36 Susan Crosland, *Tony Crosland*, p. 173.

37 Callaghan, *Time and Chance*, p. 198.

38 Hansard, House of Commons, 14 July 1966, vol. 731, cols 1733–4.

39 Castle, *Diaries 1964–70*, p. 145.

40 *The Times*, 14 October 1966.

41 Shore told Benn this on 6 August: Benn, *Out of the Wilderness*, p. 466.

42 Jenkins, *Life at the Centre*, p. 192.

43 Castle, *Diaries 1964–70*, p. 147.

44 Ibid.

45 Winstone, *Benn Diaries*, p. 160.

46 Lord Wigg, *George Wigg*, p. 334.

47 CC (66) 37th Conclusions 19th July 1966, CAB 128/46/18.

48 Castle, *Diaries 1964–70*, pp. 149–50.

49 Ibid.

50 Castle, *Diaries 1964–70*, p. 150.

51 CC (66) 38th Conclusions 20th July 1966, CAB 128/41/38.

52 Hansard, House of Commons, 20 July 1966, vol. 732, col. 629.

53 Ibid., col. 635.

54 Ibid., col. 636.

55 Ibid., col. 639.

56 *The Times*, 21 July 1966.

57 He left parliament altogether in December 1966.

58 Wilson, *Labour Government 1964–1970*, p. 262.

59 Ibid., p. 263.

60 Ibid., p. 264. The final sentence is quoted by Wilson from the *Daily Express*.

61 Wilson, *Labour Government 1964–1970*, p. 266.

62 Hansard, House of Commons, 2 August 1966, vol. 733, col. 246.

63 CC (66) 42nd Conclusions, Minute 3, 4th August 1966, CAB 128/46/20.

64 Ibid.

65 *Private Eye*, Issue 121, 5 August 1966.

66 *Report of the 65th Annual Conference*, p. 168.

67 Wilson, *Labour Government 1964–1970*, p. 272.

68 Margach, *Abuse of Power*, p. 141.

69 Castle, *Diaries 1964–70*, pp. 132–3.

70 Margach, *Abuse of Power*, pp. 145, 146.

71 Castle, *Diaries 1964–70*, p. 254.

72 It had also been chaired by the permanent secretary at the Ministry of Aviation.

73 Wilson, *Labour Government 1964–1970*, p. 373.

74 *Daily Express*, 21 February 1967.

75 Hansard, House of Commons, 21 February 1967, vol. 741, col. 1432.

76 Cmnd. 3309.

77 Cmnd. 3312.
78 Castle, *Diaries 1964–70*, p. 268.
79 Hansard, House of Commons, 22 June 1967, vol. 748, col. 2090.
80 Chapman Pincher, *The Truth About Dirty Tricks* (London: Sidgwick & Jackson Ltd, 1991), pp. 90–91.
81 *The Times*, 20 May 1967.
82 Williams, *Inside Number 10*, p. 183.
83 Pincher, *Dirty Tricks*, p. 96.
84 Margach, *Abuse of Power*, p. 29.
85 Tables in Uwe Kitzinger, *The Second Try: Labour and the EEC* (Oxford: Pergamon Press, 1968), pp. 333–4.
86 Meetings of 18 April, 20 April, 27 April, 29 April, 30 April at 10.30 a.m., 30 April at 2.45 p.m., 2 May, CAB 148/42.
87 Castle, *Diaries 1964–70*, p. 239.
88 Ibid., p. 242.
89 Ibid., p. 250.
90 Peter Jay, *The Times*, 14 June 1967.
91 C.C. (67) 52nd Conclusions, 25 July 1967; C.C. (67) 53rd Conclusions, 27 July 1967, CAB 128/42/52.
92 Hansard, House of Commons, 3 December 1968, vol. 774, col. 1241.
93 Goodman, *Tell Them I'm On My Way*, p. 253.
94 Wilson, *Chariot of Israel*, Preface.
95 Ibid., p. 381.
96 *Daily Mail*, 9 April 1970.
97 Wilson, *Labour Government 1964–1970*, p. 401.
98 Abba Eban, *An Autobiography* (Worthing: Littlehampton Book Servies Ltd, 1978), p. 346.
99 Ibid., p. 600.
100 C.C. (67) 31st Conclusions, 23 May 1967, CAB 128/42/31.
101 Ray Gunter in Hansard, House of Commons, 26 October 1967, vol. 751, col. 1889.
102 *The Times*, 13 October 1967.
103 Peter Jay, *The Times*, 21 October 1967.
104 Cairncross, *Living with the Century*, pp. 245–50.
105 Benn, *Out of the Wilderness*, p. 13.
106 Richard Crossman, *Diaries of a Cabinet Minister: Volume Two* (London: Hamish Hamilton, 1976), p. 564.
107 Wilson's Memo on the Devaluation Crisis, dictated 2–17 November 1967, in Lady Falkender Papers, in Ziegler, *Wilson*, pp. 273–4.
108 CC (66) 67th Conclusions, 16 November 1967, CAB 128/42/66.
109 Margach, *Abuse of Power*, p. 178. The group of friendly lobby journalists became known as the 'White Commonwealth'.
110 Wilson, *Labour Government 1964–1970*, pp. 463–4.
111 Winstone, *Benn Diaries*, pp. 174–5.
112 Hansard, House of Commons, 22 November 1967, vol. 754, col. 1315.
113 *The Times*, 27 November 1967.

114 Wilson, *Labour Government 1964–1970*, p. 468.

115 Jenkins, *Life at the Centre*, p. 218.

116 Wilson, *Labour Government 1964–1970*, p. 470.

117 Hansard, House of Commons, 14 December 1967, vol. 756, col. 628.

118 George Brown, *In My Way* (London: Victor Gollancz, 1971), p. 174.

119 CC (72), 72nd Conclusions, 18 December 1967, CAB 128/42/72.

120 Hansard, House of Commons, 18 December 1967, vol. 756, cols 923–4.

121 Gallup, *Volume Two*, p. 963.

Chapter 13: A moral crusade

1   *Guardian*, 6 May 1968.

2   *Guardian*, 23 February 1968.

3   Rachel Reeves with Richard Carr, *Alice in Westminster: The Political Life of Alice Bacon* (London: I.B. Tauris, 2017), p. 155.

4   Hansard, House of Commons, 22 July 1966, vol. 732, col. 1141.

5   Leo Abse, *Private Member* (Macdonald: London 1973), p. 152.

6   Ibid.

7   Crossman, *Diaries of a Cabinet Minister Volume Two*, p. 97.

8   CAB 128/41/52, C.C. (66) 52nd Conclusions, 27 October 1966.

9   *Guardian*, 17 September 2000.

10   Crossman, *Diaries of a Cabinet Minister: Volume Two*, pp. 159–60, 11 December 1966.

11   Interview with the author, 23 April 2018.

12   London: Penguin, 1959.

13   Crossman, *Diaries of a Cabinet Minister: Volume Two*, pp. 171–2, 19 December 1966.

14   *The Times*, 26 August 1967.

15   George Thomas, *Mr Speaker* (London: Century Publishing, 1985), p. 101.

16   Note to Prime Minister, 7 February 1966: University of the Air, PREM 13/740.

17   Lee to Goodman, 8 February 1966, PREM 13/740.

18   Note to Prime Minister, 8 February 1966, from D.J. Mitchell, PREM 13/740.

19   *The Times Educational Supplement*, 19 May 1967, in PREM 13/3070.

20   Edward Pearce, Obituary of Lord Glenamara, *Guardian*, 10 May 2012.

21   Prime Minister's Note, 26 January 1968, PREM 13/3070.

22   Hansard, House of Commons, 27 January 1969, vol. 776, col. 942.

23   Jenkins to Short, 6 March 1970, PREM 13/3070.

24   Mountbatten to Wilson, 20 May 1970, PREM 13/3070.

25   https://www.open.ac.uk/about/main/strategy-and-policies/facts-and-figures

26   Cmnd 3799.

27   David Butler and Gareth Butler, *British Political Facts 1900–2000* (London: Macmillan, 8th edition, 2000), p. 357.

28   From £5,144 million in the Conservatives' last year in office to £7,457 million. *Report of the 66th Annual Conference*, pp. 213–14.

29   Hansard, House of Commons, 31 October 1969, vol. 790, col. 512.

30   Nicholas Timmins, *The Five Giants: A Biography of the Welfare State* (London: Collins, 2017 edition), pp. 226–7.

Chapter 14: A new and much more hopeful phase

1   Harold Wilson, *The Labour Government 1964–1970* (Weidenfeld & Nicolson, and Michael Joseph Ltd, 1971), pp. 306–7.
2   Hansard, House of Commons, 25 January 1966, vol. 723, col. 42.
3   Record of a Meeting held in the Wardroom of HMS *Tiger* on Friday, 2 December 1966, at 2.45 p.m., in PREM 13/1737.
4   Hansard, House of Commons, 5 December 1966, vol. 737, col. 1058.
5   Ibid., cols 1059–60.
6   Ibid., col. 1060.
7   Record of a conversation between the Prime Minister and the South African Ambassador at 10 Downing Street at 12.15 p.m. on Tuesday, December 13, PREM 13/1134.
8   Castle, *Fighting All the Way*, pp. 385–6.
9   Hansard, House of Commons, 6 March 1968, vol. 760, col. 440.
10 Wilson, *Labour Government 1964–1970*, p. 92.
11 Hansard, House of Commons, 17 November 1964, vol. 702, col. 199: though existing commitments were met, including the supply of sixteen Buccaneer aircraft.
12 PREM 11/5047.
13 Harold Wilson, *The Chariot of Israel* (London: Weidenfeld & Nicolson, 1981), p. 127.
14 Record of a meeting between the Prime Minister and the Governor of Rhodesia in the Prime Minister's Cabin on HMS *Fearless* at 5.30 p.m. on October 9, 1968.
15 Record of a Meeting between the Prime Minister, with the Commonwealth Secretary and the Attorney-General, and Mr Ian Smith, with Mr Lardner-Burke and Mr Howman, in the Wardroom of HMS *Fearless* at 9.20 p.m. on Saturday, 12th October, 1968; Rhodesia: Record of talks held aboard HMS *Fearless* from 9th–13th October, 1968, PREM 13/2327.
16 Ibid.
17 Hansard, House of Commons, 22 October 1968, vol. 770, col. 1219.
18 Ibid., col. 1096.
19 Hansard, House of Commons, 1 December 1971, vol. 827, col. 468.
20 Michael Stewart, *Life & Labour: An Autobiography* (London: Sidgwick & Jackson, 1980), p. 170.
21 Interview with the author, 19 August 2020.
22 J.P.D. Dunbabin, *The Cold War: The Great Powers and their Allies* (Harlow: Pearson Education Ltd, 2008 edition), p. 295.
23 Ibid., pp. 289–90.
24 Edward Short, *Whip to Wilson* (London: Macdonald & Co. (Publishers) Ltd, 1989), p. 120.
25 Short, *Whip to Wilson*, p. 119.
26 Hansard, House of Commons, 11 May 1965, vol. 712, col. 261.
27 Short, *Whip to Wilson*, pp. 117–18.
28 *Report of the 64th Annual Conference*, p. 197.
29 Short, *Whip to Wilson*, p. 120.

30 *Report of the 65th Annual Conference*, p. 273.

31 *The Times*, 9 February 1967.

32 Brown, *In My Way*, p. 144.

33 Record of a conversation between the Prime Minister and the Vice-President of the United States of America at No. 10 Downing Street, at 12.45 p.m. on Tuesday, April 4, 1967, PREM 13/1919.

34 Extract from PM's talk with US President in June 1967, PREM 13/2459.

35 'Visiting MPs Say Wilson Will Yield to Viet Critics', *Baltimore Sun*, 14 September 1967, PREM 13/2459.

36 E.E. Tomkins at British Embassy, Washington, to Foreign Office, 'Labour MPs and Vietnam', 15 September 1967, PREM 13/2459.

37 Extract from PM's talk with US President in Melbourne, 22 December 1967, PREM 13/2459.

38 'Note by the Prime Minister of a talk with Mr Kosygin, the Soviet Prime Minister, during the second act of the Opera *Carmen* in Moscow on Tuesday evening, January 23, 1968', PREM 13/2459.

39 *The Times*, 9 February 1968.

40 *The Times*, 22 February 1968.

41 *The Times*, 23 February 1968.

42 Memo to W.W. Rostow, 'Suggested Guidance for Public and Private Discussions About Viet Nam During Your Upcoming Trip to the UK', no author marked, undated, #1, 'United Kingdom, WWR Talks With Wilson – Brfg, Bk 2/67', Country File, NSF, Box 216, LBJ Library.

43 Memo, Robert M. Sayre to Mr Walt W. Rostow, 'Possible Additional British Credit Guarantee for Castro, 17/2/67', #2a, 'United Kingdom, WWR Talks With Wilson – Brfg. Bk 2/67', Country File, NSF, Box 216, LBJ Library.

44 PREM 13/2459.

45 *The Times*, 5 August 1970, publishing from American edition of *The Times* Louis Heren's new book, *No Hail, No Farewell*, published by Harper & Row, New York.

46 Background Paper from Benjamin H. Read to Mr Walt Rostow, 'Vietnam: UK Position', 15/2/67, #10, 'United Kingdom, WWR Talks With Wilson – Brfg. Bk 2/67', Country File, NSF, Box 216, LBJ Library.

47 Memo, Thomas L. Hughes for Secretary of State, 'Wilson Plagued by Domestic Political Problems on Eve of Washington Visit, 7/2/68', #10, 'United Kingdom 2/7–9/68, Visit of PM Wilson', Country File, NSF, Box 216, LBJ Library.

48 C.M. MacLehose to P.A. Wilkinson, 6 March 1968, FCO 154/676.

49 United States Information Service, American Embassy, 2 April 1968, in PREM 13/2461.

50 Record of discussion, letter from Donald Murray to Michael Palliser, 2 April 1968, PREM 13/2461.

51 Prime Minister's Personal Message Serial No. T88/68, 31 March 1968, PREM 13/2460.

52 Telegram No. 3429, 2 April 1968, PREM 13/2461.

53 The D.R.V. Government Statement Broadcast by Hanoi Radio on April 3rd 1968 at 14.33 GMT, PREM 13/2461.

54 United States Information Service, American Embassy, 19 April 1968, in PREM 13/2461.

55 President Johnson's Press Conference of 3 May 1968, in PREM 13/2462.

56 Cypher/CAT-A – From Paris to Foreign Office, No. 450, 20 May 1968, PREM 13/2462.

57 United States Information Service, American Embassy, 'Clifford Says Hanoi is Not Responding to America's Bombing Pause', 24 May 1968, in PREM 13/2462.

58 United States Information Service, American Embassy, 'New U.S. Soviet Agreements Seen as Step to World Peace', 17 July 1968, in PREM 13/2462.

59 Cypher/CAT-A – From Washington to Foreign Office, No. 3133, 23 October 1968, PREM 13/2462.

60 United States Information Service, American Embassy, 1 November 1968, in PREM 13/2462.

61 Interview, 19 August 2020.

62 Interview, 8 July 2019.

63 Interview, 27 September 2018.

64 Wilson, *Labour Government 1964–1970*, p. 619.

Chapter 15: Tanks off my lawn

1 Jenkins, *Life at the Centre*, pp. 226–7.

2 CAB 128/43: Meetings of 4 January, 5 January, 9 January, 11 January, 12 January at 11 a.m., 12 January at 2.30 p.m., 15 January at 10 a.m., 15 January at 3.30 p.m.

3 CAB 128/43/8; CC(68), 8th Conclusions, Meeting of the Cabinet on 15th January 1968 at 3.30 p.m.

4 Peter Keating (ed.), *Rudyard Kipling: Selected Poems* (London: Penguin Books, 1993), p. 29.

5 Hansard, House of Commons, 5 March 1968, vol. 760, col. 328.

6 *Report of the 64th Annual Conference*, p. 197.

7 Background Paper from Benjamin H. Read to Mr Walt Rostow, 'UK Overseas Military Economies', #16, 'United Kingdom, WWR Talks With Wilson – Brfg. Bk 2/67', Country File, NSF, Box 216, LBJ Library.

8 Cmnd. 3203; in the vote on 28 February 1967, the Government majority fell to 39, with 62 abstentions. There was also a further defence cut with the cancellation of the F-111 aircraft. The cut that did not happen was to the Polaris nuclear deterrent: Healey argued that it now made no economic sense since 'Ninety-five per cent of the cost was spent or committed.' He added: 'If we abandoned it, it wouldn't affect the spread of nuclear weapons. And to leave France now as the only nuclear power would be an "act of stupendous irresponsibility"' (Castle, *Castle Diaries 1964–70*, p. 356: meeting of 12 January 1968). See also: Peter Hennessy, *Cabinets and the Bomb* (Oxford: Oxford University Press, published for the British Academy, 2007), p. 240.

9 Hansard, House of Commons, 17 January 1968, vol. 756, cols 1790, 1805.

10 Wilson, *Labour Government 1964–1970*, p. 508.

11 *Liverpool Daily Post*, 19 October 1970.

12 Tony Benn, *Office Without Power: Diaries 1968–72* (London: Hutchinson 1988), pp. 44–6.

13 Brown, *In My Way*, pp. 169, 175.

14 Castle, *Castle Diaries 1964–70*, p. 398.

15 Confidential interview with a Downing Street aide; Pimlott, *Wilson*, p. 332.

16 *The Sunday Times*, 17 March 1968.

17 'Implications of Devaluation for Basic Economic Policy: Progress of the Post Devaluation Studies' by Douglas Allen, 24 January 1968, CAB 164/696.

18 Hansard, House of Commons, 19 March 1968, vol. 761, cols 251–322.

19 *The Times*, 20 March 1968.

20 Castle, *Castle Diaries 1964–70*, p. 419.

21 *The Times*, 1 July 1968.

22 Richard Crossman, *Diaries of a Cabinet Minister: Volume Three* (London: Hamish Hamilton, 1977), p. 25, 25 April 1968; p. 474, 4 May 1969.

23 Ibid., p. 97, 17 June 1968.

24 CAB 128/43/32: CC(68), 32nd Conclusions, Meeting of the Cabinet on 25 June 1968 at 10 a.m. Also: Jenkins, *Life at the Centre*, p. 258.

25 Cecil King, *The Cecil King Diary* (London: Jonathan Cape Ltd, 1972), pp. 138–9. Entry of 12 August 1967.

26 Ibid., p. 323.

27 Ibid., p. 324.

28 Ibid., p. 326.

29 Ibid., pp. 26–7.

30 King, *Diary*, p. 192.

31 Robert Pearce (ed.), *Patrick Gordon Walker: Political Diaries 1932–1971* (Historians' Press, 1991), pp. 322–4.

32 Interview, 27 September 2018.

33 Interview, 23 April 2018.

34 Royal Commission on Trade Unions and Employers' Associations, Cmnd 3623.

35 Obituary in *The Times*, 19 November 1979.

36 *Sunday Telegraph*, 14 July 1968.

37 Peter Jenkins, *The Battle of Downing Street* (London: Charles Knight & Co. Ltd, 1970), p. xii.

38 Ibid., p. 31.

39 Hansard, House of Commons, 22 November 1968, vol. 773, cols 1790–97.

40 Hansard, House of Commons, 10 December 1968, vol. 775, cols 210–11.

41 Gallup, *Volume Two*, p. 1026.

42 'In Place of Strife: A Policy for Industrial Relations', Cmnd. 3888, p. 31, in LAB 44/288.

43 Ibid., p. 6.

44 CAB 129/140/3 C(69) 8 January 1969: 'Industrial Relations: The Conciliation Pause'.

45 Interview, 2 April 2020.

46 Williams, *Inside Number 10* (London: New English Library Ltd edition, 1975), p. 282

47 *The Times*, 9 January 1969.

48 CAB/128/44: Meetings of 3 January, 9 January, 14 January and 16 January 1969.

49 CAB 128/44/3: CC(69) 3rd Conclusions, Meeting of the Cabinet on 14 January 1969 at 6.30 p.m.

50 Interview, 2 April 2020.

51 Benn, *Office Without Power*, p. 157.

52 CAB 128/44/16: Meeting of 14 April 1969.

53 Hansard, House of Commons, 15 April 1969, vol. 781, cols 1005–6.

54 Tam Dalyell, Obituary of Lord Mellish, *Independent*, 11 May 1998.

55 Castle, *Diaries 1964–70*, pp. 641–2.

56 Jenkins, *Battle of Downing Street*, p. 112.

57 Wilson, *Labour Government 1964–1970*, p. 647.

58 Hansard, House of Commons, 8 May 1969, vol. 783, col. 656.

59 Richard Crossman, *Diaries of a Cabinet Minister: Volume Three* (London: Hamish Hamilton, 1977), p. 480, 8 May 1969.

60 Jenkins, *Battle of Downing Street*, p. 116.

61 Ibid., p. 138.

62 Ibid., p. 140.

63 CAB 128/44/28, CC(69) 28th Conclusions, Meeting of 17 June 1969: starting at 10.15 a.m. and resuming at 4.30 p.m.

64 Haines worked at the *Sun* prior to its takeover by Rupert Murdoch.

65 Interview, 23 April 2018.

66 *The Times*, 19 September 1972.

Chapter 16: Why did he take Charlton off?

1 Hansard, House of Commons, 26 May 1966, vol. 729, col. 721.

2 Northern Ireland House of Commons Official Report, vol. 34, col. 1095, 24 April 1934.

3 CAB 129/144/8; C (69) 108, 28th July, 1969, Northern Ireland: Memorandum by the Secretary of State for the Home Department.

4 Ibid., and CAB 128/44/39, CC(69) 39th Conclusions, Meeting of the Cabinet on Wednesday 30th July 1969.

5 CAB 128/46/6, Cabinet: Confidential Annex CC(69) 41st Conclusions, Tuesday 19th August 1969, at 2.00 p.m.

6 CAB 128/144/12, C(69) 112, Cabinet: Northern Ireland: Note by the Secretary of the Cabinet, 20 August 1969.

7 Gallup, *Volume Two*, p. 1104: poll conducted August–September 1970.

8 Ibid., pp. 1084, 1095 for April–May.

9 Hansard, House of Commons, 1 February 1968, vol. 757, col. 1572.

10 CAB 151/142.

11 Wilson, *Labour Government 1964–1970*, p. 708.

12 She had been to the Soviet Union five times in all; during a 1966 visit she paid her own fare, according to a parliamentary reply: *Punch*, April 23, 1969, pp. 601–2, Oxford, Bodleian Library [MS.Wilson.c.1612].

13 Interview, 23 April 2018.

14 Haines, *Politics of Power*, p. 166.

15 *Punch*, April 23, 1969, pp. 601–2, Oxford, Bodleian Library [MS.Wilson.c.1612].

16 Haines, *Politics of Power*, p. 167.

17 Interview with Judith Chalmers on Thames Television, 1984. Available on: https://www.youtube.com/watch?v=RBOCvVI7ltU

18 Haines, *Politics of Power*, p. 170.

19 *Punch*, April 23, 1969, pp. 601–2, Oxford, Bodleian Library [MS.Wilson.c.1612].

20 Chalmers interview on Thames Television.

21 Haines, *Politics of Power*, p. 167.

22 Ibid., p. 168.

23 PREM 16/295. The case was settled out of court.

24 Haines, *Glimmers of Twilight*, pp. 57–8.

25 Interview with Robin Wilson, 2 October 2018.

26 https://www.nytimes.com/1970/09/24/archives/mrs-wilsons-poems-a-big-hit-in-britain.html

27 Mary Wilson, *Selected Poems* (London: Hutchinson, 1970).

28 Interview with Robin Wilson, 2 October 2018.

29 Interview with Joe Haines, 2 September 2019.

30 Interview with Robin Wilson, 2 October 2018.

31 Interview with Lord Lispey, 26 March 2019.

32 https://www.bbc.co.uk/sounds/play/p009y18k

33 https://www.barnebys.co.uk/auctions/lot/harold-wilson-s-handwritten-playlist-for-desert-island-discs-harold-wilson-B-CPylMhN

34 David Butler and Michael Pinto-Duschinsky, *The British General Election of 1970* (London: The Macmillan Press Ltd, 1971), pp. 130–31.

35 Interview with Joe Haines, 3 September 2018.

36 Hansard, House of Commons, 14 April 1970, vol. 799, col. 1213.

37 Haines, *Politics of Power*, pp. 170, 172–3.

38 Roy Jenkins, *A Life at the Centre* (London: Papermac edition, 1994), p. 297.

39 *The Times*, 14 February 1969.

40 Dale, *Labour Party General Election Manifestos 1900–1997*, p. 153.

41 Butler and Pinto-Duschinsky, *General Election of 1970*, p. 408 and at p. 406 it is set out that there was strong evidence that there was a reaction against Powell that mobilised support for Labour among those who had come to Britain.

42 *Guardian*, 5 June 2021.

43 Butler and Pinto-Duschinsky, *General Election of 1970*, p. 165.

44 Ibid., p. 169.

45 Jenkins, *Life at the Centre*, p. 301.

46 Interview between Robin Wilson and the author, 2 October 2018.

47 Denis Howell, *Made in Birmingham* (London: Macdonald & Co., 1990), p. 212.

48 Butler and Pinto-Duschinsky, *British General Election of 1970*, p. 166.

49 Interview with the author, 23 April 2018.

50 'Harold Wilson: A Constituency MP' by Rt. Hon. George Howarth, November 2016, a 47-page document published on his website, pp. 24–5.

51 Wilson, *Labour Government 1964–1970*, p. 790.

52 Marcia Falkender, *Downing Street in Perspective* (London: George Weidenfeld & Nicolson Ltd, 1983), p. 12.

Chapter 17: Is Harold really necessary?

1   Interview with Joe Haines, 23 April 2018.
2   Interview with Joe Haines, 2 September 2019.
3   Haines, *Kick 'Em Back*, pp. 85, 227.
4   Tam Dalyell, Obituary of Joseph Kagan, *Independent*, 19 January 1995.
5   Haines, *Kick 'Em Back*, p. 86.
6   Ibid., p. 233.
7   Ibid., p. 84.
8   Ibid., p. 11.
9   Haines, *Glimmers of Twilight*, pp. 52–5.
10 Interview with Joe Haines, 2 September 2019.
11 Wilson, *Labour Government 1964–1970*, pp. xvii–xviii.
12 Ibid., p. 656.
13 Benn, *Office Without Power*, p. 296.
14 Howard, *Crossman Diaries*, p. 729.
15 Benn, *Office Without Power*, p. 427.
16 Howard, *Crossman Diaries*, p. 729.
17 Ibid., p. 728.
18 Jenkins, *Life at the Centre*, p. 310.
19 Ibid.
20 As quoted in Anne Perkins, *Red Queen: The Authorized Biography of Barbara Castle* (London: Pan Books, 2004), p. 347.
21 King, *Diary 1970–74*, p. 18.
22 As quoted in Perkins, *Red Queen*, p. 348.
23 Castle, *Fighting All the Way*, p. 443.
24 Interview, 22 October 2018.
25 See, for example, Roy Jenkins' address to the European Parliament as President of the Commission on 11 January 1977: https://ec.europa.eu/dorie/fileDownload. do;jsessionid=tJ13ce_ZqBHs8yDSN34Ul-u8s9t6m-ECphOskS2bMX7oLFZT3 hyW!-898031139?docId=338865&cardId=338865
26 Dick Taverne, *Against the Tide* (London: Biteback Publishing, 2014), p. 187.
27 Backbench diary, June 1970–Nov. 1973: Entry of 19 June 1970: Oxford, Bodleian Library [MS.Castle 18].
28 Callaghan, *Time and Chance*, p. 281.
29 John Campbell, *Roy Jenkins: A Well-Rounded Life* (London: Jonathan Cape, 2014), p. 374.
30 *The Times*, 19 June 1971.
31 Castle Backbench diary, 19 June 1970.
32 *Daily Mail*, 2 July 1971.
33 Cmnd 4715.
34 *Report of the 70th Annual Conference of the Labour Party*, p. 342.

35 Ibid, pp. 359–60.

36 Benn, *Against the Tide*, p. 357.

37 Hansard, House of Commons, 21 July 1971, vol. 821, col. 1471.

38 *The Times*, 22 July 1971.

39 *New Statesman*, 30 July 1971.

40 *The Times*, 18 June 1971.

41 Ibid.

42 Ibid.

43 Ibid.

44 Ibid.

45 *The Times*, 9 July 1971.

46 Interview, 3 September 2018.

47 Benn, *Against the Tide*, pp. 379–81.

48 Hansard, House of Commons, 21 October 1970, vol. 823, col. 913.

49 Ibid., col. 914.

50 Hansard, House of Lords, 26 October 1971, vol. 324, col. 566.

51 Hansard, House of Commons, 28 October 1971, vol. 823, col. 2083.

52 Ibid.

53 Ibid., col. 2084.

54 Ibid., col. 2105.

55 Ibid., col. 2106.

56 Interview, 22 October 2018.

57 Interview with the author, 11 July 2018.

58 Benn, *Office Without Power*, pp. 301, 315–16; and Callaghan, *Time and Chance*, pp. 309–10.

59 Ibid., p. 414.

60 Interview, 3 September 2018.

61 Haines, *Glimmers of Twilight*, p. 47.

62 Benn, *Office Without Power*, pp. 420–21.

63 Interview with the author, 2 April 2020.

64 *The Times*, 11 April 1972.

65 As quoted in David Butler and Dennis Kavanagh, *The British General Election of February 1974* (London: Macmillan Press Ltd, 1974), p. 19.

66 *Report of the 77th Annual Conference*, p. 268.

67 *The Times*, 27 November 1971.

68 Interview with Joe Haines, 3 September 2018.

69 Edward Heath, *The Course of My Life* (London: Hodder & Stoughton, 1998), p. 353.

70 CPI.

71 Hansard, House of Commons, 6 November 1972, vol. 845, col. 628.

72 The price freeze lasted until 28 April 1973.

73 Originally a 'pay norm' for increases of £1 per week, plus 4 per cent, with no annual increase exceeding £250; this was later relaxed to £2.25 or 7 per cent per week, with a £350 annual limit.

74 Harold Wilson, *Final Term: The Labour Government 1974–1976* (London: Weidenfeld & Nicolson, and Michael Joseph Ltd, 1979), p. 3.

75 With Shirley Williams moving to a newly created role of shadow secretary of state for prices and consumer protection.

76 Wilson, *Chariot of Israel*, p. 367. Crossman was to die of cancer on 5 April 1974.

77 Hansard, House of Commons, 18 October 1973, vol. 861, cols 440–41.

78 Heath, *Course of My Life*, p. 503.

79 Hansard, House of Commons, 13 December 1973, vol. 861, col. 651.

80 Wilson, *Final Term*, p. 30.

81 *Report of the 72nd Annual Conference*, p. 161.

82 Wilson, *Final Term*, p. 30.

83 *Report of the 72nd Annual Conference*, p. 184.

84 Dale, *Labour Party General Election Manifestos*, p. 190.

85 Wilson, *Final Term*, p. 43.

86 Heath, *Course of My Life*, p. 510.

87 David Butler and Dennis Kavanagh, *The British General Election of February 1974* (London: Macmillan Press Ltd, 1974), p. 123.

88 *The Times*, 16 February 1974.

89 Butler and Kavanagh, *General Election of February 1974*, p. 124.

90 Haines, *Politics of Power*, p. 188.

91 Bernard Donoughue, *The Heat of the Kitchen* (London: Politico's, 2003), pp. 101–2.

92 Dale, *Labour Party General Election Manifestos*, p. 181.

93 Ibid., p. 192.

94 *Report of the 72nd Annual Conference*, p. 129.

95 *The Times*, 19 February 1974.

96 Butler and Kavanagh, *General Election of February 1974*, p. 98.

97 Ibid., p. 99; *The Times*, 20 February 1974.

98 Robert Shepherd, *Enoch Powell* (London: Pimlico edition, 1997), p. 446.

99 Butler and Kavanagh, *General Election of February 1974*, pp. 104, 105.

100 Shepherd, *Powell*, p. 445, and Powell interview in Pimlott, *Wilson*, p. 612.

101 Butler and Kavanagh, *General Election of February 1974*, p. 110. Marplan and Gallup had 2 per cent; Louis Harris had 5 per cent.

102 Ibid., p. 137. The importance of those answering 'Don't Know' to pollsters was also stressed.

103 Simon Heffer, *Like the Roman: The Life of Enoch Powell* (London: Weidenfeld & Nicolson, 1998), p. 712, and footnote 1. The quote is from an interview for the book.

104 Ibid., pp. 127, 128.

Chapter 18: Herbie Roberts of the Arsenal team

1 *The Times*, 22 February 1974.

2 CMD 16194/4.

3 Jenkins, *Life at the Centre*, pp. 370–72.

4 Bernard Donoughue, *Downing Street Diary: With Harold Wilson in No. 10* (London: Pimlico edition, 2006), p. 54.

5 Bernard Donoughue, *Prime Minister: Conduct of Policy Under Harold Wilson and James Callaghan, 1974–79* (London: Jonathan Cape Ltd, 1987), pp. 47–8.

6   Wilson, *Final Term*, p. 17.

7   Callaghan, *Time and Chance*, p. 290.

8   Hansard, House of Commons, 21 May 1974 vol. 874, col. 187. Wilson also imposed an embargo on Chile, where a repressive military junta had seized power in a coup in 1973.

9   Goodman, *Bevan to Blair*, p. 159: Callaghan made an offer on Wilson's behalf at the TUC Congress in September 1974.

10   Interview, 17 April 2018.

11   Ibid.

12   Harold Wilson, *The Governance of Britain* (London: George Weidenfeld & Nicolson Ltd and Michael Joseph Ltd, 1976), p. 203: Statement made to the Commonwealth Heads of Government Conference, May 1975.

13   Interview with Lord Lispey, Special Adviser to Tony Crosland 1974–77, 26 March 2019.

14   Donoughue, *Downing Street Diary*, p. 65.

15   Falkender, *Downing Street in Perspective*, p. 131.

16   Hansard, House of Commons, 26 March 1974, vol. 871, col. 298.

17   CAB 128/54, CC(74) 3rd Conclusions: Conclusions of a Meeting of the Cabinet held at 10 Downing Street on 14 March 1974.

18   Haines, *Politics of Power*, pp. 193–4.

19   Falkender, *Downing Street in Perspective*, p. 12.

20   *The Times*, 5 April 1974.

21   *Report of the 71st Annual Conference*, p. 173.

22   Hansard, House of Commons, 4 April 1974, vol. 871, col. 1441.

23   *The Times*, 6 April 1974.

24   Barbara Castle, *The Castle Diaries 1974–76* (London: George Weidenfeld & Nicolson Ltd, 1980), p. 74.

25   Haines, *Politics of Power*, p. 202.

26   Donoughue, *Heat of the Kitchen*, pp. 204–5.

27   Haines, *Politics of Power*, p. 204.

28   Goodman, *Tell Them I'm On My Way*, pp. 250–51.

29   Donoughue, *Heat of the Kitchen*, p. 206.

30   Hansard, House of Commons, 8 April 1974, vol. 872, cols 30–31.

31   Donoughue, *Downing Street Diary*, p. 97.

32   Ibid., p. 98.

33   Falkender, *Downing Street in Perspective*, p. 138.

34   Haines, *Politics of Power*, p. 202.

35   Benn, *Against the Tide*, p. 137.

36   *The Times*, 30 April 1974, 11 May 1974.

37   *The Times*, 18 July 1974.

38   *Daily Telegraph*, 8 April 1974.

39   Haines, *Politics of Power*, p. 207.

40   *The Times*, 19 April 1974.

41   Statement to be Made in Open Court, James Harold Wilson & Beaverbrook Newspapers Ltd. Oxford, Bodleian Library [MS.Wilson.c.1627].

42 Hansard, House of Commons, 2 May 1974, vol. 872, col. 1324.

43 Donoughue, *Downing Street Diary*, p. 128.

44 Haines, *Glimmers of Twilight*, pp. 152–3.

45 Richard Ingrams and John Wells, *Mrs Wilson's Diary* (London: Private Eye Productions Ltd, 1975), entry of 26th July 1974.

46 Haines, *Glimmers of Twilight*, p. 137.

47 Donoughue, *Heat of the Kitchen*, pp. 213–14. The accounts given by Donoughue and Haines are also in Michael Cockerell, 'Unmasking Our Leaders: Confessions of a Political Documentary-Maker' (London: Biteback Publishing Ltd, 2021), p. 73.

48 Haines, *Kick 'Em Back*, p. 228.

49 Donoughue, *Downing Street Diary*, p. 76.

50 Donoughue, *Heat of the Kitchen*, pp. 215–16.

51 Interview, 10 September 2018.

52 Donoughue, *Heat of the Kitchen*, p. 219.

53 Interview, 3 July 2019.

54 Interview with Joe Haines, 18 April 2018.

55 Donoughue, *Heat of the Kitchen*, p. 178.

56 Ibid., p. 212.

57 John Warwicker, *An Outsider Inside No. 10* (Gloucestershire: The History Press, 2015), pp. 126–7.

58 Wilson, *Final Term*, p. 33.

59 David Butler and Dennis Kavanagh, *The British General Election of October 1974* (London: Macmillan Press Ltd, 1974), p. 36.

60 Benn, *Against the Tide*, p. 212.

61 Cmnd 5710.

62 Prime Minister's Personal Minute No. M95 W/74: Ministers In Charge of Departments: 'Little things that mean a lot', 8 July 1974.

63 Little Things Exercise: State of Play, written by Robin Butler, 26 July 1974, PREM 16/447.

64 Harold Lever to the Prime Minister, 24 July 1974, PREM 16/447.

65 Interview, 17 April 2018.

66 Pimlott, *Wilson*, p. 618.

67 Castle had also introduced an Employed Persons (Health and Safety) Bill in 1970 but it was dropped by the Conservatives after the election.

68 Cmnd 5034.

69 Hansard, House of Commons, 3 April 1974, vol. 871, col. 1288.

70 Section 2(1).

71 The HSC was merged into the HSE in 2008.

72 Hansard, House of Commons, 3 April 1974, vol. 871, col. 1301.

73 Hugh Robertson, 'The Health and Safety at Work Act turned 40' in *Occupational Medicine*, Volume 65, Issue 3, April 2015, pp. 176–9.

74 Kenneth O. Morgan, *Michael Foot* (London: Harper Perennial edition, 2008), pp. 310–11.

75 *Guardian*, 29 December 1975.

76 *The Times*, 20 June 1974.

77 Nicholas Henderson, *Mandarin: The Diaries of an Ambassador 1969–1982* (London: Weidenfeld & Nicholson, 1994), p. 72.

78 Donoughue, *Downing Street Diary*, p. 242.

79 Gallup, *Volume Two*, p. 1343.

80 Dale, *Labour Party General Election Manifestos*, p. 193.

81 Butler and Kavanagh, *General Election of October 1974*, p. 255.

82 Ibid., pp. 112–13.

83 Butler and Kavanagh, *General Election of October 1974*, p. 133.

84 *The Times*, 10 October 1974.

85 Butler and Kavanagh, *General Election of October 1974*, p. 274.

Chapter 19: Mary would never allow that

1 Richard Ingrams and John Wells, *Mrs Wilson's Diary* (London: Private Eye Productions Ltd, 1975), entry of 20th March 1974.

2 Falkender, *Downing Street in Perspective*, pp. 115–16.

3 Ibid., pp. 116, 127.

4 Falkender, *Downing Street in Perspective*, pp. 126–7, and photographs.

5 Ibid., p. 117.

6 CAIN Archive, Ulster University: https://cain.ulster.ac.uk/events/uwc/docs/hw25574.htm

7 Wilson, *Final Term*, p. 129.

8 CAIN Archive, Ulster University: https://cain.ulster.ac.uk/events/convention/nicc75report.htm

9 CMD 16194/5.

10 Haines, *Politics of Power*, p. 112.

11 CPI.

12 Hansard, House of Commons, 15 April 1975, vol. 890, cols 274–5.

13 CPI.

14 CAB 128/56 CC(75) 25th Conclusions, Minute 3, Confidential Annex, 22 May 1975.

15 Hansard, House of Commons, 17 June 1975, vol. 893, col. 1192.

16 Donoughue, *Heat of the Kitchen*, pp. 160–61.

17 Hansard, House of Commons, 23 June 1975, vol. 894, col. 28.

18 Anthony Sampson, *The Changing Anatomy of Britain* (London: Hodder & Stoughton Ltd, 1982), p. 188.

19 Donoughue, *Heat of the Kitchen*, p. 161.

20 Benn, *Against the Tide*, p. 302.

21 Hansard, House of Commons, 15 January 1975, vol. 884, col. 454.

22 Benn, *Against the Tide*, p. 301.

23 Donoughue, *Heat of the Kitchen*, p. 161.

24 Ibid., p. 163.

25 Ibid., p. 164.

26 Ibid., pp. 165–6.

27 CAB 128/57/1: CC(75) 31st Conclusions, Meeting of 1 July 1975.

28 Hansard, House of Commons, 1 July 1975, vol. 894, cols 1189–90.
29 Jack Jones, *Union Man* (London: William Collins, 1986), p. 296.
30 Ibid., p. 298.
31 In July 1976 it was 12.85 per cent (CPI).
32 Gallup, *Volume Two*, p. 1435.
33 Benn, *Against the Tide*, p. 305.
34 www.youtube.com/watch?v=7W67Xppg434
35 Interview, 14 November 2018.
36 Benn, *Against the Tide*, p. 305.
37 Interview, 10 September 2018.
38 EEC Referendum: Note of a Meeting held at 10 Downing Street on Friday 20th December 1974 at 9.30 a.m. PREM 16/87.
39 EEC Referendum: Meeting of Ministers, 20th December: EEC Referendum: Other Important Questions, 17 December 1974, PREM 16/87.
40 EEC Referendum: Meeting of Ministers, 20th December: Postscript by Sir John Hunt, 19 December 1974. Ref. A08483 Prime Minister, PREM 16/87.
41 Dale, *Labour Party General Election Manifestos*, pp. 186–7.
42 Interview, 10 September 2018.
43 Donoughue, *Downing Street Diary*, pp. 329–31.
44 Hansard, House of Commons, 12 March 1975, vol. 888, col. 510.
45 Ibid.
46 Ibid., col. 511.
47 Ibid.
48 CAB 129/182/8, C(75)33 14 March 1975, EEC: Renegotiation Stocktaking.
49 CAB 128/56/13, CC(75) 13th Conclusions: Conclusions of a Meeting of the Cabinet held at 10 Downing Street on Monday 17 March 1975.
50 Donoughue, *Downing Street Diary*, p. 337.
51 Benn, *Against the Tide*, p. 343.
52 Dale, *Labour Party General Election Manifestos*, p. 186.
53 Ibid., p. 211.
54 Benn, *Against the Tide*, p. 343.
55 CAB 128/56/14, CC(75) 14th Conclusions: Conclusions of a Meeting of the Cabinet held at 10 Downing Street on Tuesday 18 March 1975.
56 Benn, *Against the Tide*, p. 343.
57 CAB 128/56/14, CC(75) 14th Conclusions: Conclusions of a Meeting of the Cabinet held at 10 Downing Street on Tuesday 18 March 1975.
58 Castle, *Diaries 1974–76*, p. 342.
59 Donoughue, *Downing Street Diary*, p. 339.
60 Castle, *Diaries 1974–76*, p. 343.
61 Hansard, House of Commons, 18 March 1975, vol. 888, col. 1456.
62 See, for example, Campbell, *Jenkins*, pp. 442–3.
63 Hansard, House of Commons, 18 March 1975, vol. 888, cols 1456–65.
64 Ibid., col. 1465.
65 Ibid., col. 1467.
66 Cmnd 5999; Hansard, House of Commons, 9 April 1975, vol. 889, cols 1368–70.

67 The Referendum Campaign: Report of Official Coordinating Committee, 23 April 1975, PREM 16/407.

68 Note of a Meeting between the Prime Minister and the Federal German Chancellor at NATO on Thursday 29 May 1975 at 6.30 p.m., PREM 16/407.

69 Note from R.N. Dales at the Foreign and Commonwealth Office to Patrick Wright at 10 Downing Street, 28 May 1975. Wilson approved the draft. PREM 16/407.

70 'Britain's New Deal in Europe' issued by HM Government, printed in Great Britain for HMSO by Impress (Acton) Ltd, in PREM 16/407.

71 Ibid.

72 Interview by Llew Gardner on Thames TV, 15 May 1975, available on YouTube: https://www.youtube.com/watch?v=7W67Xppg434

73 CAB 28/56/15 CC(75), 15th Conclusions Meeting of 20 March 1975.

74 The Prime Minister, Personal Minute No. M 94/75, to the Home Secretary, 28 May 1975, PREM 16/407.

75 Stephen Wall, *The Official History of Britain and the European Community: Volume II: From Rejection to Referendum, 1963–1975* (Oxon: Routledge, 2013), p. 590: Wall's source was a letter from Ken Stowe to him dated 13 October 2011 (Endnote 221).

76 'Harold Wilson: A Flawed Political Genius?', *Lord Speaker's Lecture delivered by The Lord Donoughue Tuesday 6 March 2018*. Available at: https://www.parliament. uk/globalassets/documents/lords-information-office/2018/Lord-Donoughues-Lecture.pdf

77 Hansard, House of Commons 9 June 1975, vol. 893, cols 29–30. The speech took place during a month-long broadcasting experiment in the Commons Chamber.

78 Ibid., col. 30.

79 Ibid., col. 31.

80 Ibid.

81 'British Objectives in the European Community', QZ0122, produced on an inter-departmental basis, sent by G.R. Denman to Wilson, 14 January 1976, Annex B: 'Degree of Divergence Between the Economic Performance of the United Kingdom and Other Member States', PREM 126/863.

82 The Prime Minister, Personal Minute No. M 101/75, to the Secretary of State for Foreign and Commonwealth Affairs, 10 June 1975, PREM 16/407.

83 Ibid.

84 The Prime Minister, Personal Minute No. M 100/75, to the Home Secretary, 10 June 1975, PREM 16/407.

85 Pimlott, *Wilson*, p. 601.

86 Ibid., pp. 601–2.

87 Wilson, *Final Term*, p. 144.

88 Jenkins, *Life at the Centre*, p. 422.

89 Donoughue, *Heat of the Kitchen*, p. 159.

90 Ibid., p. 174.

91 Interview, 18 April 2018.

92 Donoughue, *Heat of the Kitchen*, p. 178.

93 Interview with Joe Haines, 18 April 2018.

94 Donoughue, *Heat of the Kitchen*, p. 179.

95 Interview with the author, 6 February 2018, and letter from Pendry to the author, 13 February 2018.

96 Donoughue, *Heat of the Kitchen*, p. 180.

97 Interview, 14 May 2019.

98 Interview, 11 July 2018.

99 Interview between Dennis Skinner and the author, 19 June 2018; interview between Margaret Beckett and the author, 15 September 2020.

100 Donoughue, *Heat of the Kitchen*, pp. 170–72.

101 CMD 16194/5.

102 Hansard, House of Commons, 4 March 1976, vol. 906, col. 1547.

103 CAB 128/58: CC(76) 1st Conclusions, Meeting of 15 January 1976.

104 Donoughue, *Heat of the Kitchen*, p. 170.

105 Hansard, House of Commons, 11 March 1976, vol. 907, col. 634.

106 Castle, *Diaries 1974–76*, p. 690.

107 Interview, 2 October 2018.

108 PREM 16/2072: 'Action Plan and Timetable'.

109 Donoughue, *Heat of the Kitchen*, p. 183; interview between Joe Haines and the author, 18 April 2018.

110 Donoughue, *Heat of the Kitchen*, p. 127.

111 CAB 128/58/10: CC (76) 10th Conclusions: Meeting of 16 March 1976.

112 Interview with Ben Pimlott as quoted in Pimlott, *Queen*, p. 430.

113 Ziegler, *Wilson*, p. 484.

114 Ibid., p. 485.

115 Wilson, *Final Term*, p. 228.

116 *The Times*, 18 March 1976.

117 *Spectator*, 20 March 1976: article reproduced in Kingsley Amis (ed.), *Harold's Years: Impressions from the New Statesman and the Spectator* (London: Quarter Books, 1977), p. 175.

118 *The Times*, 2 April 1976.

119 Falkender, *Downing Street in Perspective*, p. 271.

Chapter 20: The Wilson Plot?

1 Michael Heseltine, *Life in the Jungle* (London: Hodder & Stoughton, 2000), p. 179.

2 *The Times*, 23 April 1976.

3 *The Times*, 3 May 1976.

4 *The Times*, 27 May 1977.

5 Haines, *Politics of Power*, p. 150.

6 *The Times*, 27 May 1976.

7 *The Times*, 29 May 1976.

8 Hutchinson later penned a biography of Harold Macmillan. See bibliography.

9 Haines, *Politics of Power*, p. 153.

10 Haines, *Kick 'Em Back*, p. 226.

11 *Daily Telegraph*, 4 April 2007.

12 *The Times*, 5 July 2018.

13 *The Times*, 10 July 2018.

14 Christopher Andrew, *The Defence of the Realm: The Authorized History of MI5* (London: Penguin Books, 2010 edition), pp. 627–43.

15 Leigh, *Wilson Plot*, p. 247.

16 BBC *Panorama*, 13 October 1988.

17 Peter Wright with Paul Greengrass, *Spycatcher: The Candid Autobiography of a Senior Intelligence Officer* (New York: Viking Penguin Inc.), fifth printing, August 1987.

18 BBC *Panorama*, 13 October 1988.

19 Wright, *Spycatcher*, pp. 363–4.

20 Interview with Walter Elder, Executive Assistant to the Director of the CIA, 1961–5, interviewed on BBC *Panorama*, 13 October 1988.

21 Wright, *Spycatcher*, p. 364.

22 Ibid.

23 Andrew, *Defence of the Realm*, p. 632.

24 Leigh, *Wilson Plot*, p. 252.

25 Andrew, *Defence of the Realm*, p. 640.

26 Wright, *Spycatcher*, p. 362.

27 Ibid., p. 363.

28 Evidence of Dr Walter Somerville in BBC *Panorama*, 13 October 1988.

29 Interview with Joe Haines, 2 September 2019.

30 Barry Penrose and Roger Courtiour, *The Pencourt File* (London: Martin Secker & Warburg Ltd, 1978), p. 13.

31 Ziegler, *Wilson*, p. 501.

32 Chapman Pincher, *Inside Story: A Documentary of the Pursuit of Power* (London: Sidgwick & Jackson, 1978), p. 19.

33 Andrew, *Defence of the Realm*, p. 640: the account is a briefing from the Home Secretary, Merlyn Rees, to Callaghan.

34 Anthony Cavendish, *Inside Intelligence: The Revelations of an MI6 Officer* (London: HarperCollins; 2nd revised edition, 1997), p. 165.

35 Leigh, *Wilson Plot*, pp. 249–50.

36 Hansard, House of Commons, 6 May 1974, vol. 873, col. 22.

37 'The Hollis Affair', by Barrie Penrose, Colin Simpson and Simon Freeman, p. 17, *The Sunday Times*, 29 March 1981, Oxford, Bodleian Library [MS.Wilson.c.1627].

38 Bernard Donoughue, *Downing Street Diary: With Harold Wilson in No. 10* (London: Pimlico edition, 2006), p. 96.

39 Goodman, *Bevan to Blair*, p. 171.

40 *Panorama*, 13 October 1988.

41 Interview with the author, 19 August 2020.

42 Hain, *A Putney Plot?* (Nottingham: Spokesman, 1987), p. 150.

43 Haines, *Kick 'Em Back*, p. 103.

44 *Guardian*, 4 June 2018.

45 Hansard, House of Commons, 9 March 1976, vol. 907, col. 245.

46 John Preston, *A Very English Scandal* (London: Penguin Books edition, 2017), p. 229.

47 *The Times*, 8 June 1981.

48 Dominic Sandbrook, *Seasons in the Sun: The Battle for Britain, 1974–1979* (London: Penguin Books edition, 2013), p. 137.

49 '"Military coup was aimed at Wilson" – MI5', by Barrie Penrose, Colin Simpson and Simon Freeman, *The Sunday Times*, 29 March 1981, Oxford, Bodleian Library [MS.Wilson.c.1627].

50 Andrew, *Defence of the Realm*, p. 637.

51 Hansard, House of Commons, 28 July 1977, vol. 936, cols 1372–3.

52 Penrose and Courtiour, *Pencourt File*, p. 400.

53 Wilson's letter is in Ibid., pp. 411–12.

54 Andrew, *Defence of the Realm*, p. 632.

55 Shirley Williams, *Climbing the Bookshelves* (London: Virago Press, 2009), p. 201.

56 *Mail on Sunday*, 'Revealed: How MI5 bugged 10 Downing Street, the Cabinet and at least five Prime Ministers for 15 YEARS', 18 April 2010; Andrew, *Defence of the Realm*, p. xxi; Kenneth O. Morgan, *Callaghan: A Life* (Oxford: Oxford University Press, 1997), p. 610.

57 Andrew, *Defence of the Realm*, p. 627.

58 Wright, *Spycatcher*, p. 365.

59 Tam Dalyell, Obituary of Joseph Kagan, *Independent*, 19 January 1995.

60 Haines, *Kick 'Em Back*, p. 235.

61 Andrew, *Defence of the Realm*, pp. 628–9.

62 Ibid., p. 629.

63 Ibid., p. 630.

64 Ibid., p. 631.

65 *Private Eye*, Number 255, p. 18, quoted in Oxford, Bodleian Library [MS.Wilson.c.1627]: copy letter from Oswald Hickson, Collier & Co. to the Editor of *Private Eye*, 5 October 1971.

66 Oxford, Bodleian Library [MS.Wilson.c.1627], letter from John E. Payne to Wilson, 3 November 1971.

67 Oxford, Bodleian Library [MS.Wilson.c.1627], letter from Lawford & Co. Solicitors to Oswald, Hickson Collier & Co., 19 December 1972.

68 Cavendish, *Inside Intelligence: The Revelations of an MI6 Officer* (London: HarperCollins; 2nd revised edition, 1997), pp. 163–4.

69 Ibid., p. 165.

70 Hansard, House of Commons, 6 May 1987, vol. 115, col. 724.

71 *Panorama*, 13 October 1988.

72 Wright, *Spycatcher*, p. 369.

73 Ibid., p. 370.

74 Ibid., p. 371.

75 Castle, *Diaries 1974–76*, p. 198.

76 *The Times*, 22 February 2018. Stonehouse's biographer, Julian Hayes, points out that the dishonesty was 'Stonehouse's handling of charitable donations for an organisation he had been working for' (Julian Hayes, *Stonehouse: Cabinet Minister, Fraudster, Spy* [London: Robinson, an Imprint of Little, Brown Book Group, p. 80]). Hayes also casts doubt as to whether it was money or casual sex that turned Stonehouse, stating that the 'most compelling evidence in discrediting Stonehouse was

the money he had accepted . . .' The fabled 'honey trap . . . supposedly took place during his visit to Czechoslovakia in 1957' and Hayes questions 'whether any such event ever occurred' (Hayes, *Stonehouse*, p. 82).

77 *The Times*, 25 June 1970.

78 David Owen, *Time to Declare* (London: Michael Joseph Ltd, 1991), pp. 292–5.

79 Hansard, House of Commons, 7 November 1978, vol. 957, col. 741.

80 Ibid.

81 Ibid., col. 742.

82 Ibid., col. 744.

83 Owen, *Time to Declare*, p. 296.

84 Interview with Joe Haines, 2 September 2019.

85 Crossman, *Diaries of a Cabinet Minister Volume Two*, p. 744.

86 Hansard, House of Commons, 7 November 1978, vol. 957, col. 744.

87 https://www.theguardian.com/politics/2018/jun/07/mary-wilson-obituary

88 Oxford, Bodleian Library [MS.Wilson.c.1627], Statement to be Made in Open Court, High Court of Justice, Queen's Bench Division, 1977 W No. 3271.

89 *The Times*, 12 February 1977.

90 Richard Crossman, *Myths of Cabinet Government* (Harvard: Harvard University Press, 1972); also Richard Crossman, *Three Lectures on Prime Ministerial Government* (London: Jonathan Cape, 1972).

91 Hansard, House of Commons, 2 November 1978, vol. 906, col. 1096.

92 *The Times*, 29 July 1975; on 1 October, Widgery allowed publication to go ahead: he was not convinced banning the diaries was in the public interest, and he did not believe the material in the diaries becoming public would have an impact on the current cabinet being able to speak freely in private. *The Times*, 2 October 1975.

93 Wilson, *Governance of Britain*, p. 8.

94 Ibid., p. 10.

95 Ibid.

96 Ibid., p. xi.

97 Interview, 18 March 2020.

98 Cmnd 7937: Chapters 21 and 22 look at forms of regulation; Chapter 26 examines the cases for an extension of public ownership.

99 Interview, 18 March 2020.

100 Cmnd 7071.

101 Cmnd 9319.

102 https://britishscreenforum.co.uk

103 Harold Wilson, *A Prime Minister on Prime Ministers* (London: Weidenfeld & Nicolson and Michael Joseph, David Paradine Histories Ltd, 1977), p. 291.

104 Wilson, *Prime Minister on Prime Ministers*, p. 326.

105 Available on https://www.youtube.com/watch?v=Vlcgwp1sQw4

106 https://www.youtube.com/watch?v=OmVMeX4igPw

107 Mary Wilson, *Poems I Like* (London: Hutchinson, 1983), pp. 24–5.

108 Ibid., pp. 148–53.

109 Margaret Thatcher, *The Downing Street Years* (London: HarperCollins, 1993 paperback edition), p. 7.

110 Margaret Thatcher, *The Path to Power* (London: HarperCollins, 1995), p. 313.

111 CMD 16194/3 – draft of a review of *Another Heart and Other Pulses*.

112 Ibid.

113 Healey, *Time of My Life*, p. 478.

114 CMD 16194/4.

115 *The Times*, 7 April 1981.

116 Jenkins, *Life at the Centre*, p. 225.

117 Clip of Wilson shown in the Michael Cockerell documentary, *Roy Jenkins: A Very Social Democrat*: available at: https://www.youtube.com/watch?v=iJC-fMzBzVs

118 *The Times*, 28 February 1981.

119 CMD 16194/4.

120 Ibid.

121 Wilson, *Chariot of Israel*, Preface.

122 Ibid., p. 380.

123 Interview, 3 July 2019.

124 Ibid.

125 Interview, 14 May 2019.

126 Email to the author, 11 October 2018.

127 Interview, 3 July 2019.

128 Hansard, House of Lords, 14 March 1984, vol. 449, col. 762.

129 Ibid.

130 Hansard, House of Lords, 21 March 1984, vol. 449, col. 1244.

131 Hansard, House of Lords, 9 May 1984, vol. 451, col. 923.

132 Ibid., cols 927–8.

133 Hansard, House of Lords, 25 June 1986, vol. 477, col. 389.

134 John Preston, *Fall: The Mystery of Robert Maxwell* (London: Penguin, 2020), p. 157.

135 Roger Shashoua, *The Paper Millionaire* (London: Duckworth, 1988), p. 155.

136 Martin Waller interview with Roger Shashoua, *The Times*, 10 September 2007.

137 Shashoua, *Paper Millionaire*, p. 157.

138 Interview between the author and Ian Waitt, 31 December 2021.

139 Ibid.

140 Waitt was then the Head of the International Projects Office at the then North-East London Polytechnic.

141 Waitt himself became a board director. Interview between the author and Ian Waitt, 31 December 2021.

142 Interview between the author and Ian Waitt, 31 December 2021. Wilson himself had given former prime ministers use of a government car. Kaufman, a junior minister at the Department of the Environment from 1974 to 1975, in charge of the Government Car Service, recalled: 'I received a direct minute from the Prime Minister – it was very rare for the Prime Minister to send such a minute to a junior Minister – instructing me to write to all former Prime Ministers still living offering them a car and a chauffeur,' (Hansard, House of Commons, 24 May 1995, vol. 260, col. 914).

143 https://www.open.ac.uk/library/digital-archive/exhibition/110/theme/2/page/1

144 Ziegler, *Wilson*, pp. 515–16.

145 Hansard, House of Commons, 24 May 1995, vol. 260, col. 909.

146 Hansard, House of Commons, 24 May 1995, vol. 260, col. 913.

147 Hansard, House of Commons, 24 May 1995, vol. 260, col. 914. The party conference report actually records Wilson saying: '. . . thank you for what the BBC, if they are true to their usual form, will tonight describe as a hostile reception.' *Report of the 67th Annual Conference*, p. 164.

148 https://www.theguardian.com/politics/2018/jun/07/mary-wilson-obituary

Conclusion: Harold's Den

1   John Ramsden, *The Winds of Change: Macmillan to Heath, 1957–1975* (London: Longman, 1996), p. 317.

2   Richard Toye, *The Labour Party and the Planned Economy* (Woodbridge, Suffolk: Boydell Press, 2003), p. 239.

3   Foot, *Wilson*, p. 10.

4   *Report of the 66th Annual Conference*, p. 215.

5   Morgan Phillips, *Morgan Phillips: Labour Party Secretary* (Nottingham: Spokesman for Labour Heritage, 2017), p. 162.

6   'Harold Wilson: A Flawed Political Genius?' Lord Speaker's Lecture delivered by Donoughue.

7   Acheson was then advising President John F. Kennedy on NATO matters. He was speaking on American Affairs at the West Point Military Academy on 6 December 1962.

8   Interview, 18 March 2020.

9   Shrapnel, *Performers*, p. 39.

10 Interview with Chalmers on Thames Television, 1984.

11 Warwicker, *An Outsider*, p. 117.

12 As quoted in 'When Harold Met Marcia', by Ben Pimlott, *Independent*, 17 October 1992.

13 Haines, *Politics of Power*, p. 187.

14 Charles Moore, *Margaret Thatcher: The Authorized Biography: Volume One: Not for Turning* (London: Penguin Books, 2014 edition), p. 409, based on an interview with Lord McAlpine.

15 *The Times*, 7 April 1981.

16 Interview between Sir David Garrard and the author, 2 February 2021; for Wilson smoking a pipe in private see, for example, Kaufman's tribute to Wilson (Hansard, House of Commons, 24 May 1995, vol. 260, col. 913).

17 Introduction by Kingsley Amis in Amis (ed.), *Harold's Years*, p. 9.

Acknowledgements

I am grateful to my agent, Tracy Bohan, and to all at my publishers, Weidenfeld & Nicolson, including Jenny Lord and Ed Lake. I am also grateful to Alan Samson, who has believed in this project from the very start, and provided incredibly useful comments and edits to the first draft. Thank you to staff at the Isles of Scilly Museum, including Amanda Martin and Kate Hale; at the Bodleian Library, Oxford, including Jeremy McIlwaine; at the Lyndon Johnson Presidential Library, Texas, including Carrie Tallichet Smith; at the National Archives; and at the House of Commons Library. I am grateful to all those who granted me interviews: the late Lord (Robert) Armstrong; Dame Margaret Beckett MP; Lord (Robin) Butler; Lord (Kenneth) Clarke; Sir David Garrard; Lord (Peter) Hain; Lord (Neil) Kinnock; Lord (David) Lipsey; Rt Hon. Theresa May MP; Lord (Kenneth O.) Morgan; Lord (John) Morris; Lord (David) Owen; Lord (Tom) Pendry; Lord (William) Rodgers; Dennis Skinner; Lord (Dick) Taverne; Lord (John) Tomlinson; Sue Utting; Ian Waitt; Baroness Shirley Williams and Professor Robin Wilson. I am also grateful to Joy Crispin-Wilson for email correspondence. Robin and Joy were kind enough to invite me to Lady Wilson's Service of Thanksgiving on Monday, 26 November 2018 at St-Martin's-within-Ludgate Church, which was a solemn privilege to attend. Joe Haines was extraordinarily generous with his time and gave me a number of interviews: I am very grateful to him for his time and his insight. Thank you to Mark D'Arcy, parliamentary correspondent at *Today in Parliament* for supplying me with a key episode script. Thank you to Dame Meg Hillier MP for her email correspondence, to John Cox, Lord (Bernard) Donoughue, Lord (Paul) Murphy, Lord (Peter) Hennessy and Lord (Don) Touhig for discussions, and to Rt Hon. George Howarth MP for permission to quote from his piece on the constituency work of Harold Wilson. I am, as ever, grateful to my wife Rebecca and my family for their incredible help. Without them, the book would not have been completed. Thank you to all those who have helped me during the writing process, including Laura Jorge Harris and Rob Keenan, whose steadfast support has been invaluable. Any faults or errors in this work are, however, my responsibility alone.

Picture Credits

The author and publisher are grateful to the following for permission to reproduce illustrations.

1 (above) Young Harold on the steps of Number Ten. Getty/Hulton/Archive

1 (below) Harold as the 'Baby of the Attlee Cabinet'. Alamy/Trinity Mitttor/Mirror Pix

2 (above) Harold Wilson, George Brown and Hugh Gaitskell. Alamy/Trinity Mitttor/Mirror Pix

2 (below) Harold's 'White Heat' speech in October 1963. Alamy/PA Images

3 (above) Harold with The Beatles in March 1964. Getty Images/Keystone Press

3 (below) Harold at 10 Downing Street in October 1964. Shutterstock/Roger Jackson

4 (above) In the Scillies with his wife Mary and son Giles in August 1965. Alamy/Keystone Press

4 (below) Harold with son Robin, daughter-in-law Joy and wife Mary. Alamy/PA Images

5a (above) Harold broadcasting in November 1967. Getty Images/BBC/Reproduced by kind permission of The Labour Party

5b (below) Harold with President Lyndon B. Johnson at the White House in July 1966. Alamy/White House

6 (above) Harold negotiating with Ian Smith on HMS *Fearless* in October 1968. Getty Images/Central Press

6b (below) Harold in the House of Commons. Shutterstock/ANL

7 (above) Harold and Marcia in October 1972. Alamy/Trinity Mittor/Mirror Pix

7b (below) Bernard Donoughue and Joe Haines. Alamy/PA Images

8a (above) Harold with James Callaghan in Paris.   Alamy/The Print Collector

8b (below) The Queen at a farewell dinner for Harold at 10 Downing Street. Alamy/PA Images

Index

Index

Harold Wilson is HW throughout.